George L. Craik

A manual of English literature, and of the history of the English language

From the Norman conquest; with numerous specimens

George L. Craik

A manual of English literature, and of the history of the English language
From the Norman conquest; with numerous specimens

ISBN/EAN: 9783742804709

Manufactured in Europe, USA, Canada, Australia, Japa

Cover: Foto ©Andreas Hilbeck / pixelio.de

Manufactured and distributed by brebook publishing software (www.brebook.com)

George L. Craik

A manual of English literature, and of the history of the English language

A MANUAL

OF

ENGLISH LITERATURE,

AND OF THE HISTORY OF

THE ENGLISH LANGUAGE,

FROM

The Norman Conquest;

WITH NUMEROUS SPECIMENS.

BY

GEORGE L. CRAIK, LL.D.,

PROFESSOR OF HISTORY AND OF ENGLISH LITERATURE IN QUEEN'S COLLEGE, BELFAST.

LONDON:
CHARLES GRIFFIN AND COMPANY,
STATIONERS' HALL COURT.
1863.

ADVERTISEMENT.

The present volume consists of so much of a larger work recently published on the same subject as seemed sufficient to make a convenient and comprehensive text-book for schools and colleges, and to supply all the information needed by students in preparing themselves for the Civil Service and other competitive examinations. The concluding section is nearly all that has been added.

The reader will do well to keep in mind, or under his eye, the four following Schemes, or Synoptical Views, according to which the history of the English Language in its entire extent may be methodized:—

I.

1. Original, Pure, Simple, or First English (commonly called Saxon, or Anglo-Saxon); Synthetic, or Inflectional, in its Grammar, and Homogeneous in its Vocabulary;

2. Broken, or Second English (commonly called Semi-Saxon), —from soon after the middle of the eleventh century to about the middle of the thirteenth—when its ancient Grammatical System had been destroyed, and it had been converted from an Inflectional into a Non-Inflectional and Analytic language, by the *first* action upon it of the Norman Conquest;

3. Mixed, or Compound, or Composite, or Third English,—since the middle of the thirteenth century—about which date its Vocabulary also began to be changed by the combination of its original Gothic with a French (Romance or Neo-Latin) element, under the *second* action upon it of the Norman Conquest.

II.

1. The Original form, in which the three vowel-endings *a*, *e*, and *u* are employed in the declension of nouns and the conjugation of verbs;

2. The Second form, in which the single termination *e* represents indiscriminately the three ancient vowel-endings, but still constitutes a distinct syllable;

3. The Third form, in which this termination *e* of nouns and verbs, though still written, is no longer syllabically pronounced.

III.

1. *Saxon*, or *Anglo-Saxon*; throughout the period before the Norman Conquest;

2. *Semi-Saxon*; from about the middle of the eleventh to the middle of the thirteenth century; the period of the Infancy and Childhood of our existing national speech;

3. *Old*, or rather *Early*, *English*; from the middle of the thirteenth to the middle of the fourteenth century; the period of the Boyhood of our existing speech;

4. *Middle English*; from the middle of the fourteenth to the middle of the sixteenth century; the Youth, or Adolescence of our existing speech;

5. *Modern English*; since the middle of the sixteenth century; the Manhood of our existing speech.

IV.

A.D.
450. Commencement of the conquest and occupation of South Britain by the Angles and Saxons, bringing with them their ancestral Gothic speech;

1066. Conquest of England by the Normans; Establishment of French as the courtly and literary language of the country; Commencement of the reduction of the ancient vernacular tongue to the condition of a patois, and of its conversion from a synthetic to an analytic tongue;

1154. End of the reign of the four Norman kings and accession of the Plantagenet dynasty; Beginning of the connexion with Southern France through the marriage of Henry II. with Eleanor of Poiton; Termination of the National Chronicle, the latest considerable composition in the regular form of the ancient language; Full commencement of the intermixture of the two races;

1272. New age of the Edwards; Commencement of the connexion of the English royal family with that of France by the second marriage of Edward I. with a daughter of Philip III.; Employment, at first occasionally, afterwards habitually, of French instead of English as the language of the Statutes; Commencement of its active intermixture with the vernacular tongue;

1362. Trials at law in the King's Courts directed by the statute of 36 Edward III. to be conducted no longer in French but in English; Victory of the native tongue in its new composite form over its foreign rival, and recovery of its old position as the literary language of the country, under the impulse of the war with France, and of the genius of Minot, Langland, and Chaucer;

1455. Outbreak of the desolating War of the Roses, and complete extinction for a time of the light of literature in England;

1558. Accession of Elizabeth; Commencement of a new literary era, with the native language in sole dominion;

1660. Restoration of the Stuarts; Noonday of the Gallican age of English literature;

1760. Accession of George III.; Complete association in the national literature of Scottish and Irish writers with those of England.

CONTENTS.

INTRODUCTORY

	PAGE
The Languages of Modern Europe	1
Early Latin Literature in Britain	3
The Celtic Languages and Literatures	7
Decay of the Earliest English Scholarship	12
The English Language	16
Original English (commonly called *Saxon*, or *Anglo-Saxon*)	20
The Norman Conquest	24
Arabic and other New Learning	29
Schools and Universities	34
Rise of the Scholastic Philosophy	39
Classical Learning; Mathematics; Medicine; Law; Books	41
The Latin Language	46
Latin Chroniclers	47
The French Language in England	48
The Langue D'Oc and the Langue D'Oyl	53
Vernacular Language and Literature:—A.D. 1066—1216	56
The Thirteenth and Fourteenth Centuries:—Ascendancy of the Scholastic Philosophy	67
Mathematical and other Studies	69
Universities and Colleges	73
Cultivation and Employment of the Learned Tongues in the Thirteenth and Fourteenth Centuries	75
Last Age of the French Language in England	79
Re-emergence of the English as a Literary Tongue	82
Second English (commonly called *Semi-Saxon*)	85
The Brut of Layamon	89
The Ormulum	95
The Ancren Riwle	99
Early English Metrical Romances	102
Metrical Chronicle of Robert of Gloucester	104
Robert Mannyng, or De Brunne	105
Lawrence Minot	106
Alliterative Verse:—Piers Ploughman	110
Piers Ploughman's Creed	118

CONTENTS.

	PAGE
THIRD ENGLISH (*Mixed or Compound English*)	121
Geoffrey Chaucer	121
John Gower	155
John Barbour	157
Compound English Prose:—Sir John Mandevil; Trevisa; Wiclif; Chaucer	164
Printing in England:—Caxton	167
English Chroniclers	169
Bishop Pecock; Fortescue; Malory	169
English Poets:—Occleve; Lydgate	174
Scottish Poets:—Wyntoun; James I.; Henryson; Holland; Blind Harry	176
Prose Writers:—More; Elyot; Tyndal; Cranmer; Latimer	183
Scottish Prose Writers	190
English Poets:—Hawes; Barklay	191
Skelton	192
Roy; John Heywood	194
Scottish Poets:—Gawin Douglas; Dunbar; Lyndsay	195
Surrey; Wyatt	196
The Elizabethan Literature	198
The Mirror for Magistrates	198
Origin of the Regular Drama	200
Interludes of John Heywood	202
Udall's Ralph Roister Doister	203
Gammer Gurton's Needle	205
Misogonus	206
Chronicle Histories:—Bale's Kynge Johan, etc.	207
Tragedy of Gorboduc:—Blank Verse	208
Other Early Dramas	211
Second Stage of the Regular Drama:—Peele; Greene	212
Marlow	214
Lyly; Kyd; Lodge	215
Earlier Elizabethan Prose:—Lyly; Sidney; Spenser; Nash; etc.	219
Edmund Spenser	224
Other Elizabethan Poetry	237
William Warner	238
Samuel Daniel	242
Michael Drayton	246
Joseph Hall	249
Joshua Sylvester	249
Chapman's Homer	251
Harington; Fairfax; Fanshawe	252
William Drummond	253
Sir John Davies	253
John Donne	254
Shakespeare's Minor Poems	257
Shakespeare's Dramatic Works	258

CONTENTS.

THIRD ENGLISH—*continued.*

	PAGE
Dramatists contemporary with Shakespeare	265
Beaumont and Fletcher	268
Jonson	270
Massinger; Ford	271
Later Elizabethan Prose Writers	272
Translation of the Bible	273
Theological Writers:—Bishop Andrews; Donne; Hall; Hooker	274
Francis Bacon	275
Robert Burton	277
Historical Writers	278

MIDDLE AND LATTER PART OF THE SEVENTEENTH CENTURY 280

Shirley, and end of the Old Drama	280
Giles Fletcher; Phineas Fletcher	282
Other Religious Poets:—Quarles; Herbert; Herrick; Crashaw	283
Cartwright; Randolph; Corbet	284
Poets of the French School:—Carew; Lovelace; Suckling	286
Denham	288
Cleveland	289
Wither	290
William Browne	296
Prose Writers:—Charles I.	297
Milton's Prose Works	299
Hales; Chillingworth	301
Jeremy Taylor	302
Fuller	303
Sir Thomas Browne	306
Sir James Harrington	308
Newspapers	309
Retrospect of the Commonwealth Literature	310
Poetry of Milton	312
Cowley	321
Butler	322
Waller	323
Marvel	325
Other Minor Poets	327
Dryden	329
Dramatists	331
Prose Writers:—Clarendon	333
Hobbes	334
Henry Nevile	336
Other Prose Writers:—Cudworth; More; Barrow; Bunyan; &c.	337

CONTENTS.

	PAGE
THE CENTURY BETWEEN THE ENGLISH REVOLUTION AND THE FRENCH REVOLUTION	341
First Effects of the Revolution on our Literature	341
Surviving Writers of the preceding Period	342
Bishop Burnet	345
Thomas Burnet	346
Other Theological Writers:—Tillotson; South	346
Locke	348
Swift	349
Pope	353
Addison and Steele	357
Shaftesbury; Mandeville	359
Gay; Arbuthnot; Atterbury	362
Prior; Parnell	363
Bolingbroke	364
Garth; Blackmore	365
Defoe	366
Dramatic Writers	369
Minor Poets	370
Collins; Shenstone; Gray	376
Young; Thomson	377
Armstrong; Akenside; Wilkie; Glover	379
Scottish Poetry	380
The Novelists Richardson; Fielding; Smollett	382
Sterne	387
Goldsmith	388
Churchill	392
Falconer; Beattie; Mason	393
The Wartons; Percy; Chatterton; Macpherson	394
Dramatic Writers	396
Female Writers	397
Periodical Essayists	398
Political Writing:—Wilkes; Junius	401
Johnson	404
Burke	408
Metaphysical and Ethical Writers	421
Historical Writers:—Hume; Robertson; Gibbon	422
Political Economy; Theology; Criticism and Belles Lettres	426
THE LATTER PART OF THE EIGHTEENTH CENTURY	427
Cowper	427
Darwin	437
Burns	440

THE NINETEENTH CENTURY 457

Last Age of the Georges.—Wordsworth 459
Coleridge 474
Southey 481
Scott 482
Crabbe; Campbell; Moore 488
Byron 496
Shelley 497
Keats 501
Hunt 505
Other Poetical Writers of the earlier part of the Nineteenth Century 510
Prose Literature 511

LITERATURE OF THE PRESENT DAY. 513

Mrs. Browning 514
Tennyson 525
Browning 528
Hood 531

INDEX 533

SPECIMENS.

	PAGE
Song of Canute	87
Archbishop Aldred's Curse	87
St. Godric's Hymn	87
" Sister's Rhyme	88
" Hymn to St. Nicholas	88
Rhyme of Flemings and Normans (1173)	89
Hugh Bigott's Boast	88
The Here Prophecy	89
Layamon's Brut :—Part of Introduction	92
The Ormulum :—Part of Dedication	96
" " Injunction as to Spelling	98
The Ancren Riwle :—Eating and Fasting	101
Robert of Gloucester's Chronicle :—French Language in England	105
Minot ; First Invasion of France by Edward III.	108
Vision of Piers Ploughman :—Commencement	113
Piers Ploughman's Creed :—Description of Piers	118
Chaucer :—House of Fame ; Eagle's Address to Chaucer	138
" " " Notice of Fire-arms	140
" " " Old Mechanical Artillery	141
" Canterbury Tales ; The Prioress (from the Prologue)	142
" " " The Mendicant Friar (from the Prologue)	143
" " " Emily (from the Knight's Tale)	145
" " " Temple of Mars (from the Knight's Tale)	146
" " " Passages relating to the Host	148
" " " Part of the Clerk's Tale of Griselda	153
Barbour :—The Bruce ; Eulogy on Freedom	162
Mandevil :—Travels ; part of Prologue	164
Chaucer (Prose) :—Canterbury Tales ; Pride in Dress, etc.	166
Bishop Pecock :—Repressor ; Midsummer Eve	170
Fortescue :—Difference, etc. ; French King and People	171
Malory :—Morte Arthur ; Death of Lancelot	173
Wyntoun :—Chronicle	177
Blind Harry :—Wallace ; his Latin Original	181
" " " The same subject	181
" " " Commencement of the Poem	181

SPECIMENS.   xv

	PAGE
Blind Harry :—Wallace ; Part of Battle of Shortwoodshaw	182
" " " L'Envoy	183
Sir Thomas More :—Letter to his Wife	185
Udall ;—Ralph Roister Doister	204
Spenser :—Fairy Queen ; Belphœbe	234
Warner :—Albion's England ; Old Man and his Ass	241
" " " Fall of Richard the Third	241
" " " Fair Rosamund and Queen Eleanor	242
Daniel :—Musophilus ; Defence of Poetry	244
Drayton :—Polyolbion ; Stag-hunt	246
" " Nymphidia ; Queen of the Fairies	248
Sylvester :—Divine Weeks and Works ; Praise of Night	250
Donne :—Song	256
Cloveland :—Epitaph on Ben Jonson	260
" " Eulogy on Jonson	260
Wither :—Amygdala Britannica ; Prophecy	263
" Songs and Hymns ; Thanksgiving for Seasonable Weather	265
" " " Thanksgiving for Victory	266
Fuller :—Worthies ; Shakespeare and Ben Jonson	304
" " Philemon Holland	304
Milton :—College Exercise ; His Native Language	313
Waller :—His Last Verses	324
Marvel :—The Picture of T. C.	326
Mandeville :—Fable of the Bees ; Anticipation of Adam Smith	360
Burke :—Speech on Nabob of Arcot ; Devastation of the Carnatic	414
" Reflections on French Revolution ; Hereditary Principle	415
" Letter to Mr. Elliot ; True Reform	417
" Letters on a Regicide Peace ; Right Way of making War	419
Cowper :—Table Talk ; National Vice	432
" Truth ; Voltaire	432
" Conversation ; Meeting on the Road to Emmaus	433
" Lines on his Mother's Picture	434
Darwin :—Botanic Garden ; "Flowers of the Sky"	439
" " " The Compass	439
Burns :—To a Mouse	442
" To a Mountain Daisy	444
" Epistle to a Young Friend	446
" The Vision (part)	448
" Highland Mary	453
" Verses from various Songs	453
Wordsworth :—The Fountain, a Conversation	463
" The Affliction of Margaret	465
" "Her Eyes are wild"	467
" Laodamia	469
Coleridge :—"Maid of my Love"	475
" Time, Real and Imaginary	476
" Work without Hope	477
" Youth and Age	477
" "Yes, yes! that boon!"	479

SPECIMENS.

	PAGE
Coleridge:—Love, Hope, and Patience, in Education	480
Scott:—Marmion; The Battle (part)	484
Campbell:—Adelgitha	491
" Theodric; Letter of Constance	491
Crabbe:—Tales of the Hall; Story of the Elder Brother (part)	492
Moore:—Lalla Rookh; Calm after Storm	495
Shelley:—Ode to a Skylark	499
Keats:—Ode to a Nightingale	503
Hunt:—The Sultan Mahmoud	505
" The Fancy Concert	507
Mrs. Browning:—A Child's Grave at Florence	514
" Aurora Leigh; Pictures of England	518
" " " Paris	519
" " " Her Mother's Picture	520
Tennyson:—The Lord of Burleigh	522
" Wellington	524
R. Browning:—The Pied Piper of Hamelin (part)	526
Hood:—The Death-bed	531

MANUAL OF THE HISTORY
OF
ENGLISH LITERATURE.

THE LANGUAGES OF MODERN EUROPE.

THE existing European languages may be nearly all comprehended under five divisions. First, there are the Celtic tongues of Ireland and Wales, and their subordinate varieties. Secondly, there are the tongues founded upon the Latin spoken by the old Romans, and thence called the Romance or the Neo-Latin, that is, the New Latin, tongues; of these, the principal are the Italian, the Spanish, and the French. The Romaic, or Modern Greek, may be included under the same head. Thirdly, there are what have been variously designated the Germanic, Teutonic, or Gothic tongues, being those which were originally spoken by the various barbarian races by whom the Roman empire of the West was overthrown and overwhelmed (or at the least subjugated, revolutionized, and broken up) in the fifth and sixth centuries. Fourthly, there are the Slavonic tongues, of which the Russian and the Polish are the most distinguished. Fifthly, there are the Tschudic tongues, as they have been denominated, or those spoken by the Finnic and Laponnic races. Almost the only language which this enumeration leaves out is that still preserved by the French and Spanish Biscayans, and known as the Basque, or among those who speak it as the Euskarian, which seems to stand alone among the tongues not only of Europe but of the world. It is supposed to be a remnant of the ancient Iberian or original language of Spain.

The order in which four at least of the five sets or classes of languages have been named may be regarded as that of their probable introduction into Europe from Asia or the East, or at any rate of their establishment in the localities of which they are now severally in possession. First, apparently, came the Celtic, now driven on to the farthest west; after which followed in succession the Latin, the Gothic, and the Slavonic, pressing upon and urging forward one another like so many waves.

Their present geographical position may also be set forth in few words. Those of the Celtic type are found, as just mentioned, in the West, the Latin generally in the South, the Slavonic in the East, the Tschudic in the North, and the Gothic over the whole of the central region. The chief exception is, that one Tschudic language, the Madgyar, is spoken in Hungary, at the south-eastern extremity of Europe.

The English is essentially or fundamentally a Gothic tongue. That is to say, it is to be classed among those which were spoken by the main division of the barbaric invaders and conquerors of the Roman empire, and which are now spread over the whole of the central portion of the European continent, or what we may call the body of Europe as distinguished from its head and limbs. These Gothic tongues have been subdivided into the High-Germanic, the Low-Germanic, and the Scandinavian; and each of these subordinate groups or clusters has a certain character of its own in addition to the common character by which they are all allied and discriminated from those belonging to quite other stocks. They may be said to present different shades of the same colour. And even in their geographical distribution they lie as it were in so many successive ridges;—the High-Germanic languages farthest south; next to them, the Low-Germanic, in the middle; and then, farthest north, the Scandinavian. The High-Germanic may be considered to be principally represented by the modern classic German; the Low-Germanic by the language of the people of Holland, or what we call the Low Dutch, or simply the Dutch; the Scandinavian, by the Swedish, Danish, or Icelandic.

It may be remarked, too, that the gradation of character among the three sets of languages corresponds to their geographical position. That is to say, their resemblance is in proportion to their proximity. Thus, the High-Germanic and the Scandinavian groups are both nearer in character, as well as in position, to the Low-Germanic than they are to each other; and the Low-Germanic tongues, lying in the middle, form as it were a sort of link, or bridge, between the other two extreme groups. Climate, and the relative elevation of the three regions, may have something to do with this. The rough and full-mouthed pronunciation of the High-Germanic tongues, with their broad vowels and guttural combinations, may be the natural product of the bracing mountain air of the south; the clearer and neater articulation of the Low-Germanic ones, that of the milder influences of the plain; the thinner and sharper sounds of the Scandinavian group, that of the more chill and pinching hyperborean atmosphere in which they have grown up and been formed.

EARLY LATIN LITERATURE IN BRITAIN.

When the South of Britain became a part of the Roman empire, the inhabitants, at least of the towns, seem to have adopted generally the Latin language and applied themselves to the study of the Latin literature. The diffusion among them of this new taste was one of the first means employed by their politic conquerors, as soon as they had fairly established themselves in the island, to rivet their dominion. A more efficacious they could not have devised; and, happily, it was also the best fitted to turn their subjugation into a blessing to the conquered people. Agricola, having spent the first year of his administration in establishing in the province the order and tranquillity which is the first necessity of the social condition, and the indispensable basis of all civilization, did not allow another winter to pass without beginning the work of thus training up the national mind to a Roman character. Tacitus informs us that he took measures for having the sons of the chiefs educated in the liberal arts, exciting them at the same time by professing to prefer the natural genius of the Britons to the studied acquirements of the Gauls; the effect of which was, that those who lately had disdained to use the Roman tongue now became ambitious of excelling in eloquence. In later times, schools were no doubt established and maintained in all the principal towns of Roman Britain, as they were throughout the empire in general. There are still extant many imperial edicts relating to these public seminaries, in which privileges are conferred upon the teachers, and regulations laid down as to the manner in which they were to be appointed, the salaries they were to receive, and the branches of learning they were to teach. But no account of the British schools in particular has been preserved. It would appear, however, that, for some time at least, the older schools of Gaul were resorted to by the Britons who pursued the study of the law: Juvenal, who lived in the end of the first and the beginning of the second century, speaks, in one of his Satires, of eloquent Gaul instructing the pleaders of Britain. But even already forensic acquirements must have become very general in the latter country and the surrounding regions, if we may place any reliance on the assertion which he makes in the next line, that in Thule itself people now talked of hiring rhetoricians to manage their causes. Thule, whatever may have been the particular island or country to which that name was given, was the most northern land known to the ancients.

It is somewhat remarkable that, while a good many names of natives of Gaul are recorded in connexion with the last age of Roman literature, scarcely a British name of that period of any literary reputation has been preserved, if we except a few which figure in the history of the Christian Church. The poet Ausonius, who flourished in the fourth century, makes frequent mention of a contemporary British writer whom he calls Sylvius Bonus, and whose native name is supposed to have been Coil the Good; but of his works, or even of their titles or subjects, we know nothing. Ausonius, who seems to have entertained strong prejudices against the Britons, speaks of Sylvius with the same animosity as of the rest of his countrymen. Of ecclesiastical writers in Latin belonging to the sixth century, the heresiarch Pelagius and his disciple Celestius, St. Patrick, the apostle of Ireland, with his friend Bishop Secundinus, and the poet Sedulius, are generally regarded as having been natives of the British islands.

Gildas, our earliest historian of whom anything remains, also wrote in Latin. St. Gildas the Wise, as he is styled, was a son of Caw, Prince of Strathclyde, in the capital of which kingdom, the town of Alcluyd, now Dunbarton, he is supposed to have been born about the end of the fifth or beginning of the sixth century. Caw was also father of the famous bard Aneurin: one theory, indeed, is that Aneurin and Gildas were the same person. In his youth Gildas is said to have gone over to Ireland, and to have studied in the schools of the old national learning that still flourished there; and, like his brother Aneurin (if Aneurin was his brother), he also commenced his career as a bard, or composer of poetry in his native tongue. He was eventually, however, converted to Christianity, and became a zealous preacher of his new religion. The greater part of his life appears to have been spent in his native island; but at last he retired to Armorica, or Little Britain, on the Continent, and died there. He is said to lie buried in the Cathedral of Vannes. Gildas is the author of two declamatory effusions, the one commonly known as his History (De Excidio Britanniæ Liber Querulus), the other as his Epistle (De Excidio Britanniæ et Britonum Exulatione), which have been often printed. The latest edition is that contained in the Monumenta Historica Britannica, 1848; and there is also an edition prepared by Mr. Joseph Stevenson for the English Historical Society,

8vo. London: 1834. A translation of the Epistle was published in 1638; and both works are included in Dr. Giles's Six Old English Chronicles, 1848. They consist principally of violent invectives directed against his own countrymen as well as their continental invaders and conquerors; and throw but little light upon the obscure period to which they relate.

Our next historical writer is Nennius, said to have been a monk of Bangor, and to have escaped from the massacre of his brethren in 613. He too, like Gildas, is held to have been of Welsh or Cumbrian origin: his native name is conjectured to have been Ninian. But there is much obscurity and confusion in the accounts we have of Nennius: it appears to be probable that there were at least two early historical writers of that name. The author of a late ingenious work supposes that the true narrative of the ancient Nennius only came down to the invasion of Julius Cæsar, and is now lost, although we probably have an abridgment of it in the British History (Eulogium Britanniæ, sive Historia Britonum), published by Gale in his Scriptores Quindecim, Oxon. 1691, which, however, is expressly stated in the preface by the author himself to have been drawn up in 858. A very valuable edition of 'The Historia Britonum, commonly attributed to Nennius, from a MS. lately discovered in the Library of the Vatican Palace at Rome,' was published in 8vo. at London, in 1819, by the Rev. W. Gunn, B.D., rector of Irstead, Norfolk; and his greatly improved text has been chiefly followed in the subsequent edition prepared by Mr. Stevenson for the Historical Society (8vo. London, 1838). The most complete text, however, is probably that given in the Monumenta Historica Britannica, from a collation of no fewer than twenty-six manuscripts. An English version, originally published by Mr. Gunn in his edition of the Vatican text, is reprinted by Dr. Giles in his Six Old English Chronicles. But the most curious and important volume connected with Nennius is that published in 1847 by the Irish Archæological Society, containing an Irish version of his History executed in the fourteenth century, with a translation and Notes by Dr. Todd, together with a large mass of Additional Notes, and an Introduction, by the Hon. Algernon Herbert.

Of the Latin writers among the Angles and Saxons any of whose works remain, the most ancient is Aldhelm, abbot of Malmesbury, and afterwards the first bishop of Sherborn, who died in 700. Aldhelm was of the stock of the kings of Wessex, and was initiated in Greek and Latin learning at the school in Kent presided over by the Abbot Adrian, who, like his friend Archbishop Theodore, appears to have been a native of Asia

Minor, so that Greek was his native tongue. We are assured by one of his biographers that Aldhelm could write and speak Greek like a native of Greece. He also early associated himself with the monastic brotherhood of Malmesbury, or Meildulfesbyrig, that is, burgh or town of Moildulf, Maildulf, or Meldun, an Irish exile, by whom the monastery had been founded about half a century before the birth of Aldhelm. Among the studies of Aldhelm's after-life are mentioned the Roman law, the rules of Latin prosody, arithmetic, astronomy, and astrology.

But the English name of the times before the Norman Conquest that is most distinguished in literature is that of Beda, or Bede, upon whom the epithet of "The Venerable" has been justly bestowed by the respect and gratitude of posterity. All that we have written by Bede is in the Latin language. He was born some time between the years 672 and 677, at Jarrow, a village near the mouth of the Tyne, in the county of Durham, and was educated in the neighbouring monastery of Wearmouth under its successive abbots Benedict and Ceolfrid. He resided here, as he tells us himself, from the age of seven to that of twelve, during which time he applied himself with all diligence, he says, to the meditation of the Scriptures, the observance of regular discipline, and the daily practice of singing in the church. "It was always sweet to me," he adds, "to learn, to teach, and to write." In his nineteenth year he took deacon's orders, and in his thirtieth he was ordained priest. From this date till his death, in 735, he remained in his monastery, giving up his whole time to study and writing. His principal task was the composition of his celebrated Ecclesiastical History of England, which he brought to a close in his fifty-ninth year. It is our chief original authority for the earlier portion even of the civil history of the English nation. But Bede also wrote many other works, among which he has himself enumerated, in the brief account he gives of his life at the end of his Ecclesiastical History, Commentaries on most of the books of the Old and New Testaments and the Apocrypha, two books of Homilies, a Martyrology, a chronological treatise entitled On the Six Ages, a book on orthography, a book on the metrical art, and various other theological and biographical treatises. He likewise composed a book of hymns and another of epigrams. Most of these writings have been preserved, and have been repeatedly printed. It appears, from an interesting account of Bede's last hours by his pupil St. Cuthbert, that he was engaged at the time of his death in translating St. John's Gospel into his native tongue. Among his last utterances to his affectionate disciples watching around his bed were some recitations in the English language: "For," says the account, "he was very learned in our songs; and, putting his thoughts into English verse, he spoke it with compunction."

Another celebrated English churchman of this age was St. Boniface, originally named Winfrith, who was born in Devonshire about the year 680. Boniface is acknowledged as the Apostle of Germany, in which country he founded various monasteries, and was greatly instrumental in the diffusion both of Christianity and of civilization. He eventually became archbishop of Mentz, and was killed in East Friesland by a band of heathens in 755. Many of his letters to the popes, to the English bishops, to the kings of France, and to the kings of the various states of his native country, still remain, and are printed in the collections entitled Bibliothecæ Patrum.

THE CELTIC LANGUAGES AND LITERATURES.

No other branch of what is called the Indo-European family of languages is of higher interest in certain points of view than the Celtic. The various known forms of the Celtic are now regarded as coming under two great divisions, the Gaelic and the Cymric: Ireland being the head seat of the Gaelic (which may therefore also be called Irish), Wales being the head seat of the Cymric (which accordingly is by the English commonly called Welsh). Subordinate varieties of the Irish are the Gaelic of Scotland (often called Erse, or Ersh, that is, Irish), and the Manks, or Isle of Man tongue (now fast dying out): other Cymric dialects are the Cornish (now extinct as a spoken language), and the Armorican, or that still spoken in some parts of Bretagne.

The probability is, that the various races inhabiting the British islands when they first became known to the civilized world were mostly, if not all, of Celtic speech. Even in the parts of the country that were occupied by the Caledonians, the Picts, and the Belgian colonists, the oldest topographical names, the surest evidence that we have in all cases, and in this case almost our only evidence, are all, so far as can be ascertained, Celtic, either of the Cymric or of the Gaelic form. And then there are the great standing facts of the existence to this day of a large Cymric population in South Britain, and of a still larger Gaelic-speaking population in North Britain and in Ireland. No other account of these Celtic populations, or at least of the Welsh, has been attempted to be given, than that, as their own traditions and records are unanimous in asserting, they are the remnants of the races by which the two islands were occupied when they first attracted the attention of the Romans about half a century before the commencement of the Christian era.

And both the Welsh and the Irish possess a large mass of literature in their native tongues, much of which has been printed, in great part no doubt of comparatively modern production, but claiming some of it, in its substance if not exactly in the very form in which it now presents itself, an antiquity transcending any other native literature of which the country can boast.

Neither the Welsh nor the Irish language and literature, however, can with any propriety be included in a history of English literature and of the English language. The relationship of English to any Celtic tongue is more remote than its relationship not only to German or Icelandic or French or Italian or Latin, but even to Russian or Polish, or to Persian or Sanscrit. Irish and Welsh are opposed in their entire genius and structure to English. It has indeed been sometimes asserted that the Welsh is one of the fountains of the English. One school of last-century philologists maintained that full a third of our existing English was Welsh. No doubt, in the course of the fourteen centuries that the two languages have been spoken alongside of each other in the same country, a considerable number of vocables can hardly fail to have been borrowed by each from the other; the same thing would have happened if it had been a dialect of Chinese that had maintained itself all that time among the Welsh mountains. If, too, as is probable, a portion of the previous Celtic population chose or were suffered to remain even upon that part of the soil which came to be generally occupied after the departure of the Romans by the Angles, Saxons, and other Teutonic or Gothic tribes, the importers of the English language and founders of the English nation, something of Celtic may in that way have intermingled and grown up with the new national speech. But the English language cannot therefore be regarded as of Celtic parentage. The Celtic words, or words of Celtic extraction, that are found in it, be they some hundreds in number, or be they one or two thousands, are still only something foreign. They are products of another seed that have shot up here and there with the proper crop from the imperfectly cleared soil; or they are fragments of another mass which have chanced to come in contact with the body of the language, pressed upon by its weight, or blown upon it by the wind, and so have adhered to it or become imbedded in it. It would perhaps be going farther than known facts warrant us if we were to say that a Gothic tongue and a Celtic tongue are incapable of a true amalgamation. But undoubtedly it would require no common pressure to overcome so strong an opposition of nature and genius. The Gothic tongues, and the Latin or Romance tongues also, indeed, belong to distinct branches of what is called the Indo-European family; but the Celtic branch, though admitted to be of the same tree, has much more of a character of its own than any of the others. Probably any other two languages of the entire multitude held to be of this general stock would unite more readily than two of which only one was Celtic. It would be nearly the same case with that of the intermixture of an Indo-European with a Semitic language. It has been suggested that the Celtic branch must in all probability have diverged from the common stem at a much earlier date than any of the others. At any rate, in point of fact the English can at most be said to have been powdered or sprinkled with a little Celtic. Whatever may be the number of words which it has adopted, whether from the ancient Britons or from their descendants the Welsh, they are only single scattered words. No considerable department of the English dictionary is Welsh. No stream of words has flowed into the language from that source. The two languages have in no sense met and become one. They have not mingled as two rivers do when they join and fall into the same channel. There has been no chemical combination between the Gothic and the Celtic elements, but only more or less of a mechanical intermixture.

As the forms of the original English alphabetical characters are the same with those of the Irish, it is probable that it was from Ireland the English derived their first knowledge of letters. There was certainly, however, very little literature in the country before the arrival of Augustine, in the end of the sixth century. Augustine is supposed to have established schools at Canterbury; and, about a quarter of a century afterwards, Sigebert, king of the East Angles, who had spent part of his early life in France, is stated by Bede to have, upon his coming to the throne, founded an institution for the instruction of the youth of his dominions similar to those he had seen abroad. The schools planted by Augustine at Canterbury were afterwards greatly extended and improved by his successor, Archbishop Theodore, who obtained the see in 668. Theodore and his learned friend Adrian, Bede informs us, delivered instructions to crowds of pupils, not only in divinity, but also in astronomy, medicine, arithmetic, and the Greek and Latin languages. Bede states that some of the scholars of these accomplished foreigners were alive in his time, to whom the Greek and Latin were as familiar as their mother-tongue. Schools now began to multiply in other parts, and were generally to be found in all the monasteries and at the bishops' seats. Of these episcopal and monastic schools, that founded by Bishop Benedict in his abbey at Wearmouth, where Bede was educated, and that which Archbishop Egbert established at York, were among the most famous. But others of great reputation at a somewhat later date were superintended by learned teachers from Ireland. One was that of Maildulf at Malmesbury. At Glastonbury, also, it is related in one of the ancient lives of St. Dunstan, some Irish ecclesiastics had settled, the books belonging to whom Dunstan is recorded to have diligently studied. The northern parts of the kingdom, moreover, were indebted for the first light of learning as well as of religion to the missionaries from Iona, which was an Irish foundation.

For some ages Ireland was the chief seat of learning in Christian Europe; and the most distinguished scholars who appeared in other countries were mostly either Irish by birth or had received their education in Irish schools. We are informed by Bede that in his day, the earlier part of the eighth century, it was customary for his English fellow-countrymen of all ranks, from the highest to the lowest, to retire for study and devotion to Ireland, where, he adds, they were all hospitably received, and supplied gratuitously with food, with books, and with instruction.* The glory of this age of Irish scholarship and genius is the celebrated Joannes Scotus, or Erigena, as he is as frequently designated,—either appellative equally proclaiming his true birthplace. He is supposed to have first made his appearance in France about the year 845, and to have remained in that country till his death, which appears to have taken place before 875. Erigena is the author of a translation from the Greek of certain mystical works ascribed to Dionysius the Areopagite, which he executed at the command of his patron, the French king, Charles the Bald, and also of several original treatises on metaphysics and theology. His productions may be taken as furnishing clear and conclusive evidence that the Greek language was taught at this time in the Irish schools. Mr. Turner has given a short account of his principal work, his Dialogue De Divisione Naturæ (On the Division of Nature), which he characterises as "distinguished for its Aristotelian acuteness and extensive information." In one place "he takes occasion," it is observed, "to give concise and able definitions of the seven

* Hist. Eccles. iii. 28.

liberal arts, and to express his opinion on the composition of
things. In another part he inserts a very elaborate discussion
on arithmetic, which he says he had learnt from his infancy.
He also details a curious conversation on the elements of things,
on the motions of the heavenly bodies, and other topics of
astronomy and physiology. Among these he even gives the
means of calculating the diameters of the lunar and solar circles.
Besides the fathers Austin, the two Gregories, Chrysostom, Basil,
Epiphanius, Origen, Jerome, and Ambrosius, of whose works,
with the Platonising Dionysius and Maximus, he gives large
extracts, he also quotes Virgil, Cicero, Aristotle, Pliny, Plato,
and Boethius; he details the opinions of Eratosthenes and of
Pythagoras on some astronomical topics; he also cites Martianus
Capella. His knowledge of Greek appears almost in every
page." * The subtle speculations of Erigena have strongly
attracted the notice of the most eminent among the modern
inquirers into the history of opinion and of civilization; and the
German Tenneman agrees with the French Cousin and Guizot in
attributing to them a very extraordinary influence on the philosophy of his own and of succeeding times. To his writings
and translations it is thought may be traced the introduction into
the theology and metaphysics of Europe of the later Platonism
of the Alexandrian school. It is remarkable, as Mr. Moore has
observed, that the learned Mosheim had previously shown the
study of the scholastic or Aristotelian philosophy to have been
also of Irish origin. "That the Hibernians," says that writer,
"who were called Scots in this [the eighth] century, were
lovers of learning, and distinguished themselves in these times
of ignorance by the culture of the sciences beyond all the other
European nations, travelling through the most distant lands,
both with a view to improve and to communicate their knowledge, is a fact with which I have been long acquainted; as we
see them in the most authentic records of antiquity discharging,
with the highest reputation and applause, the function of doctor
in France, Germany, and Italy, both during this and the following century. But that these Hibernians were the first teachers
of the scholastic theology in Europe, and so early as the eighth
century illustrated the doctrines of religion by the principles of
philosophy, I learned but lately."† And then he adduces the
proofs that establish his position.

* Turner, Anglo-Sax. iii. 393.
† Translated in Moore's Ireland, i. 302.

DECAY OF THE EARLIEST ENGLISH SCHOLARSHIP.

It should seem not to be altogether correct to attribute the decline and extinction of the earliest literary civilization of the Angles and Saxons wholly to the Danish invasions. The Northmen did not make their appearance till towards the close of the eighth century, nor did their ravages occasion any considerable public alarm till long after the commencement of the ninth; but for a whole century preceding this date, learning in England appears to have been falling into decay. Bede, who died in 735, exactly ninety-seven years before that landing of the Danes in the Isle of Sheppey, in the reign of Egbert, which was followed by incessant attacks of a similar kind, until the fierce marauders at last won for themselves a settlement in the country, is the last name eminent for scholarship that occurs in this portion of the English annals. The historian William of Malmesbury, indeed, affirms that the death of Bede was fatal to learning in England, and especially to history; "insomuch that it may be said," he adds, writing in the early part of the twelfth century, "that almost all knowledge of past events was buried in the same grave with him, and hath continued in that condition even to our times." "There was not so much as one Englishman," Malmesbury declares, "left behind Bede, who emulated the glory which he had acquired by his studies, imitated his example, or pursued the path to knowledge which he had pointed out. A few, indeed, of his successors were good men, and not unlearned, but they generally spent their lives in an inglorious silence; while the far greater number sunk into sloth and ignorance, until by degrees the love of learning was quite extinguished in this island for a long time."

The devastations of the Danes completed what had probably been begun by the dissensions and confusion that attended the breaking up of the original political system established by the Angles and Saxons, and perhaps also by the natural decay of the national spirit among a race long habituated to a stirring and adventurous life, and now left in undisturbed ease and quiet before the spirit of a new and more intellectual activity had been sufficiently diffused among them. Nearly all the monasteries and the schools connected with them throughout the land were either actually laid in ashes by the northern invaders, or were deserted in the general terror and distraction occasioned by their attacks. When Alfred was a young man, about the middle of the ninth century, he could find no masters to instruct him in any of the higher branches of learning: there were at that time, according to his biographer Asser, few or none among the West Saxons who had any scholarship, or could so much as read with propriety and ease. The reading of the Latin language is probably what is here alluded to. Alfred has himself stated, in the preface to his translation of Gregory's Pastorale, that, though many of the English at his accession could read their native language well enough, the knowledge of the Latin tongue was so much decayed, that there were very few to the south of the Humber who understood the common prayers of the church, or were capable of translating a single sentence of Latin into English; and to the south of the Thames he could not recollect that there was one possessed of this very moderate amount of learning. Contrasting this lamentable state of things with the better days that had gone before, he exclaims, " I wish thee to know that it comes very often into my mind, what wise men there were in England, both laymen and ecclesiastics, and how happy those times were to England! The sacred profession was diligent both to teach and to learn. Men from abroad sought wisdom and learning in this country, though we must now go out of it to obtain knowledge if we should wish to have it."

It was not till he was nearly forty years of age that Alfred himself commenced his study of the Latin language. Before this, however, and as soon as he had rescued his dominions from the hands of the Danes, and reduced these foreign disturbers to subjection, he had exerted himself with his characteristic activity in bringing about the restoration of letters as well as of peace and order. He had invited to his court all the most learned men he could discover anywhere in his native land, and had even brought over instructors for himself and his people from other countries. Werfrith, the bishop of Worcester; Etholstan and Werwulf, two Mercian priests; and Plegmund, also a Mercian, who afterwards became archbishop of Canterbury, were some of the English of whose superior acquirements he thus took advantage. Asser he brought from the western extremity of Wales. Grimbald he obtained from France, having sent an embassy of bishops, presbyters, deacons, and religious laymen, bearing valuable presents to his ecclesiastical superior Fulco, the archbishop of Rheims, to ask permission for the great scholar to be allowed to come to reside in England. And so in other instances, like the bee, looking everywhere for honey, to quote the similitude of his biographer, this admirable prince sought abroad in all directions for the treasure which his own kingdom did not afford.

His labours in translating the various works that have been

mentioned above from the Latin, after he had acquired that language, he seems himself to have been half inclined to regard as to be justified only by the low state into which all learning had fallen among his countrymen in his time, and as likely perhaps to be rather of disservice than otherwise to the cause of real scholarship. Reflecting on the erudition which had existed in the country at a former period, and which had made those volumes in the learned languages useful that now lay unopened, "I wondered greatly," he says in the Preface to his translation of the Pastorale, "that of those good wise men who were formerly in our nation, and who had all learned fully these books, none would translate any part into their own language; but I soon answered myself, and said, they never thought that men could be so reckless, and that learning would be so fallen. They intentionally omitted it, and wished that there should be more wisdom in the land, by many languages being known." He then called to recollection, however, what benefit had been derived by all nations from the translation of the Greek and Hebrew Scriptures, first into Latin, and then into the various modern tongues; and, "therefore," he concludes, "'I think it better, if you think so (he is addressing Wulfsig, the bishop of London), that we also translate some books, the most necessary for all men to know, that we all may know them; and we may do this, with God's help, very easily, if we have peace; so that all the youth that are now in England, who are freemen, and possess sufficient wealth, may for a time apply to no other task till they first well know how to read English. Let those learn Latin afterwards, who will know more, and advance to a higher condition." In this wise and benevolent spirit he acted. The old writers seem to state that, besides the translations that have come down to us, he executed many others that are now lost.

It is probable, though there is no sufficient authority for the statement, that Alfred re-established many of the old monastic and episcopal schools in the various parts of the kingdom. Asser expressly mentions that he founded a seminary for the sons of the nobility, to the support of which he devoted no less than an eighth part of his whole revenue. Hither even some noblemen repaired who had far outgrown their youth, but nevertheless had scarcely or not at all begun their acquaintance with books. In another place Asser speaks of this school, to which Alfred is stated to have sent his own son Ethelward, as being attended not only by the sons of almost all the nobility of the realm, but also by many of the inferior classes. It was provided with several masters. A notion that has been eagerly maintained by some antiquaries is, that this seminary, instituted by Alfred, is to be considered as the foundation of the University of Oxford.

Up to this time absolute illiteracy seems to have been common even among the highest classes of the English. We have just seen that, when Alfred established his schools, they were as much needed for the nobility who had reached an advanced or mature age as for their children; and, indeed, the scheme of instruction seems to have been intended from the first to embrace the former as well as the latter, for, according to Asser's account, every person of rank or substance who, either from age or want of capacity, was unable to learn to read himself, was compelled to send to school either his son or a kinsman, or, if he had neither, a servant, that he might at least be read to by some one. The royal charters, instead of the names of the kings, sometimes exhibit their marks, used, as it is frankly explained, in consequence of their ignorance of letters.

The measures begun by Alfred for effecting the literary civilization of his subjects were probably pursued under his successors; but the period of the next three quarters of a century, notwithstanding some short intervals of repose, was on the whole too troubled to admit of much attention being given to the carrying out of his plans, or even, it may be apprehended, the maintenance of what he had set up. Dunstan, indeed, during his administration, appears to have exerted himself with zeal in enforcing a higher standard of learning as well as of morals, or of asceticism, among the clergy. But the renewal of the Danish wars, after the accession of Ethelred, and the state of misery and confusion in which the country was kept from this cause till its conquest by Canute, nearly forty years after, must have again laid in ruins the greater part of its literary as well as ecclesiastical establishments. The concluding portion of the tenth century was thus, probably, a time of as deep intellectual darkness in England as it was throughout most of the rest of Europe. Under Canute, however, who was a wise as well as a powerful sovereign, the schools no doubt rose again and flourished. We have the testimony, so far as it is to be relied upon, of the history attributed to Ingulphus, which professes to be written immediately after the Norman conquest, and the boyhood of the author of which is made to coincide with the early part of the reign of the Confessor, that at that time seminaries of the higher as well as of elementary learning existed in England. Ingulphus, according to this account, having been born in the city of London, was first sent to school at Westminster; and from Westminster he proceeded to Oxford, where he studied the

Aristotelian philosophy and the rhetorical writings of Cicero. This is the earliest express mention of the University of Oxford, if a passage in Asser's work in which the name occurs be, as is generally supposed, spurious, and if the History passing under his name was really written by Ingulphus.

The studies that were cultivated in those ages were few in number and of very limited scope. Alcuin, in a letter to his patron Charlemagne, has enumerated, in the fantastic rhetoric of the period, the subjects in which he instructed his pupils in the school of St. Martin at Paris. "To some," says he, "I administer the honey of the sacred writings; others I try to inebriate with the wine of the ancient classics. I begin the nourishment of some with the apples of grammatical subtlety. I strive to illuminate many by the arrangement of the stars, as from the painted roof of a lofty palace." In plain language, his instructions embraced grammar, the Greek and Latin languages, astronomy, and theology. In the poem in which he gives an account of his own education at York, the same writer informs us that the studies there pursued comprehended, besides grammar, rhetoric, and poetry, "the harmony of the sky, the labour of the sun and moon, the five zones, the seven wandering planets; the laws, risings, and settings of the stars, and the aërial motions of the sea; earthquakes; the nature of man, cattle, birds, and wild beasts, with their various kinds and forms; and the sacred Scriptures."

THE ENGLISH LANGUAGE.

The earliest historically known fact with regard to the English language is, that it was the language generally, if not universally, spoken by the barbaric invaders, apparently for the greater part of one race or blood, though of different tribes, who, upon the breaking up of the empire of the West in the fifth century, came over in successive throngs from the opposite continent, and, after a protracted struggle, acquired the possession and dominion of the principal portion of the province of Britain. They are stated to have consisted chiefly of Angles and Saxons. But, although it is usual to designate them rather by the general denomination of the Saxons, or Anglo-Saxons, it is probable that the Saxons were in reality only a section of the Angles. The *Angles*, of which term our modern *English* is only another form, appears to have been always recognized among themselves as the proper national appellation. They both concurred, Angles and Saxons alike, after their establishment in Britain, in calling their common country *Angle-land*, or *England*, and their common language *English*—that is, the language of the Angles,—as there can be little doubt it had been called from the time when it first became known as a distinct form of human speech.

This English language, since become so famous, is ordinarily regarded as belonging to the Low-Germanic, or middle, group of the Gothic tongues. That is to say, it is classed with the Dutch and the Flemish, and the dialects generally of the more northern and low-lying part of what was anciently called Germany, under which name were included the countries that we call Holland and the Netherlands, as well as that to which it is now more especially confined. It appears to have been from this middle region, lying directly opposite to Britain, that the Angles and Saxons and other tribes by whom the English language was brought over to that island chiefly came. At any rate, they certainly did not come from the more elevated region of Southern Germany. Nor does the language present the distinguishing characteristics of a High-Germanic tongue. What is now called the German language, therefore, though of the same Gothic stock, belongs to a different branch from our own. We are only distantly related to the Germans proper, or the race among whom the language and literature now known as the German have originated and grown up. We are, at least in respect of language, more nearly akin to the Dutch and the Flemings than we are to the Germans. It may even be doubted if the English language ought not to be regarded as having more of a Scandinavian than of a purely Germanic character,—as, in other words, more nearly resembling the Danish or Swedish than the modern German. The invading bands by whom it was originally brought over to Britain in the fifth and sixth centuries were in all probability drawn in great part from the Scandinavian countries. At a later date, too, the population of England was directly recruited from Denmark, and the other regions around the Baltic to a large extent. From about the middle of the ninth century the population of all the eastern and northern parts of the country was as much Danish as English. And soon after the beginning of the eleventh century the sovereignty was acquired by the Danes.

The English language, although reckoned among modern languages, is already of respectable antiquity. In one sense, indeed, all languages may be held to be equally ancient; for we can in no case get at the beginning of a language, any more than we can get at the beginning of a lineage. Each is merely the con-

c

tinuation of a preceding one, from which it cannot be separated in any case except by a purely arbitrary mark of distinction. Take two portions of the line at some distance from one another, and they may be very unlike; yet the change which has transformed the one into the other, or produced the one out of the other, has been, even when most active, so gradual, so perfectly free always from anything that can be called a convulsion or catastrophe, so merely a process of growth, however varying in its rate of rapidity, that there is no precise point at which it can be said to have begun. This is undoubtedly the way in which all languages have come into existence; they have all thus grown out of older forms of speech: none of them have been manufactured or invented. It would seem that human skill could as soon invent a tree as invent a language. The one as well as the other is essentially a natural production.

But, taking a particular language to mean what has always borne the same name, or been spoken by the same nation or race, which is the common or conventional understanding of the matter, the English may claim to be older than the great majority of the tongues now in use throughout Europe. The Basque, perhaps, and the various Celtic dialects might take precedence of it; but hardly any others. No one of the still spoken Germanic or Scandinavian languages could make out a distinct proof of its continuous existence from an equally early date. And the Romance tongues, the Italian, the Spanish, the French, are all, recognized as such, confessedly of much later origin.

The English language is recorded to have been known by that name, and to have been the national speech of the same race, at least since the middle of the fifth century. It was then, as we have seen, that the first settlers by whom it was spoken established themselves in the country of which their descendants have ever since retained possession. Call them either Angles (that is, English) or Saxons, it makes no difference; it is clear that, whether or no the several divisions of the invaders were all of one blood, all branches of a common stock, they spoke all substantially the same language, the proper name of which, as has been stated, was the *Anglish*, or *English*, as *England*, or *Angle-land* (the land of the Angles), was the name which the country received from its new occupants. And these names of *England* and *English* the country and the language have each retained ever since.

Nor can it be questioned that the same tongue was spoken by the same race, or races, long before their settlement in Britain. The Angles figure as one of the nations occupying the forest land of Germany in the picture of that country sketched by Tacitus in the first century of our era.

The most distinct and satisfactory record, however, of a language is afforded by what exists of it in a written form. In applying this test or measure of antiquity, the reasonable rule would seem to be, that, wherever we have the clear beginning or end of a distinct body or continuous series of literary remains, there we have the beginning or end of a language. Thus, of what is called the Mœsogothic we have no written remains of later date than the fourth century (or, at any rate, than the sixth, if we reckon from what is probably the true age of the transcripts which we actually possess); and accordingly we hold the Mœsogothic to be a language which has passed away and perished, notwithstanding that there may be some other language or languages still existing of which there is good reason to look upon it as having been the progenitor. But of the English language we have a continuous succession of written remains since the seventh century at least; that is to say, we have an array of specimens of it from that date such as that no two of them standing next to one another in the order of time could possibly be pronounced to belong to different languages, but only at most to two successive stages of the same language. They afford us a record or representation of the language in which there is no gap. This cannot be said of any other existing European tongue for nearly so great a length of time, unless we may except the two principal Celtic tongues, the Welsh and the Irish.

The movement of the language, however, during this extended existence, has been immense. No language ever ceases to move until it becomes what is called dead, which term, although commonly understood to mean merely that the language has ceased to be spoken, really signifies, here as elsewhere, that the life is gone out of it, which is indeed the unfailing accompaniment of its ceasing to be used as an oral medium of communication. It cannot grow after that, even if it should still continue to a certain extent to be used in writing, as has been the case with the Sanscrit in the East and the Latin in the West,—except perhaps as the hair and the nails are said sometimes to grow after the animal body is dead. It is only speaking that keeps a language alive; writing alone will not do it. That has no more than a conservative function and effect; the progressive power, the element of fermentation and change, in a language is its vocal utterance.

We shall find that the English language, moving now faster,

now slower, throughout the twelve or thirteen centuries over which our knowledge of it extends, although it has never been all at once or suddenly converted from one form into another—which is what the nature of human speech forbids—has yet within that space undergone at least *two* complete revolutions, or, in other words, presents itself to us in *three* distinct forms.

Original English:—
commonly called SAXON, or ANGLO-SAXON.

The English which the Angles and Saxons brought over with them from the Continent, when they came and took possession of the greater part of South Britain in the fifth and sixth centuries, differed from the English that we now speak and write in two important respects. It was an unmixed language; and it was what is called a synthetic, in contradistinction to an analytic, language. Its vocables were all of one stock or lineage; and it expressed the relations of nouns and verbs, not by separate words, called auxiliaries and particles, but by terminational or other modifications,—that is, by proper conjugation and declension,—as our present English still does when it says, *I loved* instead of *I did love*, or *The King's throne* instead of *The throne of the King*. These two characteristics are what constitute it a distinct form, or stage, of the language:—its synthetic or generally inflected grammatical structure, and its homogeneous vocabulary.

As a subject of philological study the importance of this earliest known form of the English language cannot be overestimated; and much of what we possess written in it is also of great value for the matter. But the essential element of a literature is not matter, but manner. Here too, as in everything else, the soul of the artistic is form;—beauty of form. Now of that what has come down to us written in this primitive English is, at least for us of the present day, wholly or all but wholly destitute.

There is much writing in forms of human speech now extinct, or no longer in oral use, which is still intelligible to us in a certain sort, but in a certain sort only. It speaks to us as anything that is dead can speak to us, and no otherwise. We can decipher it, rather than read it. We make it out as it were merely by the touch, getting some such notion of it as a blind man might get of a piece of sculpture by passing his hand over it. This, for instance, to take an extreme case, is the position in which we stand in reference to the hieroglyphic inscriptions on the ancient monuments of Egypt. They can be read as the multiplication table can be read. But that is all. There may be nothing more in them than there is in the multiplication table; but if there were, we could not get at it. M. Champollion, indeed, in his enthusiasm, saw a vision of an amatory or bacchanalian song laughing under the venerable veil of one of them; but it is plain that this must have been an illusion. A mummy from one of the neighbouring tombs, embalmed some three or four thousand years ago, might almost as soon be expected to give forth a living voice.

Even the ancient Assyrian inscriptions, which are in alphabetical characters, will certainly never be made to render up to us more than the dead matters of fact that may be buried in them. If there be any grace in the manner in which the facts are related, any beauty of style in the narrative, it has perished irretrievably. But this is what also appears to happen, in a greater or less degree, in the case even of a language the vocabulary of which we have completely in our possession, and which we are therefore quite able to interpret so far as regards the substance of anything written in it, whenever it has for some time—for a single generation, it may be—ceased both to be spoken and to be written. Something is thus lost, which seems to be irrecoverable. The two great classic tongues, it is to be observed, the old Greek and Latin, although they have both long passed out of popular use, have always continued to be not only studied and read by all cultivated minds throughout Europe, but to be also extensively employed by the learned, at least in writing. And this has proved enough to maintain the modern world in what may be called a living acquaintance with them—such an acquaintance as we have with a person we have conversed with, or a place where we have actually been, as distinguished from our dimmer conception of persons and places known to us only by description. The ancient classic literature charms us as well as informs us. It addresses itself to the imagination, and to our sense of the beautiful, as well as to the understanding. It has shape, and colour, and voice for us, as well as more substance. Every word, and every collocation of words, carries with it a peculiar meaning, or effect, which is still appreciated. The whole, in short, is felt and enjoyed, not simply interpreted. But a language, which has passed from what we may call its natural condition of true and full vitality as a national speech cannot, apparently, be thus far preserved, with something of the pulse of life still beating in it, merely by such a knowledge of it being kept up as enables us to read and translate it. Still less can a language, the very reading of which has been for a time suspended, and consequently all knowledge whatever of it forgotten, ever be restored to even the appearance of life. It has become a fossil, and cannot be resuscitated, but only dug up. A thousand facts warrant us in saying that languages, and even words, are subject to decay and dissolution as well as the human beings of whose combined mental and physical organizations they are the mysterious product; and that, once really dead, nothing can reanimate their dust or reclothe their dry bones with flesh.

The original form of the English language is in this state. It is intelligible, but that is all. What is written in it can, in a certain sense, be read, but not so as to bring out from the most elaborate compositions in it any artistic element, except of the most dubious and unsatisfactory kind. Either such an element is not present in any considerable degree, or the language is not now intimately enough known for any one to be able to detect it. If it is not literally dumb, its voice has for us of the present day entirely lost its music. Even of the system of measure and arrangement according to which it is ordinarily disposed for the purposes of poetry we have no proper apprehension or feeling. Certain mechanical principles or rules may have been discovered in obedience to which the versification appears to be constructed; but the verse as verse remains not the less for our ears and hearts wholly voiceless. When it can be distinguished from prose at all it is only by certain marks or characteristics which may indeed be perceived by the eye, or counted on the fingers, but which have no expression that excites in us any mental emotion. It is little better than if the composition merely had the words "This is verse" written over it or under it.

In respect of everything else appertaining to the soul of the language, our understanding of it is about equally imperfect. The consequence is, that, although it can be translated, it cannot be written. The late Mr. Conybeare, indeed, has left us a few specimens of verse in it of his own composition; but his attempts are of the slightest character, and, unadventurous as they are, nobody can undertake to say, except as to palpable points of right or wrong in grammar, whether they are well or ill done. The language, though so far in our hands as to admit of being analyzed in grammars and packed up in dictionaries, is not recoverable in such a degree as to make it possible to pronounce with certainty whether anything written in it is artistically good or bad. As for learning to speak it, that is a thing as little dreamt of as learning to speak the language of Swift's Houyhnhnms.

When the study of this original form of the national speech was revived in England in the middle of the sixteenth century, it had been for well-nigh four hundred years not only what is commonly called a dead language, but a buried and an utterly forgotten one. It may be questioned if at least for three preceding centuries any one had been able to read it. It was first recurred to as a theological weapon. Much in the same manner as the Reformers generally were drawn to the study of the Greek language in maintaining the accordance of their doctrines with those of the New Testament and of the first ages of Christianity, the English Reformers turned to the oldest writings in the vernacular tongue for evidence of the comparatively unromanized condition of the early English church. In the next age history and law began to receive illustration from the same source. It was not till a considerably later date that the recovered language came to be studied with much of a special view to its literary and philological interest. And it is only within the present century that it has either attracted any attention in other countries, or been investigated on what are now held to be sound principles. The specially theological period of its cultivation may be regarded as extending over the latter half of the sixteenth century, the legal and historical period over the whole of the seventeenth, the philological of the old school over the whole of the eighteenth, and the philological of the modern school over the nineteenth, so far as it has gone.

If the English language as it was written a thousand years ago had been left to itself, and no other action from without had interfered with that of its spontaneous growth or inherent principles of change and development, it might not have remained so stationary as some more highly-cultivated languages have done throughout an equal space of time, but its form in the nineteenth century would in all probability have been only a comparatively slight modification of what it was in the ninth. It would have been essentially the same language. As the case stands, the English of the ninth century is one language, and the English of the nineteenth century another. They differ at least as much as the Italian differs from the Latin, or as English differs from German. The most familiar acquaintance with the one leaves the other unintelligible. So much is this so that it has long been customary to distinguish them by different names, and to call the original form of the national speech Saxon, or Anglo-Saxon, as if it were not English at all. If the notion be that the dialect in which most of the ancient English that has come down to us is written in that which was in use among the specially Saxon part of the population, that would have been better indicated by calling it, not Anglo-Saxon, but Saxon English. But even such a designation would be inapplicable to those specimens of the language in which there is unquestionably nothing whatever that is specially Saxon, and which recent investigations have shown to be not inconsiderable in amount, as well as of high philological importance; and it would also leave the limitation of the name *English* to the more modern form of the language without any warrant in the facts of the case. Objectionable, however, as may be the common nomenclature, it is still indisputable that we have here, for all practicable purposes, not one language, but two languages. The one may have grown out of the other, and no doubt has done so at least in part or in the main; but in part also the modern language is of quite a distinct stock from the ancient. Of English Literature, therefore, and the English Language, commonly so called, the language and literature of the Angles and Saxons before the twelfth century make no proper part.

THE NORMAN CONQUEST.

The year 1066 is memorable as that of the Norman Conquest, —the conquest of England by the Normans. The conquests of which we read in the history of nations are of three kinds. Sometimes one population has been overwhelmed by or driven before another as it might have been by an inundation of the sea, or at the most a small number of the old inhabitants of the invaded territory have been permitted to remain on it as the bondsmen of their conquerors. This appears to have been the usual mode of proceeding of the barbarous races, as we call them, by which the greater part of Europe was occupied in early times, in their contests with one another. When the Touton or Goth from the one side of the Rhine attacked the Celt on the other side, the whole tribe precipitated itself upon what was the object at once of its hostility and of its cupidity. Or even if it was one division of the great Gothic race that made war upon another, as, for instance, the Scandinavian upon any Germanic country, the course that was taken was commonly, or at least frequently, the same. The land was cleared by driving away all who could fly, and the universal massacre of the rest. This primitive kind of invasion and conquest belonged properly to the night of barbarism, but in certain of the extreme parts of the European system something of it survived down to a comparatively late date. Much that we are told of the manner in which

Britain was wrested from its previous Celtic occupants by the Angles and Saxons in the fifth and sixth centuries of our era would lead us to think that the enterprise of these invaders was both originally conceived and conducted throughout in this spirit. Nay, for some centuries after this we have the Danes in their descents and inroads upon all parts of the British territories still acting, apparently, in the same style. But, ever from the time of the settlement of the barbarous nations in the more central provinces of the old Roman empire, another kind of conquest had come into use among them. Corrupted and enfeebled as it was, the advanced civilization which they now encountered seems to have touched them as with a spell, or rather could not but communicate to its assailants something of its own spirit. A policy of mere destruction was evidently not the course to be adopted here. The value of the conquest lay mainly in preserving as far as possible both the stupendous material structures and the other works of art by which the soil was everywhere covered and adorned, and the living intelligence and skill of which all these wonders were the product. Hence the second kind of conquest, in which for the first time the conquerors were contented to share the conquered country, usually according to a strictly defined proportional division, with its previous occupants. But this system too was only transitory. It passed away with the particular crisis which gave birth to it; and then arose the third and last kind of conquest, in which there is no general occupation of the soil of the conquered country by the conquerors, but only its dominion is acquired by them.

The first of the three kinds of conquest, then, has for its object and effect the complete displacement of the ancient inhabitants. It is the kind which is proper to the contests of barbarians with barbarians. Under the second form of conquest the conquerors, recognizing a superiority to themselves in many other things even in those whom their superior force or ferocity has subdued, feel that they will gain most by foregoing something of their right to the wholesale seizure and appropriation of the soil, and neither wholly destroying or expelling its ancient possessors, nor even reducing them to a state of slavery, but only treating them as a lower caste. This is the form proper and natural to the exceptional and rare case of the conquest of a civilized by a barbarous people. Finally, there is that kind of subjugation of one people or country by another which results simply in the overthrow of the independence of the former, and the substitution in it or over it of a foreign for a native government. This is generally the only kind of conquest which attends upon the wars of civilized nations with one another.

The conquest of England by the Normans in the year 1066 may be regarded as having been professedly a conquest of this last description. The age of both the first and the second kinds of conquest was over, at least everywhere throughout Europe except it may be only along some few portions of its extreme northern boundary. Both the English and the Normans stood indisputably within the pale of civilization, the former boasting the possession both of Christianity and of a national literature for four or five centuries, the latter, if more recently reclaimed from paganism and barbarism, nevertheless already recognized as one of the most brilliantly gifted of European races, and distinguished for their superior aptitude in the arts both of war and of peace, of polity and of song. And the Norman leader, having with him in his enterprise the approval and sanction of the Church, claimed the English crown as his by right; nor were there probably wanting many Englishmen, although no doubt the general national feeling was different, who held his claim to be fully as good in law and justice as that of his native competitor. In taking the style of the Conqueror with respect to England, as he had been wont to take that of the Bastard with reference to his ancestral Normandy, William, as has been often explained, probably meant nothing more than that he had acquired his English sovereignty for himself, by the nomination or bequest of his relation King Edward, or in whatever other way, and had not succeeded to it under the ordinary rule of descent. Such a right of property is still, in the old feudal language, technically described in the law of Scotland as acquired by conquest, and in that of England by purchase, which is etymologically of the same meaning,—the one word being the Latin *Conquæstus*, or *Conquisitio*, the other *Perquisitio*.

And in point of fact the Normans never transferred themselves in a body, or generally, to England. They did not, like the barbarous populations of a preceding age, abandon for this new country the one in which they had previously dwelt. England was never thus taken possession of by the Normans. It was never colonized by these foreigners, or occupied by them in any other than a military sense. The Norman Duke invaded it with an army, raised partly among his own subjects, partly drawn from other regions of the Continent, and so made himself master of it. It received a foreign government, but not at all a new population.

Two causes, however, meeting from opposite points, and working together, soon produced a result which was to some extent the same that would have been produced by a Norman colonization. The first was the natural demand on the part of William's followers or fellow-soldiers for a share in the profits and advantages of their common enterprise, which would probably in any case have compelled him eventually to surrender his new subjects to spoliation; the second was the equally natural restlessness of the latter under the foreign yoke that had been imposed upon them, by which they only facilitated the process of their general reduction to poverty and ruin.

And to the overthrow thus brought about of the native civilization was added, in the present case, the intrusion of another system of social organization, and of another language possessing also its own literature, to take the place of what was passing away. So that here again were two distinct forces harmoniously, though by movements in opposite directions, co-operating to a common end. At the same time that English culture shrunk and faded, Norman culture flourished and advanced. And the two forces were not balanced or in any way connected, but quite independent the one of the other. English culture went down, not under the disastrous influence of the rival light, but from the failure of its own natural aliment, or because the social structure of which it was the product had been smitten with universal disorganization. It was the withering of life throughout the whole frame that made the eye dim.

The difference, then, between the case of England conquered by the Normans in the eleventh century and that of Italy overrun by the Goths in the fifth, was twofold. First, the Normans did not settle in England, as the barbarous nations of the North did in Italy and other provinces of the subjugated Western empire; but, secondly, on the other hand, the new power which the Norman invasion and conquest of England established in the country was not a barbarism, but another civilization in most respects at least as advanced as the indigenous one;—if younger, only therefore the stronger and more aspiring, and yet, as it proved, not differing so far from that with which it was brought into competition as to be incapable of coalescing with it, if need were, as well as, in other circumstances, with its advantages of position, outshining it or casting it into the shade.

In this way it came to pass that the final result to both the language and the literature of the conquered people was pretty much the same in the two cases. What the barbaric influence, in its action upon the Latin language and literature, wanted of positive vital force it made up for by its mass and weight; the Norman influence, on the contrary, compensated by quality for its deficiency in quantity. There was considerable difference, however, in the process by which the transformation was effected in the two cases, and in the length of time which it occupied. The Gothic barbarism was in the first instance simply destructive; it was not till after some centuries that it came to be visibly or appreciably anything else. But the Norman influence, in virtue of being that, not of a barbarism, but of a civilization, and especially of a civilization still in all the radiant bloom and buoyant pride of youth, never could have been directly destructive; from the first moment of their actual contact it must have communicated to the native civilization something of new life.

One thing further may be noted. In both the cases that we have been comparing the result was the combination, both in the language and the literature, of the same two elements; namely, the Latin (or Classical) and the Gothic (or Germanic, in the largest sense). But the important difference was, that, the basis of the combination remaining in each case what it originally was,—Latin in Italy, in France, in Spain, but Gothic in England—while the language and literature that grew up in each of the former countries came to be in general spirit and character what is called Romance, which must be understood to mean modified Roman, the English language and literature retained their original fundamentally Gothic character, only modified by so much as it has absorbed of a Latin element.

And the remarkable distinction of the English language is, that it is the only one of all the languages of the European world which, thus combining the two elements of the Classic and the Gothic—that is, as we may say, of ancient and of modern civilization—is Gothic, or modern, in its skeleton, or bony system, and in its formative principle, and Classic, or antique, only in what of it is comparatively superficial and non-essential. The other living European languages are either without the Classic element altogether, as are all those of the Scandinavian and Teutonic branches, or have it as their principal and governing element, as is the case with the Italian, the French, and the Spanish, which may all be described as only modernized forms of the Latin. Even in the proportion, too, in which the two elements are combined the English has greatly the advantage over these Romance tongues, as they are called, in none of which is there more than a mere sprinkling of the modern element, whereas in English, although here that constitutes the dominant or more active portion of the compound, the counterpoising ingredient is also present in large quantity, and is influential to a very high degree upon the general character of the language.

It should seem to follow from all this, that, both in its inner spirit and in its voice, both in its constructional and in its musical genius, the English language, and, through that, English literature, English civilization or culture generally, and the whole temper of the English mind, ought to have a capacity of sympathizing at once with the Classical and the Gothic, with the antique and the modern, with the past and the present, to an extent not to be matched by any other speech or nation of Europe.

It so happens, too, that the political fortunes of this English tongue have been in singular accordance with its constitution and natural adaptation, inasmuch as, at the same time that it stands in this remarkable position in the Old World, its position is still more pre-eminent in the New World, whether that designation be confined to the continent of America or understood as including the entire field of modern colonization in every quarter of the globe. The English are the only really colonizing people now extant. As we remember Coleridge once expressing it, it is the natural destiny of their country, as an island, to be the mother of nations. Their geographical position, concurring with their peculiar genius, and with all the other favourable circumstances of the case, gives them the command of the readiest access to the most distant parts of the earth,—a universal highway, almost as free as is the air to the swarming bees. And, accordingly, all the greatest communities of the future, whether they be seated beyond the Atlantic or beyond the Pacific, promise to be communities of English blood and English speech.

Arabic and other New Learning.

The space of about a thousand years, extending from the overthrow of the Western Roman empire, in the middle of the fifth century, to that of the Eastern, in the middle of the fifteenth, may be divided into two nearly equal parts; the first of which may be considered as that of the gradual decline, the second as that of the gradual revival of letters. The former, reaching to the close of the tenth century, nearly corresponds, in its close as well as in its commencement, with the domination in England of the Angles and Saxons. In Europe generally, throughout this long space of time, the intellectual darkness, notwithstanding some brief and partial revivals, deepens more and more on the whole, in the same manner as in the natural day the gray of evening passes into the gloom of midnight. The Latin learning, properly so called, may be regarded as terminating with Boethius, who wrote in the early part of the sixth century. The Latin language, however, continued to be used in literary compositions, as well as in the services of the Church, both in our own country and in the other parts of Europe that had composed the old empire of Rome.

The Danish conquest of England, as completed by the accession of Canute, preceded the Norman by exactly half a century, and throughout this space, the country had, with little interruption, enjoyed a government which, if not always national,—and it was that too for rather more than half of the fifty years—was at any rate acknowledged and submitted to by the whole nation. The public tranquillity was scarcely ever disturbed for more than a moment by any internal commotion, and never at all by attacks from abroad. During this interval, therefore, many of the monastic and other schools that had existed in the days of Alfred, Athelstan, and Edgar, but had been swept away or allowed to fall into decay in the disastrous forty years that succeeded the decease of the last-mentioned monarch, were probably re-established. The more frequent communication with the Continent that began in the reign of the Confessor must also have been favourable to the intellectual advancement of the country. The dawn of the revival of letters in England, therefore, may be properly dated from a point about fifty years antecedent to the Norman Conquest, or from not very long after the commencement of the eleventh century.

Still at the date of the Conquest the country was undoubtedly in regard to everything intellectual in a very backward state. Ordericus Vitalis, almost a contemporary writer, and himself a native of England, though educated abroad, describes his countrymen generally as having been found by the Normans a rustic and almost illiterate people (*agrestes et pene illiteratos*). The last epithet may be understood as chiefly intended to characterize the clergy, for the great body of the laity at this time were everywhere illiterate. A few years after the Conquest, the king took advantage of the general illiteracy of the native clergy to deprive great numbers of them of their benefices, and to supply their places with foreigners. His real or his only motive for making this substitution may possibly not have been that which he avowed; but he would scarcely have alleged what was notoriously not the fact, even as a pretence.

The Norman Conquest introduced a new state of things in this as in most other respects. That event made England, as it were, a part of the Continent, where, not long before, a revival of letters had taken place scarcely less remarkable, if we take into consideration the circumstances of the time, than the next great revolution of the same kind in the beginning of the fifteenth century. In France, indeed, the learning that had flourished in the time of Charlemagne had never undergone so great a decay as had befallen that of England since the days of Alfred. The schools planted by Alcuin and the philosophy taught by Erigena had both been perpetuated by a line of the disciples and followers of these distinguished masters, which had never been altogether interrupted. But in the tenth century this learning of the West had met and been intermixed with a new learning originally from the East, but obtained directly from the Arab conquerors of Spain. The Arabs had first become acquainted with the literature of Greece in the beginning of the eighth century, and it instantly exercised upon their minds an awakening influence of the same powerful kind with that with which it again kindled Europe seven centuries afterwards. One difference, however, between the two cases is very remarkable. The mighty effects that arose out of the second revival of the ancient Greek literature in the modern world were produced almost solely by its eloquence and poetry; but these were precisely the parts of it that were neglected by the Arabs. The Greek books which they sought after with such extraordinary avidity were almost exclusively those that related either to metaphysics and mathematics on the one hand, or to medicine, chemistry, botany, and the other departments of physical knowledge, on the other. All Greek works of these descriptions that they could procure they not only translated into their own language, but in course of time illustrated with voluminous commentaries. The prodigious magnitude to which this Arabic literature eventually grew will stagger the reader who has adopted the common notion with regard to what are called the middle or the dark ages. "The royal library of the Fatimites" (sovereigns of Egypt), says Gibbon, "consisted of 100,000 manuscripts, elegantly transcribed and splendidly bound, which were lent, without jealousy or avarice, to the students of Cairo. Yet this collection must appear moderate if we can believe that the Ommiades of Spain had formed a library of 600,000 volumes, 44 of which were employed in the mere catalogues. Their capital Cordova, with the adjacent towns of Malaga, Almeria, and Murcia, had given birth to more than 300 writers, and above 70 public libraries were opened in the cities of the Andalusian kingdom."* The difficulty we have in conceiving the existence of a state of things such as that here described arises in great part

* Decline and Fall of the Rom. Emp. c. lii.

from the circumstance of the entire disappearance now, and for so long a period, of all this Arabic power and splendour from the scene of European affairs. But, long extinct as it has been, the dominion of the Arabs in Europe was no mere momentary blaze. It lasted, with little diminution, for nearly five hundred years, a period as long as from the age of Chaucer to the present day, and abundantly sufficient for the growth of a body of literature and science even of the wonderful extent that has been described. In the tenth century Arabic Spain was the fountain-head of learning in Europe. Thither students were accustomed to repair from every other country to study in the Arabic schools; and many of the teachers in the chief towns of France and Italy had finished their education in these seminaries, and were now diffusing among their countrymen the new knowledge which they had thence acquired. The writings of several of the Greek authors, also, and especially those of Aristotle, had been made generally known to scholars by Latin versions of them made from the Arabic.

There is no trace of this new literature having found its way to England before the Norman Conquest. But that revolution immediately brought it in its train. "The Conqueror himself," observes a writer who has illustrated this subject with a profusion of curious learning, "patronized and loved letters. He filled the bishoprics and abbacies of England with the most learned of his countrymen, who had been educated at the University of Paris, at that time the most flourishing school in Europe. He placed Lanfranc, abbot of the monastery of St. Stephen at Caen, in the see of Canterbury—an eminent master of logic, the subtleties of which he employed with great dexterity in a famous controversy concerning the real presence. Anselm, an acute metaphysician and theologian, his immediate successor in the same see, was called from the government of the abbey of Bec, in Normandy. Herman, a Norman, bishop of Salisbury, founded a noble library in the ancient cathedral of that see. Many of the Norman prelates preferred in England by the Conqueror were polite scholars. Godfrey, prior of St. Swithin's at Winchester, a native of Cambray, was an elegant Latin epigrammatist, and wrote with the smartness and ease of Martial; a circumstance which, by the way, shows that the literature of the monks at this period was of a more liberal cast than that which we commonly annex to their character and profession."* Geoffrey, also, another learned Norman, came over from the University of

* Warton's Dissertation on Introduction of Learning into England, prefixed to History of English Poetry, p. cxii. (edit. of 1840).

Paris, and established a school at Dunstable, where, according to Matthew Paris, he composed a play, called the Play of St. Catharine, which was acted by his scholars, dressed characteristically in copes borrowed from the sacrist of the neighbouring abbey of St. Albans, of which Geoffrey afterwards became abbot. "The king himself," Warton continues, "gave no small countenance to the clergy, in sending his son Henry Beauclerc to the abbey of Abingdon, where he was initiated in the sciences under the care of the abbot Grimbald, and Faritius, a physician of Oxford. Robert d'Oilly, constable of Oxford Castle, was ordered to pay for the board of the young prince in the convent, which the king himself frequently visited. Nor was William wanting in giving ample revenues to learning. He founded the magnificent abbeys of Battle and Selby, with other smaller convents. His nobles and their successors co-operated with this liberal spirit in erecting many monasteries. Herbert de Losinga, a monk of Normandy, bishop of Thetford in Norfolk, instituted and endowed with large possessions a Benedictine abbey at Norwich, consisting of sixty monks. To mention no more instances, such great institutions of persons dedicated to religious and literary leisure, while they diffused an air of civility, and softened the manners of the people in their respective circles, must have afforded powerful incentives to studious pursuits, and have consequently added no small degree of stability to the interests of learning."*

To this it may be added, that most of the successors of the Conqueror continued to show the same regard for learning of which he had set the example. Nearly all of them had themselves received a learned education. Besides Henry Beauclerc, Henry II., whose father Geoffrey Plantagenet, Earl of Anjou, was famous for his literary acquirements, had been carefully educated under the superintendence of his admirable uncle, the Earl of Gloucester; and he appears to have taken care that his children should not want the advantages he had himself enjoyed; for at least the three oldest, Henry, Geoffrey, and Richard, are all noted for their literary as well as their other accomplishments.

What learning existed, however, was still for the most part confined to the clergy. Even the nobility—although it cannot be supposed that they were left altogether without literary instruction—appear to have been very rarely initiated in any of those branches which were considered as properly constituting the scholarship of the times. The familiar knowledge of the

* Ibid. Some inaccuracies in Warton's account of Geoffrey and his play are corrected from a note by Mr. Douce.

Latin language in particular, which was then the key to all
other erudition, seems to have been almost exclusively confined
to churchmen, and to those few of the laity who embraced the
profession of schoolmasters, as some, at least on the Continent,
were now wont to do. The contemporary writer of a Life of
Becket relates, that when Henry II., in 1164, sent an embassy
to the Pope, in which the Earl of Arundel and three other
noblemen were associated with an archbishop, four bishops, and
three of the royal chaplains, four of the churchmen, at the
audience to which they were admitted, first delivered themselves
in as many Latin harangues; and then the Earl of Arundel stood
up, and made a speech in English, which he began with the
words, "We, who are illiterate laymen, do not understand one
word of what the bishops have said to your holiness."

The notion that learning properly belonged exclusively to the
clergy, and that it was a possession in which the laity were
unworthy to participate, was in some degree the common belief
of the age, and by the learned themselves was almost universally
held as an article of faith that admitted of no dispute. Nothing
can be more strongly marked than the tone of contempt which is
expressed for the mass of the community, the unlearned vulgar,
by the scholars of this period: in their correspondence with one
another especially, they seem to look upon all beyond their own
small circle as beings of an inferior species. This pride of theirs,
however, worked beneficially upon the whole: in the first place,
it was in great part merely a proper estimation of the advantages
of knowledge over ignorance; and, secondly, it helped to make
the man of the pen a match for him of the sword—the natural
liberator of the human race for its natural oppressor. At the
same time, it intimates very forcibly at once the comparative
rarity of the highly prized distinction, and the depth of the
darkness that still reigned far and wide around the few scattered
points of light.

Schools and Universities.

Schools and other seminaries of learning, however, were greatly
multiplied in this age, and were also elevated in their character,
in England as well as elsewhere. Both Archbishop Lanfranc
and his successor Anselm exerted themselves with great zeal in
establishing proper schools in connexion with the cathedrals and
monasteries in all parts of the kingdom; and the object was one
which was also patronized and promoted by the general voice
of the Church. In 1179 it was ordered by the third general

SCHOOLS AND UNIVERSITIES.

council of Lateran, that in every cathedral there should be appointed and maintained a head teacher, or scholastic, as was the title given to him, who, besides keeping a school of his own, should have authority over all the other schoolmasters of the diocese, and the sole right of granting licences, without which no one should be entitled to teach. In former times the bishop himself had frequently undertaken the office of scholastic of the diocese; but its duties were rarely efficiently performed under that arrangement, and at length they seem to have come to be generally altogether neglected. After the custom was introduced of maintaining it as a distinct office, it was filled in many cases by the most learned persons of the time. And besides these cathedral schools there were others established in all the religious houses, many of which were also of high reputation. It is reckoned that of religious houses of all kinds there were founded no fewer than five hundred and fifty-seven between the Conquest and the death of King John; and, besides these, there still existed many others that had been founded in earlier times. All these cathedral and conventual schools, however, appear to have been intended exclusively for the instruction of persons proposing to make the Church their profession. But mention is also made of others established both in many of the principal cities and even in the villages, which would seem to have been open to the community at large; for it may be presumed that the laity, though generally excluded from the benefits of a learned education, were not left wholly without the means of obtaining some elementary instruction. Some of these city schools, however, were eminent as institutes of the highest departments of learning. One in particular is mentioned in the History ascribed to Matthew Paris as established in the town of St. Albans, which was presided over by Matthew, a physician, who had been educated at the famous school of Salerno, in Italy, and by his nephew Garinus, who was eminent for his knowledge of the civil and canon laws, and where we may therefore suppose instructions were given both in law and in medicine. According to the account of London by William Stephanides, or Fitz-Stephen, written in the reign of Henry II., there were then three of these schools of a higher order established in London, besides several others that were occasionally opened by distinguished teachers. The London schools, however, do not seem to have been academies of science and the higher learning, like that of St. Albans: Fitz-Stephen's description would rather lead us to infer that, although they were attended by pupils of different ages and degrees of proficiency, they were merely schools of grammar, rhetoric, and dialectics. "On holidays," he says, "it is usual for these schools to hold public assemblies in the churches, in which the scholars engage in demonstrative or logical disputations, some using enthymems, and others perfect syllogisms; some aiming at nothing but to gain the victory, and make an ostentatious display of their acuteness, while others have the investigation of truth in view. Artful sophists on these occasions acquire great applause; some by a prodigious inundation and flow of words, others by their specious but fallacious arguments. After the disputations other scholars deliver rhetorical declamations, in which they observe all the rules of art, and neglect no topic of persuasion. Even the younger boys in the different schools contend against each other, in verse, about the principles of grammar, and the preterites and supines of verbs."

The twelfth century may be considered as properly the age of the institution of what we now call Universities in Europe, though many of the establishments that then assumed the regular form of universities had undoubtedly existed long before as schools or *studia*. This was the case with the oldest of the European universities, with Bologna and Paris, and also, in all probability, with Oxford and Cambridge. But it may be questioned if even Bologna, the mother of all the rest, was entitled by any organization or constitution it had received to take a higher name than a school or *studium* before the latter part of this century. It is admitted that it was not till about the year 1200 that the school out of which the University of Paris arose had come to subsist as an incorporation, divided into nations, and presided over by a rector.[*] The University of Oxford, properly so called, is probably of nearly the same antiquity. It seems to have been patronized and fostered by Richard I., as that of Paris was by his great rival, Philip Augustus. Both Oxford and Cambridge had undoubtedly been eminent seats of learning long before this time, as London, St. Albans, and other cities had also been; but there is no evidence that either the one or the other had at an earlier date become anything more than a great school, or even that it was distinguished by any assigned rank or privileges above the other great schools of the kingdom. In the reign of Richard I. we find the University of Oxford recognized as an establishment of the same kind with the University of Paris, and as the rival of that seminary.

We have the following account of what is commonly deemed the origin of the University of Cambridge in the continuation of

[*] See Crevier, Hist. de l'Univ. de Paris, I. 235.

the history of Ingulphus, attributed to Peter of Blois, under the year 1109:—" Joffrid, abbot of Croyland, sent to his manor of Cottenham, near Cambridge, Master Gislebert, his fellow monk, and professor of theology, with three other monks who had followed him into England; who, being very well instructed in philosophical theorems and other primitive sciences, went every day to Cambridge, and, having hired a certain public barn, taught the sciences openly, and in a little time collected a great concourse of scholars; for, in the very second year after their arrival, the number of their scholars from the town and country increased so much that there was no house, barn, nor church capable of containing them. For this reason they separated into different parts of the town, and, imitating the plan of the Studium of Orleans, brother Odo, who was eminent as a grammarian and satirical poet, read grammar, according to the doctrine of Priscian and of his commentator Remigius, to the boys and younger students, that were assigned to him, early in the morning. At one o'clock, brother Terricus, a most acute sophist, read the Logic of Aristotle, according to the Introductions and Commentaries of Porphyry and Averroes,* to those who were further advanced. At three, brother William read lectures on Tully's Rhetoric and Quintilian's Institutions. But Master Gislebert, being ignorant of the English, but very expert in the Latin and French languages, preached in the several churches to the people on Sundays and holidays."† The history in which this passage occurs is, as will presently be shown, as apocryphal as that of which it professes to be the continuation; but even if we waive the question of its authenticity, there is here no hint of any sort of incorporation or public establishment whatever; the description is merely that of a school set on foot and conducted by an association of private individuals. And even this private school would seem to have been first opened only in the year 1109, although there may possibly have been other schools taught in the place before. It may be gathered from what is added, that at the time when the account, if it was written by Peter of Blois, must have been drawn up (the latter part of the same century), the school founded by Gislebert and his companions had attained to great celebrity; but there is

* The works of Averroes, however, who died in 1198, were certainly not in existence at the time here referred to. Either Peter of Blois must have been ignorant of this, or—if he was really the author of the statement—the name must have been the insertion of some later transcriber of his text.

† Petri Blesensis Continuatio ad Historiam Ingulphi: in Rerum Anglicarum Script. Vet.: Oxon. 1684, p. 114. The translation is that given by Henry in his History of Britain.

nothing to lead us to suppose that it had even then become more than a very distinguished school. "From this little fountain," he says, "which hath swelled into a great river, we now behold the city of God made glad, and all England rendered fruitful, by many teachers and doctors issuing from Cambridge, after the likeness of the holy Paradise."

Notwithstanding, however, the rising reputation of Oxford and Cambridge, the most ambitious of the English students continued to resort for part of their education to the more distinguished foreign schools during the whole of the twelfth century. Thus, it is recorded that several volumes of the Arabian philosophy were brought into England by Daniel Merlac, who, in the year 1185, had gone to Toledo to study mathematics. Salerno was still the chief school of medicine, and Bologna of law, although Oxford was also becoming famous for the latter study. But, as a place of general instruction, the University of Paris stood at the head of all others. Paris was then wont to be styled, by way of pre-eminence, the City of Letters. So many Englishmen, or, to speak more strictly, subjects of the English crown, were constantly found among the students at this great seminary, that they formed one of the four nations into which the members of the university were divided. The English students are described by their countryman, the poet Nigellus Wireker, in the latter part of the twelfth century, in such a manner as to show that they were already noted for that spirit of display and expense which still makes so prominent a part of our continental reputation:—

<blockquote>
Moribus egregii, verbo vultuque venusti,
Ingenio pollent, consilioque vigent;
Dona pluunt populis, et detestantur avaros,
Fercula multiplicant, et sine lege bibunt.*
</blockquote>

<blockquote>
Of noble manners, gracious look and speech,
Strong sense, with genius brightened, shines in each.
Their free hand still rains largess; when they dine
Course follows course, in rivers flows the wine.
</blockquote>

Among the students at the University of Paris in the twelfth century are to be found nearly all the most distinguished names among the learned of every country. One of the teachers, the celebrated Abelard, is said to have alone had as pupils twenty persons who afterwards became cardinals, and more than fifty

---

* These verses are quoted by A. Wood, Antiq. Oxon., p. 55. The poem in which they occur is entitled *Speculum Stultorum*, or sometimes *Brunellus* (from its principal personage). It has been repeatedly printed.

who rose to be bishops and archbishops. Thomas à Becket received part of his education here. Several of the most eminent teachers were Englishmen. Among these may be particularly mentioned Robert of Melun (so called from having first taught in that city), and Robert White, or Pullus, as he is called in Latin Robert of Melun, who afterwards became bishop of Hereford, distinguished himself by the zeal and ability with which he opposed the novel views which the rising sect of the Nominalists were then introducing both into philosophy and theology. He is the author of several theological treatises, none of which, however, have been printed. Robert White, after teaching some years at Paris, where he was attended by crowded audiences, was induced to return to his own country, where he is said to have read lectures on theology at Oxford for five years, which greatly contributed to spread the renown of that rising seminary. After having declined a bishopric offered to him by Henry I., he went to reside at Rome in 1143, on the invitation of Celestine II., and was soon after made a cardinal and chancellor of the holy see. One work written by him has been printed, a summary of theology, under the then common title of The Book of Sentences, which has the reputation of being distinguished by the superior correctness of its style and the lucidness of its method.

Another celebrated name among the Englishmen who are recorded to have studied at Paris in those days is that of Nicolas Breakspear, who afterwards became pope by the title of Adrian IV. But, above all others, John of Salisbury deserves to be here mentioned. It is in his writings that we find the most complete account that has reached us not only of the mode of study followed at Paris, but of the entire learning of the age.

Rise of the Scholastic Philosophy.

At this time those branches of literary and scientific knowledge which were specially denominated the arts were considered as divided into two great classes,—the first or more elementary of which, comprehending Grammar, Rhetoric, and Logic, was called the Trivium: the second, comprehending Music, Arithmetic, Geometry, and Astronomy, the Quadrivium. The seven arts, so classified, used to be thus enumerated in a Latin hexameter:—

    Lingua, Tropus, Ratio, Numerus, Tonus, Angulus, Astra;

or, with definitions subjoined, in two still more singularly constructed verses,—

Gram. loquitur, *Dia.* vera docet, *Rhet.* verba colorat,
Mus. canit, *Ar.* numerat, *Geo.* ponderat, *Ast.* colit astra.

John of Salisbury speaks of this system of the sciences as an ancient one in his day. "The Trivium and Quadrivium," he says, in his work entitled Metalogicus, "were so much admired by our ancestors in former ages, that they imagined they comprehended all wisdom and learning, and were sufficient for the solution of all questions and the removing of all difficulties; for whoever understood the Trivium could explain all manner of books without a teacher; but he who was farther advanced, and was master also of the Quadrivium, could answer all questions and unfold all the secrets of nature." The present age, however, had outgrown the simplicity of this arrangement; and various new studies had been added to the ancient seven, as necessary to complete the circle of the sciences and the curriculum of a liberal education.

It was now, in particular, that Theology first came to be ranked as a science. This was the age of St. Bernard, the last of the Fathers, and of Peter Lombard, the first of the Schoolmen. The distinction between these two classes of writers is, that the latter do, and the former do not, treat their subject in a systematizing spirit. The change was the consequence of the cultivation of the Aristotelian logic and metaphysics. When these studies were first introduced into the schools of the West, they were wholly unconnected with theology. But, especially at a time when all the learned were churchmen, it was impossible that the great instrument of thought and reasoning could long remain unapplied to the most important of all the subjects of thought—the subject of religion. It has already been remarked that John Erigena and other Irish divines introduced philosophy and metaphysics into the discussion of questions of religion as early as the ninth century; and they are consequently entitled to be regarded as having first set the example of the method afterwards pursued by the schoolmen. But, although the influence of their writings may probably be traced in preparing the way for the introduction of the scholastic system, and also, afterwards, perhaps, in modifying its spirit, that system was derived immediately, in the shape in which it appeared in the eleventh and twelfth centuries, from another source. Erigena was a Platonist; the spirit of his philosophy was that of the school of Alexandria. But the first schoolmen, properly so called, were Aristotelians: they drew their logic and metaphysics originally from the Latin translations of the works of Aristotle made from the Arabic. And they may also have been indebted for some of their views to the commentaries of the Arabic doctors. But, whether they took their method of philosophy entirely from the ancient heathen sage, or in part from his modern Mahomedan interpreters and illustrators, it could in neither case have had at first any necessary or natural alliance with Christianity. Yet it very soon, as we have said, formed this alliance. Both Lanfranc and Anselm, although not commonly reckoned among the schoolmen, were imbued with the spirit of the new learning, and it is infused throughout their theological writings. Abelard soon after, before he was yet a churchman, may almost be considered to have wielded it as a weapon of scepticism. Even so used, however, religion was still the subject to which it was applied. At last came Peter Lombard, who, by the publication, about the middle of the twelfth century, of his celebrated Four Books of Sentences, properly founded the system of what is called the Scholastic Theology. The schoolmen, from the Master of the Sentences, as Lombard was designated, down to Francis Suarez, who died after the commencement of the seventeenth century, were all theologians. Although, however, religious speculation was the field of thought upon which the spirit of the Aristotelian philosophy chiefly expended itself, there was scarcely any one of the arts or sciences upon which it did not in some degree seize. The scholastic logic became the universal instrument of thought and study: every branch of human learning was attempted to be pursued by its assistance; and most branches were more or less affected by its influence in regard to the forms which they assumed.

CLASSICAL LEARNING.—MATHEMATICS.—MEDICINE.—LAW.—BOOKS.

The classical knowledge of this period, however, was almost confined to the Roman authors, and some of the most eminent of these were as yet unstudied and unknown. Even John of Salisbury, though a few Greek words are to be found in his compositions, seems to have had only the slightest possible acquaintance with that language. Both it and the Hebrew, nevertheless, were known to Abelard and Eloisa; and it is probable that there were both in England and other European countries a few students of the oriental tongues, for the acquisition of which inducements and facilities must have been presented, not only by the custom of resorting to the Arabic colleges in Spain, and the constant intercourse with the East kept up by the pilgrimages and the crusades, but also by the numbers of learned Jews that were everywhere to be found. In England the Jews had schools in London, York, Lincoln, Lynn, Norwich, Oxford, Cambridge, and other towns, which appear to have been attended by Christians as well as by those of their own persuasion. Some of these seminaries, indeed, were rather colleges than schools. Besides the Hebrew and Arabic languages, arithmetic and medicine are mentioned among the branches of knowledge that were taught in them; and the masters were generally the most distinguished of the rabbis. In the eleventh and twelfth centuries, the age of Sarchi, the Kimchis, Maimonides, and other distinguished names, rabbinical learning was in an eminently flourishing state.

There is no certain evidence that the Arabic numerals were yet known in Europe: they certainly were not in general use. Although the Elements of Euclid and other geometrical works had been translated into Latin from the Arabic, the mathematical sciences appear to have been but little studied. "The science of demonstration," says John of Salisbury, in his Metalogicus, "is of all others the most difficult, and alas! is almost quite neglected, except by a very few who apply to the study of the mathematics, and particularly of geometry. But this last is at present very little attended to amongst us, and is only studied by some persons in Spain, Egypt, and Arabia, for the sake of astronomy. One reason of this is, that those parts of the works of Aristotle that relate to the demonstrative sciences are so ill translated, and so incorrectly transcribed, that we meet with insurmountable difficulties in every chapter." The name of the mathematics at this time, indeed, was chiefly given to the science of astrology. "Mathematicians," says Peter of Blois, "are those who, from the position of the stars, the aspect of the firmament, and the motions of the planets, discover things that are to come." Astronomy, however, or the true science of the stars, which was zealously cultivated by the Arabs in the East and in Spain, seems also to have had some cultivators among the learned of Christian Europe. Latin translations existed of several Greek and Arabic astronomical works. In the History attributed to Ingulphus, is the following curious description of a sort of scheme or representation of the planetary system called the Nadir, which is stated to have been destroyed when the abbey of Croyland was burnt in 1091: "We then lost a most beautiful and precious table, fabricated of different kinds of metals, according to the variety of the stars and heavenly signs. Saturn was of copper, Jupiter of gold, Mars of iron, the Sun of latten, Mercury of amber, Venus of tin, the Moon of silver. The eyes were charmed, as well as the mind instructed, by beholding the colure circles, with the zodiac and all its signs, formed with wonderful art, of metals and precious stones, according to their several natures, forms, figures, and colours. It was the most admired and celebrated Nadir in all England." These last words would seem to imply that such tables were then not uncommon. This one, it is stated, had been presented to a former abbot of Croyland by a king of France.

John of Salisbury, in his account of his studies at Paris, makes no mention either of medicine or of law. With regard to the former, indeed, he elsewhere expressly tells us that the Parisians themselves used to go to study it at Salerno and Montpellier. By the beginning of the thirteenth century, however, we find a school of medicine established at Paris, which soon became very celebrated. Of course there were, at an earlier date, persons who practised the medical art in that city. The physicians in all the countries of Europe at this period were generally churchmen. Many of the Arabic medical works were early translated into Latin; but the Parisian professors soon began to publish treatises on the art of their own. The science of the physicians of this age, besides comprehending whatever was to be learned respecting the diagnostics and treatment of diseases from Hippocrates, Galen, and the other ancient writers, embraced a considerable body of botanical and chemical knowledge. Chemistry in particular the Arabs had carried far beyond the point at which it had been left by the ancients. Of anatomy little could as yet be accurately known, while the dissection of the human subject was not practised. Yet it would appear that physicians and surgeons were already beginning to be distinguished from each other. Both the canon and civil laws were also introduced into the routine of study at the University of Paris soon after the time when John of Salisbury studied there. The canon law was originally considered to be a part of theology, and only took the form of a separate study after the publication of the systematic compilation of it called the Decretum of Gratian, in 1151. Gratian was a monk of Bologna, and his work, not the first collection of the kind, but the most complete and the best-arranged that had yet been compiled, was immediately introduced as a text-book in that university. It may be regarded as having laid the foundation of the science of the canon law, in the same manner as the system of the scholastic philosophy was founded by Peter Lombard's Book of Sentences. Regular lecturers upon it very soon appeared at Orleans, at Paris, at Oxford, and all the other chief seats of learning in western Christendom; and before the end of the twelfth century no other study was more eagerly pursued, or attracted greater crowds of students, than that of the canon law. One of its first and most celebrated teachers at Paris was Girard la Pucelle, an Englishman, who afterwards became bishop of Lichfield and Coventry. Girard taught the canon law in Paris from 1160 to 1177; and, in consideration of his distinguished merits and what was deemed the great importance of his instructions, he received from Pope Alexander III. letters exempting him from the obligation of residing on his preferments in England while he was so engaged; this being, it is said, the first known example of such a privilege being granted to any professor.* The same professors who taught the canon law taught also, along with it, the civil law, the systematic study of which, likewise, took its rise in this century, and at the University of Bologna, where the Pandects of Justinian, of which a more perfect copy than had before been known is said to have been found in 1137 at Amalfi,† were arranged and first lectured upon by the German Irnerius,—the Lamp of the Law, as he was called,—about the year 1150. Both the canon and the civil law, however, are said to have been taught a few years before this time at Oxford by Roger, surnamed the Bachelor, a monk of Bec, in Normandy. The study was, from the first, vehemently opposed by the practitioners of the common law; but, sustained by the influence of the Church, and eventually also favoured by the government, it rose above all attempts to put it down. John of Salisbury affirms that, by the blessing of God, the more it was persecuted the more it flourished. Peter of Blois, in one of his letters, gives us the following curious account of the ardour with which it was pursued under the superintendence of Archbishop Theobald:—" In the house of my master, the Archbishop of Canterbury, there are several very learned men, famous for their knowledge of law and politics, who spend the time between prayers and dinner in lecturing, disputing, and debating causes. To us all the knotty questions of the

* Crevier, Hist. de l'Univ. de Paris, i. 244.
† "The discovery of the Pandects at Amalfi," says Gibbon, "is first noticed (in 1501) by Ludovicus Bologninus, on the faith of a Pisan Chronicle, without a name or date. The whole story, though unknown to the twelfth century, embellished by ignorant ages, and suspected by rigid criticism, is not however destitute of much internal probability."

kingdom are referred, which are produced in the common hall, and every one in his order, having first prepared himself, declares, with all the eloquence and acuteness of which he is capable, but without wrangling, what is wisest and safest to be done. If God suggests the soundest opinion to the youngest amongst us, we all agree to it without envy or detraction."*

Study in every department must have been still greatly impeded by the scarcity and high price of books; but their multiplication now went on much more rapidly than it had formerly done. We have already noticed the immense libraries said to have been accumulated by the Arabs, both in their oriental and European seats of empire. No collections to be compared with these existed anywhere in Christian Europe; but, of the numerous monasteries that were planted in every country, few were without libraries of greater or less extent. A convent without a library, it used to be proverbially said, was like a castle without an armoury. When the monastery of Croyland was burnt in 1091, its library, according to Ingulphus, consisted of 900 volumes, of which 300 were very large. "In every great abbey," says Warton, "there was an apartment called the Scriptorium; where many writers were constantly busied in transcribing not only the service-books for the choir, but books for the library. The Scriptorium of St. Albans abbey was built by Abbot Paulin, a Norman, who ordered many volumes to be written there, about the year 1080. Archbishop Lanfranc furnished the copies. Estates were often granted for the support of the Scriptorium. . . . I find some of the classics written in the English monasteries very early. Henry, a Benedictine monk of Hyde Abbey, near Winchester, transcribed in the year 1178 Terence, Boethius, Suetonius, and Claudian. Of these he formed one book, illuminating the initials, and forming the brazen bosses of the covers with his own hands." Other instances of the same kind are added. The monks were much accustomed both to illuminate and to bind books, as well as to transcribe them. "The scarcity of parchment," it is afterwards observed, "undoubtedly prevented the transcription of many other books in these societies. About the year 1120, one Master Hugh, being appointed by the convent of St. Edmondsbury, in Suffolk, to write and illuminate a grand copy of the Bible for their library, could procure no parchment for this purpose in England."† Paper made of cotton, however, was certainly in common use in the twelfth century, though no evidence exists that

* Ep. vi., as translated in Henry's History of Britain.
† Introd. of Learning into England, p cxvi.

that manufactured from linen rags was known till about the
middle of the thirteenth.

THE LATIN LANGUAGE.

During the whole of the Anglo-Norman period, and down to a
much later date, in England as in the other countries of Christendom, the common language of literary composition, in all works
intended for the perusal of the educated classes, was still the
Latin, the language of religion throughout the western world, as
it had been from the first ages of the Church. Christianity had
not only, through its monastic institutions, saved from destruction, in the breaking up of the Roman empire, whatever we
still possess of ancient literature, but had also, by its priesthood
and its ritual, preserved the language of Rome in some sort still
a living and spoken tongue—corrupted indeed by the introduction of many new and barbarous terms, and illegitimate acceptations, and by much bad taste in style and phraseology, but still
wholly unchanged in its grammatical forms, and even in its
vocabulary much less altered than it probably would have been
if it had continued all the while to be spoken and written by an
unmixed Roman population. It would almost seem as if, even
in the Teutonic countries, such as England, the services of the
church, uninterruptedly repeated in the same words since the
first ages, had kept up in the general mind something of a dim
traditionary understanding of the old imperial tongue. We read
of some foreign ecclesiastics, who could not speak English, being
accustomed to preach to the people in Latin. A passage quoted
above from the Croyland History seems to imply that Gislebert,
or Gilbert, one of the founders of the University of Cambridge,
used to employ Latin as well as French on such occasions. So,
Giraldus Cambrensis tells us that, in a progress which he made
through Wales in 1188, to assist Archbishop Baldwin in preaching a new crusade for the delivery of the Holy Land, he was
always most successful when he appealed to the people in a
Latin sermon: he asserts, indeed, that they did not understand a
word of it, although it never failed to melt them into tears, and
to make them come in crowds to take the cross. No doubt they
were acted upon chiefly through their ears and their imaginations,
and for the most part only supposed that they comprehended
what they were listening to; but it is probable that their self-deception was assisted by their catching a word or phrase here
and there the meaning of which they really understood. The
Latin tongue must in those days have been heard in common life

on a thousand occasions from which it has now passed away. It was the language of all the learned professions, of law and physic as well as of divinity, in all their grades. It was in Latin that the teachers at the Universities (many of whom, as well as of the ecclesiastics, were foreigners) delivered their prelections in all the sciences, and that all the disputations and other exercises among the students were carried on. It was the same at all the monastic schools and other seminaries of learning. The number of persons by whom these various institutions were attended was very great: they were of all ages from boyhood to advanced manhood; and poor scholars must have been found in every village, mingling with every class of the people, in some one or other of the avocations which they followed in the intervals of their attendance at the Universities, or after they had finished their education, from parish priests down to wandering beggars.

Latin Chroniclers.

By far the most valuable portion of our Latin literature of this age consists of the numerous historical works which it has bequeathed to us. These works have a double interest for the English reader, belonging to the country and the age in which they were written by their subject as well as by their authorship. All that we can do here, however, is to enumerate the principal collections that have been made in modern times of our old Latin historians or chroniclers:—

1. Rerum Britannicarum, id est, Angliæ, Scotiæ, Vicinarumque Insularum ac Regionum, Scriptores Vetustiores ac Præcipui: (a Hier. Commelino). Fol. Heidelb. & Lugd. 1587.

2. Rerum Anglicarum Scriptores post Bedam Præcipui, ex Vetustissimis MSS. nunc primum in lucem editi: (a Hen. Savile). Fol. Lon. 1596, and Francof. 1601.

3. Anglica, Normannica, Hibernica, Cambrica, a veteribus Scripta, ex Bibl. Guilielmi Camdeni. Fol. Francof. 1602 and 1603.

4. Historiæ Normannorum Scriptores Antiqui; studio Andreæ Duchesne. Fol. Paris. 1619.

5. Historiæ Anglicanæ Scriptores Decem, ex vetustis MSS. nunc primum in lucem editi: (a Rog. Twysden et Joan. Selden). Fol. Lon. 1652.

6. Rerum Anglicarum Scriptorum Veterum Tomus I^{us}: Quorum Ingulfus nunc primum integer, cæteri nunc primum prodeunt: (a Joan. Fell, vel potius Gul. Fulman). Fol. Oxon

1684. (Sometimes incorrectly cited as the 1st vol. of Gale's Collection.)

7. Historiæ Anglicanæ Scriptores Quinque, ex votustis Codd. MSS. nunc primum in lucem editi: (a THOM. GALE). Fol. Oxon. 1687. (This is properly the 2nd vol. of Gale's Collection.)

8. Historiæ Britannicæ, Saxonicæ, Anglo-Danicæ, Scriptores Quindecim, ex votustis Codd. MSS. editi, opera THOMÆ GALE. Fol. Oxon. 1691. (This is properly the 1st vol. of Gale's Collection, though often cited as the 3rd.)

9. Anglia Sacra; sive Collectio Historiarum ... de Archiepiscopis et Episcopis Angliæ; (a HENRICO WHARTON). 2 Tom. Fol. Lon. 1691.

10. Historiæ Anglicanæ Scriptores Varii, e Codd. MSS. nunc primum editi: (a JOS. SPARKE). Fol. Lon. 1723.

11. Historiæ Anglicanæ circa tempus Conquestus Angliæ a Guilielmo Notho, Normannorum Duce, selecta Monumenta; excerpta ex volumine And. Duchesne; cum Notis, &c.: (a FRANCISCO MASERES). 4to. Lon. 1807.

12. Monumenta Historica Britannica; or, Materials for the History of Britain from the earliest period to the end of the reign of King Henry VII. Published by command of her Majesty. Vol. 1st (extending to the Norman Conquest). Fol. Lon. 1848. (By PETRIE, SHARPE, and HARDY.)

To which may be added:—

13. The series of works printed by the HISTORICAL SOCIETY, from 1838 to 1856, extending to 29 vols. 8vo.; and,

14. The series entitled Rerum Britannicarum Medii Ævi Scriptores, or Chronicles and Memorials of Great Britain and Ireland during the Middle Ages. Published by authority of her Majesty's Treasury, under the direction of the Master of the Rolls. 8vo. Lon. 1857, &c.

THE FRENCH LANGUAGE IN ENGLAND.

It is commonly asserted that for some reigns after the Norman Conquest the exclusive language of government and legislation in England was the French,—that all pleadings, at least in the supreme courts, were carried on in that language,—and that in it all deeds were drawn up and all laws promulgated. "This popular notion," observes a late learned writer, "cannot be easily supported.... Before the reign of Henry III. we cannot discover a deed or law drawn or composed in French. Instead of prohibiting the English language, it was employed by the Conqueror and his successors in their charters until the reign of Henry II., when it was superseded, not by the French but by the Latin language, which had been gradually gaining, or rather regaining, ground; for the charters anterior to Alfred are invariably in Latin."* So far was the Conqueror from showing any aversion to the English language, or making any such attempt as is ascribed to him to effect its abolition, that, according to Ordericus Vitalis, when he first came over he strenuously applied himself to learn it for the special purpose of understanding, without the aid of an interpreter, the causes that were pleaded before him, and persevered in that endeavour till the tumult of many other occupations, and what the historian calls "durior netas"—a more iron time †—of necessity compelled him to give it up.‡ The common statement rests on the more than suspicious authority of the History attributed to Ingulphus, the fabricator of which, in his loose and ignorant account of the matter, has set down this falsehood along with some other things that are true or probable. Even before the Conquest, the Confessor himself, according to this writer, though a native of England, yet, from his education and long residence in Normandy, had become almost a Frenchman; and when he succeeded to the English throne he brought over with him great numbers of Normans, whom he advanced to the highest dignities in the church and the state. "Wherefore," it is added, "the whole land began, under the influence of the king and the other Normans introduced by him, to lay aside the English customs, and to imitate the manners of the French in many things; for example, all the nobility in their courts began to speak French as a great piece of gentility, to draw up their charters and other writings after the French fashion, and to grow ashamed of their old national habits in these and many other particulars."§ Further on we are told, "They [the Normans] held the language [of the natives] in such abhorrence that the laws of the land and the statutes of the English kings were drawn out in the Gallic [or French] tongue; and to boys in the schools the elements of grammar were taught in French and not in English: even the English manner of writing was dropped, and the French manner introduced in all charters and books."∥ The facts are more correctly given by other old writers, who, although not con-

* Sir F. avis Palgrave, Rise and Progress of the English Commonwealth, vol. i. p. ?

† Q. s dura refugimus notas?—Hor. Od. l. 35.

‡ Ex   x Libro iv. Orderici Vitalis, p. 217; edit. Maseres.

§ Ing   Historia, in Savile, 895; or in Fulman, 62. The translation, which ciently faithful, is Henry's.

∥ In. S vile, 901; Fulman, 71.

E

temporary with the Conquest, are probably of as early a date as the compiler of the Croyland History. The Dominican friar Robert Holcot, writing in the earlier part of the fourteenth century, informs us that there was then no institution of children in the old English—that the first language they learned was the French, and that through that tongue they were afterwards taught Latin; and he adds that this was a practice which had been introduced at the Conquest, and which had continued ever since.* About the middle of the same century Ranulf Higden, in his Polychronicon, says, as the passage is translated by Trevisa, "This apayringe (impairing) of the birthe tonge is by cause of tweye thinges; oon is for children in scole, aghenes (against) the usage and maner of alle other naciouns, beth (be) compelled for to leve her (their) owne langage, and for to construe wo her lessouns and her thingis a Frensche, and haveth siththe (have since) that the Normans come first into England. Also gentil mennes children beth ytaught (be taught) for to speke Fronsche from the time that thei beth rokked in her cradel, and cunneth (can) speke and playe with a childes brooche; and uplondish (rustic) men wol likne hem self (will liken themselves) to gentilmen, and fondeth (are fond) with grete bisynesse for to speke Frensche, for to be the more yiold of."† The teachers in the schools, in fact, were generally, if not universally, ecclesiastics; and the Conquest had Normanized the church quite as much as the state. Immediately after that revolution great numbers of foreigners were brought over, both to serve in the parochial cures and to fill the monasteries that now began to multiply so rapidly. These churchmen must have been in constant intercourse with the people of all classes in various capacities, not only as teachers of youth, but as the instructors of their parishioners from the altar, and as holding daily and hourly intercourse with them in all the relations that subsist between pastor and flock. They probably in this way diffused their own tongue throughout the land of their adoption to a greater extent than is commonly suspected. We shall have occasion, as we proceed, to mention some facts which would seem to imply that in the twelfth century the French language was very generally familiar to the middle classes in England, at least in the great towns. It was at any rate the only language spoken for some ages after the Conquest by our kings, and not

* Lect. in Libr. Sapient. Lect. ii, 4to. Paris, 1518; as referred to by Warton, Hist. Eng. Poetry, i. 5.
† Quoted from MS. Harl. 1900, by Tyrwhitt, in Essay on the Language and Versification of Chaucer, prefixed to his edition of the Canterbury Tales.

only by nearly all the nobility, but by a large proportion even
of the inferior landed proprietors, most of whom also were of
Norman birth or descent. Ritson, in his rambling, incoherent
Dissertation on Romance and Minstrelsy, prefixed to his
Ancient English Metrical Romances, has collected, but not in
the most satisfactory manner, some of the evidence we have
as to the speech of the first Norman kings. He does not
notice what Ordericus Vitalis tells us of the Conqueror's meritorious attempt, which does not seem, however, to have been
more successful than such experiments on the part of grown-up
gentlemen usually are; so that he may be allowed to be correct
enough in the assertion with which he sets out, that we have no
information " that William the Bastard, his son Rufus, his
daughter Maud, or his nephew Stephen, did or could speak the
Anglo-Saxon or English language." Reference is then made to
a story told in what is called Bromton's Chronicle respecting
Henry II., which, however, is not very intelligible in all its
parts, though Ritson has slurred over the difficulties. As
Henry was passing through Wales, the old chronicler relates,
on his return from Ireland in the spring of 1172, he found himself on a Sunday at the castle of Cardiff, and stopped there to
hear mass; after which, as he was proceeding to mount his
horse to be off again, there presented itself before him a somewhat singular apparition, a man with red hair and a round
tonsure,* lean and tall, attired in a white tunic and barefoot,
who, addressing him in the Teutonic tongue, began, " Gode
Olde Kinge,"† and proceeded to deliver a command from Christ,
as he said, and his mother, from John the Baptist and Peter,
that he should suffer no traffic or servile works to be done
throughout his dominions on the sabbath-day, except only such
as pertained to the use of food; " which command, if thou
observest," concluded the speaker, " whatever thou mayest
undertake thou shalt happily accomplish." The king immediately, speaking in French, desired the soldier who held the
bridle of his horse to ask the rustic if he had dreamed all this.
The soldier made the inquiry, as desired, in English; and then,
it is added, the man replied in the same language as before, and
addressing the king said, " Whether I have dreamed it or no,

* Tonsura rotunda. Scriptores Decem, 1079. The epithet would seem to
imply that there were still in Wales some priests of the ancient British
Church who retained the old national crescent-shaped tonsure, now deemed
heretical.

† Henry and his son of the same name were commonly distinguished as the
Old and the Young King from the date of the coronation of the latter (whom
his father survived) in 1170.

mark this day; for, unless thou shalt do what I have told thee, and amend thy life, thou shalt within a year's time hear such news as thou shalt mourn to the day of thy death." And, having so spoken, the man vanished out of sight. With the calamities which of course ensued to the doomed king we have here nothing to do. Although the chronicler reports only the three commencing words of the prophet's first address in what he calls the Teutonic tongue, there can be no doubt, we conceive, that the rest, though here translated into Latin, was also delivered in the same Teutonic (by which, apparently, can only have been meant the vernacular English, or what is commonly called Saxon). The man would not begin his speech in one language, and then suddenly break away into another. But, if this was the case, Henry, from his reply, would appear to have understood English, though he might not be able to speak it. The two languages, thus subsisting together, were probably both understood by many of those who could only speak one of them. We have another evidence of this in the fact of the soldier, as we have seen, speaking English and also understanding the king's French. It is, we suppose, merely so much affectation or bad rhetoric in the chronicler that makes him vary his phrase for the same thing from "the Teutonic tongue" (*Teutonica lingua*) in one place to "English" (*Anglicè*) in another, and immediately after to "the former language" (*lingua priori*); for the words which he gives as Teutonic are English words, and, when Henry desired the soldier to address the priest in English and the soldier did so, it must have been because that was the language in which he had addressed the king.*

"King Richard," Ritson proceeds, "is never known to have uttered a single English word, unless one may rely on the evidence of Robert Mannyng for the express words, when, of Isaac King of Cyprus, 'O dele,' said the king, 'this is a fole Breton.' The latter expression seems proverbial, whether it alludes to the Welsh or to the Armoricans, because Isaac was neither by birth, though he might be both by folly. Many great nobles of England, in this century, were utterly ignorant of the English language." As an instance, he mentions the case, before noticed by Tyrwhitt, of William Longchamp, bishop of Ely,

* A somewhat different view of this story is taken by Mr. Luders in his tract On the Use of the French Language in our ancient Laws and Acts of State. (Tracts on Various Subjects, p. 400.) He remarks: "The author does not tell why the ghost spoke German to the king in Wales, or how this German became all at once good English; nor how it happened that the groom addressed the German ghost in English." Mr. Luders, therefore, understands "the Teutonic tongue" to mean, not *English*, but *German*.

chancellor and prime minister to Richard I., who, according to a remarkable account in a letter of his contemporary Hugh bishop of Coventry, preserved by Hoveden, did not know a word of English.* The only fact relating to this subject in connexion with John or his reign that Ritson brings forward, is the speech which that king's ambassador, as related by Matthew Paris, made to the King of Morocco :—" Our nation is learned in three idioms, that is to say, Latin, French, and English." † This would go to support the conclusion that both the French and the Latin languages were at this time not unusually spoken by persons of education in England.

THE LANGUE D'OC AND THE LANGUE D'OYL.

French as well as Latin was at least extensively employed among us in literary composition. The Gauls, the original inhabitants of the country now called France, were a Celtic people, and their speech was a dialect of the same great primitive tongue which probably at one time prevailed over the whole of Western Europe, and is still vernacular in Ireland, in Wales, and among the Highlanders of Scotland. After the country became a Roman province this ancient language gradually gave place to the Latin; which, however, here as elsewhere, soon became corrupted in the mouths of a population mixing it with their own barbarous vocables and forms, or at least divesting it of many of its proper characteristics in their rude appropriation of it. But, as different depraving or obliterating influences operated in different circumstances, and a variety of kinds of bad Latin were thus produced in the several countries which had been provinces of the empire, so even within the limits of Gaul there grew up two such distinct dialects, one in the south, another in the north. All these forms of bastard Latin, wherever they arose, whether

* Linguam Anglicanam prorsus ignorabat.—Hoveden, 701. Ritson, omitting all mention either of Hoveden or Tyrwhitt, chooses to make a general reference to the chronicle called Brompton's, a later compilation, the author of which (vide col. 1227) has quietly appropriated Bishop Hugh's Letter, and made it part of his narrative.

† This was a secret mission despatched by John, the historian tells us, in 1213, "ad Admiralium Murmelium, regem tinguum Aphricæ, Marrochiæ, et Hispaniæ, quem vulgus Miramumelinum vocat." The words used by Thomas Herdington, the one of the three commissioners selected, on account of his superior gift of eloquence, to be spokesman, were "Gens nostra speciosa et ingeniosa tribus pollet idiomatibus erudita, scilicet Latino, Gallico, et Anglico."—Matt. Paris, 243.

in Italy, in Spain, or in Gaul, were known by the common name of Roman, or Romance, languages, or the Rustic Roman (Romana Rustica), and were by that generic term distinguished from the barbarian tongues, or those that had been spoken by the Celtic, German, and other uncivilized nations before they came into communication with the Romans. From them have sprung what are called the Latin languages of modern Europe—the Italian, the Spanish, and the Portuguese, as well as what we now denominate the French. The Romance spoken in the south of Gaul appears to have been originally nearly, if not altogether, identical with that spoken in the north-east of Spain; and it always preserved a close resemblance and affinity to that and the other Romance dialects of Spain and Italy. It is in fact to be accounted a nearer relation of the Spanish and Italian than of the modern French. The latter is exclusively the offspring of the Romance of northern Gaul, which, both during its first growth and subsequently, was acted upon by different influences from those which modified the formation of the southern tongue. It is probable that whatever it retained of the Celtic ingredient to begin with was, if not stronger or of larger quantity than what entered into the Romance dialect of the south, at any rate of a somewhat different character; but the peculiar form it eventually assumed may be regarded as having been mainly owing to the foreign pressure to which it was twice afterwards exposed, first by the settlement of the Franks in the north and north-east of Gaul in the fifth century (while the Visigoths and Burgundians had spread themselves over the south), and again by that of the Normans in the north-west in the tenth. What may have been the precise nature or amount of the effect produced upon the Romance tongue of Northern Gaul by either or both of these Teutonic occupations of the country, it is not necessary for our present purpose to inquire; it is sufficient to observe that that dialect could not fail to be thereby peculiarly affected, and its natural divergence from the southern Romance materially aided and promoted. The result, in fact, was that the two dialects became two distinct languages, differing from one another more than any two other of the Latin languages did —the Italian, for example, from the Spanish, or the Spanish from the Portuguese, and even more than the Romance of the south of Gaul differed from that either of Italy or of Spain. This southern Romance, it only remains further to be observed, came in course of time to be called the Provençal tongue; but it does not appear to have received this name till, in the beginning of the twelfth century, the county of Provence had fallen to be inherited by Raymond Berenger, Count of Catalonia, who thereupon transferred his court to Arles, and made that town the centre and chief seat of the literary cultivation which had previously flourished at Barcelona. There had been poetry written in the Romance of Southern Gaul before this; but it was not till now that the Troubadours, as the authors of that poetry called themselves, rose into much celebrity; and hence it has been maintained, with great appearance of reason, that what is best or most characteristic about the Provençal poetry is really not of French but of Spanish origin. In that case the first inspiration may probably have been caught from the Arabs. The greater part of Provence soon after passed into the possession of the Counts of Toulouse, and the Troubadours flocked to that city. But the glory of the Provençal tongue did not last altogether for much more than a century; and then, when it had ceased to be employed in poetry and literature, and had declined into a more provincial patois, it and the northern French were wont to be severally distinguished by the names of the Langue d'Oc (sometimes called by modern writers the Occitanian) and the Langue d'Oyl, from the words for *yes*, which were *oc* in the one, and *oyl*, afterwards *oy* or *oui*, in the other. Dante mentions them by these appellations, and with this explanation, in his treatise De Vulgari Eloquio, written in the end of the thirteenth or beginning of the fourteenth century; and one of them still gives its name to the great province of Languedoc, where the dialect formerly so called yet subsists as the popular speech, though, of course, much changed and debased from what it was in the days of its old renown, when it lived on the lips of rank and genius and beauty, and was the favourite vehicle of love and song.

The Langue d'Oyl, on the other hand, formerly spoken only to the north of the Loire, has grown up into what we now call the French language, and has become, at least for literary purposes, and for all the educated classes, the established language of the whole country. Some fond students of the remains of the other dialect have deplored this result as a misfortune to France, which they contend would have had a better modern language and literature if the Langue d'Oc, in the contest between the two, had prevailed over the Langue d'Oyl. It is probable, indeed, that accident and political circumstances have had more to do in determining the matter as it has gone than the merits of the case; but in every country as well as in France—in Spain, in Italy, in Germany, in England—some other of the old popular dialects than the one that has actually acquired the ascendancy has in like manner had its enthusiastic reclaimers against the unjust fortune which has condemned it to degradation or oblivion; and we may suspect that the partiality which the mind is apt to acquire for whatever it has made the subject of long investigation and study, especially if it be something which has been generally neglected, and perhaps in some instances a morbid sympathy with depression and defeat, which certain historical and philosophical speculators have in common with the readers and writers of sentimental novels, are at the bottom of much of this unavailing and purposeless lamentation. The question is one which we have hardly the means of solving, even if any solution of it which might now be attainable could have any practical effect. The Langue d'Oyl is now unalterably established as the French language; the Langue d'Oc is, except as a local patois, irrecoverably dead. Nor are there wanting French archæologists, quite equal in knowledge of the subject to their opponents, who maintain that in this there is nothing to regret, but the contrary—that the northern Romance tongue was as superior to the southern intrinsically as it has proved in fortune, and that its early literature was of far higher value and promise than the Provençal.*

VERNACULAR LANGUAGE AND LITERATURE:—A.D. 1066—1216.

From the Norman Conquest to the termination of the reign of the seventh Norman sovereign, King John, is almost exactly a century and a half, even to a day. The victory of Hastings was gained on the 14th of October, 1066, and John died on the 19th of October, 1216. His death, happening at the time it did, was probably an event of the greatest importance. The political constitution, or system of government, established by the Conquest, —a system of pure monarchy or absolutism—had been formally brought to an end the year before by the grant of the Great Charter wrung from the crown by the baronage, which at any rate tempered the monarchical despotism by the introduction of the aristocratic element into the theory of the constitution; but

* What has come to be called the French tongue, it may be proper to notice, has no relationship whatever to that of the proper French, or Franks, who were a Teutonic people, speaking a purely Teutonic language, resembling the German, or more nearly the Flemish. This old Teutonic French, which the Franks continued to speak for several centuries after their conquest of Gaul, is denominated by philologists the *Frankish*, or *Francic*. The modern French, which is a Latin tongue, has come to be so called from the accident of the country in which it was spoken having been conquered by the French or Franks—the conquerors, as in other cases, in contempt of time adopting the language of the conquered, and bestowing upon it their own name.

this might have proved little more than a theoretical or nominal innovation if John had lived. His death, and the non-age of his son and heir, left the actual management of affairs in the hands of those by whom the constitutional reform had been brought about; and that reform became a practical reality. At the least, its legal character and authority never were disputed; no attempt ever was made to repeal it; on the contrary it was ratified no less than six times in the single reign of Henry III., John's successor; and it has retained its proper place at the head of the Statute Book down to our own day. Its proper place; for it is indeed our first organic law, the true commencement or foundation-stone, of the constitution. Before it there was no mechanism in our political system, no balance of forces or play of counteracting elements and tendencies; nothing but the sort of life and movement that may belong to a stone or a cannon-ball or any other more mass. The royal power was all in all. With the Charter, and the death of the last despotic king, from whom it was extorted, begins another order of things both political and social. It may be likened to the passing away of the night and the dawning of a new day. In particular, the Charter may be said to have consummated by a solemn legislative fiat the blending and incorporation of the two races, the conquerors and the conquered, which had been actively going on without any such sanction, and under the natural influence of circumstances only, throughout the preceding half-century,—having commenced, we may reckon, perhaps, half a century earlier, or about the middle of the reign of Henry I. There is, at least, not a word in this law making the least reference to any distinction between the two races. Both are spoken of throughout only as English; the nation is again recognized as one, as fully as it had been before either William the Norman or Canute the Dane.

We have thus four successive periods of about half a century each:—The first, from the Danish to the Norman Conquest,— half English, half Danish; the Second, from the Norman Conquest to the middle of the reign of Henry I., in which the subjugated English and their French or Norman rulers were completely divided; the Third and Fourth extending to the date of Magna Charta, and presenting, the former the comparatively slow, the latter the accelerated, process of the intermixture and fusion of the two races. Some of our old chroniclers would make the third half-century also, as well as the first and second, to have been inaugurated by a great constitutional or political event: as the year 1016 is memorable for the Danish and the year 1066 for the Norman Conquest, so in 1116, we are told by

Stow, "on the 19th day of April, King Henry called a council of all the States of his realm, both of the Prelates, Nobles, and Commons, to Salisbury, there to consult for the good government of the Commonwealth, and the weighty affairs of the same, which council, taking the name and fame of the French, is called a Parliament;" "and this," he adds, "do the historiographers note to be the first Parliament in England, and that the kings before that time were never wont to call any of their Commons or people to council or lawmaking." This theory of the origin of our parliamentary government must, indeed, be rejected;[*] but the year 1116 will still remain notable as that in which Henry, reversing what had been done fifty years before, crossed the sea with an army of English to reduce his ancestral Normandy, or prevent it from falling into the hands of the son of his unfortunate elder brother. Even the next stage, half a century further on, when we have supposed the amalgamation of the two races to have assumed its accelerated movement, may be held to be less precisely indicated by such events as the appointment of Becket, said to be the first Englishman since the Conquest promoted to high office either in the Church or the State, to the archbishopric of Canterbury in 1161,—the enactment in 1164 of the Constitutions of Clarendon, by which the clergy, a body essentially foreign in feeling and to a great extent even of foreign birth, were brought somewhat more under subjection to the law of the land—and the Conquest of Ireland in 1172, to the vast exaltation of the English name and power.

What was the history of the vernacular language for this first century and a half after the Norman Conquest, throughout which everything native would thus seem to have been in a course of gradual re-emergence from the general foreign inundation that had overwhelmed the country? We have no historical record or statement as to this matter: the question can only be answered, in so far as it can be answered at all, from an examination of such compositions of the time in the vernacular tongue as may have come down to us.

The principal literature produced in England during this period was in the Latin and French languages. In the former were written most works on subjects of theology, philosophy, and history; in the latter most of those intended rather to amuse than to inform, and addressed, not to students and professional readers, but to the idlers of the court and the upper classes, by whom they were seldom actually read, or much expected to be read, but only listened to as they were recited

[*] See Sir H. Spelman, Concilia; ad an. 1116.

or chanted (for most of them were in verse) by others. How far over society such a knowledge of the imported tongue came to extend as was requisite for the understanding and enjoyment of what was thus written in it has been matter of dispute. The Abbé de la Rue conceives that a large proportion even of the middle classes, and of the town population generally, must have been so far frenchified; but later authorities look upon this as an extravagant supposition.

It is, at all events, this French literature only that is to be considered as having come into competition with, or to have taken the place of, the old vernacular literature. The employment of the Latin language in writing by monks, secular churchmen, and other persons who had had a learned education, was what had always gone on in England as in every other country of Western Christendom; there was nothing new in that; we continue to have it after the Conquest just as we had it before the Conquest. But it is quite otherwise with the writing of French; that was altogether a new thing in England, and indeed very much of a new thing everywhere, in the eleventh century: no specimen of composition in the Langue d'Oyl, in fact, either in verse or in prose, has come down to us from beyond that century, nor is there reason to believe that it had been much earlier turned to account for literary purposes even in France itself. The great mass of the oldest French literature that has been preserved was produced in England, or, at any rate, in the dominions of the King of England, in the twelfth century.

To whatever portion of society in England an acquaintance with this French literature was confined, it is evident that it was for some time after the Conquest the only literature of the day that, without addressing itself exclusively to the learned classes, still demanded some measure of cultivation in its readers or auditors as well as in its authors. It was the only popular literature that was not adapted to the mere populace. We might infer this even from the fact that, if any other ever existed, it has mostly perished. The various metrical chronicles, romances, and other compositions in the French tongue, a good many of which are still extant, are very nearly the only literary works which have come down to us from this age. And, while the mass of this produce that has been preserved is, as we have said, very considerable, we have distinct notices of much more which is now lost. How the French language should have acquired the position which it thus appears to have held in England for some time after the Conquest is easily explained.

The advantage which it derived from being the language of the court, of the entire body of the nobility, and of the opulent and influential classes generally, is obvious. This not only gave it the prestige and attraction of what we now call fashion, but, in the circumstances to which the country was reduced, would very speedily make it the only language in which any kind of regular or grammatical training could be obtained. With the native population almost everywhere deprived of its natural leaders, the old landed proprietary of its own blood, it cannot be supposed that schools in which the reading and writing of the vernacular tongue was taught could continue to subsist. This has been often pointed out. But what we may call the social cause, or that arising out of the relative conditions of the two races, was probably assisted by another which has not been so much attended to. The languages themselves did not compete upon fair terms. The French would have in the general estimation a decided advantage for the purposes of literature over the English. The latter was held universally to be merely a barbarous form of speech, claiming kindred with nothing except the other half-articulate dialects of the woods, hardly one of which had ever known what it was to have any acquaintance with letters, or was conceived even by those who spoke it to be fit to be used in writing except on the most vulgar occasions, or where anything like either dignity or precision of expression was of no importance; the former, although somewhat soiled and disfigured by ill usage received at the hands of the uneducated multitude, and also only recently much employed in formal or artistic eloquence, could still boast the most honourable of all pedigrees as a daughter of the Latin, and was thus besides allied to the popular speech of every more civilized province of Western Christendom. The very name by which it had been known when it first attracted attention with reference to its literary capabilities was, as we have seen, the Rustic Latin, or Roman (*Lingua Romana Rustica*). Even without being favoured by circumstances, as it was in the present case, a tongue having these intrinsic recommendations would not have been easily worsted, in a contest for the preference as the organ of fashionable literature, by such a competitor as the unknown and unconnected English.

There was only one great advantage possessed by the national tongue with which it was impossible for the other in the long run to cope. This was the fact of its being the national tongue, the speech, actual and ancestral, of the great body of the people. Even that, indeed, might not have enabled it to maintain its ground if it had been a mere unwritten form of speech. But it had been cultivated and trained for centuries both by the practice of composition, in prose as well as in verse, and by the application to it of the art of the grammarian. It already possessed a literature considerable in volume, and embracing a variety of departments. It was not merely something floating upon men's breath, but had a substantial existence in poems and histories, in libraries and parchments. In that state it might cease, in the storm of national calamity, to be generally either written or read, but even its more literary inflexions and constructions would be less likely to fall into complete and universal oblivion. The memory, at least, of its old renown would not altogether die away; and that alone would be found to be much when, after a time, it began to be again, although in a somewhat altered form, employed in writing.

The nature of the altered form which distinguishes the written vernacular tongue when it reappears after the Norman Conquest from the aspect it presents before that date (or the earliest modern English from what is commonly designated Saxon or Anglo-Saxon) is not matter of dispute. "The substance of the change," to adopt the words of Mr. Price, the late learned editor of Warton, "is admitted on all hands to consist in the suppression of those grammatical intricacies occasioned by the inflection of nouns, the seemingly arbitrary distinctions of gender, the government of prepositions, &c."* It was, in fact, the conversion of an inflectional into a non-inflectional, of a synthetic into an analytic language. The syntactical connexion of words, and the modification of the mental conceptions which they represent, was indicated, no longer, in general, by those variations which constitute what are called declension and conjugation, but by separate particles, or simply by juxtaposition; and whatever seemed to admit of being neglected without injury to the prime object of expressing the meaning of the speaker, or writer, — no matter what other purposes it might serve of a merely ornamental or artistic nature — was ruthlessly dispensed with.

A change such as this is unquestionably the breaking up of a language. In the first instance, at least, it amounts to the destruction of much that is most characteristic of the language, — of all that constitutes its beauty to the educated mind, imbued with a feeling for the literature into which it has been wrought, — of something, probably, even of its precision as well as of its expressiveness in a higher sense. It has become, in a manner, but the skeleton of what it was, or the skeleton with only the

* Preface to Warton's Hist. of Eng. Poetry, p. 80.

skin hanging loose upon it:—all the covering and rounding flesh gone. Or we may say it is the language no longer with its old natural bearing and suitable attire, but reduced to the rags and squalor of a beggar. Or it may be compared to a material edifice, once bright with many of the attractions of decorative architecture, now stripped of all its splendours and left only a collection of bare and dilapidated walls. It may be, too, that, as is commonly assumed, a synthetic tongue is essentially a nobler and more effective instrument of expression than an analytic one,—that, often comprising a whole sentence, or at least a whole clause, in a word, it presents thoughts and emotions in flashes and pictures where the other can only employ comparatively dead conventional signs. But perhaps the comparison has been too commonly made between the synthetic tongue in its perfection and the analytic one while only in its rudimentary state. The language may be considered to have changed its constitution, somewhat like a country which should have ceased to be a monarchy and become a republic. The new political system could only be fairly compared with the old one, and the balance struck between the advantages of the one and those of the other, after the former should have had time fully to develop itself under the operation of its own peculiar principles. Even if it be inferior upon the whole, and for the highest purposes, an analytic language may perhaps have some recommendations which a synthetic one does not possess. It may not be either more natural or, properly speaking, more simple, for the original constitution of most, if not of all, languages seems to have been synthetic, and a synthetic language is as easy both to acquire and to wield as an analytic one to those to whom it is native; nor can the latter be said to be more rational or philosophical than the former, for, as being in the main natural products, and not artificial contrivances, languages must be held to stand all on an equality in respect of the reasonableness at least of the principle on which they are constituted; but yet, if comparatively defective in poetical expressiveness, analytic languages will probably be found, whenever they have been sufficiently cultivated, to be capable, in pure exposition, of rendering thought with superior minuteness and distinctness of detail. With their small tenacity or cohesion, they penetrate into every chink and fold, like water or fine dust.

But the great question in every case of the apparent conversion of a synthetic into an analytic language is, how, or under the operation of what cause or causes, the change was brought about. In the particular case before us, for instance, what was it that converted the form of our vernacular tongue which we find alone employed in writing before the Norman Conquest into the comparatively uninflected form in which it appears in the generality of the compositions which have come down to us from the first ages after that great political and social catastrophe?

First, however, we may remark that there is no proof of the latter form having been really new, or of recent origin, about the time of the Conquest. All that we can assert is, that soon after that date it first appears in writing. If it was ever so employed before, no earlier specimens of it have been preserved. It was undoubtedly the form of the language popularly in use at the time when it thus first presents itself in our national literature. But did it not exist as an oral dialect long before? May it not have so existed from the remotest antiquity alongside of the more artificial form which was exclusively, or at least usually, employed in writing? It has been supposed that even the classical Greek and Latin, such as we find in books, may have always been accompanied each by another form of speech, of looser texture, and probably more of an analytical character, which served for the ordinary oral intercourse of the less educated population, and of which it has even been conjectured we may have some much disguised vestige or resemblance in the modern Romaic and Italian. The rise, at any rate, of what was long a merely oral dialect into a language capable of being employed in literature, and of thereby being gradually so trained and improved as to supplant and take the place of the ancient more highly inflected and otherwise more artificial literary language of the country, is illustrated by what is known to have happened in France and other continental provinces of the old Empire of the West, where the *Romana Rustica*, as it was called, which was a corrupted or broken-down form of the proper Latin, after having been for some centuries only orally used, came to be written as well as spoken, and, having been first taken into the service of the more popular kinds of literature, ended by becoming the language of all literature and the only national speech. So in this country there may possibly have been in use for colloquial purposes a dialect of a similar character to our modern analytic English even from the earliest days of the old synthetic English; and the two forms of the language, the regular and the irregular, the learned and the vulgar, the mother and the daughter, or rather, if you will, the elder and the younger sister, may have subsisted together for many centuries, till there came a crisis which for a time laid the entire fabric of the old national civilization in the dust, when the rude and hardy character of the one carried it through the storm which the more delicate structure of the other could not stand.

Or was the written English of the twelfth and thirteenth centuries the same English (or Anglo-Saxon) that was written in the ninth and tenth, only modified by that process of gradual change the principle of which was inherent in the constitution of the language? Was the former neither the sister nor the daughter of the latter, but the latter merely at a different stage of its natural growth? This is the view that has been maintained by some eminent authorities. The late Mr. Price, acknowledging it to be a matter beyond dispute "that some change had taken place in the style of composition and general structure of the language" from the end of the ninth to the end of the twelfth century, adds:—"But that these mutations were a consequence of the Norman invasion, or were even accelerated by that event, is wholly incapable of proof; and nothing is supported upon a firmer principle of rational induction, than that the same effects would have ensued if William and his followers had remained in their native soil."* The change, as we have seen, may be said to have amounted to the transformation of the language from one of a synthetic to one of an analytic constitution or structure; but Mr. Price contends that, whether it is to be considered as the result of an innate law of the language, or of some general law in the organization of those who spoke it, its having been in no way dependent upon external circumstances,—upon foreign influence or political disturbances,—is established by the undeniable fact that every other language of the Low-German stock displays the same simplification of its grammar. "In all these languages," he observes, "there has been a constant tendency to relieve themselves of that precision which chooses a fresh symbol for every shade of meaning, to lessen the amount of nice distinctions, and detect as it were a royal road to the interchange of opinion. Yet, in thus diminishing their grammatical forms and simplifying their rules, in this common effort to evince a striking contrast to the usual effects of civilization, all confusion has been prevented by the very manner in which the operation has been conducted; for the revolution produced has been so gradual in its progress, that it is only to be discovered on a comparison of the respective languages at periods of a considerable interval."†

The interval that Mr. Price has taken in the present case is certainly wide enough. What has to be explained is the difference that we find between the written English of the middle of the

* Preface to Warton, 85.   † Ib., 86.

twelfth century and that, not of the age of Alfred, or the end of the ninth century, but rather of the end of the eleventh. The question is, how we are to account for a great change which would appear to have taken place in the language, as employed for literary purposes, not in three centuries, but in one century, or even in half a century. The English of Alfred continues to be in all respects the English of Alfric, who lived and wrote more than a century later. The National Chronicle, still written substantially in the old language, comes down even to the year 1154. It is probable that we have here the continued employment, for the sake of uniformity, of an idiom which had now become antique, or what is called dead; but there is certainly no evidence or trace of any other form of the national speech having ever been used in writing before the year 1100 at the earliest. The overthrow of the native government and civilization by the Conquest in the latter part of the eleventh century would not, of course, extinguish the knowledge of the old literary language of the country till after the lapse of about a generation. We may fairly, then, regard the change in question as having taken place, in all probability, not in three centuries, as Mr. Price puts the case, but within at most the third part of that space. This correction, while it brings the breaking up of the language into close connexion in point of time with the social revolution, gives it also much more of a sudden and convulsionary character than it has in Mr. Price's representation. The gradual and gentle flow, assumed to have extended over three centuries, turns out to have been really a rapid precipitous descent—something almost of the nature of a cataract—effected possibly within the sixth or eighth part of that space of time.

It may be that there is a tendency in certain languages, or in all languages, to undergo a similar simplification of their grammar to that which the English underwent at this crisis. And it is conceivable that such a tendency constantly operating unchecked may at last produce such a change as we have in the present case, the conversion of the language from one of a synthetic to one of an analytic structure. That may have happened with those other languages of the Low-Germanic stock to which Mr. Price refers. But such was certainly not the case with the English. We have that language distinctly before us for three or four centuries, during which it is not pretended that there is to be detected a trace of the operation of any such tendency. The tendency, therefore, either did not exist, or must have been rendered inoperative by some counteracting influence. If, on the other hand, we are to suppose that, in our own or in any other language, the tendency suddenly developed itself or became active at a particular moment, that would necessarily imply the very operation of a new external cause which Mr. Price's theory denies. It is no matter whether we may or may not be able to point out the cause; that a cause there must have been is unquestionable.

In the case before us, the cause is sufficiently obvious. The integrity of the constitution or grammatical system of the language was preserved so long as its literature flourished; when that ceased to be read and studied and produced, the grammatical cultivation and knowledge of the language also ceased. The two things, indeed, were really one and the same. The literature and the literary form of the language could not but live and die together. Whatever killed the one was sure also to blight the other. And what was it that did or could bring the native literature of England suddenly to an end in the eleventh or twelfth century except the new political and social circumstances in which the country was then placed? What other than such a cause ever extinguished in any country the light of its ancient literature?

Of at least two similar cases we have a perfect knowledge. How long did the classical Latin continue to be a living language? Just so long as the fabric of Latin civilization in the Western Empire continued to exist; so long, and no longer. When that was overthrown, the literature which was its product and exponent, its expression and in a manner its very soul, and the highly artificial form of language which was the material in which that literature was wrought, were both at once struck with a mortal disease under which they perished almost with the generation that had witnessed the consummation of the barbaric invasion. Exactly similar is the history of the classic Greek, only that it continued to exist as a living language for a thousand years after the Latin, the social system with which it was bound up, of which it was part and parcel, lasting so much longer. When that fell, with the fall of the Eastern Empire in the fifteenth century, the language also became extinct. The ancient Greek gave place to the modern Greek, or what is called the Romaic. The conquest of Constantinople by the Turks was, so far, to the Greek language the same thing that the Norman Conquest was to the English.

THE THIRTEENTH AND FOURTEENTH CENTURIES.—ASCENDANCY OF THE SCHOLASTIC PHILOSOPHY.

Ever since the appearance of Peter Lombard's Four Books of Sentences, about the middle of the twelfth century, a struggle for ascendancy had been going on throughout Europe between the Scholastic Theology, or new philosophy, and the grammatical and rhetorical studies with which men had previously been chiefly occupied. At first the natural advantages of its position told in favour of the established learning; nay an impulse and a new inspiration were probably given to poetry and the belles-lettres for a time by the competition of logic and philosophy, and the general intellectual excitement thus produced: it was in the latter part of the twelfth century that the writing of Latin verse was cultivated with the greatest success; it was at the very end of that century, indeed, that Geoffrey de Vinsauf, as we have seen, composed and published his poem on the restoration of the legitimate mode of versification, under the title of Nova Poetria, or the New Poetry. But from about this date the tide began to turn; and the first half of the thirteenth century may be described as the era of the decline and fall of elegant literature, and the complete reduction of studious minds under the dominion of the scholastic logic and metaphysics.

In the University of Paris, and it was doubtless the same elsewhere, from about the middle of the thirteenth century, the ancient classics seem nearly to have ceased to be read; and all that was taught of rhetoric, or even of grammar, consisted of a few lessons from Priscian. The habit of speaking Latin correctly and elegantly, which had been so common an accomplishment of the scholars of the last age, was now generally lost: even at the universities, the classic tongue was corrupted into a base jargon, in which frequently all grammar and syntax were disregarded. This universal revolt from the study of words and of æsthetics to that of thoughts and of things is the most remarkable event in the intellectual history of the species. Undoubtedly all its results were not evil. On the whole, it was most probably the salvation even of that learning and elegant literature which it seemed for a time to have overwhelmed. The excitement of its very novelty awakened the minds of men. Never was there such a ferment of intellectual activity as now sprung up in Europe. The enthusiasm of the Crusades seemed to have been succeeded by an enthusiasm of study, which equally impelled its successive inundations of devotees. In the beginning of the fourteenth century there were thirty thousand students at the

University of Oxford; and that of Paris could probably boast of the attendance of a still vaster multitude. This was something almost like a universal diffusion of education and knowledge. The brief revival of elegant literature in the twelfth century was a premature spring, which could not last. The preliminary processes of vegetation were not sufficiently advanced to sustain any general or enduring efflorescence; nor was the state of the world such as to call for or admit of any extensive spread of the kind of scholarship then cultivated. The probability is, that, even if nothing else had taken its place, it would have gradually become feebler in character, as well as confined within a narrower circle of cultivators, till it had altogether evaporated and disappeared. The excitement of the new learning, turbulent and in some respects debasing as it was, saved Western Europe from the complete extinction of the light of scholarship and philosophy which would in that case have ensued, and kept alive the spirit of intellectual culture, though in the mean while imprisoned and limited in its vision, for a happier future time when it should have ampler scope and full freedom of range.

Almost the only studies now cultivated by the common herd of students were the Aristotelian logic and metaphysics. Yet it was not till after a struggle of some length that the supremacy of Aristotle was established in the schools. The most ancient statutes of the University of Paris that have been preserved, those issued by the pope's legate, Robert de Courçon, in 1215, prohibited the reading either of the metaphysical or the physical works of that philosopher, or of any abridgment of them. This, however, it has been remarked, was a mitigation of the treatment these books had met with a few years before, when all the copies of them that could be found were ordered to be thrown into the fire.* Still more lenient was a decree of Pope Gregory IX. in 1231, which only ordered the reading of them to be suspended until they should have undergone correction. Certain heretical notions in religion, promulgated or suspected to have been entertained by some of the most zealous of the early Aristotelians, had awakened the apprehensions of the Church; but the general orthodoxy of their successors quieted these fears; and in course of time the authority of the Stagirite was universally recognized both in theology and in the profane sciences.

Some of the most distinguished of the scholastic doctors of this period were natives of Britain. Such, in particular, were Alexander de Hales, styled the Irrefragable, an English Franciscan, who died at Paris in 1245, and who is famous as the master of

* Crevier, Histoire de l'Univ. de Paris, I. 313.

St. Bonaventura, and the first of the long list of commentators on the Four Books of the Sentences; the Subtle Doctor, John Duns Scotus, also a Franciscan and the chief glory of that order, who, after teaching with unprecedented popularity and applause at Oxford and Paris, died at Cologne in 1308, at the early age of forty-three, leaving a mass of writings, the very quantity of which would be sufficiently wonderful, even if they were not marked by a vigour and penetration of thought which, down to our own day, has excited the admiration of all who have examined them; and William Occam, the Invincible, another Franciscan, the pupil of Scotus, but afterwards his opponent on the great philosophical question of the origin and nature of Universals or General Terms, which so long divided, and still divides, logicians. Occam, who died at Munich in 1347, was the restorer, and perhaps the most able defender that the middle ages produced, of the doctrine of Nominalism, or the opinion that general notions are merely names, and not real existences, as was contended by the Realists. The side taken by Occam was that of the minority in his own day, and for many ages after, and his views accordingly were generally regarded as heterodox in the schools; but his high merits have been recognized in modern times, when perhaps the greater number of speculators have come over to his way of thinking.

MATHEMATICAL AND OTHER STUDIES.

In the mathematical and physical sciences, Roger Bacon is the great name of the thirteenth century, and indeed the greatest that either his country or Europe can produce for some centuries after this time. He was born at Ilchester about the year 1214, and died in 1292. His writings that are still preserved, of which the principal is that entitled his Opus Majus (or Greater Work), show that the range of his investigations included theology, grammar, the ancient languages, geometry, astronomy, chronology, geography, music, optics, mechanics, chemistry, and most of the other branches of experimental philosophy. In all these sciences he had mastered whatever was then known; and his knowledge, though necessarily mixed with much error, extended in various directions considerably farther than, but for the evidence of his writings, we should have been warranted in believing that scientific researches had been carried in that age. In optics, for instance, he not only understood the general laws of reflected and refracted light, and had at least conceived such an instrument as a telescope, but he makes some advances towards an explanation of the phenomena of the rainbow. It may be doubted whether what have been sometimes called his inventions and discoveries in mechanics and in chemistry were for the greater part more than notions he had formed of the possibility of accomplishing certain results; but, even regarded as mere speculations or conjectures, many of his statements of what might be done show that he was familiar with mechanical principles, and possessed considerable acquaintance with the powers of natural agents. He appears to have been acquainted with the effects and composition of gunpowder, which indeed there is other evidence for believing to have been then known in Europe. Bacon's notions on the right method of philosophizing are remarkably enlightened for the times in which he lived; and his general views upon most subjects evince a penetration and liberality much beyond the spirit of his age. With all his sagacity and freedom from prejudice, indeed, he was a believer both in astrology and alchemy; but, as it has been observed, these delusions did not then stand in the same predicament as now; they were " irrational only because unproved, and neither impossible nor unworthy of the investigation of a philosopher, in the absence of preceding experiments."*

Another eminent English cultivator of mathematical science in that age was the celebrated Robert Grosseteste, or Grostête, or Grosthead, bishop of Lincoln, the friend and patron of Bacon. Grostête, who died in 1253, and of whom we shall have more to say presently, is the author of a treatise on the sphere, which had been printed. A third name that deserves to be mentioned along with these is that of Sir Michael Scott, famous in popular tradition as a practitioner of the occult sciences, but whom his writings, of which several are extant, and have been printed, prove to have been possessed of acquirements, both in science and literature, of which few in those times could boast. He is commonly assumed to have been proprietor of the estate of Balwearie, in Fife, and to have survived till near the close of the thirteenth century; but all that is certain is that he was a native of Scotland, and one of the most distinguished of the learned persons

* Penny Cyclopædia, lii. 213. Bacon's principal work, the Opus Majus, was published by Dr. Jebb, in a folio volume, at London in 1733; and several of his other treatises had been previously printed at Francfort, Paris, and elsewhere. His Opus Minus has also now been edited by Professor Brewer, of King's College, London, and forms one of the volumes of the series entitled Rerum Britannicarum Medii Ævi Scriptores, or Chronicles and Memorials of Great Britain and Ireland during the Middle Ages; published by the authority of Her Majesty's Treasury, under the direction of the Master of the Rolls, 8vo. London, 1857, &c.

who flourished at the court of the Emperor Frederick II., who died in 1250.* Like Roger Bacon, Scott was addicted to the study of alchemy and astrology; but these were in his eyes also parts of natural philosophy. Among other works, a History of Animals is ascribed to him; and he is said to have translated several of the works of Aristotle from the Greek into Latin, at the command of the Emperor Frederick. He is reputed to have been eminently skilled both in astronomy and medicine; and a contemporary, John Bacon, himself known by the title of Prince of the Averroists, or followers of the Arabian doctor Averroes, celebrates him as a great theologian.†

These instances, however, were rare exceptions to the general rule. Metaphysics and logic, together with divinity—which was converted into little else than a subject of metaphysical and logical contention—so occupied the crowd of intellectual inquirers, that, except the professional branches of law and medicine, scarcely any other studies were generally attended to. Roger Bacon himself tells us that he knew of only two good mathematicians among his contemporaries—one John of Leyden, who had been a pupil of his own, and another whom he does not name, but who is supposed to have been John Peckham, a Franciscan friar, who afterwards became archbishop of Canterbury. Few students of the science, he says, proceeded farther than the fifth proposition of the first book of Euclid—the well-known asses' bridge. The study of geometry was still confounded in the popular understanding with the study of magic—a proof that it was a very rare pursuit. In arithmetic, although the Arabic numerals had found their way to Christian Europe before the middle of the fourteenth century, they do not appear to have come into general use till a considerably later date. Astronomy, however, was sufficiently cultivated at the University of Paris to enable some of the members to predict an eclipse of the sun which happened on the 31st of January, 1310.‡ This science was indebted for part of the attention it received to the belief that was universally entertained in the influence of the stars over human affairs. And, as astrology led to the cultivation and improvement of astronomy, so the other imaginary science of alchemy undoubtedly aided the progress of chemistry and medicine. Besides Roger Bacon and Michael Scott in the thirteenth century, England contributes the names of John Danstein, of Richard, and of Cremer abbot of Westminster, the disciple and friend of the famous Raymond

---

* See article in Penny Cyclopædia, xxi. 101.
† See an article on Michael Scott in Bayle.
‡ Crevier, ii. 224.

Lully, to the list of the writers on alchemy in the fourteenth. Lully himself visited England in the reign of Edward I., on the invitation of the king; and he affirms in one of his works, that, in the secret chamber of St. Katharine in the Tower of London, he performed in the royal presence the experiment of transmuting some crystal into a mass of diamond, or adamant as he calls it, of which Edward, he says, caused some little pillars to be made for the tabernacle of God. It was popularly believed, indeed, at the time, that the English king had been furnished by Lully with a great quantity of gold for defraying the expense of an expedition he intended to make to the Holy Land. Edward III. was not less credulous on the subject than his grandfather, as appears by an order which he issued in 1329, in the following terms:—" Know all men, that we have been assured that John of Rous and Master William of Dalby know how to make silver by the art of alchemy; that they have made it in former times, and still continue to make it; and, considering that these men, by their art, and by making the precious metal, may be profitable to us and to our kingdom, we have commanded our well-beloved Thomas Cary to apprehend the aforesaid John and William, wherever they can be found, within liberties or without, and bring them to us, together with all the instruments of their art, under safe and sure custody." The earliest English writer on medicine, whose works have been printed, is Gilbert English (or Anglicus), who flourished in the thirteenth century; and he was followed in the next century by John de Gaddesden. The practice of medicine had now been taken in a great measure out of the hands of the clergy; but the art was still in the greater part a mixture of superstition and quackery, although the knowledge of some useful remedies, and perhaps also of a few principles, had been obtained from the writings of the Arabic physicians (many of which had been translated into Latin) and from the instructions delivered in the schools of Spain and Italy. The distinction between the physician and the apothecary was already well understood. Surgery also began to be followed as a separate branch: some works are still extant, partly printed, partly in manuscript, by John Ardern, or Arden, an eminent English surgeon, who practised at Newark in the fourteenth century. A lively picture of the state of the surgical art at this period is given by a French writer, Guy de Cauliac, in a system of surgery which he published in 1363: " The practitioners in surgery," he says, " are divided into five sects. The first follow Roger and Roland, and the four masters, and apply poultices to all wounds and abscesses; the second follow Brunus and Theodoric, and in the same cases use wine only; the third follow Saliceto and Lanfranc, and treat wounds with ointments and soft plasters; the fourth are chiefly Germans, who attend the armies, and promiscuously use charms, potions, oil, and wool; the fifth are old women and ignorant people, who have recourse to the saints in all cases."

Yet the true method of philosophising, by experiment and the collection of facts, was almost as distinctly and emphatically laid down in this age by Roger Bacon, as it was more than three centuries afterwards by his illustrious namesake. Much knowledge, too, must necessarily have been accumulated in various departments by the actual application of this method. Some of the greatest of the modern chemists have bestowed the highest praise on the manner in which the experiments of the alchemists, or hermetic philosophers, as they called themselves, on metals and other natural substances appear to have been conducted. In another field—namely, in that of geography, and the institutions, customs, and general state of distant countries—a great deal of new information must have been acquired from the accounts that were now published by various travellers, especially by Marco Polo, who penetrated as far as to Tartary and China, in the latter part of the thirteenth century, and by our countryman, Sir John Mandevil, who also traversed a great part of the East about a hundred years later. Roger Bacon has inserted a very curious epitome of the geographical knowledge of his time in his Opus Majus.

UNIVERSITIES AND COLLEGES.

About the middle of the thirteenth century, both in England and elsewhere, the universities began to assume a new form, by the erection of colleges for the residence of their members as separate communities. The zeal for learning that was displayed in these endowments is the most honourable characteristic of the age. Before the end of the fourteenth century the following colleges were founded at Oxford:—University Hall, by William, archdeacon of Durham, who died in 1249; Baliol College, by John Baliol, father of King John of Scotland, about 1263; Merton College, by Walter Merton, bishop of Rochester, in 1268; Exeter College, by Walter Stapleton, bishop of Exeter, about 1315; Oriel College, originally called the Hall of the Blessed Virgin of Oxford, by Edward II. and his almoner, Adam de Brom, about 1324; Queen's College, by Robert Eglesfield, chaplain to Queen Philippa, in 1340; and New College, in 1379, by the celebrated William of Wykeham, bishop of Winchester, the munificent founder also of Winchester School or College. In the University of Cambridge the foundations were, Peter House, by Hugh Balsham, sub-prior and afterwards bishop of Ely, about 1256; Michael College (afterwards incorporated with Trinity College), by Herby de Stanton, Chancellor of the Exchequer to Edward II., about 1324; University Hall (soon afterwards burnt down), by Richard Badew, Chancellor of the University, in 1326; King's Hall (afterwards united to Trinity College), by Edward III.; Clare Hall, a restoration of University Hall, by Elizabeth de Clare, Countess of Ulster, about 1347; Pembroke Hall, or the Hall of Valence and Mary, in the same year, by Mary de St. Paul, widow of Aymer de Valence, Earl of Pembroke; Trinity Hall, in 1350, by William Bateman, bishop of Norwich; Gonvil Hall, about the same time, by Edmond Gonvil, parson of Terrington and Rushworth, in Norfolk; and Corpus Christi, or Ben'et (that is, Benedict) College, about 1351, by the United Guilds of Corpus Christi and St. Mary, in the town of Cambridge. The erection of these colleges, besides the accommodations which they afforded in various ways both to teachers and students, gave a permanent establishment to the universities, which they scarcely before possessed. The original condition of these celebrated seats of learning, in regard to all the conveniences of teaching, appears to have been humble in the extreme. Great disorders and scandals are also said to have arisen, before the several societies were thus assembled each within its own walls, from the intermixture of the students with the townspeople, and their exemption from all discipline. But, when the members of the University were counted by tens of thousands, discipline, even in the most favourable circumstances, must have been nearly out of the question. The difficulty would not be lessened by the general character of the persons composing the learned mob, if we may take it from the quaint historian of the University of Oxford. Many of them, Anthony à Wood affirms, were mere "varlets who pretended to be scholars;" he does not scruple to charge them with being habitually guilty of thieving and other enormities; and he adds, "They lived under no discipline. neither had any tutors, but only for fashion sake would sometimes thrust themselves into the schools at ordinary lectures, and, when they went to perform any mischiefs, then would they be accounted scholars, that so they might free themselves from the jurisdiction of the burghers." To repress the evils of this state of things, the old statutes of the University of Paris, in 1215, had ordained that no one should be reputed a scholar who had not a certain master. Another of these ancient regulations may be quoted in illustration of the simplicity of the times, and of the small measure of pomp and circumstance that the heads of the commonwealth of learning could then affect. It is ordered that every master reading lectures in the faculty of arts should have his cloak or gown round, black, and falling as low as the heels—"at least," adds the statute, with amusing *naïveté*, "while it is new." But this famous seminary long continued to take pride in its poverty as one of its most honourable distinctions. There is something very noble and affecting in the terms in which the rector and masters of the faculty of arts are found petitioning, in 1302, for a postponement of the hearing of a cause in which they were parties. "We have difficulty," they say, "in finding the money to pay the procurators and advocates, whom it is necessary for us to employ—*we whose profession it is to possess no wealth.*" * Yet, when funds were wanted for important purposes in connexion with learning or science, they were supplied in this age with no stinted liberality. We have seen with what alacrity opulent persons came forward to build and endow colleges, as soon as the expediency of such foundations came to be perceived. In almost all these establishments more or less provision was made for the permanent maintenance of a body of poor scholars, in other words, for the admission of even the humblest classes to a share in the benefits of that learned education whose temples and priesthood were thus planted in the land. It is probable, also, that the same kind of liberality was often shown in other ways. Roger Bacon tells us himself that, in the twenty years in which he had been engaged in his experiments, he had spent in books and instruments no less a sum than two thousand French livres, an amount of silver equal to about six thousand pounds of our present money, and in effective value certainly to many times that sum. He must have been indebted for these large supplies to the generosity of rich friends and patrons.

CULTIVATION AND EMPLOYMENT OF THE LEARNED TONGUES IN THE THIRTEENTH AND FOURTEENTH CENTURIES.

Notwithstanding the general neglect of its elegancies, and of the habit of speaking it correctly or grammatically, the Latin tongue still continued to be in England, as elsewhere, the common language of the learned, and that in which books were generally written that were intended for their perusal. Among

* Crevier, ii. 404.

this class of works may be included the contemporary chronicles, most of which were compiled in the monasteries, and the authors of almost all of which were churchmen.

Latin was also, for a great part of the thirteenth and fourteenth centuries, the usual language of the law, at least in writing. There may, indeed, be some doubt perhaps as to the Charter of John. It is usually given in Latin; but there is also a French text first published in the first edition of D'Achery's Spicilegium (1655-57), xii. 573, &c., which there is some reason for believing to be the original. "An attentive critical examination of the French and Latin together," says Mr. Luders, "will induce any person capable of making it to think several chapters of the latter translated from the former, and not originally composed in Latin."* Yet the Capitula, or articles on which the Great Charter is founded, are known to us only in Latin. And all the other charters of liberties are in that language. So is every statute down to the year 1275. The first that is in French is the Statute of Westminster the First, passed in that year, the 3rd of Edward I. Throughout the remainder of the reign of Edward they are sometimes in Latin, sometimes in French, but more frequently in the former language. The French becomes more frequent in the time of Edward II., and is almost exclusively used in that of Edward III. and Richard II. Still there are statutes in Latin in the sixth and eighth years of the last-mentioned king. It is not improbable that, from the accession of Edward I., the practice may have been to draw up every statute in both languages. Of the law treatises, Bracton (about 1265) and Fleta (about 1285) are in Latin; Britton (about 1280) and the Miroir des Justices (about 1320), in French.

Latin was not only the language in which all the scholastic divines and philosophers wrote, but was also employed by all writers on geometry, astronomy, chemistry, medicine, and the other branches of mathematical and natural science. All the works of Roger Bacon, for example, are in Latin; and it is worth noting that, although by no means a writer of classical purity, this distinguished cultivator of science is still one of the most correct writers of his time. He was indeed not a less zealous student of literature than of science, nor less anxious for the improvement of the one than of the other: accustomed himself to read the works of Aristotle in the original Greek, he denounces as mischievous impositions the wretched Latin trans-

* Tracts on the Law and History of England (1810), p. 399. D'Achery's French text may also be read in a more common book, Johnson's History of Magna Charta, 2nd edit. (1772), pp. 182–234.

lations by which alone they were known to the generality of his contemporaries: he warmly recommends the study of grammar and the ancient languages generally; and deplores the little attention paid to the Oriental tongues in particular, of which he says there were not in his time more than three or four persons in Western Europe who knew anything. It is remarkable that the most strenuous effort made within the present period to revive the study of this last-mentioned learning proceeded from another eminent cultivator of natural science, the famous Raymond Lully, half philosopher, half quack, as it has been the fashion to regard him. It was at his instigation that Clement V., in 1311, with the approbation of the Council of Vienne, published a constitution, ordering that professors of Greek, Hebrew, Arabic, and Chaldaic should be established in the universities of Paris, Oxford, Bologna, and Salamanca. He had, more than twenty years before, urged the same measure upon Honorius IV., and its adoption then was only prevented by the death of that pope. After all, it is doubtful if the papal ordinance was ever carried into effect. There were, however, professors of strange, or foreign, languages at Paris a few years after this time, as appears from an epistle of Pope John XXII. to his legate there in 1325, in which the latter is enjoined to keep watch over the said professors, lest they should introduce any dogmas as strange as the languages they taught.*

Many additional details are collected by Warton in his Dissertation on the Introduction of Learning into England. He is inclined to think that many Greek manuscripts found their way into Europe from Constantinople in the time of the Crusades. "Robert Grosthead, bishop of Lincoln," he proceeds, "an universal scholar, and no less conversant in polite letters than the most abstruse sciences, cultivated and patronized the study of the Greek language. This illustrious prelate, who is said to have composed almost two hundred books, read lectures in the school of the Franciscan friars at Oxford about the year 1230. He translated Dionysius the Areopagite and Damascenus into Latin. He greatly facilitated the knowledge of Greek by a translation of Suidas's Lexicon, a book in high repute among the lower Greeks, and at that time almost a recent compilation. He promoted John of Basingstoke to the archdeaconry of Leicester, chiefly because he was a Greek scholar, and possessed many Greek manuscripts, which he is said to have brought from Athens into England. He entertained, as a domestic in his palace, Nicholas, chaplain of the abbot of St. Albans, surnamed

* Crevier, Hist. de l'Univ. de Paris, II. 112, 227.

Græcus, from his uncommon proficiency in Greek; and by his assistance he translated from Greek into Latin the testaments of the twelve patriarchs. Grosthead had almost incurred the censure of excommunication for preferring a complaint to the pope that most of the opulent benefices in England were occupied by Italians. But the practice, although notoriously founded on the monopolizing and arbitrary spirit of papal imposition, and a manifest act of injustice to the English clergy, probably contributed to introduce many learned foreigners into England, and to propagate philological literature."* "Bishop Grosthead," Warton adds, "is also said to have been profoundly skilled in the Hebrew language. William the Conqueror permitted great numbers of Jews to come over from Rouen, and to settle in England, about the year 1087. Their multitude soon increased, and they spread themselves in vast bodies throughout most of the cities and capital towns in England, where they built synagogues. There were fifteen hundred at York about the year 1189. At Bury in Suffolk is a very complete remain of a Jewish synagogue of stone, in the Norman style, large and magnificent. Hence it was that many of the learned English ecclesiastics of those times became acquainted with their books and language. In the reign of William Rufus, at Oxford the Jews were remarkably numerous, and had acquired a considerable property; and some of their rabbis were permitted to open a school in the university, where they instructed not only their own people, but many Christian students, in the Hebrew literature, about the year 1054. Within two hundred years after their admission or establishment by the Conqueror, they were banished the kingdom. This circumstance was highly favourable to the circulation of their learning in England. The suddenness of their dismission obliged them, for present subsistence, and other reasons, to sell their moveable goods of all kinds, among which were large quantities of Rabbinical books. The monks in various parts availed themselves of the distribution of these treasures. At Huntingdon and Stamford there was a prodigious sale of their effects, containing immense stores of Hebrew manuscripts, which were immediately purchased by Gregory of Huntingdon, prior of the abbey of Ramsey. Gregory speedily became an adept in the Hebrew, by means of these valuable acquisitions, which he bequeathed to his monastery about the year 1250. Other members of the same convent, in consequence of these advantages, are said to have been equal proficients in the same language, soon after the death of Prior Gregory; among whom were

* Hist. of Eng. Poet, i. cxxxv.

Robert Dodford, librarian of Ramsey, and Laurence Holbeck, who compiled a Hebrew Lexicon. At Oxford, great multitudes of their books fell into the hands of Roger Bacon, or were bought by his brethren, the Franciscan friars of that university."* The general expulsion of the Jews from England did not take place till the year 1290, in the reign of Edward I.; but they had been repeatedly subjected to sudden violence, both from the populace and from the government, before that grand catastrophe.

LAST AGE OF THE FRENCH LANGUAGE IN ENGLAND.

The French language, however, was still in common use among us down to the latter part of the reign of Edward III. It is well remarked by Pinkerton that we are to date the cessation of the general use of French in this country from the breaking out of "the inveterate enmity" between the two nations in the reign of that king.† Higden, as we have seen, writing before this change had taken place, tells us that French was still in his day the language which the children of gentlemen were taught to speak from their cradle, and the only language that was allowed to be used by boys at school; the effect of which was, that even the country people generally understood it and affected its use. The tone, however, in which this is stated by Higden indicates that the public feeling had already begun to set in against these customs, and that, if they still kept their ground from use and wont, they had lost their hold upon any firmer or surer stay. Accordingly about a quarter of a century or thirty years later his translator Trevisa finds it necessary to subjoin the following explanation or correction:—
"This maner was myche yused tofore the first moreyn [before the first murrain or plague, which happened in 1349], and is siththe som dele [somewhat] ychaungide. For John Cornwaile, a mainter of gramer, chaungide the lore [learning] in gramer scole and construction of [from] Frensch into Englisch, and Richard Pencriche lerned that maner teching of him, and other men of Pencriche. So that now, the yere of owre Lord a thousand thre hundred foure score and fyve, of the secunde King Rychard after the Conquest nyne, in alle the gramer scoles of England children loveth Frensch, and construeth and lerneth an [in] Englisch, and

* Hist. of Eng. Poet., I. cxxxvi.
† Essay on the Origin of Scotish Poetry, prefixed to Ancient Scotish Poems, 1786, vol. i. p. lxiii. Some curious remarks upon the peculiar political position in which England was held to stand in relation to France in the first reigns after the Conquest may be read in Gale's Preface to his Scriptores Quindecim.

haveth thereby avauntage in oon [one] side and desavauntage in another. Her [their] avauntage is, that thei lerneth her [their] gramer in lasso tyme than children were wont to do; desavauntage is, that now children of gramer scole kunneth [know] no more Frensch than can her lifte [knows their left] heele; and that is harm for hem [them], and [if] thei schul passe the see and travaile in strange londes, and in many other places also. Also gentilmen haveth now mych ylefte for to teche her [their] children Frensch."*

A few years before this, in 1362 (the 36th of Edward III.), was passed the statute ordaining that all pleas pleaded in the king's courts should be pleaded in the English language, and entered and enrolled in Latin; the pleadings, or oral arguments, till now having been in French, and the enrolments of the judgments sometimes in French, sometimes in Latin. The reasons assigned for this change in the preamble of the act are: " Because it is often showed to the king by the prelates, dukes, earls, barons, and all the commonalty, of the great mischiefs which have happened to divers of the realm, because the laws, customs, and statutes of this realm be not commonly holden and kept in the same realm, for that they be pleaded, shewed, and judged in the French tongue, which is much unknown in the said realm, so that the people which do implead, or be impleaded, in the king's court, and in the courts of other, have no knowledge nor understanding of that which is said for them or against them by their sergeants and other pleaders; and that reasonably the said laws and customs the rather shall be perceived and known, and better understood, in the tongue used in the said realm, and by so much every man of the said realm may the better govern himself without offending of the law, and the better keep, save, and defend his heritage and possessions; and in divers regions and countries, where the king, the nobles, and other of the said realm have been, good governance and full right is done to every person, because that their laws and customs be learned and used in the tongue of the country."

Yet, oddly enough, this very statute (of which we have here quoted the old translation) is in French, which, whatever might be the case with the great body of the people, continued down to a considerably later date than this to be the mother-tongue of our Norman royal family, and probably also that generally spoken at court and at least in the upper house of parliament. Ritson asserts that there is no instance in which Henry III. is

* As quoted by Tyrwhitt, from Harl. MS. 1900, in Essay on the Language, &c., of Chaucer.

known to have expressed himself in English. "King Edward I. generally," he continues, "or, according to Andrew of Wyntoun, constantly, spoke the French language, both in the council and in the field, many of his sayings in that idiom being recorded by our old historians. When, in the council at Norham, in 1291-2, Anthony Beck had, as it is said, proved to the king, by reason and eloquence, that Bruce was too dangerous a neighbour to be king of Scotland, his Majesty replied, *Par le sung de dieu, vous aves bien eschuité,* and accordingly adjudged the crown to Baliol; of whom, refusing to obey his summons, he afterwards said, *A ce fol felon tel folie fais? S'il ne voult venir à nous, nous viendrons à lui.** There is but one instance of his speaking English; which was when the great sultan sent ambassadors, after his assassination, to protest that he had no knowledge of it. These, standing at a distance, adored the king, prone on the ground; and Edward said in English (*in Anglico*), *You, indeed, adore, but you little love, me.* Nor understood they his words, because they spoke to him by an interpreter.† King Edward II., likewise, who married a French princess, used himself the French tongue. Sir Henry Spelman had a manuscript, in which was a piece of poetry entitled *De le roi Edward le fiz roi Edward, le chanson qu'il fist mesmes,* which Lord Orford was unacquainted with. His son Edward III. always wrote his letters or despatches in French, as we find them preserved by Robert of Avesbury; and in the early part of his reign even the Oxford scholars were confined in conversation to Latin or French.‡ . . . . There is a single instance preserved of this monarch's use of the English language. He appeared in 1349 in a tournament at Canterbury with a white swan for his impress, and the following motto embroidered on his shield:—

> Hay, hay, the wythe swan!
> By Godes soul I am thy man!§

Lewis Beaumont, bishop of Durham, 1317, understood not a word of either Latin or English. In reading the bull of his appointment, which he had been taught to spell for several days before, he stumbled upon the word *metropolitice,* which he in vain endeavoured to pronounce; and, having hammered over it a

---

* For these two speeches, the latter of which, by-the-by, he points as if he did not understand it, Ritson quotes the Scotichronicon (Fordun), ll. 147, 156.
† For this anecdote Ritson quotes Hemingford (in Galo), p. 591.
‡ The authority for this last statement is a note in Warton's Hist. of Eng. Poet. l. 6 (edit. of 1824).
§ "See Warton's Hist. of Eng. Poet. ll. 251 (l. 86, in edit. of 1821). He had another, 'It is as it is;' and may have had a third, 'Ha St. Edward! Un St. George.'"

considerable time, at last cried out, in his mother tongue, *Seit pour dite! Par Seynt Loweys il ne fu pas curteis qui ceste parole ici escrit.** The first instance of the English language which Mr. Tyrwhitt had discovered in the parliamentary proceedings was the confession of Thomas, Duke of Gloucester, in 1398. He might, however, have met with a petition of the mercers of London ten years earlier (*Rot. Parl.* iii. 225). The oldest English instrument produced by Rymer is dated 1368 (vii. 526); but an indenture in the same idiom betwixt the abbot and convent of Whitby, and Robert the son of John Bustard, dated at York in 1343,† is the earliest known."‡

RE-EMERGENCE OF THE ENGLISH AS A LITERARY TONGUE.

French metrical romances and other poetry, accordingly, continued to be written in England, and in many instances by Englishmen, throughout the thirteenth and fourteenth centuries. Down to the end of the twelfth century verse was probably the only form in which romances, meaning originally any compositions in the Romance or French language, then any narrative compositions whatever, were written: in the thirteenth, a few may have appeared in prose; but before the close of the fourteenth prose had become the usual form in which such works were produced, and many of the old metrical romances had been recast in this new shape. The early French prose romances, however, do not, like their metrical predecessors, belong in any sense to the literature of this country: many of them were no doubt generally read for a time in England as well as in France; but we have no reason for believing that any of them were primarily addressed to the English public, or were written in England or by English subjects, and even during the brief space that they continued popular they seem to have been regarded as foreign importations.

For the last fifty years of the fourteenth century, however, the French language had been rapidly losing the position it had held among us from the middle of the eleventh, and becoming among all classes in England a foreign tongue. To the testi-

* "Robert de Graystanes, Anglia Sacra, i. 761—'Take it as said! By St. Lewis, he was not very civil who wrote this word here.'"
† "Charlton's History of Whitby, 247."
‡ Dissertation on Romance and Minstrelsy, pp. lxxv.-lxxxvi. We have not thought it necessary to preserve Ritson's peculiar spelling, adopted, apparently, on no principle except that of deviating from the established usage.

monies above produced of Higden writing immediately before
the commencement of this change, and of Trevisa after it had
been going on for about a quarter of a century, may be added
what Chaucer writes, probably within ten years after the date
(1385) which Trevisa expressly notes as that of his statement.
In the Prologue to his Testament of Love, a prose work, which
seems to have been far advanced, if not finished, in 1392* the
great father of our English poetry, speaking of those of his
countrymen who still persisted in writing French verse, expresses himself thus:—"Certes there ben some that speke thyr
poysy mater in Frenche, of whyche speche the Frenche men
have as good a fantasye as we have in hearing of French mennes
Englysho." And afterwards he adds, "Lot, then, clerkes
endyten in Latyn, for they have the propertye in science and the
knowinge in that facultye, and lette Frenchmen in theyr
Frenche also endyte theyr queynt termes, for it is kyndly
[natural] to theyr mouthes; and let us showe our fantasyes in
suche wordes as we learneden of our dames tonge." French, it
is evident from this, although it might still be a common acquirement among the higher classes, had ceased to be the mother-
tongue of any class of Englishmen, and was only known to those
to whom it was taught by a master. So, the Prioress in the
Canterbury Tales, although she could speak French "ful fayre
and fetisly," or neatly, spoke it only

> "After the scole of Stratford atte Bowe,
> For Frenche of Paris was to hire [her] unknowe."†

From this, as from many other passages in old writers, we learn
that the French taught and spoken in England had, as was indeed
inevitable, become a corrupt dialect of the language, or at least
very different from the French at Paris. But, as the foreign

---

* See Tyrwhitt's Account of the Works of Chaucer, prefixed to his
Glossary.

† It is impossible to believe with Sir Harris Nicolas, in his otherwise very
clear and judicious Life of Chaucer (8vo. Lond. 1843; additional note, p. 142),
that Chaucer perhaps here meant to intimate that the prioress could not
speak French at all, on the ground that the expression "French of Stratford-
at-Bow" is used in a tract published in 1586 (Ferne's Blazon of Gentrie), to
describe the language of English heraldry. In the first place the phrase is not
there "a colloquial paraphrase for *English*," but for the mixed French and
English, or, as it might be regarded, Anglicized or corrupted French, of our
heralds. But, at any rate, can it be supposed for a moment that Chaucer
would take so roundabout and fantastic a way as this of telling his readers
so simple a fact, as that his prioress could speak her native tongue? He
would never have spent three words upon such a matter, much less three
lines.

tongue lost its hold and declined in purity, the old Teutonic speech of the native population, favoured by the same circumstances and course of events which checked and depressed its rival, and having at last, after going through a process almost of dissolution and putrefaction, begun to assume a new organization, gradually recovered its ascendancy.

We have already examined the first revolution which the language underwent, and endeavoured to explain the manner in which it was brought about. It consisted in the disintegration of the grammatical system of the language, and the conversion of it from an inflectional and synthetic into a comparatively non-inflected and analytic language. The vocabulary, or what we may call the substance of the language, was not changed; that remained still purely Gothic, as it always had been; only the old form or structure was broken up or obliterated. There was no mixture or infusion of any foreign element; the language was as it were decomposed, but was not adulterated, and the process of decomposition may be regarded as having been mainly the work of the eleventh century, and as having been begun by the Danish Conquest and consummated by the Norman.

This first revolution which the language underwent is to be carefully distinguished from the second, which was brought about by the combination of the native with a foreign element, and consisted essentially in the change made in the vocabulary of the language by the introduction of numerous terms borrowed from the French. Of this latter innovation we find little trace till long after the completion of the former. For nearly two centuries after the Conquest the English seems to have been spoken and written (to the small extent to which it was written) with scarcely any intermixture of Norman. It only, in fact, began to receive such intermixture after it came to be adopted as the speech of that part of the nation which had previously spoken French. And this adoption was plainly the cause of the intermixture. So long as it remained the language only of those who had been accustomed to speak it from their infancy, and who had never known any other, it might have gradually become changed in its internal organization, but it could scarcely acquire any additions from a foreign source. What should have tempted the Saxon peasant to substitute a Norman term, upon any occasion, for the word of the same meaning with which the language of his ancestors supplied him? As for things and occasions for which new names were necessary, they must have come comparatively little in his way; and, when they did, the capabilities of his native tongue were sufficient to furnish him with appro priate forms of expression from its own resources. The corruption of the English by the intermixture of French vocables must have proceeded from those whose original language was French, and who were in habits of constant intercourse with French customs, French literature, and everything else that was French, at the same time that they, occasionally at least, spoke English. And this supposition is in perfect accordance with the historical fact. So long as the English was the language of only a part of the nation, and the French, as it were, struggled with it for mastery, it remained unadulterated;—when it became the speech of the whole people, of the higher classes as well as of the lower, then it lost its old Teutonic purity, and received a larger alien admixture from the alien lips through which it passed. Whether this was a fortunate circumstance, or the reverse, is another question. It may just be remarked, however, that the English, if it had been left to its own spontaneous and unassisted development, would probably have assumed a character resembling rather that of the Dutch or the Flemish than that of the German of the present day.

The commencement of this second revolution, which changed the very substance of the language, may most probably be dated from about the middle of the thirteenth century, or about a century and a half after the completion of the first, which affected, not the substance or vocabulary of the language, but only its form or grammatical system.

SECOND ENGLISH:—
COMMONLY CALLED *SEMI-SAXON*.

The chief remains that we have of English verse for the first two centuries after the Conquest have been enumerated by Sir Frederic Madden in a comprehensive paragraph of his valuable Introduction to the romance of Havelock, which we will take leave to transcribe:—" The notices by which we are enabled to trace the rise of our Saxon poetry from the Saxon period to the end of the twelfth century are few and scanty. We may, indeed, comprise them all in the Song of Canute recorded by the monk of Ely [Hist. Elyens. p. 505 apud Gale], who wrote about 1166; the words put into the mouth of Aldred archbishop of York, who died in 1060 [W. Malmesb. de Gest. Pontif. l. i. p. 271]; the verses ascribed to St. Godric, the hermit of Finchale, who died in 1170 [Rits. Bibliogr. Poet.]; the few lines preserved by Lambarde and Camden attributed to the same period [Rits. Anc. Songs, Diss. p. xxviii.]; and the prophecy said to have been set up at Here in the year 1189, as recorded by Benedict Abbas, Roger Hoveden, and the Chronicle of Lanercost [Rits. Metr. Rom. Diss. p. lxxiii.]. To the same reign of Henry II. are to be assigned the metrical compositions of Layamon [MS. Cott. Cal. A. ix., and Otho C. xiii.] and Orm [MS. Jun. 1], and also the legends of St. Katherine, St. Margaret, and St. Julian [MS. Bodl. 34], with some few others, from which we may learn with tolerable accuracy the state of the language at that time, and its gradual formation from the Saxon to the shape it subsequently assumed. From this period to the middle of the next century nothing occurs to which we can affix any certain date; but we shall probably not err in ascribing to that interval the poems ascribed to John de Guldevorde [MSS. Cott. Cal. A. ix., Jes. Coll. Oxon. 29], the Biblical History [MS. Bennet Cant. K. 11] and Poetical Paraphrase of the Psalms [MSS. Cott. Vesp. D. vii., Coll. Benn. Cant. O. 6, Bodl. 921] quoted by Warton, and the Moral Ode published by Hickes [MSS. Digby 4, Jes. Coll. Oxon. 29]. Between the years 1244 and 1258, we know, was written the versification of part of a meditation of St. Augustine, as proved by the age of the prior who gave the MS. to the Durham Library [MS. Eccl. Dun. A. iii. 12, and Bodl. 42]. Soon after this time also were composed the earlier Songs in Ritson and Percy (1264), with a few more pieces which it is unnecessary to particularize. This will bring us to the close of Henry III.'s reign and beginning of his successor's, the period assigned by our poetical antiquaries to the romances of Sir Tristrem, Kyng Horn, and Kyng Alexander." *

The verse that has been preserved of the song composed by Canute as he was one day rowing on the Nen, while the holy music came floating on the air and along the water from the choir of the neighbouring minster of Ely—a song which we are told by the historian continued to his day, after the lapse of a century and a half, to be a universal popular favourite †—is very nearly such English as was written in the fourteenth century. This interesting fragment properly falls to be given as the first of our specimens :—

        Merie sungen the muneches binnen Ely
        Tha Cnut Ching rew there by;
        Roweth, cnihtes, noer the lant,
        And here we thes muneches sueng.

---

* The Ancient English Romance of Havelok the Dane; Introduction, p. xlix. We have transferred the references, inclosed in brackets, from the bottom of the page to the text.

† Quæ usque hodie in choris publico cantantur, et in proverbiis memorantur.

That is, literally,—

> Merry (sweetly) sung the monks within Ely
> That (when) Cnute King rowed thereby:
> Row, knights, near the land,
> And hear we these monks' song.

Being in verse and in rhyme, it is probable that the words are reported in their original form; they cannot, at any rate, be much altered.

The not very clerical address of Archbishop Aldred to Ursus Earl of Worcester, who refused to take down one of his castles the ditch of which encroached upon a monastic churchyard, consists, as reported by William of Malmesbury (who by-the-by praises its elegance) of only two short lines:—

> Hatest thou* Urse?
> Have thou God's curse.

The hymn of St. Godric has more of an antique character. It is thus given by Ritson, who professes to have collated the Royal MS. 5 F, vii., and the Harleian MS. 322, and refers also to Matt. Parisiensis Historia, pp. 119, 120, edit. 1640, and to (MS. Cott.) Nero D. v:—

> Sainte Marie [clane] virgine,
> Moder Jhesu Cristes Nazarene,
> On fo [or fong] schild, help thin Godric,
> On fang bring hegilich with the in Godes riche.
> Sainte Marie, Christe's bur,
> Maidens clenhad, moderes flur,
> Dilie min sinne [or semnen], rix in min mod,
> Bring me to winne with the selfd God.

"By the assistance of the Latin versions," adds Ritson, "one is enabled to give it literally in English, as follows:—Saint Mary [chaste] virgin, mother of Jesus Christ of Nazareth, take, shield, help thy Godric; take, bring him quickly with thee into God's kingdom. Saint Mary, Christ's chamber, purity of a maiden, flower of a mother, destroy my sin, reign in my mind, bring me to dwell with the only God."

Two other short compositions of the same poetical eremite are much in the same style. One is a couplet said to have been sung to him by the spirit or ghost of his sister, who appeared to him after her death and thus assured him of her happiness:—

---

* That is, Hightest thou (art thou called)? Malmesbury's Latin translation is, "Vocaris Urens: habeas Dei maledictionem." But the first line seems to be interrogative.

> Crist and Sainte Marie swa on scamel me iledde
> That ic on this erde ne silde with mine bare fote itredde.

Which Ritson translates:—"Christ and Mary, thus supported, have me brought, that I on earth should not with my bare foot tread."

The other is a hymn to St. Nicholas:—

> Sainte Nicholaes, Godes druth,
> Tymbre us faire scone hus.
> At thi burth, at thi bare,
> Sainte Nicholaes, bring us wel there.

"That is," says Ritson, "Saint Nicholas, God's lover, build us a fair beautiful house. At thy birth, at thy bier, Saint Nicholas, bring us safely thither."

As for the rhymes given by Lambarde and Camden as of the twelfth century, they can hardly in the shape in which we have them be of anything like that antiquity: they are, in fact, in the common English of the sixteenth century. Lambarde (in his Dictionary of England, p. 36) tells us that a rabble of Flemings and Normans brought over in 1173 by Robert Earl of Leicester, when they were assembled on a heath near St. Edmunds Bury, "fell to dance and sing,

> Hoppe Wylikin, hoppe Wyllykin,
> Ingland is thyne and myne, &c."

Camden's story is that Hugh Bigott, Earl of Norfolk, in the reign of Stephen used to boast of the impregnable strength of his castle of Bungey after this fashion:—

> "Were I in my castle of Bungey,
> Upon the river of Waveney,
> I would ne care for the king of Cockeney."

What Sir Frederick Madden describes as "the prophecy said to have been set up at Here in the year 1189" is given by Ritson as follows:—

> Whan thu sees in Here bert yreret,
> Than sulen Engles in three be ydelct:
> That an into Yrland al to late waie,
> That other into Puille mid prude bileve,
> The thridde into Airhahen herd all wreken drechegen.

These lines, which he calls a "specimen of English poetry, apparently of the same age" (the latter part of the 12th century), Ritson says are preserved by Benedictus Abbas, by Hoveden, and by the Chronicle of Lanercost; and he professes to give them,

and the account by which they are introduced, from "the
former," by which he means the first of the three. But in truth
the verses do not occur as he has printed them in any of the
places to which he refers. And there is no ground for supposing,
that they were ever inscribed or set up upon any house at
"Here" or elsewhere. What is said both by Benedict and
Hoveden (who employ nearly the same words) is simply that
the figure of a hart was set upon the pinnacle of the house, in
order, as was believed, that the prophecy contained in the verses
might be accomplished—which prophecy, we are told immediately before, had been found engraven in ancient characters upon stone tables in the neighbourhood of the place. It is
clearly intended to be stated that the prophecy was much older
than the building of the house, and the erection of the figure of
a stag, in the year 1190.

THE BRUT OF LAYAMON.

Layamon, or, as he is also called, Laweman—for the old character represented in this instance by our modern y is really
only a guttural (and by no means either a j or a z, by which it
is sometimes rendered)—tells us himself that he was a priest,
and that he resided at Ernley, near Radstone, or Redstone,
which appears to have been what is now called Arley Regis, or
Lower Arley, on the western bank of the Severn, in Worcestershire. He seems to say that he was employed in the services of
the church at that place:—" ther he book radde" (there he
book read). And the only additional information that he gives
us respecting himself is, that his father's name was Leovenath
(or Leuca, as it is given in the later of the two texts).
His Brut, or Chronicle of Britain (from the arrival of Brutus
to the death of King Cadwalader in A.D. 689), is in the main,
though with many additions, a translation of the French Brut
d'Angleterre of Wace, which is itself, as has been stated above,
a translation, also with considerable additions from other
sources, of Geoffrey of Monmouth's Latin Historia Britonum,
which again professes, and probably with truth, to be translated from a Welsh or Breton original. So that the genealogy
of the four versions or forms of the narrative is:—first, a Celtic
original, believed to be now lost; secondly, the Latin of
Geoffrey of Monmouth; thirdly, the French of Wace; fourthly,
the English of Layamon. The Celtic or British version is of
unknown date; the Latin is of the earlier, the French of the

latter, half of the twelfth century; and that of Layamon would appear to have been completed in the first years of the thirteenth. We shall encounter a second English translation from Wace's French before the middle of the fourteenth.

The existence of Layamon's Chronicle had long been known, but it had attracted very little attention till comparatively recent times. It is merely mentioned even by Warton and Tyrwhitt—the latter only remarking (in his Essay on the Language and Versification of Chaucer), that, "though the greatest part of this work of Layamon resembles the old Saxon poetry, without rhyme or metre, yet he often intermixes a number of short verses of unequal lengths, but rhyming together pretty exactly, and in some places he has imitated not unsuccessfully the regular octosyllabic measure of his French original." George Ellis, in his Specimens of the Early English Poets, originally published in 1790, was, we believe, the first to introduce Layamon to the general reader, by giving an extract of considerable length, with explanatory annotations, from what he described as his "very curious work," which, he added, never had been, and probably never would be, printed. Subsequently another considerable specimen, in every way much more carefully and learnedly edited, and accompanied with a literal translation throughout into the modern idiom, was presented by Mr. Guest in his History of English Rhythms, 1838 (ii. 113-123). But now the whole work has been edited by Sir Frederic Madden, for the Society of Antiquaries of London, in three volumes 8vo. 1847. This splendid publication, besides a Literal Translation, Notes, and a Grammatical Glossary, contains the Brut in two texts, separated from each other by an interval apparently of about half a century, and, whether regarded in reference to the philological, to say nothing of the historical, value and importance of Layamon's work, or to the admirable and altogether satisfactory manner in which the old chronicle is exhibited and illustrated, may fairly be characterized as by far the most acceptable present that has been made to the students of early English literature in our day.

His editor conceives that we may safely assume Layamon's English to be that of North Worcestershire, the district in which he lived and wrote. But this western dialect, he contends, was also that of the southern part of the island, having in fact originated to the south of the Thames, whence, he says, it gradually extended itself "as far as the courses of the Severn, the Wye, the Tame, and the Avon, and more or less pervaded the counties of Gloucestershire, Worcestershire, Herefordshire,

Warwickshire, and Oxfordshire,"—besides prevailing "throughout the channel counties from east to west,"—notwithstanding that several of the counties that have been named, and that of Worcester especially, had belonged especially to the non-Saxon kingdom of Mercia. "The language of Layamon," he farther holds, "belongs to that transition period in which the groundwork of Anglo-Saxon phraseology and grammar still existed, although gradually yielding to the influence of the popular forms of speech. We find in it, as in the later portion of the Saxon Chronicle, marked indications of a tendency to adopt those terminations and sounds which characterise a language in a state of change, and which are apparent also in some other branches of the Teutonic tongue." As showing "the progress made in the course of two centuries in departing from the ancient and purer grammatical forms, as found in Anglo-Saxon manuscripts," he mentions "the use of *a* as an article;—the change of the Anglo-Saxon terminations *a* and *an* into *e* and *en*, as well as the disregard of inflexions and genders;—the masculine forms given to neuter nouns in the plural;—the neglect of the feminine terminations of adjectives and pronouns, and confusion between the definite and indefinite declensions; the introduction of the preposition *to* before infinitives, and occasional use of weak preterites of verbs and participles instead of strong;—the constant occurrence of *en* for *on* in the plurals of verbs, and frequent elision of the final *e*;—together with the uncertainty in the rule for the government of prepositions." In the earlier text one of the most striking peculiarities is what has been termed the *nunnation*, defined by Sir Frederic as "consisting of the addition of a final *n* to certain cases of nouns and adjectives, to some tenses of verbs, and to several other parts of speech." The western dialect, of which both texts, and especially the earlier, exhibit strong marks, is further described as perceptible in the "termination of the present tense plural in *th*, and infinitives in *i*, *ie*, or *y*; the forms of the plural personal pronouns, *heo, heore, heom*; the frequent occurrence of the prefix *i* before past participles; the use of *v* for *f*; and prevalence of the vowel *u* for *i* or *y*, in such words as *dude, huddle, hulle, putte, hure*, &c." "But," it is added, "on comparing the two texts carefully together, some remarkable variations are apparent in the later, which seem to arise, not from its having been composed at a more recent period, but from the infusion of an Anglian or Northern element into the dialect." From these indications the learned editor is disposed to think that the later text "may have been composed or transcribed in one of the counties conterminous to the Anglian border, and he suggests that "perhaps we might fix on the eastern side of Leicestershire as the locality."

One thing in the English of Layamon that is eminently deserving of notice with reference to the history of the language is the very small amount of the French or Latin element that is found in it. "The fact itself," Sir F. Madden observes, "of a translation of Wace's poem by a priest of one of the midland counties is sufficient evidence how widely the knowledge of the writings of the *trouvères* was dispersed, and it would appear a natural consequence, that not only the outward form of the Anglo-Norman versification, but also that many of the terms used in the original would be borrowed. This, however, is but true in a very trifling degree, compared with the extent of the work; for, if we number the words derived from the French (even including some that may have come directly from the Latin), we do not find in the earlier text of Layamon's poem so many as fifty, several of which were in usage, as appears by the Saxon Chronicle, previous to the middle of the twelfth century. Of this number the later text retains about thirty, and adds to them rather more than forty which are not found in the earlier version; so that, if we reckon ninety words of French origin in both texts, containing together more than 56,800 lines, we shall be able to form a tolerably correct estimate how little the English language was really affected by foreign converse, even as late as the middle of the thirteenth century."*

Layamon's poem extends to nearly 32,250 lines, or more than double the length of Wace's Brut. This may indicate the amount of the additions which the English chronicler has made to his French original. That, however, is only one, though the chief, of several preceding works to which he professes himself to have been indebted. His own account is:—

> He nom tha Englisca boc
> Tha makede Seint Beda;
> An other he nam on Latin,
> Tha makede Sainte Albin,
> And the feire Austin,
> The fulluht broute hider in.
> Boc he nom the thridde,
> Leide ther amidden,

---

* Preface xxlii.

Tha makede a Frenchis clerc,
Wace was ihoten,
The wel conthe writen,
And he hoe yef thare aetheler.
Aelienor, the wes Henries quene,
Thes heyes kinges.
Layamon leide theos boe,
And tha leaf wende.
He heom leofliche bi-hoold
IJthe him beo Drihten.
Fetheren he nom mid fingren,
And ficrle on boc-felle,
And tha sothe word
Sette to-gathere,
And tha thre boo
Thrumde to ane.

That is, literally:—

He took the English book
That Saint Bede made;
Another he took in Latin,
That Saint Albin made,
And the fair Austin,
That baptism brought hither in.
The third book he took,
[And] laid there in midst,
That made a French clerk.
Wace was [he] called,
That well could write,
And he it gave to the noble
Eleanor, that was Henry's queen,
The high king's.
Layamon laid [before him] these books
And the leaves turned.
He them lovingly beheld;
Merciful to him be [the] Lord.
Feather (pen) he took with fingers,
And wrote on book-skin,
And the true words
Set together,
And the three books
Compressed into one.

His English book was no doubt the translation into the vernacular tongue, commonly attributed to King Alfred, of Bede's Ecclesiastical History, which Layamon does not seem to have known to have been originally written in Latin. What he says about his Latin book is unintelligible. St. Austin died in

A.D. 604; and the only Albin of whom anything is known was Albin abbot of St. Austin's at Canterbury, who is mentioned by Bede as one of the persons to whom he was indebted for assistance in the compilation of his History; but he lived more than a century after St. Austin (or Augustine). Some Latin chronicle, however, Layamon evidently had; and his scholarship, therefore, extended to an acquaintance with two other tongues in addition to the now obsolete classic form of his own.

The principal, and indeed almost the only, passage in Layamon's poem from which any inference can be drawn as to the precise time when it was written, is one near the end (p. 31, 979-80) in which, speaking of the tax called Rome-feoh, Rome-scot, or Peter-pence, he seems to express a doubt whether it will much longer continue to be paid:—

> Drihte wat hu longe
> Theo lagen scullen ilaeste
> (The Lord knows how long
> The law shall last).

This his learned editor conceives to allude to a resistance which it appears was made to the collection of the tax by King John and the nobility in the year 1205; and that supposition, he further suggests, may be held to be fortified by the manner in which Queen Eleanor, who had retired to Aquitaine on the accession of John, and died abroad at an advanced age in 1204, is spoken of in the passage quoted above from what we may call the Preface, written, no doubt, after the work was finished—
" Aelienor, the *wes* Henries quene."

" The structure of Layamon's poem," Sir Frederic observes, " consists partly of lines in which the alliterative system of the Anglo-Saxons is preserved, and partly of couplets of unequal length rhiming together. Many couplets, indeed, occur which have both of these forms, whilst others are often met with which possess neither. The latter, therefore, must have depended wholly on accentuation, or have been corrupted in transcription. The relative proportion of each of these forms is not to be ascertained without extreme difficulty, since the author uses them everywhere intermixed, and slides from alliteration to rhime, or from rhime to alliteration, in a manner perfectly arbitrary. The alliterative portion, however, predominates on the whole greatly over the lines rhiming together, even including the imperfect or assonant terminations, which are very frequent." Mr. Guest, Sir Frederic notes, has shown by the specimen which he has given with the accents marked in his English Rhythms (ii. 114-

124), "that the rhiming couplets of Layamon are founded on the models of accentuated Anglo-Saxon rhythms of four, five, six, or seven accents."

Layamon's poetical merit, and also his value as an original authority, are rated rather high by his editor. His additions to and amplifications of Wace, we are told, consist in the earlier part of the work "principally of the speeches placed in the mouths of different personages, which are often given with quite a dramatic effect." "The text of Wace," it is added, "is enlarged throughout, and in many passages to such an extent, particularly after the birth of Arthur, that one line is dilated into twenty; names of persons and localities are constantly supplied, and not unfrequently interpolations occur of entirely new matter, to the extent of more than an hundred lines. Layamon often embellishes and improves on his copy; and the meagre narrative of the French poet is heightened by graphic touches and details, which give him a just claim to be considered, not as a mere translator, but as an original writer."

The Ormulum.

Another metrical work of considerable extent, that known as the Ormulum, from Orm, or Ormin, which appears to have been the name of the writer, has been usually assigned to the same, or nearly the same age with the Brut of Layamon. It exists only in a single manuscript, which there is some reason for believing to be the author's autograph, now preserved in the Bodleian Library among the books bequeathed by the great scholar Francis Junius, who appears to have purchased it at the Hague in 1659 at the sale of the books of his deceased friend Janus Ulitius, or Vlitius (van Vliet), also an eminent philologist and book-collector. It is a folio volume, consisting of 90 parchment leaves, besides 29 others inserted, upon which the poetry is written in double columns, in a stiff but distinct hand, and without division into verses, so that the work had always been assumed to be in prose till its metrical character was pointed out by Tyrwhitt in his edition of Chaucer's Canterbury Tales, 1775. Accordingly no mention is made of it by Warton, the first volume of whose History was published in 1774. But it had previously been referred to by Hickes and others; and it has attracted a large share of the attention of all recent investigators of the history of the language. It has now been printed in full, under the title of The Ormulum; Now first edited from the

Original Manuscript in the Bodleian, with Notes and a glossary, by Robert Meadows White, D.D., late Fellow of St. Mary Magdalene College, and formerly Professor of Anglo-Saxon in the University of Oxford; 2 vols. 8vo. Oxford, at the University Press, 1852.

The Ormulum is described by Dr. White as being "a series of Homilies, in an imperfect state, composed in metre without alliteration, and, except in very few cases, also without rhyme: the subject of the Homilies being supplied by those portions of the New Testament which were read in the daily service of the Church." The plan of the writer is, we are further told, "first to give a paraphrastic version of the Gospel of the day, adapting the matter to the rules of his verse, with such verbal additions as were required for that purpose. He then adds an exposition of the subject in its doctrinal and practical bearings, in the treatment of which he borrows copiously from the writings of St. Augustine and Ælfric, and occasionally from those of Beda." "Some idea," it is added, "may be formed of the extent of Ormin's labours when we consider that, out of the entire series of Homilies, provided for nearly the whole of the yearly service, nothing is left beyond the text of the thirty-second." We have still nearly ten thousand long lines of the work, or nearly twenty thousand as Dr. White prints them, with the fifteen syllables divided into two sections, the one of eight the other of seven syllables,—the latter, which terminates in an unaccented syllable, being prosodically equivalent to one of six, so that the whole is simply our still common alternation of the eight-syllabled and the six-syllabled line, only without either rhyme or even alliteration, which makes it as pure a species of blank verse, though a different species, as that which is now in use.

The list of the texts, or subjects of the Homilies, as preserved in the manuscript, extends to 242, and it appears to be imperfect. Ormin plainly claims to have completed his long self-imposed task. Here is the beginning of the Dedication to his brother Walter, which stands at the head of the work:—

  Nu, brotherr Wallterr, brotherr min
   [Now, brother Walter, brother mine]
  Afterr the flæshes kinde;
   [After the flesh's kind (or nature)]
  Annd brotherr min i Crisstenndom
   [And brother mine in Christendom (or Christ's kingdom)]
  Thurrh fulluhht and thurrh trowwthe;
   [Through baptism and through truth]
  Aund brotherr min i Godess hus,
   [And brother mine in God's house]

THE ORMULUM.

Yet o the thride wiſe,
  [Yet on (in) the third wiſe]
Thurrh thatt witt hafenn takenn ba
  [Though that we two have taken both]
An reghellboc to folghenn,
  [Our rule-book to follow]
Unnderr kanunnkess had and lif,
  [Under canonle's (canon's) rank and life]
Swa summ Sannt Awwſtin ſette;
  [So as St. Austin ſet (or ruled)]
Icc hafe don awa summ thu badd
  [I have done ſo as thou bade]
Annd forthedd te thin wille;
  [And performed thee thine will (wiſh)]
Icc hafe weund inntill Ennglissh
  [I have wended (turned) into Engliſh]
Goddspelless hallghe lare,
  [Goſpel's holy lore]
Affterr thatt little witt tatt me
  [After that little wit that me]
Min Drihhtin hafethth lenedd.
  [My Lord hath lent]

One remarkable feature in this English is evidently something very peculiar in the spelling. And the same system is observed throughout the work. It is found on a slight examination to consist in the duplication of the consonant whenever it follows a vowel having any other than the sound which is now for the most part indicated by the annexation of a silent *e* to the single consonant, or what may be called the *name* sound, being that by which the vowel is commonly named or spoken of in our modern English. Thus *pane* would by Ormin be written *pan*, but *pan panu*; *mean men*, but *men menn*; *pine pin*, but *pin pinn*; *own on*, but *on onn*; *tune tun*, but *tun tunn*. This, as Mr. Guest has pointed out, is, after all, only a rigorous carrying out of a principle which has always been applied to a certain extent in English orthography,—as in *tally*, or *tall*, *berry*, *witty*, *folly*, *dull*, as compared with *tale*, *beer*, *white*, *lone*, *mule*. The effect, however, in Ormin's work is on a hasty inspection to make his English seem much more rude and antique than it really is. The entry of the MS. in the catalogue of Vliet's library, as quoted by Dr. White, describes it as an old Swedish or Gothic book. Other early notices speak of it as ſemi-Saxon, or half Danish, or possibly old Scottish. Even Hickes appears to have regarded it as belonging to the first age after the Conquest.

Ormin attaches the highest importance to his peculiar system of orthography. Nevertheless, in quoting what he says upon the subject in a subsequent passage of his Dedication we will take the liberty, for the sake of giving a clear and just idea of his language to a reader of the present day, to strip it of a disguise which so greatly exaggerates its apparent antiquity:—

And whase willen shall this book
  [And whoso shall wish this book]
Eft other sithe writen,
  [After (wards) (an) other time (to) write]
Him bidde icc that he't write right,
  [Him bid I that he it write right]
Swa sum this book him teacheth,
  [So as this book him teacheth]
All thwert out after that it is
  [All athwart (or through) out after that (or what) it is]
Upo this firste bisne.
  [Upon this first example]
With all suilk rime als here is set
  [With all such rhyme as here is set]
With all se sele wordes
  [With all so many words]
And tat he looke well that he
  [And that he look well that he]
An bookstaff write twies
  [A letter write twice]
Eywhere there it upo this book
  [Wherever there (or where) it upon this book]
Is written o that wise.
  [Is written on (or in) that wise]
Looke he well that he't write sway
  [Look he well that he it write so]
For he ne may nought elles
  [For he may not else]
On English writen right te word,
  [On (or in) English write right the word]
That wite he well to soothe.
  [That wot (or know) he well to (or for) sooth (or truth)]

Thus presented, Ormin's English certainly seems to differ much less from that of the present day than Layamon's. His vocabulary may have as little in it of any foreign admixture; but it appears to contain many fewer words that have now become obsolete; and both his grammar and his construction have much more of a modern character and air.

On the whole, it may be assumed that, while we have a dialect founded on that of the Saxons specially so called in Layamon, we have a specially Anglian form of the national language in the Ormulum; and perhaps that distinction will be enough, without supposing any considerable difference of date, to explain the

linguistic differences between the two. There is good reason for
believing that the Anglian part of the country shook off the
shackles of the old inflectional system sooner than the Saxon,
and that our modern comparatively uninflected and analytic
English was at least in its earliest stage more the product of
Anglian than of purely Saxon influences, and is to be held as
having grown up rather in the northern and north-eastern parts
of the country than in the southern or south-western.

The Ancren Riwle.

There is also to be mentioned, along with the Brut of Layamon
and the Ormulum, a work of considerable extent in prose which
has been assigned to the same interesting period in the history of
the language, the Ancren Riwle, that is, the Anchorites', or
rather Anchoresses', Rule, being a treatise on the duties of the
monastic life, written evidently by an ecclesiastic, and probably
one in a position of eminence and authority, for the direction of
three ladies to whom it is addressed, and who, with their domestic
servants or lay sisters, appear to have formed the entire community of a religious house situated at Tarente (otherwise called
Tarrant-Kaines, Kaineston, or Kingston) in Dorsetshire. This
work too has now been printed, having been edited for the
Camden Society in 1853 by the Rev. James Morton, B.D. It is
preserved in four manuscripts, three of them in the Cottonian
Collection, the other belonging to Corpus Christi College, Cambridge; and there is also in the Library of Magdalen College,
Oxford, a Latin text of the greater part of it. The entire work
extends to eight Parts, or Books, which in the printed edition
cover 215 quarto pages. Mr. Morton, who has appended to
an apparently careful representation of the ancient text both a
glossary and a version in the language of the present day, has
clearly shown, in opposition to the commonly received opinion,
that the work was originally written in English, and that the
Latin in so far as it goes is only a translation. This, indeed,
might have been inferred as most probable in such a case, on the
mere ground that we have here a clergyman, however learned,
drawing up a manual of practical religious instruction for
readers of the other sex, even without the special proofs which
Mr. Morton has brought forward. The conclusion to which he
states himself to have come, after carefully examining and comparing the text which he prints with the Oxford MS., is, that
the Latin is " a translation, in many parts abridged and in some

enlarged, made at a comparatively recent period, when the language in which the whole had been originally written was becoming obsolete." In many instances, in fact, the Latin translator has misunderstood his original. Mr. Morton has also thrown great doubts upon the common belief that the authorship of the work is to be ascribed to a certain Simon de Gandavo, or Simon de Ghent, who died Bishop of Salisbury in 1315. This belief rests solely on the authority of an anonymous note prefixed to the Latin version of the work preserved in Magdalen College, Oxford; and Mr. Morton conceives that Simon is of much too late a date. It might have been thought that the fact of the work having been written in English would of itself be conclusive against his claim; but the Bishop of Salisbury, it seems, was born in London or Westminster; it was only his father who was a native of Flanders. On the whole, Mr. Morton is inclined to substitute in place of Bishop Simon a Richard Poor, who was successively Bishop of Chichester, of Salisbury, and of Durham, and who was a native of Tarente, where also, it seems, he died in 1237. Of this prelate Matthew Paris speaks in very high terms of commendation.

Two other mistakes in the old accounts are also disposed of:— that the three recluses to whom the work is addressed belonged to the monastic order of St. James, and that they were the sisters of the writer. He merely directs them, if any ignorant person should ask them of what order they were, to say that they were of the order of St. James, who in his canonical epistle has declared that pure religion consists in visiting and relieving the widow and the orphan, and in keeping ourselves unspotted from the world; and in addressing them as his dear sisters, "he only," as Mr. Morton explains, "uses the form of speech commonly adopted in convents, where nuns are usually spoken of as sisters or mothers, and monks as brothers or fathers."

Upon what is the most important question relating to the work, regarded as a documentary monument belonging to the history of the language, the learned editor has scarcely succeeded in throwing so much light. Of the age of the manuscripts, or the character of the handwriting, not a word is said. It does not even appear whether any one of the copies can be supposed to be of the antiquity assumed for the work upon either the new or the old theory of its authorship. The question is left to rest entirely upon the language, which, it is remarked, is evidently that of the first quarter of the thirteenth century, not greatly differing from that of Layamon, which has been clearly shown by Sir F. Madden to have been written not later than 1205.

THE ANCREN RIWLE.

The English of the Ancren Rule is, indeed, rude enough for the highest antiquity that can be demanded for it. "The spelling," Mr. Morton observes, "whether from carelessness or want of system, is of an uncommon and unsettled character, and may be pronounced barbarous and uncouth." The inflections which originally marked the oblique cases of substantive nouns, and also the distinctions of gender, are, it is added, for the most part discarded.

In one particular, however, the English of the Rule differs remarkably from Layamon's. In that, as we have seen, Sir F. Madden found in above 32,000 verses of the older text only about 50 words of French derivation, and only about 90 in all in the 57,000 of both texts; whereas in the present work the infusion of Norman words is described as large. But this, as Mr. Morton suggests, is "owing probably to the peculiar subjects treated of in it, which are theological and moral, in speaking of which terms derived from the Latin would readily occur to the mind of a learned ecclesiastic much conversant with that language, and with the works on similar subjects written in it."

A few sentences from the Eighth or last Part, which treats of domestic matters, will afford a sufficient specimen of this curious work:—

Ye ne schulen eten vlesche ne seim buten ine muchele secnesse; other hwoso is ener feble eteth potage blitheliche; and wunieth ou to lutel drunch. Notheleas, leoue sustren, ower mete and ower drunch haueth ithuht me lesse then ich wolde. Ne ueste ye nenne dei to bread and to watere, bute ye habbeth leue. Sum ancre maketh hire bord mid hire gistes withuten. Thet is to muche ureondschipe, uor, of alle ordres theonne is hit unkaindelukest and meast ayean ancre ordre, thet is al dead to the worlde. Me haueth i-herd ofte siggen thet deade men speken mid cwike men; auh thet heo eten mid cwike men ne uond ich neuer yete. Ne makie ye none gistninges; ne ne tulle ye to the yete non unkuthe harloz; thauh ther nere non other vuel of [hit?] bute hore methleuse muth, hit wolde other hwole letten heouendliche thouhtes.

[That is, literally:—Ye not shall eat flesh nor lard but in much sickness; or whoso is ever feeble may eat potage blithely; and accustom yourselves to little drink. Nevertheless, dear sisters, your meat and your drink have seemed to me less than I would (have it). Fast ye not no day to bread and to water but ye have leave. Some anchoresses make their board (or meals) with their friends without. That is too much friendship, for, of all orders, then is it most unnatural and most against anchoress order, that is all dead to the world. One has heard oft say that dead men speak with quick (living) men; but that they eat with quick men not found I never yet. Make not ye no banquetings, nor allure ye not to the gate no strange vagabonds; though there were not none other evil of it but their measureless mouth (or talk), it would (or might) other while (sometimes) hinder heavenly thoughts.]

EARLY ENGLISH METRICAL ROMANCES.

From the thirteenth century also we are probably to date the origin or earliest composition of English metrical romances; at least, none have descended to the present day which seem to have a claim to any higher antiquity. There is no absolutely conclusive evidence that all our old metrical romances are translations from the French; the French original cannot in every case be produced; but it is at least extremely doubtful if any such work was ever composed in English except upon the foundation of a similar French work. It is no objection that the subjects of most of these poems are not French or continental, but British—that the stories of some of them are purely English or Saxon: this, as has been shown, was the case with the early northern French poetry generally, from whatever cause, whether simply in consequence of the connection of Normandy with this country from the time of the Conquest, or partly from the earlier intercourse of the Normans with their neighbours the people of Armorica, or Bretagne, whose legends and traditions, which were common to them with their kindred the Welsh, have unquestionably served as the fountain-head to the most copious of all the streams of romantic fiction. French seems to have been the only language of popular literature (apart from mere songs and ballads) in England for some ages after the Conquest; if even a native legend, therefore, was to be turned into a romance, it was in French that the poem would at that period be written. It is possible, indeed, that some legends might have escaped the French trouveurs, to be discovered and taken up at a later date by the English minstrels; but this is not likely to have happened with any that were at all popular or generally known; and of this description, it is believed, are all those, without any exception, upon which our existing early English metrical romances are founded. The subjects of these compositions—Tristrem, King Horn, Havelok, &c.—could hardly have been missed by the French poets in the long period during which they had the whole field to themselves: we have the most conclusive evidence with regard to some of the legends in question that they were well known at an early date to the writers in that language;—the story of Havelok, for instance, is in Gaimar's Chronicle;—upon this general consideration alone, therefore, which is at least not contradicted by either the internal or historical evidence in any particular case, it seems reasonable to infer that, where we have both an English and a French metrical romance upon the same subject, the French is the earlier of the two, and the original of the other. From this it is, in the circumstances, scarcely a step to the conclusion come to by Tyrwhitt, who has intimated his belief " that we have no English romance prior to the age of Chaucer which is not a translation or imitation of some earlier French romance." * Certainly, if this judgment has not been absolutely demonstrated, it has not been refuted, by the more extended investigation the question has since received.

The history of the English metrical romance appears shortly to be, that at least the first examples of it were translations from the French;—that there is no evidence of any such having been produced before the close of the twelfth century;—that in the thirteenth century were composed the earliest of those we now possess in their original form;—that in the fourteenth the English took the place of the French metrical romance with all classes, and that this was the era alike of its highest ascendancy and of its most abundant and felicitous production;—that in the fifteenth it was supplanted by another species of poetry among the more educated classes, and had also to contend with another rival in the prose romance, but that, nevertheless, it still continued to be produced, although in less quantity and of an inferior fabric,— mostly, indeed, if not exclusively, by the mere modernization of older compositions—for the use of the common people;—and that it did not altogether cease to be read and written till after the commencement of the sixteenth. From that time the taste for this earliest form of our poetical literature (at least counting from the Norman Conquest) lay asleep in the national heart till it was re-awakened in our own day by Scott, after the lapse of three hundred years. But the metrical romance was then become quite another sort of thing than it had been in its proper era, throughout the whole extent of which, while the story was generally laid in a past age, the manners and state of society described were, notwithstanding, in most respects those of the poet's and of his readers' or hearers' own time. This was strictly the case with the poems of this description which were produced in the thirteenth, fourteenth, and fifteenth centuries; and even in those which were accommodated to the popular taste

* Essay on the Language of Chaucer, note 55.

of a later day much more than the language had to be partially modernized to preserve them in favour. When this could no longer be done without too much violence to the composition, or an entire destruction of its original character, the metrical romance lost its hold of the public mind, and was allowed to drop into oblivion. There had been very little of more antiquarianism in the interest it had inspired for three centuries. It had pleased principally as a picture or reflection of manners, usages, and a general spirit of society still existing, or supposed to exist. And this is perhaps the condition upon which any poetry must ever expect to be extensively and permanently popular. We need not say that the temporary success of the metrical romance, as revived by Scott, was in great part owing to his appeal to quite a different, almost an opposite, state of feeling.

Metrical Chronicle of Robert of Gloucester.

Nearly what Biography is to History are the metrical romances to the versified Chronicle of Robert of Gloucester, a narrative of British and English affairs from the time of Brutus to the end of the reign of Henry III., which, from events to which it alludes, must have been written after 1297.[*] All that is known of the author is that he was a monk of the abbey of Gloucester. His Chronicle was printed—"faithfully, I dare say," says Tyrwhitt, "but from incorrect manuscripts"—by Hearne, in 2 vols. 8vo., at Oxford, in 1724; and a re-impression of this edition was produced at London in 1810. The work in the earlier part of it may be considered a free translation of Geoffroy of Monmouth's Latin History; but it is altogether a very rude and lifeless composition. "This rhyming chronicle," says Warton, "is totally destitute of art or imagination. The author has clothed the fables of Geoffroy of Monmouth in rhyme, which have often a more poetical air in Geoffrey's prose." Tyrwhitt refers to Robert of Gloucester in proof of the fact that the English language had already acquired a strong tincture of French; Warton observes that the language of this writer is full of Saxonisms, and not more easy or intelligible than that of what he calls "the Norman Saxon poems" of Kyng Horn and others which he believes to belong to the preceding century.

Robert of Gloucester's Chronicle, as printed, is in long lines of fourteen syllables, which, however, are generally divisible

[*] This has been shown by Sir F. Madden in his Introduction to Havelok the Dane, p. lii.

into two of eight and six, and were perhaps intended to be so written and read. The language appears to be marked by the peculiarities of West Country English. Ample specimens are given by Warton and Ellis; we shall not encumber our limited space with extracts which are recommended by no attraction either in the matter or manner. We will only transcribe, as a sample of the language at the commencement of the reign of Edward I., and for the sake of the curious evidence it supplies in confirmation of a fact to which we have more than once had occasion to draw attention, the short passage about the prevalence of the French tongue in England down even to this date, more than two centuries after the conquest:—

"Thus come lo! Engelonde into Normannes honde,
And the Normans ne couthe speke tho bote her owe speche,
And speke French as dude atom, and here chyldren dude al so teche,
So that beynen of thys lond, that of her blod come,
Holdeth alle thulke speche that hii of hem nome.
Vor bote a man couthe French, me tolth of hym well lute:
Ac lowe men holdeth to Englyss and to her kunde speche yute.
Ich wene ther be no man in world contreyes none
That ne holdeth to her kunde speche, but Engelond one.
Ac wel me wot vor to conne bothe wel yt ys,
Vor the more that a man con the more worth he ys."

That is, literally:—Thus lo! England came into the hand of the Normans: and the Normans could not speak then but their own speech, and spoke French as they did at home, and their children did all so teach; so that high men of this land, that of their blood come, retain all the same speech that they of them took. For, unless a man know French, one talketh of him little. But low men hold to English, and to their natural speech yet. I imagine there be no people in any country of the world that do not hold to their natural speech, but in England alone. But well I wot it is well for to know both; for the more that a man knows, the more worth he is.

A short composition of Robert of Gloucester's on the Martyrdom of Thomas à Becket was printed by the Percy Society in 1845.

ROBERT MANNYNG, OR DE BRUNNE.

Along with this chronicle may be mentioned the similar performance of Robert Mannyng, otherwise called Robert de Brunne (from his birthplace,* Bruune, or Bourne, near Deping, or

* See a valuable note on De Brunne in Sir Frederic Madden's Havelok, Introduction, p. xlii.

Market Deeping, in Lincolnshire), belonging as it does to a date not quite half a century later. The work of Robert de Brunne is in two parts, both translated from the French; the first, coming down to the death of Cadwalader, from Wace's Brut; the second, extending to the death of Edward I., from the French or Romance chronicle written by Piers, or Peter, de Langtoft, a canon regular of St. Austin, at Bridlington, in Yorkshire, who wrote various works in French, and who appears to have lived at the same time with De Brunne. Langtoft, whose chronicle, though it has not been printed, is preserved in more than one manuscript, begins with Brutus; but De Brunne, for sufficient reasons it is probable, preferred Wace for the earlier portion of the story, and only took to his own countryman and contemporary when deserted by his older Norman guide. It is the latter part of his work, however, which, owing to the subject, has been thought most valuable or interesting in modern times; it has been printed by Hearne, under the title of Peter Langtoft's Chronicle (as illustrated and improved by Robert of Brunne), from the death of Cadwalader to the end of K. Edward the First's reign; transcribed, and now first published, from a MS. in the Inner Temple Library, 2 vols. 8vo. Oxford, 1725; [reprinted London, 1810.] This part, like the original French of Langtoft, is in Alexandrine verse of twelve syllables; the earlier part, which remains in manuscript, is in the same octosyllabic verse in which its original, Wace's chronicle, is written. The work is stated in a Latin note at the end of the MS. to have been finished in 1338. Ritson (Bibliographia Poetica, p. 33) is very wroth with Warton for describing De Brunne as having "scarcely more poetry than Robert of Gloucester;"—"which only proves," Ritson says, "his want of taste or judgment." It may be admitted that De Brunne's chronicle exhibits the language in a considerably more advanced state than that of Gloucester, and also that he appears to have more natural fluency than his predecessor; his work also possesses greater interest from his occasionally speaking in his own person, and from his more frequent expansion and improvement of his French original by new matter; but for poetry, it would probably require a "taste or judgment" equal to Ritson's own to detect much of it.

LAWRENCE MINOT.

Putting aside the authors of some of the best of the early metrical romances, whose names are generally or universally unknown, perhaps the earliest writer of English verse subsequent to the Conquest who deserves the name of a poet is Lawrence Minot, who lived and wrote about the middle of the fourteenth century, and of the reign of Edward III. His ten poems in celebration of the battles and victories of that king, preserved in the Cotton MS. Galba E. ix., which the old catalogue had described as a manuscript of Chaucer, the compiler having been misled by the name of some former proprietor, Richard Chawfer, inscribed on the volume, were discovered by Tyrwhitt while collecting materials for his edition of the Canterbury Tales, in a note to the Essay on the Language and Versification of Chaucer prefixed to which work their existence was first mentioned. This was in 1775. In 1781 some specimens of them were given (out of their chronological place) by Warton in the third volume of his History of Poetry. Finally, in 1796, the whole were published by Ritson under the title of Poems written anno MCCCLII., by Lawrence Minot; with Introductory Dissertations on the Scottish Wars of Edward III., on his claim to the throne of France, and Notes and Glossary. 8vo. London; and a reprint of this volume appeared in 1825. Of the 250 pages, or thereby, of which it consists, only about 50 are occupied by the poems, which are ten in number, their subjects being the Battle of Halidon Hill (fought 1333); the Battle of Bannockburn (1314), or rather the manner in which that defeat, sustained by his father, had been avenged by Edward III.; Edward's first Invasion of France (1339); the Sea-fight in the Swine, or Zwin* (1340); the siege of Tournay (the same year); the Landing of the English King at La Hogue, on his Expedition in 1346; the Siege of Calais (the same year); the Battle of Neville's Cross (the same year); the Sea-fight with the Spaniards off Winchelsea (1350); and the Taking of the Guisnes (1352). It is from this last date that Ritson, somewhat unwarrantably, assumes that all the poems were written in that year. As they are very various in their form and manner, it is more probable that they were produced as the occasions of them arose, and therefore that they ought rather to be assigned to the interval between 1333 and 1352. They are remarkable, if not for any poetical qualities of a high order, yet for a precision and selectness, as well as a force, of expression, previously, so far as is known, unexampled in English verse. There is a true martial tone and spirit too in them, which reminds us of the best of our old heroic ballads, while it is better sustained, and accompanied with more refinement of style, than it usually is in these popular and anony-

* To the south of the Isle of Cadsand, at the mouth of the West Scheldt.

mous compositions. As a sample we will transcribe the one on
Edward's first expedition to France, omitting a prologue, which
is in a different measure, and modernizing the spelling where it
does not affect the rhyme or rhythm:—

  Edward, owre comely king,
  In Braband has his woning[1]
   With many comely knight;
  And in that land, truely to tell,
  Ordains he still for to dwell
   To time[2] he think to fight.

  Now God, that is of mightés mast,[3]
  Grant him grace of the Holy Ghast
   His heritage to win;
  And Mary Moder, of mercy free,
  Save our king and his meny[4]
   Fro sorrow, shame, and sin.

  Thus in Braband has he been,
  Where he before was seldom seen
   For to prove their japes;[5]
  Now no langer will he spare,
  Bot unto France fast will he fare
   To comfort him with grapes.

  Furth he fared into France;
  God save him fro mischance,
   And all his company!
  The noble Duke of Braband
  With him went into that land,
   Ready to live or die.

  Then the rich flower de lice[6]
  Was there full little price;
   Fast he fled for feared:
  The right heir of that countree
  Is comen,[7] with all his knightes free,
   To shake him by the beard.

  Sir Philip the Valays[8]
  Wit his men in tho days
   To battle had he thought:[9]
  He bade his men them purvey
  Withouten langer delay;
   But he ne held it nought.

---

[1] Dwelling.   [2] Till the time.   [3] Most of might.
[4] Followers.   [5] Jeers.   [6] Fleur de lis.
[7] Come.   [8] Philip VI. de Valois, king of France.
[9] The meaning seems to be, "Informed his men in those days that he had
a design to fight." Unless, indeed, *wit* be a mistranscription of *with*.

LAWRENCE MINOT.

He brought folk full great won,[1]
Aye seven agains[2] one,
 That full well weaponed were,
Bot soon when he heard ascry[3]
That king Edward was near thereby,
 Then durst he nought come near.

In that morning fell a mist,
And when our Englishmen it wist,
 It changed all their cheer;
Our king unto God made his boon,[4]
And God sent him good comfort soon;
 The weader wex full clear.

Our king and his men held the field
Stalworthly with spear and shield,
 And thought to win his right;
With lordes and with knightes keen,
And other doughty men bydeen[5]
 That war full frek[6] to fight.

When Sir Philip of France heard tell
That king Edward in field wald[7] dwell,
 Then gained him no glee:[8]
He traisted of no better boot,[9]
Bot both on horse and on foot
 He hasted him to flee.

It seemed he was feared for strokes
When he did fell his greate oaks
 Obout[10] his pavilions;
Abated was then all his pride,
For langer there durst he nought bide;
 His boast was brought all down.

The king of Beme[11] had cares cold,
That was full hardy and bold
 A steed to umstride:[12]
He and the king als[13] of Naverne[14]
War fair feored[15] in the fern
 Their hovids[16] for to hide.

---

[1] Number.   [2] Against.   [3] Report.
[4] Prayer, request.—*Ritz.* Perhaps, rather, vow or *bond.*
[5] Perhaps "besides." The word is of common occurrence, but of doubtful or various meaning.   [6] Were full eager.   [7] Would (was dwelling).
[8] The meaning seems to be, "then no glee, or joy, was given him" (*accusit of*).   [9] He trusted in no better expedient, or alternative.
[10] About.   [11] Bohemia.   [12] Bestride.   [13] Also.
[14] Navarre.   [15] Were fairly frightened.   [16] Heads.

And leves¹ well it is no lie,
And field hat² Flemangry³
  That king Edward was in,
With princes that were stiff and bold,
And dukes that were doughty told⁴
  In battle to begin.

The princes, that were rich on raw,⁵
Gent⁶ nakers⁷ strike, and trumpes blaw,
  And made mirth at their might,
Both alblast⁸ and many a bow
War ready railed⁹ upon a row,
  And full frek for to fight.

Gladly they gave meat and drink,
So that they mild the better awink,¹⁰
  The wight¹¹ men that there were.
Sir Philip of France fled for doubt,
And hied him hame with all his rout:
  Coward! God Give him care!

For there then had the lily flower
Lorn all halely¹² his honour,
  That so gat fled¹³ for feard;
But our king Edward come full still¹⁴
When that he trowed no harm him till,¹⁵
  And keeped him in the beard.¹⁶

ALLITERATIVE VERSE.—PIERS PLOUGHMAN.

It may be observed that Minot's verses are thickly sprinkled with what is called *alliteration*, or the repetition of words having the same commencing letter, either immediately after one another, or with the intervention only of one or two other words generally unemphatic or of subordinate importance. Alliteration, which we find here combined with rhyme, was in an earlier stage of our poetry employed, more systematically, as the substitute for that decoration—the recurrence, at certain regular intervals, of like beginnings, serving the same purpose which is now accom-

¹ Believe.   ⁵ Was called.   ³ The village of La Flamengrie.
⁴ Reckoned.   ² Apparently, "arranged richly clad in a row."
⁶ Caused.   ⁷ Tymbals.   ⁸ Arblast, or crossbow.
⁹ Placed.   ¹⁰ Should the better labour.
¹¹ Stout.   ¹³ Lost wholly.   ¹³ Got put to flight?
¹⁴ Came back quietly at his ease.
¹⁵ When he perceived there was no harm intended him.
¹⁶ Perhaps, "kept his beard untouched."

plished by what Milton has contemptuously called "the jingling sound of like endings." To the English of the period before the Conquest, until its very latest stage, rhyme was unknown, and down to the tenth century our verse appears to have been constructed wholly upon the principle of alliteration. Hence, naturally, even after we had borrowed the practice of rhyme from the French or Romance writers, our poetry retained for a time more or less of its original habit. In Layamon, as we have seen, alliterative and rhyming couplets are intermixed; in other cases, as in Minot, we have the rhyme only pretty liberally bespangled with alliteration. At this date, in fact, the difficulty probably would have been to avoid alliteration in writing verse; all the old customary phraseologies of poetry had been moulded upon that principle; and indeed alliterative expression has in every age, and in many other languages as well as our own, had a charm for the popular ear, so that it has always largely prevailed in proverbs and other such traditional forms of words, nor is it yet by any means altogether discarded as an occasional embellishment of composition, whether in verse or in prose. But there is one poetical work of the fourteenth century, of considerable extent, and in some respects of remarkable merit, in which the verse is without rhyme, and the system of alliteration is almost as regular as what we have in the poetry of the times before the Conquest. This is the famous Vision of Piers Ploughman, or, as the subject is expressed at full length in the Latin title, Visio Willielmi de Petro Ploughman, that is, The Vision of William concerning Piers or Peter Ploughman. The manuscripts of this poem, which long continued to enjoy a high popularity, are very numerous, and it has also been repeatedly printed: first in 1550, at London, by Robert Crowley, "dwelling in Elye rentes in Holburne," who appears to have produced three successive impressions of it in the same year; again in 1561, by Owen Rogers, "dwellyng neare unto great Saint Bartolmewes gate, at the sygne of the Spred Egle;" next in 1813, under the superintendence of the late Thomas Dunham Whitaker, LL.D.; lastly, in 1842, under the care of Thomas Wright, Esq., M.A., F.R.S., &c.

Of the author of Piers Ploughman scarcely anything is known. He has commonly been called Robert Langland: but there are grounds for believing that his Christian name was William, and it is probable that it is himself of whom he speaks under that name throughout his work. He is supposed to have been a monk, and he seems to have resided in the West of England, near the Malvern Hills, where he introduces himself at the commencement of his poem as falling asleep "on a May morwenynge," and entering upon his dreams or visions. The date may be pretty nearly fixed. In one place there is an allusion to the treaty of Bretigny made with France in 1360, and to the military disasters of the previous year which led to it: in another passage mention is made of a remarkable tempest which occurred on the 15th of January, 1362, as of a recent event. "It is probable," to quote Mr. Wright, "that the poem of Piers Ploughman was composed in the latter part of this year, when the effects of the great wind were fresh in people's memory, and when the treaty of Bretigny had become a subject of popular discontent."* We may assume, at least, that it was in hand at this time.

We cannot attempt an analysis of the work. It consists, in Mr. Wright's edition, where the long line of the other editions is divided into two, of 14,696 verses, distributed into twenty sections, or *Passus* as they are called. Each *passus* forms, or professes to form, a separate vision; and so inartificial or confused is the connection of the several parts of the composition (notwithstanding Dr. Whitaker's notion that it had in his edition "for the first time been shown that it was written after a regular and consistent plan"), that it may be regarded as being in reality not so much one poem as a succession of poems. The general subject may be said to be the same with that of Bunyan's Pilgrim's Progress, the exposition of the impediments and temptations which beset the crusade of this our mortal life; and the method, too, like Bunyan's, is the allegorical; but the spirit of the poetry is not so much picturesque, or even descriptive, as satirical. Vices and abuses of all sorts come in for their share of the exposure and invective; but the main attack throughout is directed against the corruptions of the church, and the hypocrisy and worldliness, the ignorance, indolence, and sensuality, of the ecclesiastical order. To this favourite theme the author constantly returns with new affection and sharper zest from any less high matter which he may occasionally take up. Hence it has been commonly assumed that he must have himself belonged to the ecclesiastical profession, that he was probably a priest or monk. And his Vision has been regarded not only as mainly a religious poem, but as almost a puritanical and Protestant work, although produced nearly two centuries before either Protestanism or Puritanism was ever heard of. In this notion, as we have seen, it was brought into such repute at the time of the Reformation that three editions of it were printed in one year. There is nothing, however, of anti-Romanism, properly

* Introduction, p. xii.

so called, in Langland, either doctrinal or constitutional; and even the anti-clerical spirit of his poetry is not more decided than what is found in the writings of Chaucer, and the other popular literature of the time. In all ages, indeed, it is the tendency of popular literature to erect itself into a power adverse to that of the priesthood, as has been evinced more especially by the poetical literature of modern Europe from the days of the Provençal troubadours. In the Canterbury Tales, however, and in most other works where this spirit appears, the puritanism (if so it is to be called) is merely one of the forms of the poetry; in Piers Ploughman the poetry is principally a form or expression of the puritanism.

The rhythm or measure of the verse in this poem must be considered as accentual rather than syllabical—that is to say, it depends rather upon the number of the accents than of the syllables. This is, perhaps, the original principle of all verse; and it still remains the leading principle in various kinds of verse, both in our own and in other languages. At first, probably, only the accented syllables were counted, or reckoned of any rhythmical value; other syllables upon which there was no emphasis went for nothing, and might be introduced in any part of the verse, one, two, or three at a time, as the poet chose. Of course it would at all times be felt that there were limits beyond which this licence could not be carried without destroying or injuring the metrical character of the composition; but these limits would not at first be fixed as they now for the most part are. The elementary form of the verse in Piers Ploughman demands a succession of four accented syllables—two in the first hemistich or short line, and two in the second; but, while each of those in the first line is usually preceded by either one or two unaccented syllables, commonly only one of those in the second line is so preceded. The second line, therefore, is for the most part shorter than the first. And they also differ in regard to the alliteration: it being required that in the first both the accented or emphatic syllables, which are generally initial syllables, should begin with the same letter, but that in the second only the first accented syllable should begin with that letter. This is the general rule; but, either from the text being corrupt or from the irregularity of the composition, the exceptions are very numerous.

The poem begins as follows:—

        In a summer season,
        When soft was the sun,

I shoop me into shrowds[1]
  As I a sheep[2] were;
In habit as an hermit
  Unholy of werkes,[3]
Went wide in this world
  Wonders to hear;
Ac[4] on a May morwening
  On Malvern hills
Me befel a ferly,[5]
  Of fairy me thought.
I was weary for-wandered,[6]
  And went me to rest
Under a brood[7] bank,
  By a burn's[8] side;
And as I lay and leaned,
  And looked on the waters,
I slombered into a sleeping,
  It swayed so mury.[9]
Then gan I meten[10]
  A marvellous sweven,[11]
That I was in a wilderness,
  Wist I never where;
And, as I beheld into the east
  On high to the sun,
I seigh[12] a tower on a toft[13]
  Fræliche ymaked,[14]
A deep dale beneath,
  A donjon therein,
With deep ditches and darke,
  And dreadful of sight.
A fair field full of folk
  Found I there between,
Of all manner of men,
  The mean and the rich,
Werking[15] and wandering
  As the world asketh.
Some putten hem[16] to the plough,
  Playden full seld.[17]

---

[1] I put myself into clothes.   [2] A shepherd.
[3] Whitaker's interpretation is, "in habit, not like an anchorite who keeps his cell, but like one of those unholy hermits who wander about the world to see and hear wonders." He reads, "That went forth in the worl," &c.
[4] And.   [5] Wonder.   [6] Worn out with wandering.
[7] Broad.   [8] Stream's.   [9] It sounded so pleasant.
[10] Meet.   [11] Dream.   [12] Saw.
[13] An elevated ground.   [14] Handsomely built.   [15] Working.
[16] Put them.   [17] Played full seldom.

In setting and sowing
  Swonken[1] full hard,
And wonnen that wasters
  With gluttony destroyeth.[2]
And some putten hem to pride,
  Apparelled hem thereafter,
In countenance of clothing
  Comen deguised,[3]
In prayers and penances
  Putten hem many,[4]
All for the love of our Lord
  Liveden full strait,[5]
In hope to have after
  Heaven-riche bliss ;[6]
As anchors and heremites[7]
  That holden hem in hir[8] cells,
And coveten nought in country
  To carryen about,
For no likerous liflode
  Hir likame to please.[9]
And some chosen chaffer :[10]
  They cheveden[11] the better,
As it seemeth to our sight
  That swich me thriveth.[12]
And some murthes to make
  As minstralles con,[13]
And geten gold with hir glee,[14]
  Guiltless, I leve.[15]
Ac japers and jaugellers[16]
  Judas' children,
Feignen hem fantasies
  And fools hem maketh,
And han hir[17] wit at will
  To werken if they wold.
That Poul preacheth of hem
  I wol not preve[18] it here:
But *qui loquitur turpiloquium*[19]
  Is Jupiter's hine.[20]

---

[1] Laboured. [2] Was that which wasters with gluttony destroy.
[3] Came disguised. Whitaker reads, "In countenance and in clothing."
[4] Many put them, applied themselves to, engaged in.
[5] Lived full strictly. [6] The bliss of the kingdom of heaven.
[7] Anchorites and eremites or hermits. [8] Hold them in their.
[9] By no likerous living their body to please. [10] Merchandise.
[11] Achieved their end. [12] That such men thrive.
[13] And some are skilled to make mirths, or amusements, as minstrels.
[14] And get gold with their minstrelsy. [15] Believe.
[16] But jesters and jugglers. [17] Have their. [18] Will not prove.
[19] Whoso speaketh ribaldry. [20] Our modern *hind*, or servant.

Bidders[1] and beggars
　Fast about yede,[2]
With hir bellies and hir bags
　Of bread full y-crammed,
Faiteden[3] for hir food,
　Foughten at the ale:
In gluttony, God wot,
　Go they to bed,
And risen with ribaudry,[4]
　The Roberd's knaves;[5]
Sleep and sorry slewth[6]
　Sueth[7] hem ever.
Pilgrims and palmers
　Plighten hem togider[8]
For to seeken Saint Jame
　And saintes at Rome:
They wenten forth in hir way[9]
　With many wise tales,
And hadden leave to lien[10]
　All hir life after.
I seigh some that seiden[11]
　They had y-sought saints:
To each a tale that they told
　Hir tongue was tempered to lie[12]
More than to say sooth,
　It seemed by hir speech.
Hermits on an heap,[13]
　With hooked staves,
Wenten to Walsingham,
　And hir wenches after;
Great loobies and long,
　That loath were to swink,[14]
Clothed hem in copes
　To be knowen from other,
And shopen hem[15] hermits
　Hir ease to have.
I found there freres,
　All the four orders,
Preaching the people
　For profit of hem selve

---

[1] Petitioners.　[2] Went.　[3] Flattered.　[4] Rise with ribaldry.
[5] Those Robertsmen—a class of malefactors mentioned in several statutes of the fourteenth century. The same may have meant originally Robin Hood's men, as Whitaker conjectures.
[6] Sloth.　　　　　　　　　[7] Pursue.
[8] Gather them together.　　[9] They went forth on their way.
[10] To lie.　　　　　　　　[11] I saw some that said.
[12] In every tale that they told their tongue was trained to lie.
[13] In a crowd.　[14] Labour.　[15] Made themselves.

Glosed the gospel
 As hem good liked;[1]
For coveitise of copes[2]
 Construed it as they would.
Many of these master freres
 Now clothen hem at liking,[3]
For his money and his merchandize
 Marchen togeders.
For sith charity hath been chapman,
 And chief to shrive lords,
Many ferlies han fallen[4]
 In a few years:
But holy church and hi[5]
 Hold better togeders,
The most mischief on mould[6]
 Is mounting well fast.
There preached a pardoner,
 As he a priest were;
Broughte forth a bull
 With many bishops' seals,
And said that himself might
 Assoilen hem all,
Of falsehede of fasting,[7]
 Of avowes y-broken.
Lewed[8] men leved[9] it well,
 And liked his words;
Comen up kneeling
 To kissen his bulls:
He bouched[10] hem with his brevet,[11]
 And bleared his eyen,[12]
And raught with his ragman[13]
 Ringes and brooches.

Here it will be admitted, we have both a well-filled canvas and a picture with a good deal of life and stir in it. The satiric touches are also natural and effective; and the expression clear, easy, and not deficient in vigour.

[1] As it seemed to them good. [2] Covetousness of copes or rich clothing.
[3] Clothe themselves to their liking. [4] Many wonders have happened.
[5] Unless holy church and they. [6] The greatest mischief on earth.
[7] Of breaking fast-days. [8] Ignorant. [9] Loved.
[10] Stopped their mouths. [11] Little brief. [12] Bedimmed their eyes.
[13] Reached, drew in, with his catalogue or roll of names?

PIERS PLOUGHMAN'S CREED.

The popularity of Langland's poem appears to have brought alliterative verse into fashion again even for poems of considerable length: several romances were written in it, such as that of William and the Worwolf, that of Alexander, that of Jerusalem, and others; and the use of it was continued throughout the greater part of the fifteenth century. But the most remarkable imitation of the Vision is the poem entitled Piers the Ploughman's Creed, which appears to have been written about the end of the fourteenth century: it was first printed separately at London, in 4to. by Reynold Wolfe, in 1553; then by Rogers, along with the Vision, in 1561. In modern times it has also been printed separately, in 1814, as a companion to Whitaker's edition of the Vision; and, along with the Vision, in Mr. Wright's edition of 1842. The Creed is the composition of a follower of Wyclif, and an avowed opponent of Romanism. Here, Mr. Wright observes, "Piers Ploughman is no longer an allegorical personage: he is the simple representative of the peasant rising up to judge and act for himself—the English *sans-culotte* of the fourteenth century, if we may be allowed the comparison." The satire, or invective, in this effusion (which consists only of 1697 short lines), is directed altogether against the clergy, and especially the monks or friars; and Piers or Peter is represented as a poor ploughman from whom the writer receives that instruction in Christian truth which he had sought for in vain from every order of these licensed teachers. The language is quite as antique as that of the Vision, as may appear from the following passage, in which Piers is introduced:—

> Then turned I me forth,
> And talked to myself
> Of the falsehede of this folk,
> How faithless they weren
> And as I went by the way
> Weeping for sorrow,
> I see a seely[1] man me by
> Upon the plough hongen.[2]
> His coat was of a clout[3]
> That cary[4] was y-called;
> His hood was full of holes,
> And his hair out;

---
[1] Simple.   [2] Hung, bent, over.   [3] Cloth.
[4] This is probably the same word that we have elsewhere in carry mary. It would seem to be the name of a kind of cloth.

With his knopped shoon[1]
  Clouted full thick,
His ton[2] toteden[3] out
  As he the lond treaded:
His hosen overhongen his hoo-shynes[4]
  On overich a side,
All beslomered[5] in fen[6]
  As he the plough followed.
Twey[7] mittens as meter[8]
  Made all of clouts,
The fingers weren for-weard[9]
  And full of fen honged.
This whit[10] wasled[11] in the fenn[12]
  Almost to the anclo:
Four rotheren[13] him beforn,
  That feeble were worthy;[14]
Men might reckon each a rib[15]
  So rentful[16] they weren.
His wife walked him with,
  With a long goad,
In a cutted coat
  Cutted full high,
Wrapped in a winnow[17] sheet
  To wearen her fro weders,[18]
Barefoot on the bare ice,
  That the blood followed.
And at the lond's end[19] lath[20]
  A little crum-bolle,[21]
And thereon lay a little child
  Lapped in clouts,
And tweyn of twey years old[22]
  Upon another side.
And all they songen[23] o[24] song,
  That sorrow was to hearen;
They crieden all o cry,
  A careful note.

---

[1] Knobbed shoes. [2] Toes. [3] Peeped.
[4] Neither of Mr. Wright's explanations seems quite satisfactory: "crooked shins;" or "the shin towards the hock or ankle?"
[5] Bedaubed. [6] Mud. [7] Two.
[8] Mr. Wright suggests *fitter*; which does not seem to make sense.
[9] Were worn out. [10] Wight. [11] Dirtied himself.
[12] Fen, mud. [13] Oxen (the Four Evangelists).
[14] Become? Perhaps the true reading is *forthy*, that is, *for that*.
[15] Each rib. [16] Meagre? [17] Winnowing.
[18] The meaning seems to be, "to protect her from the weather."
[19] The end of the field. [20] Lieth?
[21] Mr. Wright explains by "crum-bowl."
[22] Two of two years old. [23] Sang. [24] One.

The seely man sighed sore,
  And said, "Children, beth[1] still."
This man looked opon me,
  And leet the plough stonden;[2]
And said, "Seely man,
  Why sighest thou so hard?
Gif thee lack lifelode,[3]
  Lene thee ich will[4]
Swich[5] good as God hath sent:
  Go we, leve brother."[6]

---

[1] Be.   [2] Let the plough stand.
[3] If livelihood lack, or be wanting to, thee.
[4] Give or lend thee I will.   [5] Such.
[6] Let us go, dear brother.

THIRD ENGLISH.

(MIXED OR COMPOUND ENGLISH.)

GEOFFREY CHAUCER.

The Vision of Piers Ploughman is our earliest poetical work of any considerable extent that may still be read with pleasure; but not much of its attraction lies in its poetry. It interests us chiefly as rather a lively picture (which, however, would have been nearly as effective in prose) of much in the manners and general social condition of the time, and of the new spirit of opposition to old things which was then astir; partly, too, by the language and style, and as a monument of a peculiar species of versification. Langland, or whoever was the author, probably contributed by this great work to the advancement of his native tongue to a larger extent than he has had credit for. The grammatical forms of his English will be found to be very nearly, if not exactly the same with those of Chaucer's; his vocabulary, if more sparingly admitting the non-Teutonic element, still does not abjure the principle of the same composite constitution; nor is his style much inferior in mere regularity and clearness. So long a work was not likely to have been undertaken except by one who felt himself to be in full possession of the language as it existed: the writer was no doubt prompted to engage in such a task in great part by his gift of ready expression; and he could not fail to gain additional fluency and skill in the course of the composition, especially with a construction of verse demanding so incessant an attention to words and syllables. The popularity of the poem, too, would diffuse and establish whatever improvements in the language it may have introduced or exemplified. In addition to the ability displayed in it, and the popular spirit of the day with which it was animated, its position in the national literature naturally and deservedly gave to the Vision of Piers Ploughman an extraordinary influence: for it has the distinction (so far as is either known or probable) of being the earliest original work, of any magnitude, in the present form of the language. Robert of Gloucester and Robert de Brunne, Langland's predecessors, were both, it may be remembered, only translators or paraphrasts.

If Langland, however, is our earliest original writer, Chaucer is still our first great poet, and the true father of our literature, properly so called. Compared with his productions, all that precedes is barbarism. But what is much more remarkable is, that very little of what has followed in the space of nearly five centuries that has elapsed since he lived and wrote is worthy of being compared with what he has left us. He is in our English poetry almost what Homer is in that of Greece, and Dante in that of Italy—at least in his own sphere still the greatest light.

Although, therefore, according to the scheme of the history of the language which has been propounded, the third form of it, or that which still subsists, may be regarded as having taken its commencement perhaps a full century before the date at which we are now arrived, and so as taking in the works, not only of Langland, but of his predecessors from Robert of Gloucester inclusive, our living English Literature may be most fitly held to begin with the poetry of Chaucer. It will thus count an existence already of above five centuries. Chaucer is supposed to have been born about the beginning of the reign of Edward III.—in the year 1328, if we may trust what is said to have been the ancient inscription on his tombstone; so that he had no doubt begun to write, and was probably well known as a poet, at least as early as Langland. They may indeed have been contemporaries in the strictest sense of the word, for anything that is ascertained. If Langland wrote the Creed of Piers Ploughman, as well as the Vision, which (although it has not, we believe, been suggested) is neither impossible nor very unlikely, he must have lived to as late, or very nearly as late, a date as Chaucer, who is held to have died in 1400. At the same time, as Langland's greatest, if not only, work appears to have been produced not long after the middle of the reign of Edward III., and the composition of Chaucer's Canterbury Tales not to have been begun till about the middle of that of Richard II., the probability certainly is, regard being had to the species and character of these poems, each seemingly impressed with a long experience of life, that Langland, if not the earlier writer, was the elder man.

The writings of Chaucer are very voluminous; comprising, in so far as they have come down to us, in verse, The Canterbury Tales; the Romaunt of the Rose, in 7701 lines, a translation from the French Roman de la Rose of Guillaume de Lorris and Jean de Meun; Troilus and Creseide, in Five Books, on the same subject as the Filostrato of Boccaccio; The House of Fame, in Three Books; Chaucer's Dream, in 2235 lines; the Book of the Duchess (sometimes called the Dream of Chaucer), 1334 lines; the Assembly of Fowls, 694 lines; the Flower and the Leaf, 595 lines; the Court of Love, 1442 lines; together with many ballads and other minor pieces: and in prose (besides portions of the Canterbury Tales), a translation of Boethius' De Consolatione Philosophiæ; the Testament of Love, an imitation of the same treatise; and a Treatise on the Astrolabe, addressed to his son Lewis in 1391, of which, however, we have only two out of five parts of which it was intended to consist. All these works have been printed, most of them more than once; and a good many other pieces have also been attributed to Chaucer which are either known to be the compositions of other poets, or of which at least there is no evidence or probability that he is the author. Only the Canterbury Tales, however, have as yet enjoyed the advantage of anything like careful editing. Tyrwhitt's elaborate edition was first published, in 4 vols. 8vo., in 1775, his Glossary to all the genuine works of Chaucer having followed in 1778; and another edition, presenting a new text, and also accompanied with notes and a Glossary, was brought out by Mr. T. Wright for the Percy Society in 1847.

In his introductory Essay on the Language and Versification of Chaucer, Tyrwhitt observes, that at the time when this great writer made his first essays the use of rhyme was established in English poetry, not exclusively (as we have seen by the example of the Vision of Piers Ploughman), but very generally, " so that in this respect he had little to do but to imitate his predecessors." But the metrical part of our poetry, the learned editor conceives, " was capable of more improvement, by the polishing of the measures already in use, as well as by the introduction of new modes of versification." " With respect," he continues, " to the regular measures then in use, they may be reduced, I think, to four. First, the long Iambic metre, consisting of not more than fifteen nor less than fourteen syllables, and broken by a cæsura at the eighth syllable. Secondly, the Alexandrine metre, consisting of not more than thirteen syllables nor less than twelve, with a cæsura at the sixth. Thirdly, the Octosyllable metre, which was in reality the ancient dimeter Iambic. Fourthly, the stanza of six verses, of which the first, second, fourth, and fifth were in the complete octosyllable metre, and the third and last cataloctic—that is, wanting a syllable, or even two." The first of these metres Tyrwhitt considers to be exemplified in the Ormulum, and probably also in the Chronicle of Robert of Gloucester, if the genuine text could be recovered; the second, apparently, by Robert de Brunne, in imitation of his French original, although his verse in Hearne's edition is frequently defective: the third and fourth were very common, being then generally used in lighter compositions, as they still are. "In the first of these metres," he proceeds, "it does not appear that Chaucer ever composed at all (for I presume no one can imagine that he was the author of Gamelyn), or in the second; and in the fourth we have nothing of his but the Rhyme of Sire Thopas, which, being intended to ridicule the vulgar romancers, seems to have been purposely written in their favourite metre. In the third, or octosyllable metre, he has left several compositions, particularly an imperfect translation of the Roman de la Rose, which was probably one of his earliest performances, The House of Fame, The Dethe of the Duchesse Blanche, and a poem called his Dreme: upon all which it will be sufficient here to observe in general, that, if he had given no other proofs of his poetical faculty, these alone must have secured to him the preeminence above all his predecessors and contemporaries in point of versification. But by far the most considerable part of Chaucer's works is written in that kind of metre which we now call the Heroic, either in distichs or stanzas; and, as I have not been able to discover any instance of this metre being used by any English poet before him, I am much inclined to suppose that he was the first introducer of it into our language." It had been long practised by the writers both in the northern and southern French; and within the half century before Chaucer wrote it had been successfully cultivated, in preference to every other metre, by the great poets of Italy—Dante, Petrarch, and Boccaccio. Tyrwhitt argues, therefore, that Chaucer may have borrowed his new English verse either from the French or from the Italian.

That the particular species of verse in which Chaucer has written his Canterbury Tales and some of his other poems had not been used by any other English poet before him, has not, we believe, been disputed, and does not appear to be disputable, at least from such remains of our early poetical literature as we now possess. Here, then, is one important fact. It is certain, also, that the French, if not likewise the Italian, poets who employed the decasyllabic (or more properly hendecasyllabic *)

---

* In the Italian language, at least, the original and proper form of the verse appears to have consisted of eleven syllables; whence the generical name of the metro is endecasyllabo, and a verse of ten syllables is called endecasyllabo tronco, and one of twelve, endecasyllabo sdrucciolo. But these variations do not affect the prosodical character of the verse, which requires only that the tenth

metre were well known to Chaucer. The presumption, therefore, that his new metre is, as Tyrwhitt asserts, this same Italian or French metre of ten or eleven syllables (our present heroic verse) becomes very strong.

Moreover, if Chaucer's verse be not constructed upon the principle of syllabical as well as accentual regularity, when was this principle, which is now the law and universal practice of our poetry, introduced? It will not be denied to have been completely established ever since the language acquired in all material respects its present form and pronunciation—that is to say, at least since the middle of the sixteenth century: if it was not by Chaucer at the end of the fourteenth, by whom among his followers in the course of the next hundred and fifty years was it first exemplified?

At present it is sufficient to say that no one of his successors throughout this space has hinted that any improvement, any change, had been made in the construction of English verse since Chaucer wrote. On the contrary, he is generally recognized by them as the great reformer of our language and our poetry, and as their master and instructor in their common art. By his friend and disciple Occleve he is called " the first finder of our fair langage." So Lydgate, in the next generation, celebrates him as his master—as " chief poet of Britain "—as

> — "he that was of making soverain,
> Whom all this lande of right ought prefer,
> Sith of our langage he was the lode-ster"—

and as—

> "The noble rhethor poet of Britain,
> That worthy was the laurer to have

---

should be in all cases the last *accented* syllable. The modern English heroic, or, as we commonly call it, ten-syllabled verse, still admits of being extended by an eleventh or even a twelfth *unaccented* syllable; although, from the constitution of our present language as to syllabic emphasis, such extension is with us the exception, not the rule, as it is (at least to the length of eleven syllables) in Italian. It may be doubted whether Chaucer's type or model line is to be considered as decasyllabic or hendecasyllabic; Tyrwhitt was of opinion that the greater number of his verses, when properly written and pronounced, would be found to consist of eleven syllables; and this will seem probable, if we look to what is assumed, on the theory of his versification which we are considering, to have been the pronunciation of the language in his day. At the same time many of his lines evidently consist (even on this theory) of ten syllables only; and such a construction of verse for ordinary purposes is become so much more agreeable to modern usage and taste that his poetry had better be so read whenever it can be done, even at the cost of thereby somewhat violating the exactness of the ancient pronunciation.

> Of poetrye, and the palm attain;
> That made first to distil and rain
> The gold dew-drops of speech and eloquence
> Into our tongue through his excellence,
> And found the flowres first of rhetoric
> Our rude speech only to enlumine," &c.

A later writer, Gawin Douglas, sounds his praise as—

> "Venerable Chaucer, principal poet but [1] peer,
> Heavenly trumpet, orlege,[2] and regulere;[3]
> In eloquence balm, condict,[4] and dial,
> Milky fountain, clear strand, and rose rial,"[5]

in a strain, it must be confessed, more remarkable for enthusiastic vehemence than for poetical inspiration. The learned, and at the same time elegant, Leland, in the next age describes him as the writer to whom his country's tongue owes all its beauties:—

> "Anglia Chaucerum veneratur nostra poetam,
> Cui veneres debet patria lingua suas;"

and again, in another tribute, as having first reduced the language into regular form:—

> "Linguam qui patriam redegit illam
> In formam."

And such seems to have been the unbroken tradition down to Spenser, who, looking back through two centuries, hails his great predecessor as still the "well of English undefiled."

If now we proceed to examine Chaucer's verse, do we find it actually characterized by this regularity, which indisputably has at least from within a century and a half of his time been the law of our poetry? Not, if we assume that the English of Chaucer's time was read in all respects precisely like that of our own day. But are we warranted in assuming this? We know that some changes have taken place in the national pronunciation within a much shorter space. The accentuation of many words is different even in Shakespeare and his contemporaries from what it now is: even since the language has been what we may call settled, and the process of growth in it nearly stopped, there has still been observable a disposition in the accent or syllabic emphasis to project itself with more precipitation than formerly, to seize upon a more early enunciated part in dissyllables and other polysyllabic words than that to which it was

---

[1] Without.
[2] Regulator.
[3] Horologe, clock or watch.
[4] Condiment.
[5] Royal.

wont to be attached. For example, we now always pronounce the word *aspect* with the accent on the first syllable; in the time of Shakespeare it was always accented on the last. We now call a certain short composition an *essáy*; but only a century ago it was called an *essáy*: "And write next winter," says Pope, "more essáys on man." Probably at an earlier period, when this change was going on more actively, it was part of that general process by which the Teutonic, or native, element in our language eventually, after a long struggle, acquired the ascendancy over the French element; and, if so, for a time the accentuation of many words would be unfixed, or would oscillate between the two systems—the French habit of reserving itself for the final syllable, and the native tendency to cling to a prior portion of the word. This appears to have been the case in Chaucer's day: many words are manifestly in his poetry accented differently from what they are now (as is proved, upon either theory of his prosody, when they occur at the end of a verse), and in many also he seems to vary the accent—pronouncing, for instance, *lángage* in one line, *langáge* in another—as suits his convenience. But again, under the tendency to elision and abbreviation, which is common to all languages in a state of growth, there can be no doubt that, in the progress of the English tongue, from its first subjection to literary cultivation in the middle of the thirteenth century to its final settlement in the middle of the seventeenth, it dropt and lost altogether many short or unaccented syllables. Some of these, indeed, our poets still assert their right to revive in pressing circumstances: thus, though we now almost universally elide or suppress the *e* before the terminating *d* of the preterites and past participles of our verbs, it is still sometimes called into life again to make a distinct syllable in verse. Two centuries ago, when perhaps it was generally heard in the common speech of the people (as it still is in some of our provincial dialects), and when its suppression in reading prose would probably have been accounted an irregularity, it was as often sounded in verse as not, and the licence was probably considered to be taken when it was elided. The elision, when it took place, was generally marked by the omission of the vowel in the spelling. If we go back another century, we find the pronunciation of the termination as a distinct syllable to be clearly the rule and the prevailing practice, and the suppression of the vowel to be the rare exception. But even at so late a date as the end of the sixteenth and the beginning of the seventeenth century, other short vowels as well as this were still occasionally pronounced, as they were almost always written. Both the genitive or possessive singular and the nominative plural of nouns were, down to this time, made by the addition not of *s* only, as now, but of *es* to the nominative singular; and the *es* makes a distinct syllable sometimes in Shakespeare, and often in Spenser. In Chaucer, therefore, it is only what we should expect that it should generally be so pronounced: it is evident that originally, or when it first appeared in the language, it always was, and that the practice of running it and the preceding syllable together, as we now do, has only been gradually introduced and established.

The deficiencies of Chaucer's metre, Tyrwhitt contends, are to be chiefly supplied by the pronunciation of what he calls "the *e* feminine;" by which he means the *e* which still terminates so many of our words, but is now either totally silent and inoffective in the pronunciation, or only lengthens or otherwise alters the sound of the preceding vowel—in either case is entirely inoperative upon the syllabication. Thus, such words as *large*, *strange*, *time*, &c., he conceives to be often dissyllables, and such words as *Romaine*, *sentence*, often trisyllables, in Chaucer. Some words also he holds to be lengthened a syllable by the intervention of such an *e*, now omitted both in speaking and writing, in the middle—as in *jug-e-ment*, *command-e-ment*, *vouch-e-safe*, &c.

Wallis, the distinguished mathematician, in his Grammar of the English Language (written in Latin, and published about the middle of the seventeenth century) had suggested that the origin of this silent *e* probably was, that it had originally been pronounced, though somewhat obscurely, as a distinct syllable, like the French *e* feminine, which still counts for such in the prosody of that language. Wallis adds, that the surest proof of this is to be found in our old poets, with whom the said *e* sometimes makes a syllable, sometimes not, as the verse requires. "With respect to words imported directly from France," observes Tyrwhitt, "it is certainly quite natural to suppose that for some time they retained their native pronunciation." "We have not indeed," he continues, "so clear a proof of the original pronunciation of the Saxon part of our language; but we know, from general observation, that all changes of pronunciation are generally made by small degrees; and, therefore, when we find that a great number of those words which in Chaucer's time ended in *e* originally ended in *a*, we may reasonably presume that our ancestors first passed from the broader sound of *a* to the thinner sound of *e* feminine, and not at once from *a* to *e* mute. Besides, if the final *e* in such words was not pronounced, why was it added? From the time that it has confessedly ceased to be pronounced it has been gradually omitted in them, except where it may be supposed of use to lengthen or soften the preceding syllable, as in *hope, name*, &c. But according to the ancient orthography it terminates many words of Saxon original where it cannot have been added for any such purpose, as *herte, childe, olde, wilde*, &c. In these, therefore, we must suppose that it was pronounced as *e* feminine, and made part of a second syllable, and so, by a parity of reason, in all others in which, as in those, it appears to have been substituted for the Saxon *a*." From all this Tyrwhitt concludes that "the pronunciation of the *e* feminine is founded on the very nature of both the French and Saxon parts of our language," and therefore that "what is generally considered as an *e* mute, either at the end or in the middle of words, was anciently pronounced, but obscurely, like the *e* feminine of the French." In a note, referring to an opinion expressed by Wallis, who, observing that the French very often suppressed this short *e* in their common speech, was led to think that the pronunciation of it would perhaps shortly be in all cases disused among them, as among ourselves, he adds: "The prediction has certainly failed; but, notwithstanding, I will venture to say that when it was made it was not unworthy of Wallis's sagacity. Unluckily for its success, a number of eminent writers happened at that very time to be growing up in France, whose works, having since been received as standards of style, must probably fix for many centuries the ancient usage of the *e* feminine in poetry, and of course give a considerable check to the natural progress of the language. If the age of Edward III. had been as favourable to letters as that of Louis XIV.; if Chaucer and his contemporary poets had acquired the same authority here that Corneille, Molière, Racine, and Boileau have obtained in France; if their works had been published by themselves, and perpetuated in a genuine state by printing; I think it probable that the *e* feminine would still have preserved its place, in our poetical language at least, and certainly without any prejudice to the smoothness of our versification."

In supporting his views by these reasons, Tyrwhitt avoids having recourse to any arguments that might be drawn from the practice of Chaucer himself—that being in fact the matter in dispute; but his main proposition, to the extent at least of the alleged capacity of the now silent final *e* to make a distinct syllable in Chaucer's day, appears to be demonstrated by some instances in the poet's works. Thus, for example, in the following couplet from the Prologue to the Canterbury Tales, unless the word *Rome* which ends the first line be pronounced as a dissyllable, there will be no rhyme:—

"That straight was comen from the court of Rome;
Full loud he sang—Come hither, love, to me."

So again, in the Canon Yeoman's Tale, we have the following lines:—

"And when this alchymister saw his time,
Ris'th up, Sir Priest, quod he, and stondeth by me,"

in the first of which *time* must evidently in like manner be read as a word of two syllables. The same rhyme occurs in a quatrain in the Second Book of the Troilus and Creseide:—

"All easily now, for the love of Marte,
Quod Pandarus, for every thing hath time,
So long abide, till that the night departe
For all so sicker as thou liest here by me."

Finding *Rome* and *time* to be clearly dissyllables in these passages, it would seem that we ought, as Tyrwhitt remarks (Note on Prol. to Cant. Tales, 674), to have no scruple so to pronounce them and other similar words wherever the metre requires it.

"The notion, probably, which most people have of Chaucer," to borrow a few sentences of what we have written elsewhere, "is merely that he was a remarkably good poet for his day; but that, both from his language having become obsolete, and from the advancement which we have since made in poetical taste and skill, he may now be considered as fairly dead and buried in a literary, as well as in a literal, sense. This, we suspect, is the common belief even of educated persons and of scholars who have not actually made acquaintance with Chaucer, but know him only by name or by sight;—by that antique-sounding dissyllable that seems to belong to another nation and tongue, as well as to another age; and by that strange costume of diction, grammar, and spelling, in which his thoughts are clothed, fluttering about them, as it appears to do, like the rags upon a scarecrow.

"Now, instead of this, the poetry of Chaucer is really, in all essential respects, about the greenest and freshest in our language. We have some higher poetry than Chaucer's—poetry that has more of the character of a revelation, or a voice from another world: we have none in which there is either a more abounding or a more bounding spirit of life, a truer or fuller natural inspiration. He may be said to verify, in another sense, the remark of Bacon, that what we commonly call antiquity was really the youth of the world: his poetry seems to breathe of a time when humanity was younger and more joyous-hearted than it now is. Undoubtedly he had an advantage as to this matter, in having been the first great poet of his country. Occupying this position, he stands in some degree between each of his successors and nature. The sire of a nation's minstrelsy is of necessity, though it may be unconsciously, regarded by all who come after him as almost a portion of nature—as one whose utterances are not so much the echo of hers as in very deed her own living voice—carrying in them a spirit as original and divine as the music of her running brooks, or of her breezes among the leaves. And there is not wanting something of reason in this idolatry. It is he alone who has conversed with nature directly, and without an interpreter—who has looked upon the glory of her countenance unveiled, and received upon his heart the perfect image of what she is. Succeeding poets, by reason of his intervention, and that imitation of him into which, in a greater or less degree, they are of necessity drawn, see her only, as it were, wrapt in hazy and metamorphosing adornments, which human hands have woven for her, and are prevented from perfectly discerning the outline and the movements of her form by that encumbering investiture. They are the fallen race, who have been banished from the immediate presence of the divinity, and have been left only to conjecture from afar off the brightness of that majesty which sits throned to them behind impenetrable clouds: he is the First Man, who has seen God walking in the garden, and communed with him face to face.

"But Chaucer is the Homer of his country, not only as having been the earliest of her poets (deserving to be so called), but also as being still one of her greatest. The names of Spenser, of Shakspeare, and of Milton are the only other names that can be placed on the same line with his.

"His poetry exhibits, in as remarkable a degree perhaps as any other in any language, an intermixture and combination of what are usually deemed the most opposite excellences. Great poet as he is, we might almost say of him that his genius has as much about it of the spirit of prose as of poetry, and that, if he had not sung so admirably as he has done of flowery meadows, and summer skies, and gorgeous ceremonials, and high or tender passions, and the other themes over which the imagination loves best to pour her vivifying light, he would have won to himself the renown of a Montaigne or a Swift by the originality and penetrating sagacity of his observations on ordinary life, his insight into motives and character, the richness and peculiarity of his humour, the sharp edge of his satire, and the propriety, flexibility, and exquisite expressiveness of his refined yet natural diction. Even like the varied visible creation around us, his poetry too has its earth, its sea, and its sky, and all the "sweet vicissitudes" of each. Here you have the clear-eyed observer of man as he is, catching 'the manners living as they rise,' and fixing them in pictures where not their minutest lineament is or ever can be lost: here he is the inspired dreamer, by whom earth and all its realities are forgotten, as his spirit soars and sings in the finer air and amid the diviner beauty of some far-off world of its own. Now the riotous verse rings loud with the turbulence of human merriment and laughter, casting from it, as it dashes on its way, flash after flash of all the forms of wit and comedy; now it is the tranquillizing companionship of the sights and sounds of inanimate nature of which the poet's heart is full—the springing herbage, and the dew-drops on the leaf, and the rivulets glad beneath the morning ray and dancing to their own simple music. From mere narrative and playful humour up to the heights of imaginative and impassioned song, his genius has exercised itself in all styles of poetry, and won imperishable laurels in all."*

It has been commonly believed that one of the chief sources from which Chaucer drew both the form and the spirit of his poetry was the recent and contemporary poetry of Italy—that eldest portion of what is properly called the literature of modern Europe, the produce of the genius of Petrarch and Boccaccio and their predecessor and master, Dante. But, although this may have been the case, it is by no means certain that it was so; and some circumstances seem to make it rather improbable that Chaucer was a reader or student of Italian. Of those of his poems which have been supposed to be translations from the Italian, it must be considered very doubtful if any one was really derived by him from that language. The story of his Palamon and Arcite, which, as the Knight's Tale, begins the Canterbury Tales, but which either in its present or another form appears to have been originally composed as a separate work, is substantially the same with that of Boccaccio's heroic poem in twelve books entitled Le Teseide—a fact which, we believe, was first pointed out by Warton. But an examination of the two poems leads rather to the conclusion that they are both founded upon a common original than that the one was taken from the other. Boccaccio's poem extends to about 12,000 octosyllabic, Chaucer's to not many more than 2000 decasyllabic,

* Printing Machine, No. 37 (1835).

verses; and not only is the story in the one much less detailed than in the other, but the two versions differ in some of the main circumstances.* Chaucer, moreover, nowhere mentions Boccaccio as his original; on the contrary, as Warton has himself noticed, he professes to draw his materials, not from the works of any contemporary, but from "olde Stories," and "olde bookes that all this story telleth more plain."† Tyrwhitt, too, while holding, as well as Warton, that Chaucer's original was Boccaccio, admits that the latter was in all probability not the inventor of the story.‡ Boccaccio himself, in a letter relating to his poem, describes the story as very ancient, and as existing in what he calls *Latino volgare*, by which he may mean rather the Provençal than the Italian.§ In fact, as both Warton and Tyrwhitt have shown, there is reason to believe that it had previously been one of the themes of romantic poetry in various languages. The passages pointed out by Tyrwhitt in his notes to Chaucer's poem, as translated or imitated from that of Boccaccio, are few and insignificant, and the resemblances they present would be sufficiently accounted for on the supposition of both writers having drawn from a common source. Nearly the same observations apply to the supposed obligations of Chaucer in his Troilus and Creseide to another poetical work of Boccaccio's, his Filostrato. The discovery of these was first announced by Tyrwhitt in his Essay prefixed to the Canterbury Tales. But Chaucer himself tells us (ii. 14) that he translates his poem "out of Latin;" and in other passages (i. 394, and v. 1653), he expressly declares his "auctor" or author,

* See this pointed out by Dr. Nott (who nevertheless assumes the one poem to be a translation from the other), in a note to his Dissertation on the State of English Poetry before the Sixteenth Century, p. cclxxiv.
† Warton's Hist. Eng. Poetry, ii. 179.
‡ Introductory Discourse to Canterbury Tales, Note (13).
§ The letter is addressed to his mistress (la Fiametta), Mary of Aragon, a natural daughter of Robert king of Naples. "Trovata," he says, "una antichissima storia, et al più delle genti non manifesta, in Latino volgare," &c. The expression here has a curious resemblance to the words used by Chaucer in enumerating his own works in the Legende of Good Women, v. 420,—

"He made the boke that hight the House of Fame, &c.
And all the love of Palamon and Arcite
Of Thebes, *though the story is knowen lite.*"

Tyrwhitt's interpretation of these last words is, that they seem to imply that the poem to which they allude, the Palamon and Arcite (as first composed), had not made itself very popular. Both he and Warton understand the *Latino volgare*, as meaning the Italian language in this passage of the letter to La Fiametta, as well as in a stanza which he quotes from the Teseide in Discourse, Note (9).

to be named *Lollius*. In a note to the Parson's Tale, in the Canterbury Tales, Tyrwhitt assumes that Lollius is another name for Boccaccio, but how this should be he confesses himself unable to explain. In his Glossary (a later publication), he merely describes Lollius as "a writer from whom Chaucer professes to have translated his poem of Troilus and Creseide," adding, "I have not been able to find any further account of him." It is remarkable that he should omit to notice that Lollius is mentioned by Chaucer in another poem, his House of Fame (iii. 378), as one of the writers of the Trojan story, along with Homer, Dares Phrygius, Livy (whom he calls Titus), Guido of Colonna, and "English Galfrid," that is, Geoffrey of Monmouth. The only writer of the name of Lollius of whom anything is now known appears to be Lollius Urbicus, who is stated to have lived in the third century, and to have composed a history of his own time, which, however, no longer exists.* But our ignorance of who Chaucer's Lollius was does not entitle us to assume that it is Boccaccio whom he designates by that name. Besides, the two poems have only that general resemblance which would result from their subject being the same, and their having been founded upon a common original. Tyrwhitt (note to Parson's Tale), while he insists that the fact of the one being borrowed from the other "is evident, not only from the fable and characters, which are the same in both poems, but also from a number of passages in the English which are literally translated from the Italian," admits that "at the same time there are several long passages, and even episodes, in the Troilus of which there are no traces in the Filostrato;" and Warton makes the same statement almost in the same words.† Tyrwhitt acknowledges elsewhere, too, that the form of Chaucer's stanza in the Troilus does not appear ever to have been used by Boccaccio, nor does he profess to have been able to find such a stanza in any early Italian poetry.‡ The only other composition of Chaucer's for which he can be imagined to have had an Italian original is his Clerk's Tale in the Canterbury Tales, the matchless story of Griselda. This is one of the stories of the Decameron; but it was not from Boccaccio's Italian that Chaucer took it, but from Petrarch's Latin, as he must be understood to intimate in the Prologue, where he says, or makes the narrator say—

* See Warton, Hist. Eng. Poetry, ii. 220; and Vossius, de Historicis Latinis, ed. 1651, p. 176.
† Hist. Eng. Poetry, ii. p. 221, note.
‡ Essay, § 8.

> "I woll you tell a tale which that I
> Learned at Padowe of a worthy clerk,
> As preved by his wordes and his werk:
> He is now dead and nailed in his chest;
> I pray to God so yeve his soule rest.
> Francis Petrarch, the laureat poet,
> Highte this clerk, whose rhethoricke sweet
> Enlumined all Itaille of poetrie."

Petrarch's Latin translation of Boccaccio's tale is, as Tyrwhitt states, printed in all the editions of his works, under the title of *De Obedientia et Fide Uxoria Mythologia* (a Myth on Wifely Obedience and Faithfulness). But, indeed, Chaucer may not have even had Petrarch's translation before him; for Petrarch, in his letter to Boccaccio, in which he states that he had translated it from the Decameron, only recently come into his hands, informs his friend also that the story had been known to him many years before. He may therefore have communicated it orally to Chaucer, through the medium of what was probably their common medium of communication, the Latin tongue, if they ever met, at Padua or elsewhere, as it is asserted they did. All that we are concerned with at present, is the fact that it does not appear to have been taken by Chaucer from the Decameron: he makes no reference to Boccaccio as his authority, and, while it is the only one of the Canterbury Tales which could otherwise have been suspected with any probability to have been derived from that work, it is at the same time one an acquaintance with which we know he had at least the means of acquiring through another language than the Italian. To these considerations may be added a remark made by Sir Harris Nicolas:—"That Chaucer was not acquainted with Italian," says that writer, "may be inferred from his not having introduced any Italian quotation into his works, redundant as they are with Latin and French words and phrases." To which he subjoins in a note: "Though Chaucer's writings have not been examined for the purpose, the remark in the text is not made altogether from recollection; for at the end of Speght's edition of Chaucer's works translations are given of the Latin and French words in the poems, but not a single Italian word is mentioned."*

---

* Life of Chaucer, p. 25. Sir Harris had said before:—"Though Chaucer undoubtedly knew Latin and French, it is by no means certain, notwithstanding his supposed obligations to the Decameron, that he was as well acquainted with Italian. There may have been a common Latin original of the main incidents of many if not of all the Tales for which Chaucer is supposed to have been wholly indebted to Boccaccio, and from which original Boccaccio himself may have taken them." Beside the Clerk's Tale, which has been

It may be questioned, then, if much more than the fame of Italian song had reached the ear of Chaucer; but, at all events, the foreign poetry with which he was most familiar was certainly that of France. This, indeed, was probably still accounted everywhere the classic poetical literature of the modern world; the younger poetry of Italy, which was itself a derivation from that common fountain-head, had not yet, with all its real superiority, either supplanted the old lays and romances of the trouvères and troubadours, or even taken its place by their side. The earliest English, as well as the earliest Italian, poetry was for the most part a translation or imitation of that of France. Of the poetry written in the French language, indeed, in the eleventh, twelfth, and thirteenth centuries, the larger portion, as we have seen, was produced in England, for English readers, and to a considerable extent by natives of this country. French poetry was not, therefore, during this era, regarded among us as a foreign literature at all; and even at a later date it must have been looked back upon by every educated Englishman as rather a part of that of his own land. For a century, or perhaps more, before Chaucer arose, the greater number of our common versifiers had been busy in translating the French romances and other poetry into English, which was now fast becoming the ordinary or only speech even of the educated classes; but this work had for the most part been done with little pains or skill, and with no higher ambition than to convey the mere sense of the French original to the English reader. By the time when Chaucer began to write, in the latter half of the fourteenth century, the French language appears to have almost gone out of use as a common medium of communication; the English on the other hand, as we may see by the poetry of Langland and Minot as compared with that of Robert of Gloucester, had, in the course of the preceding hundred years, thrown off much of its primitive rudeness, and acquired a considerable degree of regularity and flexibility, and general fitness for literary composition. In these

---

noticed above, the only stories in the Canterbury Tales which are found in the Decameron are the Reeve's Tale, the Shipman's Tale, and the Franklin's Tale; but both Tyrwhitt and Warton, while maintaining Chaucer's obligations in other respects to the Italian writers, admit that the two former are much more probably derived from French Fabliaux (the particular fabliau, indeed, on which the Reeve's Tale appears to be founded has been published by Le Grand); and the Franklin's Tale is expressly stated by Chaucer himself to be a Breton lay. He nowhere mentions Boccaccio or his Decameron, or any other Italian authority. Of the Pardoner's Tale, "the mere outline," as Tyrwhitt states, is to be found in the *Cento Novelle Antiche*; but the greater part of that collection is borrowed from the Contes and Fabliaux of the French.

circumstances, writing in French in England was over for any good purpose: Chaucer himself observes in the prologue to his prose treatise entitled the Testament of Love:—"Certes there ben some that speak their poesy matter in French, of which speech the Frenchmen have as good a fantasy as we have in hearing of Frenchmen's English." And again:—"Let, then, clerks enditen in Latin, for they have the property of science and the knowinge in that faculty; and let Frenchmen in their French also endite their quaint terms, for it is kindly [natural] to their mouths; and let us show our fantasies in such words as we learneden of our dames' tongue." The two languages, in short, like the two nations, were now become completely separated, and in some sort hostile: as the Kings of England were no longer either Dukes of Normandy or Earls of Poitou, and recently a fierce war had sprung up still more effectually to divide the one country from the other, and to break up all intercourse between them, so the French tongue was fast growing to be almost as strange and distinctly foreign among us as the English had always been in France. Chaucer's original purpose and aim may be supposed to have been that of the generality of his immediate predecessors, to put his countrymen in possession of some of the best productions of the French poets, so far as that could be done by translation; and with his genius and accomplishments, and the greater pains he was willing to take with it, we may conjecture that he hoped to execute his task in a manner very superior to that in which such work had hitherto been performed. With these views he undertook what was probably his earliest composition of any length, his translation of the *Roman de la Rose*, begun by Guillaume de Lorris, who died about 1260, and continued and finished by Jean de Meun, whose date is about half a century later. "This poem," says Warton, "is esteemed by the French the most valuable piece of their old poetry. It is far beyond the rude efforts of all their preceding romancers; and they have nothing equal to it before the reign of Francis the First, who died in the year 1547. But there is a considerable difference in the merit of the two authors. William of Lorris, who wrote not one quarter of the poem, is remarkable for his elegance and luxuriance of description, and is a beautiful painter of allegorical personages. John of Meun is a writer of another cast. He possesses but little of his predecessor's inventive and poetical vein; and in that respect, he was not properly qualified to finish a poem begun by William of Lorris. But he has strong satire and great liveliness. He was one of the wits of the court of Charles le Bel. The difficulties and dangers of a lover in pursuing and obtaining the object of his desires are the literal argument of this poem. This design is couched under the argument of a rose, which our lover after frequent obstacles gathers in a delicious garden. He traverses vast ditches, scales lofty walls, and forces the gates of adamantine and almost impregnable castles. These enchanted fortresses are all inhabited by various divinities; some of which assist, and some oppose, the lover's progress."* The entire poem consists of no fewer than 22,734 verses, of which only 4,149 are the composition of William of Lorris. All this portion has been translated by Chaucer, and also about half of the 18,588 lines written by De Meun: his version comprehends 13,105 lines of the French poem. These, however, he has managed to comprehend in 7701 (Warton says 7699) English verses: this is effected by a great compression and curtailment of De Meun's part; for, while the 4149 French verses of De Lorris are fully and faithfully rendered in 4432 English verses, the 8956 that follow by De Meun are reduced in the translation to 3269. Warton, who exhibits ample specimens both of the translation and of the original, considers that Chaucer has throughout at least equalled De Lorris, and decidedly surpassed and improved De Meun.

No verse so flowing and harmonious as what we have in this translation, no diction at once so clear, correct, and expressive, had, it is probable, adorned and brought out the capabilities of his native tongue when Chaucer began to write. Several of his subsequent poems are also in whole or in part translations; the Troilus and Creseide, the Legend of Good Women (much of which is borrowed from Ovid's Epistles), and others. But we must pass over these, and will take our first extract from his House of Fame, no foreign original of which has been discovered, although Warton is inclined to think that it may have been translated or paraphrased from the Provençal. Chaucer, however, seems to appear in it in his own person; at least the poet or dreamer is in the course of it more than once addressed by the name of Geoffrey. And in the following passage he seems to describe his own occupation and habits of life. It is addressed to him by the golden but living Eagle, who has carried him up into the air in his talons, and by whom the marvellous sights he relates are shown and explained to him:—

> First, I, that in my feet have thee,
> Of whom thou hast great fear and wonder,

---

* Hist. Eng. Poetry, II. 209.

Am dwelling with the God of Thunder,
Which men yeallen Jupiter,
That doth me flyen full oft fer[1]
To do all his commandement;
And for this cause he hath me sent
To thee; harken now by thy trouth;
Certain he hath of thee great routh,[2]
For that thou hast so truëly
So long served entuntifly[3]
His blinde nephew Cupido,
And the fair queen Venus also,
Withouten guerdon ever yet;
And natheless[4] hast set thy wit
Althoughe in thy head full lit is
To make bokes, songs, and dittes,
In rhime or elles in cadence,
As thou best canst, in reverence
Of Love and of his servants eke,
That have his service sought and seek;
And painest thee to praise his art,
Although thou haddest never part;
Wherefore, so wisely God me bless,
Jovis yhalt[5] it great humbless,
And virtue eke, that thou wilt make
Anight[6] full oft thine head to ache
In thy study, so thou ywritest,
And ever more of Love enditest,
In honour of him and praisings,
And in his folkes furtherings,
And in their matter all devisest,
And not him ne his folk despisest,
Although thou may'st go in the dance
Of them that him list not avance:
Wherefore, as I now said, ywis,
Jupiter considreth well this,
And als, beau sire,[7] of other things,
That is, that thou hast no tidings
Of Loves folk if they be glade,
Ne of nothing else that God made,
And not only fro[8] fer countree
That no tidinges comen to thee,
Not of thy very neighebores,
That dwellen almost at thy dores,
Thou hearest neither that ne this;
For, when thy labour all done is,

[1] Far.	[3] Ruth, pity.	[5] Attentively.
[2] Nevertheless.	[4] Jove held.	[6] O'nights, at night
	[7] Fair sir.	[8] From.

> And hast made all thy reckonings,
> Instead of rest and of new things,
> Thou goest home to thine house anon,
> And, all so dumb as any stone,
> Thou sittest at another book,
> Till fully dazed is thy look,
> And livest thus as an hermit,
> Although thine abstinence is lit;
> And therefore Jovis, through his grace,
> Will that I bear thee to a place
> Which that yhight the House of Fame, &c.

From the mention of his *reckonings* in this passage, Tyrwhitt conjectures that Chaucer probably wrote the House of Fame while he held the office of Comptroller of the Customs of Wools, to which he was appointed in 1374. It may be regarded, therefore, as one of the productions of the second or middle stage of his poetical life, as the Romaunt of the Rose is supposed to have been of the first. The House of Fame is in three books, comprising in all 2190 lines, and is an exceedingly interesting poem on other accounts, as well as for the reference which Chaucer seems to make in it to himself, and the circumstances of his own life. In one place, we have an illustration drawn from a novelty which we might have thought had hardly yet become familiar enough for the purposes of poetry. The passage, too, is a sample of the wild, almost grotesque imagination, and force of expression, for which the poem is remarkable:—

> What did this Æolus? but he
> Took out his blacke trompe of brass,
> That fouler than the devil was,
> And gan this trompe for to blow
> As all the world should overthrow.
> Throughout every region
> Ywent this foule trompes soun,
> *As swift as pellet out of gun*
> *When fire is in the powder run:*
> And such a smoke gan out wend
> Out of the foule trompes end,
> Black, blue, and greenish, swartish, red,
> As doeth where that men melt lead,
> Lo all on high from the tewel:[1]
> And thereto one thing saw I well,
> That aye the ferther that it ran
> The greater wexen it began,
> As doth the river from a well;
> And it stank as the pit of hell.

---

[1] Funnel.

The old mechanical artillery, however, is alluded to in another passage as if also still in use:—

> And the noise which that I heard,
> For all the world right so it fered [1]
> As doth the routing [2] of the stone
> That fro the engine is letten gone.

Through such deeper thinking and bolder writing as we have in the House of Fame, Chaucer appears to have advanced from the descriptive luxuriance of the Romaunt of the Rose to his most matured style in the Canterbury Tales. This is not only his greatest work, but it towers above all also that he has written, like some palace or cathedral ascending with its broad and lofty dimensions from among the common buildings of a city. His genius is another thing here altogether from what it is in his other writings. Elsewhere he seems at work only for the day that is passing over him; here, for all time. All his poetical faculties put forth a strength in the Canterbury Tales they have nowhere else shown; not only is his knowledge of life and character greater, his style firmer, clearer, more flexible, and more expressive, his humour more subtle and various, but his fancy is more nimble-winged, his imagination far richer and more gorgeous, his sensibility infinitely more delicate and more profound. And this great work of Chaucer's is nearly as remarkably distinguished by its peculiar character from the great works of other poets as it is from the rest of his own compositions. Among ourselves at least, if we except Shakespeare, no other poet has yet arisen to rival the author of the Canterbury Tales in the entire assemblage of his various powers. Spenser's is a more aerial, Milton's a loftier song; but neither possesses the wonderful combination of contrasted and almost opposite characteristics which we have in Chaucer:—the sportive fancy, painting and gilding everything, with the keen, observant, matter-of-fact spirit that looks through whatever it glances at; the soaring and creative imagination, with the homely sagacity, and healthy relish for all the realities of things; the unrivalled tenderness and pathos, with the quaintest humour and the most exuberant merriment; the wisdom at once and the wit; the all that is best, in short, both in poetry and in prose, at the same time.

The Canterbury Tales is an unfinished, or at least, as we have it, an imperfect work; but it contains above 17,000 verses, besides more than a fourth of that quantity of matter in prose. The Tales (including the two in prose) are twenty-four in

[1] Fared, proceeded.   [2] Roared.

number; and they are interspersed with introductions to each, generally short, called prologues, besides the Prologue to the whole work, in which the pilgrims or narrators of the tales are severally described, and which consists of between 800 and 900 lines. The Prologue to the Wife of Bath's Tale is fully as long. All the twenty-four tales are complete, except only the Cook's Tale, of which we have only a few lines, the Squire's Tale, which remains "half-told," and the burlesque Tale of Sir Thopas, which is designedly broken off in the middle. Of the nineteen complete tales in verse, the longest are the Knight's Tale of 2250 verses, the Clerk's Tale of 1156, and the Merchant's Tale of 1172. The entire work, with the exception of the prose tales and the Rime of Sir Thopas (205 lines), is in decasyllabic (or hendecasyllabic) verse, arranged either in couplets or in stanzas.

The general Prologue is a gallery of pictures almost unmatched for their air of life and truthfulness. Here is one of them:—

> There was also a nun, a Prioress
> That of her smiling was full simple and coy,
> Her greatest oathe n'as but by Saint Loy;[1]
> And she was cleped[2] Madame Eglantine.
> Full well she sange the service divine,
> Entuned in her nose full sweetely;
> And French she spake full fair and fetisly[3]
> After the school of Stratford atte Bow,
> For French of Paris was to her unknow.[4]
> At meate was she well ytaught withal;
> She let no morsel from her lippes fall,
> Ne wet her fingers in her sauce deep;
> Well could she carry a morsel and well keep
> Thatte no droppe ne fell upon her breast;
> In curtesy was set full much her lest.[5]
> Her over-lippe wiped she so clean
> That in her cuppe was no ferthing[6] seen
> Of grease when she dronken had her draught.
> Full semely after her meat she raught.[7]
> And sickerly[8] she was of great disport,
> And full pleasant and amiable of port,
> And pained[9] her to counterfeiten cheer
> Of court, and been estatelich of manere,

---

[1] That is, Saint Eloy or Eligius. Oaths here, according to Mr. Guest is the old genitive plural (originally atha), meaning of oaths.
[2] Called.   [3] Neatly.   [4] Unknown.
[5] Pleasure.   [6] Smallest spot.
[7] Reached.   [8] Surely.   [9] Took pains.

And to been holden digne[1] of reverence
But for to speaken of her conscience,
She was so charitable and so pitous
She wolde weep if that she saw a mouse
Caught in a trap, if it were dead or bled.
Of smale houndes had she that she fed
With roasted flesh, and milk, and wastel bread;
But sore wept she if one of them were dead,
Or if men smote it with a yerde[2] smart:
And all was conscience and tender heart.
  Full semely her wimple ypinched was;
Her nose tretis,[3] her eyen grey as glass;
Her mouth full small, and thereto[4] soft and red,
But sickerly she had a fair forehead;
It was almost a spanne broad, I trow;
For hardily[5] she was not undergrow.[6]
  Full fetise[7] was her cloak, as I was ware.
Of smale coral about her arm she bare
A pair of beades gauded all with green;[8]
And thereon heng[9] a brooch of gold full sheen,
On which was first ywritten a crowned A,
And after, *Amor vincit omnia*.

As a companion to this perfect full length, we will add that of the Mendicant Friar:—

A Frere there was, a wanton and a merry,
A limitour,[10] a full solemne man;
In all the orders four is none that can
So much of dalliance and fair langage.
He had ymade full many a marriage
Of younge women at his owen cost;
Until[11] his order he was a noble post.
Full well beloved and familier was he
With frankline[12] over all in his countree,
And eke with worthy women of the town;
For he had power of confessioun,
As said him selfe, more than a curat,
For of his order he was a licenciat.
Full sweetly hearde he confession,
And pleasant was his absolution.
He was an easy man to give penance
There as he wist to han a good pitance;[13]

---

[1] Worthy. [2] Yard, rod. [3] Long and well proportioned.
[4] In addition to that. [5] Certainly. [6] Undergrown, of a low stature.
[7] Neat. [8] Having the gauds or beads coloured green.
[9] Hung. [10] A friar licensed to beg within a certain district.
[11] Unto. [12] Freeholders of the superior class.
[13] Where he knew he should have a good pittance or fee.

For unto a poor order for to give
Is signe that a man is well yshrive;[1]
For, if he gave, he durste make avant,[2]
He wiste that a man was repentant;
For many a man so hard is of his heart
He may not weep although him sore smart;
Therefore, instead of weeping and prayeres,
Men mote give silver to the poore freres.
  His tippet was aye farsed[3] full of knives
And pinnes for to given faire wives:
And certainly he had a merry note;
Well could he sing and playen on a rote.[4]
Of yeddings[5] he bare utterly the pris.[6]
His neck was white as is the flower de lis;[7]
Thereto he strong was as a champioun,
And knew well the taverns in every town,
And every hosteler and gay tapstere,
Better than a lazar or a beggere;
For unto swich[8] a worthy man as he
Accordeth nought[9] as,[10] by his facultee,[11]
To haven with sick lazars acquaintance;
It is not honest, it may not avance,[12]
As[13] for to dealen with no swich poorall[14]
But all with rich and sellers of vitail.[15]
And, over[16] all, there as[17] profit should arise,
Curteis[18] he was, and lowly of service;
There n'as no man no where so virtuous;
He was the best beggar in all his house;
And gave a certain ferme[19] for the grant
None of his brethren came in his haunt;
For, though a widow hadde but a shoe,
So pleasant was his *In principio*,
Yet would he have a ferthing or he went;
His purchase[20] was well better than his rent.
And rage he could as it had been a whelp;
In lovedays[21] there could he mochel[22] help;
For there was he nat[23] like a cloisterere
With threadbare cope, as is a poor scholere;

---

[1] Shriven. [2] Boast. [3] Stuffed.
[4] A musical instrument so called. [5] Stories, romances. [6] Prize.
[7] Fleur de lis, lily. [8] Such. [9] It suits not, is not fitting.
[10] As in this and in other forms seems to have the effect of merely generalizing or giving indefiniteness to the expression.
[11] Having regard to his quality or functions? [12] Profit.
[13] As in the fourth line preceding. [14] Poor people.
[15] Victual. [16] In addition to. [17] Wherever. [18] Courteous.
[19] Farm. [20] What he got by begging and the exercise of his profession.
[21] Days formerly appointed for the amicable settlement of differences.
[22] Much. [23] Not.

> But he was like a maister or a pope:
> Of double worsted was his semi-cope,
> That round was as a bell out of the press.[1]
> Somewhat he lisped for his wantonness,
> To make his English sweet upon his tongue;
> And in his harping, when that he had sung,
> His eyen twinkled in his head aright,
> As don the sterres[2] in a frosty night.
> This worthy limitour, was clep'd Huberd.

It may be observed in all these extracts how fond Chaucer is of as it were welding one couplet and one paragraph to another, by allowing the sense to flow on from the last line of the one through the first of the other, thus producing an alternating movement of the sense and the sound, instead of making the one accompany the other, as is the general practice of our modern poetry. This has been noticed, and a less obvious part of the effect pointed out, by a poet of our own day, who has shown how well he felt Chaucer by something more and much better than criticism. "Chaucer," observes Leigh Hunt, "took the custom from the French poets, who have retained it to this day. It surely has a fine air, both of conclusion and resumption; as though it would leave off when it thought proper, knowing how well it could recommence."[3] It is so favourite a usage with Chaucer, that it may be sometimes made available to settle the reading, or at least the pointing and sense of a doubtful passage. And it is also common with his contemporary Gower.

The following is the first introduction to the reader of Emily, the heroine of the Knight's Tale of Palamon and Arcite:—

> Thus passeth year by year, and day by day,
> Till it fell ones in a morrow of May
> That Emily, that fairer was to seen
> Than is the lilly upon his stalke green,
> And fresher than the May with floures new
> (For with the rose colour strof[4] her hue;
> I n'ot[5] which was the finer of them two)
> Ere it was day, as she was wont to do,
> She was arisen and all ready dight,
> For May wol have no slogardy[6] a night;

---

[1] Not understood. It is the bell or the semicope that is described as *out of the press*? [2] As do the stars.

[3] Preface to Poetical Works, 8vo. Lon. 1832. See also Mr. Hunt's fine Imitation and continuation of the Squire's Tale in the Fourth Number of the Liberal. Lon. 1823.

[4] Strove.   [5] Wot not, know not.   [6] Sloth.

The season pricketh every gentle heart,
And maketh him out of his sleep to start,
And saith, Arise, and do thine observance.
  This maketh Emily han[1] remembrance
To don honour to May, and for to rise.
Yclothed was she fresh for to devise:[2]
Her yellow hair was broided[3] in a tress
Behind her back, a yerde long I guess;
And in the garden as the sun uprist[4]
She walketh up and down where as her list:[5]
She gathereth floures partie[6] white and red
To make a sotel[7] gerlond[8] for her head:
And as an angel heavenlich she sung.

Of the many other noble passages in this Tale we can only present a portion of the description of the Temple of Mars:—

Why should I not as well eke tell you all
The portraiture that was upon the wall
Within the Temple of mighty Mars the Red?
All painted was the wall in length and bred[9]
Like to the estres[10] of the grisley place
That hight[11] the great Temple of Mars in Trace,[12]
In thilke[13] cold and frosty region
There as Mars hath his sovereign mansion.
  First on the wall was painted a forest,
In which there wonneth[14] neither man ne beast;
With knotty knarry barren trees old,
Of stubbes sharp and hidous to behold,
In which there ran a rumble and a swough,[15]
As though a storm should bresten[16] every bough;
And downward from an hill under a bent[17]
There stood the Temple of Mars Armipotent,
Wrought all of burned[18] steel, of which the entree
Was long, and strait, and ghastly for to see;
And thereout came a rage and swich a vise[19]
That it made all the gates for to rise.
The northern light in at the dore shone;
For window on the wall ne was there none
Through which men mighten any light discern.
The door was all of athamant[20] etern,

---

[1] Have.   [2] With exactness (point devise).   [3] Braided.
[4] Uprises.   [5] Where it pleaseth her.   [6] Mixed of.
[7] Subtle, artfully contrived.   [8] Garland.   [9] Breadth.
[10] The interior.   [11] Is called.   [12] Thrace.
[13] That same.   [14] Dwelleth.
[15] A long sighing noise, such as in Scotland is called a *sugh*.
[16] Was going to break.   [17] A declivity.   [18] Burnished.
[19] A violent blast?   [20] Adamant.

Yclenched overthwart and endelong [1]
With iron tough, and, for to make it strong,
Every pillar the temple to sustene
Was tonne-grent,[2] of iron bright and shene.
There saw I first the dark imagining
Of Felony, and all the compassing;
The cruel Ire, red as any gled;[3]
The Picke-purse, and eke the pale Dread;
The Smiler with the knife under the cloak;
The shepen[4] brenning[5] with the blake smoke;
The treason of the murdering in the bed;
The open wer,[6] with woundes all bebled;
Contek[7] with bloody knife and sharp menace;
All full of chirking[8] was that sorry place.
The sleer[9] of himself yet saw I there;
His hearte-blood hath bathed all his hair;
The nail ydriven in the shod[10] on hight;
The colde death, with mouth gaping upright.
Amiddes of the Temple sat Mischance,
With discomfort and sorry countenance:
Yet saw I Woodness[11] laughing in his rage,
Armed Complaint, Outhees,[12] and fierce Outrage;
The carrain[13] in the bush, with throat ycorven;[14]
A thousand slain, and not of qualm ystorven;[15]
The tyrant, with the prey by force yraft;[16]
The town destroyed;—there was nothing laft.[17]

 . . . .

The statue of Mars upon a carte[18] stood
Armed, and looked grim as he were wood;[19]
And over his head there shineu two figures
Of sterres, that been cleped in scriptures[20]
That one Puella, that other Rubeus.
This God of Armes was arrayed thus:
A wolf there stood beforn him at his feet
With eyen red, and of a man he eat.

Chaucer's merriment, at once hearty and sly, has of course
the freedom and unscrupulousness of his time; and much of the
best of it cannot be produced in our day without offence to our
greater sensitiveness, at least in the matter of expression.
Besides, humour in poetry, or any other kind of writing, can

---

[1] Across and lengthways. [2] Of the circumference of a tun.
[3] Burning coal. [4] Stable. [5] Burning. [6] War.
[7] Contention. [8] Disagreeable sound. [9] Slayer.
[10] Hair of the head. [11] Madness. [12] Outcry.
[13] Carrion. [14] Cut. [15] Dead (starved).
[16] Reft. [17] Left. [18] Car, chariot. [19] Mad.
[20] Stars that are called in books.

least of all qualities be effectively exemplified in extract: its subtle life, dependent upon the thousand minutiæ of place and connection, perishes under the process of excision; it is to attempt to exhibit, not the building by the brick, but the living man by a "pound of his fair flesh." We will venture, however, to give one or two short passages. Nothing is more admirable in the Canterbury Tales than the manner in which the character of the Host is sustained throughout. He is the moving spirit of the poem from first to last. Here is his first introduction to us presiding over the company at supper in his own

gentle hostelry,
That highte the Tabard faste by the Bell,

in Southwark, on the evening before they set out on their pilgrimage:—

> Great cheere made our Host us everich one,
> And to the supper set he us anon,
> And served us with vitail of the best;
> Strong was the wine, and well to drink us lest.[1]
> A seemly man our Hoste was with all
> For to han been a marshal in an hall;
> A large man he was, with eyen steep;
> A fairer burgess is there none in Cheap;
> Bold of his speech, and wise, and well ytaught,
> And of manhood ylaked[2] right him naught:
> Eke thereto[3] was he a right merry man;
> And after supper played he began,
> And spake of mirth amonges other things,
> When that we hadden made our reckonings,
> And said thus: Now, Lordings, truely
> Ye been to me welcome right heartily;
> For, by my troth, if that I shall not lie,
> I saw nat this yer swich[4] a company
> At ones in this berberwe[5] as is now;
> Fain would I do you mirth an I wist how;
> And of a mirth I am right now bethought
> To don you ease, and it shall cost you nought.
> Ye gon to Canterbury; God you speed,
> The blissful martyr quite you your meed:
> And well I wot as ye gon by the way
> Ye shapen[6] you to talken and to play;
> For truely comfort ne mirth is none
> To riden by the way dumb as the stone;
> And therefore would I maken you disport,

---

[1] It pleased us. [2] Lacked. [3] In addition, besides, also.
[4] Such. [5] Inn. [6] Prepare yourselves, intend.

As I said erst, and don you some comfort.
And if you liketh all by one assent
Now for to stonden¹ at my judgement,
And for to werchen² as I shall you say
To morrow, when ye riden on the way,
Now, by my fader's soule that is dead,
But ye be merry³ smiteth⁴ off my head:
Hold up your hondes withouten more speech.

They all gladly assent; upon which mine Host proposes further that each of them (they were twenty-nine in all, besides himself) should tell two stories in going, and two more in returning, and that, when they got back to the Tabard, the one who had told the "tales of best sentence and most solace" should have a supper at the charge of the rest. And, adds the eloquent, sagacious, and large-hearted projector of the scheme,

—for to make you the more merry
I woll my selven gladly with you ride
Right at mine owen cost, and be your guide.
And who that woll my judgement withsay⁵
Shall pay for all we spenden by the way.

Great as the extent of the poem is, therefore, what has been executed, or been preserved, is only a small part of the design; for this liberal plan would have afforded us no fewer than a hundred and twenty tales. Nothing can be better than the triumphant way in which mine Host of the Tabard is made to go through the duties of his self-assumed post;—his promptitude, his decision upon all emergencies, and at the same time his good feeling never at fault any more than his good sense, his inexhaustible and unflagging fun and spirit, and the all-accommodating humour and perfect sympathy with which, without for a moment stooping from his own frank and manly character, he bears himself to every individual of the varied cavalcade. He proposes that they should draw cuts to decide who was to begin; and with how genuine a courtesy, at once encouraging and reverential, he first addresses himself to the modest Clerk, and the gentle Lady Prioress, and the Knight, who also was "of his port as meek as is a maid:"—

Sir Knight, quod he, my maister and my lord,
Now draweth cut, for that is mine accord.

---

¹ Stand.   ² Work, do.   ³ If ye shall not be merry.
⁴ Smite. The imperative has generally this termination.
⁵ Resist, oppose, withstand.

Cometh near, quod he, my Lady Prioress;
And ye, Sir Clerk, let be your shamefastness,
Ne studieth nought; lay hand to, every man.

But for personages of another order, again, he is another man, giving and taking jibe and jeer with the hardest and boldest in their own style and humour, only more nimbly and happily than any of them, and without ever compromising his dignity. And all the while his kindness of heart, simple and quick, and yet considerate, is as conspicuous as the cordial appreciation and delight with which he enters into the spirit of what is going forward, and enjoys the success of his scheme. For example,—

When that the Knight had thus his tale told,
In all the company n'as there young ne old
That he ne said it was a noble storie,
And worthy to be drawen to memorie,[1]
And namely[2] the gentles everich one.
Our Hoste lough[3] and swore, So mote I gone,[4]
This goth aright; unbokeled is the male;[5]
Let see now who shall tell another tale,
For truely this game is well begonne:
Now telleth ye, Sir Monk, if that ye conne,[6]
Somewhat to quiten with[7] the Knighte's tale.
    The Miller, that for-dronken[8] was all pale,
So that uneathes[9] upon his horse he sat,
He n'old avalen[10] neither hood ne hat,
Ne abiden[11] no man for his courtesy,
But in Pilate's voice[12] he gan to cry,
And swore, By armes, and by blood and bones,
I can[13] a noble tale for the nones,[14]
With which I wol now quite the Knightes tale.
    Our Hoste saw that he was dronken of ale,
And said, Abide, Robin, my leve[15] brother;
Some better man shall tell us first another;
Abide and let us werken[16] thriftily.
By Goddes soul, quod he, that woll not I,
For I woll speak, or elles go my way.
    Our Host answered, Tell on a devil way;

---

[1] Probably pronounced *stó-ri-e* and *me-mó-ri-e*. [2] Especially.
[3] Laughed. [4] So may I fare well. [5] Unbuckled is the budget.
[6] Can. [7] To requite. [8] Very drunk.
[9] With difficulty. [10] Would not doff or lower. [11] Stop for.
[12] "In such a voice as Pilate was used to speak with in the Mysteries. Pilate, being an odious character, was probably represented as speaking with a harsh disagreeable voice."—*Tyrwhitt*.
[13] Know. [14] For the nonce, for the occasion. [15] Dear.
[16] Go to work.

> Thou art a fool; thy wit is overcome.
> Now, hearkeneth, quod the Miller, all and some;
> But first I make a protestatioun
> That I am drunk, I know it by my soun,
> And therefore, if that I misspeak or say,
> Wite it¹ the ale of Southwark, I you pray.

The Miller is at last allowed to toll his tale—which is more accordant with his character, and the condition he was in, than with either good morals or good manners;—as the poet observes:—

> What should I more say, but this Millere
> He n'old his wordes for no man forbere,
> But told his cherle's² tale in his manere;
> Methinketh that I shall rehearse it here:
> And therefore every gentle wight I pray
> For Goddes love, as deem not that I say,
> Of evil intent, but that I mote rehearse
> Their tales all, al be they better or werse,
> Or elles falsen some of my matere:
> And, therefore, whoso list it not to hear,
> Turn over the leaf, and chese³ another tale;
> For he shall find enow, both great and smale,
> Of storial thing that toucheth gentiless,
> And eke morality and holiness.

The Miller's Tale is capped by another in the same style from his fellow "churl" the Reve (or Bailiff)—who before he begins, however, avails himself of the privilege of his advanced years to prelude away for some time in a preaching strain, till his eloquence is suddenly cut short by the voice of authority:—

> When that our Host had heard this sermoning,
> He gan to speak as lordly as a king,
> And said, What amounteth all this wit?
> What, shall we speak all day of holy writ?
> The devil made a Reve for to preach,
> Or of a souter⁴ a shipman or a leech.⁵
> Say forth thy tale, and tarry not the time;
> Lo Depeford,⁶ and it is half way prime;⁷
> Lo Greenowich, there many a shrew is in:⁸
> It were all time thy Tale to begin.

¹ Lay the blame of it on.   ² Churl's.   ³ Choose.
⁴ Cobbler.   ⁵ Physician.   ⁶ Deptford.
⁷ Tyrwhitt supposes this means half-past seven in the morning.
⁸ In which (wherein) is many a shrew.

The last specimen we shall give of "our Host" shall be from the Clerk's Prologue:—

> Sir Clerk of Oxenford, our Hoste said,
> Ye ride as still and coy as doth a maid
> Were newe spoused, sitting at the bourd;
> This day ne heard I of your tongue a word.
> I trow ye study abouten some sophime,[1]
> But Salomon saith that every thing hath time.
> For Goddé's sake as beth[2] of better cheer;
> It is no time for to studien here.
> Tell us some merry tale by your fay;[3]
> For what man that is entered in a play
> He needes must unto the play assent,
> But preacheth not, as freres don in Lent,
> To make us for our olde sinnes weep,
> No that thy tale make us not to sleep.
> Tell us some merry thing of aventures;
> Your terms, your coloures, and your figures,
> Keep them in store till so be ye indite
> High style, as when that men to kinges write.
> Speaketh so plain at this time, I you pray,
> That we may understonden what ye say.
>
> This worthy Clerk benignely answerd;
> Hoste, quod he, I am under your yerde;
> Ye have of us as now the governance,
> And therefore would I do you obeisance,
> As fer as reason asketh hardily.[4]
> I wol you tell a tale which that I
> Learned at Padow of a worthy clerk,
> As preved[5] by his wordes and his werk:
> He is now dead and nailed in his chest;
> I pray to God so yeve his soule rest.
> Francis Petrarch, the laureat poete
> Highte this clerk, whose rhethoricke sweet
> Enlumined all Itaille of poetry,
> As Linian[6] did of philosophy,
> Or law, or other art particulere;
> But death, that wol not suffre us dwellen here
> But as it were a twinkling of an oye,
> Them both hath slain, and alle we shall die.

And our last specimen of the Canterbury Tales, and also of Chaucer, being a passage exhibiting that power of pathos in the delicacy as well as in the depth of which he is unrivalled, shall

---

[1] Sophism, perhaps generally for a logical argument.
[2] Be.   [3] Faith.   [4] Surely.
[5] Proved.   [6] A great lawyer of the fourteenth century.

be taken from this tale told by the Clerk, the exquisite tale of Griselda. Her husband has carried his trial of her submission and endurance to the last point by informing her that she must return to her father, and that his new wife is "coming by the way:"—

And she again answerd in patience:
My lord, quod she, I wot, and wist alway,
How that betwixen your magnificence
And my povert no wight ne can ne may
Maken comparison: it is no nay:
I ne held me never digne[1] in no manere
To be your wife, ne yet your chamberere.[2]

And in this house there[3] ye me lady made
(The highe God take I for my witness,
And all so wisly[4] he my soule glade)
I never held me lady ne maistresse,
But humble servant to your worthinesse,
And ever shall, while that my life may dure,
Aboven every worldly creature.

That ye so long, of your benignity,
Han[5] holden me in honour and nobley,[6]
Whereas[7] I was not worthy for to be,
That thank I God and you, to whom I pray
Foryeld[8] it you: there is no more to say.
Unto my fader gladly wol I wend,
And with him dwell unto my lives end.

God shielde swich a lordes wife to take
Another man to husband or to make.[9]

And of your newe wife God of his grace
So grant you weale and prosperity;
For I wol gladly yielden her my place,
In which that I was blissful wont to be:
For, sith it liketh you, my lord, quod she,
That whilome weren all my heartes rest,
That I shall gon, I wol go where you list.

But, thereas[10] ye me profer swich dowair[11]
As I first brought, it is well in my mind
It were my wretched clothes, nothing fair,
The which to me were hard now for to find.
O goode God! how gentle and how kind
Ye seemed by your speech and your visage
The day that maked was our marriage!

---

[1] Worthy.   [2] Chambermaid.   [3] Where.   [4] Surely.
[5] Have.   [6] Nobility.   [7] Where.   [8] Repay.
[9] Mate.   [10] Whereas.   [11] Such dower.

But sooth is said, algate[1] I find it true,
For in effect it preved[2] is on me,
Love is not old as when that it is new.
But certes, Lord, for non adversity[3]
To dien in this case, it shall not be
That ever in word or werk I shall repent
That I you yave mine heart in whole intent.

My lord, yo wot that in my fader's place
Yo did me strip out of my poore weed,
And richely ye clad me of your grace:
To you brought I nought elles, out of drede,[4]
But faith, and nakedness, and maidenhede:
And here again your clothing I restore,
And eke your wedding ring, for evermore.

The remnant of your jewels ready be
Within your chamber, I dare it safely sayn.
Naked out of my fader's house, quod she,
I came, and naked I mote turn again.
All your pleasance wold I follow fain:
But yet I hope it be not your intent
That I smockless out of your palace went.

. . . . . .

Let me not like a worm go by the way:
Remember you, mine owen lord so dear,
I was your wife, though I unworthy were.

. . . . . .

The smock, quod he, that thou hast on thy back
Let it be still, and bear it forth with thee.
But well unneathes[5] thilke[6] word he spake,
But went his way for ruth and for pitee.
Before the folk herselven strippeth she,
And in her smock, with foot and head all bare,
Toward her father's house forth is she fare.[7]

The folk her followen weeping in her way,
And Fortune aye they cursen as they goue:
But she fro weeping kept her eyen drey,[8]
Ne in this time word ne spake she none.
Her fader, that this tiding heard anon,
Curseth the day and time that nature
Shope him[9] to been a lives[10] creature.

---

[1] In every way.   [2] Proved.
[3] For no unhappiness that may be my lot, were it even to die?
[4] Doubt.   [5] With great difficulty.   [6] This same.
[7] Gone.   [8] Dry.   [9] Formed.   [10] Living.

There is scarcely perhaps to be found anywhere in poetry a finer burst of natural feeling than in the lines we have printed in italics.

John Gower.

Contemporary with Chaucer, and probably born a few years earlier, though of the two he survived to the latest date, for his death did not take place till the year 1408, was John Gower. Moral Gower, as he is commonly designated, is the author of three great poetical works (sometimes spoken of as one, though they do not seem to have had any connection of plan or subject):—the Speculum Meditantis, which is, or was, in French; the Vox Clamantis, which is in Latin; and the Confessio Amantis, which is in English. But the first, although an account of it, founded on a mistake, has been given by Warton, has certainly not been seen in modern times, and has in all probability perished. The Vox Clamantis was edited for the Roxburghe Club in 1850 by the Rev. H. G. Coxe. It consists of seven Books in Latin elegiacs. "The greater bulk of the work," says Dr. Pauli, "the date of which its editor is inclined to fix between 1382 and 1384, is rather a moral than an historical essay; but the First Book describes the insurrection of Wat Tyler in an allegorical disguise; the poet having a dream on the 11th of June 1381, in which men assumed the shape of animals. The Second Book contains a long sermon on fatalism, in which the poet shows himself no friend to Wiclif's tenets, but a zealous advocate for the reformation of the clergy. The Third Book points out how all orders of society must suffer for their own vices and demerits; in illustration of which he cites the example of the secular clergy. The Fourth Book is dedicated to the cloistered clergy and the friars, the Fifth to the military; the Sixth contains a violent attack on the lawyers; and the Seventh subjoins the moral of the whole, represented in Nebuchadnezzar's dream, as interpreted by Daniel."[*] The allusion in the title seems to be to St. John the Baptist, and to the general clamour then abroad in the country. The Confessio Amantis has been several times printed;—by Caxton in 1483, by Bertholet in 1532 and again in 1554; and by Alexander Chalmers in the second volume of his English poets, 1810; but all these previous editions have been superseded by the very commodious and beautiful one of Dr. Reinhold Pauli, in 3 vols. 8vo., London, 1857.

We will avail ourselves of Dr. Pauli's account of the course in

[*] Introd. Essay to Confessio Amantis.

which the work proceeds:—"The poem opens by introducing the author himself, in the character of an unhappy lover in despair. Venus appears to him, and, after having heard his prayer, appoints her priest called Genius, like the mystagogue in the picture of Cebes, to hear the lover's confession. This is the frame of the whole work, which is a singular mixture of classical notions, principally borrowed from Ovid's Ars Amandi, and of the purely medieval idea, that as a good Catholic the unfortunate lover must state his distress to a father confessor. This is done with great regularity and even pedantry; all the passions of the human heart, which generally stand in the way of love, being systematically arranged in the various books and subdivisions of the work. After Genius has fully explained the evil affection, passion, or vice under consideration, the lover confesses on that particular point; and frequently urges his boundless love for an unknown beauty, who treats him cruelly, in a tone of affectation which would appear highly ridiculous in a man of more than sixty years of age, were it not a common characteristic of the poetry of the period. After this profession the confessor opposes him, and exemplifies the fatal effects of each passion by a variety of opposite stories, gathered from many sources, examples being then, as now, a favourite mode of inculcating instruction and reformation. At length, after a frequent and tedious recurrence of the same process, the confession is terminated by some final injunctions of the priest—the lover's petition in a strophic poem addressed to Venus—the bitter judgment of the goddess, that he should remember his old age and leave off such fooleries . . . . his cure from the wound caused by the dart of love, and his absolution, received as if by a pious Roman Catholic." *

Such a scheme as this, pursued through more than thirty thousand verses, promises perhaps more edification than entertainment; but the amount of either that is to be got out of the Confessio Amantis is not considerable. Ellis, after charitably declaring that so long as Moral Gower keeps to his morality he is "wise, impressive, and sometimes almost sublime," is compelled to add, "But his narrative is often quite petrifying; and, when we read in his work the tales with which we had been familiarized in the poems of Ovid, we feel a mixture of surprise and despair at the perverse industry employed in removing every detail on which the imagination had been accustomed to fasten. The author of the Metamorphoses was a poet, and at least sufficiently fond of ornament; Gower considers him as a mere

* Introductory Essay, p. xxxiv.

annalist; scrupulously preserves his facts; relates them with great perspicuity; and is fully satisfied when he has extracted from them as much morality as they can be reasonably expected to furnish."* In many cases this must be little enough.

BARBOUR.

This latter part of the fourteenth century is also the age of the birth of Scottish poetry; and Chaucer had in that dialect a far more worthy contemporary and rival than his friend and fellow-Englishman Gower, in John Barbour. Of Barbour's personal history but little is known. He was a churchman, and had attained to the dignity of Archdeacon of Aberdeen by the year 1357; so that his birth cannot well be supposed to have been later than 1320. He is styled Archdeacon of Aberdeen in a passport granted to him in that year by Edward III. at the request of David de Bruce (that is, King David II. of Scotland), to come into England with three scholars in his company, for the purpose, as it is expressed, of studying in the University of Oxford; and the protection is extended to him and his companions while performing their scholastic exercises, and generally while remaining there, and also while returning to their own country. It may seem strange that an Archdeacon should go to college; but Oxford appears to have been not the only seat of learning to which Barbour resorted late in life with the same object. Three other passports, or safe-conducts, are extant which were granted to him by Edward at later dates:—the first, in 1364, permitting him to come, with four horsemen, from Scotland, by land or sea, into England, to study at Oxford, or elsewhere, as he might think proper; the second, in 1365, by which he is authorized to come into England, and travel throughout that kingdom, with six horsemen as his companions, as far as to St. Denis in France; and the third, in 1368, securing him protection in coming, with two valets and two horses, into England, and travelling through the same to the king's other dominions, on his way to France (*versus Franciam*) for the purpose of studying there, and in returning thence. Yet he had also been long before this employed, and in a high capacity, in civil affairs. In 1357 he was appointed by the Bishop of Aberdeen one of his two Commissioners deputed to attend a meeting at Edinburgh about the ransom of the king. Nothing more is heard of him till 1373, in which year he appears as one of the

* Specimens of the Early English Poets, L 179.

anditors of Exchequer, being styled Archdeacon of Aberdeen, and clerk of probation (*clerico probacionis*) of the royal household. In his later days he appears to have been in the receipt of two royal pensions, both probably bestowed upon him by Robert II., who succeeded David II. in 1370; the first one of 10*l*. Scots from the customs of Aberdeen, the other one of 20*s*. from the *borough mails*, or city rents, of the same town. An entry in the records of Aberdeen for 1471 states on the authority of the original roll, now lost, that the latter was expressly granted to him " for the compilation of the book of the Acts of King Robert the First." In a passage occurring in the latter part of this work, he himself tells us that he was then compiling it in the year 1375. All that is further known of him is, that his death took place towards the close of 1395. Besides his poem commonly called The Bruce, another metrical work of his entitled The Broite or The Brute, being a deduction of the history of the Scottish kings from Brutus, is frequently referred to by the chronicler Wynton in the next age; but no copy of it is now believed to exist. Of the Bruce the first critical edition was that by Pinkerton, published in 3 vols. 8vo. at London in 1790; the last and best, is that by the Rev. Dr. John Jamieson, forming the first volume of The Bruce and Wallace, 2 vols. 4to. Edinburgh, 1820.

The Scotch in which Barbour's poem is written was undoubtedly the language then commonly in use among his countrymen, for whom he wrote and with whom his poem has been a popular favourite ever since its first appearance. By his countrymen, of course, we mean the inhabitants of southern and eastern, or Lowland Scotland, not the Celts or Highlanders, who have always been and still are as entirely distinct a race as the native Irish are, and always have been, from the English in Ireland, and to confound whom either in language or in any other respect with the Scottish Lowlanders is the same sort of mistake that it would be to speak of the English as being either in language or lineage identical with the Welsh. Indeed, there is a remarkable similarity as to this matter in the circumstances of the three countries: in each a primitive Celtic population, which appears to have formerly occupied the whole soil, has been partially expelled by another race, but still exists, inhabiting its separate locality (in all the three cases the maritime and mountainous wilds of the west), and retaining its own ancient and perfectly distinct language. The expulsion has been the most sweeping in England, where it took place first, and where the Welsh form now only about a sixteenth of the general population; it has been carried to a less extent in Scotland, where it was not effected till a later age, and where the numbers of the Highlanders are still to those of the Lowlanders in the proportion of one to five or six; in Ireland, where it happened last of all, the new settlers have scarcely yet ceased to be regarded as foreigners and intruders, and the ancient Celtic inhabitants, still covering, although not possessing, by far the greater part of the soil, the larger proportion of them, however, having relinquished their ancestral speech, continue to be perhaps six or eight times as numerous as the Saxons or English. For in all the three cases it is the same Saxon, or at least Teutonic, race before which the Celts have retired or given way: the Welsh, the Scottish Highlanders, and the native Irish, indeed, all to this day alike designate the stranger who has set himself down beside them by the common epithet of the Saxon. We know that other Teutonic or northern races were mixed with the Angles and Saxons in all the three cases: not only were the English, who settled in Scotland in great numbers, and conquered Ireland, in the eleventh and twelfth centuries, in part French Normans, but the original Normans or Danes had in the eighth and ninth centuries effected extensive settlements in each of the three countries. Besides, the original English were themselves a mixed people; and those of them who were distinctively Saxons were even the old hereditary enemies of the Danes. Still, as the Saxons, Angles, and Jutes were as one people against the Scandinavian Danes, or their descendants the French Normans, so even Saxons and Danes, or Normans, were united everywhere against the Celts. As for the language spoken by the Lowland Scots in the time of Barbour, it must have sprung out of the same sources, and been affected by nearly the same influences, with the English of the same age. Nobody now holds that any part of it can have been derived from the Picts, who indeed originally occupied part of the Lowlands of Scotland, but who were certainly not a Teutonic but a Celtic people. Lothian, or all the eastern part of Scotland to the south of the Forth, was English from the seventh century, as much as was Northumberland or Yorkshire: from this date the only difference that could have distinguished the language there used from that spoken in the south of England was probably a larger infusion of the Danish forms; but this characteristic must have been shared in nearly the same degree by all the English then spoken to the north of the Thames. Again, whatever effect may have been produced by the Norman Conquest, and the events consequent upon that revolution, would probably be pretty equally diffused over the two countries. In the twelfth and thirteenth centuries both the Normans themselves and their literature appear to have acquired almost the same establishment and ascendancy in Scotland as in England. We have seen that French was the language of the court in the one country as well as in the other, and that Scottish as well as English writers figure among the imitators of the Norman trouveurs and romance poets. Afterwards the connexion of Scotland with France became much more intimate and uninterrupted than that of England; and this appears to have affected the Scottish dialect in a way which will be presently noticed. But in Barbour's day, the language of Teutonic Scotland was distinguished from that of the south of England (which had now acquired the ascendancy over that of the northern counties as the literary dialect), by little more than the retention, perhaps, of a good many vocables which had become obsolete among the English, and a generally broader enunciation of the vowel sounds. Hence Barbour never supposes that he is writing in any other language than English any more than Chaucer; that is the name by which not only he, but his successors Dunbar and even Lyndsay, always designate their native tongue: down to the latter part of the sixteenth century, by the term *Scotch* was generally understood what is now called the *Gaelic*, or the *Erse* or *Ersh* (that is, Irish), the speech of the Celts or Highlanders. Divested of the grotesque and cumbrous spelling of the old manuscripts, the language of Barbour is quite as intelligible at the present day to an English reader as that of Chaucer; the obsolete words and forms are not more numerous in the one writer than in the other, though some that are used by Barbour may not be found in Chaucer, as many of Chaucer's are not in Barbour; the chief general distinction, as we have said, is the greater breadth given to the vowel sounds in the dialect of the Scottish poet. The old termination of the present participle in *and* is also more frequently used than in Chaucer, to whom however it is not unknown, any more than its modern substitute *ing* is to Barbour. The most remarkable peculiarity of the more recent form of the Scottish dialect that is not found in Barbour is the abstraction of the final *l* from syllables ending in that consonant preceded by a vowel or diphthong: thus he never has *a'*, *fa'*, *fu'* or *fou'*, *pow*, *how*, for *all*, *fall*, *full*, *poll*, *hole*, &c. The subsequent introduction of this habit into the speech of the Scotch is perhaps to be attributed to their imitation of the liquefaction of the *l* in similar circumstances by the French, from whom they have also borrowed a considerable number of their modern vocables, never used in England, and to whose accentuation, both of individual words and of sentences, theirs has much general resemblance, throwing the emphasis, contrary, as already noticed, to the tendency of the English language, upon one of the latter syllables, and also running into the rising in many cases where the English use the falling intonation.

The Bruce is a very long poem, comprising between twelve and thirteen thousand lines, in octosyllabic metre, which the two last editors have distributed, Pinkerton into twenty, Jamieson into fourteen, Books. It relates the history of Scotland, and especially the fortunes of the great Bruce, from the death of Alexander III. in 1286, or rather, from the competition for the crown, and the announcement of the claims of Edward I. as lord paramount, on that of his daughter, Margaret the Maiden of Norway, in 1290—the events of the first fifteen or sixteen years, however, before Bruce comes upon the stage, being very succinctly given—to the death of Bruce (Robert I.) in 1320, and that of his constant associate and brother of chivalry, Lord James Douglas, the bearer of the king's heart to the Holy Land, in the year following. The 12,500 verses, or thereby, may be said therefore to comprehend the events of about twenty-five years; and Barbour, though he calls his work a "romaunt," as being a narrative poem, professes to relate nothing but what he believed to be the truth, so that he is to be regarded not only as the earliest poet but also as the earliest historian of his country. Fordun, indeed, was his contemporary, but the Latin chronicle of that writer was probably not published till many years after his death. And to a great extent Barbour's work is and has always been regarded as being an authentic historical monument; it has no doubt some incidents or embellishments which may be set down as fabulous; but these are in general very easily distinguished from the main texture of the narrative, which agrees substantially with the most trustworthy accounts drawn from other sources, and has been received and quoted as good evidence by all subsequent writers and investigators of Scottish history, from Andrew of Wynton to Lord Hailes inclusive.

Barbour is far from being a poet equal to Chaucer; but there is no other English poet down to a century and a half after their day who can be placed by the side of the one any more than of the other. He has neither Chaucer's delicate feeling of the beautiful, nor his grand inventive imagination, nor his wit or humour; but in mere narrative and description he is, with his clear, strong, direct diction, in a high degree both animated and picturesque, and his poem is pervaded by a glow of generous sentiment, well befitting its subject, and lending grace as well as additional force to the ardent, bounding spirit of life with which it is instinct from beginning to end. The following passage, which occurs near the commencement, has been often quoted (at least in part); but it is too remarkable to be omitted in any exemplification of the characteristics of Barbour's poetry. He is describing the oppressions endured by the Scots during the occupation of their country by the English king, Edward I., after his deposition of his puppet Baliol:—

    And gif that ony man them by
    Had ony thing that wes worthy,
    As horse, or hund, or other thing,
    That war pleasand to their liking!
    With right or wrang it wald have they.
    And gif ony wald them withsay,
    They suld swa do, that they suld tine[1]
    Other[2] land or life, or live in pine.
    For they dempt[3] them efter their will,
    Takand na kepe[4] to right na skill.[5]
    Ah! what they dempt them felonly![6]
    For gud knightes that war worthy,
    For little enchesoun[7] or then[8] nane
    They hangit be the neckbane.
    Als[9] that folk, that ever was free,
    And in freedom wont for to be,
    Through their great mischance and folly,
    Wor treated then sa wickedly,
    That their faes[10] their judges ware:
    What wretchedness may man have mair?[11]
      Ah! Freedom is a noble thing!
    Freedom mays[12] man to have liking;[13]
    Freedom all solace to man gives:
    He lives at ease that freely lives!
    A noble heart may have nane ease,
    Ne elles nought that may him please
    Giff freedom failye: for free liking
    Is yarnit[14] ower[15] all other thing.
    Na he that aye has livit free
    May nought knaw well the property.[16]

---

[1] Lose.   [2] Either.   [3] Doomed, judged.
[4] Taking no heed, paying no regard.   [5] Reason.
[6] Ah! how cruelly they judged them!   [7] Cause.
[8] Both the sense and the metre seem to require that this then (in orig. than should be transferred to the next line; "they hangit then."
[9] Also, thus.   [10] Foes.   [11] More.   [12] Makes.
[13] Pleasure.   [14] Yearned for, desired.   [15] Over, above.
[16] The quality, the peculiar state or condition?

> The anger, na the wretched doom,
> That is couplit[1] to foul thirldoom.[2]
> But gif he had assayit it,
> Then all perquer[3] he suld it wit;
> And suld think freedom mair to prise
> Than all the gold in warld that is.

It is, he goes on to observe, by its contrary, or opposite, that the true nature of everything is best discovered:—the value and blessing of freedom, for example, are only to be fully felt in slavery; and then the worthy archdeacon, who, although the humorous is not his strongest ground, does not want slyness or a sense of the comic, winds up with a very singular illustration, which, however, is more suited to his own age than to ours, and may be suppressed here without injury to the argument.

But Barbour's design, no doubt, was to effect by means of this light and sportive conclusion an easy and harmonious descent from the height of declamation and passion to which he had been carried in the preceding lines. Throughout his long work he shows, for his time, a very remarkable feeling of the *art* of poetry, both by the variety which he studies in the disposition and treatment of his subject, and by the rare temperance and self-restraint which prevents him from ever overdoing what he is about either by prosing or raving. Even his patriotism, warm and steady as it is, is wholly without any vulgar narrowness or ferocity: he paints the injuries of his country with distinctness and force, and celebrates the heroism of her champions and deliverers with all admiration and sympathy; but he never runs into either the gasconading exaggerations or the furious depreciatory invectives which would, it might be thought, have better pleased the generality of those for whom he wrote. His understanding was too enlightened, and his heart too large, for that. His poem stands in this respect in striking contrast to that of Harry, the blind minstrel, on the exploits of Wallace, to be afterwards noticed; but each poet suited his hero—Barbour, the magnanimous, considerate, and far-seeing king; Blind Harry, the indomitable popular champion, with his one passion and principle, hatred of the domination of England, occupying his whole soul and being.

[1] Coupled, attached. [2] Thraldom. [3] Exactly.

Compound English Prose.—Mandevil; Trevisa; Wiclif; Chaucer.

To the fourteenth century belong the earliest specimens of prose composition in our present mixed English that have been preserved.

Our oldest Mixed English prose author is Sir John Mandevil, whose Voyages and Travels, a singular repertory of the marvellous legends of the middle ages, have been often printed. The best editions are that published in 8vo., at London, in 1725, and the reprint of it in the same form in 1839, "with an introduction, additional notes, and a glossary, by J. O. Halliwell, Esq., F.S.A., F.R.A.S." The author's own account of himself and of his book is given in an introductory address, or Prologue:—

And, for als moch as it is long time passed that there was no general passage ne vyage over the sea, and many men desiren for to hear speak of the Holy Lond, and han[1] thereof great solace and comfort, I, John Maundeville, knight, all be it I be not worthy, that was born in Englond, in the town of Saint Albons, passed the sea in the year of our Lord Jesu Christ 1322, in the day of Saint Michel; and hider-to have ben[2] longtime over the sea, and have seen and gone thorough many divers londs, and many provinces, and kingdoms, and isles, and have passed thorough Tartary, Persie, Ermonie[3] the Little and the Great; thorough Libye, Chaldee, and a great part of Ethiop; thorough Amazoyn, Ind the Less and the More, a great party; and thorough out many other isles, that ben abouten Ind; where dwellen many divers folks, and of divers manners and laws, and of divers shappe of men. Of which londs and isles I shall speak more plainly hereafter. And I shall devise you some party of things that there ben,[4] when time shall ben after it may best come to my mind; and specially for hem[5] that will[6] and are in purpose for to visit the Holy City of Jerusalem, and the holy places that are thereabout. And I shall tell the way that they should holden thider. For I have often times passed and ridden the way, with good company of many lords, God be thonked.

And ye shull understond that I have put this book out of Latin into French, and translated it agen out of French into English, that every man of my nation may understond it. But lords and knights, and other noble and worthy men, that con[7] Latin but little, and han ben beyond the sea, knowen and understonden gif I err in devising, for forgetting or else; that they mowe[8] redress it and amend it. For things passed out, of long time, from a man's mind, or from his sight, turnen soon into forgetting; because that mind of man no may not ben comprehended no withholden for the freelty of mankind.

| [1] Have. | [2] Been. | [3] Armenia. | [4] Be. |
| [5] Them ('em). | [6] Wish. | [7] Know. | [8] May. |

Mandevil is said to have returned to England in 1356, or after an absence of thirty-four years; and, as he is recorded to have died at Liege in 1371, his book must have been written early in the latter half of the fourteenth century.

The oldest English translation we have of the Bible is that of Wiclif. John de Wiclif, or Wycliffe, died at about the age of sixty in 1384, and his translation of the Scriptures from the Vulgate appears to have been finished two or three years before. The New Testament has been several times printed; first in folio in 1731 under the care of the Rev. John Lewis; next in 4to. in 1810 under that of the Rev. H. H. Baber; lastly in 4to. in 1841, and again in 1846, in Bagster's English Hexapla. And now the Old Testament has also been given to the world from the Clarendon press, at the expense of the University of Oxford, admirably edited by the Rev. J. Forshall and Sir Frederick Madden, in four magnificent quartos, Oxford, 1850. Wiclif is also the author of many original writings in his native language, in defence of his reforming views in theology and church government, some of which have been printed, but most of which that are preserved still remain in manuscript. His style is everywhere coarse and slovenly, though sometimes animated by a popular force or boldness of expression.

Chaucer is the author of three separate works in prose; a translation of Boethius de Consolatione Philosophiæ, printed by Caxton, in folio, without date, under the title of The Boke of Consolacion of Philosophie, wich that Boecius made for his Comforte and Consolacion; a Treatise on the Astrolabe, addressed to his son Lewis, in 1391, and printed (at least in part) in the earlier editions of his works; and The Testament of Love, an apparent imitation of the treatise of Boethius, written towards the end of his life, and also printed in the old editions of his collected works. But, perhaps, the most highly finished, and in other respects also the most interesting, of the great poet's prose compositions are the Tale of Melibœus and the Parson's Tale, in the Canterbury Tales. The Parson's Tale, which winds up the Canterbury Tales, as we possess the work, is a long moral discourse, which, for the greater part, is not very entertaining, but which yet contains some passages curiously illustrative of the age in which it was written. Here is part of what occurs in the section headed De Superbia (Of Pride), the first of the seven mortal sins. Tyrwhitt justly recommends that the whole " should be read carefully by any antiquary who may mean to write De re Vestiaria of the English nation in the fourteenth century."

Now ben there two manner of prides: that on of hem[1] is within the heart of a man, and that other is without; of which soothly these foresaid things, and mo[2] than I have said, appertainen to pride that is within the heart of man. And there be other spices[3] that ben withouten; but, natheless, that on of these spices of pride is sign of that other, right as the gay levesell[4] at the tavern is sign of the wine that is in the cellar. And this is in many things, as in speech and countenance, and outrageous array of clothing; for certes if there had ben no sin in clothing Christ wold not so soon have noted and spoken of the clothing of thilk rich man in the Gospel: and, as Saint Gregory saith, that precious clothing is culpable, for the dearth of it, and for his softness, and for his strangeness and disguising, and for the superfluity or for the inordinate scantiness of it. Alas! may not a man see as in our days the sinful costlew array of clothing, and namely[5] in too much superfluity, or else in too disordinate scantness.

As to the first sin, in superfluity of clothing, which that maketh it so dear, to the harm of the people, not only the cost of the embrouding,[6] the disguising, indenting or barring, ownding,[7] paling,[8] winding, or bending, and semblable waste of cloth in vanity; but there is also the costlew furring in hir gowns, so moch pounsoning[9] of chisel to maken holes, so moch dagging[10] of shears, with the superfluity in length of the foresaid gowns, trailing in the dong and in the mire, on horse and eke on foot, as well of man as of woman, that all thilk training is verily (as in effect) wasted, consumed, threadbare, and rotten with dong, rather than it is yeven to the poor, to great damage of the foresaid poor folk, and that in sondry wise; this is to sayn, the more that cloth is wasted, the more must it cost to the poor people, for the scarceness; and, furthermore, if so be that they wolden yeve swich pounsoned and dagged clothing to the poor people, it is not convenient to wear for hir estate, ne suffisant to bote[11] hir necessity, to keep hem fro the distemperance of the firmament....

Also the sin of ornament or of apparel is in things that appertain to riding, as in too many delicate horse that ben holden for delight, that ben so fair, fat, and costlew; and also in many a vicious knave that is sustained because of hem; in curious harness, as in saddles, croppers, peitrels, and bridles, covered with precious cloth and rich, barred and plated of gold and of silver; for which God saith by Zachary the prophet, I wol confound the riders of swich horse. These folk taken little regard of the riding of God's son of heaven, and of his harness, whan he rode upon the ass, and had none other harness but the poor clothes of his disciples, ne we read not that ever he rode on ony other beast. I speak this for the sin of superfluity, and not for honesty whan reason it requireth. And, moreover,

---

[1] The one of them. [2] More. [3] Species, kinds.
[4] The meaning of this word, which at a later date appears to have been pronounced and written lesell, is unknown. See Tyrwhitt's note to Cant. Tales, v. 4059, and Glossary, ad verbum; and note by the editor, Mr. Albert Way, on pp. 300, 301, of the Promptorium Parvulorum, vol. i., printed for the Camden Society, 4to. Lond. 1843. [5] Especially.
[6] Embroidering. [7] Imitating waves. [8] Imitating pales.
[9] Punching. [10] Slitting. [11] Help (boot).

cartes pride is greatly notified in holding of great meiny,[1] whan they ben of little profit, or of right no profit, and namely whan that meiny is falonious and damageous to the people by hardiness of high lordship, or by way of office; for certes swich lords sell than hir lordship to the devil of hell, whan they sustain the wickedness of hir meiny; or else whan these folk of low degree, as they that holden hostelries, sustainen theft of hir hostellers, and that is in many manner of deceits; thilk manner of folk ben the flies that followen the honey, or else the hounds that followen the carrain; swich foresaid folk stranglen spiritually hir lordships; for which thus saith David the prophet, Wicked death mot come unto thilk lordships, and God yeve that they mot descend into hell all down, for in hir houses is iniquity and shrewedness, and not God of heaven: and certes, but if they done amendment, right as God yave his benison to Laban by the service of Jacob, and to Pharaoh by the service of Joseph, right so wol God yeve his malison to swich lordships as sustain the wickedness of hir servants, but they come to amendment. Pride of the table appeareth eke full oft; for certes rich men be cleped[2] to feasts, and poor folk be put away and rebuked; and also in excess of divers meats and drinks, and namely swich manner bake meats and dish meats brenning[3] of wild fire, and painted and castled with paper, and semblable waste, so that it is abusion to think; and eke in too great preciousness of vessel, and curiosity of minstrelsy, by which a man is stirred more to the delights of luxury.

PRINTING IN ENGLAND.—CAXTON.

The art of printing had been practised nearly thirty years in Germany before it was introduced either into England or France —with so tardy a pace did knowledge travel to and fro over the earth in those days, or so unfavourable was the state of these countries for the reception of even the greatest improvements in the arts. At length a citizen of London secured a conspicuous place to his name for ever in the annals of our national literature, by being, so far as is known, the first of his countrymen that learned the new art, and certainly the first who either practised it in England, or in printing an English book. William Caxton was born, as he tells us himself, in the Weald of Kent, it is supposed about the year 1412. Thirty years after this date his name is found among the members of the Mercers' Company in London. Later in life he appears to have repeatedly visited the Low Countries, at first probably on business of his own, but afterwards in a sort of public capacity,—having in 1464 been commissioned, along with another person, apparently also a merchant, by Edward IV. to negotiate a commercial treaty with the Duke of Burgundy. He was afterwards taken into the house-

[1] Body of menials.   [2] Called, invited.   [3] Burning.

hold of Margaret Duchess of Burgundy. It was probably while resident abroad, in the Low Countries or in Germany, that he commenced practising the art of printing. He is commonly supposed to have completed before the end of the year 1471 impressions of Raoul le Fevre's Recueil des Histoires de Troyes, in folio; of the Latin oration of John Russell on Charles Duke of Burgundy being created a Knight of the Garter, in quarto; and of an English translation by himself of Le Fevre's above-mentioned history, in folio; "whyche sayd translacion and werke," says the title, "was begonne in Brugis in 1468, and ended in the holy cyte of Colen, 19 Sept. 1471." But these words undoubtedly refer only to the translation; and sufficient reasons have lately been advanced by Mr. Knight for entertaining the strongest doubts of any one of the above-mentioned books having been printed by Caxton.[*] The earliest work now known, which we have sufficient grounds for believing to have been printed by Caxton, is another English translation by himself, from the French, of a moral treatise entitled The Game and Playe of the Chesse, a folio volume, which is stated to have been "finished the last day of March, 1474." It is generally supposed that this work was printed in England; and the year 1474 accordingly is assumed to have been that of the introduction of the art into this country. It is certainly known that Caxton was resident in England in 1477, and had set up his press in the Almonry, near Westminster Abbey, where he printed that year, in folio, The Dictes and Notable Wyse Sayenges of the Phylosophers, translated from the French by Anthony Woodville, Earl Rivers. From this time Caxton continued both to print and translate with indefatigable industry for about a dozen years, his last publication with a date having been produced in 1490, and his death having probably taken place in 1491, or 1492. Before he died he saw the admirable art which he had introduced into his native country already firmly established there, and the practice of it extensively diffused. Theodore Rood, John Lettow, William Machelinn, and Wynkyn de Worde, foreigners, and Thomas Hunt, an Englishman, all printed in London both before and after Caxton's death. It is probable that the foreigners had been his assistants, and were brought into the country by him. A press was also set up at St. Albans by a schoolmaster of that place, whose name has not been preserved; and books began to be printed at Oxford so early as the year 1478.

[*] See William Caxton, a Biography, 12mo. Lond. 1844. pp. 103, &c. This work has since been expanded into The Old Printer and the Modern Press, 8vo. 1854.

ENGLISH CHRONICLERS.

The series of our Modern English chronicles may perhaps be most properly considered as commencing with John de Trevisa's translation of Higden, with various additions, which, as already mentioned, was finished in 1387, and was printed, with a continuation to 1460, by Caxton, in 1482. After Trevisa comes John Harding, who belongs to the fifteenth century; his metrical Chronicle of England coming down to the reign of Edward IV.* The metre is melancholy enough; but the part of the work relating to the author's own times is not without value. Harding is chiefly notorious as the author, or at least the collector and producer, of a great number of charters and other documents attesting acts of fealty done by the Scottish to the English kings, which are now generally admitted to be forgeries. Caxton himself must be reckoned our next English chronicler, as the author both of the continuation of Trevisa and also of the concluding part of the volume entitled The Chronicles of England, published by him in 1480,—the body of which is translated from a Latin chronicle by Douglas, a monk of Glastonbury, who lived in the preceding century. Neither of these performances, however, is calculated to add to the fame of the celebrated printer. To this period we may also in part assign the better known Concordance of Historics of Robert Fabyan, citizen and draper of London; though the author only died in 1512, nor was his work printed till a few years later. Fabyan's history, which begins with Brutus and comes down to his own time, is in the greater part merely a translation from the preceding chroniclers; its chief value consists in a number of notices it has preserved relating to the city of London.†

BISHOP PECOCK; FORTESCUE; MALORY.

Of the English theological writers of the age immediately following that of Wiclif, the most noteworthy is Reynold Pecock, Bishop of Asaph and afterwards of Chichester. As may be inferred from these ecclesiastical dignities, Pecock was no Wiclifite, but a defender of the established system both of doctrine and of church government: he tells us himself, in one of his

* First printed by Grafton in 1543. The most recent edition is that by Sir H. Ellis, 4to. Lond. 1812.
† First published in 1516. The last edition is that of Sir H. Ellis, Lond. 4to. 1811.

books, that twenty years of his life had been spent for the greater part in writing against the Lollards. But, whatever effect his arguments may have produced upon those against whom they were directed, they gave little satisfaction to the more zealous spirits on his own side, who probably thought that he was too fond of reasoning with errors demanding punishment by a cautery sharper than that of the pen ; and the end was that he was himself, in the year 1457, charged with heresy, and, having been found guilty, was first compelled to read a recantation, and to commit fourteen of his books, with his own hands, to the flames at St. Paul's Cross, and then deprived of his bishopric, and consigned to an imprisonment in which he was allowed the use neither of writing materials nor of books, and in which he is supposed to have died about two years after. One especial heresy alleged to be found in his writings was, that in regard to matters of faith the church was not infallible. Bishop Pecock's Life has been ably and learnedly written by the Rev. John Lewis, to whom we also owe biographies of Wiclif and of Caxton. His numerous treatises are partly in English, partly in Latin. Of those in English the most remarkable is one entitled The Repressor, which he produced in 1449. A short specimen, in which the spelling, but only the spelling, is modernized, will give some notion of his manner of writing, and of the extent to which the language had been adapted to prose eloquence or reasoning of the more formal kind in that age :—

"Say to me, good sir, and answer hereto : when men of the country upland bringen into London in Midsummer eve branches of trees fro Bishop's Wood, and flowers fro the field, and betaken tho[1] to citizens of London for to therewith array her[2] houses, shoulden men of London, receiving and taking tho branches and flowers, say and hold that the branches grewen out of the carts which broughten hem[3] to London, and that the carts or the hands of the bringers weren grounds and fundaments of tho branches and flowers? God forbid so little wit be in her heads. Certes, though Christ and his apostles weren now living at London, and would bring, so as is now said, branches from Bishop's Wood, and flowers from the fields, into London, and woulden hem deliver to men, that they make therewith her houses gay, into remembrance of St. John Baptist, and of this that it was prophesied of him, that many shoulden joy of his birth, yet the men of London, receiving so tho branches and flowers, oughten not say and feel that the branches and flowers grewen out of Christ's hands. The branches grewen out of the boughs upon which they in Bishop's Wood stooden, and the boughs grewen out of stocks or

---

[1] Take them, or those.   [2] Their.   [3] Them.

truncheons, and the truncheons or shafts grewen out of the root, and the root out of the next earth thereto, upon which and in which the root is buried. So that neither the cart, neither the hands of the bringers, neither the bringers ben the grounds or fundaments of the branches."

The good bishop, we see, has a popular and lively as well as clear and precise way of putting things. It may be doubted, nevertheless, if his ingenious illustrations would be quite as convincing to the earnest and excited innovators to whom they were addressed as they were satisfactory to himself.

Another eminent English prose writer of this date was Sir John Fortescue, who was Lord Chief Justice of the King's Bench under Henry VI., and to whom the king is supposed to have also confided the great seal at some time during his expulsion from the throne. Fortescue is the author of various treatises, some in English, some in Latin, most of which, however, still remain in manuscript. One in Latin, which was first sent to press in the reign of Henry VIII., and has been repeatedly reprinted since, is commonly referred to under the title of De Laudibus Legum Angliæ. It has also been several times translated into English. This treatise is drawn up in the form of a dialogue between the author and Henry's unfortunate son, Edward Prince of Wales, so barbarously put to death after the battle of Towkesbury. Fortescue's only English work that has been printed was probably written at a later date, and would appear to have had for its object to secure for him, now that the Lancastrian cause was beaten to the ground, the favour of the Yorkist king, Edward IV. It was first published, in 1714, by Mr. John Fortescue Aland, of the Middle Temple, with the title of The Difference between an Absolute and Limited Monarchy, as it more particularly regards the English Constitution,—which, of course, is modern, but has been generally adopted to designate the work. The following passage (in which the spelling is again reformed) will enable the reader to compare Fortescue as a writer with his contemporary Pecock, and is also curious both for its matter and its spirit:—

And how so be it that the French king reigneth upon his people *dominio regali*, yet St. Lewis, sometime king there, ne any of his predecessors set never tallies ne other impositions upon the people of that land without the consent of the three estates, which, when they may be assembled, are like to the court of Parliament in England. And this order kept many of his successors till late days, that Englishmen kept such a war in France that the three estates durst not come together. And then, for that cause, and for great necessity which the French king had of goods for the defence of that land, he took upon him to set tallies and other impositions upon the commons without the assent of the three estates; but yet he would not set any such charges, nor hath set, upon the nobles, for fear of rebellion. And, because the commons, though they have grudged, have not rebelled, nor be hardy to rebel, the French kings have yearly sithen[1] set such charges upon them, and so augmented the same charges as the same commons be so impoverished and destroyed that they may uneath[2] live. They drink water, they eat apples, with bread, right brown, made of rye. They eat no flesh, but if it be selden[3] a little lard, or of the entrails or heads of beasts slain for the nobles and merchants of the land. They wear no woollen, but if it be a poor coat under their uttermost garment, made of great canvas, and passen not their knee; wherefore they be gartered and their thighs bare. Their wives and children gone barefoot. They may in none otherwise live; for some of them that was wont to pay to his landlord for his tenement which he hireth by the year a scute[4] payeth now to the king, over[5] that scute, five scutes. Where-through they be artied[6] by necessity, so to watch, labour, and grub in the ground for their sustenance, that their nature is much wasted, and the kind of them brought to nought. They gone crooked, and are feeble, not able to fight nor to defend the realm; nor have they weapon, nor money to buy them weapon, withal; but verily they live in the most extreme poverty and misery; and yet they dwell in one of the most fertile realms of the world. Where-through the French king hath not men of his own realm able to defend it, except his nobles, which bearen not such impositions, and therefore they are right likely of their bodies; by which cause the king is compelled to make his armies, and retinues for defence of his land, of strangers, as Scots, Spaniards, Aragoners, men of Almayne,[7] and of other nations; else all his enemies might overrun him; for he hath no defence of his own, except his castles and fortresses. Lo! this the fruit of his *jus regale*.

It is in the same spirit that the patriotic chief justice elsewhere boasts, that there were more Englishmen hanged for robbery in one year than Frenchmen in seven, and that "if an Englishman be poor, and see another having riches which may be taken from him by might, he will not spare to do so."

Fortescue was probably born not much more than thirty years after Pecock; but the English of the judge, in vocabulary, in grammatical forms, in the modulation of the sentences, and in its air altogether, might seem to exhibit quite another stage of the language.

Although both Pecock and Fortescue lived to see the great invention of printing, and the latter at any rate survived the introduction of the new art into his native country, no production

---

[1] Since. [2] Scarcely, with difficulty (uneasily).
[3] Seldom, on rare occasions.
[4] An *ecut*, or *ecu* (d'or), about three shillings and fourpence.
[5] In addition to, over and above.   [6] Compelled.
[7] Germany.

of either appears to have been given to the world through the press in the lifetime of the writer. Perhaps this was also the case with another prose writer of this date, who is remembered, however, less by his name than by the work of which he is the author, and which still continues to be read, the famous history of King Arthur, commonly known under the name of the Morte Arthur. This work was first printed by Caxton in the year 1485. He tells us in his prologue, or preface, that the copy was given him by Sir Thomas Malory, Knight, who took it, out of certain books in French, and reduced it into English. Malory himself states at the end, that he finished his task in the ninth year of King Edward IV., which would be in 1469 or 1470. The Morte Arthur was several times reprinted in the course of the following century and a half, the latest of the old editions having appeared in a quarto volume in 1634. From this, two reprints were brought out by different London booksellers in the same year, 1816; one in three duodecimos, the other in two. But the standard modern edition is that which appeared in two volumes quarto in the following year, 1817, exactly reprinted from Caxton's original edition, with the title of The Byrth, Lyfe, and Actes of Kyng Arthur; of his noble Knyghtes of the Rounde Table, &c., with an Introduction and Notes, by Robert Southey. Malory, whoever he may have been (Leland says he was Welsh), and supposing him to have been in the main only a translator, must be admitted to show considerable mastery of expression; his English is always animated and flowing, and, in its earnestness and tenderness, occasionally rises to no common beauty and eloquence. The concluding chapters in particular have been much admired. We extract a few sentences:—

Then Sir Lancelot, ever after, eat but little meat, nor drank, but continually mourned until he was dead; and then he sickened more and more, and dried and dwindled away. For the bishop, nor none of his fellows, might not make him to eat, and little he drank, that he was soon waxed shorter by a cubit than he was, that the people could not know him. For evermore day and night he prayed [taking no rest], but needfully as nature required; sometimes he slumbered a broken sleep; and always he was lying grovelling upon King Arthur's and Queen Guenever's tomb; and there was no comfort that the bishop, nor Sir Bors, not none of all his fellows could make him; it availed nothing.

Oh! ye mighty and pompous lords, winning in the glorious transitory of this unstable life, as in reigning over great realms and mighty great countries, fortified with strong castles and towers, edified with many a rich city; yea also, ye fierce and mighty knights, so valiant in adventurous deeds of arms, behold! behold! see how this mighty conqueror, King

Arthur, whom in his human life all the world doubted,[1] yea also the noble Queen Guenever, which sometime sat in her chair adorned with gold, pearls, and precious stones, now lie full low in obscure foss, or pit, covered with clods of earth and clay! Behold also this mighty champion, Sir Lancelot, peerless of all knighthood; see now how he lieth grovelling upon the cold mould; now being so feeble and faint, that sometime was so terrible: how, and in what manner, ought ye to be so desirous of worldly honour so dangerous? Therefore, me thinketh this present book is right necessary often to be read; for in all[2] ye find the most gracious, knightly, and virtuous war, of the most noble knights of the world, whereby they got praising continually; also me seemeth, by the oft reading thereof, ye shall greatly desire to accustom yourself in following of those gracious knightly deeds; that is to say, to dread God and to love righteousness, faithfully and courageously to serve your sovereign prince; and, the more that God hath given you the triumphal honour, the meeker ought ye to be, ever fearing the unstableness of this deceitful world.

. . . . . .

And so, within fifteen days, they came to Joyous Guard, and there they laid his corpse in the body of the quire, and sung and read many psalters and prayers over him and about him; and even his visage was laid open and naked, that all folk might behold him. For such was the custom in those days, that all men of worship should so lie with open visage till that they were buried. And right thus as they were at their service there came Sir Ector de Maris, that had sought seven years all England, Scotland, and Wales, seeking his brother Sir Lancelot. . . .
And then Sir Ector threw his shield, his sword, and his helm from him; and when he beheld Sir Lancelot's visage, he fell down in a swoon; and, when he awoke, it were hard for any tongue to tell the doleful complaints that he made for his brother. "Ah, Sir Lancelot," said he, "thou wert head of all Christian knights."—"And now, I dare say," said Sir Bors, "that Sir Lancelot, there thou liest, thou wert never matched of none earthly knight's hands. And thou wert the courtliest knight that ever bare shield; and thou wert the truest friend to thy lover that ever bestrode horse; and thou wert the truest lover, of a sinful man, that ever loved woman; and thou wert the kindest man that ever stroke with sword; and thou wert the goodliest person that ever came among press of knights; and thou wert the meekest man, and the gentlest, that ever eat in hall among ladies; and thou wert the sternest knight to thy mortal foe that ever put spear in rest."

ENGLISH POETS.—OCCLEVE; LYDGATE.

The most numerous class of writers in the mother tongue belonging to this time, are the poets, by courtesy so called. We must refer to the learned and curious pages of Warton, or to the still more elaborate researches of Ritson,[*] for the names of a

[1] Dreaded (held as *redoubtable*).   [2] It?
[*] *Bibliographia Poetica*.

crowd of worthless and forgotten versifiers that fill up the annals of our national minstrelsy from Chaucer to Lord Surrey. The last-mentioned antiquary has furnished a list of about seventy English poets who flourished in this interval. The first known writer of any considerable quantity of verse after Chaucer is Thomas Occleve. Warton places him about the year 1420. He is the author of many minor pieces, which mostly remain in manuscript—although "six of peculiar stupidity," says Ritson, "were selected and published" by Dr. Askew in 1796;—and also of a longer poem, entitled De Regimine Principum (On the Government of Princes), chiefly founded on a Latin work, with the same title, written in the thirteenth century by an Italian ecclesiastic Egidius, styled the Doctor Fundatissimus, and on the Latin treatise on the game of chess of Jacobus de Casulis, another Italian writer of the same age—the latter being the original of the Game of the Chess, translated by Caxton from the French, and printed by him in 1474. Occleve's poem has never been published—and is chiefly remembered for a drawing of Chaucer by the hand of Occleve, which is found in one of the manuscripts of it now in the British Museum.* Occleve repeatedly speaks of Chaucer as his master and poetic father, and was no doubt personally acquainted with the great poet. All that Occleve appears to have gained, however, from his admirable model is some initiation in that smoothness and regularity of diction of which Chaucer's writings set the first great example. His own endowment of poetical power and feeling was very small—the very titles of his pieces, as Warton remarks, indicating the poverty and frigidity of his genius.

By far the most famous of these versifiers of the fifteenth century is John Lydgate, the monk of Bury, whom the Historian of our Poetry considers to have arrived at his highest point of eminence about the year 1430. Ritson has given a list of about 250 poems attributed to Lydgate. Indeed he seems to have followed the manufacture of rhymes as a sort of trade, furnishing any quantity to order whenever he was called upon. On one occasion, for instance, we find him employed by the historian Whethamstede, who was abbot of St. Albans, to make a translation into English, for the use of that convent, of the Latin legend of its patron saint. "The chronicler who records a part of this anecdote," observes Warton, "seems to consider Lydgate's translation as a matter of mere manual mechanism; for he adds,

* Harl. MS. 4866. This portrait, which is a half-length, is coloured. There is a full-length portrait in another copy of Occleve's Poems in Royal MS. 17 D. vi.—See Life of Chaucer, by Sir Harris Nicolas, pp. 104, &c.

that Whethamstede paid for the translation, the writing, and illuminations, one hundred shillings."* Lydgate, however, though excessively diffuse, and possessed of very little strength or originality of imagination, is a considerably livelier and more expert writer than Occleve. His memory was also abundantly stored with the learning of his age; he had travelled in France and Italy, and was intimately acquainted with the literature of both these countries; and his English makes perhaps a nearer approach to the modern form of the language than that of any preceding writer. His best-known poem consists of nine books of Tragedies, as he entitles them, respecting the falls of princes, translated from a Latin work of Boccaccio's: it was printed at London in the reign of Henry VIII. A Selection from the Minor Poems of Dan John Lydgate, edited by Mr. Halliwell, has been printed for the Percy Society, 8vo. Lon. 1840.

SCOTTISH POETS.—WYNTON; JAMES I.; HENRYSON; HOLLAND; BLIND HENRY.

The most remarkable portion of our poetical literature belonging to the fifteenth century (as also, we shall presently find, of that belonging to the first half of the sixteenth), was contributed by Scottish writers. The earliest successor of Barbour was Andrew of Wyntown, or Wynton, a canon regular of the Priory of St. Andrews, and Prior of the Monastery of St. Serf's Inch in Lochleven, one of the establishments subordinate to that great house, who is supposed to have been born about 1350, and whose Originale Cronykil of Scotland appears to have been finished in the first years of the fifteenth century. It is a long poem, of nine books, written in the same octosyllabic rhyme with the Bruce of Barbour, to which it was no doubt intended to serve as a kind of introduction. Wynton, however, has very little of the old archdeacon's poetic force and fervour; and even his style, though in general sufficiently simple and clear, is, if anything, rather ruder than that of his predecessor—a difference which is probably to be accounted for by Barbour's frequent residences in England and more extended intercourse with the world. The Chronykil is principally interesting in an historical point of view, and in that respect it is of considerable value and authority, for Wynton, besides his merits as a distinct narrator, had evidently taken great pains to obtain the best information within his reach with regard to the events both of his own and

* Hist. Eng. Poetry, vol. ii. p. 363.

of preceding times. The work begins (as was then the fashion), with the creation of the world, and comes down to the year 1408; but the first five books are occupied rather with general than with Scottish history. The last four books, together with such parts of the preceding ones as contain anything relating to British affairs, were very carefully edited by the late Mr. David Macpherson (the author of the well-known Annals of Commerce and other works), in two volumes 8vo. Lon. 1795. It is deserving of notice that a considerable portion of Wynton's Chronicle is not his own composition, but was the contribution of another contemporary poet.; namely, all from the 19th chapter of the Eighth to the 10th chapter of the Ninth Book inclusive, comprising the space from 1324 to 1390, and forming about a third of the four concluding books. This he conscientiously acknowledges, in very careful and explicit terms, both at the beginning and end of the insertion. We may give what he says in the latter place, as a short sample of his style:—

> This part last treated beforn,
> Fra Davy the Brus our king was born,
> While [1] his sister son Robert
> The Second, our king, than called Stuert,
> That next[2] him reigned successive,
> His days had endd of his live,
> Wit ye well, wes nought my dite;[3]
> Thereof I dare me well acquite.
> Wha that it dited, nevertheless,
> He showed him of mair cunnandness
> Than me commendis[4] his treatise,
> But[5] favour, wha[6] will it clearly prize.
> This part wes written to me send;
> And I, that thought for to mak end
> Of that purpose I took on hand,
> Saw it was well accordand
> To my matere; I wes right glad;
> For I was in my travail sad;
> I eked[7] it here to this dite,
> For to mak me some respite.

This is interesting as making it probable that poetical, or a least metrical, composition in the national dialect was common in Scotland at this early date.

Of all our poets of the early part of the fifteenth century the one of greatest eminence must be considered to be King

[1] Till. [2] Next. [3] Writing.
[4] He showed himself of more cunning (skill) than I who commend.
[5] Without. [6] Whosoever. [7] Added.

James I. of Scotland, even if he be only the author of The King's Quair (that is, the King's *quire* or *book*), his claim to which has scarcely been disputed. It is a serious poem, of nearly 1400 lines, arranged in seven-line stanzas; the style in great part allegorical; the subject, the love of the royal poet for the lady Joanna Beaufort, whom he eventually married, and whom he is said to have first beheld walking in the garden below from the window of his prison in the Round Tower of Windsor Castle. The poem was in all probability written during his detention in England, and previous to his marriage, which took place in February 1424, a few months before his return to his native country. In the concluding stanza James makes grateful mention of his—

> maisters dear
> Gower and Chaucer, that on the steppes sate
> Of rhetorick while they were livand here,
> Superlative as poets laureate,
> Of morality and eloquence ornate;

and he is evidently an imitator of the great father of English poetry. The poem too must be regarded as written in English rather than in Scotch, although the difference between the two dialects, as we have seen, was not so great at this early date as it afterwards became, and although James, who was in his eleventh year when he was carried away to England in 1405 by Henry IV., may not have altogether avoided the peculiarities of his native idiom. The Quair was first published from the only manuscript (one of the Selden Collection in the Bodleian Library), by Mr. W. Tytler at Edinburgh, in 1783; there have been several editions since. Two other poems of considerable length, in a humorous style, have also been attributed to James I. —Peebles to the Play, and Christ's Kirk on the Green, both in the Scottish dialect; but they are more probably the productions of his equally gifted and equally unfortunate descendant James V. (b. 1511, d. 1542). Chalmers, however, assigns the former to James I. As for the two famous comic ballads of The Gaberlunyie Man, and the Jolly Beggar, which it has been usual among recent writers to speak of as by one or other of these kings, there seems to be no reasonable ground — not even that of tradition of any antiquity—for assigning them to either.

Chaucer, we have seen, appears to have been unknown to his contemporary Barbour; but after the time of James I. the Scottish poetry for more than a century bears evident traces of the imitation of the great English master. It was a consequence

of the relative circumstances of the two countries, that, while
the literature of Scotland, the poorer and ruder of the two, could
exert no influence upon that of England, the literature of England
could not fail powerfully to affect and modify that of its more
backward neighbour. No English writer would think of studying or imitating Barbour; but every Scottish poet who arose
after the fame of Chaucer had passed the border would seek, or,
even if he did not seek, would still inevitably catch, some
inspiration from that great example. If it could in any circumstances have happened that Chaucer should have remained
unknown in Scotland, the singular fortunes of James I. were
shaped as if on purpose to transfer the manner and spirit of his
poetry into the literature of that country. From that time forward the native voice of the Scottish muse was mixed with this
other foreign voice. One of the earliest Scottish poets after
James I. is Robert Henryson, or Henderson, the author of the
beautiful pastoral of Robin and Makyne, which is popularly
known from having been printed by Bishop Percy in his
Reliques. He has left us a continuation or supplement to
Chaucer's Troilus and Cresseide, which is commonly printed
along with the works of that poet under the title of The Testament of Fair Cresseide. All that is known of the era of Henryson
is that he was alive and very old about the close of the fifteenth
century. He may therefore probably have been born about the
time that James I. returned from England. Henryson is also
the author of a translation into English or Scottish verse of
Æsop's Fables, of which there is a MS. in the Harleian Collection (No. 3865), and which was printed at Edinburgh in 8vo. in
1621, under the title of The Moral Fables of Æsop the Phrygian,
compyled into eloquent and ornamental meter, by Robert Hen-
rison, schoolemaster of Dumforling. To Henryson, moreover.
as has been already noticed, Mr. Laing attributes the tale of
Orpheus and Eurydice contained in the collection of old poetry,
entitled The Knightly Tale of Golagrus and Gawane, &c., reprinted by him in 1827.

Contemporary, too, with Henryson, if not perhaps rather before
him, was Sir John or Richard Holland. His poem entitled The
Buke of the Howlat (that is, the owl), a wild and rugged effusion in alliterative metre, cannot be charged as an imitation of
Chaucer, or of any other English writer of so late a date.

Another Scottish poet of this time the style and spirit as well
as the subject of whose poetry must be admitted to be exclusively
national is Henry the Minstrel, commonly called Blind Harry,
author of the famous poem on the life and acts of Wallace. The

testimony of the historian John Major to the time at which Henry wrote is sufficiently express: "The entire book of William Wallace," he says, "Henry, who was blind from his birth, composed in the time of my infancy (*meae infantiae tempore cudit*), and what things used popularly to be reported wove into popular verse, in which he was skilled." Major is believed to have been born about 1469; so that Henry's poem may be assigned to the end of the third quarter of the fifteenth century. The standard edition is that published from a manuscript dated 1488 by Dr. Jamieson along with Barbour's poem, 4to. Edin. 1820. The Wallace, which is a long poem of about 12,000 decasyllabic lines, used to be a still greater favourite than was The Bruce with the author's countrymen; and Dr. Jamieson does not hesitate to place Harry as a poet before Barbour. In this judgment, however, probably few critical readers will concur, although both Warton and Ellis, without going so far, have also acknowledged in warm terms the rude force of the Blind Minstrel's genius. It may be remarked, by the way, that were it not for Major's statement, and the common epithet that has attached itself to his name, we should scarcely have supposed that the author of Wallace had been either blind from his birth or blind at all. He nowhere himself alludes to any such circumstance. His poem, besides, abounds in descriptive passages, and in allusions to natural appearances and other objects of sight: perhaps, indeed, it might be said that there is an ostentation of that kind of writing, such as we meet with also in the modern Scotch poet Blacklock's verses, and which it may be thought is not unnatural to a blind person. Nor are his apparent literary acquirements to be very easily reconciled with Major's account, who represents him as going about reciting his verses among the nobility (*coram principibus*), and thereby obtaining food and raiment, of which, says the historian, he was worthy (*victum, et vestitum, quo dignus erat, nactus est*). "He seems," as Dr. Jamieson observes, "to have been pretty well acquainted with that kind of history which was commonly read in that period." The Doctor refers to allusions which he makes in various places to the romance histories of Hector, of Alexander the Great, of Julius Cæsar, and of Charlemagne; and he conceives that his style of writing is more richly strewed with the more peculiar phraseology of the writers of romance than that of Barbour. But what is most remarkable is that he distinctly declares his poem to be throughout a translation from the Latin. The statement, which occurs toward the conclusion, seems too express and particular to be a mere imitation of the usage of the romance-writers, many of whom appeal, but generally in very vague terms, to a Latin original for their marvels:—

> Of Wallace life wha has a further feel[1]
> May show furth mair with wit and eloquence;
> For I to this have done my diligence,
> Efter the proof given fra the Latin book
> Whilk Maister Blair in his time undertook,
> In fair Latin compiled it till ane end:
> With thir witness the mair is to commend.[2]
> Bishop Sinclair than lord was of Dunkell;
> He gat this book, and confirmed it himsell
> For very true; therefore he had no drede;[3]
> Himsell had seen great part of Wallace deed.
> His purpose was till have sent it to Rome,
> Our fader of kirk thereon to give his doom.
> But Maistre Blair and als Shir Thomas Gray
> Efter Wallace they lestit[4] mony day:
> Thir twa[5] knew best of Gud Schir Williams's deed,
> Fra sixteen year while[6] nine and twenty yeid.[7]

In another place (Book V. v. 538 *et seq.*) he says:—

> Maistre John Blair was oft in that message,
> A worthy clerk, baith wise and right savage,
> Lewit[8] he was before in Paris town
> Amang maisters in science and renown.
> Wallace and he at hame in schul had been:
> Soon efterwart, as verity is seen,
> He was the man that principal undertook,
> That first compiled in dite[9] the Latin book
> Of Wallace life, right famous in renown;
> And Thomas Gray, person of Libertown.

Blind Harry's notions of the literary character are well exemplified by his phrase of a "worthy clerk, baith wise and right savage." He himself, let his scholarship have been what it may, is in spirit as thorough a Scot as if he had never heard the sound of any other than his native tongue. His gruff patriotism speaks out in his opening lines:—

> Our antecessors, that we suld of read,
> And hold in mind their noble worthy deed,

---

[1] Knowledge.
[2] We do not profess to understand this line. *Thir* is Scotch for *these*. *Mair* is *mar* in Jamieson.
[3] Doubt.
[4] Survived (lasted).
[5] These two.
[6] Till.
[7] Went, passed.
[8] Dr. Jamieson's only interpretation is "allowed, left."
[9] Writing.

We let oweralide,[1] through very sleuthfulness,
And casts us ever till other business.
Till honour enemies is our hail[2] intent;
It has been seen in thir times bywent:
Our auld enemies comen of Saxons blud,
That never yet to Scotland wald do gud,
But ever on force and contrar hail their will,
How great kindness there has been kythe[3] them till.
It is weil known on mony divers side
How they have wrought into their mighty pride
To hald Scotland at under evermair:
But God above has made their might to pair.[4]

Of the fighting and slaying, which makes up by far the greater part of the poem, it is difficult to find a sample that is short enough for our purpose. The following is a small portion of what is called the battle of Shortwoodshaw:—

On Wallace set a bicker bauld and keen;
A bow he bare was big and well besoen,
And arrows als, baith lang and sharp with aw;[5]
No man was there that Wallace bow might draw.
Right stark he was, and in to souer gear;[6]
Bauldly he shot amang they[7] men of wer.[8]
Ane angel heade[9] to the buiks he drew
And at a shot the foremost soon he slew.
Inglis archers, that hardy war and wight,
Amang the Scots bickered with all their might;
Their aweful shot was felon[10] for to bide;
Of Wallace men they woundit sore that tide;
Few of them was sicker[11] of archery;
Better they were, all they gat even party,
In field to bide either with swerd or spear.
Wallace perceivit his men tuk mickle deir;[12]
He gart[13] them change, and stund nought in to stead;[14]
He cast all ways to save them fra the dead.[15]
Full great travail upon himself tuk he;
Of Southron men feil[16] archers he gart dee.[17]
Of Longcashier[18] bowmen was in that place
A snir[19] archer aye waitit on Wallace,

[1] Allow to slip out of memory. [2] Whole.
[3] Shown. [4] Diminish, impair.
[5] Dr. Jamieson's only interpretation is *ow*. It would almost seem as if we had here the modern Scottish *witha'* for *withall*.
[6] In sure warlike accoutrements. [7] These.
[8] War. [9] The barbed head of an arrow. [10] Terrible.
[11] Sure. [12] Took much hazard, ran much risk. [13] Caused.
[14] Stand not in their place. Perhaps it should be "o stead," that is, one place. [15] Death. [16] Many.
[17] Caused die. [18] Lancashire. [19] Skilful.

> At ane opine,[1] whar he uait to repair;
> At him he drew a sicker shot and sair
> Under the chin, through a collar of steel
> On the left side, and hurt his halse[2] some deal.
> Astonied he was, but nought greatly aghast;
> Out fra his men on him he followit fast;
> In the turning with gud will has him ta'en
> Upon the crag,[3] in sunder straik the bain.

It will be seen from this specimen that the Blind Minstrel is a vigorous versifier. His descriptions, however, though both clear and forcible, and even not unfrequently animated by a dramatic abruptness and boldness of expression, want the bounding airy spirit and flashing light of those of Barbour. As a specimen of his graver style we may give his Envoy or concluding lines:—

> Go, noble book, fulfillit of gud sentence,
> Suppose thou be barren of eloquence:
> Go, worthy book, fulfillt of suthfast deed;
> But in langage of help thou hast great need.
> Whan gud makers[4] rang weil into Scotland,
> Great harm was it that nane of them ye fand.[5]
> Yet there is part that can thee weil avance;
> Now bide thy time, and be a remembrance.
> I you besek of your benevolence,
> Wha will nought lou,[6] lak nought[7] my eloquence;
> (It is weil knawn I am a burel[8] man)
> For here is said as gudly as I can;
> My sprite feeles ne termes asperans.[9]
> Now beseek God, that giver is of grace,
> Made hell and erd,[10] and set the heaven above,
> That he us grant of his dear lastand[11] love.

PROSE WRITERS:—MORE; ELYOT; TYNDAL; CRANMER; LATIMER.

The fact most deserving of remark in the progress of English literature, for the first half of the sixteenth century, is the cultivation that now came to be bestowed upon the language in the form of prose composition,—a form always in the order of time subsequent to that of verse in the natural development of a

---

[1] Open place? [2] Neck. [3] Throat.
[4] Poets. [5] Found. [6] Love?
[7] Scoff not at. [8] Boorish, clownish.
[9] Understands no lofty (aspiring) terms. But it seems impossible that *asperans* can rhyme to *grace*.
[10] Earth. [11] Lasting.

national language and literature. Long before this date, indeed, Chaucer, in addition to what he did in his proper field, had given proof of how far his genius preceded his age by several examples of composition in prose, in which may be discerned the presence of something of the same high art with which he first elevated our poetry; but, besides that his genius drew him with greatest force to poetry, and that the foreign models upon which he seems chiefly to have formed himself led him in the same direction, the state of the English language at that day perhaps fitted it better for verse than for prose, or rather, it had not yet arrived at the point at which it could be so advantageously employed in prose as in verse. At all events Chaucer had no worthy successor as a writer of prose, any more than as a writer of poetry, till more than a century after his death. Meanwhile, however, the language, though not receiving much artificial cultivation, was still undergoing a good deal of what, in a certain sense, might be called application to literary purposes, by its employment both in public proceedings and documents, and also in many popular writings, principally on the subject of the new opinions in religion, both after and previous to the invention of printing. In this more extended use and exercise, by persons of some scholarship at least, if not bringing much artistic feeling and skill to the task of composition, it must, as a mere language, or system of vocables and grammatical forms, have not only sustained many changes and modifications, but, it is probable, acquired on the whole considerable enlargement of its capacities and powers, and been generally carried forward towards maturity under the impulse of a vigorous principle of growth and expansion. But it is not till some time after the commencement of the sixteenth century that we can properly date the rise of our classical prose literature. Perhaps the earliest compositions that are entitled to be included under that name are some of those of Sir Thomas More, especially his Life and Reign of King Edward V., which Rastell, his brother-in-law, by whom it was first printed in 1557, from, as he informs us, a copy in More's handwriting, states to have been written by him when he was under-sheriff of London, in the year 1513.* Most of More's other English writings are

* Sir Henry Ellis, however, in the Preface to his edition of Harding's Chronicle (4to. 1812), has called attention to what had not before been noticed, namely, that the writer speaks as if he had been present with Edward IV. in his last sickness, which More could not have been, being then (in 1483) only a child of three years old; and Sir Henry infers that the manuscript from which the tract was printed by Rastell, although in More's handwriting, could have been only a copy made by him of a narrative drawn up by some one else, very probably Cardinal Morton. But, of a controversial character, and are occupied about subjects both of very temporary importance, and that called up so much of the eagerness and bitterness of the author's party zeal as considerably to disturb and mar both his naturally gentle and benignant temper and the oily eloquence of his style; but this historic piece is characterized throughout by an easy narrative flow which rivals the sweetness of Herodotus. It is certainly the first English historic composition that can be said to aspire to be more than a mere chronicle.

The letter which Sir Thomas More wrote to his wife in 1528, after the burning of his house at Chelsea, affords one of the best specimens of the epistolary style of this period:—

Maistres Alyce, in my most harty wise I recommend me to you; and, whereas I am enfourmed by my son Heron of the losse of our barnes and of our neighbourn also, with all the corn that was therein, albeit (saving God's pleasure) it is gret pitie of so much good corne lost, yet sith it hath liked hym to sende us such a chaunce, we must and are bounden, not only to be content, but also to be glad of his visitacion. He sent to us all that we have loste: and, sith he hath by such a chaunce taken it away againe, his pleasure be fulfilled. Let us never grudge ther at, but take it in good worth, and hartely thank him, as well for adversitie as for prosperite. And peradventure we have more cause to thank him for our losse then for our winning; for his wisdome better seeth what is good for vs then we do our selves. Therfore I pray you be of good chere, and take all the howsold with you to church, and there thanke God, both for that he hath given us, and for that he hath taken from us, and for that he hath left us, which if it please hym he can encrease when he will. And if it please hym to leave us yet lesse, at his pleasure be it.

I pray you to make some good ensearche what my poore neighbours have loste, and bid them take no thought therfore: for and I shold not leave myself a spone, ther shal no pore neighbour of mine here no losse by any chaunce happened in my house. I pray you be with my children and your houshold merry in God. And devise some what with your frendes, what wayes wer best to take, for provision to be made for corne for our household, and for sede thys yere comming, if ye thinke it good that we kepe the ground stil in our handes. And whether ye think it good that we so shall do or not, yet I think it were not best sodenlye thus to leave it all up, and to put away our folke of our farme till we have somwhat advised us thereon. How beit if we have more nowe then ye shall nede, and which can get them other maisters, ye may then discharge us of them. But I would not that any man were sodenly sent away he wote nere wether.

---

although Morton was a person of distinguished eloquence, the style is surely far too modern to have proceeded from a writer who was born within ten years after the close of the fourteenth century, the senior of More by seventy years.

At my commlng hither I perceived none other but that I shold tary still with the Kinges Grace. But now I shal (I think), because of this chance, get leave this next weke to come home and se you : and then shall we further devyse together uppon all thinges what order shalbe best to take. And thus as hartely fare you well with all our children as ye can wishe. At Woodstok the thirde daye of Septembre by the hand of

your louing husbande
Thomas More Knight.*

Along with More, as one of the earliest writers of classic English prose, may be mentioned his friend Sir Thomas Elyot, the author of the political treatise entitled The Governor, and of various other works, one of which is a Latin and English Dictionary, the foundation of most of the compilations of the same kind that were published for a century afterwards. More was executed in 1535, and Elyot also died some years before the middle of the century. William Tyndal's admirable translations of the New Testament and of some portions of the Old, and also numerous tracts by the same early reformer in his native tongue, which he wrote with remarkable correctness as well as with great vigour and eloquence, appeared between 1520 and his death in 1536. Next in the order of time among our more eminent prose writers may be placed some of the distinguished leaders of the Reformation in the latter part of the reign of Henry VIII. and in that of Edward VI., more especially Archbishop Cranmer, whose compositions in his native tongue are of considerable volume, and are characterized, if not by any remarkable strength of expression or weight of matter, yet by a full and even flow both of words and thought. On the whole, Cranmer was the greatest writer among the founders of the English Reformation. His friends and fellow-labourers, Ridley and Latimer, were also celebrated in their day for their ready popular elocution ; but the few tracts of Ridley's that remain are less eloquent than learned, and Latimer's discourses are rather quaint and curious than either learned or eloquent in any lofty sense of that term. Latimer is stated to have been one of the first English students of the Greek language ; but this could hardly be guessed from his Sermons, which, except a few scraps of Latin, show scarcely a trace of scholarship or literature of any kind. In addressing the people from the pulpit, this honest, simple-minded bishop, feeling no exaltation either from his position or his subject, expounded the most sublime doctrines of religion in the same familiar and homely language in which the humblest or most rustic of his hearers were accustomed to chaffer

* Sir Thomas More's Works, by Rastell, 4to. 1557, pp. 1418, 1419.

with one another in the market-place about the price of a yard of cloth or a pair of shoes. Nor, indeed, was he more fastidious as to matter than as to manner: all the preachers of that age were accustomed to take a wide range over things in general, but Latimer went beyond everybody else in the miscellaneous assortment of topics he used to bring together from every region of heaven and earth,—of the affairs of the world that now is as well as of that which is to come. Without doubt his sermons must have been lively and entertaining far beyond the common run of that kind of compositions; the allusions with which they abounded to public events, and to life in all its colours and grades, from the palace to the cottage, from the prince to the peasant,—the anecdotes of his own experience and the other stories the old man would occasionally intersperse among his strictures and exhortations,—the expressiveness of his unscrupulous and often startling phraseology,—all this, combined with the earnestness, piety, and real goodness and simplicity of heart that breathed from every word he uttered, may well be conceived to have had no little charm for the multitudes that crowded to hear his living voice; even as to us, after the lapse of three centuries, these sermons of Latimer's are still in the highest degree interesting both for the touches they contain in illustration of the manners and social condition of our forefathers, and as a picture of a very peculiar individual mind. They are also of some curiosity and value as a monument of the language of the period; but to what is properly to be called its literature, as we have said, they can hardly be considered as belonging at all.

Generally it may be observed, with regard to the English prose of the earlier part of the sixteenth century that it is both more simple in its construction, and of a more purely native character in other respects, than the style which came into fashion in the latter years of the Elizabethan period. When first made use of in prose composition, the mother-tongue was written as it was spoken; even such artifices and embellishments as are always prompted by the nature of verse were here scarcely aspired after or thought of; that which was addressed to and specially intended for the instruction of the people was set down as far as possible in the familiar forms and fashions of the popular speech, in genuine native words, and direct unincumbered sentences; no painful imitation of any learned or foreign model was attempted, nor any species of elaboration whatever, except what was necessary for mere perspicuity, in a kind of writing which was scarcely regarded as partaking of the character of literary composition at all. The delicacy of a scholarly taste no doubt influenced even the English style of such writers as More and his more eminent contemporaries or immediate followers; but whatever eloquence or dignity their compositions thus acquired was not the effect of any professed or conscious endeavour to write in English as they would have written in what were called the learned tongues.

The age, indeed, of the critical cultivation of the language for the purposes of prose composition had already commenced; but at first that object was pursued in the best spirit and after the wisest methods. Erasmus, in one of his Letters, mentions that his friend Dean Colet laboured to improve his English style by the diligent perusal and study of Chaucer and the other old poets, in whose works alone the popular speech was to be found turned with any taste or skill to a literary use; and doubtless others of our earliest classic prose writers took lessons in their art in the same manner from these true fathers of our vernacular literature. And even the first professed critics and reformers of the language that arose among us proceeded in the main in a right direction and upon sound principles in the task they undertook. The appearance of a race of critical and rhetorical writers in any country is, in truth, always rather a symptom or indication than, what it has frequently been denounced as being, a cause of the corruption and decline of the national literature. The writings of Dionysius of Halicarnassus and of Quintilian, for instance, certainly did not hasten, but probably rather contributed to retard, the decay of the literature of ancient Greece and Rome. The first eminent English writer of this class was the celebrated Roger Ascham, the tutor of Queen Elizabeth, whose treatise entitled Toxophilus, the School or Partitions of Shooting, was published in 1545. The design of Ascham, in this performance, was not only to recommend to his countrymen the use of their old national weapon, the bow, but to set before them an example and model of a pure and correct English prose style. In his dedication of the work, To all the Gentlemen and Yeomen of England, he recommends to him that would write well in any tongue the counsel of Aristotle,—"To speak as the common people do, to think as wise men do." From this we may perceive that Ascham had a true feeling of the regard due to the great fountain-head and oracle of the national language—the vocabulary of the common people. He goes on to reprobate the practice of many English writers, who by introducing into their compositions, in violation of the Aristotelian precept, many words of foreign origin, Latin, French, and Italian, made all things dark and hard. "Once," he says, "I communed with a man which reasoned the English tongue to be enriched and increased thereby, saying. Who will not praise that feast where a man shall drink at a dinner both wine, ale, and beer? Truly, quoth I, they be all good, every one taken by himself alone: but if you put malmsey and sack, red wine and white, ale and beer and all, in one pot, you shall make a drink neither easy to be known, nor yet wholesome for the body." The English language, however, it may be observed, had even already become too thoroughly and essentially a mixed tongue for this doctrine of purism to be admitted to the letter; nor, indeed, to take up Ascham's illustration, is it universally true, even in regard to liquids, that a salutary and palatable beverage can never be made by the interfusion of two or more different kinds. Our tongue is now, and was many centuries ago, not, indeed, in its grammatical structure, but in its vocabulary, as substantially and to as great an extent Neo-Latin as Gothic; it would be as completely torn in pieces and left the mere tattered rag of a language, useless for all the purposes of speaking as well as of writing, by having the foreign as by having the native element taken out of it. Ascham in his own writings uses many words of French and Latin origin (the latter mostly derived through the medium of the French); nay, the common people themselves of necessity did in his day, as they do still, use many such foreign words, or words not of English origin, and could scarcely have held communication with one another on the most ordinary occasions without so doing. It is another question whether it might not have been more fortunate if the original form of the national speech had remained in a state of celibacy and virgin purity; by the course of events the Gothic part of the language has, in point of fact, been married to the Latin part of it; and what God or nature has thus joined together it is now beyond the competency of man to put asunder. The language, while it subsists, must continue to be the product of that union, and nothing else. As for Ascham's own style, both in his Toxophilus, and in his Schoolmaster, published in 1571, three years after the author's death, it is not only clear and correct, but idiomatic and muscular. That it is not rich or picturesque is the consequence of the character of the writer's mind, which was rather rhetorical than poetical. The publication of Ascham's Toxophilus was soon followed by an elaborate treatise expressly dedicated to the subject of English composition—The Art of Rhetorick, for the use of all such as are studious of Eloquence, set forth in English, by Thomas Wilson. Wilson, whose work appeared in 1553, takes pains to impress the same principles that Ascham had laid down before him with regard to purity of style and the general rule of writing well. But the very solicitude thus shown by the ablest and most distinguished of those who now assumed the guardianship of the vernacular tongue to protect it from having its native character overlaid and debased by an intermixture of terms borrowed from other languages, may be taken as evidence that such debasement was actually at this time going on; that our ancient English was beginning to be oppressed and half suffocated by additions from foreign sources brought in upon it faster than it could absorb and assimilate them. Wilson, indeed, proceeds to complain that this was the case. While some "powdered their talk with over-sea language," others, whom he designates as "the unlearned or foolish fantastical, that smell but of learning," were wont, he says, "so to Latin their tongues," that simple persons could not but wonder at their talk, and think they surely spake by some revelation from heaven. It may be suspected, however, that this affectation of unnecessary terms, formed from the ancient languages, was not confined to mere pretenders to learning. Another well-known critical writer of this period, Webster Puttenham, in his Art of English Poesy, published in 1582, but believed to have been written a good many years earlier, in like manner advises the avoidance in writing of such words and modes of expression as are used "in the marches and frontiers, or in port towns where strangers haunt for traffic sake, or yet in universities, where scholars use much peevish affectation of words out of the primitive languages;" and he warns his readers that in some books were already to be found "many inkhorn terms so ill affected, brought in by men of learning, as preachers and schoolmasters, and many strange terms of other languages by secrotaries, and merchants, and travellers, and many dark words, and not usual nor well-sounding, though they be daily spoken at court." On the whole, however, Puttenham considers the best standard both for speaking and writing to be "the usual speech of the court, and that of London and the shires lying about London within sixty miles, and not much above." This judgment is probably correct, although the writer was a gentleman pensioner, and perhaps also a cockney by birth.

Scottish Prose Writers.

Before the middle of the sixteenth century a few prose writers had also appeared in the Scottish dialect. The Scottish History of Hector Boethius, or Boecius (Boece or Boyce), translated from the Latin by John Bellenden, was printed at Edinburgh in 1537; and a translation by the same person of the first Five Books of Livy remained in MS. till it was published at Edinburgh, in 4to. in 1829; a second edition of the translation of Boecius having also been brought out there, in two vols. 4to., the same year. But the most remarkable composition in Scottish prose of this era is The Complaynt of Scotland, printed at St. Andrews in 1548, which has been variously assigned to Sir James Inglis, knight, a country gentleman of Fife, who died in 1554; to Wedderburn, the supposed author of the Compendious Book of Godly and Spiritual Sangs and Ballats (reprinted from the edition of 1621 by Sir John Grahame Dalzell, 8vo. Edinburgh, 1801); and by its modern editor, the late John Leyden, in the elaborate and ingenious Dissertation prefixed to his reprint of the work, 8vo. Edinburgh, 1801, to the famous poet, Sir David Lyndsay.

It is worthy of remark, that, although in this work we have unquestionably the Scottish dialect, distinctly marked by various peculiarities (indeed the author in his prologue or preface expressly and repeatedly states that he has written in Scotch, "in our Scottis-langage," as he calls it), yet one chief characteristic of the modern Scotch is still wanting—the suppression of the final *l* after a vowel or diphthong—just as it is in Barbour and Blind Harry. This change, as we before remarked, is probably very modern. It has taken place in all likelihood since Scotch ceased to be generally used in writing; the principle of growth, which, after a language passes under the government of the pen, is to a great extent suspended, having recovered its activity on the dialect being abandoned again to the comparatively lawless liberty, or at least looser guardianship, of the lips.

ENGLISH POETS:—HAWES; BARKLAY.

The English poetical literature of the first half of the sixteenth century may be fairly described as the dawn of a new day. Two poetic names of some note belong to the reign of Henry VII.—Stephen Hawes and Alexander Barklay. Hawes is the author of many pieces, but is chiefly remembered for his Pastime of Pleasure, or History of Grand Amour and La Belle Pucelle, first printed by Wynkyn de Worde in 1517, but written about two years earlier. Warton holds this performance to be almost the only effort of imagination and invention which had appeared in our poetry since Chaucer, and eulogizes it as containing no common touches of romantic and allegoric fiction.

Hawes was both a scholar and a traveller, and was perfectly familiar with the French and Italian poetry as well as with that of his own country. It speaks very little, however, for his taste, that, among the preceding English poets, he has evidently made Lydgate his model, even if it should be admitted that, as Warton affirms, he has added some new graces to the manner of that cold and wordy versifier. Lydgate and Hawes may stand together as perhaps the two writers who, in the century and a half that followed the death of Chaucer, contributed most to carry forward the regulation and modernisation of the language which he began. Barklay, who did not die till 1552, when he had attained a great age, employed his pen principally in translations, in which line his most celebrated performance is his Ship of Fools, from the German of Sebastian Brandt, which was printed in 1508. Barklay, however, besides consulting both a French and a Latin version of Brandt's poem, has enlarged his original with the enumeration and description of a considerable variety of follies which he found flourishing among his own countrymen. This gives the work some value as a record of the English manners of the time; but both its poetical and its satirical pretensions are of the very humblest order. At this date most of our writers of what was called poetry seem to have been occupied with the words in which they were to clothe their ideas almost to the exclusion of all the higher objects of the poetic art. And that, perhaps, is what of necessity happens at a particular stage in the progress of a nation's literature—at the stage corresponding to the transition state in the growth of the human being between the termination of free rejoicing boyhood and the full assurance of manhood begun; which is peculiarly the season not of achievement but of preparation, not of accomplishing ends, but of acquiring the use of means and instruments, and also, it may be added, of the aptitude to mistake the one of these things for the other.

SKELTON.

But the poetry with the truest life in it produced in the reign of Henry the Seventh and the earlier part of that of his son is undoubtedly that of Skelton. John Skelton may have been born about or soon after 1460; he studied at Cambridge, if not at both universities; began to write and publish compositions in verse between 1480 and 1490; was graduated as poet laureat (a degree in grammar, including versification and rhetoric) at Oxford before 1490; was admitted *ad eundem* at Cambridge in 1493; in 1498 took holy orders; was probably about the same time appointed tutor to the young prince Henry, afterwards Henry the Eighth; was eventually promoted to be rector of Diss in Norfolk; and died in 1529 in the sanctuary at Westminster Abbey, where he had taken refuge to escape the vengeance of Cardinal Wolsey, originally his patron, but latterly the chief butt at which he had been wont to shoot his satiric shafts. As a scholar Skelton had a European reputation in his own day; and the great Erasmus has styled him *Britannicarum literarum decus et lumen* (the light and ornament of English letters). His Latin verses are distinguished by their purity and classical spirit. As for his English poetry, it is generally more of a mingled yarn, and of a much coarser fabric. In many of his effusions indeed, poured forth in sympathy with or in aid of some popular cry of the day, he is little better than a rhyming buffoon; much of his ribaldry is now nearly unintelligible; and it may be doubted if a considerable portion of his grotesque and apparently incoherent jingle ever had much more than the sort of half meaning with which a half-tipsy writer may satisfy readers as far gone as himself. Even in the most reckless of these compositions, however, he rattles along, through sense and nonsense, with a vivacity that had been a stranger to our poetry for many a weary day; and his freedom and spirit, even where most unrefined, must have been exhilarating after the long fit of somnolency in which the English muse had dozed away the last hundred years. But much even of Skelton's satiric verse is instinct with genuine poetical vigour, and a fancy alert, sparkling, and various, to a wonderful degree. The charm of his writing lies in its natural ease and freedom, its inexhaustible and untiring vivacity; and these qualities are found both in their greatest abundance and their greatest purity where his subject is suggestive of the simplest emotions and has most of a universal interest. His Book of Philip Sparrow, for instance, an elegy on the sparrow of fair Jane Scroop, slain by a cat in the nunnery of Carow, near Norwich, extending (with the "commendation" of the "goodly maid") to nearly 1400 lines, is unrivalled in the language for elegant and elastic playfulness, and a spirit of whim that only kindles into the higher blaze the longer it is kept up. The second part, or "Commendation," in particular, is throughout animated and hilarious to a wonderful degree:—the *refrain*,—

> For this most goodly flower,
> This blossom of fresh colour,
> So Jupiter me succour,
> She flourisheth new and new
> In beauty and virtue;
> *Hac claritate genuina,*
> *O Gloriosa femina,* &c.—

recurring often so suddenly and unexpectedly, yet always so naturally, has an effect like that of the harmonious evolutions of some lively and graceful dance. Have we not in this poem, by-the-by, the true origin of Skelton's peculiar dancing verse? Is it not Anacreontic, as the spirit also of the best of his poetry undoubtedly is?*

ROY; JOHN HEYWOOD.

Along with Skelton, viewed as he commonly has been only as a satirist, is usually classed William Roy, a writer who assisted Tyndal in his translation of the New Testament, and who is asserted by Bale to be the author of a singular work entitled, Read me and be not wroth, For I say nothing but troth, which is supposed to have been first printed abroad about 1525.† This is also a satire upon Wolsey and the clergy in general, and is as bitter as might be expected from the supposed author, who, having begun his life as a friar, spent the best part of it in the service of the Reformation, and finished it at the stake. Among the buffoon-poets of this age, is also to be reckoned John Heywood, styled the Epigrammatist, from the six centuries of Epigrams, or versified jokes, which form a remarkable portion of his works. Heywood's conversational jocularity has the equivocal credit of having been exceedingly consoling both to the old age of Henry VIII. and to his daughter Queen Mary : it must have been strong jesting that could stir the sense of the ludicrous in either of those terrible personages. Besides a number of plays, which are the most important of his productions, Heywood also wrote a long burlesque allegory, which fills a thick quarto volume, on the dispute between the old and the new religions, under the title of A Parable of the Spider and the Fly; where it appears that by the spider is intended the Pro-

---

* A most valuable and acceptable present has been made to the lovers of our old poetry in a collected edition of Skelton's Poetical Works, 2 vols. 8vo. Lond. Rodd. 1843, by the Rev. Alexander Dyce, who has performed his difficult task in a manner to leave little or nothing further to be desired.

† Ritson's Bibliog. Poet. p. 318.

testant party, by the fly the Catholic, but in which, according to the judgment of old Harrison, "he dealeth so profoundly, and beyond all measure of skill, that neither he himself that made it, neither any one that readeth it, can reach unto the meaning thereof."*

SCOTTISH POETS:—GAWIN DOUGLAS; DUNBAR; LYNDSAY.

But, while in England the new life to which poetry had awakened had thus as yet produced so little except ribaldry and buffoonery, it is remarkable that in Scotland, where general social civilization was much less advanced, the art had continued to be cultivated in its highest departments with great success, and the language had already been enriched with some compositions worthy of any age. Perhaps the Scottish poetry of the earlier part of the sixteenth century may be regarded as the same spring which had visited England in the latter part of the fourteenth,—the impulse originally given by the poetry of Chaucer only now come to its height in that northern clime. Gawin Douglas, Bishop of Dunkeld, who flourished in the first quarter of the sixteenth century, and who is famous for his translation of the Æneid, the first metrical version of any ancient classic that had yet appeared in the dialect of either kingdom, affects great anxiety to eschew "Southron," or English, and to write his native tongue in all its breadth and plainness; but it does not follow, from his avoidance of English words, that he may not have formed himself to a great extent on the study of English models. At the same time it may be admitted that neither in his translation nor in his original works of King Hart, and the Palace of Honour,—which are two long allegories, full, the latter especially, of passages of great descriptive beauty,—does Douglas convict himself of belonging to the school of Chaucer. He is rather, if not the founder, at least the chief representative, of a style of poetry which was attempted to be formed in Scotland by enriching and elevating the simplicity of Barbour and his immediate followers with an infusion of something of what was deemed a classic manner, drawn in part directly from the Latin writers, but more from those of the worst than those of the best age, in part from the French poetry, which now began in like manner to aspire towards a classic tone. This preference, by the Scottish poets, of Latin and French to "Southron," as a source from which to supply the

* Description of England.

deficiencies of their native dialect, had probably no more reasonable origin than the political circumstances and feelings of the nation: the spirit of the national genius was antagonistic to it, and it therefore never could become more than a temporary fashion. Yet it infected more or less all the writers of this age; and amongst the rest, to a considerable extent, by far the greatest of them all, William Dunbar. This admirable master, alike of serious and of comic song, may justly be styled the Chaucer of Scotland, whether we look to the wide range of his genius, or to his eminence in every style over all the poets of his country who preceded and all who for ages came after him. That of Burns is certainly the only name among the Scottish poets that can yet be placed on the same line with that of Dunbar; and even the inspired ploughman, though the equal of Dunbar in comic power, and his superior in depth of passion, is not to be compared with the elder poet either in strength or in general fertility of imagination. Finally, to close the list, comes another eminent name, that of Sir David Lyndsay, whose productions are not indeed characterised by any high imaginative power, but yet display infinite wit, spirit, and variety in all the forms of the more familiar poetry. Lyndsay was the favourite, throughout his brief reign and life, of the accomplished and unfortunate James V., and survived to do perhaps as good service as any in the war against the ancient church by the tales, plays, and other products of his abounding satiric vein, with which he fed, and excited, and lashed up the popular contempt for the now crazy and tumbling fabric once so imposing and so venerated. Perhaps he also did no harm by thus taking off a little of the acrid edge of mere resentment and indignation with the infusion of a dash of merriment, and keeping alive a genial sense of the ludicrous in the midst of such serious work. If Dunbar is to be compared to Burns, Lyndsay may be said to have his best representative among the more recent Scottish poets in Allan Ramsay, who does not, however, come so near to Lyndsay by a long way as Burns does to Dunbar.

SURREY; WYATT.

Lyndsay is supposed to have survived till about the year 1567. Before that date a revival of the higher poetry had come upon England like the rising of a new day. Two names are commonly placed together at the head of our new poetical literature, Lord Surrey and Sir Thomas Wyatt. Henry Howard, Earl of Surrey, memorable in our history as the last victim of the capricious and sanguinary tyranny of Henry VIII., had already, in his short life, which was terminated by the axe of the executioner in his twenty-seventh year, carried away from all his countrymen the laurels both of knighthood and of song. The superior polish alone of the best of Surrey's verses would place him at an immeasurable distance in advance of all his immediate predecessors. So remarkable, indeed, is the contrast in this respect which his poetry presents to theirs, that in modern times there has been claimed for Surrey, as we have seen, the honour of having been the first to introduce our existing system of rhythm into the language. The true merit of Surrey is, that, proceeding upon the same system of versification which had been introduced by Chaucer, and which, indeed, had in principle been followed by all the writers after Chaucer, however rudely or imperfectly some of them may have succeeded in the practice of it, he restored to our poetry a correctness, polish, and general spirit of refinement such as it had not known since Chaucer's time, and of which, therefore, in the language as now spoken, there was no previous example whatever. To this it may be added that he appears to have been the first, at least in this age, who sought to modulate his strains after that older poetry of Italy, which thenceforward became one of the chief fountainheads of inspiration to that of England throughout the whole space of time over which is shed the golden light of the names of Spenser, of Shakespeare, and of Milton. Surrey's own imagination was neither rich nor soaring; and the highest qualities of his poetry, in addition to the facility and general mechanical perfection of the versification, are delicacy and tenderness. It is altogether a very light and bland Favonian breeze. The poetry of his friend Wyatt is of a different character, neither so flowing in form nor so uniformly gentle in spirit, but perhaps making up for its greater ruggedness by a force and a depth of sentiment occasionally which Surrey does not reach. The poems of Lord Surrey and Sir Thomas Wyatt were first published together in 1557.

To Surrey we owe the introduction into the language of our present form of blank verse, the suggestion of which he probably took from the earliest Italian example of that form of poetry, a translation of the First and Fourth Books of the Æneid by the Cardinal Hippolito de' Medici (or, as some say, by Francesco Maria Molsa), which was published at Venice in 1541. A translation of the same two Books into English blank verse appeared in the collection of Surrey's Poems published by Tottel in 1557. Dr. Nott has shown that this translation was founded upon the metrical Scottish version of Gawin Douglas, which, although not published till 1553, had been finished, as the author himself informs us, in 1513. But it ought not to be forgotten that, as already remarked, we have one example at least of another form of blank verse in the Ormulum, centuries before Surrey's day.

THE ELIZABETHAN LITERATURE.

Of what is commonly called our Elizabethan literature, the greater portion appertains to the reign, not of Elizabeth, but of James—to the seventeenth, not to the sixteenth century. The common name, nevertheless, is the fair and proper one. It sprung up in the age of Elizabeth, and was mainly the product of influences which belonged to that age, although their effect extended into another. It was born of and ripened by that sunny morning of a new day,—"great Eliza's golden time,"— when a general sense of security had given men ease of mind and disposed them to freedom of thought, while the economical advancement of the country put life and spirit into everything, and its growing power and renown filled and elevated the national heart. But such periods of quiet and prosperity seem only to be intellectually productive when they have been preceded and ushered in by a time of uncertainty and struggle which has tried men's spirits: the contrast seems to be wanted to make the favourable influences be felt and tell; or the faculty required must come in part out of the strife and contention. The literature of our Elizabethan age, more emphatically, may be said to have had this double parentage: if that brilliant day was its mother, the previous night of storm was its father.

THE MIRROR FOR MAGISTRATES.

Our classical Elizabethan poetry and other literature dates only from about the middle of the reign; most of what was produced in the earlier half of it, constrained, harsh, and immature, still bears upon it the impress of the preceding barbarism. Nearly coincident with its commencement is the first appearance of a singular work, The Mirror for Magistrates. It is a collection of narratives of the lives of various remarkable English historical personages, taken, in general, with little more embellishment than their reduction to a metrical form, from the common popular chronicles; and the idea of it appears to have been borrowed from a Latin work of Boccaccio's, which had been translated and versified many years before by Lydgate, under the title of The Fall of Princes. It was planned and begun (it is supposed about the year 1557) by Thomas Sackville, afterwards distinguished as a statesman, and ennobled by the titles of Lord Buckhurst and Earl of Dorset. But Sackville soon found himself obliged to relinquish the execution of his extensive design, which contemplated a survey of the whole range of English history from William the Conqueror to the end of the wars of the Roses, to other hands. The two writers to whom he recommended the carrying on of the work were Richard Baldwynne, who was in orders, and had already published a metrical version of the Song of Solomon, and George Ferrers, who was a person of some rank, having sat in parliament in the time of Henry VIII., but who had latterly been chiefly known as a composer of occasional interludes for the diversion of the Court. It is a trait of the times that, although a member of Lincoln's Inn, and known both as a legal and an historical author, Ferrers was in 1552-3 appointed by Edward VI. to preside over the Christmas revels at the royal palace of Greenwich in the office of Lord of Misrule: Stow tells us that upon this occasion he "so pleasantly and wisely behaved himself, that the king had great delight in his pastimes." Baldwynne and Ferrers called other writers to their assistance, among whom were Thomas Churchyard, Phaer, the translator of Virgil, &c.; and the book, in its first form and extent, was published in a quarto volume in 1559. The Mirror for Magistrates immediately acquired and for a considerable time retained great popularity; a second edition of it was published in 1563; a third in 1571; a fourth, with the addition of a series of new lives from the fabulous history of the early Britons, by John Higgins, in 1574; a fifth, in 1587; a sixth, with further additions, in 1610, by Richard Nichols, assisted by Thomas Blenerhasset (whose contributions, however, had been separately printed in 1578).* The copiousness of the plan, into which any narrative might be inserted belonging to either the historical or legendary part of the national annals, and that without any trouble in the way of connexion or adaptation, had made the work a receptacle for the contributions of all the ready versifiers of the day—a common, or parish green, as it were, on which a fair was held to which any one who chose might bring his wares

* A reprint of the Mirror for Magistrates, in 2 (sometimes divided into 3) vols. 4to., was brought out by the late Mr. Haslewood in 1815.

—or rather a sort of continually growing monument, or cairn, to which every man added his stone, or little separate specimen of brick and mortar, who conceived himself to have any skill in building the lofty rhyme. There were scarcely any limits to the size to which the book might have grown, except the mutability of the public taste, which will permit no one thing, good or bad, to go on for ever. The Mirror for Magistrates, however, for all its many authors, is of note in the history of our poetry for nothing else which it contains, except the portions contributed by its contriver Sackville, consisting only of one legend, that of Henry, Duke of Buckingham (Richard the Third's famous accomplice and victim, and grandfather of Lord Stafford, the great patron of the work), and the introduction, or Induction, as it is called, prefixed to that narrative, which however is said to have been originally intended to stand at the head of the whole work. Both for his poetical genius, and in the history of the language, Sackville and his two poems in the Mirror for Magistrates—more especially this Induction—must be considered as forming the connecting link or bridge between Chaucer and Spenser, between the Canterbury Tales and the Fairy Queen.

Nothing is wanting to Sackville that belongs to force either of conception or of expression. In his own world of the sombre and sad, also, he is almost as great an inventor as he is a colourist; and Spenser has been indebted to him for many hints, as well as for example and inspiration in a general sense: what most marks the immaturity of his style is a certain operose and constrained air, a stiffness and hardness of manner, like what we find in the works of the earliest school of the Italian painters, before Raphael and Michael Angelo arose to convert the art from a painful repetition or mimicry of reality into a process of creation—from the timid slave of nature into her glorified rival. Of the flow and variety, the genuine spirit of light and life, that we have in Spenser and Shakespeare, there is little in Sackville; his poetry—ponderous, gloomy, and monotonous—is still oppressed by the shadows of night; and we see that, although the darkness is retiring, the sun has not yet risen.

Origin of the Regular Drama.

From the first introduction of dramatic representations in England, probably as early, at least, as the beginning of the twelfth century, down to the beginning of the fifteenth, or perhaps somewhat later, the only species of drama known was that styled the

Miracle, or Miracle-play. The subjects of the miracle-plays were all taken from the histories of the Old and New Testament, or from the legends of saints and martyrs; and, indeed, it is probable that their original design was chiefly to instruct the people in religious knowledge. They were often acted as well as written by clergymen, and were exhibited in abbeys, in churches, and in churchyards, on Sundays or other holidays. It appears to have been not till some time after their first introduction that miracle-plays came to be annually represented under the direction and at the expense of the guilds or trading companies of towns, as at Chester and elsewhere. The characters, or *dramatis personæ*, of the miracle-plays, though sometimes supernatural or legendary, were always actual personages, historical or imaginary; and in that respect these primitive plays approached nearer to the regular drama than those by which they were succeeded—the Morals, or Moral-plays, in which, not a history, but an apologue was represented, and in which the characters were all allegorical. The moral-plays are traced back to the early part of the reign of Henry VI., and they appear to have gradually arisen out of the miracle-plays, in which, of course, characters very nearly approaching in their nature to the impersonated vices and virtues of the new species of drama must have occasionally appeared. The Devil of the Miracles, for example, would very naturally suggest the Vice of the Morals; which latter, however, it is to be observed, also retained the Devil of their predecessors, who was too amusing and popular a character to be discarded. Nor did the moral-plays altogether put down the miracle-plays: in many of the provincial towns, at least, the latter continued to be represented almost to as late a date as the former. Finally, by a process of natural transition very similar to that by which the sacred and supernatural characters of the religious drama had been converted into the allegorical personifications of the moral-plays, these last, gradually becoming less and less vague and shadowy, at length, about the middle of the sixteenth century, boldly assumed life and reality, giving birth to the first examples of regular tragedy and comedy.

Both moral-plays, however, and even the more ancient miracle-plays, continued to be occasionally performed down to the very end of the sixteenth century. One of the last dramatic representations at which Elizabeth was present, was a moral-play, entitled The Contention between Liberality and Prodigality, which was performed before her majesty in 1600, or 1601. This production was printed in 1602, and was probably written not long before that time: it has been said to have been the joint production of

Thomas Lodge and Robert Greene, the last of whom died in 1592. The only three manuscripts of the Chester miracle-plays now extant were written in 1600, 1604, and 1607, most probably while the plays still continued to be acted. There is evidence that the ancient annual miracle-plays were acted at Tewkesbury at least till 1585, at Coventry till 1591, at Newcastle till 1598, and at Kendal down even to the year 1603.

As has been observed, however, by Mr. Collier, the latest and best historian of the English drama, the moral-plays were enabled to keep possession of the stage so long as they did, partly by means of the approaches they had for some time been making to a more improved species of composition, "and partly because, under the form of allegorical fiction and abstract character, the writers introduced matter which covertly touched upon public events, popular prejudices, and temporary opinions."* He mentions, in particular, the moral entitled The Three Ladies of London, printed in 1584, and its continuation, The Three Lords and Three Ladies of London, which appeared in 1590 (both by R. W.), as belonging to this class.

INTERLUDES OF JOHN HEYWOOD.

Meanwhile, long before the earliest of these dates, the ancient drama had, in other hands, assumed wholly a new form. Mr. Collier appears to consider the Interludes of John Heywood, the earliest of which must have been written before 1521, as first exhibiting the moral-play in a state of transition to the regular tragedy and comedy. "John Heywood's dramatic productions," he says, "almost form a class by themselves: they are neither miracle-plays nor moral-plays, but what may be properly and strictly called interludes, a species of writing of which he has a claim to be considered the inventor, although the term interlude was applied generally to theatrical productions in the reign of Edward IV." A notion of the nature of these compositions may be collected from the plot of one of them, A Merry Play betwene the Pardoner and the Frere, the Curate and neighbour Pratte, printed in 1533, of which Mr. Collier gives the following account:—"A pardoner and a friar have each obtained leave of the curate to use his church,—the one for the exhibition of his relics, and the other for the delivery of a sermon—the object of both being the same, that of procuring money. The friar arrives first, and is about to commence his discourse, when the pardoner enters

* Hist. of Dramatic Poetry, ii. 413.

and disturbs him; each is desirous of being heard, and, after many vain attempts by force of lungs, they proceed to force of arms, kicking and cuffing each other unmercifully. The curate, called by the disturbance in his church, endeavours, without avail, to part the combatants; he therefore calls in neighbour Pratte to his assistance, and, while the curate seizes the friar, Pratte undertakes to deal with the pardoner, in order that they may set them in the stocks. It turns out that both the friar and the pardoner are too much for their assailants; and the latter, after a sound drubbing, are glad to come to a composition, by which the former are allowed quietly to depart."* Here, then, we have a dramatic fable, or incident at least, conducted not by allegorical personifications, but by characters of real life, which is the essential difference that distinguishes the true tragedy or comedy from the mere moral. Heywood's interludes, however, of which there are two or three more of the same description with this (besides others partaking more of the allegorical character), are all only single acts, or, more properly, scenes, and exhibit, therefore, nothing more than the mere rudiments or embryo of the regular comedy.

UDALL'S RALPH ROISTER DOISTER.

The earliest English comedy, properly so called, that has yet been discovered, is commonly considered to be that of Ralph Roister Doister, the production of Nicholas Udall, an eminent classical scholar in the earlier part of the sixteenth century, and one of the masters, first at Eton, and afterwards at Westminster. Its existence was unknown till a copy was discovered in 1818, which perhaps (for the title-page is gone) was not printed earlier than 1566, in which year Thomas Hackett is recorded in the register of the Stationers' Company to have had a licence for printing a play entitled Rauf Ruyster Duster; but the play is quoted in Thomas Wilson's Rule of Reason, first printed in 1551, so that it must have been written at least fifteen or sixteen years before.† This hypothesis would carry it back to about the same date with the earliest of Heywood's interludes; and it certainly was produced while that writer was still alive and in the height of his popularity. It may be observed that Wilson calls Udall's play an interlude, which would therefore seem to have been at this time the common name for any dramatic composition, as, indeed, it appears to have been for nearly a century preceding.

* Hist. of Dramatic Poetry, ii. 386. † See Collier, ii. 446.

The author himself, however, in his prologue, announces it as a Comedy, or Interlude, and as an imitation of the classical models of Plautus and Terence.

And, in truth, both in character and in plot, Ralph Roister Doister has every right to be regarded as a true comedy, showing indeed, in its execution, the rudeness of the age, but in its plan, and in reference to the principle upon which it is constructed, as regular and as complete as any comedy in the language. It is divided into acts and scenes, which very few of the moral-plays are; and, according to Mr. Collier's estimate, the performance could not have been concluded in less time than about two hours and a half, while few of the morals would require more than about an hour for their representation.* The dramatis personæ are thirteen in all, nine male and four female; and the two principal ones at least—Ralph himself, a vain, thoughtless, blustering fellow, whose ultimately baffled pursuit of the gay and rich widow Custance forms the action of the piece; and his servant, Matthew Merrygreek, a kind of flesh-and-blood representative of the Vice of the old moral-plays—are strongly discriminated, and drawn altogether with much force and spirit. The story is not very ingeniously involved, but it moves forward through its gradual development, and onwards to the catastrophe, in a sufficiently bustling, lively manner; and some of the situations, though the humour is rather farcical than comic, are very cleverly conceived and managed. The language also may be said to be on the whole, racy and characteristic, if not very polished. A few lines from a speech of one of the widow's handmaidens, Tibet Talkapace, in a conversation with her fellow-servants on the approaching marriage of their masters, may be quoted as a specimen:—

> And I heard our Nourse speake of an husbande to-day
> Ready for our mistresse; a rich man and a gay:
> And we shall go in our French hoodes every day;
> In our silke cassocks (I warrant you) freshe and gay;
> In our tricke ferdigews, and billiments of golde,
> Brave in our sutes of chaunge, seven double folde.
> Then shall ye see Tibet, sirs, treade the mowe so trimme;
> Nay, why sald I treade? ye shall see hir glide and swimme,
> Not lumperdee, clomperdee, like our spaniell Rig.

---

* See Collier, ii. 45.

GAMMER GURTON'S NEEDLE.

Ralph Roister Doister is in every way a very superior production to Gammer Gurton's Needle, which, before the discovery of Udall's piece, had the credit of being the first regular English comedy. At the same time, it must be admitted that the superior antiquity assigned to Ralph Roister Doister is not very conclusively made out. All that we know with certainty with regard to the date of the play is, that it was in existence in 1551. The oldest edition of Gammer Gurton's Needle is dated 1575 : but how long the play may have been composed before that year is uncertain. The title-page of the 1575 edition describes it as "played on the stage not long ago in Christ's College, in Cambridge;" and Warton, on the authority of a manuscript memorandum by Oldys, the eminent antiquary of the early part of the last century, says that it was written and first printed in 1551. Wright also, in his Historia Histrionica, first printed in 1660, states it as his opinion that it was written in the reign of Edward VI. In refutation of all this it is alleged that "it could not have been produced so early, because John Still (afterwards bishop of Bath and Wells), the author of it, was not born until 1543; and, consequently, in 1552, taking Warton's latest date, would only have been nine years old.* But the evidence that Bishop Still was the author of Gammer Gurton's Needle is exceedingly slight. The play is merely stated on the title-page to have been "made by Mr. S., Master of Arts;" and even if there was, as is asserted, no other Master of Arts of Christ's College whose name began with S. at the time when this title-page was printed, the author of the play is not stated to have been of that college, nor, if he were, is it necessary to assume that he was living in 1575. On the whole, therefore, while there is no proof that Ralph Roister Doister is older that the year 1551, it is by no means certain that Gammer Gurton's Needle was not written in that same year.

This "right pithy, pleasant, and merie comedie," as it is designated on the title-page, is, like Udall's play, regularly divided into acts and scenes, and, like it too, is written in rhyme—the language and versification being, on the whole, perhaps rather more easy than flowing—a circumstance which, more than any external evidence that has been produced, would incline us to assign it to a somewhat later date. But it is in all respects a very tame and poor performance—the plot, if so it can be

* Collier, ii. 444.

called, meagre to insipidity and silliness, the characters only a few slightly distinguished varieties of the lowest life, and the dialogue in general as feeble and undramatic as the merest monotony can make it. Its merriment is of the coarsest and most boisterous description, even where it is not otherwise offensive; but the principal ornament wherewith the author endeavours to enliven his style is a brutal filth and grossness of expression, which is the more astounding when we consider that the piece was the production, in all probability, of a clergyman at least, if not of one who afterwards became a bishop, and that it was certainly represented before a learned and grave university. There is nothing of the same high seasoning in Ralph Roister Doister, though that play seems to have been intended only for the amusement of a common London audience. The Second Act of Gammer Gurton's Needle is introduced by a song,

> I cannot eat but little meat,
> My stomach is not good, &c.

which is the best thing in the whole play, and which is well known from having been quoted by Warton, who describes it as the earliest *chanson à boire*, or drinking ballad, of any merit in the language; and observes that "it has a vein of ease and humour which we should not expect to have been inspired by the simple beverage of those times." But this song is most probably not by the author of the play: it appears to be merely a portion of a popular song of the time, which is found elsewhere complete, and has recently been so printed, from a MS. of the sixteenth century, by Dr. Dyce, in his edition of Skelton.*

MISOGONUS.

Probably of earlier date than Gammer Gurton's Needle, is another example of the regular drama, which, like Ralph Roister Doister, has been but lately recovered, a play entitled Misogonus, the only copy of which is in manuscript, and is dated 1577. An allusion, however, in the course of the dialogue, would seem to prove that the play must have been composed about the year 1560. To the prologue is appended the name of Thomas Rychardes, who has therefore been assumed to be the author. The play, as contained in the manuscript, consists only of the

* See Account of Skelton and his Writings, vol. i. pp. 7—9. Mr. Dyce states that the MS. from which he has printed the song is certainly of an earlier date than the oldest-known edition of the play (1575).

unusual number of four acts, but the story, nevertheless, appears to be completed. The piece is written throughout in rhyming quatrains, not couplets, and the language would indicate it to be of about the same date with Gammer Gurton's Needle. It contains a song, which for fluency and spirit may very well bear to be compared with the drinking-song in that drama. Neither in the contrivance and conduct of the plot, however, nor in the force with which the characters are exhibited, does it evince the same free and skilful hand with Ralph Roister Doister, although it is interesting for some of the illustrations which it affords of the manners of the time.

CHRONICLE HISTORIES:—BALE'S KYNGE JOHAN; ETC.

If the regular drama thus made its first appearance among us in the form of comedy, the tragic muse was at least not far behind. There is some ground for supposing, indeed, that one species of the graver drama of real life may have begun to emerge rather sooner than comedy out of the shadowy world of the old allegorical representations; that, namely, which was long distinguished from both comedy and tragedy by the name of History, or Chronicle History, consisting, to adopt Mr. Collier's definition, "of certain passages or events detailed by annalists put into a dramatic form, often without regard to the course in which they happened; the author sacrificing chronology, situation, and circumstance, to the superior object of producing an attractive play."* Of what may be called at least the transition from the moral-play to the history, we have an example in Bale's lately recovered drama of Kynge Johan,† written in all probability some years before the middle of the sixteenth century, in which, while many of the characters are still allegorical abstractions, others are real personages; King John himself, Pope Innocent, Cardinal Pandulphus, Stephen Langton, and other historical figures moving about in odd intermixture with such mere notional spectres as the Widowed Britannia, Imperial Majesty, Nobility, Clergy, Civil Order, Treason, Verity, and Sedition. The play is accordingly described by Mr. Collier, the editor, as occupying an intermediate place between moralities and historical plays; and "it is," he adds, "the only known existing specimen of that species of composition of so early a date."

* Hist. Dram. Poet. ii. p. 414.
† Published by the Camden Society, 4to. 1838, under the care of Mr. Collier.

Tragedy of Gorboduc.—Blank Verse.

But the era of genuine tragedies and historical plays had already commenced some years before these last-mentioned pieces saw the light. On the 18th of January, 1562, was "shown before the Queen's most excellent Majesty," as the old title-pages of the printed play inform us, "in her Highness' Court of Whitehall, by the Gentlemen of the Inner Temple," the Tragedy of Gorboduc, otherwise entitled the Tragedy of Ferrex and Porrex, the production of the same Thomas Sackville who has already engaged our attention as by far the most remarkable writer in The Mirror for Magistrates, and of Thomas Norton, who is said to have been a puritan clergyman, and who had already acquired a poetic reputation, though in a different province of the land of song, as one of the coadjutors of Sternhold and Hopkins in their metrical version of the Psalms. On the title-page of the first edition, printed in 1565, which, however, was surreptitious, it is stated that the three first acts were written by Norton, and the two last by Sackville; and, although this announcement was afterwards withdrawn, it was never expressly contradicted, and it is not improbable that it may have a general foundation of truth. It must be confessed, however, that no change of style gives any indication which it is easy to detect of a succession of hands; and that, judging by this criterion, we should rather be led to infer that, in whatever way the two writers contrived to combine their labours, whether by the one retouching and improving what the other had rough-sketched, or by the one taking the quieter and humbler, the other the more impassioned, scenes or portions of the dialogue, they pursued the same method throughout the piece. Charles Lamb expresses himself "willing to believe that Lord Buckhurst supplied the more vital parts."* At the same time he observes that "the style of this old play is stiff and cumbersome, like the dresses of its times;" and that, though there may be flesh and blood underneath, we cannot get at it. In truth, Gorboduc is a drama only in form. In spirit and manner it is wholly undramatic. The story has no dramatic capabilities, no evolution either of action or of character, although it affords some opportunities for description and eloquent declamation; neither was there anything of specially dramatic aptitude in the genius of Sackville (to whom we may safely attribute whatever is most meritorious in the composition), any more than there would appear to have been in Spenser or in Milton, illustrious as they both stand in

* Specimens of Eng. Dram. Poets, I. 6 (edit. of 1835).

the front line of the poets of their country and of the world. Gorboduc, accordingly, is a most unaffecting and uninteresting tragedy; as would also be the noblest book of the Fairy Queen or of Paradise Lost—the portion of either poem that soars the highest—if it were to be attempted to be transformed into a drama by merely being divided into acts and scenes, and cut up into the outward semblance of dialogue. In whatever abundance all else of poetry might be outpoured, the spirit of dialogue and of dramatic action would not be there. Gorboduc, however, though a dull play, is in some other respects a remarkable production for the time. The language is not dramatic, but it is throughout singularly correct, easy, and perspicuous; in many parts it is even elevated and poetical; and there are some passages of strong painting not unworthy of the hand to which we owe the Induction to the Legend of the Duke of Buckingham in the Mirror for Magistrates. The piece has accordingly won much applause in quarters where there was little feeling of the true spirit of dramatic writing as the exposition of passion in action, and where the chief thing demanded in a tragedy was a certain orderly pomp of expression, and monotonous respectability of sentiment, to fill the ear, and tranquillize rather than excite and disturb the mind. One peculiarity of the more ancient national drama retained in Gorboduc is the introduction, before every act, of a piece of machinery called the Dumb Show, in which was shadowed forth, by a sort of allegorical exhibition, the part of the story that was immediately to follow. This custom survived on the English stage down to a considerably later date: the reader may remember that Shakespeare, though he rejected it in his own dramas, has introduced the play acted before the King and Queen in Hamlet by such a prefigurative dumb show.*

Another expedient, which Shakespeare has also on two occasions made use of, namely, the assistance of a chorus, is also adopted in Gorboduc: but rather by way of mere decoration, and to keep the stage from being at any time empty, as in the old Greek drama, than to carry forward or even to explain the

* Besides the original 1565 edition of Gorboduc, there was another in 1569 or 1570, and a third in 1590. It was again reprinted in 1736; and it has also appeared in all the editions of Dodsley's Old Plays, 1744, 1780, and 1825. It has now been edited for the Shakespearian Society by Mr. W. D. Cooper, in the same volume with Ralph Roister Doister. Mr. Cooper has shown that the edition of 1590 was not, as had been supposed, an exact reprint of that of 1565. He has also given us elaborate biographies both of Norton and of Sackville, in the latter of which he has shown that Sackville, who died suddenly at the Council-table in 1608, was born in 1536, and not in 1527, as commonly supposed.

action, as in Henry the Fifth and Pericles. It consists, to quote the description given by Warton, "of Four Ancient and Sage Men of Britain, who regularly close every act, the last excepted, with an ode in long-lined stanzas, drawing back the attention of the audience to the substance of what has just passed, and illustrating it by recapitulatory moral reflections and poetical or historical allusions."* These effusions of the chorus are all in rhyme, as being intended to be of the same lyrical character with those in the Greek plays; but the dialogue in the rest of the piece is in blank verse, of the employment of which in dramatic composition it affords the earliest known instance in the language. The first modern experiment in this "strange metro," as it was then called, had, as has already been noticed, been made only a few years before by Lord Surrey, in his translation of the Second and Fourth Books of the Æneid, which was published in 1557, but must have been written more than ten years before, Surrey having been put to death in January, 1547. In the mean time the new species of verse had been cultivated in several original compositions by Nicholas Grimoald, from whom, in the opinion of Warton, the rude model exhibited by Surrey received "now strength, elegance, and modulation."† Grimoald's pieces in blank verse were first printed in 1557, along with Surrey's translation, in Tottel's collection entitled Songs and Sonnets of Uncertain Authors; and we are not aware that there was any more English blank verse written or given to the world till the production of Gorboduc. In that case, Sackville would stand as our third writer in this species of verse; in the use of which also, he may be admitted to have surpassed Grimoald fully as much as the latter improved upon Surrey. Indeed, it may be said to have been Gorboduc that really established blank verse in the language; for its employment from the time of the appearance of that tragedy became common in dramatic composition, while in other kinds of poetry, notwithstanding two or three early attempts, it never made head against rhyme, nor acquired any popularity, till it was brought into repute by the Paradise Lost, published a full century after Sackville's play. Even in dramatic composition the use of blank verse appears to have been for some time confined to pieces not intended for popular representation.

* Hist. of Eng. Poet. iv. 181.   † Ibid. III. 346.

OTHER EARLY DRAMAS.

Among the very few original plays of this period that have come down to us is one entitled Damon and Pythias, which was acted before the queen at Christ Church, Oxford, in September, 1566, the production of Richard Edwards, who, in the general estimation of his contemporaries, seems to have been accounted the greatest dramatic genius of his day, at least in the comic style. His Damon and Pythias does not justify their laudation to a modern taste; it is a mixture of comedy and tragedy, between which it would be hard to decide whether the grave writing or the gay is the rudest and dullest. The play is in rhyme, but some variety is produced by the measure or length of the line being occasionally changed. Mr. Collier thinks that the notoriety Edwards attained may probably have been in great part owing to the novelty of his subjects; Damon and Pythias being one of the earliest attempts to bring stories from profane history upon the English stage. Edwards, however, besides his plays, wrote many other things in verse, some of which have an ease, and even an elegance, that neither Surrey himself nor any other writer of that age has excelled. Most of these shorter compositions are contained in the miscellany called the Paradise of Dainty Devices, which, indeed, is stated on the title-page to have been "devised and written for the most part" by Edwards, who had, however, been dead ten years when the first edition appeared in 1576. Among them are the very beautiful and tender lines, which have been often reprinted, in illustration of Terence's apophthegm,—

"Amantium iræ amoris redintegratio est;"

or, as it is here rendered in the burthen of each stanza,—

"The falling out of faithful friends renewing is of love."

Edwards, who, towards the end of his life, was appointed one of the gentlemen of the Chapel Royal and master of the queen's singing-boys, "united," says Warton, "all those arts and accomplishments which minister to popular pleasantry: he was the first fiddle, the most fashionable sonnetteer, the readiest rhymer, and the most facetious mimic, of the court."[*] Another surviving play produced during this interval is the Tragedy of Tancred and Gismund, founded upon Boccaccio's well-known story, which was presented before Elizabeth at the Inner Temple in 1568, the

[*] Hist. of Eng. Poet. iv. 110.

five acts of which it consists being severally written by five gentlemen of the society, of whom one, the author of the third act, was Christopher Hatton, afterwards the celebrated dancing lord chancellor. The play, however, was not printed till 1592, when Robert Wilmot, the writer of the fifth act, gave it to the world, as the title-page declares, "newly revived, and polished according to the decorum of these days." The meaning of this announcement, Mr. Collier conceives to be, that the piece was in the first instance composed in rhyme; but, rhymed plays having by the year 1592 gone out of fashion even on the public stage, Wilmot's reviving and polishing consisted chiefly in cutting off many of the "tags to the lines," or turning them differently. The tragedy of Tancred and Gismund, which, like Gorboduc, has a dumb show at the commencement and a chorus at the close of every act, is, he observes, "the earliest English play extant the plot of which is known to be derived from an Italian novel."*
To this earliest stage in the history of the regular drama belong, finally, some plays translated or adapted from the ancient and from foreign languages, which doubtless also contributed to excite and give an impulse to the national taste and genius in this department.

SECOND STAGE OF THE REGULAR DRAMA:—PEELE; GREENE.

It thus appears that numerous pieces entitled by their form to be accounted as belonging to the regular drama had been produced before the year 1580; but nevertheless no dramatic work had yet been written which can be said to have taken its place in our literature, or to have almost any interest for succeeding generations on account of its intrinsic merits and apart from its mere antiquity. The next ten years disclose a new scene. Within that space a crowd of dramatists arose whose writings still form a portion of our living poetry, and present the regular drama, no longer only painfully struggling into the outward shape proper to that species of composition, but having the breath of life breathed into it, and beginning to throb and stir with the pulsations of genuine passion. We can only here shortly notice some of the chief names in this numerous company of our early dramatists, properly so called. One to whom much attention has been recently directed is George Peele, the first of whose dramatic productions, The Arraignment of Paris, a sort

* Hist. Dram. Poet. iii. 13.

of masque or pageant which had been represented before the queen, was printed anonymously in 1584. But Peele's most celebrated drama is his Love of King David and Fair Bethsabe, first published in 1599, two or three years after the author's death. This play Mr. Campbell has called " the earliest fountain of pathos and harmony that can be traced in our dramatic poetry;" and he adds, " there is no such sweetness of versification and imagery to be found in our blank verse anterior to Shakespeare."* David and Bethsabe was, in all probability, written not anterior to Shakespeare, but after he had been at least six or seven years a writer for the stage, and had produced perhaps ten or twelve of his plays, including some of those in which, to pass over all other and higher things, the music of the verse has ever been accounted the most perfect and delicious. We know at least that The Midsummer Night's Dream, Romeo and Juliet, The Merchant of Venice, Richard II., King John, and Richard III., were all written and acted, if not all printed, before Peele's play was given to the world. But, independently of this consideration, it must be admitted that the best of Peele's blank verse, though smooth and flowing, and sometimes tastefully decorated with the embellishments of a learned and imitative fancy, is both deficient in richness or even variety of modulation, and without any pretensions to the force and fire of original poetic genius. Contemporary with Peele was Robert Greene, the author of five plays, besides one written in conjunction with a friend. Greene died in 1592, and he appears only to have begun to write for the stage about 1587. Mr. Collier thinks that, in facility of expression, and in the flow of his blank verse, he is not to be placed below Peele. But Greene's most characteristic attribute is his turn for merriment, of which Peele in his dramatic productions shows little or nothing. His comedy, or farce rather, is no doubt usually coarse enough, but the turbid stream flows at least freely and abundantly. Among his plays is a curious one on the subject of the History of Friar Bacon and Friar Bungay, which is supposed to have been written in 1588 or 1589, though first published in 1594. This, however, is not so much a story of diablerie as of mere legerdemain, mixed, like all the rest of Greene's pieces, with a good deal of farcical incident and dialogue; even the catastrophe, in which one of the characters is carried off to hell, being so managed as to impart no supernatural interest to the drama.

* Spec. of Eng. Poet. L 110.

MARLOW.

Of a different and far higher order of poetical and dramatic character is another play of this date upon a similar subject, the Tragical History of the Life and Death of Doctor Faustus, by Christopher Marlow. Marlow died at an early age in 1593, the year after Greene, and three or four years before Peele. He had been a writer for the stage at least since 1586, in which year, or before, was brought out the play of Tamburlaine the Great, his claim to the authorship of which has been conclusively established by Mr. Collier, who has further shown that this was the first play written in blank verse that was exhibited on the public stage.* "Marlow's mighty line" has been celebrated by Ben Jonson in his famous verses on Shakespeare; but Drayton, the author of the Polyolbion, has extolled him in the most glowing description,—in words the most worthy of the theme:—

> Next Marlow, bathed in the Thespian springs,
> Had in him those brave translunary things
> That the first poets had: his raptures were
> All air and fire, which made his verses clear:
> For that fine madness still he did retain,
> Which rightly should possess a poet's brain.†

Marlow is, by nearly universal admission, our greatest dramatic writer before Shakespeare. He is frequently, indeed, turgid and bombastic, especially in his earliest play, Tamburlaine the Great, which has just been mentioned, where his fire, it must be confessed, sometimes blazes out of all bounds and becomes a mere wasting conflagration—sometimes only raves in a furious storm of sound, filling the ear without any other effect. But in his fits of truer inspiration, all the magic of terror, pathos, and beauty flashes from him in streams. The gradual accumulation of the agonies of Faustus, in the concluding scene of that play, as the moment of his awful fate comes nearer and nearer, powerfully drawn as it is, is far from being one of those coarse pictures of wretchedness that merely oppress us with horror: the most admirable skill is applied throughout in balancing that emotion by sympathy and even respect for the sufferer,—

> ———— for he was a scholar once admired
> For wondrous knowledge in our German schools,—

---

* Hist. Dram. Poet. III. pp. 107—126.
† Elegy, "To my dearly beloved friend Henry Reynolds, Of Poets and Poesy."

and yet without disturbing our acquiescence in the justice of his doom; till we close the book, saddened, indeed, but not dissatisfied, with the pitying but still tributary and almost consoling words of the Chorus on our hearts,—

> Cut is the branch that might have grown full straight,
> And burned is Apollo's laurel-bough
> That sometime grew within this learned man.

Still finer, perhaps, is the conclusion of another of Marlow's dramas—his tragedy of Edward the Second. "The reluctant pangs of abdicating royalty in Edward," says Charles Lamb, "furnished hints which Shakespeare scarce improved in his Richard the Second; and the death-scene of Marlow's king moves pity and terror beyond any scene, ancient or modern, with which I am acquainted."* Much splendour of poetry, also, is expended upon the delineation of Barabas, in The Rich Jew of Malta; but Marlow's Jew, as Lamb has observed, "does not approach so near to Shakespeare's [in the Merchant of Venice] as his Edward the Second." We are more reminded of some of Barabas's speeches by the magnificent declamation of Mammon in Jonson's Alchymist.

LYLY; KYD; LODGE.

Marlow, Greene, and Peele are the most noted names among those of our dramatists who belong exclusively to the age of Elizabeth; but some others that have less modern celebrity may perhaps be placed at least on the same line with the two latter. John Lyly, the Euphuist, as he is called, from one of his prose works, which will be noticed presently, is, as a poet, in his happiest efforts, elegant and fanciful; but his genius was better suited for the lighter kinds of lyric poetry than for the drama. He is the author of nine dramatic pieces, but of these seven are in prose, and only one in rhyme and one in blank verse. All of them, according to Mr. Collier, "seem to have been written for court entertainments, although they were also performed at theatres, most usually by the children of St. Paul's and the Revels." They were fitter, it might be added, for beguiling the listlessness of courts than for the entertainment of a popular audience, athirst for action and passion, and very indifferent to mere ingenuities of style. All poetical readers, however, remember some songs and other short pieces of verse with which some of

* Spec. of Eng. Dram. Poets, I. 31.

them are interspersed, particularly a delicate little anacreontic in that entitled Alexander and Campaspe, beginning—

> Cupid and my Campaspe played
> At cards for kisses, &c.

Mr. Collier observes that Malone must have spoken from a very superficial acquaintance with Lyly's works when he contends that his plays are comparatively free from those affected conceits and remote allusions that characterise most of his other productions. Thomas Kyd, the author of the two plays of Jeronimo and the Spanish Tragedy (which is a continuation of the former), besides a translation of another piece from the French, appears to be called Sporting Kyd by Jonson, in his verses on Shakespeare, in allusion merely to his name. There is, at least, nothing particularly sportive in the little that has come down to us from his pen. Kyd was a considerable master of language; but his rank as a dramatist is not very easily settled, seeing that there is much doubt as to his claims to the authorship of by far the most striking passages in the Spanish Tragedy, the best of his two plays. Lamb, quoting the scenes in question, describes them as "the very salt of the old play," which, without them, he adds, "is but a *caput mortuum.*" It has been generally assumed that they were added by Ben Jonson, who certainly was employed to make some additions to this play; and Mr. Collier attributes them to him as if the point did not admit of a doubt—acknowledging, however, that they represent Jonson in a new light, and that "certainly there is nothing in his own entire plays equalling in pathetic beauty some of his contributions to the Spanish Tragedy." Nevertheless, it does not seem to be perfectly clear that the supposed contributions by another hand might not have been the work of Kyd himself. Lamb says, "There is nothing in the undoubted plays of Jonson which would authorise us to suppose that he could have supplied the scenes in question. I should suspect the agency of some 'more potent spirit.' Webster might have furnished them. They are full of that wild, solemn, preternatural cast of grief which bewilders us in the Duchess of Malfy." The last of these early dramatists we shall notice, Thomas Lodge, who was born about 1556, and began to write for the stage about 1580, is placed by Mr. Collier "in a rank superior to Greene, but in some respects inferior to Kyd." His principal dramatic work is entitled The Wounds of Civil War, lively set forth in the true Tragedies of Marius and Sylla; and is written in blank verse with a mixture of rhyme. It shows him, Mr. Collier thinks, to have unquestionably the advantage ever Kyd as a drawer of character, though not equalling that writer in general vigour and boldness of poetic conception. His blank verse is also much more monotonous than that of Kyd. Another strange drama in rhyme, written by Lodge in conjunction with Greene, is entitled A Looking-glass for London and England, and has for its object to put down the puritanical outcry against the immorality of the stage, which it attempts to accomplish by a grotesque application to the city of London of the Scriptural story of Nineveh. The whole performance, in Mr. Collier's opinion, "is wearisomely dull, although the authors have endeavoured to lighten the weight by the introduction of scenes of drunken buffoonery between 'a clown and his crew of ruffians,' and between the same clown and a person disguised as the devil, in order to frighten him, but who is detected and well beaten." Mr. Hallam, however, pronounces that there is great talent shown in this play, "though upon a very strange canvass."* Lodge, who was an eminent physician, has left a considerable quantity of other poetry besides his plays, partly in the form of novels or tales, partly in shorter pieces, many of which may be found in the miscellany called England's Helicon, from which a few of them have been extracted by Mr. Ellis, in his Specimens. They are, perhaps, on the whole, more creditable to his poetical powers than his dramatic performances. He is also the author of several short works in prose, sometimes interspersed with verse. One of his prose tales, first printed in 1590, under the title of Rosalynde: Euphues' Golden Legacie, found in his cell at Silextra (for Lodge was one of Lyly's imitators), is famous as the source from which Shakespeare appears to have taken the story of his As You Like It. "Of this production it may be said," observes Mr. Collier, "that our admiration of many portions of it will not be diminished by a comparison with the work of our great dramatist."†

It is worthy of remark, that all these founders and first builders-up of the regular drama in England were, nearly if not absolutely without an exception, classical scholars and men who had received a university education. Nicholas Udall was of Corpus Christi College, Oxford; John Still (if he is to be considered the author of Gammer Gurton's Needle) was of Christ's College, Cambridge; Sackville was educated at both universities; so was Gascoigne; Richard Edwards was of Corpus Christi, Oxford; Marlow was of Bonet College, Cambridge; Greene, of

* Literature of Eur. ii. 271.
† Hist. of Dram. Poet. iii. 213.—See upon this subject the Introductory Notice to As You Like It in Knight's Shakspere, vol. iii. 247—263.

St. John's, Cambridge; Peele, of Christ's Church, Oxford; Lyly, of Magdalen College, and Lodge of Trinity College, in the same university. Kyd was also probably a university man, though we know nothing of his private history. To the training received by these writers the drama that arose among us after the middle of the sixteenth century may be considered to owe not only its form, but in part also its spirit, which had a learned and classical tinge from the first, that never entirely wore out. The diction of the works of all these dramatists betrays their scholarship; and they have left upon the language of our higher drama, and indeed of our blank verse in general, of which they were the main creators, an impress of Latinity, which, it can scarcely be doubted, our vigorous but still homely and unsonorous Gothic speech needed to fit it for the requirements of that species of composition. Fortunately, however, the greatest and most influential of them were not mere men of books and readers of Greek and Latin. Greene and Peele and Marlow all spent the noon of their days (none of them saw any afternoon) in the busiest haunts of social life, sounding in their reckless course all the depths of human experience, and drinking the cup of passion, and also of suffering, to the dregs. And of their great successors, those who carried the drama to its height among us in the next age, while some were also accomplished scholars, all were men of the world—men who knew their brother-men by an actual and intimate intercourse with them in their most natural and open-hearted moods, and over a remarkably extended range of conditions. We know, from even the scanty fragments of their history that have come down to us, that Shakespeare and Jonson and Beaumont and Fletcher all lived much in the open air of society, and mingled with all ranks from the highest to the lowest; some of them, indeed, having known what it was actually to belong to classes very far removed from each other at different periods of their lives. But we should have gathered, though no other record or tradition had told us, that they must have been men of this genuine and manifold experience from the drama alone which they have bequeathed to us,—various, rich, and glowing as that is, even as life itself.

EARLIER ELIZABETHAN PROSE:—LYLY; SIDNEY; SPENSER; NASH; ETC.

Before leaving the earlier part of the reign of Elizabeth, a few of the more remarkable writers in prose who had risen into notice before the year 1590 may be mentioned. The singular affectation known by the name of *Euphuism* was, like some other celebrated absurdities, the invention of a man of true genius— John Lyly, noticed above as a dramatist and poet—the first part of whose prose romance of Euphues appeared in 1578 or 1579. "Our nation," says Sir Henry Blount, in the preface to a collection of some of Lyly's dramatic pieces which he published in 1632, "are in his debt for a new English which he taught them. Euphues and his England* began first that language; all our ladies were then his scholars; and that beauty in court which could not parley Euphuism—that is to say, who was unable to converse in that pure and reformed English, which he had formed his work to be the standard of—was as little regarded as she which now there speaks not French." Some notion of this "pure and reformed English" has been made familiar to the reader of our day by the great modern pen that has called back to life so much of the long-vanished past, though the discourse of Sir Piercie Shafton, in the Monastery, is rather a caricature than a fair sample of Euphuism. Doubtless, it often became a purely silly and pitiable affair in the mouths of the courtiers, male and female; but in Lyly's own writings, and in those of his lettered imitators, of whom he had several, and some of no common talent, it was only fantastic and extravagant, and opposed to truth, nature, good sense, and manliness. Pedantic and far-fetched allusion, elaborate indirectness, a cloying smoothness and drowsy monotony of diction, alliteration, punning, and other such puerilities,—these are the main ingredients of Euphuism; which do not, however, exclude a good deal of wit, fancy, and prettiness, occasionally, both in the expression and the thought. Although Lyly, in his verse as well as in his prose, is always artificial to excess, his ingenuity and finished elegance are frequently very captivating. Perhaps, indeed, our language is, after all, indebted to this writer and his Euphuism for not a little of its present euphony. From the strictures Shakespeare, in Love's Labour's Lost, makes Holofernes pass on the mode of speaking of his Euphuist, Don Adriano de Armado

* This is the title of the second part of the Euphues, published in 1581. The first part is entitled Euphues, the Anatomy of Wit.

—"a man of fire-new words, fashion's own knight—that hath a mint of phrases in his brain—one whom the music of his own vain tongue doth ravish like enchanting harmony"—it should almost seem that the now universally adopted pronunciation of many of our words was first introduced by such persons as this refining "child of fancy:"—"I abhor such fanatical fantasms, such insociable and point-device companions; such rackers of orthography as to speak *dout*, fine, when he should say *doubt*; *det*, when he should pronounce *debt*, d, e, b, t; not d, e, t: he clepeth a *calf, cauf; half, hauf; neighbour* vocatur *nebour; neigh*, abbreviated *ne*; this is abhominable (which he would call *abominable*): it insinuateth me of insanie." Here, however, the all-seeing poet laughs rather at the pedantic schoolmaster than at the fantastic knight; and the euphuistic pronunciation which he makes Holofernes so indignantly criticise was most probably his own and that of the generality of his educated contemporaries.

A renowned English prose classic of this age, who made Lyly's affectations the subject of his ridicule some years before Shakespeare, but who also perhaps was not blind to his better qualities, and did not disdain to adopt some of his reforms in the language, if not to imitate even some of the peculiarities of his style, was Sir Philip Sidney, the illustrious author of the Arcadia. Sidney, who was born in 1554, does not appear to have sent anything to the press during his short and brilliant life, which was terminated by the wound he received at the battle of Zutphen, in 1586; but he was probably well known, nevertheless, at least as a writer of poetry, some years before his lamented death. Puttenham, whose Art of English Poesy, at whatever time it may have been written, was published before any work of Sidney's had been printed, so far as can now be discovered, mentions him as one of the best and most famous writers of the age "for eclogue and pastoral poesy." The Countess of Pembroke's Arcadia, as Sidney's principal work had been affectionately designated by himself, in compliment to his sister, to whom it was inscribed—the "fair, and good, and learned" lady, afterwards celebrated by Ben Jonson as "the subject of all verse"—was not given to the world even in part till 1590, nor completely till 1593. His collection of sonnets and songs entitled Astrophel and Stella, first appeared in 1591, and his other most celebrated piece in prose, The Defence of Poesy, in 1595. The production in which he satirises the affectation and pedantry of the modern corrupters of the vernacular tongue is a sort of masque, supposed to pass before Queen Elizabeth in Wanstead garden, in which, among other characters, a village schoolmaster called Rombus appears, and declaims in a jargon not unlike that of Shakespeare's Holofernes. Sidney's own prose is the most flowing and poetical that had yet been written in English; but its graces are rather those of artful elaboration than of a vivid natural expressiveness. The thought, in fact, is generally more poetical than the language; it is a spirit of poetry encased in a rhetorical form. Yet, notwithstanding the conceits into which it frequently runs—and which, after all, are mostly rather the frolics of a nimble wit, somewhat too solicitous of display, than the sickly perversities of a coxcombical or effeminate taste—and, notwithstanding also some want of animation and variety, Sidney's is a wonderful style, always flexible, harmonious, and luminous, and on fit occasions rising to great stateliness and splendour; while a breath of beauty and noble feeling lives in and exhales from the whole of his great work, like the fragrance from a garden of flowers.

Among the most active occasional writers in prose, also, about this time were others of the poets and dramatists of the day, besides Lodge, who has been already mentioned as one of Lyly's imitators. Another of his productions, besides his tale of Rosalynd, which has lately attracted much attention, is a Defence of Stage Plays, which he published, probably in 1579, in answer to Stephen Gosson's School of Abuse, and of which only two copies are known to exist, both wanting the title-page. Greene was an incessant pamphleteer upon all sorts of subjects; the list of his prose publications, so far as they are known, given by Mr. Dyce extends to between thirty and forty articles, the earliest being dated 1584, or eight years before his death. Morality, fiction, satire, blackguardism, are all mingled together in the stream that thus appears to have flowed without pause from his ready pen. "In a night and a day," says his friend Nash, "would he have yarked up a pamphlet as well as in seven years: and glad was that printer that might be so blest to pay him dear for the very dregs of his wit."* His wit, indeed, often enough appears to have run to the dregs, nor is it very sparkling at the best; but Greene's prose, though not in general very animated, is more concise and perspicuous than his habits of composition might lead us to expect. He has generally written from a well-informed or full mind, and the matter is interesting even when there is no particular attraction in the manner. Among his most curious pamphlets are his several tracts on the rogueries of London, which he describes under the name of Coney-catching—a favourite subject also with other popular writers of that day.

* Strange News, in answer to Gabriel Harvey's Four Letters.

But the most remarkable of all Greene's contributions to our literature are his various publications which either directly relate or are understood to shadow forth the history of his own wild and unhappy life—his tale entitled Never too Late; or, A Powder of Experience, 1590; the second part entitled Francesco's Fortunes, the same year; his Groatsworth of Wit, bought with a Million of Repentance, and The Repentance of Robert Greene, Master of Arts, which both appeared, after his death, in 1592. Greene, as well as Lodge, we may remark, is to be reckoned among the Euphuists; a tale which he published in 1587, and which was no less than five times reprinted in the course of the next half-century, is entitled Menaphon; Camilla's Alarum to slumbering Euphues, in his melancholy cell at Silexedra, &c.; and the same year he produced Euphues his Censure to Philantus; wherein is presented a philosophical combat between Hector and Achilles, &c. But he does not appear to have persisted in this fashion of style. It may be noticed as curiously illustrating the spirit and manner of our fictitious literature at this time, that in his Pandosto, or, History of Dorastus and Fawnia, Greene, a scholar, and a Master of Arts of Cambridge, does not hesitate to make Bohemia an island, just as is done by Shakespeare in treating the same story in his Winter's Tale. The critics have been accustomed to instance this as one of the evidences of Shakespeare's ignorance, and Ben Jonson is recorded to have, in his conversation with Drummond of Hawthornden, quoted it as a proof that his great brother-dramatist "wanted art,[*] and sometimes sense." The truth is, as has been observed,[†] such deviations from fact, and other incongruities of the same character, were not minded, or attempted to be avoided, either in the romantic drama, or in the legends out of which it was formed. They are not blunders, but part and parcel of the fiction. The making Bohemia an island is not nearly so great a violation of geographical truth as other things in the same play are of all the proprieties and possibilities of chronology and history—for instance, the co-existence of a kingdom of Bohemia at all, or of that modern barbaric name, with anything so entirely belonging to the old classic world as the Oracle of Delphi. The story (though no earlier record of it has yet been discovered) is not improbably much older than either Shakespeare or Greene: the latter no doubt expanded and

[*] Yet Jonson has elsewhere expressly commended Shakespeare for his art. See his well-known verses prefixed to the first folio edition of the Plays.
[†] See Notice on the Costume of the Winter's Tale in Knight's Shakspere, vol. iv.

adorned it, and mainly gave it its present shape; but it is most likely that he had for his groundwork some rude popular legend or tradition, the characteristic middle age geography and chronology of which he most properly did not disturb.

But the most brilliant pamphleteer of this age was Thomas Nash. Nash is the author of one slight dramatic piece, mostly in blank verse, but partly in prose, and having also some lyrical poetry interspersed, called Summer's Last Will and Testament, which was exhibited before Queen Elizabeth at Nonsuch in 1592; and he also assisted Marlow in his Tragedy of Dido, Queen of Carthage, which, although not printed till 1594, is supposed to have been written before 1590. But his satiric was of a much higher order than his dramatic talent. There never perhaps was poured forth such a rushing and roaring torrent of wit, ridicule, and invective, as in the rapid succession of pamphlets which he published in the course of the year 1589 against the Puritans and their famous champion (or rather knot of champions) taking the name of Martin Mar-Prelate; unless in those in which he began two years after to assail poor Gabriel Harvey, his persecution of and controversy with whom lasted a much longer time—till indeed the Archbishop of Canterbury (Whitgift) interfered in 1597 to restore the peace of the realm by an order that all Harvey's and Nash's books should be taken wherever they might be found, "and that none of the said books be ever printed hereafter." Mr. D'Israeli has made both these controversies familiar to modern readers by his lively accounts of the one in his Quarrels, of the other in his Calamities, of Authors; and ample specimens of the criminations and recriminations hurled at one another by Nash and Harvey have also been given by Mr. Dyce in the Life of Greene prefixed to his edition of that writer's dramatic and poetical works. Harvey too was a man of eminent talent; but it was of a kind very different from that of Nash. Nash's style is remarkable for its airiness and facility; clear it of its old spelling, and, unless it be for a few words and idioms which have now dropt out of the popular speech, it has quite a modern air. This may show, by-the-by, that the language has not altered so much since the latter part of the sixteenth century as the ordinary prose of that day would lead us to suppose; the difference is rather that the generality of writers were more pedantic then than now, and sought, in a way that is no longer the fashion, to brocade their composition with what were called ink-horn terms, and outlandish phrases never used except in books. If they had been satisfied to write as they spoke, the style of that day (as we may perceive from the example of Nash) would have in its general character considerably more resembled that of the present. Gabriel Harvey's mode of writing exhibits all the peculiarities of his age in their most exaggerated form. He was a great scholar—and his composition is inspired by the very genius of pedantry; full of matter, full often of good sense, not unfrequently rising to a tone of dignity, and even eloquence, but always stiff, artificial, and elaborately unnatural to a degree which was even then unusual. We may conceive what sort of chance such a heavy-armed combatant, encumbered and oppressed by the very weapons he carried, would have in a war of wit with the quick, elastic, inexhaustible Nash, and the showering jokes and sarcasms that flashed from his easy, natural pen. Harvey, too, with all his merits, was both vain and envious; and he had some absurdities which afforded tempting game for satire.

EDMUND SPENSER.

Edmund Spenser has been supposed to have come before the world as a poet so early as the year 1569, when some sonnets translated from Petrarch, which long afterwards were reprinted with his name, appeared in Vander Noodt's Theatre of Worldlings: on the 20th of May in that year he was entered a sizer of Pembroke Hall, Cambridge; and in that same year, also, an entry in the Books of the Treasurer of the Queen's Chamber records that there was "paid upon a bill signed by Mr. Secretary, dated at Windsor 18° Octobris, to Edmund Spenser, that brought letters to the Queen's Majesty from Sir Henry Norris, Knight, her Majesty's ambassador in France, being at Thouars in the said realm, for his charges the sum of 6l. 13s. 4d., over and besides 9l. presented to him by Sir Henry Norris."* It has been supposed that this entry refers to the poet. The date 1510, given as that of the year of his birth upon his monument in Westminster Abbey, erected long after his death, is out of the question; but the above-mentioned facts make it probable that he was born some years before 1553, the date commonly assigned.

He has himself commemorated the place of his birth: "At length," he says in his Prothalamion, or poem on the marriages of the two daughters of the Earl of Worcester,

* First published in Mr. Cunningham's Introduction (p. xxx.) to his Extracts from the Accounts of the Revels at Court, printed for the Shakespeare Society, 8vo. Lond. 1842.

> At length they all to merry London came,
> To merry London, my most kindly nurse,
> That to me gave this life's first native source,
> Though from another place I take my name,
> An house of ancient fame.

It is commonly said, on the authority of Oldys, that he was born in East Smithfield by the Tower. It appears from the register of the University that he took his degree of Bachelor of Arts in 1572, and that of Master of Arts in 1576. On leaving Cambridge he retired for some time to the north of England. Here he appears to have written the greater part of his Shepherd's Calendar, which, having previously come up to London, he published in 1579. In the beginning of August, 1580, on the appointment of Arthur Lord Grey of Wilton as Lord Deputy of Ireland, he accompanied his lordship to that country as his secretary; in March, the year following, he was appointed to the office of Clerk in the Irish Court of Chancery; but on Lord Grey being recalled in 1582 Spenser probably returned with him to England.

Of how he was employed for the next three or four years nothing is known; but in 1586 he obtained from the crown a grant of above 3000 acres of forfeited lands in Ireland: the grant is dated the 27th of July, and, if it was procured, as is not improbable, through Sir Philip Sidney, it was the last kindness of that friend and patron, whose death took place in October of this year. Spenser proceeded to Ireland to take possession of his estate, which was a portion of the former domain of the Earl of Desmond in the county of Cork; and here he remained, residing in what had been the earl's castle of Kilcolman, till he returned to England in 1590, and published at London, in 4to., the first three Books of his Fairy Queen. If he had published anything else since the Shepherd's Calendar appeared eleven years before, it could only have been a poem of between four and five hundred lines, entitled Muiopotmos, or the Fate of the Butterfly, which he dedicated to the Lady Carey. He has himself related, in his Colin Clout's Come Home Again, how he had been visited in his exile by the Shepherd of the Ocean, by which designation he means Sir Walter Raleigh, and persuaded by him to make this visit to England for the purpose of having his poem printed. Raleigh introduced him to Elizabeth, to whom the Fairy Queen was dedicated, and who in February, 1591, bestowed on the author a pension of 50*l*. This great work immediately raised Spenser to such celebrity, that the publisher hastened to collect whatever of his other poems he could find, and, under the general title of Complaints; Containing sundry small poems of the

World's Vanity; printed together, in a 4to. volume, The Ruins of Time, The Tears of the Muses, Virgil's Gnat, Mother Hubberd's Tale, The Ruins of Rome (from the French of Bellay), Muiopotmos (which is stated to be the only one of the pieces that had previously appeared), and The Visions of Petrarch, &c., already mentioned. Many more, it is declared, which the author had written in former years were not to be found.

Spenser appears to have remained in England till the beginning of the year 1592: his Daphnaida, an elegy on the death of Douglas Howard, daughter of Lord Howard, and wife of Arthur Gorges, Esq., is dedicated to the Marchioness of Northampton in an address dated the 1st of January in that year, and it was published soon after. He then returned to Ireland, and, probably in the course of 1592 and 1593, there composed the series of eighty-eight sonnets in which he relates his courtship of the lady whom he at last married,* celebrating the event by a splendid Epithalamion. But it appears from the eightieth sonnet that he had already finished six Books of his Fairy Queen. His next publication was another 4to. volume which appeared in 1595, containing his Colin Clout's Come Home Again, the dedication of which to Raleigh is dated "From my house at Kilcolman, December the 27th, 1591," no doubt a misprint for 1594; and also his Astrophel, an elegy upon Sir Philip Sidney, dedicated to his widow, now the Countess of Essex; together with The Mourning Muse of Thestylis, another poem on the same subject. The same year appeared, in 8vo., his sonnets, under the title of Amoretti, accompanied by the Epithalamion. In 1596 he paid another visit to England, bringing with him the Fourth, Fifth, and Sixth Books of his Fairy Queen, which were published, along with a new edition of the preceding three books, in 4to., at London in that year. In the latter part of the same year appeared, in a volume of the same form, a reprint of his Daphnaida, together with his Prothalamion, or spousal verse on the marriages of the Ladies Elizabeth and Catharine Somerset, and his Four Hymns in honour of Love, of Beauty, of Heavenly Love, and of Heavenly Beauty, dedicated to the Countesses of Cumberland and Warwick, in an address dated Greenwich, the 1st of September, 1596. The first two of these Hymns he states had been composed in the greener times of his youth; and, although he had been moved by one of the two ladies to call in the same, as "having

* She was not, as has been commonly assumed, a peasant girl, but evidently a gentlewoman, a person of the same social position with Spenser himself. I have shown this, for the first time, in Spenser and his Poetry, vol. III. pp. 223, &c.

too much pleased those of like age and disposition, which, being too vehemently carried with that kind of affection, do rather suck out poison to their strong passion than honey to their honest delight," he "had been unable so to do, by reason that many copies thereof were formerly scattered abroad." At this time it was still common for literary compositions of all kinds to be extensively circulated in manuscript, as used to be the mode of publication before the invention of printing. These Hymns were the last of his productions that he sent to the press. It was during this visit to England that he presented to Elizabeth, and probably wrote, his prose treatise entitled A View of the State of Ireland, written dialogue-wise between Eudoxus and Irenaeus; but that work remained unprinted, till it was published at Dublin by Sir James Ware in 1633.

Spenser returned to Ireland probably early in 1597; and was the next year recommended by the Queen to be sheriff of Cork; but, soon after the breaking out of Tyrone's rebellion in October, 1598, his house of Kilcolman was attacked and burned by the rebels, and, one child having perished in the flames, it was with difficulty that he made his escape with his wife and two sons. He arrived in England in a state of destitution; but it seems unlikely that, with his talents and great reputation, his powerful friends, his pension, and the rights he still retained, although deprived of the enjoyment of his Irish property for the moment, he could have been left to perish, as has been commonly said, of want: the breaking up of his constitution was a natural consequence of the sufferings he had lately gone through. All that we know, however, is that, after having been ill for some time, he died at an inn in King Street, Westminster, on the 16th of January, 1599. Two Cantos, undoubtedly genuine, of a subsequent Book of the Fairy Queen, and two stanzas of a third Canto, entitled Of Mutability, and forming part of the Legend of Constancy, were published in an edition of his collected works, in a folio volume, in 1609; and it may be doubted if much more of the poem was ever written.

The most remarkable of Spenser's poems written before his great work, The Fairy Queen, are his Shepherd's Calendar and his Mother Hubberd's Tale. Both of these pieces are full of the spirit of poetry, and his genius displays itself in each in a variety of styles.

The Shepherd's Calendar, though consisting of twelve distinct poems denominated Æclogues, is less of a pastoral, in the ordinary acceptation, than it is of a piece of polemical or party divinity. Spenser's shepherds are, for the most part, pastors of the church, or clergymen, with only pious parishioners for sheep. One is a good shepherd, such as Algrind, that is, the puritanical archbishop of Canterbury, Grindall. Another, represented in a much less favourable light, is Morell, that is, his famous antagonist, Elmore, or Aylmer, bishop of London. The puritanical spirit of some parts of the Shepherd's Calendar, probably contributed to the popularity which the poem long retained. It was reprinted four times during the author's lifetime, in 1581, 1586, 1591, and 1597. Yet it is not only a very unequal composition, but is, in its best executed or most striking parts, far below the height to which Spenser afterwards learned to rise. This earliest work of Spenser's, however, betrays his study of our elder poetry as much by its diction as by other indications: he has thickly sprinkled it with words and phrases which had generally ceased to be used at the time when it was written. This he seems to have done, not so much that the antiquated style might give the dialogue an air of rusticity proper to the speech of shepherds, but rather in the same spirit and design (though he has carried the practice much farther) in which Virgil has done the same thing in his heroic poetry, that his verse might thereby be the more distinguished from common discourse, that it might fall upon the ears of men with something of the impressiveness and authority of a voice from other times, and that it might seem to echo, and, as it were, continue and prolong, the strain of the old national minstrelsy; thus at once expressing his love and admiration of the preceding poets who had been his examples, and, in part, his instructors and inspirers, and making their compositions reflect additional light and beauty upon his own. This is almost the only advantage which the later poets in any language have over the earlier; and Spenser has availed himself of it more or less in most of his writings, though not in any later work to the same extent as in this first publication.

Executed in a firmer and more matured style, and, though with more regularity of manner, yet also with more true boldness and freedom, is the admirable Prosopopoia, as it is designated, of the adventures of the Fox and the Ape, or Mother Hubberd's Tale, notwithstanding that this, too, is stated to have been an early production—" long sithens composed," says the author in his dedication of it to the Lady Compton and Montcagle, " in the raw conceit of my youth." Perhaps, however, this was partly said to avert the offence that might be taken at the audacity of the satire. It has not much the appearance, either in manner or in matter, of the production of a very young writer. We should say that Mother Hubberd's Tale represents the middle age of Spenser's genius, if not of his life—the stage in his mental and poetical progress when his relish and power of the energetic had attained perfection, but the higher sense of the beautiful had not yet been fully developed. Such appears to be the natural progress of every mind that is capable of the highest things in both these directions: the feeling of force is first awakened, or at least is first matured; the feeling of beauty is of later growth. With even poetical minds of a subordinate class, indeed, it may sometimes happen that a perception of the beautiful, and a faculty of embodying it in words, acquire a considerable development without the love and capacity of the energetic having ever shown themselves in any unusual degree: such may be said to have been the case with Petrarch, to quote a remarkable example. But the greatest poets have all been complete men, with the sense of beauty, indeed, strong and exquisite, and crowning all their other endowments, which is what makes them the greatest; but also with all other passions and powers correspondingly vigorous and active. Homer, Dante, Chaucer, Spenser, Shakespeare, Milton, Goethe, were all of them manifestly capable of achieving any degree of success in any other field as well as in poetry. They were not only poetically, but in all other respects, the most gifted intelligences of their times; men of the largest sense, of the most penetrating insight, of the most general research and information; nay, even in the most worldly arts and dexterities, able to cope with the ablest, whenever they chose to throw themselves into that game. They may not any of them have attained the highest degree of what is called worldly success; some of them may have even been crushed by the force of circumstances or evil days; Milton may have died in obscurity, Dante in exile; "the vision and the faculty divine" may have been all the light that cheered, all the estate that sustained, the old age of Homer; but no one can suppose that in any of these cases it was want of the requisite skill or talent that denied a different fortune. As for Spenser, we shall certainly much mistake his character if we suppose, from the romantic and unworldly strain of much—and that, doubtless, the best and highest—of his poetry, that he was anything resembling a mere dreamer. In the first place, the vast extent of his knowledge, comprehending all the learning of his age, and his voluminous writings, sufficiently prove that his days were not spent in idleness. Then, even in the matter of securing a livelihood and a position in the world, want of activity or eagerness is a fault of which he can hardly be accused. Bred, for-whatever reason, to no profession, it may be doubted if he had any other course to take, in that age, upon the whole so little objectionable as the one he adopted. The scheme of life with which he set out seems to have been to endeavour, first of all, to procure for himself, by any honourable means, the leisure necessary to enable him to cultivate and employ his poetical powers. With this view he addressed himself to Sidney, the chief professed patron of letters in that day (when, as yet, letters really depended to a great extent for encouragement and support upon the patronage of the great), hoping, through his interest, to obtain such a provision as he required from the bounty of the crown. In thus seeking to be supported at the public expense, and to withdraw a small portion of a fund, pretty sure to be otherwise wasted upon worse objects, for the modest maintenance of one poet, can we say that Spenser, being what he was, was much, or at all, to blame? Would it have been wiser, or more highminded, or in any sense better, for him to have thrown himself, like Greene and Nash, and the rest of that crew, upon the town, and, like them, wasted his fine genius in pamphleteering and blackguardism? He knew that he would not eat that public bread without returning to his country what she gave him a hundred and a thousand fold; he who must have felt and known well that no man had yet uttered himself in the English tongue so endowed for conferring upon the land, the language, and the people what all future generations would prize as their best inheritance, and what would contribute more than laws or victories, or any other glory, to maintain the name of England in honour and renown so long as it should be heard of among men.

But he did not immediately succeed in his object. It is probably true, as has been commonly stated, that Burghley looked with but small regard upon the poet and his claims. However, he at last contrived to overcome this obstacle; and eventually, as we have seen, he obtained from the crown both lands, offices, and a considerable pension. It is not at all likely that, circumstanced as he was at the commencement of his career, Spenser could in any other way have attained so soon to the same comparative affluence that he thus acquired. Probably the only respect in which he felt much dissatisfied or disappointed was in being obliged to take up his residence in Ireland, without which, it may have been, he would have derived little or no benefit from his grant of land. Mother Hubberd's Tale must be supposed to have been written before he obtained that grant. It is a sharp and shrewd satire upon the common modes

of rising in the church and state; not at all passionate or declamatory,—on the contrary, pervaded by a spirit of quiet
humour, which only occasionally gives place to a tone of greater
elevation and solemnity, but assuredly, with all its high-minded
and even severe morality, evincing in the author anything rather
than either ignorance of the world or indifference to the ordinary
objects of human ambition. No one will rise from its perusal
with the notion that Spenser was a mere rhyming visionary, or
singing somnambulist. No; like every other greatest poet, he
was an eminently wise man, exercised in every field of thought,
and rich in all knowledge—above all, in knowledge of mankind,
the proper study of man. In this poem of Mother Hubberd's
Tale we still find also both his puritanism and his imitation of
Chaucer, two things which disappear altogether from his later
poetry. Indeed, he has written nothing else so much in
Chaucer's manner and spirit; nor have we nearly so true a
reflection, or rather revival, of the Chaucerian narrative
style—at once easy and natural, clear and direct, firm and
economical, various and always spirited—in any other modern
verse.

The Fairy Queen was designed by its author to be taken as an
allegory—"a continued allegory, or dark conceit," as he calls it
in his preliminary Letter to Raleigh "expounding his whole
intention in the course of this work." The allegory was even
artificial and involved to an unusual degree; for not only was
the Fairy Queen, by whom the knights are sent forth upon their
adventures, to be understood as meaning Glory in the general
intention, but in a more particular sense she was to stand for
"the most excellent and glorious person" of Queen Elizabeth;
and some other eminent individual of the day appears in like
manner to have been shadowed forth in each of the other figures.
The most interesting allegory that was ever written carries us
along chiefly by making us forget that it is an allegory at all.
The charm of Bunyan's Pilgrim's Progress is that all the persons
and all the places in it seem real—that Christian, and Evan-
gelist, and Mr. Worldly Wiseman, and Mr. Greatheart, and the
Giant Despair, and all the rest, are to our apprehension not
shadows, but beings of flesh and blood; and the Slough of
Despond, Vanity Fair, Doubting Castle, the Valley of Humiliation, and the Enchanted Ground, all so many actual
scenes or localities which we have as we read before us or
around us. For the moral lessons that are to be got out of the
parable, it must no doubt be considered in another manner; but
we speak of the delight it yields as a work of imagination.

That is not increased, but impaired, or destroyed, by regarding it as an allegory—just as would be the humour of Don Quixote, or the marvels of the Arabian Nights' Entertainments, by either work being so regarded. In the same manner, whoever would enjoy the Fairy Queen as a poem must forget that it is an allegory, either single or double, either compound or simple. Nor in truth is it even much of a story. Neither the personages that move in it, nor the adventures they meet with, interest us much. For that matter, the most ordinary novel, or a police report in a newspaper, may often be much more entertaining. One fortunate consequence of all this is, that the poem scarcely loses anything by the design of the author never having been completed, or its completion at least not having come down to us. What we have of it is not injured in any material respect by the want of the rest. This Spenser himself no doubt felt when he originally gave it to the world in successive portions;—and it would not have mattered much although of the six Books he had published the three last before the three first.

These peculiarities—the absence of an interesting story or concatenation of incidents, and the want of human character and passion in the personages that carry on the story, such as it is—are no defects in the Fairy Queen. On the contrary, the poetry is only left thereby so much the purer. Without calling Spenser the greatest of all poets, we may still say that his poetry is the most poetical of all poetry. Other poets are all of them something else as well as poets, and deal in reflection, or reasoning, or humour, or wit, almost as largely as in the proper product of the imaginative faculty; his strains alone, in the Fairy Queen, are poetry, all poetry, and nothing but poetry. It is vision unrolled after vision, to the sound of endlessly varying music. The "*shaping* spirit of imagination," considered apart from moral sensibility—from intensity of passion on the one hand, and grandeur of conception on the other—certainly never was possessed in the like degree by any other writer; nor has any other evinced a deeper feeling of all forms of the beautiful; nor have words ever been made by any other to embody thought with more wonderful art. On the one hand invention and fancy in the creation or conception of his thoughts; on the other the most exquisite sense of beauty, united with a command over all the resources of language, in their vivid and musical expression—those are the great distinguishing characteristics of Spenser's poetry. What of passion is in it lies mostly in the melody of the verse; but that is often thrilling and subduing in the highest degree. Its moral tone, also, is very captivating: a soul of nobleness, gentle and tender as the spirit of its own chivalry, modulates every cadence.

Spenser's extraordinary faculty of vision-seeing and picture-drawing can fail to strike none of his readers; but he will not be adequately appreciated or enjoyed by those who regard verse either as a non-essential or as a very subordinate element of poetry. Such minds, however, must miss half the charm of all poetry. Not only all that is purely sensuous in poetry must escape them, but likewise all the pleasurable excitement that lies in the harmonious accordance of the musical expression with the informing idea or feeling, and in the additional force or brilliancy that in such inter-union is communicated by the one to the other. All beauty is dependent upon form: other things may often enter into the beautiful, but this is the one thing that can never be dispensed with; all other ingredients, as they must be contained by, so must be controlled by this; and the only thing that standing alone may constitute the beautiful is form or outline. Accordingly, whatever addresses itself to or is suited to gratify the imagination takes this character: it falls into more or less of regularity and measure. Mere passion is of all things the most unmeasured and irregular, naturally the most opposed of all things to form. But in that state it is also wholly unfitted for the purposes of art; before it can become imaginative in any artistic sense it must have put off its original merely volcanic character, and worn itself into something of measure and music. Thus all impassioned composition is essentially melodious, in a higher or lower degree; measured language is the appropriate and natural expression of passion or deep feeling operating artistically in writing or speech. The highest and most perfect kind of measured language is verse; and passion expressing itself in verse is what is properly called poetry. Take away the verse, and in most cases you take away half the poetry, sometimes much more. The verse, in truth, is only one of several things by the aid of which the passion seeks to give itself effective expression, or by which the thought is endowed with additional animation or beauty; nay, it is only one ingredient of the musical expression of the thought or passion. If the verse may be dispensed with, so likewise upon the same principle may every decoration of the sentiment or statement, everything else that would do more than convey the bare fact. Let the experiment be tried, and see how it will answer. Take a single instance. "Immediately through the obscurity a great number of flags were seen to be raised, all richly coloured:" out of these words, no doubt, the reader or hearer might, after some meditation, extract the conception of a very imposing scene. But, although they intimate with sufficient exactness and distinctness the same literal fact, they are nevertheless the deadest prose compared with Milton's glorious words:—

> "All in a moment through the gloom were seen
> Ten thousand banners rise into the air,
> With orient colours waving."

And so it would happen in every other case in which true poetry was divested of its musical expression: a part, and it might be the greater part, of its life, beauty, and effect, would always be lost; and it would, in truth, cease to be what is distinctively called poetry or song, of which verse is as much one of the necessary constituents as passion or imagination itself. Those who dispute this will never be able to prove more than that their own enjoyment of the sensuous part of poetry, which is really that in which its peculiar character resides, is limited or feeble; which it may very well be in minds otherwise highly gifted, and even endowed with considerable imaginative power. The feeling of the merely beautiful, however, or of beauty unimpregnated by something of a moral spirit or meaning, is not likely in such minds to be very deep or strong. High art, therefore, is not their proper region, in any of its departments. In poetry they will probably not very greatly admire or enjoy either Spenser or Milton—and perhaps would prefer Paradise Lost in the prose version which Osborne the bookseller in the last century got a gentleman of Oxford to execute for the use of readers to whom the sense was rather obscured by the verse.

Passing over several of the great passages towards the commencement of the poem—such as the description of Queen Lucifera and her Six Counsellors in the Fourth Canto of the First Book, that of the visit of the Witch Duessa to Hell in the Fifth, and that of the Cave of Despair in the Ninth—which are probably more familiarly known to the generality of readers, we will take as a specimen of the Fairy Queen the escape of the Enchanter Archimage from Bragadoccio and his man Trompart, and the introduction and description of Belphoebe, in the Third Canto of Book Second:—

> He stayed not for more bidding, but away
> Was sudden vanished out of his sight:
> The northern wind his wings did broad display
> At his command, and reared him up light,
> From off the earth to take his airy flight.

SPENSER.

They looked about, but nowhere could espy
Tract of his foot; then dead through great affright
They both nigh were, and each bade other fly;
Both fled at once, ne ever back returned eye;

Till that they come unto a forest green,
In which they shrowd themselves from causeless fear;
Yet fear them follows still, whereso they been;
Each trembling leaf and whistling wind they hear
As ghastly bug¹ does greatly them afear;
Yet both do strive their fearfulness to feign.²
At last they heard a horn, that shrilled clear
Throughout the wood, that echoed again,
And made the forest ring, as it would rive in twain.

Eft³ through the thick they heard one rudely rush,
With noise whereof he from his lofty steed
Down fell to ground, and crept into a bush,
To hide his coward head from dying dread;
But Trompart stoutly stayed, to taken heed
Of what might hap. Eftsoon there stepped foorth
A goodly lady clad in hunter's weed,
That seemed to be a woman of great worth,
And by her stately portance⁴ born of heavenly birth.

Her face so fair as flesh it seemed not,
But heavenly portrait of bright angels' hue,
Clear as the sky, withouten blame or blot,
Through goodly mixture of complexions due;
And in her cheeks the vermeil red did show
Like roses in a bed of lillies shed,
The which ambrosial odours from them threw,
And gazers' sense with double pleasure fed,
Able to heal the sick, and to revive the dead.

In her fair eyes two living lamps did flame,
Kindled above at the heavenly Maker's light,
And darted fiery beams out of the same,
So passing persant and so wondrous bright
That quite bereaved the rash beholder's sight:
In them the blinded god his lustful fire
To kindle oft assayed, but had no might;
For with dread majesty and awful ire
She broke his wanton darts, and quenched base desire.

Her ivory forehead, full of bounty brave,
Like a broad table did itself disprend
For Love his lofty triumphs to engrave,
And write the battles of his great godhead:

---

¹ Bugbear. ² Conceal. ³ Soon. ⁴ Carriage.

All good and honour might therein be read,
For there their dwelling was; and, when she spake,
Sweet words like dropping honey she did shed,
And twixt the pearls and rubins[1] softly brake
A silver sound, that heavenly music seemed to make.

Upon her eyelids many graces sate,
Under the shadow of her even brows,
Working belgardes[2] and amorous retrate;[3]
And every one her with a grace endows,
And every one with meekness to her bows:
So glorious mirror of celestial grace,
And sovereign moniment of mortal vows,
How shall frail pen descrive[4] her heavenly face,
For fear through want of skill her beauty to disgrace?

So fair, and thousand thousand times more fair,
She seemed, when she presented was to sight;
And was yclad, for heat of scorching air,
All in a silken camus[5] lilly white,
Purfled[6] upon with many a folded plight;[7]
Which all above besprinkled was throughout
With golden aigulets, that glistened bright,
Like twinkling stars; and all the skirt about
Was hemmed with golden fringe.

Below her ham her weed[8] did somewhat train;[9]
And her straight legs most bravely were embailed[10]
In gilden[11] buskins of costly cordwain,[12]
All barred with golden bends, which were entailed[13]
With curious anticks,[14] and full fair aumailed;[15]
Before they fastened were under her knee
In a rich jewel, and therein entrailed[16]
The ends of all the knots, that none might see
How they within their foldings close enwrapped be.

Like two fair marble pillars they were seen,
Which do the temple of the gods support,
Whom all the people deck with girlonds[17] green,
And honour in their festival resort;
Those same with stately grace and princely port
She taught to tread, when she herself would grace;
But with the woody nymphs when she did sport,
Or when the flying libbard[18] she did chase,
She could them nimbly move, and after fly apace.

---

[1] Rubies.   [2] Beautiful looks.   [3] Aspect.   [4] Describe.
[5] Thin gown.   [6] Gathered.   [7] Plait.   [8] Dress.
[9] Hang.   [10] Enclosed.   [11] Gilded.   [12] Spanish leather.
[13] Engraved, marked.   [14] Figures.   [15] Enamelled.
[16] Interwoven.   [17] Garlands.   [18] Leopard.

And in her hand a sharp boar-spear she held,
And at her back a bow and quiver gay
Stuffed with steel-headed darts, wherewith she quelled
The salvage beasts in her victorious play,
Knit with a golden baldric, which forelay
Athwart her snowy breast, and did divide
Her dainty paps; which, like young fruit in May,
Now little, gan to swell, and, being tied,
Through her thin weed their places only signified.

Her yellow locks, crisped like golden wire,
About her shoulders weren loosely shed,
And, when the wind amongst them did inspire,
They waved like a penon wide dispread,
And low behind her back were scattered;
And, whether art it were or heedless hap,
As through the flowering forest rash she fled,
In her rude hairs sweet flowers themselves did lap,
And flourishing fresh leaves and blossoms did enwrap.

Such as Diana, by the sandy shore
Of swift Eurotas, or on Cynthus green,
Where all the nymphs have her unwares forlore,[1]
Wandereth alone, with bow and arrows keen,
To seek her game; or as that famous queen
Of Amazons, whom Pyrrhus did destroy,
The day that first of Priam she was seen
Did show herself in great triumphant joy,
To succour the weak state of sad afflicted Troy.

OTHER ELIZABETHAN POETRY.

In the six or seven years from 1590 to 1596, what a world of wealth had thus been added to our poetry by Spenser alone! what a different thing from what it was before had the English language been made by his writings to natives, to foreigners, to all posterity! But England was now a land of song, and the busiest and most productive age of our poetical literature had fairly commenced. What are commonly called the minor poets of the Elizabethan age are to be counted by hundreds, and few of them are altogether without merit. If they have nothing else, the least gifted of them have at least something of the freshness and airiness of that balmy morn, some tones caught from their greater contemporaries, some echoes of the spirit of music that then filled the universal air. For the most part the minor

---

[1] Forsaken.

Elizabethan poetry is remarkable for ingenuity and elaboration, often carried to the length of quaintness, both in the thought and the expression; but, if there be more in it of art than of nature, the art is still that of a high school, and always consists in something more than the mere disguising of prose in the dress of poetry. If it is sometimes unnatural, it is at least very seldom simply insipid, like much of the well-sounding verse of more recent eras. The writers are always in earnest, whether with their nature or their art; they never write from no impulse, and with no object except that of stringing commonplaces into rhyme or rhythm; even when it is most absurd, what they produce is still fanciful, or at the least fantastical. The breath of some sort of life or other is almost always in it. The poorest of it is distinguished from prose by something more than the mere sound.

WARNER.

The three authors of the poems of most pretension, with the exception of the Fairy Queen, that appeared during the period now under review, are Warner, Drayton, and Daniel. William Warner is supposed to have been born about the year 1558; he died in 1609. He has told us himself (in his Eleventh Book, chapter 62), that his birthplace was London, and that his father was one of those who sailed with Chancellor to Muscovy, in 1555: this, he says, was before he himself was born. Warner's own profession was the not particularly poetical one of an attorney of the Common Pleas. According to Anthony Wood, who makes him to have been a Warwickshire man, he had, before 1586 written several pieces of verse, "whereby his name was cried up among the minor poets;" but this is probably a mistake; none of this early poetry imputed to Warner is now known to exist; and in the Preface to his Albion's England, he seems to intimate that that was his first performance in verse. In the Dedication to his poem he explains the meaning of the title, which is not very obvious: "This our whole island," he observes, "anciently called Britain, but more anciently Albion, presently containing two kingdoms, England and Scotland, is cause (right honourable) that, to distinguish the former, whose only occurronts [occurrences] I abridge from our history, I entitle this my book Albion's England." Albion's England first appeared, in thirteen Books, in 1586: and was reprinted in 1589, in 1592, in 1596, in 1597, and in 1602. In 1606 the author added a

Continuance, or continuation, in three Books; and the whole work was republished (without, however, the last three Books having been actually reprinted) in 1612. In this last edition it is described on the title-page as "now revised, and newly enlarged [by the author] a little before his death." It thus appears that, so long as its popularity lasted, Albion's England was one of the most popular long poems ever written. But that was only for about twenty years: although the early portion of it had in less than that time gone through half a dozen editions, the Continuation, published in 1606, sold so indifferently that enough of the impression still remained to complete the book when the whole was republished in 1612, and after that no other edition was ever called for, till the poem was reprinted in Chalmers's collection in 1810. The entire neglect into which it so soon fell, from the height of celebrity and popular favour, was probably brought about by various causes. Warner, according to Anthony Wood, was ranked by his contemporaries on a level with Spenser, and they were called the Homer and Virgil of their age. If he and Spenser were ever equally admired, it must have been by very different classes of readers. Albion's England is undoubtedly a work of very remarkable talent of its kind. It is in form a history of England, or Southern Britain, from the Deluge to the reign of James I., but may fairly be said to be, as the title-page of the last edition describes it, "not barren in variety of inventive intermixtures." Or, to use the author's own words in his Preface, he certainly, as he hopes, has no great occasion to fear that he has grossly failed "in verity, brevity, invention, and variety, profitable, pathetical, pithy, and pleasant." In fact, it is one of the liveliest and most amusing poems ever written. Every striking event or legend that the old chronicles afford is seized hold of, and related always clearly, often with very considerable spirit and animation. But it is far from being a mere compilation; several of the narratives are not to be found anywhere else, and a large proportion of the matter is Warner's own, in every sense of the word. In this, as well as in other respects, it has greatly the advantage over the Mirror for Magistrates, as a rival to which work it was perhaps originally produced, and with the popularity of which it could scarcely fail considerably to interfere. Though a long poem (not much under 10,000 verses), it is still a much less ponderous work than the Mirror, absolutely as well as specifically. Its variety, though not obtained by any very artificial method, is infinite: not only are the stories it selects, unlike those in the Mirror, generally of a merry cast, and much more briefly and smartly told, but the reader is never kept long even on the same track or ground: all subjects, all departments of human knowledge or speculation, from theology down to common arithmetic, are intermixed, or rather interlaced, with the histories and legends in the most extraordinary manner. The verse is the favourite fourteen-syllable line of that age, the same in reality with that which has in modern times been commonly divided into two lines, the first of eight, the second of six syllables, and which in that form is still most generally used for short compositions in verse, more especially for those of a narrative or otherwise popular character. What Warner was chiefly admired for in his own day was his style. Meres in his Wit's Treasury mentions him as one of those by whom the English tongue in that age had been "mightily enriched, and gorgeously invested in rare ornaments and resplendent habiliments." And for fluency, combined with precision and economy of diction, Warner is probably unrivalled among the writers of English verse. We do not know whether his professional studies and habits may have contributed to give this character to his style; but, if the poetry of attorneys be apt to take this curt, direct, lucid, and at the same time flowing shape, it is a pity that we had not a little more of it. His command of the vulgar tongue, in particular, is wonderful. This indeed is perhaps his most remarkable poetical characteristic; and the tone which was thus given to his poem (being no doubt that of his own mind) may be conjectured to have been in great part the source both of its immense popularity for a time, and of the neglect and oblivion into which it was afterwards allowed to drop. Nevertheless, the poem, as we have said, has very remarkable merit in some respects, and many passages, or rather portions of passages, in it may still be read with pleasure. It is also in the highest degree curious both as a repository of our old language, and for many notices of the manners and customs of our ancestors which are scattered up and down in it. All that is commonly known of Warner is from the story of Argentile and Curan, which has been reprinted from his Fourth Book by Mrs. Cooper in The Muses' Library (1738), and by Percy in his Reliques, and that of The Patient Countess, which Percy has also given from his Eighth Book.

The following passage from the Third Book, being the conclusion of the 17th Chapter, is a specimen of Warner's very neatest style of narration.—He has related Cæsar's victory over the Britons, which he says was won with difficulty, the conquest of the country having been only accomplished through the submission of that "traitorous knight, the Earl of London," whose disloyal example in yielding his charge and city to the foe was followed by the other cities; and then he winds up thus:—

But he, that won in every war, at Rome in civil robe
Was stabbed to death : no certainty is underneath this globe;
The good are envied of the bad, and glory finds disdain,
And people are in constancy as April is in rain;
Whereof, amidst our serious pen, this fable entertain:—
An Ass, an Old Man, and a Boy did through the city pass;
And, whilst the wanton Boy did ride, the[1] Old Man led the Ass.
See yonder doting fool, said folk, that crawleth scarce for age,
Doth set the boy upon his ass, and makes himself his page.
Anon the blamed Boy alights, and lets the Old Man ride,
And, as the Old Man did before, the Boy the Ass did guide.
But, passing so, the people then did much the Old Man blame,
And told him, Churl, thy limbs be tough; let ride the boy, for shame.
The fault thus found, both Man and Boy did back the ass and ride;
Then that the ass was over-charged each man that met them cried.
Now both alight and go on foot, and lead the empty beast;
But then the people laugh, and say that one might ride at least.
The Old Man, seeing by no ways he could the people please,
Not blameless then, did drive the ass and drown him in the seas.
Thus, whilst we be, it will not be that any pleaseth all;
Else had been wanting, worthily, the noble Cæsar's fall.

The end of Richard the Third, in the Sixth Book (Chapter 26th), is given with much spirit:—

Now Richard heard that Richmond was assisted, and on shore,
And like unkenneled Cerberus the crooked tyrant swore,
And all complexions act at once confusedly in him;
He studieth, striketh, rareats, entreats, and looketh mildly grim;
Mistrustfully he trusteth, and he dreadingly doth[2] dare,
And forty passions in a trice in him consort and square.
But when, by his convented force, his foes increased more,
He hastened battle, finding his corrival apt therefore.
When Richmond orderly in all had battailed his aid,
Enringed by his complices, their cheerful leader said:—
Now is the time and place, sweet friends, and we the persons be
That must give England breath, or else unbreathe for her must we.
No tyranny is fabled, and no tyrant was indeed,
Worse than our foe, whose works will act my words if well be speed.
For ills[s] to ills superlative are easily enticed,
But entertain amendment as the Gergesites did Christ.

---

[1] In the printed copy "a." The edition before us, that of 1612, abounds with typographical errata.
[2] There can be no question that this is the true word, which is misprinted "did" in the edition before us.   [s] Misprinted "ill."

R

Be valiant then; he biddeth so that would not be outbid
For courage, yet shall honour him, though base, that better did.
I am right heir Lancastrian, he in York's destroyed right
Usurpeth; but, through either source,[1] for neither claim I fight,
But for our country's long-lacked weal, for England's peace, I war;
Wherein He speed us, unto whom I all events refer.
    Meanwhile had furious Richard set his armies in array,
And then, with looks even like himself, this or the like did say:—
Why, lads? shall yonder Welshman, with his stragglers, overmatch?
Disdain ye not such rivals, and defer ye their dispatch?
Shall Tudor from Plantagenet the crown by craking snatch?
Know Richard's very thoughts (he touched the diadem he wore)
Be metal of this metal: then believe I love it more
Than that for other law than life to supersede my claim;
And lesser must not be his plea that counterpleads the same.
    The weapons overtook his words, and blows they bravely change,
When like a lion, thirsting blood, did moody Richard range,
And made large slaughters where he went, till Richmond he espied,
Whom singling, after doubtful swords, the valorous tyrant died.

There are occasionally touches of true pathos in Warner, and one great merit which he has is, that his love of brevity generally prevents him from spoiling any stroke of this kind by multiplying words and images with the view of heightening the effect, as many of his contemporaries are prone to do. His picture of Fair Rosamond in the hands of Queen Eleanor is very touching:—

Fair Rosamond, surprised thus ere thus she did expect,
Fell on her humble knees, and did her fearful hands erect:
She blushed out beauty, whilst the tears did wash her pleasing face,
And begged pardon, meriting no less of common grace.
So far, forsooth, as in me lay, I did, quoth she, withstand;
But what may not so great a king by means or force command?
And dar'st thou, minion, quoth the Queen, thus article to me?
    .   .   .   .   .
With that she dashed her on the lips, so dyed double red:
Hard was the heart that gave the blow; soft were those lips that bled.
Then forced she her to swallow down, prepared for that intent,
A poisoned potion . . . . .

DANIEL.

The great work of Samuel Daniel, who was born at Taunton, in Somersetshire, in 1562, and died in 1619, is his Civil Wars between the Two Houses of Lancaster and York, in eight Books.

[1] This is the only reading like sense we can make out of "through either ours," which is the nonsense of the edition before us.

the first four published in 1595, the fifth in 1599, the sixth in 1602, the two last in 1609; the preceding Books being always, we believe, republished along with the new edition. He is also the author of various minor poetical productions, of which the principal are a collection of fifty-seven Sonnets entitled Delia, his Musophilus, containing a General Defence of Learning, some short epistles, and several tragedies and court masques. And he wrote, besides, in prose, a History of England, from the Conquest to the end of the reign of Edward III., as well as a Defence of Rhyme. Very opposite judgments have been passed upon Daniel. Ben Jonson, in his conversations with Drummond, declared him to be no poet: Drummond, on the contrary, pronounces him "for sweetness of rhyming second to none." His style, both in prose and verse, has a remarkably modern air: if it were weeded of a few obsolete expressions, it would scarcely seem more antique than that of Waller, which is the most modern of the seventeenth century. Bishop Kennet, who has republished Daniel's History, after telling us that the author had a place at Court in the reign of King James I., being groom of the privy chambers to the Queen, observes, that he "seems to have taken all the refinement a court could give him;" and probably the absence of pedantry in his style, and its easy and natural flow, are to be traced in great part to the circumstance of his having been a man of the world. His verse, too, always careful and exact, is in many passages more than smooth; even in his dramatic writings (which, having nothing dramatic about them except the form, have been held in very small estimation) it is frequently musical and sweet, though always artificial. The highest quality of his poetry is a tone of quiet, pensive reflection in which he is fond of indulging, and which often rises to dignity and eloquence, and has at times even something of depth and originality. Daniel's was the not uncommon fate of an attendant upon courts and the great: he is believed to have experienced some neglect from his royal patrons in his latter days, or at least to have been made jealous by Ben Jonson being employed to furnish part of the poetry for the court entertainments, the supply of which he used to have all to himself; upon which he retired to a life of quiet and contemplation in the country. It sounds strange in the present day to be told that his favourite retreat from the gaiety and bustle of London was a house which he rented in Old Street, St. Luke's. In his gardens here, we are informed by the writer of the Life prefixed to his collected poems, he would often indulge in entire solitude for many months, or at most receive the visits of only a few select friends. It is said to have been here that he composed most of his dramatic pieces. Towards the end of his life he retired to a farm which he had at Beckington, near Philip's Norton, in Somersetshire, and his death took place there. "He was married," says the editor of his works, "but whether to the person he so often celebrates under the name of Delia, is uncertain." Fuller, in his Worthies, tells us that his wife's name was Justina. They had no children. Daniel is said to have been appointed to the honorary post of Poet Laureate after the death of Spenser.

In his narrative poetry, Daniel is in general wire-drawn, flat, and feeble. He has no passion, and very little descriptive power. His Civil Wars has certainly as little of martial animation in it as any poem in the language. There is abundance, indeed, of "the tranquil mind;" but of "the plumed troops," and the rest of "the pride, pomp, and circumstance of glorious war," Daniel seems, in composing this work (we had nearly written in this composing work) to have taken as complete a farewell as Othello himself. It is mostly a tissue of long-winded disquisition and cold and languid declamation, and has altogether more of the qualities of a good opiate than of a good poem. We will therefore take the few extracts for which we can make room from some of his other productions, where his vein of reflection is more in place, and also better in itself. His Musophilus is perhaps upon the whole his finest piece. The poem, which is in the form of a dialogue between Philocosmus (a lover of the world) and Musophilus (a lover of the Muse), commences thus:—

Philocosmus.

Fond man, Musophilus, that thus dost spend
In an ungainful art thy dearest days,
Tiring thy wits, and toiling to no end
But to attain that idle smoke of praise!
Now, when this busy world cannot attend
The untimely music of neglected lays,
Other delights than these, other desires,
This wiser profit-seeking age requires.

Musophilus.

Friend Philocosmus, I confess indeed
I love this sacred art thou set'st so light:
And, though it never stand my life in stead,
It is enough it gives myself delight,
The whilst my unafflicted mind doth feed
On no unholy thoughts for benefit.

Be it that my unseasonable song
Come out of time, that fault is in the time;

And I must not do virtue so much wrong
As love her aught the worse for others' crime;
And yet I find some blessed spirits among
That cherish me, and like and grace my rhyme.

A gain that[1] I do more in soul esteem
Than all the gain of dust the world doth crave;
And, if I may attain but to redeem
My name from dissolution and the grave,
I shall have done enough; and better deem
To have lived to be than to have died to have.

Short-breathed mortality would yet extend
That span of life so far forth as it may,
And rob her fate; seek to beguile her end
Of some few lingering days of after-stay;
That all this Little All might not descend
Into the dark an universal prey;
And give our labours yet this poor delight
That, when our days do end, they are not done,
And, though we die, we shall not perish quite,
But live two lives where others have but one.

Afterwards Musophilus replies very finely to an objection of Philocosmus to the cultivation of poetry, from the small number of those who really cared for it:—

And for the few that only lend their ear,
That few is all the world; which with a few
Do ever live, and move, and work, and stir.
This is the heart doth feel, and only know;
The rest, of all that only bodies bear,
Roll up and down, and fill up but the row;

And serve as others' members, not their own,
The instruments of those that do direct.
Then, what disgrace is this, not to be known
To those know not to give themselves respect?
And, though they swell, with pomp of folly blown,
They live ungraced, and die but in neglect.

And, for my part, if only one allow
The care my labouring spirits take in this,
He is to me a theatre large enow,
And his applause only sufficient is;
All my respect is bent but to his brow;
That is my all, and all I am is his.

---

[1] Erroneously printed in the edition before us (2 vols. 12mo. 1718, "Again that."

> And, if some worthy spirits be pleased too,
> It shall more comfort breed, but not more will.
> But what if none? It cannot yet undo
> The love I bear unto this holy skill:
> This is the thing that I was born to do;
> This is my scene; this part must I fulfil.

It is in another poem, his Epistle to the Lady Margaret Countess of Cumberland (mother of Lady Anne Clifford, afterwards Countess of Pembroke, Dorset, and Montgomery, to whom Daniel had been tutor), that we have the stanza ending with the striking exclamation—

> —— Unless above himself he can
> Erect himself, how poor a thing is man!

DRAYTON.

Michael Drayton, who is computed to have been born in 1563, and who died in 1631, is one of the most voluminous of our old poets; being the author, besides many minor compositions, of three works of great length:—his Barons' Wars (on the subject of the civil wars of the reign of Edward II.), originally entitled Mortimeriados, under which name it was published in 1596; his England's Heroical Epistles, 1598; and his Polyolbion, the first eighteen Books of which appeared in 1612, and the whole, consisting of thirty Books, and extending to as many thousand lines, in 1622. This last is the work on which his fame principally rests. It is a most elaborate and minute topographical description of England, written in Alexandrine rhymes; and is a very remarkable work for the varied learning it displays, as well as for its poetic merits. The genius of Drayton is neither very imaginative nor very pathetic; but he is an agreeable and weighty writer, with an ardent, if not a highly creative, fancy. From the height to which he occasionally ascends, as well as from his power of keeping longer on the wing, he must be ranked, as he always has been, much before both Warner and Daniel. He has greatly more elevation than the former, and more true poetic life than the latter. The following is from the commencement of the Thirteenth Book, or Song, of the Polyolbion, the subject of which is the County of Warwick, of which Drayton, as he here tells us, was a native:—

> Upon the mid-lands now the industrious muse doth fall;
> That shire which we the heart of England well may call,

As she herself extends (the midst which is decreas'd),
Betwixt St. Michael's Mount and Berwick bordering Tweed,
Brave Warwick, that abroad so long advanced her Bear,
By her illustrious Earls renowned every where;
Above her neighbouring shires which always bore her head.
  My native country, then, which so brave spirits hast bred,
If there be virtues yet remaining in thy earth,
Or any good of thine thou bred'st into my birth,
Accept it as thine own, whilst now I sing of thee,
Of all thy later brood the unworthiest though I be.

When Phœbus lifts his head out of the water's[1] wave,
No sooner doth the earth her flowery bosom brave,
At such time as the year brings on the pleasant spring
But Hunt's up to the morn the feathered sylvans sing;
And, in the lower grove as on the rising knowl,
Upon the highest spray of every mounting pole
These quiristers are perched, with many a speckled breast:
Then from her burnished gate the goodly glittering East
Gilds every mountain-top, which late the humorous night
Bespangled had with pearl, to please the morning's sight;
On which the mirthful quires, with their clear open throats,
Unto the joyful morn so strain their warbling notes
That hills and valleys ring, and even the echoing air
Seems all composed of sounds about them every where.
The throstle with shrill sharps, as purposely he sung
To awake the lustless sun, or chiding that so long
He was in coming forth that should the thickets thrill;
The woosel near at hand; that hath a golden bill,
As nature him had marked of purpose t' let us see
That from all other birds his tunes should different be:
For with their vocal sounds they sing to pleasant May;
Upon his dulcet pipe the merle doth only play.
When in the lower brake the nightingale hard by
In such lamenting strains the joyful hours doth ply
As though the other birds she to her tunes would draw
And, but that Nature, by her all-constraining law,
Each bird to her own kind this season doth invite,
They else, alone to hear that charmer of the night
(The more to use their ears) their voices sure would spare,
That moduleth her notes so admirably rare
As man to set in parts at first had learned of her.
To Philomel the next the linnet we prefer;
And by that warbling the bird woodlark place we then,
The red-sparrow, the nope, the redbreast, and the wren;
The yellow-pate, which, though she hurt the blooming tree,
Yet scarce hath any bird a finer pipe than she.

---

[1] Or, perhaps, "watery." The common text gives "winter's."

And, of these chanting fowls, the goldfinch not behind,
That hath so many sorts descending from her kind.
The tydy, for her notes as delicate as they;
The laughing hecco; then, the counterfeiting jay.
The softer with the shrill, some hid among the leaves,
Some in the taller trees, some in the lower greaves,
Thus sing away the morn, until the mounting sun
Through thick exhaled fogs his golden head hath run,
And through the twisted tops of our close covert creeps
To kiss the gentle shade, this while that sweetly sleeps.

We will add a short specimen of Drayton's lighter style from his Nymphidia—the account of the equipage of the Queen of the Fairies, when she set out to visit her lover Pigwiggen. The reader may compare it with Mercutio's description in Romeo and Juliet:—

> Her chariot ready straight is made;
> Each thing therein is fitting laid,
> That she by nothing might be stayed,
>   For nought must be her letting;
> Four nimble gnats the horses were,
> Their harnesses of gossamer,
> Fly Cranion, her charioteer,
>   Upon the coach-box getting.
>
> Her chariot of a snail's fine shell,
> Which for the colours did excel,
> The fair Queen Mab becoming well,
>   So lively was the limning;
> The seat the soft wool of the bee,
> The cover (gallantly to see)
> The wing of a pied butterflee;
>   I trow 'twas simple trimming.
>
> The wheels composed of cricket's bones,
> And daintily made for the nonce;
> For fear of rattling on the stones
>   With thistle down they shod it;
> For all her maidens much did fear
> If Oberon had chanced to hear
> That Mab his queen should have been there,
>   He would not have abode it.
>
> She mounts her chariot with a trice,
> Nor would she stay for no advice
> Until her maids, that were so nice,
>   To wait on her were fitted;
> But ran herself away alone;
> Which when they heard, there was not one
> But hasted after to be gone,
>   As she had been diswitted.

Hop, and Mop, and Drab so clear,
Pip and Trip, and Skip, that were
To Mab their sovereign so dear,
 Her special maids of honour;
Fib, and Tib, and Pink, and Pin,
Tick, and Quick, and Jill, and Jin,
Tit, and Nit, and Wap, and Win,
 The train that wait upon her.

Upon a grasshopper they got,
And, what with amble and with trot,
For hedge nor ditch they spared not,
 But after her they hie them:
A cobweb over them they throw,
To shield the wind if it should blow;
Themselves they wisely could bestow
 Lest any should espy them.

JOSEPH HALL.

Joseph Hall was born in 1574, and was successively bishop of Exeter and Norwich, from the latter of which sees having been expelled by the Long Parliament, he died, after protracted sufferings from imprisonment and poverty, in 1656. Hall began his career of authorship by the publication of Three Books of Satires, in 1597, while he was a student at Cambridge, and only in his twenty-third year. A continuation followed the next year under the title of Virgidemiarum the Three last Books; and the whole were afterwards republished together, as Virgidemiarum Six Books; that is, six books of bundles of rods. "These satires," says Warton, who has given an elaborate analysis of them, "are marked with a classical precision to which English poetry had yet early attained. They are replete with animation of style and sentiment. . . . The characters are delineated in strong and lively colouring, and their discriminations are touched with the masterly traces of genuine humour. The versification is equally energetic and elegant, and the fabric of the couplets approaches to the modern standard."* Hall's Satires have been repeatedly reprinted in modern times.

SYLVESTER.

One of the most popular poets of this date was Joshua Sylvester, the translator of The Divine Weeks and Works, and

* Hist. of Eng. Poet. iv. 338.

other productions, of the French poet Du Bartas. Sylvester has the honour of being supposed to have been one of the early favourites of Milton. In one of his publications he styles himself a Merchant-Adventurer, and he seems to have belonged to the Puritan party, which may have had some share in influencing Milton's regard. His translation of Du Bartas was first published in 1605; and the seventh edition (beyond which, we believe, its popularity did not carry it) appeared in 1641. Nothing can be more uninspired than the general run of Joshua's verse, or more fantastic and absurd than the greater number of its more ambitious passages; for he had no taste or judgment, and, provided the stream of sound and the jingle of the rhyme were kept up, all was right in his notion. His poetry consists chiefly of translations from the French; but he is also the author of some original pieces, the title of one of which, a courtly offering from the poetical Puritan to the prejudices of King James, may be quoted as a lively specimen of his style and genius:—" Tobacco battered, and the pipes shattered, about their ears that idly idolize so base and barbarous a weed, or at leastwise overlove so loathsome a vanity, by a volley of holy shot thundered from Mount Helicon."* But, with all his general flatness and frequent absurdity, Sylvester has an uncommon flow of harmonious words at times, and occasionally even some fine lines and felicitous expressions. His contemporaries called him the " Silver-tongued Sylvester," for what they considered the sweetness of his versification—and some of his best passages justify the title. Indeed, even when the substance of what he writes approaches nearest to nonsense, the sound is often very graceful, soothing the ear with something like the swing and ring of Dryden's heroics. The commencement of the following passage from his translation of Du Bartas may remind the reader of Milton's " Hail, holy light! offspring of heaven first-born ":—

> All hail, pure lamp, bright, sacred, and excelling;
> Sorrow and care, darkness and dread repelling;
> Thou world's great taper, wicked man's just terror,
> Mother of truth, true beauty's only mirror,
> God's eldest daughter; O! how thou art full
> Of grace and goodness! O! how beautiful!
>   .   .   .   .   .   .
> But yet, because all pleasures wax unpleasant
> If without pause we still possess them present,
> And none can right discern the sweets of peace
> That have not felt war's irksome bitterness,

---

* 8vo. Lond. 1615.

And swans seem whiter if swart crows be by
(For contraries each other best descry),
The All's architect alternately decreed
That Night the Day, the Day should Night succeed.
  The Night, to temper Day's exceeding drought,
Moistens our air, and makes our earth to sprout:
The Night is she that all our travails eases,
Buries our cares, and all our griefs appeases:
The Night is she that, with her sable wing
In gloomy darkness hushing every thing,
Through all the world dumb silence doth distil,
And wearied bones with quiet sleep doth fill.
  Sweet Night! without thee, without thee, alas!
Our life were loathsome, even a hell, to pass;
For outward pains and inward passions still,
With thousand deaths, would soul and body thrill.
O Night, thou pullest the proud masque away
Wherewith vain actors, in this world's great play,
By day disguise them. For no difference
Night makes between the peasant and the prince,
The poor and rich, the prisoner and the judge,
The foul and fair, the master and the drudge,
The fool and wise, Barbarian and the Greek;
For Night's black mantle covers all alike.

Chapman's Homer.

  George Chapman was born at Hitching Hill, in the county of Hertford, in 1557, and lived till 1634. Besides his plays, which will be afterwards noticed, he is the author of several original poetical pieces; but he is best and most favourably known by his versions of the Iliad and the Odyssey. "He would have made a great epic poet," Charles Lamb has said, in his Specimens of the English Dramatic Poets, turning to these works after having characterized his dramas, "if, indeed, he has not abundantly shown himself to be one: for his Homer is not so properly a translation as the stories of Achilles and Ulysses re-written. The earnestness and passion which he has put into every part of these poems would be incredible to a reader of mere modern translations. His almost Greek zeal for the honour of his heroes is only paralleled by that fierce spirit of Hebrew bigotry with which Milton, as if personating one of the zealots of the old law, clothed himself when he sat down to paint the acts of Samson against the uncircumcised. The great obstacle to Chapman's translations being read is their unconquerable quaintness. He pours out in the same breath the most just and natural, and the most violent and forced expressions. He seems to grasp whatever words come first to hand during the impetus of inspiration, as if all other must be inadequate to the divine meaning. But passion (the all in all in poetry) is everywhere present, raising the low, dignifying the mean, and putting sense into the absurd. He makes his readers glow, weep, tremble, take any affection which he pleases, be moved by words or in spite of them, be disgusted and overcome that disgust." Chapman's Homer is, in some respects, not unworthy of this enthusiastic tribute. Few writers have been more copiously inspired with the genuine frenzy of poetry. With more judgment and more care he might have given to his native language, in his version of the Iliad, one of the very greatest of the poetical works it possesses. In spite, however, of a hurry and impetuosity which betray him into many mistranslations, and, on the whole, have the effect perhaps of giving a somewhat too tumultuous and stormy representation of the Homeric poetry, the English into which Chapman transfuses the meaning of the mighty ancient is often singularly and delicately beautiful. He is the author of nearly all the happiest of the compound epithets which Pope has adopted, and of many others equally musical and expressive. "Far-shooting Phœbus," —"the ever-living gods,"—"the many-headed hill,"—"the ivory-wristed queen,"—are a few of the felicitous combinations with which he has enriched his native tongue. Carelessly executed, indeed, as the work for the most part is, there is scarcely a page of it that is not irradiated by gleams of the truest poetic genius. Often in the midst of a long paragraph of the most chaotic versification, the fatigued and distressed ear is surprised by a few lines,—or it may be sometimes only a single line,—"musical as is Apollo's lute,"—and sweet and graceful enough to compensate for ten times as much ruggedness.

HARINGTON; FAIRFAX; FANSHAWE.

Of the translators of foreign poetry which belong to this period, three are very eminent. Sir John Harington's translation of the Orlando Furioso first appeared in 1591, when the author was in his thirtieth year. It does not convey all the glow and poetry of Ariosto; but it is, nevertheless, a performance of great ingenuity and talent. The translation of Tasso's great epic by Edward Fairfax was first published, under the title of Godfrey of Bulloigne, or the Recoverie of Jerusalem, in 1600. This is a work of true genius, full of passages of great beauty; and, although by no means a perfectly exact or servile version of the Italian original, is throughout executed with as much care as taste and spirit.* Sir Richard Fanshawe is the author of versions of Camoens's Lusiad, of Guarini's Pastor Fido, of the Fourth Book of the Æneid, of the Odes of Horace, and of the Querer por Solo Querer (To love for love's sake) of the Spanish dramatist Mendoza. Some passages from the last-mentioned work, which was published in 1649, may be found in Lamb's Specimens,† the ease and flowing gaiety of which never have been excelled even in original writing. The Pastor Fido is also rendered with much spirit and elegance. Fanshawe is, besides, the author of a Latin translation of Fletcher's Faithful Shepherdess, and of some original poetry. His genius, however, was sprightly and elegant rather than lofty, and perhaps he does not succeed so well in translating poetry of a more serious style.

DRUMMOND.

One of the most graceful poetical writers of the reign of James I. is William Drummond, of Hawthornden, near Edinburgh; and he is further deserving of notice as the first of his countrymen, at least of any eminence, who aspired to write in English. He has left us a quantity of prose as well as verse; the former very much resembling the style of Sir Philip Sidney in his Arcadia,—the latter, in manner and spirit, formed more upon the model of Surrey, or rather upon that of Petrarch and the other Italian poets whom Surrey and many of his English successors imitated. No early English imitator of the Italian poetry, however, has excelled Drummond, either in the sustained melody of his verse, or its rich vein of thoughtful tenderness.

DAVIES.

A remarkable poem of this age, first published in 1599, is the Nosce Teipsum of Sir John Davies, who was successively solicitor- and attorney-general in the reign of James, and had been appointed to the place of Chief Justice of the King's Bench, when he died, before he could enter upon its duties, in 1626.

* Reprinted in the Tenth and Fourteenth Volumes of KNIGHT'S WEEKLY VOLUME.   † Vol. ii. pp. 242—253.

Davies is also the author of a poem on dancing entitled Orchestra, and of some minor pieces, all distinguished by vivacity as well as precision of style; but he is only now remembered for his philosophical poem, the earliest of the kind in the language. It is written in rhyme, in the common heroic ten-syllable verse, but disposed in quatrains. No other writer has managed this difficult stanza so successfully as Davies: it has the disadvantage of requiring the sense to be in general closed at certain regularly and quickly recurring turns, which yet are very ill adapted for an effective pause; and even all the skill of Dryden has been unable to free it from a certain air of monotony and languor,—a circumstance of which that poet may be supposed to have been himself sensible, since he wholly abandoned it after one or two early attempts. Davies, however, has conquered its difficulties; and, as has been observed, "perhaps no language can produce a poem, extending to so great a length, of more condensation of thought, or in which fewer languid verses will be found."* In fact, it is by this condensation and sententious brevity, so carefully filed and elaborated, however, as to involve no sacrifice of perspicuity or fullness of expression, that he has attained his end. Every quatrain is a pointed expression of a separate thought, like one of Rochefoucault's Maxims; each thought being, by great skill and painstaking in the packing, made exactly to fit and to fill the same case. It may be doubted, however, whether Davies would not have produced a still better poem if he had chosen a measure which would have allowed him greater freedom and real variety; unless, indeed, his poetical talent was of a sort that required the suggestive aid and guidance of such artificial restraints as he had to cope with in this, and what would have been a bondage to a more fiery and teeming imagination was rather a support to his.

Donne.

The title of the Metaphysical School of poetry, which in one sense of the words might have been given to Davies and his imitators, has been conferred by Dryden upon another race of writers, whose founder was a contemporary of Davies, the famous Dr. John Donne, Dean of St. Paul's. Donne, who died at the age of fifty-eight, in 1631, is said to have written most of his poetry before the end of the sixteenth century, but none of it was published till late in the reign of James. It consists of

* Hallam, Lit. of Europe, ii. 227.

lyrical pieces (entitled Songs and Sonnets), epithalamions or marriage songs, funeral and other elegies, satires, epistles, and divine poems. On a superficial inspection, Donne's verses look like so many riddles. They seem to be written upon the principle of making the meaning as difficult to be found out as possible—of using all the resources of language, not to express thought, but to conceal it. Nothing is said in a direct, natural manner; conceit follows conceit without intermission; the most remote analogies, the most far-fetched images, the most unexpected turns, one after another, surprise and often puzzle the understanding; while things of the most opposite kinds—the harsh and the harmonious, the graceful and the grotesque, the grave and the gay, the pious and the profane—meet and mingle in the strangest of dances. But, running through all this bewilderment, a deeper insight detects not only a vein of the most exuberant wit, but often the sunniest and most delicate fancy, and the truest tenderness and depth of feeling. Donne, though in the latter part of his life he became a very serious and devout poet as well as man, began by writing amatory lyrics, the strain of which is anything rather than devout; and in this kind of writing he seems to have formed his poetic style, which, for such compositions, would, to a mind like his, be the most natural and expressive of any. The species of lunacy which quickens and exalts the imagination of a lover, would, in one of so seething a brain as he was, strive to expend itself in all sorts of novel and wayward combinations, just as Shakespeare has made it do in his Romeo and Juliet, whose rich intoxication of spirit he has by nothing else set so livingly before us, as by making them thus exhaust all the eccentricities of language in their struggle to give expression to that inexpressible passion which had taken captive the whole heart and being of both. Donne's later poetry, in addition to the same abundance and originality of thought, often running into a wildness and extravagance not so excusable here as in his erotic verses, is famous for the singular movement of the versification, which has been usually described as the extreme degree of the rugged and tuneless. Pope has given us a translation of his four Satires into modern language, which he calls The Satires of Dr. Donne Versified. Their harshness, as contrasted with the music of his lyrics, has also been referred to as proving that the English language, at the time when Donne wrote, had not been brought to a sufficiently advanced state for the writing of heroic verse in perfection.* That this last notion is wholly unfounded, numerous examples sufficiently testify;

* See article on Donne in Penny Cyclopædia, vol. ix. p. 85.

not to speak of the blank verse of the dramatists, the rhymed heroics of Shakespeare, of Fletcher, of Jonson, of Spenser, and of other writers contemporary with and of earlier date than Donne, are, for the most part, as perfectly smooth and regular as any that have since been written; at all events, whatever irregularity may be detected in them, if they be tested by Pope's narrow gamut, is clearly not to be imputed to any immaturity in the language. These writers evidently preferred and cultivated, deliberately and on principle, a wider compass, and freer and more varied flow, of melody than Pope had a taste or an ear for. Nor can it be questioned, we think, that the peculiar construction of Donne's verse in his satires and many of his other later poems was also adopted by choice and on system. His lines, though they will not suit the see-saw style of reading verse,—to which he probably intended that they should be invincibly impracticable,—are not without a deep and subtle music of their own, in which the cadences respond to the sentiment, when enunciated with a true feeling of all that they convey. They are not smooth or luscious verses, certainly; nor is it contended that the endeavour to raise them to as vigorous and impressive a tone as possible, by depriving them of all oversweetness or liquidity, has not been carried too far; but we cannot doubt that whatever harshness they have was designedly given to them, and was conceived to infuse into them an essential part of their relish.

Here is one of Donne's Songs:—

  Sweetest love, I do not go
   For weariness of thee,
  Nor in hope the world can show
   A fitter love for me;
   But, since that I
  Must die at last, 'tis best
  Thus to use myself in jest
   By feigned death to die.

  Yesternight the sun went hence,
   And yet is here to-day;
  He hath no desire nor sense,
   Nor half so short a way:
   Then fear not me,
  But believe that I shall make
  Hastier journeys, since I take
   More wings and spurs than he.

  O how feeble is man's power!
   That, if good fortune fall,
  Cannot add another hour,
   Nor a lost hour recall;

But come bad chance,
And we join to it our strength,
And we teach it art and length
Itself o'er us to advance.

When thou sigh'st thou sigh'st not wind,
But sigh'st my soul away;
When thou weep'st, unkindly kind,
My life's blood doth decay.
It cannot be
That thou lov'st me as thou may'st,
If in thine my life thou waste,
Which art the life of me.

Let not thy divining heart
Forethink me any ill;
Destiny may take thy part
And may thy fears fulfil;
But think that we
Are but laid aside to sleep:
They who one another keep
Alive ne'er parted be.

Somewhat fantastic as this may be thought, it is surely, notwithstanding, full of feeling; and nothing can be more delicate than the execution. Nor is it possible that the writer of such verses can have wanted an ear for melody, however capriciously he may have sometimes experimented upon language, in the effort, as we conceive, to bring a deeper, more expressive music out of it than it would readily yield.

SHAKESPEARE'S MINOR POEMS.

In the long list of the minor names of the Elizabethan poetry appears the bright name of William Shakespeare. Shakespeare published his Venus and Adonis in 1593, and his Tarquin and Lucrece in 1594; his Passionate Pilgrim did not appear till 1599; the Sonnets not till 1609. It is probable, however, that the first mentioned of these pieces, which, in his dedication of it to the Earl of Southampton, he calls the first heir of his invention, was written some years before its publication; and, although the Tarquin and Lucrece may have been published immediately after it was composed, it, too, may be accounted an early production. But, although this minor poetry of Shakespeare sounds throughout like the utterance of that spirit of highest invention and sweetest song before it had found its proper theme, much is here also, immature as it may be, that is still all Shakespearian

—the vivid conception, the inexhaustible fertility and richness of thought and imagery, the glowing passion, the gentleness withal that is ever of the poetry as it was of the man, the enamoured sense of beauty, the living words, the ear-delighting and heart-enthralling music; nay, even the dramatic instinct itself, and the idea at least, if not always the realization, of that sentiment of all subordinating and consummating art of which his dramas are the most wonderful exemplification in literature.

SHAKESPEARE'S DRAMATIC WORKS.

Shakespeare, born in 1564, is enumerated as one of the proprietors of the Blackfriars Theatre in 1589; is sneered at by Robert Greene in 1592, in terms which seem to imply that he had already acquired a considerable reputation as a dramatist and a writer in blank verse, though the satirist insinuates that he was enabled to make the show he did chiefly by the plunder of his predecessors;* and in 1598 is spoken of by a critic of the day as indisputably the greatest of English dramatists, both for tragedy and comedy, and as having already produced his Two Gentlemen of Verona, Comedy of Errors, Love's Labours Lost, Love's Labours Won (generally supposed to be All's Well that Ends Well),† Midsummer Night's Dream, Merchant of Venice, Richard II., Richard III., Henry IV., King John, Titus Andronicus, and Romeo and Juliet.‡ There is no ground, however, for feeling assured, and, indeed, it is rather improbable, that we have here a complete catalogue of the plays written by Shakespeare up to this date; nor is the authority of so evidently loose a statement, embodying, it is to be supposed, the mere report of the town, sufficient even to establish absolutely the authenticity of every one of the plays enumerated. It is very possible, for

---

* "There is an upstart crow, beautified with our feathers, that, with his tiger's heart wrapt in a player's hide, supposes he is as well able to bombast out a blank verse as the best of you; and, being an absolute Johannes Factotum, is, in his own conceit, the only Shake-scene in a country."—Greene's Groatsworth of Wit, 1592.

† But the Rev. Joseph Hunter, in the Second Part of New Illustrations of the Life, Studies, and Writings of Shakespeare, 8vo. Lond. 1844, and previously in a Disquisition on the Tempest, separately published, has contended that it must be the Tempest; and I have more recently stated some reasons for supposing that it may be the Taming of the Shrew (see The English of Shakespeare, 1857; Prolegomena, pp. 8, 9).

‡ Palladis Tamia; Wit's Treasury. Being the Second Part of Wit's Commonwealth. By Francis Meres, 1598, p. 282.

example, that Meres may be mistaken in assigning Titus Andronicus to Shakespeare; and, on the other hand, he may be the author of Pericles, and may have already written that play and some others, although Meres does not mention them. The only other direct or positive information we possess on this subject is, that a History called Titus Andronicus, presumed to be the play afterwards published as Shakespeare's, was entered for publication at Stationers' Hall in 1593; that the Second Part of Henry VI. (if it is by Shakespeare), in its original form of The First Part of the Contention betwixt the Two Famous Houses of York and Lancaster, was published in 1594; the Third Part of Henry VI. (if by Shakespeare), in its original form of The True Tragedy of Richard Duke of York, in 1595; his Richard II., Richard III., and Romeo and Juliet, in 1597; Love's Labours Lost and the First Part of Henry IV. in 1598 (the latter, however, having been entered at Stationers' Hall the preceding year); "a corrected and augmented" edition of Romeo and Juliet in 1599; Titus Andronicus (supposing it to be Shakespeare's), the Second Part of Henry IV., Henry V., in its original form, the Midsummer Night's Dream, Much Ado about Nothing, and the Merchant of Venice, in 1600 (the last having been entered at Stationers' Hall in 1598); the Merry Wives of Windsor, in its original form, in 1602 (but entered at Stationers' Hall the year before*); Hamlet in 1603 (entered likewise the year before); a second edition of Hamlet, "enlarged to almost as much again as it was, according to the true and perfect copy," in 1604; Lear in 1608, and Troilus and Cressida, and Pericles, in 1609 (each being entered the preceding year); Othello not till 1622, six years after the author's death; and all the other plays, namely, the Two Gentlemen of Verona, the Winter's Tale, the Comedy of Errors, King John, All's Well that Ends Well, As You Like It, King Henry VIII., Measure for Measure, Cymbeline, Macbeth, the Taming of the Shrew, Julius Cæsar, Antony and Cleopatra, Coriolanus, Timon of Athens, the Tempest, Twelfth Night, the First Part of Henry VI. (if Shakespeare had anything to do with that play†), and also the perfect editions of Henry V., the Merry Wives of Windsor, and the Second and Third Parts of Henry VI.,

---

* This first sketch of the Merry Wives of Windsor has been reprinted for the Shakespeare Society, under the care of Mr. Halliwell, 1842.

† See upon this question Mr. Knight's Essay upon the Three Parts of King Henry VI. and King Richard III., in the Seventh Volume of his Library Edition of Shakspere, pp. 1—119. And see also Mr. Halliwell's Introduction to the reprint of The First Sketches of the Second and Third Parts of King Henry the Sixth (the First Part of the Contention and the True Tragedy), edited by him for the Shakespeare Society, 1843.

not, so far as is known, till they appear, along with those formerly printed, in the first folio, in 1623.

Such then is the sum of the treasure that Shakespeare has left us; but the revolution which his genius wrought upon our national drama is placed in the clearest light by comparing his earliest plays with the best which the language possessed before his time. He has made all his predecessors obsolete. While his Merchant of Venice, and his Midsummer Night's Dream, and his Romeo and Juliet, and his King John, and his Richard II., and his Henry IV., and his Richard III., all certainly produced, as we have seen, before the year 1598, are still the most universally familiar compositions in our literature, no other dramatic work that had then been written is now popularly read, or familiar to anybody except to a few professed investigators of the antiquities of our poetry. Where are now the best productions even of such writers as Greene, and Peele, and Marlow, and Decker, and Marston, and Webster, and Thomas Heywood, and Middleton? They are to be found among our Select Collections of Old Plays,—publications intended rather for the mere preservation of the pieces contained in them, than for their diffusion among a multitude of readers. Or, if the entire works of a few of those elder dramatists have recently been collected and republished, this has still been done only to meet the demand of a comparatively very small number of curious students, anxious to possess and examine for themselves whatever relics are still recoverable of the old world of our literature. Popularly known and read the works of these writers never again will be: there is no more prospect or probability of this than there is that the plays of Shakespeare will over lose their popularity among his countrymen. In that sense, overlasting oblivion is their portion, as everlasting life is his. In one form only have they any chance of again attracting some measure of the general attention—namely, in the form of such partial and very limited exhibition as Lamb has given us an example of in his Specimens. And herein we see the first great difference between the plays of Shakespeare and those of his predecessors, and one of the most immediately conspicuous of the improvements which he introduced into dramatic writing. He did not create our regular drama, but he regenerated and wholly transformed it, as if by breathing into it a new soul. We possess no dramatic production anterior to his appearance that is at once a work of high genius and of anything like equably sustained power throughout. Very brilliant flights of poetry there are in many of the pieces of our earlier dramatists; but the higher they soar in one scene, the lower they generally seem to think it expedient to sink in the next. Their great efforts are made only by fits and starts: for the most part it must be confessed that the best of them are either merely extravagant and absurd, or do nothing but trifle or doze away over their task with the expenditure of hardly any kind of faculty at all. This may have arisen in part from their own want of judgment or want of painstaking, in part from the demands of a very rude condition of the popular taste; but the effect is to invest all that they have bequeathed to us with an air of barbarism, and to tempt us to take their finest displays of successful daring for more capricious inspirations, resembling the sudden impulses of fury by which the listless and indolent man of the woods will sometimes be roused for the instant from his habitual laziness and passiveness to an exhibition of superhuman strength and activity. From this savage or savage-looking state our drama was first redeemed by Shakespeare. Even Milton has spoken of his "wood-notes wild;" and Thomson, more unceremoniously, has baptized him "wild Shakespeare,"*—as if a sort of half insane irregularity of genius were the quality that chiefly distinguished him from other great writers. If he be a "wild" writer, it is in comparison with some dramatists and poets of succeeding times, who, it must be admitted, are sufficiently tame: compared with the dramatists of his own age and of the age immediately preceding,—with the general throng of the writers from among whom he emerged, and the coruscations of whose feebler and more desultory genius he has made pale,—he is distinguished from them by nothing which is more visible at the first glance than by the superior regularity and elaboration that mark his productions. Marlow, and Greene, and Kyd may be called wild, and wayward, and careless; but the epithets are inapplicable to Shakespeare, by whom, in truth, it was that the rudeness of our early drama was first refined, and a spirit of high art put into it, which gave it order and symmetry as well as elevation. It was the union of the most consummate judgment with the highest creative power that made Shakespeare the miracle that he was,—if, indeed, we ought not rather to say that such an endowment as his of the poetical faculty necessarily implied the clearest and truest discernment as well as the utmost productive energy,—even as the most intense heat must illuminate as well as warm.

But, undoubtedly, his dramas are distinguished from those of his predecessors by much more than merely this superiority in

* "Is not wild Shakespeare thine and Nature's boast?"—Thomson's *Summer*.

the general principles upon which they are constructed. Such rare passages of exquisite poetry, and scenes of sublimity or true passion, as sometimes brighten the dreary waste of their productions, are equalled or excelled in almost every page of his;— "the highest heaven of invention," to which they ascend only in far distant flights, and where their strength of pinion never sustains them long, is the familiar home of his genius. Other qualities, again, which charm us in his plays are nearly unknown in theirs. He first informed our drama with true wit and humour. Of boisterous, uproarious, blackguard merriment and buffoonery there is no want in our earlier dramatists, nor of mere gibing and jeering and vulgar personal satire; but of true airy wit there is little or none. In the comedies of Shakespeare the wit plays and dazzles like dancing light. This seems to have been the excellence, indeed, for which he was most admired by his contemporaries; for quickness and felicity of repartee they placed him above all other play-writers. But his humour was still more his own than his wit. In that rich but delicate and subtile spirit of drollery, moistening and softening whatever it touches like a gentle oil, and penetrating through all enfoldings and rigorous encrustments into the kernel of the ludicrous that is in everything, which mainly created Malvolio, and Shallow, and Slender, and Dogberry, and Verges, and Bottom, and Lancelot, and Launce, and Costard, and Touchstone, and a score of other clowns, fools, and simpletons, and which, gloriously overflowing in Falstaff, makes his wit exhilarate like wine, Shakespeare has had almost as few successors as he had predecessors.

And in these and all his other delineations he has, like every other great poet, or artist, not merely observed and described, but, as we have said, created, or invented. It is often laid down that the drama should be a faithful picture or representation of real life; or, if this doctrine be given up in regard to the tragic or more impassioned drama, because even kings and queens in the actual world never do declaim in the pomp of blank verse, as they do on the stage, still it is insisted that in comedy no character is admissible that is not a transcript,—a little embellished perhaps,—but still substantially a transcript from some genuine flesh and blood original. But Shakespeare has shown that it belongs to such an imagination as his to create in comedy, as well as in tragedy or in poetry of any other kind. Most of the characters that have just been mentioned are as truly the mere creations of the poet's brain as are Ariel, or Caliban, or the Witches in Macbeth. If any modern critic will have it that Sahkespeare must have actually seen Malvolio, and Launce, and

Touchstone, before he could or at least would have drawn them, we would ask the said critic if he himself has ever seen such characters in real life; and, if he acknowledge, as he needs must, that he never has, we would then put it to him to tell us why the contemporaries of the great dramatist might not have enjoyed them in his plays without ever having seen them elsewhere, just as we do,—or, in other words, why such delineations might not have perfectly fulfilled their dramatic purpose then as well as now, when they certainly do not represent anything that is to be seen upon earth, any more than do Don Quixote and Sancho Panza. There might have been professional clowns and fools in the age of Shakespeare such as are no longer extant; but at no time did there ever actually exist such fools and clowns as his. These and other similar personages of the Shakespearian drama are as much mere poetical phantasmata as are the creations of the kindred humour of Cervantes. Are they the less amusing or interesting, however, on that account?—do we the less sympathize with them?—nay, do we feel that they are the less naturally drawn? that they have for us less of a truth and life than the most faithful copies from the men and women of the real world?

But in the region of reality, too, there is no other drama so rich as that of Shakespeare. He has exhausted the old world of our actual experience as well as imagined for us new worlds of his own.* What other anatomist of the human heart has searched its hidden core, and laid bare all the strength and weakness of our mysterious nature, as he has done in the gushing tenderness of Juliet, and the "fine frenzy" of the discrowned Lear, and the sublime melancholy of Hamlet, and the wrath of the perplexed and tempest-torn Othello, and the eloquent misanthropy of Timon, and the fixed hate of Shylock? What other poetry has given shape to anything half so terrific as Lady Macbeth, or so winning as Rosalind, or so full of gentlest womanhood as Desdemona? In what other drama do we behold so living a humanity as in his? Who has given us a scene either so crowded with diversities of character, or so stirred with the heat and hurry of actual existence? The men and the manners of all countries and of all ages are there: the lovers and warriors, the priests and prophetesses, of the old heroic and kingly times of Greece,—the Athenians of the days of Pericles and Alcibiades,—the proud patricians and turbulent commonalty of the earliest period of republican Rome,—Cæsar, and Brutus,

* { "Each change of many-coloured life he drew, Exhausted worlds, and then imagined new."—Johnson.

and Cassius, and Antony, and Cleopatra, and the other splendid figures of that later Roman scene,—the kings, and queens, and princes, and courtiers of barbaric Denmark, and Roman Britain, and Britain before the Romans,—those of Scotland in the time of the English Heptarchy,—those of England and France at the era of Magna Charta,—all ranks of the people of almost every reign of our subsequent history from the end of the fourteenth to the middle of the sixteenth century,—not to speak of Venice, and Verona, and Mantua, and Padua, and Illyria, and Navarre, and the Forest of Arden, and all the other towns and lands which he has peopled for us with their most real inhabitants.

Nor even in his plays is Shakespeare merely a dramatist. Apart altogether from his dramatic power he is the greatest poet that ever lived. His sympathy is the most universal, his imagination the most plastic, his diction the most expressive, ever given to any writer. His poetry has in itself the power and varied excellences of all other poetry. While in grandeur, and beauty, and passion, and sweetest music, and all the other higher gifts of song, he may be ranked with the greatest,—with Spenser, and Chaucer, and Milton, and Dante, and Homer,—he is at the same time more nervous than Dryden, and more sententious than Pope, and more sparkling and of more abounding conceit, when he chooses, than Donne, or Cowley, or Butler. In whose handling was language ever such a flame of fire as it is in his? His wonderful potency in the use of this instrument would alone set him above all other writers.* Language has been called the costume of thought: it is such a costume as leaves are to the tree or blossoms to the flower, and grows out of what it adorns. Every great and original writer accordingly has distinguished, and as it were individualised, himself as much by his diction as by even the sentiment which it embodies; and the invention of such a distinguishing style is one of the most unequivocal evidences of genius. But Shakespeare has invented twenty styles. He has a style for every one of his great characters, by

* Whatever may be the extent of the vocabulary of the English language, it is certain that the most copious writer has not employed more than a fraction of the entire number of words of which it consists. It has been stated that some inquiries set on foot by the telegraph companies have led to the conclusion that the number of words in ordinary use does not exceed 3000. A rough calculation, founded on Mrs. Clarke's Concordance, gives about 21,000 as the number to be found in the Plays of Shakespeare, without counting inflectional forms as distinct words. Probably the vocabulary of no other of our great writers is nearly so extensive. Todd's Verbal Index would not give us more than about 7000 for Milton; so that, if we were to add even fifty per cent. to compensate for Milton's inferior voluminousness, the Miltonic vocabulary would still be not more than half as copious as the Shakespearian.

which that character is distinguished from every other as much as Pope is distinguished by his style from Dryden, or Milton from Spenser. And yet all the while it is he himself with his own peculiar accent that we hear in every one of them. The style, or manner of expression, that is to say,—and, if the manner of expression, then also the manner of thinking, of which the expression is always the product—is at once both that which belongs to the particular character and that which is equally natural to the poet, the conceiver and creator of the character. This double individuality, or combination of two individualities, is inherent of necessity in all dramatic writing; it is what distinguishes the imaginative here from the literal, the artistic from the real, a scene of a play from a police report. No more in this than in any other kind of literature, properly so called, can we dispense with that infusion of the mind from which the work has proceeded, of something belonging to that mind and to no other, which is the very life or constituent principle of all art, the one thing that makes the difference between a creation and a copy, between the poetical and the mechanical.

Dramatists Contemporary with Shakespeare.

Shakespeare died in 1616. The space of a quarter of a century, or more, over which his career as a writer for the stage extends, is illustrated also by the names of a crowd of other dramatists, many of them of very remarkable genius; but Shakespeare is distinguished from the greater number of his contemporaries nearly as much as he is from his immediate predecessors. With regard to the latter, it has been well observed by a critic of eminent justness and delicacy of taste, that, while they "possessed great power over the passions, had a deep insight into the darkest depths of human nature, and were, moreover, in the highest sense of the word, poets, of that higher power of creation with which Shakespeare was endowed, and by which he was enabled to call up into vivid existence all the various characters of men and all the events of human life, Marlow and his contemporaries had no great share,—so that their best dramas may be said to represent to us only gleams and shadowings of mind, confused and hurried actions, from which we are rather led to guess at the nature of the persons acting before us than instantaneously struck with a perfect knowledge of it; and, even amid their highest efforts, with them the fictions of the drama are felt to be but faint semblances of reality. If we seek for a poetical image, a burst of passion, a beautiful sentiment, a trait of nature, we seek not in vain in the works of our very oldest dramatists. But none of the predecessors of Shakespeare must be thought of along with him, when he appears before us, like Prometheus, moulding the figures of men, and breathing into them the animation and all the passions of life."* "The same," proceeds this writer, "may be said of almost all his illustrious contemporaries. Few of them ever have conceived a consistent character, and given a perfect drawing and colouring of it; they have rarely, indeed, inspired us with such belief in the existence of their personages as we often feel towards those of Shakespeare, and which makes us actually unhappy unless we can fully understand everything about them, so like are they to living men. . . . The plans of their dramas are irregular and confused, their characters often wildly distorted, and an air of imperfection and incompleteness hangs in general over the whole composition; so that the attention is wearied out, the interest flags, and we rather hurry on, than are hurried, to the horrors of the final catastrophe."† In other words, the generality of the dramatic writers who were contemporary with Shakespeare still belong to the semi-barbarous school which subsisted before he began to write.

BEAUMONT AND FLETCHER.

Of the dramatic writers of the present period that hold rank the nearest to Shakespeare, the names of Beaumont and Fletcher must be regarded as indicating one poet rather than two, for it is impossible to make anything of the contradictory accounts that have been handed down as to their respective shares in the plays published in their conjoint names, and the plays themselves furnish no evidence that is more decisive. The only ascertained facts relating to this point are the following:—that John Fletcher was about ten years older than his friend Francis Beaumont, the former having been born in 1576, the latter in 1585; that Beaumont, however, so far as is known, came first before the world as a writer of poetry, his translation of the story of Salmacis and Hermaphroditus, from the Fourth Book of Ovid's Metamorphoses, having been published in 1602, when he was only in his seventeenth year; that the Masque of the Inner Temple and Gray's Inn (consisting of only a few pages), pro-

* Analytical Essays on the Early English Dramatists (understood to be by the late Henry Mackenzie), in Blackwood's Magazine, vol. ii. p. 657.
† Blackwood's Magazine, vol. ii. p. 657.

duced in 1612, was written by Beaumont alone; that the
pastoral drama of the Faithful Shepherdess is entirely Fletcher's;
that the first published of the pieces which have been ascribed
to the two associated together, the comedy of The Woman-Hater,
appeared in 1607; that Beaumont died in March, 1616; and
that, between that date and the death of Fletcher, in 1625, there
were brought out, as appears from the note-book of Sir Henry
Herbert, Deputy Master of the Revels, at least eleven of the
plays found in the collection of their works, besides two others
that were brought out in 1626, and two more that are lost.
Deducting the fourteen pieces which thus appear certainly to
belong to Fletcher exclusively (except that in one of them, The
Maid in the Mill, he is said to have been assisted by Rowley),
there still remain thirty-seven or thirty-eight which it is possible
they may have written together in the nine or ten years over
which their poetical partnership is supposed to have extended.*
Eighteen of Beaumont and Fletcher's plays, including the
Masque by the former and the Pastoral by the latter, were pub-
blished separately before 1640; thirty-four more were first pub
lished together in a folio volume in 1647; and the whole were
reprinted, with the addition of a comedy, supposed to have been
lost ('The Wild Goose Chase),† making a collection of fifty-three
pieces in all, in another folio, in 1679. Beaumont and Fletcher
want altogether that white heat of passion by which Shakespeare
fuses all things into life and poetry at a touch, often making a
single brief utterance flash upon us a full though momentary
view of a character, which all that follows deepens and fixes,
and makes the more like to actual seeing with the eyes and
hearing with the ears. His was a deeper, higher, in every way
more extended and capacious nature than theirs. They want his
profound meditative philosophy as much as they do his burning
poetry. Neither have they avoided nearly to the same degree
that he has done the degradation of their fine gold by the intermixture of baser metal. They have given us all sorts of writing,
good, bad, and indifferent, in abundance. Without referring in
particular to what we now deem the indecency and licentiousness which pollutes all their plays, but which, strange to say,
seems not to have been looked upon in that light by anybody in
their own age, simply because it is usually wrapped in very
transparent *double entendre*, they might, if judged by nearly one-

* One, the comedy of The Coronation, is also attributed to Shirley.
† This play, one of the best of Fletcher's comedies, for it was not produced
till some years after Beaumont's death, had been previously recovered and
printed by itself in 1652.

half of all they have left us, be held to belong to almost the lowest rank of our dramatists instead of to the highest. There is scarcely one of their dramas that does not bear marks of haste and carelessness, or of a blight in some part or other from the playhouse tastes or compliances to which they were wont too easily to give themselves up when the louder applause of the day and the town made them thoughtless of their truer fame. But fortunately, on the other hand, in scarcely any of their pieces is the deformity thus occasioned more than partial: the circumstances in which they wrote have somewhat debased the produce of their fine genius, but their genius itself suffered nothing from the unworthy uses it was often put to. It springs up again from the dust and mud, as gay a creature of the element as ever, soaring and singing at heaven's gate as if it had never touched the ground. Nothing can go beyond the flow and brilliancy of the dialogue of these writers in their happier scenes; it is the richest stream of real conversation, edged with the fire of poetry. For the drama of Beaumont and Fletcher is as essentially poetical and imaginative, though not in so high a style, as that of Shakespeare; and they, too, even if they were not great dramatists, would still be great poets. Much of their verse is among the sweetest in the language; and many of the lyrical passages, in particular, with which their plays are interspersed, have a diviner soul of song in them than almost any other compositions of the same class. As dramatists they are far inferior to Shakespeare, not only, as we have said, in striking development and consistent preservation of character, —in other words, in truth and force of conception,—but also both in the originality and the variety of their creations in that department; they have confined themselves to a comparatively small number of broadly distinguished figures, which they delineate in a dashing, scene-painting fashion, bringing out their peculiarities rather by force of situation, and contrast with one another, than by the form and aspect with which each individually looks forth and emerges from the canvas. But all the resources of this inferior style of art they avail themselves of with the boldness of conscious power, and with wonderful skill and effect. Their invention of plot and incident is fertile in the highest degree; and in the conduct of a story for the mere purposes of the stage,—for keeping the attention of an audience awake and their expectation suspended throughout the whole course of the action,—they excel Shakespeare, who, aiming at higher things, and producing his more glowing pictures by fewer strokes, is careless about the mere excitement of curiosity, whereas they are tempted to linger as long as possible over every scene, both for that end, and because their proper method of evolving character and passion is by such delay and repetition of touch upon touch. By reason principally of this difference, the plays of Beaumont and Fletcher, in the great days of the stage, and so long as the state of public manners tolerated their licence and grossness, were much greater favourites than those of Shakespeare in our theatres; two of theirs, Dryden tells us, were acted in his time for one of Shakespeare's; their intrigues,—their lively and florid but not subtle dialogue,—their strongly-marked but somewhat exaggerated representations of character,—their exhibitions of passion, apt to run a little into the melodramatic,—were more level to the general apprehension, and were found to be more entertaining, than his higher art and grander poetry. Beaumont and Fletcher, as might be inferred from what has already been said, are, upon the whole, greater in comedy than in tragedy; and they seem themselves to have felt that their genius led them more to the former,—for, of their plays, only ten are tragedies, while their comedies amount to twenty-four or twenty-five, the rest being what were then called tragi-comedies—in many of which, however, it is true, the interest is, in part at least, of a tragic character, although the story ends happily.* But, on the other hand, all their tragedies have also some comic passages; and, in regard to this matter, indeed, their plays may be generally described as consisting, in the words of the prologue to one of them,† of

"Passionate scenes mixed with no vulgar mirth."

Undoubtedly, taking them all in all, they have left us the richest and most magnificent drama we possess after that of Shakespeare; the most instinct and alive both with the true dramatic spirit and with that of general poetic beauty and power; the most brilliantly lighted up with wit and humour; the freshest and most vivid, as well as various, picture of human manners and passions; the truest mirror, and at the same time the finest embellishment, of nature.

* The following definition of what was formerly understood by the term tragi-comedy, or tragic-comedy, is given by Fletcher in the preface to his Faithful Shepherdess:—"A tragic-comedy is not so called in respect of mirth and killing, but in respect it wants deaths (which is enough to make it no tragedy): yet brings some near to it (which is enough to make it no comedy): which [viz. tragic-comedy] must be a representation of familiar people, with such kind of trouble as no life can be without; so that a god is as lawful in this as in a tragedy; and mean people as in a comedy.'

† The Custom of the Country.

JONSON.

Ben Jonson was born in 1574, or two years before Fletcher, whom he survived twelve years, dying in 1637. He is supposed to have begun to write for the stage so early as 1593; but nothing that he produced attracted any attention till his Comedy of Every Man in his Humour was brought out at the Rose Theatre in 1596. This play, greatly altered and improved, was published in 1598; and between that date and his death Jonson produced above fifty more dramatic pieces in all, of which ten are comedies, three what he called comical satires, only two tragedies, and all the rest masques, pageants, or other court entertainments. His two tragedies of Sejanus and Catiline are admitted on all hands to be nearly worthless; and his fame rests almost entirely upon his first comedy, his three subsequent comedies of Volpone or The Fox, Epicoene or The Silent Woman, and The Alchemist, his court Masques, and a Pastoral entitled The Sad Shepherd, which was left unfinished at his death. Ben Jonson's comedies admit of no comparison with those of Shakespeare or of Beaumont and Fletcher; he belongs to another school. His plays are professed attempts to revive, in English, the old classic Roman drama, and aim in their construction at a rigorous adherence to the models afforded by those of Plautus, and Terence, and Seneca. They are admirable for their elaborate art, which is, moreover, informed by a power of strong conception of a decidedly original character; they abound both in wit and eloquence, which in some passages rises to the glow of poetry; the figures of the scene stand out in high relief, every one of them, from the most important to the most insignificant, being finished off at all points with the minutest care; the dialogue carries on the action, and is animated in many parts with the right dramatic reciprocation; and the plot is in general contrived and evolved with the same learned skill, and the same attention to details, that are shown in all other particulars. But the execution, even where it is most brilliant, is hard and angular; nothing seems to flow naturally and freely; the whole has an air of constraint, and effort, and exaggeration; and the effect that is produced by the most arresting passages is the most undramatic that can be,—namely, a greater sympathy with the performance as a work of art than as anything else. It may be added that Jonson's characters, though vigorously delineated, and though not perhaps absolutely false to nature, are most of them rather of the class of her occasional excrescences or eccentricities than samples of any general humanity; they are the oddities and perversions of a particular age or state of manners, and have no universal truth or interest. What is called the humour of Jonson consists entirely in the exhibition of the more ludicrous kinds of these morbid aberrations; like everything about him, it has force and raciness enough, but will be most relished by those who are most amused by dancing bears and other shows of that class. It seldom or never makes the heart laugh, like the humour of Shakespeare,—which is, indeed, a quality of altogether another essence. • As a poet, Jonson is greatest in his masques and other court pageants. The airy elegance of these compositions is a perfect contrast to the stern and rugged strength of his other works; the lyrical parts of them especially have often a grace and sportiveness, a flow as well as a finish, the effect of which is very brilliant. Still, even in these, we want the dewy light and rich coloured irradiation of the poetry of Shakespeare and Fletcher: the lustre is pure and bright, but at the same time cold and sharp, like that of crystal. In Jonson's unfinished pastoral of The Sad Shepherd there is some picturesque description and more very harmonious verse, and the best parts of it (much of it is poor enough) are perhaps in a higher style than anything else he has written; but to compare it, as has sometimes been done, either as a poem or as a drama, with The Faithful Shepherdess of Fletcher seems to us to evince a deficiency of true feeling for the highest things, equal to what would be shown by preferring, as has also been done by some critics, the humour of Jonson to that of Shakespeare. Fletcher's pastoral, blasted as it is in some parts by fire not from heaven, is still a green and leafy wilderness of poetical beauty; Jonson's, deformed also by some brutality more elaborate than anything of the same sort in Fletcher, is at the best but a trim garden, and, had it been ever so happily finished, would have been nothing more.

MASSINGER; FORD.

After Shakespeare, Beaumont and Fletcher, and Jonson, the next great name in our drama is that of Philip Massinger, who was born in 1584, and is supposed to have begun to write for the stage soon after 1606, although his first published play, his tragedy of The Virgin Martyr, in which he was assisted by Decker, did not appear till 1622. Of thirty-eight dramatic pieces which he is said to have written, only eighteen have been preserved; eight others were in the collection of Mr. Warburton, which his servant destroyed. Massinger, like Jonson, had received a learned education, and his classic reading has coloured his style and manner; but he had scarcely so much originality of genius as Jonson. He is a very eloquent writer, but has little power of high imagination or pathos, and still less wit or comic power. He could rise, however, to a vivid conception of a character moved by some single aim or passion; and he has drawn some of the darker shades of villany with great force. His Sir Giles Overreach, in A New Way to Pay Old Debts, and his Luke in the City Madam, are perhaps his most successful delineations in this style. In the conduct of his plots, also, he generally displays much skill. In short, all that can be reached by mere talent and warmth of susceptibility he has achieved; but his province was to appropriate and decorate rather than to create.

John Ford, the author of about a dozen plays that have survived, and one of whose pieces is known to have been acted so early as 1613, has one quality, that of a deep pathos, perhaps more nearly allied to high genius than any Massinger has shown; but the range of the latter in the delineation of action and passion is so much more extensive, that we can hardly refuse to regard him as the greater dramatist. Ford's blank verse is not so imposing as Massinger's; but it has often a delicate beauty, sometimes a warbling wildness and richness, beyond anything in Massinger's fuller swell.

LATER ELIZABETHAN PROSE WRITERS.

By the end of the sixteenth century, our prose, as exhibited in its highest examples, if it had lost something in ease and clearness, had gained considerably in copiousness, in sonorousness, and in splendour. In its inferior specimens, also, a corresponding change is to be traced, but of a modified character. In these the ancient simplicity and directness had given place only to a long-winded wordiness, and an awkwardness and intricacy, sometimes so excessive as to be nearly unintelligible, produced by piling clause upon clause, and involution upon involution, in the endeavour to crowd into every sentence as much meaning or as many particulars as possible. Here the change was nearly altogether for the worse; the loss in one direction was compensated by hardly anything that could be called a gain in another. It ought also to be noticed that towards the close of the reign of Elizabeth a singularly artificial mode of composition became fashionable, more especially in sermons and other theological writings, consisting mainly in the remotest or most recondite analogies of thought and the most elaborate verbal ingenuities or conceits. This may be designated the opposite pole in popular preaching to what we have in the plainness and simplicity, natural sometimes even to buffoonery, of Latimer.

Translation of the Bible.

The authorized translation of the Bible, on the whole so admirable both for correctness and beauty of style, is apt, on the first thought, to be regarded as exhibiting the actual state of the language in the time of James I., when it was first published. It is to be remembered, however, that the new translation was formed, by the special directions of the king, upon the basis of that of Parker's, or the Bishops' Bible, which had been made nearly forty years before, and which had itself been founded upon that of Cranmer, made in the reign of Henry VIII. The consequence is, as Mr. Hallam has remarked, that, whether the style of King James's translation be the perfection of the English language or no, it is not the language of his reign. "It may, in the eyes of many," adds Mr. Hallam, "be a better English, but it is not the English of Daniel, or Raleigh, or Bacon, as any one may easily perceive. It abounds, in fact, especially in the Old Testament, with obsolete phraseology, and with single words long since abandoned, or retained only in provincial use."* This is, perhaps, rather strongly put; for although the preceding version served as a general guide to the translators, and was not needlessly deviated from, they have evidently modernized its style, not perhaps quite up to that of their own day, but so far, we apprehend, as to exclude nearly all words and phrases that had then passed out even of common and familiar use. In that theological age, indeed, few forms of expression found in the Bible could well have fallen altogether into desuetude, although some may have come to be less apt and significant than they once were, or than others that might now be substituted for them. But we believe the new translators, in any changes they made, were very careful to avoid the employment of any mere words of yesterday, the glare of whose recent coinage would have contrasted offensively with the general

* Lit. of Eur. ii. 464.

antique colour of diction which they desired to retain. If ever their version were to be revised, whether to improve the rendering of some passages by the lights of modern criticism, or to mend some hardness and intricacy of construction in others, it ought to be retouched in the same spirit of affectionate veneration for the genius and essential characteristics of its beautiful diction; and a good rule to be laid down might be, that no word should be admitted in the improved renderings which was not in use in the age when the translation was originally made. The language was then abundantly rich enough to furnish all the words that could be wanted for the purpose.

THEOLOGICAL WRITERS:—BISHOP ANDREWS; DONNE; HALL; HOOKER.

Besides the translation of the Bible, the portion of the English literature of the present period that is theological is very great in point of quantity, and a part of it also possesses distinguished claims to notice in a literary point of view. Religion was the great subject of speculation and controversy in this country throughout the entire space of a century and a half between the Reformation and the Revolution.

One of the most eminent preachers, perhaps the most eminent, of the age of Elizabeth and James, was Dr. Lancelot Andrews, who, after having held the sees of Chichester and Ely, died bishop of Winchester in 1626. Bishop Andrews was one of the translators of the Bible, and is the author, among other works, of a folio volume of Sermons published, by direction of Charles I., soon after his death; of another folio volume of Tracts and Speeches, which appeared in 1629; of a third volume of Lectures on the Ten Commandments, published in 1642; and of a fourth, containing Lectures delivered at St. Paul's and at St. Giles's, Cripplegate, published in 1657. Both the learning and ability of Andrews are conspicuous in everything he has written; but his eloquence, nevertheless, is to a modern taste grotesque enough. In his more ambitious passages he is the very prince of verbal posture-masters,—if not the first in date, the first in extravagance, of the artificial, quibbling, syllable-tormenting school of our English pulpit rhetoricians; and he undoubtedly contributed more to spread the disease of that manner of writing than any other individual.

Donne, the poet, was also a voluminous writer in prose; having left a folio volume of Sermons, besides a treatise against

Popery entitled The Pseudo-Martyr, another singular performance, entitled Biathanatos, in confutation of the common notion about the necessary sinfulness of suicide, and some other professional disquisitions. His biographer, Izaak Walton, says that he preached "as an angel, *from* a cloud, but not in a cloud;" but most modern readers will probably be of opinion that he has not quite made his escape from it. His manner is fully as quaint in his prose as in his verse, and his way of thinking as subtle and peculiar.

Another of the most learned theologians and eloquent preachers of those times was as well as Donne an eminent poet, Bishop Joseph Hall. Hall's English prose works, which are very voluminous, consist of sermons, polemical tracts, paraphrases of Scripture, casuistical divinity, and some pieces on practical religion, of which his Contemplations, his Art of Divine Meditation, and his Enochismus, or Treatise on the Mode of Walking with God, are the most remarkable. The poetic temperament of Hall reveals itself in his prose as well as in his verse, by the fervour of his piety, and the forcible and often picturesque character of his style.

Last of all may be mentioned, among the great theological writers of this great theological time, one who stands alone, Richard Hooker, the illustrious author of the Eight Books of the Laws of Ecclesiastical Polity; of which the first four were published in 1594, the fifth in 1597, the three last not till 1632, many years after the author's death. Hooker's style is almost without a rival for its sustained dignity of march; but that which makes it most remarkable is its union of all this learned gravity and correctness with a flow of genuine, racy English, almost as little tinctured with pedantry as the most familiar popular writing. The effect also of its evenness of movement is the very reverse of tameness or languor; the full river of the argument dashes over no precipices, but yet rolls along without pause, and with great force and buoyancy.

BACON.

Undoubtedly the principal figure in English prose literature, as well as in philosophy, during the first quarter of the seventeenth century, is Francis Bacon. Bacon, born in 1561, published the first edition of his Essays in 1597; his Two Books of the Advancement of Learning in 1605; his Wisdom of the Ancients (in Latin) in 1610; a third edition of his Essays, greatly extended, in 1612; his Two Books of the Novum Organum, or Second Part of the Instauratio Magna, designed to consist of Six Parts (also in Latin), in 1620; his History of the Reign of Henry VII., in 1622; his Nine Books De Augmentis Scientiarum, a Latin translation and extension of his Advancement of Learning, in 1623. He died in 1626. The originality of the Baconian or Inductive method of philosophy, the actual service it has rendered to science, and even the end which it may be most correctly said to have in view, have all been subjects of dispute almost ever since Bacon's own day; but, notwithstanding all differences of opinion upon these points, the acknowledgment that he was intellectually one of the most colossal of the sons of men has been nearly unanimous. They who have not seen his greatness under one form have discovered it in another; there is a discordance among men's ways of looking at him, or their theories respecting him; but the mighty shadow which he projects athwart the two bygone centuries lies there immovable, and still extending as time extends. The very deductions which are made from his merits in regard to particular points thus only heighten the impression of his general eminence,—of that something about him not fully understood or discerned, which, spite of all curtailment of his claims in regard to one special kind of eminence or another, still leaves the sense of his eminence as strong as ever. As for his Novum Organum, or so-called new instrument of philosophy, it may be that it was not really new when he announced it as such, either as a process followed in the practice of scientific discovery, or as a theory of the right method of discovery. Neither may Bacon have been the first writer, in his own or the immediately preceding age, who recalled attention to the inductive method, or who pointed out the barrenness of what was then called philosophy in the schools. Nor can it be affirmed that it was really he who brought the reign of that philosophy to a close: it was falling fast into disrepute before he assailed it, and would probably have passed away quite as soon as it did although his writings had never appeared. Nor possibly has he either looked at that old philosophy with a very penetrating or comprehensive eye, or even shown a perfect understanding of the inductive method in all its applications and principles. As for his attempts in the actual practice of the inductive method, they were, it must be owned, either insignificant or utter failures; and that, too, while some of his contemporaries, who in no respect acknowledged him as their teacher, were turning it to account in extorting from nature the most brilliant revelations. But this was not Bacon's proper province. He belongs not to mathematical or natural science, but to literature and to moral science in its most extensive acceptation,—to the realm of imagination, of wit, of eloquence, of æsthetics, of history, of jurisprudence, of political philosophy, of logic, of metaphysics and the investigation of the powers and operations of the human mind. He is either not at all or in no degree worth mentioning an investigator or expounder of mathematics, or of mechanics, or of astronomy, or of chemistry, or of any other branch of geometrical or physical science; but he is a most penetrating and comprehensive investigator, and a most magnificent expounder, of that higher wisdom in comparison with which all these things are but a more intellectual sort of legerdemain. All his works, his essays, his philosophical writings, commonly so called, and what he has done in history, are of one and the same character; reflective and, so to speak, poetical, not simply demonstrative, or elucidatory of mere matters of fact. What, then, is his glory?—in what did his greatness consist? In this, we should say;—that an intellect at once one of the most capacious and one of the most profound ever granted to a mortal—in its powers of vision at the same time one of the most penetrating and one of the most far-reaching—was in him united and reconciled with an almost equal endowment of the imaginative faculty; and that he is, therefore, of all philosophical writers, the one in whom are found together, in the largest proportions, depth of thought and splendour of eloquence. His intellectual ambition, also,—a quality of the imagination,—was of the most towering character; and no other philosophic writer has taken up so grand a theme as that on which he has laid out his strength in his greatest works. But with the progress of scientific discovery that has taken place during the last two hundred years, it would be difficult to show that these works have had almost anything to do. His Advancement of Learning and his Novum Organum have more in them of the spirit of poetry than of science; and we should almost as soon think of fathering modern physical science upon Paradise Lost as upon them.

Burton.

A remarkable prose work of this age, which ought not to be passed over without notice, is Burton's Anatomy of Melancholy. Robert Burton, who, on his title-page, takes the name of Democritus Junior, died in 1640, and his book was first published in 1621. It is an extraordinary accumulation of out-of-the-way learning, interspersed, somewhat in the manner of Montaigne's Essays, with original matter, but with this among other differences,— that in Montaigne the quotations have the air of being introduced, as we know that in fact they were, to illustrate the original matter, which is the web of the discourse, they but the embroidery; whereas in Burton the learning is rather the web, upon which what he has got to say of his own is worked in by way of forming a sort of decorative figure. Burton is far from having the variety or abundance of Montaigne; but there is considerable point and penetration in his style, and he says many striking things in a sort of half-splenetic, half-jocular humour, which many readers have found wonderfully stimulating. Dr. Johnson declared that Burton's Anatomy of Melancholy was the only book that ever drew him out of bed an hour sooner than he would otherwise have got up.

HISTORICAL WRITERS.

Among the historical writers of the reign of James may be first mentioned the all-accomplished Sir Walter Raleigh. Raleigh is the author of a few short poems, and of some miscellaneous pieces in prose; but his great work is his History of the World, composed during his imprisonment in the Tower, and first published in a folio volume in 1614. It is an unfinished work, coming down only to the first Macedonian war; and there is no reason to suppose that any more of it was ever written, although it has been asserted that a second volume was burnt by the author. Raleigh's History, as a record of facts, has long been superseded; the interest it possesses at the present day is derived almost entirely from its literary merits, and from a few passages in which the author takes occasion to allude to circumstances that have fallen within his own experience. Much of it is written without any ambition of eloquence; but the style, even where it is most careless, is still lively and exciting, from a tone of the actual world which it preserves, and a certain frankness and heartiness coming from Raleigh's profession and his warm impetuous character. It is not disfigured by any of the petty pedantries to some one or other of which most of the writers of books in that day gave way more or less, and it has altogether comparatively little of the taint of age upon it; while in some passages the composition, without losing anything of its natural grace and heartiness, is wrought up to great rhetorical polish and elevation.

Another celebrated historical work of this time is Richard

Knolles's History of the Turks, published in 1610. Johnson, in one of his Ramblers, has awarded to Knolles the first place among English historians; and Mr. Hallam concurs in thinking that his style and power of narration have not been too highly extolled by that critic. "His descriptions," continues Mr. Hallam, "are vivid and animated; circumstantial, but not to feebleness; his characters are drawn with a strong pencil..... In the style of Knolles there is sometimes, as Johnson has hinted, a slight excess of desire to make every phrase effective; but he is exempt from the usual blemishes of his age; and his command of the language is so extensive, that we should not err in placing him among the first of our elder writers."* Much of this praise, however, is to be considered as given to the uniformity or regularity of Knolles's style; the chief fault of which perhaps is, that it is too continuously elaborated and sustained for a long work. We have already mentioned Samuel Daniel's History of England from the Conquest to the reign of Edward III., which was published in 1618. It is of little historical value, but is remarkable for the same simple ease and purity of language which distinguish Daniel's verse. The contribution to this department of literature of all those that the early part of the seventeenth century produced, which is at the same time the most valuable as an original authority and the most masterly in its execution, is undoubtedly Bacon's History of the reign of Henry VII.

* Lit. of Eur. iii. 572.

MIDDLE AND LATTER PART OF THE SEVENTEENTH CENTURY.

EXCLUDING from our view the productions of the last fifty or sixty years, as not yet ripe for the verdict of history, we may affirm that our national literature, properly so called, that is, whatever of our literature by right of its poetic shape or spirit is to be held as peculiarly belonging to the language and the country, had its noonday in the period comprehending the last quarter of the sixteenth and the first of the seventeenth century. But a splendid afternoon flush succeeded this meridian blaze, which may be said to have lasted for another half century, or longer. Down almost to the Revolution, or at least to the middle of the reign of Charles II., our higher literature continued to glow with more or less of the coloured light and the heart of fire which it had acquired in the age of Elizabeth and James. Some of the greatest of it indeed—as the verse of Milton and the prose poetry of Jeremy Taylor—was not given to the world till towards the close of the space we have just indicated. But Milton, and Taylor, and Sir Thomas Browne, and Cudworth, and Henry More, and Cowley, the most eminent of our English writers in the interval from the Restoration to the Revolution (if we except Dryden, the founder of a new school, and Barrow, whose writings, full as they are of thought, have not much of the poetical or untranslatable) were all of them, it is worthy of observation, born before the close of the reign of James I. Nor would the stormy time that followed be without its nurture for such minds. A boyhood or youth passed in the days of Shakespeare and Bacon, and a manhood in those of the Great Rebellion, was a training which could not fail to rear high powers to their highest capabilities.

SHIRLEY, AND THE END OF THE OLD DRAMA.

The chief glory of our Elizabethan literature, however, belongs almost exclusively to the time we have already gone over. The only other name that remains to be mentioned to complete our sketch of the great age of the Drama, is that of James Shirley, who was born about the year 1594, and whose first play, the comedy of The Wedding, was published in 1629. He is the author of about forty dramatic pieces which have come down to us. "Shirley," observes Lamb, "claims a place among the worthies of this period, not so much for any transcendent genius in himself, as that he was the last of a great race, all of whom spoke nearly the same language, and had a set of moral feelings and notions in common. A new language and quite a new turn of tragic and comic interest came in with the Restoration."* Of this writer, who survived till 1666, the merits and defects have been well stated, in a few comprehensive words, by Mr. Hallam:—"Shirley has no originality, no force in conceiving or delineating character, little of pathos, and less, perhaps, of wit; his dramas produce no deep impression in reading, and of course can leave none in the memory. But his mind was poetical: his better characters, especially females, express pure thoughts in pure language; he is never tumid or affected, and seldom obscure; the incidents succeed rapidly; the personages are numerous, and there is a general animation in the scenes, which causes us to read him with some pleasure." †

A preface by Shirley is prefixed to the first collection of part of the plays of Beaumont and Fletcher, which, as already mentioned, appeared in 1647. "Now, reader," he says, "in this tragical age, where the theatre hath been so much outacted, congratulate thy own happiness that, in this silence of the stage, thou hast a liberty to read these inimitable plays,—to dwell and converse in these immortal groves,—which were only showed our fathers in a conjuring-glass, as suddenly removed as represented." At this time all theatrical amusements were prohibited; and the publication of these and of other dramatic productions which were their property, or rather the sale of them to the booksellers, was resorted to by the players as a way of making a little money when thus cut off from the regular gains of their profession; the eagerness of the public to possess the said works in print being of course also sharpened by the same cause.

The permanent suppression of theatrical entertainments was the act of the Long Parliament. An ordinance of the Lords and Commons passed on the 2nd of September, 1642,—after setting forth that "public sports do not well agree with public calamities, nor public stage-plays with the seasons of humiliation, this being an exercise of sad and pious solemnity, and the other being spectacles of pleasure, too commonly expressing lascivious mirth and levity,"—ordained, "that, while these sad causes and

* Specimens, ii. 110.   † Lit. of Eur. iii. 345.

set times of humiliation do continue, public stage-plays shall cease and be forborne." It has been plausibly conjectured that this measure originated, "not merely in a spirit of religious dislike to dramatic performances, but in a politic caution, lest playwriters and players should avail themselves of their power over the minds of the people to instil notions and opinions hostile to the authority of a puritanical parliament."* This ordinance certainly put an end at once to the regular performance of plays; although it is known to have been occasionally infringed.

GILES FLETCHER; PHINEAS FLETCHER.

Nor is the poetical produce other than dramatic of the quarter of a century that elapsed from the death of James to the establishment of the Commonwealth, of very considerable amount. Giles and Phineas Fletcher were brothers, cousins of the dramatist, and both clergymen. Giles, who died in 1623, is the author of a poem entitled Christ's Victory and Triumph in Heaven and Earth over and after Death, which was published in a quarto volume in 1610. It is divided into four parts, and is written in stanzas somewhat like those of Spenser, only containing eight lines each instead of nine: both the Fletchers, indeed, were professed disciples and imitators of the great author of the Fairy Queen. Phineas, who survived till 1650, published in 1633, along with a small collection of Piscatory Eclogues and other Poetical Miscellanies, a long allegorical poem, entitled The Purple Island, in twelve Books or Cantos, written in a stanza of seven lines. The idea upon which this performance is founded is one of the most singular that ever took possession of the brain even of an allegorist: the *purple island* is nothing else than the human body, and the poem is, in fact, for the greater part, a system of anatomy, nearly as minute in its details as if it were a scientific treatise, but wrapping up everything in a fantastic guise of double meaning, so as to produce a languid sing-song of laborious riddles, which are mostly unintelligible without the very knowledge they make a pretence of conveying. After he has finished his anatomical course, the author takes up the subject of psychology, which he treats in the same luminous and interesting manner. Such a work as this has no claim to be considered a poem even of the same sort with the Fairy Queen. In Spenser, the allegory, whether historical or moral, is little more than formal: the poem, taken in its natural and obvious import, as a

* Collier, Hist. Dram. Poet. ii. 106.

tale of "knights' and ladies' gentle deeds"—a song of their "fierce wars and faithful loves"—has meaning and interest enough, without the allegory at all, which, indeed, except in a very few passages, is so completely concealed behind the direct narrative, that we may well suppose it to have been nearly as much lost sight of and forgotten by the poet himself as it is by his readers: here, the allegory is the soul of every stanza and of every line—that which gives to the whole work whatever meaning, and consequently whatever poetry, it possesses—with which, indeed, it is sometimes hard enough to be understood, but without which it would be absolute inanity and nonsense. The Purple Island is rather a production of the same species with Dr. Darwin's Botanic Garden; but, forced and false enough as Darwin's style is in many respects, it would be doing an injustice to his poem to compare it with Phineas Fletcher's, either in regard to the degree in which nature and propriety are violated in the principle and manner of the composition, or in regard to the spirit and general success of the execution. Of course, there is a good deal of ingenuity shown in Fletcher's poem; and it is not unimpregnated by poetic feeling, nor without some passages of considerable merit. But in many other parts it is quite grotesque; and, on the whole, it is fantastic, puerile, and wearisome.

OTHER RELIGIOUS POETS:—QUARLES; HERBERT; HERRICK; CRASHAW.

The growth of the religious spirit in the early part of the seventeenth century is shown in much more of the poetry of the time as well as in that of the two Fletchers. Others of the most notable names of this age are Quarles, Herrick, Herbert, and Crashaw. Francis Quarles, who died in 1644, was one of the most popular as well as voluminous writers of the day, and is still generally known by his volume of Emblems. His verses are characterized by ingenuity rather than fancy, but, although often absurd, he is seldom dull or languid. There is a good deal of spirit and coarse vigour in some of his pieces, as for instance in his well-known Song of Anarchus, portions of which have been printed both by Ellis and Campbell, and which may perhaps have suggested to Cowper, the great religious poet of a later day, his lines called The Modern Patriot. Quarles, however, though he appears to have been a person of considerable literary acquirement, must in his poetical capacity be regarded as mainly a writer for the populace. George Herbert, a younger brother of the celebrated Edward Lord Herbert of Cherbury, was a clergyman. His volume, entitled The Temple, was first published soon after his death in 1633, and was at least six or seven times reprinted in the course of the next quarter of a century. His biographer, Izaak Walton, tells us that when he wrote, in the reign of Charles II., twenty thousand copies of it had been sold. Herbert was an intimate friend of Donne, and no doubt a great admirer of his poetry; but his own has been to a great extent preserved from the imitation of Donne's peculiar style, into which it might in other circumstances have fallen, in all probability by its having been composed with little effort or elaboration, and chiefly to relieve and amuse his own mind by the melodious expression of his favourite fancies and contemplations. His quaintness lies in his thoughts rather than in their expression, which is in general sufficiently simple and luminous. Robert Herrick, who was also a clergyman, is the author of a thick octavo volume of verse, published in 1648, under the title of Hesperides. It consists, like the poetry of Donne, partly of love verses, partly of pieces of a devotional character, or, as the two sorts are styled in the title-page, Works Human and Divine. The same singular licence which even the most reverend persons, and the purest and most religious minds, in that age allowed themselves to take in light and amatory poetry is found in Herrick as well as in Donne, a good deal of whose singular manner, and fondness for conceits both of sound and sense, Herrick has also caught. Yet some both of his hymns and of his anacreontics—for of such strange intermixture does his poetry consist—are beautifully simple and natural, and full of grace as well as fancy. Richard Crashaw was another clergyman, who late in life became a Roman Catholic, and died a canon of Loretto in 1650. He is perhaps, after Donne, the greatest of these religious poets of the early part of the seventeenth century. He belongs in manner to the same school with Donne and Herrick, and in his lighter pieces he has much of their lyrical sweetness and delicacy; but there is often a force and even occasionally what may be called a grandeur of imagination in his more solemn poetry which Herrick never either reaches or aspires to.

CARTWRIGHT; RANDOLPH; CORBET.

All the poetical clergymen of this time, however, had not such pious muses. The Rev. William Cartwright, who died at an early age in 1643, is said by Anthony Wood to have been "a most florid and seraphic preacher;" but his poetry, which is mostly amatory, is not remarkable for its brilliancy. He is the author of several plays, and he was one of the young writers who were honoured with the title of his sons by Ben Jonson, who said of him, "My son Cartwright writes all like a man." Another of Ben's poetical sons was Thomas Randolph, who was likewise a clergyman, and is also the author of several plays, mostly in verse, as well as of a quantity of other poetry. Randolph has a good deal of fancy, and his verse flows very melodiously; but his poetry has in general a bookish and borrowed air. Much of it is on subjects of love and gallantry; but the love is chiefly of the head, or, at most, of the senses—the gallantry, it is easy to see, that merely of a fellow of a college and a reader of Ovid. Randolph died under thirty in 1634, and his poems were first collected after his death by his brother. The volume, which also contains his Plays, was frequently reprinted in the course of the next thirty or forty years; the edition before us, dated 1668, is called the fifth.

One of the most remarkable among the clerical poets of this earlier half of the seventeenth century was Dr. Richard Corbet, successively Bishop of Oxford and of Norwich. Corbet, who was born in 1582, became famous both as a poet and as a wit early in the reign of James; but very little, if any, of his poetry was published till after his death, which took place in 1635. It is related, that after Corbet was a doctor of divinity he once sang ballads at the Cross at Abingdon: "On a market day," Aubrey writes, "he and some of his comrades were at the tavern by the Cross (which, by the way, was then the finest in England; I remember it when I was a freshman; it was admirable curious Gothic architecture, and fine figures in the niches; 'twas one of those built by King . . . . for his Queen). The ballad-singer complained he had no custom—he could not put off his ballads. The jolly doctor puts off his gown, and puts on the ballad-singer's leathern jacket, and, being a handsome man, and a rare full voice, he presently vended a great many, and had a great audience." Aubrey had heard, however, that as a bishop "he had an admirable grave and venerable aspect." Corbet's poetry, too, is a mixture or alternation of gravity and drollery. But it is the subject or occasion, rather than the style or manner, that makes the difference; he never rises to anything higher than wit; and he is as witty in his elegies as in his ballads. As that ingredient, however, is not so suitable for the former as for the latter, his graver performances are worth very little. Nor is his merriment of a high order; when it is most elaborate it is strained and fantastic, and when more natural it is apt to run into buffoonery. But much of his verse, indeed, is merely prose in rhyme, and very different rhyme for the most part. His happiest effusions are the two that are best known, his Journey into France and his ballad of The Fairies' Farewell. His longest and most curious poem is his Iter Boreale, describing a journey which he took in company with other three university men, probably about 1620, from Oxford as far north as Newark and back again.

POETS OF THE FRENCH SCHOOL:—CAREW; LOVELACE; SUCKLING.

Both our poetry and our prose eloquence continued to be generally infected by the spirit of quaintness and conceit, or over-refinement and subtlety of thought, for nearly a century after the first introduction among us of that fashion of writing. Even some of the highest minds did not entirely escape the contagion. If nothing of it is to be found in Spenser or Milton, neither Shakespeare nor Bacon is altogether free from it. Of our writers of an inferior order, it took captive not only the greater number, but some of the greatest, who lived and wrote from the middle of the reign of Elizabeth to nearly the middle of that of Charles II.—from Bishop Andrews, whom we have already mentioned, in prose, and Donne both in prose and verse, to Cowley inclusive. The style in question appears to have been borrowed from Italy: it came in, at least, with the study and imitation of the Italian poetry, being caught apparently from the school of Petrarch, or rather of his later followers, about the same time that a higher inspiration was drawn from Tasso and Ariosto. It is observable that the species or departments of our poetry which it chiefly invaded were those which have always been more or less influenced by foreign models: it made comparatively little impression upon our dramatic poetry, the most truly native portion of our literature; but our lyrical and elegiac, our didactic and satirical verse, was overrun and materially modified by it, as we have said, for nearly a whole century. The return to a more natural manner, however, was begun to be made long before the expiration of that term. And, as we had received the malady from one foreign literature, so we were indebted for the cure to another. It is commonly assumed that our modern English poetry first evinced a disposition to imitate that of France after the Restoration. But the truth is that the influence of French literature had begun to be felt by our own at a considerably earlier date. The court of Charles I. was far from being so thoroughly French as that of Charles II.; but the connexion established between the two kingdoms through Queen Henrietta could not fail to produce a partial imitation of French models both in writing and in other things. The distinguishing characteristic of French poetry (and indeed of French art generally), neatness in the dressing of the thought, had already been carried to considerable height by Malherbe, Racan, Malleville, and others; and these writers are doubtless to be accounted the true fathers of our own Waller, Carew, Lovelace, and Suckling, who all began to write about this time, and whose verses may be said to have first exemplified in our lighter poetry what may be done by correct and natural expression, smoothness of flow, and all that lies in the *ars celare artem*—the art of making art itself seem nature. Of the four, Waller was perhaps first in the field; but he survived almost till the Revolution, and did not rise to his greatest celebrity till after the Restoration, so that he will more fitly fall to be noticed in a subsequent page. The other three all belong exclusively to the times of Charles I. and of the Commonwealth.

Thomas Carew, styled on the title-page "One of the Gentlemen of the Privy Chamber, and Sewer in Ordinary to His Majesty," is the author of a small volume of poetry first printed in 1640, the year after his death. In polish and evenness of movement, combined with a diction elevated indeed in its tone, as it must needs be by the very necessities of verse, above that of mere good conversation, but yet in ease, lucidity, and directness rivalling the language of ordinary life, Carew's poetry is not inferior to Waller's; and, while his expression is as correct and natural, and his numbers as harmonious, the music of his verse is richer, and his imagination is warmer and more florid. But the texture of his composition is in general extremely slight, the substance of most of his pieces consisting merely of the elaboration of some single idea; and, if he has more tenderness than Waller, he is far from having so much dignity, variety, or power of sustained effort.

The poems of Colonel Richard Lovelace are contained in two small volumes, one entitled Lucasta, published in 1649; the other entitled Posthume Poems, published by his brother in 1659, the year after the author's death. They consist principally of songs and other short pieces. Lovelace's songs, which are mostly amatory, are many of them carelessly enough written, and there are very few of them not defaced by some harshness or deformity;

but a few of his best pieces are as sweetly versified as Carew's, with perhaps greater variety of fancy as well as more of vital force; and a tone of chivalrous gentleness and honour gives to some of them a pathos beyond the reach of any more poetic art.

Lovelace's days, darkened in their close by the loss of everything except honour, were cut short at the age of forty; his contemporary, Sir John Suckling, who moved gaily and thoughtlessly through his short life as through a dance or a merry game, died, in 1641, at that of thirty-two. Suckling, who is the author of a small collection of poems, as well as of four plays, has none of the pathos of Lovelace or Carew, but he equals them in fluency and natural grace of manner, and he has besides a sprightliness and buoyancy which is all his own. His poetry has a more impulsive air than theirs; and, while, in reference to the greater part of what he has produced, he must be classed along with them and Waller as an adherent to the French school of propriety and precision, some of the happiest of his effusions are remarkable for a cordiality and impetuosity of manner which has nothing foreign about it, but is altogether English, although there is not much resembling it in any of his predecessors any more than of his contemporaries, unless perhaps in some of Skelton's pieces. His famous ballad of The Wedding is the very perfection of gaiety and archness in verse; and his Session of the Poets, in which he scatters about his wit and humour in a more careless style, may be considered as constituting him the founder of a species of satire, which Cleveland and Marvel and other subsequent writers carried into new applications, and which only expired among us with Swift.

DENHAM.

To this date belongs a remarkable poem, the Cooper's Hill of Sir John Denham, first published in 1642. It immediately drew universal attention. Denham, however, had the year before made himself known as a poet by his tragedy of The Sophy, on the appearance of which Waller remarked that he had broken out like the Irish rebellion, threescore thousand strong, when nobody was aware or in the least suspected it. Cooper's Hill may be considered as belonging in point of composition to the same school with Sir John Davies's Nosce Teipsum: and, if it has not all the concentration of that poem, it is equally pointed, correct, and stately, with, partly owing to the subject, a warmer tone of imagination and feeling, and a fuller swell of verse. The spirit of the same classical style pervades both; and they are the two greatest poems in that style which had been produced down to the date at which we are now arrived. Denham is the author of a number of other compositions in verse, and especially of some songs and other shorter pieces, several of which are very spirited; but the fame of his principal poem has thrown everything else he has written into the shade. It is remarkable that many biographical notices of this poet make him to have survived nearly till the Revolution, and relate various stories of the miseries of his protracted old age; when the fact is, that he died in 1668, at the age of fifty-three.

CLEVELAND.

But, of all the cavalier poets, the one who did his cause the heartiest and stoutest service, and who, notwithstanding much carelessness or ruggedness of execution, possessed perhaps, even considered simply as a poet, the richest and most various faculty, was John Cleveland, the most popular verse-writer of his own day, the most neglected of all his contemporaries ever since. Cleveland was the eldest son of the Rev. Thomas Cleveland, vicar of Hinckley and rector of Stoke, in Leicestershire, and he was born at Loughborough in that county in 1613. Down to the breaking out of the civil war, he resided at St. John's College, Cambridge, of which he was a Fellow, and seems to have distinguished himself principally by his Latin poetry. But, when every man took his side, with whatever weapons he could wield, for king or parliament, Anthony Wood tells us that Cleveland was the first writer who came forth as a champion of the royal cause in English verse. To that cause he adhered till its ruin; at last in 1655, after having led for some years a fugitive life, he was caught and thrown into prison at Yarmouth; but, after a detention of a few months, Cromwell, on his petition, allowed him to go at large. The transaction was honourable to both parties.

Cleveland is commonly regarded as a mere dealer in satire and invective, and as having no higher qualities than a somewhat rude force and vehemence. His prevailing fault is a straining after vigour and concentration of expression; and few of his pieces are free from a good deal of obscurity, harshness, or other disfigurement, occasioned by this habit or tendency, working in association with an alert, ingenious, and fertile fancy, a neglect of and apparently a contempt for neatness of finish, and the turn for quaintness and quibbling characteristic of the school to which he belongs—for Cleveland must be considered as essentially one of the old wit poets. Most of his poems seem to have been thrown off in haste, and never to have been afterwards corrected or revised. There are, however, among them some that are not without vivacity and sprightliness; and others of his more solemn verses have considerable dignity.

The following epitaph on Ben Jonson is the shortest and best of several tributes to the memory of that poet, with whose masculine genius that of Cleveland seems to have strongly sympathised:—

> The Muses' fairest light in no dark time;
> The wonder of a learned age; the line
> Which none can pass; the most proportioned wit
> To nature; the best judge of what was fit;
> The deepest, plainest, highest, clearest pen;
> The voice most echoed by consenting men;
> The soul which answered best to all well said
> By others, and which most requital made;
> Tuned to the highest key of ancient Rome,
> Returning all her music with his own;
> In whom with Nature Study claimed a part,
> Yet who unto himself owed all his art;
> Here lies Ben Jonson: every age will look
> With sorrow here, with wonder on his book.

Elsewhere he thus expresses his preference for Jonson, as a dramatist, over the greatest of his contemporaries:—

> Shakespeare may make griefs, merry Beaumont's style
> Ravish and melt anger into a smile;
> In winter nights or after meals they be,
> I must confess, very good company;
> But thou exact'st our best hours' industry;
> We may read them, we ought to study thee;
> Thy scenes are precepts; every verse doth give
> Counsel, and teach us, not to laugh, but live.

WITHER.

These last-mentioned writers — Carew, Lovelace, Suckling, Denham, and Cleveland — were all, as we have seen, cavaliers: but the cause of puritanism and the parliament had also its poets as well as that of love and loyalty. Of these the two most eminent were Marvel and Wither. Marvel's era, however, is rather after the Restoration. George Wither, who was born in 1588, covers nearly seventy years of the seventeenth century with his life, and not very far from sixty with his works: his first publication, his volume of satires entitled Abuses Stript and Whipt, having appeared in 1611, and some of his last pieces only a short time before his death in 1667. The entire number of his separate works, as they have been reckoned up by modern bibliographers, exceeds a hundred.

One excellence for which all Wither's writings are eminent, his prose as well as his verse, is their genuine English. His unaffected diction, even now, has scarcely a stain of age upon it, —but flows on, ever fresh and transparent, like a pebbled rill.

Down to the breaking out of the war between the king and the parliament, Wither, although his pious poetry made him a favourite with the puritans, had always professed himself a strong church and state man; even at so late a date as in 1639, when he was above fifty, he served as a captain of horse in the expedition against the Scotch Covenanters; and when two or three years after he took arms on the other side, he had yet his new principles in a great measure to seek or make. It appears not to have been till a considerable time after this that his old admiration of the monarchy and the hierarchy became suddenly converted into the conviction that both one and other were, and had been all along, only public nuisances—the fountains of all the misrule and misery of the nation. What mainly instigated him to throw himself into the commencing contest with such eagerness seems to have been simply the notion, which possessed and tormented him all his life, that he was born with a peculiar genius for public affairs, and that things had very little chance of going right unless he were employed. With his head full of this conceit, it mattered comparatively little on which side he took his stand to begin with: he would speedily make all even and right; the one thing needful in the first instance was, that his services should be taken advantage of. Of course, Wither's opinions, like those of other men, were influenced by his position, and he was no doubt perfectly sincere in the most extreme of the new principles which he was ultimately led to profess. The defect of men of his temper is not insincerity. But they are nevertheless apt to be almost as unstable as if they had no strong convictions at all. Their convictions, in truth, however strong, do not rest so much upon reason or principle, as upon mere passion. They see everything through so thick and deeply coloured an atmosphere of self, that its real shape goes for very little in their conception of it; change only the hue of the haze, or the halo, with which it is thus invested, and you altogether change to them the thing itself—making the white appear black, the bright dim, the round square, or the reverse. Wither, with all his ardour and real honesty, appears never in fact to have acquired any credit for reliability, or steadiness in the opinions he hold, either from friends or opponents. He very naively lets out this himself in a prose pamphlet which he published in 1624, entitled The Scholar's Purgatory, being a vindication of himself addressed to the Bishops, in which, after stating that he had been offered more money and better entertainment if he would have employed himself in setting forth heretical fancies than he had any chance of ever obtaining by the profession of the truth, he adds, "Yea, sometimes I have been wooed to the profession of their wild and ill-grounded opinions by the sectaries of so many several separations, that, had I liked, or rather had not God been the more merciful to me, I might have been Lieutenant, if not Captain, of some new band of such volunteers long ere this time." Overtures of this kind are, of course, only made to persons who are believed to be open to them. It is plain from his own account that Wither was thus early notorious as a speculator or trader in such securities—as one ready, not precisely to sell himself, his opinions, and his conscience, to the highest bidder, but yet to be gained over if the offer were only made large enough to convert as well as purchase him. There is a great deal of very passable wearing and working honesty of this kind in the world.

The history of Wither's numerous publications has been elaborately investigated by the late Mr. Park in the first and second volumes of the British Bibliographer; many of his poems have been reprinted by Sir Egerton Brydges, and others of his admirers; and an ample account of his life and writings, drawn up with a large and intimate knowledge, as well as affectionate zeal and painstaking, which make it supersede whatever had been previously written on the subject, forms the principal article (extending over more than 130 pages) of Mr. Wilmott's Lives of Sacred Poets (8vo. Lon. 1834). Much injustice, however, has been done to Wither by the hasty judgment that has commonly been passed, even by his greatest admirers, upon his later political poetry, as if it consisted of mere party invective and fury, and all that he had written of any enduring value or interest was to be found in the productions of the early part of his life. Some at least of his political pieces are very remarkable for their vigour and terseness. As a specimen we will give a portion of a poem which he published without his name in 1647, under the title of "Amygdala Britannica; Almonds for Parrots; a dish of Stone-fruit, partly shelled and partly unshelled; which, if cracked, picked, and well digested, may be wholesome against those epidemic distempers of the brain now predominant, and prevent some malignant diseases likely to ensue: composed heretofore by a well-known modern author, and now published according to a copy found written with his own hand. *Qui bene latuit bene vixit.*" This fantastic title-page (with the manufacture of which the bookseller may have had more to do than Wither himself) was suited to the popular taste of the day, but would little lead a modern reader to expect the nervous concentration and passionate earnestness of such verses as the following:—

> The time draws near, and hasteth on,
> In which strange works shall be begun;
> And prosecutions, whereon shall
> Depend much future bliss or bale.
> If to the left hand you decline,
> Assured destruction they divine;
> But, if the right-hand course ye take,
> This island it will happy make.
>
> A time draws nigh in which you may
> As you shall please the chess-men play;
> Remove, confine, check, leave, or take,
> Dispose, depose, undo, or make,
> Pawn, rook, knight, bishop, queen, or king,
> And act your wills in every thing:
> But, if that time let slip you shall,
> For yesterday in vain you call.
>
> A time draws nigh in which the sun
> Will give more light than he hath done:
> Then also you shall see the moon
> Shine brighter than the sun at noon;
> And many stars now seeming dull
> Give shadows like the moon at full.
> Yet then shall some, who think they see,
> Wrapt in Egyptian darkness be.
>
> A time draws nigh when with your blood
> You shall preserve the viper's brood,
> And starve your own; yet fancy than [1]
> That you have played the pelican;
> But, when you think the frozen snakes
> Have changed their natures for your sakes,
> They, in requital, will contrive
> Your mischief who did them revive.
>
> A time will come when they that wake
> Shall dream; and sleepers undertake

---

[1] Then.

The grand affairs; yet,[1] few men know
Which are the dreamers of these two ·
And fewer care by which of these
They guided be, so they have ease:
But an alarum shall advance
Your drowsy spirits from that trance.

   A time shall come ere long in which
Mere beggars shall grow soonest rich;
The rich with wants be pinched more
Than such as go from door to door;
The honourable by the base
Shall be despited to their face;
The truth defamed be with lies;
The fool preferred before the wise;
And he that fighteth to be free,
By conquering enslaved shall be.

   . . . . .

   A time will come when see you shall
Toads fly aloft and eagles crawl;
Wolves walk abroad in human shapes;
Men turn to asses, hogs, and apes:
But, when that cursed time is come,
Well 's he that is both deaf and dumb;
That nothing speaketh, nothing hears,
And neither hopes, desires, nor fears.

   . . . . .

   When men shall generally confess
Their folly and their wickedness;
Yet act as if there neither were
Among them conscience, wit, or fear;
When they shall talk as if they had
Some brains, yet do as they were mad;
And nor by reason, nor by noise,
By human or by heavenly voice,
By being praised or reproved,
By judgments or by mercies, moved:
Then look for so much sword and fire
As such a temper doth require.

   . . . . .

   Ere God his wrath on Balaam wreaks,
First by his ass to him he speaks;
Then shows him in an angel's hand
A sword, his courage to withstand;
But, seeing still he forward went,
Quite through his heart a sword he sent.

---

[1] As yet.

And God will thus, if thus they do,
Still deal with kings, and subjects too;
That, where his grace despised is grown,
He by his judgments may be known.

Neither Churchhill nor Cowper ever wrote anything in the same style better than this. The modern air, too, of the whole, with the exception of a few words, is wonderful. But this, as we have said, is the character of all Wither's poetry—of his earliest as well as of his latest. It is nowhere more conspicuous than in his early religious verses, especially in his collection entitled Songs and Hymns of the Church, first published in 1624. There is nothing of the kind in the language more perfectly beautiful than some of these. We subjoin two of them:—

Thanksgiving for Seasonable Weather. Song 85.

Lord, should the sun, the clouds, the wind,
  The air, and seasons be
To us so froward and unkind
  As we are false to thee;
All fruits would quite away be burned,
  Or lie in water drowned,
Or blasted be or overturned,
  Or chilled on the ground.

But from our duty though we swerve,
  Thou still dost mercy show,
And deign thy creatures to preserve,
  That men might thankful grow:
Yea, though from day to day we sin,
  And thy displeasure gain,
No sooner we to cry begin
  But pity we obtain.

The weather now thou changed hast
  That put us late to fear,
And when our hopes were almost past
  Then comfort did appear.
The heaven the earth's complaints hath heard;
  They reconciled be;
And thou such weather hast prepared
  As we desired of thee.

For which, with lifted hands and eyes,
  To thee we do repay
The due and willing sacrifice
  Of giving thanks to-day;
Because such offerings we should not
  To render thee be slow,
Nor let that mercy be forgot
  Which thou art pleased to show.

Thanksgiving for Victory. Song 68.

We love thee, Lord, we praise thy name,
  Who, by thy great almighty arm,
Hast kept us from the spoil and shame
  Of those that sought our causeless harm:
Thou art our life, our triumph-song,
  The joy and comfort of our heart;
To thee all praises do belong,
  And thou the God of Armies art.

We must confess it is thy power
  That made us masters of the field;
Thou art our bulwark and our tower,
  Our rock of refuge and our shield:
Thou taught'st our hands and arms to fight;
  With vigour thou didst gird us round;
Thou mad'st our foes to take their flight,
  And thou didst beat them to the ground.

With fury came our armed foes,
  To blood and slaughter fiercely bent;
And perils round did us inclose,
  By whatsoever way we went;
That, hadst not thou our Captain been,
  To lead us on, and off again,
We on the place had dead been seen,
  Or masked in blood and wounds had lain.

This song we therefore sing to thee,
  And pray that thou for evermore
Would'st our Protector deign to be,
  As at this time and heretofore;
That thy continual favour shown
  May cause us more to thee incline,
And make it through the world be known
  That such as are our foes are thine.

BROWNE.

Along with Wither ought to be mentioned a contemporary poet of a genius, or at least of a manner, in some respects kindred to his, and whose fate it has been to experience the same long neglect, William Browne, the author of Britannia's Pastorals, of which the first part was published in 1613, the second in 1616, and of The Shepherd's Pipe in Seven Eclogues, which appeared in 1614. Browne was a native of Tavistock in Devonshire, where he was born in 1590, and he is supposed to have died in 1645. It is remarkable that, if he lived to so late a date, he should not have written more than he appears to have done: the two parts of his Britannia's Pastorals were reprinted together in 1625; and a piece called The Inner Temple Masque, and a few short poems, were published for the first time in an edition of his works brought out, under the care of Dr. Farmer, in 1772; but the last thirty years of his life would seem, in so far as regards original production, to have been a blank. Yet a remarkable characteristic of his style, as well as of Wither's, is its ease and fluency; and it would appear, from what he says in one of the songs of his Pastorals, that he had written part of that work before he was twenty. His poetry certainly does not read as if its fountain would be apt soon to run dry. His facility of rhyming and command of harmonious expression are very great; and, within their proper sphere, his invention and fancy are also extremely active and fertile. His strength, however, lies chiefly in description, not the thing for which poetry or language is best fitted, and a species of writing which cannot be carried on long without becoming tiresome; he is also an elegant didactic declaimer; but of passion, or indeed of any breath of actual living humanity, his poetry has almost none. This, no doubt, was the cause of the neglect into which after a short time it was allowed to drop; and this limited quality of his genius may also very probably have been the reason why he so soon ceased to write and publish. From the time when religious and political contention began to wax high, in the latter years of King James, such poetry as Browne's had little chance of acceptance: from about that date Wither, as we have seen, who also had previously written his Shepherd's Hunting, and other similar pieces, took up a new strain; and Browne, if he was to continue to be listened to, must have done the same, which he either would not or could not. Yet, although without the versatility of Wither, and also with less vitality than Wither even in the kind of poetry which is common to the two, Browne rivals that writer both in the abundance of his poetic vein and the sweetness of his verse; and the English of the one has nearly all the purity, perspicuity, and unfading freshness of style which is so remarkable in the other.

PROSE WRITERS:—CHARLES I.

Most of the prose that was written and published in England in the middle portion of the seventeenth century, or the twenty years preceding the Restoration, was political and theological, but very little of it has any claim to be considered as belonging to the national literature. A torrent of pamphlets and ephemeral polemics supplied the ravenous public appetite with a mental sustenance which answered the wants of the moment, much as the bakers' ovens did with daily bread for the body. It was all devoured, and meant to be devoured, as fast as it was produced —devoured in the sense of being quite used up and consumed, so far as any good was to be got out of it. It was in no respect intended for posterity, any more than the linen and broad-cloth then manufactured were intended for posterity. Still even this busy and excited time produced some literary performances which still retain more or less of interest.

The writings attributed to Charles I. were first collected and published at the Hague soon after his death, in a folio volume without date, under the title of Reliquiæ Sacræ Carolinæ, and twice afterwards in England, namely, in 1660 and 1687, with the title of ΒΑΣΙΛΙΚΑ: The Works of King Charles the Martyr. If we except a number of speeches to the parliament, letters, despatches, and other political papers, the contents of this collection are all theological, consisting of prayers, arguments, and disquisitions on the controversy about church government, and the famous Eikon Basilikè, or, The Portraiture of his Sacred Majesty in his Solitude and Sufferings; which, having been printed under the care of Dr. Gauden (after the Restoration successively bishop of Exeter and Worcester), had been first published by itself immediately after the king's execution. It is now generally admitted that the Eikon was really written by Gauden, who, after the Restoration, openly claimed it as his own. Mr. Hallam, however, although he has no doubt of Gauden being the author, admits that it is, nevertheless, superior to his acknowledged writings. "A strain of majestic melancholy," he observes, "is well kept up; but the personated sovereign is rather too theatrical for real nature; the language is too rhetorical and amplified, the periods too artificially elaborated. None but scholars and practised writers employ such a style as this."* It is not improbable that the work may have been submitted to Charles's revisal, and that it may have received both his approval and his corrections. Charles, indeed, was more in the habit of correcting what had been written by others than of writing anything himself. "Though he was of as slow a pen as of speech," says Sir Philip Warwick, "yet both were very significant; and he had that modest esteem of his own parts, that he would usually say, he would willingly make his

* Lit. of Eur. iii. 376.

own despatches, but that he found it better to be a cobbler than
a shoemaker. I have been in company with very learned men,
when I have brought them their own papers back from him with
his alterations, who ever confessed his amendments to have been
very material. And I once, by his commandment, brought him
a paper of my own to read, to see whether it was suitable to his
directions, and he disallowed it slightingly: I desired him I
might call Dr. Sanderson to aid me, and that the doctor might
understand his own meaning from himself; and, with his
majesty's leave, I brought him whilst he was walking and
taking the air; whereupon we two went back; but pleased him
as little when we returned it: for, smilingly, he said, a man
might have as good ware out of a chandler's shop; but afterwards
he set it down with his own pen very plainly, and suitably to
his own intentions." The most important of the literary productions which are admitted to be wholly Charles's own, are his
papers in the controversy which he carried on at Newcastle in
June and July, 1646, with Alexander Henderson, the Scotch
clergyman, on the question between episcopacy and presbytery,
and those on the same subject in his controversy with the parliamentary divines at Newport in October, 1648. These papers
show considerable clearness of thinking and logical or argumentative talent; but it cannot be said that they are written
with any force or elegance.

MILTON'S PROSE WORKS.

We have already mentioned Bishop Hall, both as a poet and
as a writer of prose. A part which Hall took in his old age in
the grand controversy of the time brought him into collision
with one with whose name in after ages the world was to
resound. John Milton, then in his thirty-third year, and recently returned from his travels in France and Italy, had
already, in 1641, lent the aid of his pen to the war of the
Puritans against the established church by the publication of
his treatise entitled Of Reformation, in Two Books. The same
year Hall published his Humble Remonstrance in favour of
Episcopacy; which immediately called forth an Answer by
Smectymnuus,—a word formed from the initial letters of the
names of five Puritan ministers by whom the tract was written
—Stephen Marshall, Edmund Calamy, Thomas Young, Matthew
Newcomen, and William (or, as he was on this occasion reduced
to designate himself, Uuilliam) Spurstow. The Answer pro-

duced a Confutation by Archbishop Usher; and to this Milton replied in a treatise entitled Of Prelatical Episcopacy. Hall then published a Defence of the Humble Remonstrance; and Milton wrote Animadversions upon that. About the same time he also brought out a performance of much greater pretension, under the title of The Reason of Church Government urged against Prelaty, in Two Books. This is the work containing the magnificent passage in which he makes the announcement of his intention to attempt something in one of the highest kinds of poetry "in the mother-tongue," long afterwards accomplished in his great epic. Meanwhile a Confutation of the Animadversions having been published by Bishop Hall, or his son, Milton replied, in 1642, in an Apology for Smectymnuus, which was the last of his publications in this particular controversy. But, nearly all his other prose writings were given to the world within the period with which we are now engaged:—namely, his Tractate of Education, addressed to his friend Hartlib, and his noble Areopagitica, a Speech for the Liberty of Unlicensed Printing, in 1644; his Doctrine and Discipline of Divorce, and his Judgment of Martin Bucer concerning Divorce, the same year; his Tetrachordon, and Colasterion (both on the same subject) in 1645; his Tenure of Kings and Magistrates, his Eikonoclastes, in answer to the Eikon Basilike, and one or two other tracts of more temporary interest, all after the execution of the king, in 1649; his Defence for the People of England, in answer to Salmasius (in Latin), in 1651; his Second Defence (also in Latin), in reply to a work by Peter du Moulin, in 1654; two additional Latin tracts in reply to rejoinders of Du Moulin, in 1655; his treatises on Civil Power in Ecclesiastical Cases, and on The Means of Removing Hirelings out of the Church, in 1659; his Letter concerning the Ruptures of the Commonwealth, and Brief Delineation of a Free Commonwealth, the same year; and, finally, his Ready and Easy Way to establish a Free Commonwealth, and his Brief Notes upon a Sermon preached by Dr. Griffith, called The Fear of God and the King, in the spring of 1660, immediately before the king's return. Passages of great poetic splendour occur in some of these productions, and a fervid and fiery spirit breathes in all of them, though the animation is as apt to take the tone of mere coarse objurgation and abuse as of lofty and dignified scorn or of vigorous argument; but, upon the whole, it cannot be said that Milton's English prose is a good style. It is in the first place, not perhaps in vocabulary, but certainly in genius and construction, the most Latinized of English styles; but it does not merit the commendation bestowed by Pope on another style which he conceived to be formed after the model of the Roman eloquence, of being "so Latin, yet so English all the while." It is both soul and body Latin, only in an English dress. Owing partly to this principle of composition upon which he deliberately proceeded, or to the adoption of which his education and tastes or habits led him, partly to the character of his mind, fervid, gorgeous, and soaring, but having little involuntary impulsiveness or self-abandonment, rich as his style often is, it never moves with any degree of rapidity or easy grace even in passages where such qualities are most required, but has at all times something of a stiff, cumbrous, oppressive air, as if every thought, the lightest and most evanescent as well as the gravest and stateliest, were attired in brocade and whalebone. There is too little relief from constant straining and striving; too little repose and variety; in short, too little nature. Many things, no doubt, are happily said; there is much strong and also some brilliant expression; but even such imbedded gems do not occur so often as might be looked for from so poetical a mind. In fine, we must admit the truth of what he has himself confessed—that he was not naturally disposed to "this manner of writing;" "wherein," he adds, "knowing myself inferior to myself, led by the genial power of nature to another task, I have the use, as I may account it, but of my left hand." * With all his quick susceptibility for whatever was beautiful and bright, Milton seems to have needed the soothing influences of the regularity and music of verse fully to bring out his poetry, or to sublimate his imagination to the true poetical state. The passion which is an enlivening flame in his verse half suffocates him with its smoke in his prose.

HALES; CHILLINGWORTH.

Two other eminent names of theological controversialists belonging to this troubled age of the English church may be mentioned together—those of John Hales and William Chillingworth. Hales, who was born in 1584, and died in 1656, the same year with Hall and Usher, published in his lifetime a few short tracts, of which the most important is a Discourse on Schism, which was printed in 1642, and is considered to have been one of the works that led the way in that bold revolt

* Reason of Church Government, Book II.

against the authority of the fathers, so much cried up by the preceding school of Andrews and Laud, upon which has since been founded what many hold to be the strongest defence of the Church of England against that of Rome. All Hales's writings were collected and published after his death, in 1659, in a quarto volume, bearing the title of Golden Remains of the Ever-Memorable Mr. John Hales,—a designation which has stuck to his name. The main idea of his treatise on Schism had, however, been much more elaborately worked out by his friend Chillingworth—the Immortal Chillingworth, as he is styled by his admirers—in his famous work entitled The Religion of Protestants a Safe Way to Salvation, published in 1637. This is one of the most closely and keenly argued polemical treatises ever written: the style in which Chillingworth presses his reasoning home is like a charge with the bayonet. He was still only in his early manhood when he produced this remarkably able work; and he died in 1644 at the age of forty-two.

Jeremy Taylor.

But the greatest name by far among the English divines of the middle of the seventeenth century is that of Jeremy Taylor. He was born in 1613, and died bishop of Down and Connor in 1667; but most of his works were written, and many of them were also published, before the Restoration. In abundance of thought; in ingenuity of argument; in opulence of imagination; in a soul made alike for the feeling of the sublime, of the beautiful, and of the picturesque; and in a style, answering in its compass, flexibility, and sweetness to the demands of all these powers, Taylor is unrivalled among the masters of English eloquence. He is the Spenser of our prose writers; and his prose is sometimes almost as musical as Spenser's verse. His Sermons, his Golden Grove, his Holy Living, and, still more, his Holy Dying, all contain many passages, the beauty and splendour of which are hardly to be matched in any other English prose writer. Another of his most remarkable works, Theologia Eclectica, a Discourse of the Liberty of Prophesying, first published in 1647, may be placed beside Milton's Areopagitica, published three years before, as doing for liberty of conscience the same service which that did for the liberty of the press. Both remain the most eloquent and comprehensive defences we yet possess of these two great rights.

FULLER.

The last of the theological writers of this era that we shall notice is Fuller. Dr. Thomas Fuller was born in 1604, and died in 1661; and in the course of his not very extended life produced a considerable number of literary works, of which his Church History of Britain from the Birth of Jesus Christ until the Year 1648, which appeared in 1656, and his History of the Worthies of England, which was not published till the year after his death, are the most important. He is a most singular writer, full of verbal quibbling and quaintness of all kinds, but by far the most amusing and engaging of all the rhetoricians of this school, inasmuch as his conceits are rarely mere elaborate feats of ingenuity, but are usually informed either by a strong spirit of very peculiar humour and drollery, or sometimes even by a warmth and depth of feeling, of which too, strange as it may appear, the oddity of his phraseology is often a not ineffective exponent. He was certainly one of the greatest and truest wits that ever lived: he is witty not by any sort of effort at all, but as it were in spite of himself, or because he cannot help it. But wit, or the faculty of looking at and presenting things in their less obvious relations, is accompanied in him, not only by humour and heart, but by a considerable endowment of the irradiating power of fancy. Accordingly, what he writes is always lively and interesting, and sometimes even eloquent and poetical, though the eccentricities of his characteristic manner are not favourable, it must be confessed, to dignity or solemnity of style when attempted to be long sustained. Fuller, and it is no wonder, was one of the most popular writers, if not the most popular, of his own day: he observes himself, in the opening chapter of his Worthies, that hitherto no stationer (or publisher) had lost by him; and what happened in regard to one of his works, his Holy State, is perhaps without example in the history of book-publishing:—it appeared originally in a folio volume in 1642, and is believed to have been four times reprinted before the Restoration; but the publisher continued to describe the two last impressions on the title-page as still only the *third* edition, as if the demand had been so great that he felt (for whatever reason) unwilling that its extent should be known. It is conjectured that his motive probably was " a desire to lull suspicion, and not to invite prohibition from the ruling powers."[*]

[*] Preface by the Editor, Mr. James Nichols, to The Holy State. 8vo. Lon. 1841.

Hardly anything can be found in Fuller that is dull or wearisome. The following interesting passage, often referred to, makes part of the account of Warwickshire in the Worthies:—

William Shakespeare was born at Stratford on Avon in this county; in whom three eminent poets may seem in some sort to be compounded: 1. Martial, in the warlike sound of his surname (whence some may conjecture him of a military extraction), Hastivibrans, or Shakespeare. 2. Ovid, the most natural and witty of all poets; and hence it was that Queen Elizabeth, coming into a grammar-school, made this extemporary verse,

"Persius a Crabstaff, Bawdy Martial, Ovid a fine wag."

3. Plautus, who was an exact comedian, yet never any scholar; as our Shakespeare, if alive, would confess himself. Add to all these, that, though his genius generally was jocular, and inclining him to festivity, yet he could, when so disposed, be solemn and serious, as appears by his tragedies; so that Heraclitus himself (I mean if secret and unseen) might afford to smile at his comedies, they were so merry; and Democritus scarce forbear to sigh at his tragedies, they were so mournful.

He was an eminent instance of the truth of that rule, *Poeta non fit, sed nascitur*; one is not made, but born a poet. Indeed his learning was very little, so that, as Cornish diamonds are not polished by any lapidary, but are pointed, and smoothed even, as they are taken out of the earth, so nature itself was all the art which was used upon him.

Many were the wit combats betwixt him and Ben Jonson. Which two I behold like a Spanish great galleon and an English man-of-war. Master Jonson, like the former, was built far higher in learning; solid, but slow, in his performances. Shakespeare, with the English man-of-war, lesser in bulk, but lighter in sailing, could turn with all tides, tack about, and take advantage of all winds, by the quickness of his wit and invention. He died anno Domini 16.., and was buried at Stratford upon Avon, the town of his nativity.

We may add another Warwickshire worthy, of a different order :—

Philemon Holland, where born is to me unknown, was bred in Trinity College in Cambridge a Doctor in Physic, and fixed himself in Coventry. He was the translator general in his age, so that those books alone of his turning into English will make a country gentleman a competent library for historians; in so much that one saith,

"Holland with his translations doth so fill us,
He will not let *Suetonius* be *Tranquillus*."

Indeed, some decry all translators as interlopers, spoiling the trade of learning, which should be driven amongst scholars alone. Such also allege that the best translations are works rather of industry than judgment, and, in easy authors, of faithfulness rather than industry; that many be but bunglers, forcing the meaning of the authors they translate, "forcing the lock when they cannot open it."

But their opinion resents too much of envy, that such gentlemen who cannot repair to the fountain should be debarred access to the stream. Besides, it is unjust to charge all with the faults of some; and a distinction must be made amongst translators betwixt cobblers and workmen, and our Holland had the true *knack* of translating.

Many of these his books he wrote with one pen, whereon he himself thus pleasantly versified:—

  "With one sole pen I writ this book,
   Made of a grey goose quill;
  A pen it was when it I took,
   And a pen I leave it still."

This monumental pen he solemnly kept, and showed to my reverend tutor, Doctor Samuel Ward. It seems he leaned very lightly on the neb thereof, though weightily enough in another sense, performing not slightly but solidly what he undertook.

But what commendeth him most to the praise of posterity is his translating Camden's Britannia, a translation more than a translation, with many excellent additions not found in the Latin, done fifty years since in Master Camden's lifetime, not only with his knowledge and consent, but also, no doubt, by his desire and help. Yet such additions (discoverable in the former part with asterisks in the margent) with some antiquaries obtain not equal authenticalness with the rest. This eminent translator was translated to a better life anno Domini 16 . . .

The translation of the translator took place in fact in 1636, when he had reached the venerable age of eighty-five, so that translating would seem to be not an unhealthy occupation. The above sketch is Fuller all over, in heart as well as in head and hand—the last touch especially, which, jest though it be, and upon a solemn subject, falls as gently and kindly as a tear on good old Philemon and his labours. The effect is as if we were told that even so gently fell the touch of death itself upon the ripe old man—even so easy, natural, and smiling, his labours over, was his leave-taking and exchange of this earth of many languages, the confusion or discord of which he had done his best to reduce, for that better world, where there is only one tongue, and translation is not needed or known. And Fuller's wit and jesting are always of this character; they have not in them a particle either of bitterness or of irreverence. No man ever (in writing at least) made so many jokes, good, bad, and indifferent; be the subject what it may, it does not matter; in season and out of season he is equally facetious; he cannot let slip an occasion of saying a good thing any more than a man who is tripped can keep himself from falling; the habit is as irresistible with him as the habit of breathing; and yet there is probably neither an ill-natured nor a profane witticism to be found in all that he has written. It is the sweetest-blooded wit that was ever infused into man or book. And how strong and weighty, as well as how gentle and beautiful, much of his writing is! The work perhaps in which he is oftenest eloquent and pathetic is that entitled The Holy State and the Profane State, the former great popularity of which we have already noticed. Almost no writer whatever tells a story so well as Fuller—with so much life and point and gusto.

Sir Thomas Browne.

Another of the most original and peculiar writers of the middle portion of the seventeenth century is Sir Thomas Browne, the celebrated author of the Religio Medici, published in 1642; the Pseudodoxia Epidemica, or Inquiries into Vulgar and Common Errors, in 1646; and the Hydriotaphia, Urn Burial, or a Discourse on the Sepulchral Urns found in Norfolk; and The Garden of Cyrus, or the Quincuncial Lozenge, or Network Plantations of the Ancients, Artificially, Naturally, Mystically Considered, which appeared together in 1658. Browne died in 1682, at the age of seventy-seven; but he published nothing after the Restoration, though some additional tracts found among his papers were given to the world after his death. The writer of a well-known review of Browne's literary productions, and of the characteristics of his singular genius, has sketched the history of his successive acts of authorship in a lively and striking passage: —" He had no sympathy with the great business of men. In that awful year when Charles I. went in person to seize five members of the Commons' House,—when the streets resounded with shouts of ' Privilege of Parliament,' and the king's coach was assailed by the prophetic cry, ' To your tents, O Israel.'— in that year, in fact, when the civil war first broke out, and when most men of literary power were drawn by the excitement of the crisis into patriotic controversy on either side,—appeared the calm and meditative reveries of the Religio Medici. The war raged on. It was a struggle between all the elements of government. England was torn by convulsion and red with blood. But Browne was tranquilly preparing his Pseudodoxia Epidemica: as if errors about basilisks and griffins were the paramount and fatal epidemic of the time; and it was published in due order in that year when the cause which the author advocated, as far as he could advocate anything political, lay at its last gasp. The king dies on the scaffold. The Protectorate succeeds. Men are again fighting on paper the solemn cause already decided in the field. Drawn from visions more sublime,—forsaking studies more intricate and vast than those of the poetical Sage of Norwich,—diverging from a career bounded by the most splendid goal,—foremost in the ranks shines the flaming sword of Milton: Sir Thomas Browne is lost in the quincunx of the ancient gardens; and the year 1658 beheld the death of Oliver Cromwell, and the publication of the Hydriotaphia."* The writings of Sir Thomas Browne, to be relished or rightly appreciated, must of course be read in the spirit suited to the species of literature to which they belong. If we look for matter-of-fact information in a poem, we are likely to be disappointed; and so are we likewise, if we go for the passionate or pictured style of poetry to an encyclopædia. Browne's works, with all their varied learning, contain very little positive information that can now be accounted of much value; very little even of direct moral or economical counsel by which any person could greatly profit; very little, in short, of anything that will either put money in a man's pocket, or actual knowledge in his head. Assuredly the interest with which they were perused, and the charm that was found to belong to them, could not at any time have been due, except in very small part indeed, to the estimation in which their readers held such pieces of intelligence as that the phœnix is but a fable of the poets, and that the griffin exists only in the zoology of the heralds. It would fare ill with Browne if the worth of his books were to be tried by the amount of what they contain of this kind of information, or, indeed, of any other kind of what is commonly called useful knowledge; for, in truth, he has done his best to diffuse a good many vulgar errors as monstrous as any he had corrected. For that matter, if his readers were to continue to believe with him in astrology and witchcraft, we shall all agree that it was of very little consequence what faith they may hold touching the phœnix and the griffin. Mr. Hallam, we think, has, in a manner which is not usual with him, fallen somewhat into this error of applying a false test in the judgment he has passed upon Browne. It is, no doubt, quite true that the Inquiry into Vulgar Errors "scarcely raises a high notion of Browne himself as a philosopher, or of the state of physical knowledge in England;"† that the Religio Medici shows its author to have been "far removed from real philosophy, both by his turn of mind and by the nature of his erudition;" and likewise that

* Article in Edinburgh Review for October, 1836; No. 129, p. 34. (Understood to be by Sir Edward Bulwer Lytton.)
† Lit. of Eur. III. 461.

"he seldom reasons," that "his thoughts are desultory," that "sometimes he appears sceptical or paradoxical," but that "credulity and deference to authority prevail" in his habits of thinking.* Understanding *philosophy* in the sense in which the term is here used, that is to say, as meaning the sifting and separation of fact from fiction, it may be admitted that there is not much of that in Sir Thomas Browne; his works are all rather marked by a very curious and piquant intermixture of the two. Of course, such being the case, what he writes is not to be considered solely or even principally with reference to its absolute truth or falsehood, but rather with reference to its relative truth and significance as an expression of some feeling or notion or other idiosyncracy of the very singular and interesting mind from which it has proceeded. Read in this spirit, the works of Sir Thomas Browne, more especially his Religio Medici, and his Urn Burial, will be found among the richest in our literature—full of uncommon thoughts, and trains of meditation leading far away into the dimmest inner chambers of life and death—and also of an eloquence, sometimes fantastic, but always striking, not seldom pathetic, and in its greatest passages gorgeous with the emblazoury of a warm imagination. Out of such a writer the rightly attuned and sympathizing mind will draw many things more precious than any mere facts.

Sir James Harrington.

We can merely mention Sir James Harrington's political romance entitled Oceana, which was published in 1056. Harrington's leading principles are, that the natural element of power in states is property; and that, of all kinds of property, that in land is the most important, possessing, indeed, certain characteristics which distinguish it, in its natural and political action, from all other property. "In general," observes Mr. Hallam, "it may be said of Harrington that he is prolix, dull, pedantic, yet seldom profound; but sometimes redeems himself by just observations."† This is true in so far as respects the style of the Oceana; but it hardly does justice to the ingenuity, the truth, and the importance of certain of Harrington's views and deductions in the philosophy of politics. If he has not the merit of absolute originality in his main propositions, they had at least never been so clearly expounded and demonstrated by any preceding writer.

* Lit. of Eur. iii. 153. † Id. iv. 200.

NEWSPAPERS.

It has now been satisfactorily shown that the three newspapers, entitled The English Mercurie, Nos. 50, 51, and 54, preserved among Dr. Birch's historical collections in the British Museum, professing to be "published by authority, for the contradiction of false reports," at the time of the attack of the Spanish Armada, on the credit of which the invention of newspapers used to be attributed to Lord Burleigh, are modern forgeries,—*jeux d'esprit*, in fact, of the reverend Doctor.[*] Occasional pamphlets, containing foreign news, began to be published in England towards the close of the reign of James I. The earliest that has been met with is entitled News out of Holland, dated 1619; and other similar papers of news from different foreign countries are extant which appeared in 1620, 1621, and 1622. The first of these news-pamphlets which came out at regular intervals appears to have been that entitled The News of the Present Week, edited by Nathaniel Butler, which was started in 1622, in the early days of the Thirty Years' War, and was continued, in conformity with its title, as a weekly publication. But the proper era of English newspapers, at least of those containing domestic intelligence, commences with the Long Parliament. The earliest that has been discovered is a quarto pamphlet of a few leaves, entitled The Diurnal Occurrences, or Daily Proceedings of Both Houses, in this great and happy parliament, from the 3rd of November, 1640, to the 3rd of November, 1641; London, printed for William Cooke, and are to be sold at his shop at Furnival's Inn Gate, in Holborn, 1641.[†] More than a hundred newspapers, with different titles, appear to have been published between this date and the death of the king, and upwards of eighty others between that event and the Restoration.[‡] "When hostilities commenced," says the writer from whom we derive this information, "every event, during a most eventful period, had its own historian, who communicated *News* from *Hull*, *Truths* from *York*, *Warranted Tidings* from *Ireland*, and *Special Passages* from *several places*. These were all occasional papers. Impatient, however, as a distracted people were for information, the news were never distributed daily. The various newspapers were published weekly at first;

[*] See A Letter to Antonio Panizzi, Esq. By Thomas Watts, of the British Museum. 8vo. Lond. 1839.
[†] See Chronological List of Newspapers from the Epoch of the Civil Wars, in Chalmers's Life of Ruddiman, pp. 404—442.
[‡] See Chalmers's Life of Ruddiman, p. 114.

but in the progress of events, and the ardour of curiosity, they were distributed twice or thrice in every week.* Such were the French Intelligencer, the Dutch Spy, the Irish Mercury, and the Scots Dove, the Parliament Kite, and the Secret Owl. *Mercurius Acherontieus* brought them hebdomadal *News from Hell*; *Mercurius Democritus* communicated wonderful news from the World in the Moon; the *Laughing Mercury* gave perfect news from the Antipodes; and *Mercurius Mastix* faithfully lashed all Scouts, Mercuries, Posts, Spies, and other Intelligencers."† Besides the newspapers, also, the great political and religious questions of the time were debated, as already mentioned, in a prodigious multitude of separate pamphlets, which appear to have been read quite as universally and as eagerly. Of such pamphlets printed in the twenty years from the meeting of the Long Parliament to the Restoration there are still preserved in the British Museum, forming the collection called the King's Pamphlets, no fewer than thirty thousand, which would give a rate of four or five new ones every day.

Where our modern newspapers begin, the series of our old chroniclers closes with Sir Richard Baker's Chronicle of the Kings of England, written while its author was confined for debt in the Fleet Prison, where he died in 1645, and first published in a folio volume in 1641. It was several times reprinted, and was a great favourite with our ancestors for two or three succeeding generations; but it has now lost all interest, except for a few passages relating to the author's own time. Baker, however, himself declares it to be compiled "with so great care and diligence, that, if all others were lost, this only will be sufficient to inform posterity of all passages memorable or worthy to be known." Sir Richard and his Chronicle are now popularly remembered principally as the trusted historical guides and authorities of Addison's incomparable Sir Roger de Coverley.‡

RETROSPECT OF THE COMMONWEALTH LITERATURE.

It thus appears that the age of the Civil War and the Commonwealth does not present an absolute blank in the history of our highest literature; but, unless we are to except the Areopa-

* In December, 1642, however, Spalding, the Aberdeen annalist, in a passage which Mr. Chalmers has quoted, tells us that "now printed papers *daily* came from London, called *Diurnal Occurrences*, declaring what is done in parliament."—Vol. I. p. 336.

† Chalmers, p. 110.   ‡ See Spectator, No. 329.

gitics of Milton, the Liberty of Prophesying, and a few other controversial or theological treatises of Jeremy Taylor, some publications by Fuller, and the successive apocalypses of the imperturbable dreamer of Norwich, no work of genius of the first class appeared in England in the twenty years from the meeting of the Long Parliament to the Restoration; and the literary productions having any enduring life in them at all, that are to be assigned to that space, make but a very scanty sprinkling. It was a time when men wrote and thought, as they acted, merely for the passing moment. The unprinted plays of Beaumont and Fletcher, indeed, were now sent to the press, as well as other dramatic works written in the last age; the theatres, by which they used to be published in another way, being shut up—a significant intimation, rather than anything else, that the great age of the drama was at an end. A new play continued to drop occasionally from the commonplace pen of Shirley—almost the solitary successor of the Shakespeares, the Fletchers, the Jonsons, the Massingers, the Fords, and the rest of that bright throng. All other poetry, as well as dramatic poetry, was nearly silent—hushed partly by the din of arms and of theological and political strife, more by the frown of triumphant puritanism, boasting to itself that it had put down all the other fine arts as well as poetry, never again to lift their heads in England. It is observable that even the confusion of the contest that lasted till after the king's death did not so completely banish the Muses, or drown their voice, as did the grim tranquillity under the sway of the parliament that followed. The time of the war, besides the treatises just alluded to of Milton, Taylor, Fuller, and Browne, produced the Cooper's Hill, and some other poetical pieces, by Denham, and the republication of the Comus and other early poems of Milton; the collection of the plays of Beaumont and Fletcher, and Cowley's volume entitled The Mistress, appeared in 1647, in the short interval of doubtful quiet between the first and the second war; the volume of Herrick's poetry was published the next year, while the second war was still raging, or immediately after its close; Lovelace's first volume, in 1649, probably before the execution of the king. Hobbes's Leviathan, and one or two other treatises of his, all written some time before, were printed at London in 1650 and 1651, while the author was resident in Paris. For some years from this date the blank is nearly absolute. Then, when the more liberal despotism of Cromwell had displaced the Presbyterian moroseness of the parliament, we have Fuller's Church History printed in 1655; Harrington's Oceana, and the collection of Cowley's poetry, in 1656; Browne's Hydriotaphia and Garden of Cyrus, in 1658; Lovelace's second volume, and Hales's Remains, in 1659; together with two or three philosophical publications by Hobbes, and a few short pieces in verse by Waller, of which the most famous is his Panegyric on Oliver Cromwell, written after the Protector's death, an occasion which also afforded its first considerable theme to the ripening genius of Dryden. It is to be noted, moreover, that, with one illustrious exception, none of the writers that have been named belonged to the prevailing faction. If Waller and Dryden took that side in their verses for a moment, it must be admitted that they both amply made up for their brief conformity; Denham, Browne, Taylor, Herrick, Lovelace, Fuller, Hales, Hobbes, Cowley, were all consistent, most of them ardent, royalists; Harrington was a theoretical republican, but even he was a royalist by personal attachments; Milton alone was in life and heart a Commonwealth-man and a Cromwellian.

POETRY OF MILTON.

From the appearance of his minor poems, in 1645, Milton had published no poetry, with the exception of a sonnet to Henry Lawes, the musician, prefixed to a collection of Psalm tunes by that composer in 1648, till he gave to the world his Paradise Lost, in Ten Books, in 1667. In 1671 appeared his Paradise Regained and Samson Agonistes; in 1673 a new edition of his minor poems, with nine new sonnets and other additions; and in 1674, what is properly the second edition of the Paradise Lost, now distributed (by the bisection of the seventh and tenth) into twelve books. He died on Sunday the 8th of November, in that year, when within about a month of completing the sixty-sixth year of his age. His prose writings have been already noticed. Verse, however, was the form in which his genius had earliest expressed itself, and also that in which he had first come forth as an author. Passing over his paraphrases of one or two Psalms, done at a still earlier age, we have abundant promise of the future great poet in his lines On the Death of a Fair Infant, beginning,

O fairest flower, no sooner blown but blasted,

written in his seventeenth year; and still more in the College Exercise, written in his nineteenth year. A portion of this latter is almost as prophetic as it is beautiful; and, as the verses have not been much noticed,* we will here give a few of them:—

> Hail, native Language, that by sinews weak
> Didst move my first endeavouring tongue to speak,
> And mad'st imperfect words with childish trips,
> Half-unpronounced, slide through my infant lips:
>
> . . . . . .
>
> I have some naked thoughts that rove about,
> And loudly knock to have their passage out;
> And, weary of their place, do only stay
> Till thou hast deck'd them in their best array.
>
> . . . . . .
>
> Yet I had rather, if I were to choose,
> Thy service in some graver subject use,
> Such as may make thee search thy coffers round,
> Before thou clothe my fancy in fit sound;
> Such where the deep transported mind may soar
> Above the wheeling poles, and at heaven's door
> Look in, and see each blissful deity
> How he before the thunderous throne doth lie,
> Listening to what unshorn Apollo sings
> To the touch of golden wires, while Hebe brings
> Immortal nectar to her kingly sire:
> Then, passing through the spheres of watchful fire,
> And misty regions of wide air next under,
> And hills of snow, and lofts of piled thunder,
> May tell at length how green-eyed Neptune raves,
> In heaven's defiance mustering all his waves;
> Then sing of secret things that came to pass
> When beldame Nature in her cradle was;
> And last of kings, and queens, and heroes old,
> Such as the wise Demodocus once told
> In solemn songs at King Alcinous' feast,
> While sad Ulysses' soul and all the rest
> Are held with his melodious harmony
> In willing chains and sweet captivity.

This was written in 1627. Fourteen years later, after his return from Italy, where some of his juvenile Latin compositions, and some others in the same language, which, as he tells us, he "had shifted in scarcity of books and conveniences to patch up amongst them, were received with written encomiums, which the Italian is not forward to bestow on men of this side the Alps;" and when assenting in so far to these commendations, and not less

---

* Mr. Hallam, in his work on the Literature of Europe (iii. 269), inadvertently assumes that we have no English verse of Milton's written before his twenty-second year.

to an inward prompting which now grew daily upon him, he had ventured to indulge the hope that, by labour and study—"which I take," he nobly says, "to be my portion in this life"—joined with the strong propensity of nature, he "might perhaps leave something so written in after-times as they should not willingly let it die"—he continued still inclined to fix all the industry and art he could unite to the adorning of his native tongue—or, as he goes on to say, "to be an interpreter and relater of the best and sagest things among mine own citizens, throughout this island, in the mother-dialect;—that what the greatest and choicest wits of Athens, Rome, or modern Italy, and those Hebrews of old, did for their country, I, in my proportion, with this over and above of being a Christian, might do for mine; not caring to be once named abroad, though perhaps I could attain to that, but content with these British islands as my world;" and he again, more distinctly than before, though still only in general expressions, announced the great design, "of highest hope and hardest attempting," which he proposed to himself one day to accomplish—whether in the epic form, as exemplified by Homer, Virgil, and Tasso, or after the dramatic, "wherein Sophocles and Euripides reign"—or in the style of "those magnific odes and hymns" of Pindarus and Callimachus; not forgetting that of all these kinds of writing the highest models are to be found in the Holy Scriptures—in the Book of Job, in the Song of Solomon and the Apocalypse of St. John, in the frequent songs interspersed throughout the Law and the Prophets. "The thing which I had to say," concluded this remarkable announcement, "and those intentions which have lived within me ever since I could conceive myself anything worth to my country, I return to crave excuse that urgent reason hath plucked from me by an abortive and foredated discovery. And the accomplishment of them lies not but in a power above man's to promise; but that none hath by more studious ways endeavoured, and with more unwearied spirit that none shall, that I dare almost aver of myself, as far as life and free leisure will extend; and that the land had once enfranchised herself from this impertinent yoke of prelaty, under whose inquisitorious and tyrannical duncery no free and splendid wit can flourish. Neither do I think it shame to covenant with any knowing reader, that for some few years yet I may go on trust with him toward the payment of what I am now indebted; as being a work not to be raised from the heat of youth or the vapours of wine, like that which flows at waste from the pen of some vulgar amourist, or the trencher fury of a rhyming parasite; nor to be obtained by the invocation of dame Memory and her Siren daughters; but by devout prayer to that eternal Spirit, who can enrich with all utterance and knowledge, and sends out his seraphim, with the hallowed fire of his altar, to touch and purify the lips of whom he pleases. To this must be added industrious and select reading, steady observation, insight into all seemly and generous arts and affairs. Till which in some measure be accomplished, at mine own peril and cost I refuse not to sustain this expectation from as many as are not loth to hazard as much credulity upon the best pledges that I can give them."*

Before this, there had appeared in print of Milton's poetry only his Comus and Lycidas; the former in 1637, the latter with some other Cambridge verses on the same occasion, the loss at sea of his friend Edward King, in 1638: but, besides some of his sonnets and other minor pieces, he had also written the fragment entitled Arcades, and the two companion poems the L'Allegro and the Il Penseroso. These productions already attested the worthy successor of the greatest writers of English verse in the preceding age—recalling the fancy and the melody of the minor poems of Spenser and Shakespeare, and of the Faithful Shepherdess of Fletcher. The Comus, indeed, might be considered as an avowed imitation of the last-mentioned production. The resemblance in poetical character between the two sylvan dramas of Fletcher and Milton is very close; and they may be said to stand apart from all else in our literature—for Ben Jonson's Sad Shepherd is not for a moment to be compared with either, and in the Midsummer Night's Dream, Shakespeare, ever creative, passionate, and dramatic beyond all other writers, has soared so high above both, whether we look to the supernatural part of his fable or to its scenes of human interest, that we are little reminded of his peopled woodlands, his fairies, his lovers, or his glorious "rude mechanicals," either by the Faithful Shepherdess or the Comus. Of these two compositions, Milton's must be admitted to have the higher moral inspiration, and it is also the more elaborate and exact as a piece of writing; but in all that goes to make up dramatic effect, in the involvement and conduct of the story, and in the eloquence of natural feeling, Fletcher's is decidedly superior. It has been remarked that even in Shakespeare's early narrative poems—his Venus and Adonis, and his Tarquin and Lucrece—we may discern the future great dramatist by the full and unwithholding abandonment with which he there projects himself into whatever character he brings forward, and

* The Reason of Church Government urged against Prelaty (published in 1641).

the power of vivid conception with which he realizes the visionary scene, and brings it around him almost in the distinctness of broad daylight, as shown by a peculiar directness and life of expression evidently coming everywhere unsought, and escaping from his pen, one might almost say without his own consciousness,—without apparently any feeling, at least, of either art exercised or feat achieved.* In the case of Milton, on the contrary, his first published poem and earliest poetical attempt of any considerable extent, although in the dramatic form, affords abundant evidence that his genius was not dramatic. Comus is an exquisitely beautiful poem, but nearly destitute of everything we more especially look for in a drama—of passion, of character, of story, of action or movement of any kind. It flows on in a continued stream of eloquence, fancy, and most melodious versification; but there is no dialogue, properly so called, no replication of diverse emotions or natures; it is Milton alone who sings or declaims all the while,—sometimes of course on one side of the argument, sometimes on the other, and not, it may be, without changing his attitude and the tone of his voice, but still speaking only from one head, from one heart, from one ever-present and over-dominant constitution of being. And from this imprisonment within himself Milton never escapes, either in his dramatic or in his other poetry; it is the characteristic which distinguishes him not only from our great dramatists, but also from other great epic and narrative poets. His poetry has been sometimes described as to an unusual degree wanting in the expression of his own personal feelings; and, notwithstanding some remarkable instances of exception, not only in his minor pieces, but in his great epic, the remark is true in a certain sense. He is no habitual brooder over his own emotions, no self-dissector, no systematic resorter for inspiration to the accidents of his own personal history. His subject in some degree forbade this; his proud and lofty nature still more withheld him from it. But, although disdaining thus to picture himself at full length either for our pity or admiration, he has yet impressed the stamp of his own individuality—of his own character, moral as well as intellectual—as deep on all he has written as if his theme had been ever so directly himself. Compare him in this respect with Homer. We scarcely conceive of the old Greek poet as having a sentient existence at all, any more than we do of the sea or the breezes of heaven, whose music his continuous, undulating verse, ever various, ever the same, resembles. Who in the delineation of

* See this illustrated in Coleridge's Biographia Literaria, vol. II.

the wrath of Achilles finds a trace of the temper or character of the delineator? Who in Milton's Satan does not recognize much of Milton himself? But, although the spirit of his poetry is thus essentially egotistic, the range of his poetic power is not thereby confined within narrow limits. He had not the "myriad-minded" nature of Shakespeare—the all-penetrating sympathy by which the greatest of dramatists could transform himself for the time into any one of the other existences around him, no matter how high, no matter how low: conceive the haughty genius of Milton employed in the task of developing such a character as Justice Shallow, or Bottom the weaver, or a score of others to be found in the long, various, brilliant procession headed by Falstaff and ending with Dogberry! Anything of this kind he could scarcely have performed much better than the most ordinarily gifted of the sons of men; he had no more the wit or humour requisite for it than he had the power of intense and universal sympathy. But his proper region was still a vast one; and there, his vision, though always tinged with the colour of his own passions and opinions, was, notwithstanding, both as far reaching and as searching as any poet's ever was. In its style or form his poetry may be considered to belong rudimentally to the same Italian school with that of the greatest of his predecessors—of Spenser and of Shakespeare, if not also of Chaucer. But, as of these others, so it is true of him, that the inspiration of his Italian models is most perceptible in his earlier and minor verses, and that in his more mature and higher efforts he enriched this original basis of his poetic manner with so much of a different character, partly derived from other foreign sources, partly peculiar to himself, that the mode of conception and expression which he ultimately thus worked out is most correctly described by calling it his own. Conversant as he was with the language and literature of Italy, his poetry probably acquired what it has of Italian in its character principally through the medium of the elder poets of his own country; and it is, accordingly, still more English than Italian. Much of its inner spirit, and something also of its outward fashion, is of Hebrew derivation: it may be affirmed that from the fountain of no other foreign literature did Milton drink with so much eagerness as from this, and that by no other was his genius so much nourished and strengthened. Not a little, also, one so accomplished in the lore of classic antiquity must needs have acquired from that source; the touch of the poetry of Greece and Rome are heard more or less audibly everywhere in that of the great epic poet of England. But do we go too far in holding that in what he has actually achieved in his proper domain, the modern writer rises high "above all Greek, above all Roman fame?" Where in the poetry of the ancient world shall we find anything which approaches the richness and beauty, still less the sublimity, of the most triumphant passages in Paradise Lost? The First Book of that poem is probably the most splendid and perfect of human compositions—the one, that is to say, which unites these two qualities in the highest degree; and the Fourth is as unsurpassed for grace and luxuriance as that is for magnificence of imagination. And, though these are perhaps the two greatest books in the poem, taken each as a whole, there are passages in every one of the other books equal or almost equal to the finest in these. And worthy of the thoughts that breathe are the words that burn. A tide of gorgeous eloquence rolls on from beginning to end, like a river of molten gold; outblazing, we may surely say, everything of the kind in any other poetry. Finally, Milton's blank verse, both for its rich and varied music and its exquisite adaptation, would in itself almost deserve to be styled poetry, without the words: alone of all our poets, before or since, he has brought out the full capabilities of the language in that form of composition. Indeed, out of the drama, he is still our only great blank verse writer. Compared to his, the blank verse of no other of our narrative or didactic poets, unless we are to except a few of the happiest attempts at the direct imitation of his pauses and cadences, reads like anything else than a sort of muffled rhyme—rhyme spoilt by the ends being blunted or broken off. Who remembers, who can repeat, any narrative blank verse but his? In whose ear does any other linger? What other has the true organ tone which makes the music of this form of verse—either the grandeur or the sweetness?

It is natural, in comparing, or contrasting, Milton's Paradise Lost with his Paradise Regained, to think of the two great Homeric epics; the Iliad commonly believed by antiquity to have proceeded from the inspired poet in the vigour and glow of his manhood or middle age, the Odyssey to reflect the milder radiance of his imagination in the afternoon or evening of his life. It has been common accordingly to apply to the case of the English poet also the famous similitude of Longinus, and to say that in the Paradise Regained we have the sun on his descent, the same indeed as ever in majesty (τὸ μέγεθος), but deprived of his overpowering ardour (δίχα τῆς σφοδρότητος). Some have gone farther, not claiming for the Paradise Regained the honour of being sunshine at all, but only holding it worthy of being applauded in the spirit and after the fashion in which Pope has eulogized the gracious though not dazzling qualities of his friend Martha Blount:—

> So, when the sun's broad beam has tired the sight,
> All mild ascends the moon's more sober light;
> Serene in virgin modesty she shines,
> And unobserved the glaring orb declines.

An ingenious theory has been put forth by one of the editors of the Paradise Regained, Mr. Charles Dunster; he conceives that Milton designed this poem for an example of what he has himself in the remarkable passage of his Reason of Church Government, to which we have already had occasion to refer, spoken of as the *brief epic*, and distinguished from the *great and diffuse epic*, such as those of Homer and of Virgil, and his own Paradise Lost. Milton's words in full are:—"Time serves not now, and, perhaps, I might seem too profuse, to give any certain account of what the mind at home, in the spacious circuits of her musing, hath liberty to propose to herself, though of highest hope and hardest attempting; whether that epic form, whereof the two poems of Homer, and those other two of Virgil and Tasso, are a diffuse, and the book of Job a brief, model." Dunster accordingly thinks that we may suppose the model which Milton set before him in his Paradise Regained to have been in a great measure the book of Job.*

But surely the comparison which the companionship or sequence of the two Miltonic epics most forcibly suggests to a true feeling of both their resemblance and their difference, and of the prevailing spirit that animates each, is that of the Old and the New Testament. The one is distinctively Hebrew, the other as distinctively Christian. With much in common, they have also, like the two religions, and the two collections of sacred books, much in which they are unlike, and in a certain sense opposed to one another, both in manner and in sentiment. The poetry of the Paradise Lost, all life and movement, is to that of the Paradise Regained what a conflagration is to a sunlit landscape. In the one we have the grandeur of the old worship, in the other the simplicity of the new. The one addresses itself more to the sense, the other to the understanding. In respect either of force or of variety, either of intense and burning passion or of imaginative power mingling and blending all the wonders of brightness and gloom, there can be no comparison between them. There is the same poetic art, it is true, in both poems; they are more unmistakeably products of the same mind, perhaps, than are

* Paradise Regained; with notes. By Charles Dunster, M.A. 4to. Lond. 1795. p. 2.

the Iliad and the Odyssey; and yet the difference between them in tone and character is greater than that between the two Greek epics. It is in some respects like the difference between an oil-painting and a painting in water-colours. The more brevity of the one as compared with the other would stamp it as a work of inferior pretension, and it is still more limited in subject or scope than it is in dimensions. The Paradise Regained must be considered, in fact, as only an appendage to the Paradise Lost. Yet, comparatively short as it is, the thread of the narrative is felt to be spun out and over-much attenuated. It contains some highly finished and exquisite passages; but perhaps the only poetical quality in which it can be held to match, if it does not sometimes even surpass, the Paradise Lost, is picturesqueness. In that it more resembles the L'Allegro and the Il Penseroso than it does its companion epic. Even the argumentative eloquence, of which it is chiefly made up, brilliant as it is, is far from being equal to the best of that in the Paradise Lost. It has the same ingenuity and logic, with as much, or perhaps even more, concentration in the expression; but, unavoidably, it may be, from the circumstances of the case, it has not either the same glow and splendour or even the same tone of real feeling. The fallen spirits thronging Pandemonium, or stretched on the burning lake before that gorgeous pile "rose like an exhalation," consult and debate, in their misery and anxious perplexity, with an accent of human earnestness which it was impossible to give either to the conscious sophistry of their chief in that other scene or to the wisdom more than human by which he is refuted and repelled.

It is commonly said that Milton himself professed to prefer the Paradise Regained to the Paradise Lost. The probability is that, if he asserted the former to be the better poem of the two, it was only in a qualified sense, or with reference to something else than its poetical merits, and in the same feeling with which he explained the general prevalence of the opposite opinion by attributing it to most people having a much stronger feeling of regret for the loss of Paradise than desire for the recovery of it, or at least inclination for the only way in which it was to be recovered. It was very characteristic of him, however, to be best pleased with what he had last produced, as well as to be only confirmed in his partiality by having the general voice against him and by his contempt for what of extravagance and injustice there was in the popular depreciation of the new poem. He was in all things by temper and mental constitution essentially a partisan; seeing clearly, indeed, all that was to be said on both sides of any question, but never for all that remaining in suspense between them, or hesitating to make up his mind and to take his place distinctly on one side. This is shown by the whole course of his life. Nor is it less expressively proclaimed not only by the whole tone and manner of his poetry, everywhere so ardent, impetuous, and dogmatical, and so free from the faintest breath either of suspicion or of any kind of self-distrust, but even in that argumentative eloquence which is one of its most remarkable characteristics. For one of the chief necessary conditions of the existence of oratorical or debating power, and, indeed, of every kind of fighting ability, is that it should, at one and the same time, both feel passionately in favour of its own side of the question and discern clearly the strength of the adverse position. Whatever may be the fact as to his alleged preference of the Paradise Regained to the Paradise Lost, Milton has, at any rate, pronounced judgment in a sufficiently decisive and uncompromising way upon another point in regard to which both these works stand contrasted with much of his earlier poetry. We refer to his vehement denunciation, in a notice prefixed to the Paradise Lost,* of rhyme as being, in all circumstances, for he makes no exception, "a thing of itself, to all judicious ears, trivial and of no true musical delight," and as having no claim to be regarded as anything else than the barbarous invention of a barbarous age, and a mere jingle and life-repressing bondage. We certainly rejoice that the Paradise Lost is not written in rhyme; but we are very glad that these strong views were not taken up by the great poet till after he had produced his L'Allegro and Il Penseroso, his Lycidas and his Sonnets.

COWLEY.

The poetry of Milton, though principally produced after the Restoration, belongs in everything but in date to the preceding age; and this is also nearly as true of that of Cowley. Abraham Cowley, born in London in 1618, published his first volume of verse, under the title of Poetic Blossoms, in 1633, when he was yet only a boy of fifteen: one piece contained in this publication, indeed—The Tragical History of Pyramus and Thisbe—was written when he was only in his tenth year. The four books of his unfinished epic entitled Davideis were mostly written while he was a student at Trinity College, Cambridge. His pastoral

---

* This notice, commonly headed *The Verse* in modern editions of the poem, is found in three of the five various forms of the first edition (1667, 1668, and 1669), and there bears the superscription *The Printer to the Reader*; but there can be no doubt that it is Milton's own.

drama of Love's Riddle, and his Latin comedy called Naufragium Jocularo, were both published in 1638. In 1647 appeared his collection of amatory poems entitled The Mistress, and in 1653 his comedy of The Guardian, afterwards altered, and republished as The Cutter of Coleman Street. After the Restoration he collected such of his pieces as he thought worth preserving, and republished them, together with some additional productions, of which the most important were his Davideis, and his Pindarique Odes.

Few poets have been more popular, or more praised, in their own time than Cowley. Milton is said to have declared that the three greatest English poets were Spenser, Shakespeare, and Cowley; though it does not follow that he held all three to be equally great. Sir John Denham, in some verses on Cowley's Death and Burial amongst the Ancient Poets in Westminster Abbey, sets him above all the English poets that had gone before him, and prophesies that posterity will hold him to have been equalled by Virgil alone among those of antiquity. For a long time, too, his works appear to have been more generally read than those of any other English poet, if a judgment may be formed from the frequency with which they were reprinted, and the numerous copies of them in various forms that still exist.[*] This popular favour they seem to have shared with those of Donne, whose legitimate successor Cowley was considered to be; or rather, when the poetry of Donne became obsolete or unfashionable, that of Cowley took its place in the reading and admiration of the poetical part of the public. Cowley, indeed, is in the main a mere modernization and dilution of Donne. With the same general characteristics of manner, he is somewhat less forced and fantastical, a good deal less daring in every way, but unfortunately also infinitely less poetical. Everything about him, in short, is less deep, strong, and genuine. His imagination is tinsel, or mere surface gilding, compared to Donne's solid gold; his wit little better than word-catching, to the profound meditative quaintness of the elder poet; and of passion, with which all Donne's finest lines are tremulous, Cowley has none. Considerable grace and dignity occasionally distinguish his Pindaric Odes (which, however, are Pindaric only in name); and he has shown much elegant playfulness of style and fancy in his translations from and imitations of Anacreon, and in some other verses written in the same manner. As for what he intends for love verses, some of them are pretty enough frost-work; but the only sort of love there is in them is the love of point and sparkle.

[*] A twelfth edition of the collection formed by Cowley himself was published by Tonson in 1721.

BUTLER.

This manner of writing is more fitly applied by another celebrated poet of the same date, Samuel Butler, the immortal author of Hudibras. Butler, born in 1612, is said to have written most of his great poem during the interregnum; but the first part of it was not published till 1663. The poetry of Butler has been very happily designated as merely the comedy of that style of composition which Donne and Cowley practised in its more serious form—the difference between the two modes of writing being much the same with that which is presented by a countenance of a peculiar cast of features when solemnized by deep reflection, and the same countenance when lighted up by cheerfulness or distorted by mirth.* And it may be added, that the gayer and more animated expression is here, upon the whole, the more natural. The quantity of explosive matter of all kinds which Butler has contrived to pack up in his verses is amazing; it is crack upon crack, flash upon flash, from the first line of his long poem to the last. Much of this incessant bedazzlement is, of course, merely verbal, or otherwise of the humblest species of wit; but an infinite number of the happiest things are also thrown out. And Hudibras is far from being all mere broad farce. Butler's power of arguing in verse, in his own way, may almost be put on a par with Dryden's in his; and, perseveringly as he devotes himself upon system to the exhibition of the ludicrous and grotesque, he sometimes surprises us with a sudden gleam of the truest beauty of thought and expression breaking out from the midst of the usual rattling fire of smartnesses and conundrums— as when in one place he exclaims of a thin cloud drawn over the moon—

> Mysterious veil; of brightness made,
> At once her lustre and her shade!

He must also be allowed to tell his story and to draw his characters well, independently of his criticisms.

WALLER.

The most celebrated among the minor poets of the period between the Restoration and the Revolution was Waller. Edmund Waller, born in 1605, had, as already noticed, announced himself as a writer of verse before the close of the reign of James I., by

* Scott, in Life of Dryden.

his lines on the escape of Prince Charles at the port of San
Andero, in the Bay of Biscay, on his return from Spain, in September, 1623; and he continued to write till after the accession
of James II., in whose reign he died, in the year 1687. His last
production was the little poem concluding with one of his
happiest, one of his most characteristic, and one of his best-
known passages:—

> The soul's dark cottage, battered and decayed,
> Lets in new light through chinks that time has made:
> Stronger by weakness, wiser men become
> As they draw near to their eternal home:
> Leaving the old, both worlds at once they view,
> That stand upon the threshold of the new.

Fenton, his editor, tells us that a number of poems on religious
subjects, to which these verses refer, were mostly written when
he was about [above] eighty years old; and he has himself
intimated that his bodily faculties were now almost gone:—

> When we for age could neither read nor write,
> The subject made us able to indite.

Waller, therefore, as well as Milton, Cowley, and Butler, may be
considered to have formed his manner in the last age; but his
poetry does not belong to the old English school even so much as
that of either Butler or Cowley. The contemporaries of the
earlier portion of his long career were Carew and Lovelace; and
with them he is properly to be classed in respect of poetical style
and manner. Both Lovelace and Carew, however, as has been
already intimated, have more passion than Waller, who, with all
his taste and elegance, was incapable of either expressing or feeling anything very lofty or generous—being, in truth, poet as he
was, a very mean-souled description of person, as his despicable
political course sufficiently evinced. His poetry accordingly is
beyond the reach of critical animadversion on the score of such
extravagance as is sometimes prompted by strong emotion.
Waller is always perfectly master of himself, and idolizes his
mistress with quite as much coolness and self-possession as he
flatters his prince. But, although cold and unaffecting at all
times, he occasionally rises to much dignity of thought and
manner. His panegyric on Cromwell, the offering of his gratitude to the Protector for the permission granted to him of returning to England after ten years' exile, is one of the most
graceful pieces of adulation ever offered by poetry to power; and
the poet is here probably more sincere than in most of his
effusions, for the occasion was one on which he was likely to be

moved to more than usual earnestness of feeling. A few years after he welcomed Charles II. on his restoration to the throne of his ancestors in another poem, which has been generally considered a much less spirited composition: Fenton accounts for the falling off by the author's advance in the meanwhile from his forty-ninth to his fifty-fifth year—"from which time," he observes, "his genius began to decline apace from its meridian;" but the poet himself assigned another reason:—when Charles frankly told him that he thought his own panegyric much inferior to Cromwell's, "Sir," replied Waller, "we poets never succeed so well in writing truth as in fiction." Perhaps the true reason, after all, might be that his majesty's return to England was not quite so exciting a subject to Mr. Waller's muse as his own return had been. One thing must be admitted in regard to Waller's poetry; it is free from all mere verbiage and empty sound; if he rarely or never strikes a very powerful note, there is at least always something for the fancy or the understanding, as well as for the ear, in what he writes. He abounds also in ingenious thoughts, which he dresses to the best advantage, and exhibits with great transparency of style. Eminent, however, as he is in his class, he must be reckoned among that subordinate class of poets who think and express themselves chiefly in similitudes, not among those who conceive and write passionately and metaphorically. He had a decorative and illuminating, but not a transforming imagination.

MARVEL.

The chief writer of verse on the popular side after the Restoration was Andrew Marvel, the noble-minded member for Hull, the friend of Milton, and, in that age of brilliant profligacy, renowned alike as the first of patriots and of wits. Marvel, the son of the Rev. Andrew Marvel, master of the grammar-school of Hull, was born there in 1620, and died in 1678. His poetical genius has scarcely had justice done to it. He is the author of a number of satires in verse, in which a rich vein of vigorous, though often coarse, humour runs through a careless, extemporaneous style, and which did prodigious execution in the party warfare of the day; but some of his other poetry, mostly perhaps written in the earlier part of his life, is eminent both for the delicate bloom of the sentiment and for grace of form. His Song of the Exiles, beginning "Where the remote Bermudas ride," is a gem of melody, picturesqueness, and sentiment, nearly without a flaw, and is familiar to every lover of poetry. The following verses, which are less known, are exquisitely elegant and tuneful. They are entitled The Picture of T. C. in a Prospect of Flowers:—

> See with what simplicity
> This nymph begins her golden days!
> In the green grass she loves to lie,
> And there with her fair aspect tames
> The wilder flowers, and gives them names;
> But only with the roses plays,
> And them does tell
> What colour best becomes them, and what smell.
>
> Who can foretell for what high cause
> This darling of the gods was born?
> See this is she whose cluster laws
> The wanton Love shall one day fear,
> And, under her command severe,
> See his bow broke and ensigns torn.
> Happy who can
> Appease this virtuous enemy of man!
>
> O then let me in time compound,
> And parley with those conquering eyes;
> Ere they have tried their force to wound,
> Ere with their glancing wheels they drive
> In triumph over hearts that strive,
> And them that yield but more despise.
> Let me be laid
> Where I may see the glory from some shade.
>
> Meantime, whilst every verdant thing
> Itself does at thy beauty charm,[1]
> Reform the errors of the spring:
> Make that the tulips may have share
> Of sweetness, seeing they are fair;
> And roses of their thorns disarm:
> But most procure
> That violets may a longer age endure.
>
> But oh, young beauty of the woods,
> Whom nature courts with fruits and flowers,
> Gather the flowers, but spare the buds;
> Lest Flora, angry at thy crime
> To kill her infants in their prime,
> Should quickly make the example yours;
> And, ere we see,
> Nip in the blossom all our hopes in thee.

---

[1] *Charm itself*, that is, delight itself.

Certainly neither Carew, nor Waller, nor any other court poet of that day, has produced anything in the same style finer than these lines. But Marvel's more elaborate poetry is not confined to love songs and other such light exercises of an ingenious and elegant fancy. Witness his verses on Milton's Paradise Lost—"When I beheld the poet blind, yet bold"— which have throughout almost the dignity, and in parts more than the strength, of Waller.

Other Minor Poets.

Of the other minor poets of this date we shall only mention the names of a few of the most distinguished. Sir Charles Sedley is the Suckling of the time of Charles II., with less impulsiveness and more insinuation, but a kindred gaiety and sprightliness of fancy, and an answering liveliness and at the same time courtly ease and elegance of diction. King Charles, a good judge of such matters, was accustomed to say that Sedley's style, either in writing or discourse, would be the standard of the English tongue; and his contemporary, the Duke of Buckingham (Villiers) used to call his exquisite art of expression *Sedley's witchcraft*. Sedley's genius early ripened and bore fruit: he was born only two or three years before the breaking out of the Civil War; and he was in high reputation as a poet and a wit within six or seven years after the Restoration. He survived both the Revolution and the century, dying in the year 1701. Sedley's fellow debauchee, the celebrated Earl of Rochester (Wilmot)—although the brutal grossness of the greater part of his verse has deservedly made it and its author infamous—was perhaps a still greater genius. There is immense strength and pregnancy of expression in some of the best of his compositions, careless and unfinished as they are. Rochester had not completed his thirty-third year when he died, in July 1680. Of the poetical productions of the other court wits of Charles's reign the principal are, the Duke of Buckingham's satirical comedy of the Rehearsal, which was very effective when first produced, and still enjoys a great reputation, though it would probably be thought but a heavy joke now by most readers not carried away by the prejudice in its favour; the Earl of Roscommon's very commonplace Essay on Translated Verse; and the Earl of Dorset's lively and well-known song, "To all you ladies now on land," written at sea the night before the engagement with the Dutch on the 3rd of June, 1665, or rather professing to have been then written, for the asserted poetic tranquillity of the noble author in expectation of the morrow's fight has been disputed. The Marquis of Halifax and Lord Godolphin were also writers of verse at this date; but neither of them has left anything worth remembering. Among the minor poets of the time, however, we ought not to forget Charles Cotton, best known for his humorous, though somewhat coarse, travesties of Virgil and Lucian, and for his continuation of Izaak Walton's Treatise on Angling, and his fine idiomatic translation of Montaigne's Essays, but also the author of some short original pieces in verse, of much fancy and liveliness. One entitled an Ode to Winter, in particular, has been highly praised by Wordsworth.

Dryden.

By far the most illustrious name among the English poets of the latter half of the seventeenth century — if we exclude Milton as belonging properly to the preceding age — is that of John Dryden. Born in 1632, Dryden produced his first known composition in verse in 1649, his lines on the death of Lord Hastings, a young nobleman of great promise, who was suddenly cut off by small-pox, on the eve of his intended marriage, in that year. This earliest of Dryden's poems is in the most ambitious style of the school of Donne and Cowley: Donne himself, indeed, has scarcely penned anything quite so extravagant as one passage, in which the fancy of the young poet runs riot among the phenomena of the loathsome disease to which Lord Hastings had fallen a victim:—

> So many spots, like naeves on Venus' soil,
> One jewel set off with so many a foil:
> Blisters with pride swell'd, which through 's flesh did sprout
> Like rose-buds stuck i' the lily skin about.
> Each little pimple had a tear in it,
> To wail the fault its rising did commit:—

and so forth. Almost the only feature of the future Dryden which this production discloses is his deficiency in sensibility or heart; exciting as the occasion was, it does not contain an affecting line. Perhaps, on comparing his imitation with Donne's own poetry, so instinct with tenderness and passion, Dryden may have seen or felt that his own wanted the very quality which was the light and life of that of his master; at any rate, wiser than Cowley, who had the same reason for shunning a competition with Donne, he abandoned this style with his first attempt, and, indeed, for anything that appears, gave up the writing of poetry for some years altogether. His next verses of any consequence are dated nine years later,—his Heroic Stanzas on the death of Oliver Cromwell,—and, destitute as they are of the vigorous conception and full and easy flow of versification which he afterwards attained, they are free from any trace of the elaborate and grotesque absurdity of the Elegy on Lord Hastings. His Astræa Redux, or poem on the return of the king, produced two years after, evinces a growing freedom and command of style. But it is in his Annus Mirabilis, written in 1666, that his genius breaks forth for the first time with any promise of that full effulgence at which it ultimately arrived; here, in spite of the incumbrance of a stanza (the quatrain of alternately rhyming heroics) which he afterwards wisely exchanged for a more manageable kind of verse, we have much both of the nervous diction and the fervid fancy which characterize his latest and best works. From this date to the end of his days Dryden's life was one long literary labour; eight original poems of considerable length, many shorter pieces, twenty-eight dramas, and several volumes of poetical translation from Chaucer, Boccaccio, Ovid, Theocritus, Lucretius, Horace, Juvenal, Persius, and Virgil, together with numerous discourses in prose, some of them very long and elaborate, attest the industry as well as the fertility of a mind which so much toil and so many draughts upon its resources were so far from exhausting, that its powers continued not only to exert themselves with unimpaired elasticity, but to grow stronger and brighter to the last. The genius of Dryden certainly did not, as that of Waller is said to have done, begin "to decline apace from its meridian" after he had reached his fifty-fifth year. His famous Alexander's Feast and his Fables, which are among his happiest performances, were the last he produced, and were published together in the year 1700, only a few months before his death, at the age of sixty-eight.

Dryden has commonly been considered to have founded a new school of English poetry; but perhaps it would be more strictly correct to regard him as having only carried to higher perfection —perhaps to the highest to which it has yet been brought— a style of poetry which had been cultivated long before his day. The satires of Hall and of Marston, and also the Nosce Teipsum of Sir John Davies, all published before the end of the sixteenth century, not to refer to other less eminent examples, may be classed as of the same school with his poetry. It is a school very distinguishable from that to which Milton and the greatest of our older poets belong, deriving its spirit and character, as it does, chiefly from the ancient Roman classic poetry, whereas the other is mainly the offspring of the middle ages, of Gothic manners and feelings and the Romance or Provençal literature. The one therefore may be called, with sufficient propriety, the classic, the other the romantic school of poetry. But it seems to be a mistake to assume that the former first arose in England after the Restoration, under the influence of the imitation of the French, which then became fashionable; the most that can be said is, that the French taste which then became prevalent among us may have encouraged its revival; for undoubtedly what has been called the classic school of poetry had been cultivated by English writers at a much earlier date; nor is there any reason to suppose that the example of the modern poetry of France had had any share in originally turning our own into that channel. Marston and Hall, and Sackville in his Ferrex and Porrex, and Ben Jonson in his comedies and tragedies, and the other early writers of English poetry in the classic vein, appear not to have imitated any French poets, but to have gone to the fountain-head, and sought in the productions of the Roman poets themselves,—in the plays of Terence and Seneca, and the satires of Juvenal and Persius, —for examples and models. Nay, even Dryden, at a later period, probably formed himself almost exclusively upon the same originals and upon the works of these his predecessors among his own countrymen, and was little, if at all, indebted to or influenced by any French pattern. His poetry, unlike as it is to that of Milton or Spenser, has still a thoroughly English character—an English force and heartiness, and, with all its classicality, not a little even of the freedom and luxuriance of the more genuine English style. Smooth Waller, who preceded him, may have learned something from the modern French poets; and so may Pope, who came after him; but Dryden's fiery energy and "full-resounding line" have nothing in common with them in spirit or manner. Without either creative imagination or any power of pathos, he is in argument, in satire, and in declamatory magnificence, the greatest of our poets. His poetry, indeed, is not the highest kind of poetry, but in that kind he stands unrivalled and unapproached. Pope, his great disciple, who, in correctness, in neatness, and in the brilliancy of epigrammatic point, has outshone his master, has not come near him in easy flexible vigour, in indignant vehemence, in narrative rapidity, any more than he has in sweep and variety of versification. Dryden never writes coldly, or timidly, or drowsily. The movement of verse always sets him on fire, and whatever he produces is a coinage hot from the brain, not slowly scraped or pinched into shape, but struck out as from a die with a few stout blows or a single wrench of the screw. It is this fervour especially which gives to his personal sketches their wonderful life and force: his Absalom and Achitophel is the noblest portrait-gallery in poetry.

It is chiefly as a dramatic writer that Dryden can be charged with the imitation of French models. Of his plays, nearly thirty in number, the comedies for the most part in prose, the tragedies in rhyme, few have much merit considered as entire works, although there are brilliant passages and spirited scenes in most of them. Of the whole number, he has told us that his tragedy of All for Love, or the World well Lost (founded on the story of Antony and Cleopatra), was the only play he wrote for himself; the rest, he admits, were sacrifices to the vitiated taste of the age. His Almanzor, or the Conquest of Granada (in two parts), although extravagant, is also full of genius. Of his comedies, the Spanish Friar is perhaps the best; it has some most effective scenes.

Dramatists.

Many others of the poets of this age whose names have been already noticed were also dramatists. Milton's Comus was never acted publicly, nor his Samson Agonistes at all. Cowley's Love's Riddle and Cutter of Coleman Street were neither of them originally written for the stage; but the latter was brought out in one of the London theatres after the Restoration, and was also revived about the middle of the last century. Waller altered the fifth act of Beaumont and Fletcher's Maid's Tragedy, making his additions to the blank verse of the old dramatists in rhyme, as he states in a prologue:—

> In this old play what's new we have expressed
> In rhyming verse distinguish'd from the rest;
> That, as the Rhone its hasty way does make
> (Not mingling waters) through Geneva's lake,
> So, having here the different styles in view,
> You may compare the former with the new.

Villiers, Duke of Buckingham, besides his Rehearsal, wrote a farce entitled the Battle of Sedgmoor, and also altered Beaumont and Fletcher's comedy of The Chances. The tragedy of Valentinian of the same writers was altered by the Earl of Rochester. Sedley wrote three comedies, mostly in prose, and three tragedies, one in rhyme and two in blank verse. And Davenant is the author of twenty-five tragedies, comedies, and masques, produced between 1629 and his death, in 1668. But the most eminent dramatic names of this era are those of Thomas Otway, Nathaniel Lee, John Crowne, Sir George Etheridge, William Wycherly, and Thomas Southerne. Of six tragedies and four comedies written by Otway, his tragedies of the Orphan and Venice Preserved still sustain his fame and popularity as the most pathetic and tear-drawing of all our dramatists. Their licentiousness has necessarily banished his comedies from the stage, with most of those of his contemporaries. Lee has also great tenderness, with much more fire and imagination than Otway; of his pieces, eleven in number—all tragedies—his Theodosius, or the Force of Love, and his Rival Queens, or Alexander the Great, are the most celebrated. Crowne, though several of his plays were highly successful when first produced, was almost forgotten, till Mr. Lamb reprinted some of his scenes in his Dramatic Specimens, and showed that no dramatist of that age had written finer things. Of seventeen pieces produced by Crowne between 1671 and 1698, his tragedy of Thyestes and his comedy of Sir Courtley Nice are in particular of eminent merit, the first for its poetry, the second for plot and character. Etheridge is the author of only three comedies, the Comical Revenge (1664), She Would if She Could (1668), and the Man of Mode, or Sir Fopling Flutter (1676); all remarkable for the polish and fluency of the dialogue, and entitled to be regarded as having first set the example of that modern style of comedy which was afterwards cultivated by Wycherly, Farquhar, Vanbrugh, and Congreve. Wycherly, who was born in 1640, and lived till 1715, produced his only four plays, Love in a Wood, The Gentleman Dancing Master, The Country Wife, and The Plain Dealer, all comedies, between the years 1672 and 1677. The two last of these pieces are written with more elaboration than anything of Etheridge's, and both contain some bold delineation of character and strong satiric writing, reminding us at times of Ben Jonson; but, like him, too, Wycherly is deficient in ease and nature. Southerne, who was only born in the year of the Restoration, and lived till 1746, had produced no more than his two first plays before the Revolution of 1688, —his tragedy of the Loyal Brother in 1682, and his comedy of the Disappointment in 1684. Of ten dramatic pieces of which he is the author, five are comedies, and are of little value; but his tragedies of The Fatal Marriage (1692), Oroonoko (1696), and The Spartan Dame (1719), are interesting and affecting.

PROSE WRITERS:—CLARENDON.

Eminent as he is among the poets of his age, Dryden is also one of the greatest of its prose writers. In ease, flexibility, and variety, indeed, his English prose has scarcely ever been excelled. Cowley, too, is a charming writer of prose: the natural, pure, and flowing eloquence of his Essays is better than anything in his poetry. Waller, Suckling, and Sedley, also, wrote all well in prose; and Marvel's literary reputation is founded more upon his prose than upon his verse. Of writers exclusively in prose belonging to the space between the Restoration and the Revolution, Clarendon may be first mentioned, although his great work, his History of the Rebellion and Civil Wars, was not published till the year 1702, nor his Life and Continuation of his History, before 1759. His style cannot be commended for its correctness; the manner in which he constructs his sentences, indeed, often sets at defiance all the rules of syntax; but yet he is never unintelligible or obscure—with such admirable expository skill is the matter arranged and spread out, even where the mere verbal sentence-making is the most negligent and entangled. The style, in fact, is that proper to speaking rather than to writing, and had, no doubt, been acquired by Clarendon, not so much from books as from his practice in speaking at the bar and in parliament; for, with great natural abilities, he does not seem to have had much acquaintance with literature, or much acquired knowledge of any kind resulting from study. But his writing possesses the quality that interests above all the graces or artifices of rhetoric —the impress of a mind informed by its subject, and having a complete mastery over it; while the broad full stream in which it flows makes the reader feel as if he were borne along on its tide. The abundance, in particular, with which he pours out his stores of language and illustration in his characters of the eminent persons engaged on both sides of the great contest seems inexhaustible. The historical value of his history, however, is not very considerable; it has not preserved very many facts which are not to be found elsewhere; and, whatever may be thought of its general bias, the inaccuracy of its details is so great throughout, as demonstrated by the authentic evidences of the time, that there is scarcely any other contemporary history which is so little trustworthy as an authority with regard to minute particulars. Clarendon, in truth, was far from being placed in the most favourable circumstances for giving a perfectly correct account of many of the events he has undertaken to record: he was not, except for a very short time, in the midst of the busy scene: looking to it, as he did, from a distance, while the mighty drama was still only in progress, he was exposed to some chances of misconception to which even those removed from it by a long interval of time are not liable; and, without imputing to him any further intention to deceive than is implied in the purpose which we may suppose be chiefly had in view in writing his work, the vindication of his own side of the question, his position as a partisan, intimately mixed up with the affairs and interests of one of the two contending factions, could not fail both to bias his own judgment, and even in some measure to distort or colour the reports made to him by others. On the whole, therefore, this celebrated work is rather a great literary performance than a very valuable historical monument.

Hobbes.

Another royalist history of the same times and events to which Clarendon's work is dedicated, the Behemoth of Thomas Hobbes of Malmesbury, introduces one of the most distinguished names both in English literature and in modern metaphysical, ethical, and political philosophy. Hobbes, born in 1588, commenced author in 1628, at the age of forty, by publishing his translation of Thucydides, but did not produce his first original work, his Latin treatise entitled De Cive, till 1642. This was followed by his treatises entitled Human Nature and De Corpore Politico, in 1650; his Leviathan, in 1651; his translations in verse of the Iliad and Odyssey, in 1675; and his Behemoth, or History of the Causes of the Civil Wars of England, and of the counsels and artifices by which they were carried on, from the year 1640 to the year 1660, a few months after his death, at the age of ninety-two, in 1679. Regarded merely as a writer of English, there can be little difference of opinion about the high rank to be assigned to Hobbes. He has been described as our first uniformly careful and correct writer;[*] and he may be admitted to have at least set the first conspicuous and influential example in

---
[*] Hallam, Lit. of Eur. iv. 316.

what may be called our existing English (for Roger Ascham, Sir Thomas Elyot, and one or two other early writers, seem to have aimed at the same thing in a preceding stage of the language), of that regularity of style which has since his time been generally attended to. This, however, is his least merit. No writer has succeeded in making language a more perfect exponent of thought than it is as employed by Hobbes. His style is not poetical or glowingly eloquent, because his mind was not poetical, and the subjects about which he wrote would have rejected the exaggerations of imaginative or passionate expression if he had been capable of supplying such. But in the prime qualities of precision and perspicuity, and also in economy and succinctness, in force and in terseness, it is the very perfection of a merely expository style. Without any affectation of point, also, it often shapes itself easily and naturally into the happiest aphoristic and epigrammatic forms. Hobbes's clearness and aptness of expression, the effect of which is like that of reading a book with a good light, never forsake him—not even in that most singular performance, his version of Homer, where there is scarcely a trace of ability of any other kind. There are said to be only two lines in that work in which he is positively poetical; those which describe the infant Astyanax in the scene of the parting of Hector and Andromache, in the Sixth Book of the Iliad:—

> Now Hector met her with her little boy,
> That in the nurse's arms was carried;
> And like a star upon her bosom lay
> His beautiful and shining golden head.

But there are other passages in which by dint of mere directness and transparency of style he has rendered a line or two happily enough—as, for instance, in the description of the descent of Apollo at the prayer of Chryses, in the beginning of the poem:—

> His prayer was granted by the deity,
> Who, with his silver bow and arrows keen,
> Descended from Olympus silently,
> In likeness of the sable night unseen.

As if expressly to proclaim and demonstrate, however, that this momentary success was merely accidental, immediately upon the back of this stanza comes the following:—

> His bow and quiver both behind him hang,
> The arrows chink as often as he jogs,
> And as he shot the bow was heard to twang,
> And first his arrows flew at mules and dogs.

For the most part, indeed, Hobbes's Iliad and Odyssey are no better than travesties of Homer's, the more ludicrous as being undesigned and unconscious. Never was there a more signal revenge than that which Hobbes afforded to imagination and poetry over his own unbelieving and scoffing philosophism by the publication of this work. It was almost as if the man born blind, who had all his lifetime been attempting to prove that the sense which he himself wanted was no sense at all, and that that thing, colour, which it professed peculiarly to discern, was a mere delusion, should have himself at last taken the painter's brush and pallet in hand, and attempted, in confirmation of his theory, to produce a picture by the mere senses of touch, taste, smell, and hearing.*

Nevile.

The most remarkable treatise on political philosophy which appeared in the interval between the Restoration and the Revolution is Henry Nevile's Plato Redivivus, or a Dialogue concerning Government; which was first published in 1681, and went through at least a second edition the same year. Nevile, who was born in 1620, and survived till 1694, had in the earlier part of his life been closely connected with Harrington, the author of the Oceana, and also with the founders of the Commonwealth, and he is commonly reckoned a republican writer; but the present work professes to advocate a monarchical form of government. Its leading principle is the same as that on which Harrington's work is founded, the necessity of all stable government being based upon property; but, in a Preface, in the form of an Address from the Publisher to the Reader, pains are taken to show that the author's application of this principle is different from Harrington's. It is observed, in the first place, that the principle in question is not exclusively or originally Harrington's; it had been discoursed upon and maintained in very many treatises and pamphlets before ever the Oceana came out; in particular in A Letter from an Officer in Ireland to His Highness the Lord Protector, printed in 1653, "which was more than three years before Oceana was written." Besides, continues the writer,

---

* It is right, however, to state that Coleridge, in a note to the second (1818) edition of the Friend, Introd. Essay iv., admits that in the original edition of that work he had spoken too contemptuously of Hobbes's Odyssey, which when he so wrote of it he had not seen. "It is doubtless," he adds, "as much too ballad-like as the later versions are too epic; but still, on the whole, it leaves a much truer impression of the original."

who is evidently Nevile himself, "Oceana was written (it being thought lawful so to do in those times) to evince out of these principles that England was not capable of any other government than a democracy. And this author, out of the same maxims or aphorisms of politics, endeavours to prove that they may be applied, naturally and fitly, to the redressing and supporting one of the best monarchies in the world, which is that of England." The tenor of the work is throughout in conformity with this declaration.

OTHER PROSE WRITERS:—CUDWORTH, MORE; BARROW; BUNYAN; &c.

The most illustrious antagonist of metaphysical Hobbism, when first promulgated, was Dr. Ralph Cudworth, the First Part of whose True Intellectual System of the Universe, wherein all the Reason and Philosophy of Atheism is Confuted, was first published in 1678. As a vast storehouse of learning, and also as a display of wonderful powers of subtle and far-reaching speculation, this celebrated work is almost unrivalled in our literature; and it is also written in a style of elastic strength and compass which places its author in a high rank among our prose classics. Along with Cudworth may be mentioned his friend and brother Platonist, Dr. Henry More, the author of numerous theological and philosophical works, and remarkable for the union of some of the most mystic notions with the clearest style, and of the most singular credulity with powers of reasoning of the highest order. Other two great theological writers of this age were the voluminous Richard Baxter and the learned and eloquent Dr. Robert Leighton, Archbishop of Glasgow. "Baxter," says Bishop Burnet, "was a man of great piety; and, if he had not meddled in too many things, would have been esteemed one of the learned men of the age. He writ near two hundred books; of these three are large folios: he had a very moving and pathetical way of writing, and was his whole life long a man of great zeal and much simplicity; but was most unhappily subtle and metaphysical in everything."* Of Leighton, whom he knew intimately, the same writer has given a much more copious account, a few sentences of which we will transcribe:—"His preaching had a sublimity both of thought and expression in it. The grace and gravity of his pronunciation was such that few heard him without a very sensible emotion.... It was so different from all others, and indeed from everything that one

* Own Time, i. 180.

could hope to rise up to, that it gave a man an indignation at himself and all others. . . . His style was rather too fine; but there was a majesty and beauty in it that left so deep an impression that I cannot yet forget the sermons I heard him preach thirty years ago."* The writings of Archbishop Leighton that have come down to us have been held by some of the highest minds of our own day—Coleridge for one—to bear out Burnet's affectionate panegyric. But perhaps the greatest genius among the theological writers of this age was the famous Dr. Isaac Barrow, popularly known chiefly by his admirable Sermons, but renowned also in the history of modern science as, next to Newton himself, the greatest mathematician of his time. "As a writer," the late Professor Dugald Stewart has well said of Barrow, "he is equally distinguished by the redundancy of his matter and by the pregnant brevity of his expression; but what more peculiarly characterizes his manner is a certain air of powerful and of conscious facility in the execution of whatever he undertakes. Whether the subject be mathematical, metaphysical, or theological, he seems always to bring to it a mind which feels itself superior to the occasion, and which, in contending with the greatest difficulties, puts forth but half its strength. He has somewhere spoken of his Lectiones Mathematicæ (which it may, in passing, be remarked, display *metaphysical* talents of the highest order) as extemporaneous effusions of his pen; and I have no doubt that the same epithet is still more literally applicable to his pulpit discourses. It is, indeed, only thus that we can account for the variety and extent of his voluminous remains, when we recollect that the author died at the age of forty-six."† But the name that in popular celebrity transcends all others, among the theological writers of this age, is that of John Bunyan, the author of various religious works, and especially of the Pilgrim's Progress. One critic has in our time had the courage to confess in print, that to him this famous allegory appeared "mean, jejune, and wearisome." Our late brilliant essayist, Lord Macaulay, on the other hand, in a paper published in 1830, has written:—"We are not afraid to say, that, though there were many clever men in England during the latter half of the seventeenth century, there were only two minds which possessed the imaginative faculty in a very eminent degree. One of those minds produced the Paradise Lost, the other the Pilgrim's Progress." And, to the

---

* Own Time, I. 135.
† Dissertation on the Progress of Philosophy, p. 43.

end of his life, we find him faithful to the same enthusiasm.* He conceives it to be the characteristic peculiarity of the Pilgrim's Progress "that it is the only work of its kind which possesses a strong human interest." The pilgrimage of the great Italian poet through Hell, Purgatory, and Paradise is of course regarded as not properly an allegory. But high poetry is treated somewhat unceremoniously throughout this paper. Of the Fairy Queen it is said:—"Of the persons who read the first canto, not one in ten reaches the end of the first book, and not one in a hundred perseveres to the end of the poem. Very few and very weary are those who are in at the death of the Blatant Beast. If the last six books, which are said to have been destroyed in Ireland, had been preserved, we doubt whether any heart less stout than that of a commentator would have held out to the end." It must be admitted that, as a story, the Pilgrim's Progress is a great deal more interesting than the Fairy Queen. And we suspect that, if we are to take the verdict of the most numerous class of readers, it will carry off the palm quite as decidedly from the Paradise Lost. Very few, comparatively, and very weary, we apprehend, are the readers of that great poem, too, who have made their way steadily through it from the beginning of the First Book to the end of the Twelfth. Still, although Bunyan had undoubtedly an ingenious, shaping, and vivid imagination, and his work, partly from its execution, partly from its subject, takes a strong hold, as Macaulay has well pointed out, of minds of very various kinds, commanding the admiration of the most fastidious critics, such, for instance, as Doctor Johnson, while it is loved by those who are too simple to admire it, we must make a great distinction between the power by which such general attraction as this is produced and what we have in the poetry of Milton and Spenser. The difference is something of the same kind with that which exists between any fine old popular ballad and a tragedy of Sophocles or of Shakespeare. Bunyan could rhyme too, when he chose; but he has plenty of poetry without that, and we cannot agree with the opinion expressed by good Adam Clarke, "that the Pilgrim's Progress would be more generally read, and more abundantly useful to a particular class of readers, were it turned into decent rhyme." We suspect the ingenious gentleman, who, in the early part of the last century, published an edition of Paradise Lost turned into prose, had a more correct notion of what would

* See the Paper on Ranke's History of the Popes (1840); and again the lively, though slight, sketch of Bunyan's history in the Biographies.

be most useful, and also most agreeable, to a pretty numerous class of readers.

What Lord Macaulay says of Bunyan's English, though his estimate is, perhaps, a little high-pitched, is worth quoting:—
"The style of Bunyan is delightful to every reader, and invaluable as a study to every person who wishes to obtain a wide command over the English language. The vocabulary is the vocabulary of the common people. There is not an expression, if we except a few technical terms of theology, which would puzzle the rudest peasant. We have observed several pages which do not contain a single word of more than two syllables. Yet no writer has said more exactly what he meant to say. For magnificence, for pathos, for vehement exhortation, for subtle disquisition, for every purpose of the poet, the orator, and the divine, this homely dialect, the dialect of plain working men, was perfectly sufficient. There is no book in our literature on which we would so readily stake the fame of the old unpolluted English language, no book which shows so well how rich that language is in its own proper wealth, and how little it has been improved by all that it has borrowed."

To the names that have been mentioned may be added those of Izaak Walton, the mild-tempered angler and biographer; Sir William Temple, the lively, agreeable, and well-informed essayist and memoirist; and many others that might be enumerated if it were our object to compile a catalogue instead of noticing only the principal lights of our literature.

ENGLISH LITERATURE SINCE THE REVOLUTION OF 1688.

First Effects of the Revolution on our Literature.

The Revolution, brought on by some of the same causes that had given birth to the Commonwealth, and restoring something of the same spirit and condition of things, came like another nightfall upon our higher literature, putting out the light of poetry in the land still more effectually than had even that previous triumph of the popular principle. Up to this date English literature had grown and flourished chiefly in the sunshine of court protection and favour; the public appreciation and sympathy were not yet sufficiently extended to afford it the necessary warmth and shelter. Its spirit, consequently, and affections were in the main courtly; it drooped and withered when the encouragement of the court was withdrawn, from the deprivation both of its customary support and sustenance and of its chief inspiration. And, if the decay of this kind of light at the Revolution was, as we have said, still more complete than that which followed upon the setting up of the Commonwealth, the difference seems to have been mainly owing to there having been less of it to extinguish at the one epoch than at the other. At the Restoration the impulse given by the great poets of the age of Elizabeth and James was yet operating, without having been interrupted and weakened by any foreign influence, upon the language and the national mind. Doubtless, too, whatever may be thought of the literary tendencies of puritanism and republicanism when they had got into the ascendant, the nurture both for head and heart furnished by the ten years of high deeds, and higher hopes and speculations, that ushered in the Commonwealth, must have been of a far other kind than any that was to be got out of the thirty years, or thereby, of laxity, frivolity, denationalization, and insincerity of all sorts, down the comparatively smooth stream of which men slid, without effort and without thought, to the Revolution. No wonder that some powerful minds were trained by the former, and almost none by the latter.

SURVIVING WRITERS OF THE PRECEDING PERIOD.

With the exception of some two or three names, none of them of the highest class, to be presently mentioned, almost the only writers that shed any lustre on the first reign after the Revolution are those of a few of the survivors of the preceding era. Dryden, fallen on what to him were evil days and evil tongues, and forced in his old age to write for bread with less rest for his wearied head and hand than they had ever had before, now produced some of his most laborious and also some of his most happily executed works: his translation of Virgil, among others, his Fables, and his Alexander's Feast. Lee, the dramatic poet, discharged from Bedlam, finished two more tragedies, his Princess of Cleve and his Massacre of Paris, before, "returning one night from the Bear and Harrow, in Butcher-Row, through Clare Market, to his lodgings in Duke Street, overladen with wine, he fell down on the ground as some say, according to others on a bulk, and was killed or stifled in the snow," early in the year 1692. The comic Etheredge also outlived the deposition of his patron James II., but is not known to have written anything after that event; he followed James to France, and is reported to have died characteristically at Ratisbon a year or two after: "having treated some company with a liberal entertainment at his house there, where he had taken his glass too freely, and, being, through his great complaisance, too forward in waiting on his guests at their departure, flushed as he was, he tumbled down stairs and broke his neck, and so fell a martyr to jollity and civility." Wycherley, who at the date of the Revolution was under fifty, lived to become a correspondent of Pope, and even saw out the reign of Anne; but he produced nothing in that of William, although he published a volume of poems in 1704, and left some other trifles behind him, which were printed long afterwards by Theobald. Southerne, indeed, who survived till 1746, continued to write and publish till within twenty years of his death; his two best dramas—his Fatal Marriage and his Oroonoko—were both produced in the reign of William. Southerne, though not without considerable pathetic power, was fortunate in a genius on the whole not above the appreciation of the unpoetical age he lived in: "Dryden once took occasion to ask him how much he got by one of his plays; to which he answered that he was really ashamed to inform him. But, Mr. Dryden being a little importunate to know, he plainly told him that by his last play he cleared seven hundred pounds, which appeared astonishing to Dryden, as he himself had never been able to acquire more than one hundred by his most successful pieces."* Southerne, who, whatever estimate may be formed of his poetry, was not, we may gather from this anecdote, without some conscience and modesty, had worse writers than himself to keep him in countenance by their preposterous prosperity, in this lucky time for mediocrity and dulness. Shadwell was King William's first poet-laureate, and Nahum Tate his next. Tate, indeed, and his friend Dr. Nicholas Brady, were among the most flourishing authors and greatest public favourites of this reign : it was now that they perpetrated in concert their version, or perversion, of the Psalms, with which we are still afflicted. Brady also published a play, and, at a later date, some volumes of sermons and a translation of the Æneid, which, fortunately, not having been imposed or recommended by authority, are all among the most forgotten of books. Elkanah Settle, too, was provided for as City poet.

Among writers of another class, perhaps the most eminent who, having been distinguished before the Revolution, survived and continued to write after that event, was Sir William Temple. His Miscellanies, by which he is principally known, though partly composed before, were not published till then. John Evelyn, who, however, although a very miscellaneous as well as voluminous writer, has hardly left any work that is held in esteem for either style or thought, or for anything save what it may contain of positive information or mere matter of fact, also published one or two books in the reign of William, which he saw to an end : for he died at the age of eighty-five, in 1706. Bishop Stillingfleet, who had been known as an author since before the Restoration, for his Irenicum appeared in 1659, when he was only in his twenty-fourth year, and who had kept the press in employment by a rapid succession of publications during the next five-and-twenty years, resumed his pen after the Revolution, which raised him to the bench, to engage in a controversy with Locke about some of the principles of his famous essay ; but, whether it was that years had abated his powers, or that he had a worse cause to defend, or merely that the public taste was changed, he gained much less applause for his dialectic skill on this than on most former occasions. Stillingfleet lived to the year 1699.

John Norris, also, one of the last of the school of English Platonists, which may be considered as having been founded in the latter part of the seventeenth century by Cudworth and Henry More, had, we believe, become known as a writer some years before the Revolution ; but the greater number of his publications first appeared in the reign of William, and he may be reckoned

* Biog. Dram.

one of the best writers properly or principally belonging to that reign. Yet he is not for a moment to be compared for learning, compass of thought, or power and skill of expression, to either Cudworth or More. Norris's principal work is his Essay on the Ideal World, published in two parts in 1701 and 1702. He is also the author of a volume of religious poetry, of rather a feeble character, which has been often reprinted. Bishop Spratt, though a clergyman, and a writer both of prose and verse, cannot be called a divine; he had in earlier life the reputation of being the finest writer of the day, but, although he lived till very nearly the end of the reign of Anne, he published nothing, we believe, after the Revolution, nor indeed for a good many years before it. His style, which was so much admired in his own age, is a Frenchified English, with an air of ease and occasionally of vivacity, but without any true grace or expressiveness.

Good old Richard Baxter, who had been filling the world with books for half a century, just lived to see the Revolution. He died, at the age of seventy-six, in the beginning of December, 1691. And in the end of the same month died, a considerably younger man, Robert Boyle, another of the most voluminous writers of the preceding period, and famous also for his services in the cause of religion, as well as of science. In the preceding May, at a still less advanced age, had died the most eminent Scotch writer of the period between the Restoration and the Revolution, Sir George Mackenzie, lord-advocate under both Charles II. and his successor; the author of the Institution of the Laws of Scotland, and many other professional, historical, and antiquarian works, but the master also of a flowing pen in moral speculation, the belles lettres, and even in the department of fancy and fiction—as may be gathered from the titles of his Aretina, or the Serious Romance, 1660; Religio Stoici, or the Virtuoso, 1663; Solitude preferred to Public Employment, 1665; Moral Gallantry, 1667. Mackenzie may be regarded as the first successor of his countryman Drummond of Hawthornden in the cultivation of an English style; he was the correspondent of Dryden and other distinguished English writers of his day: but he has no pretensions of his own to any high rank either for the graces of his expression or the value of his matter. Whatever may have been his professional learning, too, his historical disquisitions are as jejune and uncritical as his attempts at fine writing are, with all their elaboration, at once pedantic and clownish. He has nothing either of the poetry or the elegance of Drummond.

BISHOP BURNET.

The most active and conspicuous undoubtedly of the prose writers who, having acquired distinction in the preceding period, continued to prosecute the business of authorship after the Revolution, was the celebrated Dr. Gilbert Burnet, now Bishop of Salisbury. Of 145 distinct publications (many of them, however, only single sermons and other short pamphlets), which are enumerated as having proceeded from his incessant pen between 1669 and his death, at the age of seventy-two, in 1715 (including, indeed, his History of his Own Time, and his Thoughts on Education, which did not appear till after his death), we find that 71, namely 21 historical works and 50 sermons and tracts, belong to the period before the Revolution; 36, namely 5 historical works and 31 sermons and tracts, to the reign of William; and the remaining 38, namely one historical work and 37 pamphlets, to a later date. Many of what we have called historical works, however, are more pamphlets: in fact Burnet's literary performances of any considerable extent are only three in number:—his Memoirs of James and William, Dukes of Hamilton, published, in one volume folio, in 1676; his History of the Reformation of the Church of England, 3 volumes folio, 1679, 1681, and 1714; and his History of his Own Time, in two volumes folio, published after his death in 1723 and 1734. There is enough of literary labour, as well as of historical value, in these works to preserve to the author a very honourable name; each of them contains much matter now nowhere else to be found, and they must always continue to rank among the original sources of our national history, both ecclesiastical and civil. In regard to their execution, too, it must be admitted that the style is at least straightforward and unaffected, and generally as unambiguous as it is unambitious; the facts are clearly enough arranged; and the story is told not only intelligibly, but for the most part in rather a lively and interesting way. On the other hand, to any high station as a writer Burnet can make no claim; he is an industrious collector of intelligence, and a loquacious and moderately lively gossip: but of eloquence, or grace, or refinement of any sort, he is as destitute as he is (and that is altogether) of imagination, and wit, and humour, and subtlety, and depth and weight of thought, and whatever other qualities give anything either of life or lustre to what a man utters out of his own head or heart. We read him for the sake of his facts only; he troubles us with but few reflections, but of that no reader will complain. He does not see far into anything, nor indeed, properly speaking, into it at all; for that matter he is little more, to adopt a modern term, than a penny-a-liner on a large scale, and best performs his task when he does not attempt to be anything else. Nor is he a neat-handed workman even of that class; in his History of his Own Time, in particular, his style, with no strength, or flavour, or natural charm of any kind, to redeem its rudeness, is the most slovenly undress in which a writer ever wrapt up what he had to communicate to the public. Its only merit, as we have observed, is that it is without any air of pretension, and that it is evidently as extemporaneous and careless as it is unelevated, shapeless, and ungrammatical. Among the most important and best known of Burnet's other works are, that entitled Some Passages of the Life and Death of the Right Honourable John Wilmot, Earl of Rochester, 1680; his Life of Bishop Bedel, 1685; his Travels through France, Italy, Germany, and Switzerland, 1685; and his Exposition of the Thirty-Nine Articles, 1699. The first mentioned of these is the best written of all his works.

Thomas Burnet.

In the same year with Bishop Burnet, but at a more advanced age, died Dr. Thomas Burnet, the learned and eloquent author of the Telluris Sacra Theoria, first published in Latin in 1680, and afterwards translated into English by the author; of the Archæologia Philosophica, published in 1692; and of two or three other treatises, also in Latin, which did not appear till after his death. Burnet's system of geology has no scientific value whatever; indeed, it must be considered as a mere romance, although, from the earnestness of the author's manner and his constant citation of texts of Scripture in support of his positions, as well as from more than one answer which he afterwards published to the attacks made upon his book, it is evident that he by no means intended it to be so received. But, with his genius and imagination and consummate scholarship, he is a very different species of writer from his garrulous and mitred namesake: his English style is singularly flowing and harmonious, as well as perspicuous and animated, and rises on fit occasions to much majesty and even splendour.

Other Theological Writers:—Tillotson; South.

Another name that may be here mentioned is that of Archbishop Tillotson, who was a very popular preacher among the

Presbyterians before the Restoration, and began publishing sermons so early as in the year 1661, while he still belonged to that sect. He died in 1694, in his sixty-fourth year. Tillotson's Sermons, still familiarly known by reputation, long continued to be the most generally esteemed collection of such compositions in the language; but are probably now very little read. They are substantial performances, such as make the reader feel, when he has got through one of them, that he has accomplished something of a feat; and, being withal as free from pedantry and every other kind of eccentricity or extravagance as from flimsiness, and exceedingly sober in their strain of doctrine, with a certain blunt cordiality in the expression and manner, they were in all respects very happily addressed to the ordinary peculiarities of the national mind and character. But, having once fallen into neglect, Tillotson's writings have no qualities that will ever revive attention to them. There is much more of a true vitality in the sermons of Dr. Robert South, whose career of authorship commenced in the time of the Protectorate, though his life was extended till after the accession of George I. He died in 1716, at the age of eighty-three. South's sermons, the first of which dates even before the earliest of Tillotson's, and the last after Tillotson's latest, are very well characterised by Mr. Hallam:— "They were," he observes, "much celebrated at the time, and retain a portion of their renown. This is by no means surprising. South had great qualifications for that popularity which attends the pulpit, and his manner was at that time original. Not diffuse, nor learned, nor formal in argument like Barrow, with a more natural structure of sentences, a more pointed though by no means a more fair and satisfactory turn of reasoning, with a style clear and English, free from all pedantry, but abounding with those colloquial novelties of idiom, which, though now become vulgar and offensive, the age of Charles II. affected, sparing no personal or temporary sarcasm, but, if he seems for a moment to tread on the verge of buffoonery, recovering himself by some stroke of vigorous sense and language: such was the worthy Dr. South, whom the courtiers delighted to hear. His sermons want all that is called unction, and sometimes even earnestness; but there is a masculine spirit about them, which, combined with their peculiar characteristics, would naturally fill the churches where he might be heard."* Both South and Tillotson are considered to belong as divines to the Arminian, or, as it was then commonly called, the Latitudinarian school—as well as Cudworth, More, and Stillingfleet.

* Lit. of Europe, iv. 56.

LOCKE.

The only considerable literary name that belongs exclusively, or almost exclusively, to the first reign after the Revolution is that of Locke. John Locke, born in 1632, although his Adversariorum Methodus, or New Method of a Common-Place-Book, had appeared in French in Leclerc's Bibliothèque for 1686, and an abridgment of his celebrated Essay, and his first Letter on Toleration, both also in French, in the same publication for 1687 and 1688, had published nothing in English, or with his name, till he produced in 1690 the work which has ever since made him one of the best known of English writers, both in his own and in other countries, his Essay concerning Human Understanding. This was followed by his Second Letter on Toleration, and his two Treatises on Government, in the same year; his Considerations on Lowering the Interest of Money, in 1691; his Third Letter on Toleration, in 1692; his Thoughts concerning Education, in 1693; his Reasonableness of Christianity, in 1695; and various controversial tracts in reply to his assailants, Dr. Edwards and Bishop Stillingfleet, between that date and his death in 1704. After his death appeared his Conduct of the Understanding, and several theological treatises, the composition of which had been the employment of the last years of his industrious and productive old age. Locke's famous Essay was the first work, perhaps in any language, which professedly or systematically attempted to popularise metaphysical philosophy. It is the first comprehensive survey that had been attempted of the whole mind and its faculties; and the very conception of such a design argued an intellect of no common reach, originality, and boldness. It will remain also of very considerable value as an extensive register of facts, and a storehouse of acute and often suggestive observations on psychological phenomena, whatever may be the fate of the views propounded in it as aspiring to constitute a metaphysical system. Further, it is not to be denied that this work has exercised a powerful influence upon the course of philosophical inquiry and opinion ever since its appearance. At first, in particular, it did good service in putting finally to the rout some fantastic notions and methods that still lingered in the schools; it was the loudest and most comprehensive proclamation that had yet been made of the liberation of philosophy from the dominion of authority; but Locke's was a mind stronger and better furnished for the work of pulling down than of building up: he had enough of clearsightedness and independence of mental character for the one; whatever endowments of a different kind he pos-ceased, he had too little imagination, or creative power, for the other. Besides, the very passionless character of his mind would have unfitted him for going far into the philosophy of our complex nature, in which the passions are the revealers and teachers of all the deepest truths, and alone afford us any intimation of many things which, even with the aid of their lurid light, we discern but as fearful and unfathomable mysteries. What would Shakespeare's understanding of the philosophy of human nature have been, if he had had no more imagination and passion in his own nature than Locke?

SWIFT.

His renowned Tale of a Tub and a tract entitled The Battle of the Books, published together in 1704, were the first announcement of the greatest master of satire at once comic and caustic that has yet appeared in our language. Swift, born in Dublin in 1667, had already, in the last years of the reign of King William, made himself known by two volumes of Letters selected from the papers of his friend Temple (who died in 1699), and also by a political pamphlet in favour of the ministry of the day, which attracted little notice, and gave as little promise of his future eminence as a writer. To politics as well as satire, however, he adhered throughout his career—often blending the two, but producing scarcely anything, if we may not except some of his effusions in verse, that was not either satirical or political. His course of authorship as a political writer may be considered properly to begin with his Letter concerning the Sacramental Test, and another high Tory and high Church tract, which he published in 1708; in which same year he also came forward with his ironical Argument for the Abolition of Christianity, and, in his humorous Predictions first assumed his *nom de guerre* of Isaac Bickerstaff, Esquire, subsequently made so famous by other *jeux d'esprit* in the same style, and by its adoption soon after by the wits of the Tatler. Of his other most notable performances, his Conduct of the Allies was published in 1712; his Public Spirit of the Whigs, in 1714; his Drapier's Letters, in 1724; his immortal Gulliver's Travels, in 1727; and his Polite Conversation, which, however, had been written many years before, in 1738. His poem of Cadenus and Vanessa, besides, had appeared, without his consent, in 1723, soon after the death of Miss Hester Vanhomrigh, its heroine. The History of the Four Last Years of Queen Anne (if his, which there can hardly

be a doubt that it is), the Directions for Servants, many of his
verses and other shorter pieces, and his Diary written to Stella
(Miss Johnson, whom he eventually married), were none of them
printed till after, some of them not till long after, his death,
which took place in 1745.

"O thou!" exclaims his friend Pope,

> ——" whatever title please thine ear,
> Dean, Drapier, Bickerstaff, or Gulliver!
> Whether thou choose Cervantes' serious air,
> Or laugh and shake in Rabelais' easy chair,
> Or praise the court, or magnify mankind,
> Or thy grieved country's copper chains unbind,"—

lines that describe comprehensively enough the celebrated dean's
genius and writings—what he did and what he was. And the
first remark to be made about Swift is, that into everything that
came from his pen he put a strong infusion of himself; that in
his writings we read the man—not merely his intellectual ability,
but his moral nature, his passions, his principles, his prejudices,
his humours, his whole temper and individuality. The common
herd of writers have no individuality at all; those of the very
highest class can assume at will any other individuality as perfectly as their own—they have no exclusiveness. Next under
this highest class stand those whose individuality is at once
their strength and their weakness;—their strength, inasmuch
as it distinguishes them from and lifts them far above the multitude of writers of mere talent or expository skill; their weakness
and bondage, in that it will not be thrown off, and that it with-
holds them from over going out of themselves, and rising from
the merely characteristic, striking, or picturesque, either to the
dramatic or to the beautiful, of both of which equally the spirit is
unegotistic and universal. To this class, which is not the
highest but the next to it, Swift belongs. The class, however,
like both that which is above and that which is below it, is one
of wide comprehension, and includes many degrees of power, and
even many diversities of gifts. Swift was neither a Cervantes
nor a Rabelais; but yet, with something that was peculiar to
himself, he combined considerable portions of both. He had
more of Cervantes than Rabelais had, and more of Rabelais than
was given to Cervantes. There cannot be claimed for him the
refinement, the humanity, the pathos, the noble elevation of the
Spaniard—all that irradiates and beautifies his satire and drollery
as the blue sky does the earth it bends over; neither, with all his
ingenuity and fertility, does our English wit and humourist

anywhere display either the same inexhaustible abundance of grotesque invention, or the same gaiety and luxuriance of fancy, with the historian of the Doings and Sayings of the Giant Gargantua. Yet neither Cervantes nor Rabelais, nor both combined, could have written the Tale of a Tub. The torrent of triumphant merriment is broader and more rushing than anything of the same kind in either. When we look indeed to the perfection and exactness of the allegory at all points, to the biting sharpness and at the same time the hilarity and comic animation of the satire, to its strong and unpausing yet easy and natural flow, to the incessant blaze of the wit and humour, and to the style so clear, so vivid and expressive, so idiomatic, so English, so true and appropriate in all its varieties, narrative, didactic, rhetorical, colloquial, as we know no work of its class in our own language that as a whole approaches this, so we doubt if there be another quite equal to it in any language.

Swift was undoubtedly the most masculine intellect of his age, the most earnest thinker of a time in which there was less among us of earnest and deep thinking than in any other era of our literature. In its later and more matured form, his wit itself becomes earnest and passionate, and has a severity, a fierceness, a *sæva indignatio*, that are all his own, and that have never been blended in any other writer with so keen a perception of the ludicrous and so much general comic power. The breath of his rich, pungent, original jocularity is at the same time cutting as a sword and consuming as fire. Other masters of the same art are satisfied if they can only make their readers laugh; this is their main, often their sole aim: with Swift, to excite the emotion of the ludicrous is, in most of his writings, only a subordinate purpose,—a means employed for effecting quite another and a much higher end; if he labours to make anything ridiculous, it is because he hates it, and would have it trodden into the earth or extirpated. This, at least, became the settled temper of all the middle and latter portion of his life. No sneaking kindness for his victim is to be detected in his crucifying raillery; he is not a mere admirer of the comic picturesque, who will sometimes rack or gibbet an unhappy individual for the sake of the fantastic grimaces he may make, or the capers he may cut in the air; he has the true spirit of an executioner, and only loves his joke as sauce and seasoning to more serious work. Few men have been more perversely prejudiced and self-willed than Swift, and therefore of absolute truth his works may probably contain less than many others not so earnestly written; but of what was truth to the mind of the writer, of what he actually believed and desired, no works contain more. Here, again, as well as in the other respect noticed some pages back, Swift is in the middle class of writers; far above those whose whole truth is truth of expression—that is, correspondence between the words and the thoughts (possibly without any between the thoughts and the writer's belief); but below those who both write what they think, and whose thoughts are pre-eminently valuable for their intrinsic beauty or profoundness. Yet in setting honestly and effectively before us even his own passions and prejudices a writer also tells us the truth—the truth, at least, respecting himself, if not respecting anything else. This much Swift does always; and this is his great distinction among the masters of wit and humour;—the merriest of his jests is an utterance of some real feeling of his heart at the moment, as much as the fiercest of his invectives. Alas! with all his jesting and merriment, he did not know what it was to have a mind at ease, or free from the burden and torment of dark, devouring passions, till, in his own words, the cruel indignation that tore continually at his heart was laid at rest in the grave. In truth, the insanity which ultimately fell down upon and laid prostrate his fine faculties had cast something of its black shadow athwart their vision from the first—as he himself probably felt or suspected when he determined to bequeath his fortune to build an hospital in his native country for persons afflicted with that calamity; and sad enough, we may be sure, he was at heart, when he gaily wrote that he did so merely

<blockquote>
To show, by one satiric touch,
No nation wanted it so much.*
</blockquote>

Yet the madness, or predisposition to madness, was also part and parcel of the man, and possibly an element of his genius—which might have had less earnestness and force, as well as less activity, productiveness, and originality, if it had not been excited and impelled by that perilous fervour. Nay, something of their power and peculiar character Swift's writings may owe to the exertions called forth in curbing and keeping down the demon which, like a proud steed under a stout rider, would have mastered him, if he had not mastered it, and, although support and strength to him so long as it was held in subjection, would,

---

* "I have often," says Lord Orrery, "heard him lament the state of childhood and idiotism to which some of the greatest men of this nation were reduced before their death. He mentioned, as examples within his own time, the Duke of Marlborough and Lord Somers: and, when he cited these melancholy instances, it was always with a heavy sigh, and with gestures that showed great uneasiness, as if he felt an impulse of what was to happen to him before he died."—Remarks, p. 188.

dominant over him, have rent him in pieces, as in the end it did. Few could have maintained the struggle so toughly and so long.

Swift would probably have enjoyed a higher reputation as a poet if he had not been so great a writer in prose. His productions in verse are considerable in point of quantity, and many of them admirable of their kind. But those of them that deserve to be so described belong to the humblest kind of poetry—to that kind which has scarcely any distinctively poetical quality or characteristic about it except the rhyme. He has made some attempts in a higher style, but with little success. His Pindaric Odes, written and published when he was a young man, drew from Dryden (who was his relation) the emphatic judgment, "Cousin Swift, you will never be a poet:" and, though Swift, never forgave this frankness, he seems to have felt that the prognostication was a sound one, for he wrote no more Pindaric Odes. Nor indeed did he ever afterwards attempt anything considerable in the way of serious poetry, if we except his Cadenus and Vanessa (the story of Miss Vanhomrigh), his effusion entitled Poetry, a Rhapsody, and that on his own death —and even these are chiefly distinguished from his other productions by being longer and more elaborate, the most elevated portions of the first mentioned scarcely rising above narrative and reflection, and whatever there is of more dignified or solemn writing in the two others being largely intermixed with comedy and satire in his usual easy ambling style. With all his liveliness of fancy, he had no grandeur of imagination, as little feeling of the purely graceful or beautiful, no capacity of tender emotion, no sensibility to even the simplest forms of music. With these deficiencies it was impossible that he should produce anything that could be called poetical in a high sense. But of course he could put his wit and fancy into the form of verse—and so as to make the measured expression and the rhyme give additional point and piquancy to his strokes of satire and ludicrous narratives or descriptions. Some of his lighter verses are as good as anything of the kind in the language.

POPE.

Of Swift's contemporaries, by far the most memorable name is that of Alexander Pope. If Swift was at the head of the prose writers of the early part of the last century, Pope was as incontestably the first of the writers in verse of that day, with no other either equal or second to him. Born a few months before the

Revolution, he came forth as a poet, by the publication of his Pastorals in Tonson's Miscellany in 1709, when he was yet only in his twenty-first year; and they had been written five years before. Nor were they the earliest of his performances; his Ode on Solitude, his verses upon Silence, his translations of the First Book of the Thebais and of Ovid's Epistle from Sappho to Phaon, and his much more remarkable paraphrases of Chaucer's January and May and the Prologue to the Wife of Bath's Tale, all preceded the composition of the Pastorals. His Essay on Criticism (written in 1709) was published in 1711; the Messiah the same year (in the Spectator); the Rape of the Lock in 1712; the Temple of Fame (written two years before) the same year; his Windsor Forest (which he had commenced at sixteen) in 1713; the first four books of his translation of the Iliad in 1715; his Epistle from Eloisa to Abelard (written some years before) we believe in 1717, when he published a collected edition of his poems; the remaining portions of the Iliad at different times, the last in 1720; his translation of the Odyssey (in concert with Fenton and Broome) in 1725; the first three books of the Dunciad in 1728; his Essay on Man in 1733 and 1734; his Imitations of Horace, various other satirical pieces, the Prologue and Epilogue to the Satires, his four epistles styled Moral Essays, and his modernised version of Donne's Satires between 1730 and 1740; and the fourth book of the Dunciad in 1742. Besides all this verse, collections of his Letters were published, first surreptitiously by Curl, and then by himself in 1737; and, among other publications in prose, his clever *jeu d'esprit* entitled a Narrative of the Frenzy of John Dennis appeared in 1713; his Preface to Shakespeare, with his edition of the works of that poet, in 1721; his Treatise of the Bathos, or Art of Sinking in Poetry, and his Memoirs of P. P., Clerk of This Parish (in ridicule of Burnet's History of his Own Time), in 1727. He died in May, 1744, about a year and a half before his friend Swift, who, more than twenty years his senior, had naturally anticipated that he should be the first to depart, and that, as he cynically, and yet touchingly too, expressed it, while Arbuthnot grieved for him a day, and Gay a week, he should be lamented a whole month by "poor Pope,"—whom, of all those he best knew, he seems to have the most loved.

Pope, with talent enough for anything, might deserve to be ranked among the most distinguished prose writers of his time, if he were not its greatest poet; but it is in the latter character that he falls to be noticed in the history of our literature. And what a broad and bright region would be cut off from our poetry if he had never lived! If we even confine ourselves to his own works, without regarding the numerous subsequent writers who have formed themselves upon him as an example and model, and may be said to constitute the school of which he was the founder, how rich an inheritance of brilliant and melodious fancies do we not owe to him! For what would any of us resign the Rape of the Lock, or the Epistle of Eloisa, or the Essay on Man, or the Moral Essays, or the Satires, or the Epistle to Dr. Arbuthnot, or the Dunciad? That we have nothing in the same style in the language to be set beside or weighed against any one of these performances will probably be admitted by all; and, if we could say no more, this would be to assign to Pope a rank in our poetic literature which certainly not so many as half a dozen other names are entitled to share with him. Down to his own day at least, Chaucer, Spenser, Shakespeare, Milton, and Dryden alone had any pretensions to be placed before him or by his side. It is unnecessary to dilate upon what has been sufficiently pointed out by all the critics, and is too obvious to be overlooked, the general resemblance of his poetry, in both its form and spirit, to that of Dryden rather than to that of our elder great writers. A remarkable external peculiarity of it is, that he is probably the only one of our modern poets of eminence who has written nothing in blank verse; while even in rhyme he has nearly confined himself to that one decasyllabic line upon which it would almost seem to have been his purpose to impress a new shape and character. He belongs to the classical school as opposed to the romantic, to that in which a French rather than to that in which an Italian inspiration may be detected. Whether this is to be attributed principally to his constitutional temperament and the native character of his imagination, or to the influences of the age in which he lived and wrote, we shall not stop to inquire. It is enough that such is the fact. But, though he may be regarded as in the main the pupil and legitimate successor of Dryden, the amount of what he learned or borrowed from that master was by no means so considerable as to prevent his manner from having a great deal in it that is distinctive and original. If Dryden has more impetuosity and a freer flow, Pope has far more delicacy, and, on fit occasions, far more tenderness and true passion. Dryden has written nothing in the same style with the Rape of the Lock on the one hand, or with the Epistle to Abelard and the Elegy on the Death of an Unfortunate Lady on the other. Indeed, these two styles may be said to have been both, in so far as the English tongues is concerned, invented by Pope. In what preceding writer had he an example of either? Nay, did either the French or the Italian language furnish him with anything to copy from nearly so brilliant and felicitous as his own performances? In the sharper or more severe species of satire, again, while in some things he is inferior to Dryden, in others he excels him. It must be admitted that Dryden's is the nobler, the more generous scorn; it is passionate, while Pope's is frequently only peevish: the one is vehement, the other venomous. But, although Pope does not wield the ponderous, fervid scourge with which his predecessor tears and mangles the luckless object of his indignation or derision, he knows how, with a lighter touch, to inflict a torture quite as maddening at the moment, and perhaps more difficult to heal. Neither has anything of the easy elegance, the simple natural grace, the most exquisite artifice simulating the absence of all art, of Horace; but the care, and dexterity, and superior refinement of Pope, his neatness, and concentration, and point, supply a better substitute for these charms than the ruder strength, and more turbulent passion, of Dryden. If Dryden, too, has more natural fire and force, and rises in his greater passages to a stormy grandeur to which the other does not venture to commit himself, Pope in some degree compensates for that by a dignity, a quiet, sometimes pathetic, majesty, which we find nowhere in Dryden's poetry. Dryden has translated the Æneid, and Pope the Iliad; but the two tasks would apparently have been better distributed if Dryden had chanced to have taken up Homer, and left Virgil to Pope. Pope's Iliad, in truth, whatever may be its merits of another kind, is, in spirit and style, about the most unhomeric performance in the whole compass of our poetry, as Pope had, of all our great poets, the most unhomeric genius. He was emphatically the poet of the highly artificial age in which he lived; and his excellence lay in, or at least was fostered and perfected by, the accordance of all his tastes and talents, of his whole moral and intellectual constitution, with the spirit of that condition of things. Not touches of natural emotion, but the titillation of wit and fancy,—not tones of natural music, but the tone of good society,—make up the charm of his poetry; the polish, pungency, and brilliance of which, however, in its most happily executed passages leave nothing in that style to be desired. Pope, no doubt, wrote with a care and elaboration that were unknown to Dryden; against whom, indeed, it is a reproach made by his pupil, that, copious as he was, he

———— wanted or forgot
The last and greatest art—the art to blot.

And so perhaps, although the expression is a strong and a startling one, may the said art, not without some reason, be called in reference to the particular species of poetry which Dryden and Pope cultivated, dependent as that is for its success in pleasing us almost as much upon the absence of faults as upon the presence of beauties. Such partial obscuration or distortion of the imagery as we excuse, or even admire, in the expanded mirror of a lake reflecting the woods and hills and overhanging sky, when its waters are ruffled or swayed by the fitful breeze, would be intolerable in a looking-glass, were it otherwise the most splendid article of the sort that upholstery every furnished.

Addison and Steele.

Next to the prose of Swift and the poetry of Pope, perhaps the portion of the literature of the beginning of the last century that was both most influential at the time, and still lives most in the popular remembrance, is that connected with the names of Addison and Steele. These two writers were the chief boast of the Whig party, as Swift and Pope were of the Tories. Addison's poem, The Campaign, on the victory of Blenheim, his imposing but frigid tragedy of Cato, and some other dramatic productions, besides various other writings in prose, have given him a reputation in many departments of literature; and Steele also holds a respectable rank among our comic dramatists as the author of the Tender Husband and the Conscious Lovers; but it is as the first, and on the whole the best, of our English essayists, the principal authors (in every sense) of the Tatler, the Spectator, and the Guardian, that these two writers have sent down their names with most honour to posterity, and have especially earned the love and gratitude of their countrymen. Steele was in his thirty-ninth, and his friend Addison in his thirty-eighth year, when the Tatler was started by the former in April, 1709. The paper, published thrice a week, had gone on for about six weeks before Addison took any part in it; but from that time he became, next to Steele, the chief contributor to it, till it was dropped in January, 1711. "I have only one gentleman," says Steele in his preface to the collected papers, "who will be nameless, to thank for any frequent assistance to me, which indeed it would have been barbarous in him to have denied to one with whom he has lived in an intimacy from childhood, considering the great ease with which he is able to dispatch the most entertaining pieces of this nature." The person alluded to is Addison.

"This good office," Steele generously adds, "he performed with such force of genius, humour, wit, and learning, that I fared like a distressed prince who calls in a powerful neighbour to his aid: I was undone by my auxiliary; when I had once called him in, I could not subsist without dependence on him." By far the greater part of the Tatler, however, is Steele's. Of 271 papers of which it consists, above 200 are attributed either entirely or in the greater part to him, while those believed to have been written by Addison are only about fifty. Among the other contributors Swift is the most frequent. The Spectator was begun within two months after the discontinuance of the Tatler, and was carried on at the rate of six papers a week till the 6th of December, 1712, on which day Number 555 was published. In these first seven volumes of the Spectator Addison's papers are probably more numerous than Steele's; and between them they wrote perhaps four-fifths of the whole work. The Guardian was commenced on the 12th of March, 1713, and, being also published six times a week, had extended to 175 numbers, when it was brought to a close on the 1st of October in the same year. There is only one paper by Addison in the first volume of the Guardian, but to the second he was rather a more frequent contributor than Steele. This was the last work in which the two friends joined; for Addison, we believe, wrote nothing in the Englishman, the fifty-seven numbers of which were published, at the rate of three a week, between the 0th of October, 1713, and the 15th of February following; nor Steele any of the papers, eighty in number, forming the eighth volume of the Spectator, of which the first was published on the 18th of June, 1714, the last on the 20th of December in the same year, the rate of publication being also three times a week. Of these additional Spectators twenty-four are attributed to Addison. The friendship of nearly half a century which had united these two admirable writers was rent asunder by political differences some years before the death of Addison, in 1719: Steele survived till 1729.

Invented or introduced among us as the periodical essay may be said to have been by Steele and Addison, it is a species of writing, as already observed, in which perhaps they have never been surpassed, or on the whole equalled, by any one of their many followers. More elaboration and depth, and also more brilliancy, we may have had in some recent attempts of the same kind; but hardly so much genuine liveliness, ease, and cordiality, anything so thoroughly agreeable, so skilfully adapted to interest without demanding more attention than is naturally and spontaneously given to it. Perhaps so large an admixture of the speculative and didactic was never made so easy of apprehension and so entertaining, so like in the reading to the merely narrative. But, besides this constant atmosphere of the pleasurable arising simply from the lightness, variety, and urbanity of these delightful papers, the delicate imagination and exquisite humour of Addison, and the vivacity, warmheartedness, and altogether generous nature of Steele, give a charm to the best of them, which is to be enjoyed, not described. We not only admire the writers, but soon come to love them, and to regard both them and the several fictitious personages that move about in the other little world they have created for us as among our best and best-known friends.

SHAFTESBURY; MANDEVILLE.

Among the prose works of the early part of the last century which used to have the highest reputation for purity and elegance of style, is that by Lord Shaftesbury entitled Characteristics of Men, Manners, Opinions, and Things. Its author, Anthony Ashley Cooper, third Earl of Shaftesbury (grandson of the first Earl, the famous meteoric politician of the reign of Charles II.), was born in 1671 and died in 1713; and the Characteristics, which did not appear in its present form, or with that title, till after his death, consists of a collection of disquisitions on various questions in moral, metaphysical, and critical philosophy, most of which he had previously published separately.

But the most remarkable philosophical work of this time, at least in a literary point of view, is Mandeville's Fable of the Bees. Bernard de Mandeville was a native of Holland, in which country he was born about the year 1670; but, after having studied medicine and taken his doctor's degree, he came over to England about the end of that century, and he resided here till his death in 1733. His Fable of the Bees originally appeared in 1708, in the form of a poem of 400 lines in octosyllabic verse, entitled The Grumbling Hive, or Knaves turned Honest, and it was not till eight years afterwards that he added the prose notes which make the bulk of the first volume of the work as we now have it. The second volume, or part, which consists of a series of six dialogues, was not published till 1729. The leading idea of the book is indicated by its second title, Private Vices Public Benefits;—in other words, that what are called and what really are vices in themselves, and in the individual indulging in them, are nevertheless, in many respects, serviceable to the community. Mandeville holds in fact, to quote the words in which he sums up his theory at the close of his first volume, "that neither the friendly qualities and kind affections that are natural to man, nor the real virtues he is capable of acquiring by reason and self-denial, are the foundation of society; but that what we call evil in this world, moral as well as natural, is the grand principle that makes us sociable creatures, the solid basis, the life and support, of all trades and employments without exception; that there we must look for the true origin of all arts and sciences; and that the moment evil ceases the society must be spoiled, if not totally destroyed." The doctrine had a startling appearance thus nakedly announced; and the book occasioned a great commotion; but it is now generally admitted that, whatever may be the worth, or worthlessness, of the philosophical system propounded in it, the author's object was not an immoral one. Independently altogether of its general principles and conclusions, the work is full both of curious matter and of vigorous writing.

Mandeville, certainly, is no flatterer of human nature; his book, indeed, is written throughout in a spirit not only satirical, but cynical. Every page, however, bears the stamp of independent thinking; and many of the remarks he throws out indicate that he had at least glimpses of views which were not generally perceived or suspected at that day. It would probably be found that the Fable of the Bees has been very serviceable in the way of suggestion to various subsequent writers who have not adopted the general principles of the work. The following paragraphs, for example, are remarkable as an anticipation of a famous passage in the Wealth of Nations:—

If we trace the most flourishing nations in their origin, we shall find, that, in the remote beginnings of every society, the richest and most considerable men among them were a great while destitute of a great many comforts of life that are now enjoyed by the meanest and most humble wretches; so that many things which were once looked upon as the inventions of luxury are now allowed even to those that are so miserably poor as to become the objects of public charity, nay counted so necessary that we think no human creature ought to want them. . . . . A man would be laughed at that should discover luxury in the plain dress of a poor creature that walks along in a thick parish gown, and a coarse shirt underneath it; and yet what a number of people, how many different trades, and what a variety of skill and tools must be employed to have the most ordinary Yorkshire cloth! What depth of thought and ingenuity, what toil and labour, and what length of time must it have cost, before man could learn from a seed to raise and prepare so useful a product as linen!—Remark T, vol. i. pp. 182-183 (edit. of 1724).

What a bustle is there to be made in several parts of the world before a fine scarlet or crimson cloth can be produced; what multiplicity of trades and artificers must be employed? Not only such as are obvious, as wool-combers, spinners, the weaver, the cloth-worker, the scourer, the dyer, the setter, the drawer, and the packer; but others that are more remote, and might seem foreign to it,—as the mill-wright, the pewterer, and the chemist, which yet are all necessary, as well as a great number of other handicrafts, to have the tools, utensils, and other implements belonging to the trades already named. But all these things are done at home, and may be performed without extraordinary fatigue or danger; the most frightful prospect is left behind, when we reflect on the toil and hazard that are to be undergone abroad, the vast seas we are to go over, the different climates we are to endure, and the several nations we must be obliged to for their assistance. Spain alone, it is true, might furnish us with wool to make the finest cloth; but what skill and pains, what experience and ingenuity, are required to dye it of those beautiful colours! How widely are the drugs and other ingredients dispersed through the universe that are to meet in one kettle! Alum, indeed, we have of our own; argot we might have from the Rhine, and vitriol from Hungary: all this is in Europe. But then for saltpetre in quantity we are forced to go as far as the East Indies. Cochenil, unknown to the ancients, is not much nearer to us, though in a quite different part of the earth; we buy it, 'tis true, from the Spaniards: but, not being their product, they are forced to fetch it for us from the remotest corner of the new world in the West Indies. Whilst so many sailors are broiling in the sun and sweltered with heat in the East and West of us, another set of them are freezing in the North to fetch potashes from Russia.—Search into the Nature of Society (appended to the second edition), pp. 411-413.

In another place, indeed (Remark Q, pp. 213-216), Mandeville almost enunciates one of the great leading principles of Smith's work: after showing how a nation might be undone by too much money, he concludes, "Let the value of gold and silver either rise or fall, the enjoyment of all societies will ever depend upon the fruits of the earth and the *labour* of the people; both which joined together are a more certain, a more inexhaustible, and a more real treasure than the gold of Brazil or the silver of Potosi." It might be conjectured also from some of his other writings that Smith was a reader of Mandeville: the following sentence, for instance (Remark C, p. 55), may be said almost to contain the germ of the Theory of the Moral Sentiments:—"That we are often ashamed and blush for others . . . is nothing else but that sometimes we make the case of others too nearly our own;—so people shriek out when they see others in danger:—whilst we are reflecting with too much earnest on the effect which such a blameable action, if it was ours, would produce in us, the spirits, and consequently the blood, are insensibly moved after the same manner as if the action was our own, and so the same symptoms must appear."

GAY; ARBUTHNOT; ATTERBURY.

Along with Pope, as we have seen, Swift numbers among those who would most mourn his death, Gay and Arbuthnot. He survived them both, Gay having died, in his forty-fourth year, in 1732, and Arbuthnot at a much more advanced age in 1735.

John Gay, the author of a considerable quantity of verse and of above a dozen dramatic pieces, is now chiefly remembered for his Beggar's Opera, his Fables, his mock-heroic poem of Trivia, or the Art of Walking the Streets of London, and some of his ballads. He has no pretensions to any elevation of genius, but there is an agreeable ease, nature, and sprightliness in everything he has written; and the happiest of his performances are animated by an archness, and light but spirited raillery, in which he has not often been excelled. His celebrated English opera, as it was the first attempt of the kind, still remains the only one that has been eminently successful. Now, indeed, that much of the wit has lost its point and application to existing characters and circumstances, the dialogue of the play, apart from the music, may be admitted to owe its popularity in some degree to its traditionary fame; but still what is temporary in it is intermixed with a sufficiently diffused, though not very rich, vein of general satire, to allow the whole to retain considerable piquancy. Even at first the Beggar's Opera was probably indebted for the greater portion of its success to the music; and that is so happily selected that it continues still as fresh and as delightful as ever.

Dr. John Arbuthnot, a native of Scotland, besides various professional works of much ability, is generally regarded as the author of the Memoirs of Martinus Scriblerus, printed in the works of Pope and Swift, and said to have been intended as the commencement of a general satire on the abuses of learning, of which, however, nothing more was ever written except Pope's treatise already mentioned on the Bathos, and one or two shorter fragments. The celebrated political satire, entitled The History of John Bull, which has been the model of various subsequent imitations, but of none in which the fiction is at once so apposite and so ludicrous, is also attributed to Arbuthnot. Pope's highly wrought and noble Prologue to his Satires, which is addressed to Arbuthnot, or rather in which the latter figures as the poet's interlocutor, will for ever preserve both the memory of their friendship, and also some traits of the character and manner of the learned, witty, and kind-hearted physician.

The commencement of the reign of the Whigs at the accession

of the House of Hanover, which deprived Arbuthnot of his appointment of one of the physicians extraordinary—leaving him, however, in the poet's words,

> social, cheerful, and serene,
> And just as rich as when he served a queen—

was more fatal to the fortunes of another of Pope's Tory or Jacobite friends, Francis Atterbury, the celebrated Bishop of Rochester, already mentioned as the principal author of the reply to Bentley's Dissertation on Phalaris. Atterbury also took a distinguished part in the professional controversies of his day, and his sermons and letters, and one or two short copies of verse by him, are well known; but his fervid character probably flashed out in conversation in a way of which we do not gather any notion from his writings. Atterbury was deprived and outlawed in 1722; and he died abroad in 1731, in his sixty-ninth year.

PRIOR; PARNELL.

Matthew Prior is another distinguished name in the band of the Tory writers of this age, and he was also an associate of Pope and Swift, although we hear less of him in their epistolary correspondence than of most of their other friends. Yet perhaps no one of the minor wits and poets of the time has continued to enjoy higher or more general favour with posterity. Much that he wrote, indeed, is now forgotten; but some of the best of his comic tales in verse will live as long as the language, which contains nothing that surpasses them in the union of ease and fluency with sprightliness and point, and in all that makes up the spirit of humorous and graceful narrative. They are our happiest examples of a style that has been cultivated with more frequent success by French writers than by our own. In one poem, his Alma, or The Progress of the Mind, extending to three cantos, he has even applied this light and airy manner of treatment with remarkable felicity to some of the most curious questions in mental philosophy. In another still longer work, again, entitled Solomon on the Vanity of the World, in three Books, leaving his characteristic archness and pleasantry, he emulates not unsuccessfully the dignity of Pope, not without some traces of natural eloquence and picturesqueness of expression which are all his own. Prior, who was born in 1664, commenced author before the Revolution, by the publication in 1688 of his City Mouse and Country Mouse, written in concert with Charles Montagu, afterwards Earl of Halifax, in ridicule of Dryden's Hind and Panther; and he continued a Whig nearly to the end of the reign of William; but he then joined the most extreme section of the Tories, and acted cordially with that party down to his death in 1721. Such also was the political course of Parnell, only that, being a younger man, he did not make his change of party till some years after Prior. The Rev. Dr. Thomas Parnell was born at Dublin in 1679, and left his original friends the Whigs at the same time with Swift, on the ejection of Lord Godolphin's ministry, in 1710. He died in 1718. Parnell is always an inoffensive and agreeable writer; and sometimes, as, for example, in his Nightpiece on Death, which probably suggested Gray's more celebrated Elegy, he rises to considerable impressiveness and solemn pathos. But, although his poetry is uniformly fluent and transparent, and its general spirit refined and delicate, it has little warmth or richness, and can only be called a sort of water-colour poetry. One of Parnell's pieces, we may remark,—his Fairy Tale of Edwin and Sir Topaz, —may have given some hints to Burns for his Tam o' Shanter.

BOLINGBROKE.

The mention of Prior naturally suggests that of his friend and patron, and also the friend of Swift and Pope—Henry St. John, better known by his title of the Lord Viscount Bolingbroke, although his era comes down to a later date, for he was not born till 1678, and he lived to 1751. Bolingbroke wrote no poetry, but his collected prose works fill five quarto volumes (without including his letters), and would thus entitle him by their quantity alone to be ranked as one of the most considerable writers of his time; of which we have abundant testimony that he was one of the most brilliant orators and talkers, and in every species of mere cleverness one of the most distinguished figures. His writings, being principally on subjects of temporary politics, have lost much of their interest; but a few of them, especially his Letters on the Study and Use of History, his Idea of a Patriot King, and his account and defence of his own conduct in his famous Letter to Sir William Windham, will still reward perusal even for the sake of their matter, while in style and manner almost everything he has left is of very remarkable merit. Bolingbroke's style, as we have elsewhere observed, "was a happy medium between that of the scholar and that of the man of society—or rather it was a happy combination of the best qualities of both, heightening the ease, freedom, fluency, and liveliness of elegant conversation with many of the deeper and richer tones of the eloquence of formal orations and of books. The example he thus set has probably had a very considerable effect in moulding the style of popular writing among us since his time."*

GARTH; BLACKMORE.

In one of the passages in which he commemorates the friendship of Swift, Atterbury, and Bolingbroke, Pope records also the encouragement his earliest performances in rhyme received from a poet and man of wit of the opposite party, "well-natured Garth."† Sir Samuel Garth, who was an eminent physician and a zealous Whig, is the author of various poetical pieces published in the reigns of William and Anne, of which the one of greatest pretension is that entitled The Dispensary, a mock epic, in six short cantos, on the quarrels of his professional brethren, which appeared in 1699. The wit of this slight performance may have somewhat evaporated with age, but it cannot have been at any time very pungent. A much more voluminous, and also more ambitious, Whig poet of this Augustan age, as it is sometimes called, of our literature, was another physician, Sir Richard Blackmore. Blackmore made his début as a poet so early as the year 1696, by the publication of his Prince Arthur, which was followed by a succession of other epics, or long poems of a serious kind, each in six, ten, or twelve books, under the names of King Arthur, King Alfred, Eliza, the Redeemer, the Creation, &c., besides a Paraphrase of the Book of Job, a new version of the Psalms, a Satire on Wit, and various shorter effusions both in verse and prose. The indefatigable rhymester—" the everlasting Blackmore," as Pope calls him—died at last in 1729. Nothing can be conceived wilder or more ludicrous than this incessant discharge of epics; but Blackmore, whom Dryden charged with writing "to the rumbling of his coach's wheels," may be pronounced, without any undue severity, to have been not more a fool than a blockhead. His Creation, indeed, has been praised both by Addison and Johnson; but the politics of the author may be supposed to have blinded or mollified the one critic, and his piety the other; at least the only thing an ordinary reader

* Article on Bolingbroke in Penny Cyclopædia, v. 78.
† See Prologue to the Satires, 135, &c.

will be apt to discover in this his *chef-d'œuvre*, that is not the flattest commonplace, is an occasional outbreak of the most ludicrous extravagance and bombast. Altogether this knight, droning away at his epics for above a quarter of a century, is as absurd a phenomenon as is presented to us in the history of literature. Pope has done him no more than justice in assigning him the first place among the contending "brayers" at the immortal games instituted by the goddess of the Dunciad:—

> But far o'er all, sonorous Blackmore's strain:
> Walls, steeples, skies, bray back to him again.
> In Tot'nam fields the brethren, with amaze,
> Prick all their ears up, and forget to graze;
> Long Chancery-lane retentive rolls the sound,
> And courts to courts return it round and round;
> Thames wafts it thence to Rufus' roaring hall,
> And Hungerford re-echoes bawl for bawl.
> All hail him victor in both gifts of song,
> Who sings so loudly and who sings so long.

DEFOE.

The Whigs, however, had to boast of one great writer of prose fiction, if, indeed, one who, although taking a frequent and warm part in the discussion of political subjects, really stood aloof from and above all parties, and may be said to have been in enlargement of view far in advance of all the public men of his time, can be properly claimed by any party. Nor does Daniel Defoe seem to have been recognized as one of themselves by the Whigs of his own day. He stood up, indeed, from first to last, for the principles of the Revolution against those of the Jacobites; but in the alternating struggle between the Whig and Tory parties for the possession of office he took little or no concern; he served and opposed administrations of either colour without reference to anything but their measures: thus we find him in 1706 assisting Godolphin and his colleagues to compass the union with Scotland; and in 1713 exerting himself with equal zeal in supporting Harley and Bolingbroke in the attempt to carry through their commercial treaty with France. He is believed to have first addressed himself to his countrymen through the press in 1683, when he was only in his twenty-third year. From this time for a space of above thirty years he may be said never to have laid down his pen as a political writer; his publications in prose and verse, which are far too numerous to be here particularized, embracing nearly every subject which either the progress of events made of prominent importance during that time, or which was of eminent popular or social interest independently of times and circumstances. Many of these productions, written for a temporary purpose, or on the spur of some particular occasion, still retain a considerable value, even for their matter, either as directories of conduct or accounts of matters of fact; some, indeed, such as his History of the Union, are the works of highest authority we possess respecting the transactions to which they relate; all of them bear the traces of a sincere, earnest, manly character, and of an understanding unusually active, penetrating, and well-informed. Evidence enough there often is, no doubt, of haste and precipitation, but it is always the haste of a full mind: the subject may be rapidly and somewhat rudely sketched out, and the matter not always very artificially disposed, or set forth to the most advantage; but Defoe never wrote for the mere sake of writing, or unless when he really had something to state which he conceived it important that the public should know. He was too thoroughly honest to make a trade of politics.

Defoe's course and character as a political writer bear a considerable resemblance in some leading points to those of one of the most remarkable men of our own day, the late William Cobbett, who, however, had certainly much more passion and wilfulness than Defoe, whatever we may think of his claims to as much principle. But Defoe's political writings make the smallest part of his literary renown. At the age of fifty-eight—an age when other writers, without the tenth part of his amount of performance to boast of, have usually thought themselves entitled to close their labours—he commenced a new life of authorship with all the spirit and hopeful alacrity of five-and-twenty. A succession of works of fiction, destined, some of them, to take and keep the highest rank in that department of our literature, and to become popular books in every language of Europe, now proceeded from his pen with a rapidity evincing the easiest flow as well as the greatest fertility of imagination. Robinson Crusoe appeared in 1719; the Dumb Philosopher, the same year; Captain Singleton, in 1720; Duncan Campbell, the same year; Moll Flanders, in 1721; Colonel Jacque, in 1722; the Journal of the Plague, and probably, also, the Memoirs of a Cavalier (to which there is no date), the same year; the Fortunate Mistress, or Roxana, in 1724; the New Voyage Round the World, in 1725; and the Memoirs of Captain Carleton, in 1728. But these effusions of his inventive faculty seem to have been, after all, little more than the amusements of his leisure. In the course of the twelve years from 1719 to his death in 1731, besides his novels, he produced about twenty miscellaneous works, many of them of considerable extent. It may be pretty safely affirmed that no one who has written so much has written so well. No writer of fictitious narrative has ever excelled him in at least one prime excellence—the air of reality which he throws over the creations of his fancy; an effect proceeding from the strength of conception with which he enters into the scenes, adventures, and characters he undertakes to describe, and his perfect reliance upon his power of interesting the reader by the plainest possible manner of relating things essentially interesting. Truth and nature are never either improved by flowers of speech in Defoe, or smothered under that sort of adornment. In some of his political writings there are not wanting passages of considerable height of style, in which, excited by a fit occasion, he employs to good purpose the artifices of rhetorical embellishment and modulation; but in his works of imagination his almost constant characteristic is a simplicity and plainness, which, if there be any affectation about it at all, is chargeable only with that of a homeliness sometimes approaching to rusticity. His writing, however, is always full of idiomatic nerve, and in a high degree graphic and expressive; and even its occasional slovenliness, whether the result of carelessness or design, aids the illusion by which the fiction is made to read so like a matter of fact. The truthful air of Defoe's fictions, we may just remark, is of quite a different character from that of Swift's, in which, although there is also much of the same vivid conception, and therefore minutely accurate delineation, of every person and thing introduced, a discerning reader will always perceive a smile lurking beneath the author's assumed gravity, telling him intelligibly enough that the whole is a joke. It is said, indeed, that, as the Journal of the Plague is quoted as an authentic narrative by Dr. Mead, and as Lord Chatham was, in all simplicity, in the habit of recommending the Memoirs of a Cavalier to his friends as the best account of the Civil Wars, and as those of Captain Carleton were read even by Samuel Johnson without a suspicion of their being other than a true history, so some Irish bishop was found with faith enough to believe in Gulliver's Travels, although not a little amazed by some things stated in the book. But it is not probable that there ever was any second instance, even on the Irish episcopal bench, of so high a pitch of innocence.

DRAMATIC WRITERS.

To this age, also, belong three of our comic dramatists. Congreve, Vanbrugh, and Farquhar were born in the order in which we have named them, and also, we believe, successively presented themselves before the public as writers for the stage in the same order, although they reversed it in making their exits from the stage of life,—Farquhar dying in 1707 at the age of twenty-nine, Vanbrugh in 1726 at that of fifty-four, Congreve not till 1729 in his fifty-ninth or sixtieth year.

Congreve's first play, The Old Bachelor, was brought out in 1693, the author having already, two or three years before, made himself known in the literary world by a novel called The Incognita, or Love and Duty Reconciled. The Old Bachelor was followed by The Double Dealer in 1694, and by Love for Love in 1695; the tragedy of The Mourning Bride was produced in 1697; and the comedy of The Way of the World, in 1700: a masquerade and an opera, both of slight importance, were the only dramatic pieces he wrote during the rest of his life. The comedy of Congreve has not much character, still less humour, and no nature at all; but blazes and crackles with wit and repartee, for the most part of an unusually pure and brilliant species,—not quaint, forced, and awkward, like what we find in some other attempts, in our dramatic literature and elsewhere, at the same kind of display, but apparently as easy and spontaneous as it is pointed, polished, and exact. His plots are also constructed with much artifice.

Sir John Vanbrugh is the author of ten or twelve comedies, of which the first, The Relapse, was produced in 1697, and of which The Provoked Wife, The Confederacy, and The Journey to London (which last, left unfinished by the author, was completed by Colley Cibber), are those of greatest merit. The wit of Vanbrugh flows rather than flashes; but its copious stream may vie in its own way with the dazzling fire-shower of Congreve's; and his characters have much more of real flesh and blood in their composition, coarse and vicious as almost all the more powerfully drawn among them are.

George Farquhar, the author of The Constant Couple and The Beaux' Stratagem, and of five or six other comedies, was a native of Ireland, in which country Congreve also spent his childhood and boyhood. Farquhar's first play, his Love in a Bottle, was brought out with great success at Drury Lane in 1698; The Beaux' Stratagem, his last, was in the midst of its run when the illness during which it had been written terminated in the poor author's early death. The thoughtless and volatile, but good natured and generous, character of Farquhar is reflected in his comedies, which, with less sparkle, have more natural life and airiness, and are animated by a finer spirit of whim, than those of either Vanbrugh or Congreve. His morality, like theirs, is abundantly free and easy; but there is much more heart about his profligacy than in theirs, as well as much less grossness or hardness.

To these names may be added that of Colley Cibber, who has, however, scarcely any pretensions to be ranked as one of our classic dramatists, although, of about two dozen comedies, tragedies, and other pieces of which he is the author, his Careless Husband and one or two others may be admitted to be lively and agreeable. Cibber, who was born in 1671, produced his first play, the comedy of Love's Last Shift, in 1696, and was still an occasional writer for the stage after the commencement of the reign of George II.; one of his productions, indeed, his tragedy entitled Papal Tyranny, was brought out so late as the year 1745, when he himself performed one of the principal characters; and he lived till 1757. His well-known account of his own life, or his Apology for his Life, as he modestly or affectedly calls it, is an amusing piece of something higher than gossip; the sketches he gives of the various celebrated actors of his time are many of them executed, not perhaps with the deepest insight, but yet with much graphic skill in so far as regards those mere superficial characteristics that meet the ordinary eye.

The chief tragic writer of this age was Nicholas Rowe, the author of The Fair Penitent and Jane Shore, of five other tragedies, one comedy, and a translation in rhyme of Lucan's Pharsalia. Rowe, who was born in 1673, and died in 1718, was esteemed in his own day a great master of the pathetic, but is now regarded as little more than a smooth and occasionally sounding versifier.

MINOR POETS.

The age of the first two Georges, if we put aside what was done by Pope, or consider him as belonging properly to the preceding reign of Anne, was not very prolific in poetry of a high order; but there are several minor poets belonging to this time whose names live in our literature, and some of whose productions are still read. Matthew Green's poem entitled The Spleen originally appeared, we believe, in his lifetime in the first volume of Dodsley's Collection—although his other pieces, which are

few in number and of little note, were only published by his
friend Glover after the death of the author in 1737, at the age
of forty-one. The Spleen, a reflective effusion in octo-syllabic
verse, is somewhat striking from an air of originality in the
vein of thought, and from the laboured concentration and epigrammatic point of the language; but, although it was much
cried up when it first appeared, and the laudation has continued
to be duly echoed by succeeding formal criticism, it may be
doubted if many readers could now make their way through
it without considerable fatigue, or if it be much read in fact at
all. With all its ingenious or energetic rhetorical posture-
making, it has nearly as little real play of fancy as charm of
numbers, and may be most properly characterized as a piece of
bastard or perverted Hudibrastic—an imitation of the manner of
Butler to the very dance of his verse, only without the comedy
—the same antics, only solemnized or made to carry a moral
and serious meaning. The Grongar Hill of Dyer was published
in 1726, when its author was in his twenty-seventh year; and
was followed by The Ruins of Rome in 1740, and his most
elaborate performance, The Fleece, in 1757, the year before his
death. Dyer's is a natural and true note, though not one of
much power or compass. What he has written is his own;
not borrowed from or suggested by "others' books," but what
he has himself seen, thought, and felt. He sees, too, with an
artistic eye—while at the same time his pictures are full of the
moral inspiration which alone makes description poetry. There
is also considerable descriptive power in Somervile's blank verse
poem of The Chase, in four Books, which was first published
in 1735. Somervile, who was a Warwickshire squire, and the
intimate friend of Shenstone, and who, besides his Chase, wrote
various other pieces, now for the most part forgotten, died in
1742. Tickell, Addison's friend, who was born in 1686 and
lived till 1740, is the author of a number of compositions, of
which his Elegy on Addison and his ballad of Colin and Lucy
are the best known. The ballad Gray has called "the prettiest
in the world"—and if prettiness, by which Gray here probably
means a certain easy simplicity and trimness, were the soul of
ballad poetry, it might carry away a high prize. Nobody writes
better grammar than Tickell. His style is always remarkably
clear and exact, and the mere appropriateness and judicious
collocation of the words, aided by the swell of the verse in his
more elaborate or solemn passages, have sometimes an imposing effect. Of his famous Elegy, the most opposite opinions
have been expressed. Goldsmith has called it "one of the

finest in our language;" and Johnson has declared that "a more sublime or elegant funeral poem is not to be found in the whole compass of English literature." So Lord Macaulay:—"Tickell bewailed his friend in an Elegy which would do honour to the greatest name in our literature, and which unites the energy and magnificence of Dryden to the tenderness and purity of Cowper."* Steele on the other hand has denounced it as being nothing more than "prose in rhyme." And it must be admitted that it is neither very tender nor very imaginative; yet rhyme too is part and parcel of poetry, and solemn thoughts, vigorously expressed and melodiously enough versified, which surely we have here, cannot reasonably be refused that name, even though the informing power of passion or imagination may not be present in any very high degree.

The notorious Richard Savage is the author of several poetical compositions, published in the last fifteen or twenty years of his tempestuous and unhappy life, which he closed in Bristol jail in 1743, at the age of forty-six. Savage's poem called The Bastard has some vigorous lines, and some touches of tenderness as well as bursts of more violent passion; but, as a whole, it is crude, spasmodic, and frequently wordy and languid. His other compositions, some of which evince a talent for satire, of which assiduous cultivation might have made something, have all passed into oblivion. The personal history of Savage, which Johnson's ardent and expanded narrative has made universally known, is more interesting than his verse; but even that owes more than half its attraction to his biographer. He had, in fact, all his life, apparently, much more of another kind of madness than he ever had of that of poetry.

Fenton and Broome—the former of whom died in 1730 at the age of forty-seven, the latter in 1745, at what age is not known,—are chiefly remembered as Pope's coadjutors in his translation of the Odyssey. Johnson observes, in his Life of Fenton, that the readers of poetry have never been able to distinguish their Books from those of Pope; but the account he has given here and in the Life of Broome of the respective shares of the three, on the information, as he says, of Mr. Langton, who had got it from Spence, may be reasonably doubted. It differs, indeed, in some respects from that given in Spence's Anecdotes, since published. A critical reader will detect very marked varieties of style and manner in the different parts of the work. It is very clear, for instance, that the nineteenth and twentieth Books are not by Pope, and have not even received much of his revi-

* Essay on Addison.

sion: they are commonly attributed to Fenton, and we should
think rightly. But it is impossible to believe, on the other
hand, that the translator of these two Books is also the translator of the whole of the fourth Book, which is likewise
assigned to Fenton in Johnson's statement. Could any one
except Pope have written the following lines, which occur in
that Book?—

> But, oh, beloved by heaven, reserved to thee,
> A happier lot the smiling fates decree;
> Free from that law, beneath whose mortal sway
> Matter is changed, and varying forms decay,
> Elysium shall be thine; the blissful plains
> Of utmost earth, where Rhadamanthus reigns.
> Joys ever young, unmixed with pain or fear,
> Fill the wide circle of the eternal year:
> Stern winter smiles on that auspicious clime,
> The fields are florid with unfading prime;
> From the bleak pole no winds inclement blow,
> Mould the round hail, or flake the fleecy snow;
> But from the breezy deep the bless'd inhale
> The fragrant murmurs of the western gale.
> This grace peculiar will the Gods afford
> To thee, the son of Jove, the beauteous Helen's lord.

Pope, indeed, may have inserted this and other passages in this
and other Books, of which he did not translate the whole.
Broome was a much more dexterous versifier than Fenton, and
would come much nearer to Pope's ordinary manner: still we
greatly doubt if the twenty-third Book in particular (which
passes for Broome's) be not entirely Pope's, and also many parts
of the second, the eighth, the eleventh, and the twelfth. On the
other hand, the thirteenth, fourteenth, fifteenth, and twenty-
fourth seem to us to be throughout more likely to be by him
than by Pope. Pope himself seems to have looked upon Broome
as rather a clever mimic of his own manner than as anything
much higher. When they had quarrelled a few years after
this, he introduced his old associate in the Dunciad, in a
passage which originally ran:—

> See under Ripley rise a new Whitehall,
> While Jones and Boyle's united labours fall;
> While Wren with sorrow to the grave descends,
> Gay dies unpensioned with a hundred friends;
> Hibernian politics, O Swift, thy doom,
> And Pope's, translating ten whole years with Broome.

It was pretended, indeed, in a note, that no harm was meant to
poor Broome by this delicate crucifixion of him. Yet he is

understood to be the W. B. who, in the sixth chapter of the Art of Sinking in Poetry, entitled "Of the several kinds of geniuses in the Profound, and the marks and characters of each," heads the list of those described as "the Parrots, that repeat another's words in such a hoarse, odd voice, as makes them seem their own." And Broome, as Johnson has observed, is quoted more than once in the treatise as a proficient in the Bathos. Johnson adds, "I have been told that they were afterwards reconciled; but I am afraid their peace was without friendship." The couplet in the Dunciad, at least, was ultimately altered to—

Hibernian politics, O Swift! thy fate,
And Pope's, ten years to comment and translate.

Both Broome and Fenton published also various original compositions in verse, but nothing that the world has not very willingly let die. Fenton, however, although his contributions to the translation of the Odyssey neither harmonize well with the rest of the work, nor are to be commended taken by themselves, had more force and truth of poetical feeling than many of his verse-making contemporaries: one of his pieces, his ode to Lord Gower, is not unmusical, nor without a certain lyric glow and elevation.

Another small poet of this age is Ambrose Philips, whose Six Pastorals and tragedy of The Distressed Mother brought him vast reputation when they were first produced, but whose name has been kept in the recollection of posterity, perhaps, more by Pope's vindictive satire. An ironical criticism on the Pastorals in the Guardian, which took in Steele, who published it in the 40th number of that paper (for 27th April, 1713), was followed long afterwards by the unsparing ridicule of the Treatise on the Art of Sinking in Poetry, in which many of the illustrations are taken from the rhymes of poor Philips, who is held up in one place as the great master both of the infantine and the inane in style, and is elsewhere placed at the head of the clan of writers designated the Tortoises, who are described as slow and dull, and, like pastoral writers, delighting much in gardens: "they have," it is added, "for the most part, a fine embroidered shell, and underneath it a heavy lump."* Philips, in some of his later effusions, had gone, in pursuit of what he conceived to be nature

* According to Johnson, Gay's Pastorals were written at Pope's instigation, in ridicule of those of Philips; "but," it is added, "the effect of reality and truth became conspicuous, even when the intention was to show them grovelling and degraded. These Pastorals became popular, and were read with delight, as just representations of rural manners and occupations, by those who had no interest in the rivalry of the poets, nor knowledge of the critical dispute."—Life of Gay.

and simplicity, into a style of writing in short verses with not overmuch meaning, which his enemies parodied under the name of Namby-pamby. On the whole, however, he had no great reason to complain: if his poetry was laughed at by Pope and the Tories, it was both lauded, and very substantially rewarded, by the Whigs, who not only made Philips a lottery commissioner and a justice of peace for Westminster, but continued to push him forward till he became member for the county of Armagh in the Irish parliament, and afterwards judge of the Irish Prerogative Court. His success in life is alluded to in the same part of the Dunciad where Broome is brought in—in the line,

Lo! Ambrose Philips is preferred for wit!

This Namby-pamby Philips, who was born in 1671 and lived till 1749, must not be confounded with John Philips, the author of the mock-heroic poem of The Splendid Shilling (published in 1703), and also of a poem in two books, in serious blank verse, entitled Cider, which has the reputation of being a good practical treatise on the brewing of that drink. John Philips, who published likewise a poem on the battle of Blenheim, in rivalry of Addison, was a Tory poet, and the affectation of simplicity, at least, cannot be laid to his charge, for what he aims at imitating or appropriating is not what is called the language of nature, but the swell and pomp of Milton. His serious poetry, however, is not worth much, at least as poetry. John Philips was born in 1676, and died in 1708.

Two or three more names may be merely mentioned. Leonard Welsted, who was born in 1689, and died in 1747, also, like Ambrose Philips, figures in the Dunciad and in the Treatise of Martinus Scriblerus, and produced a considerable quantity both of verse and prose, all now utterly forgotten. Thomas Yalden, who died a Doctor of Divinity in 1736, was a man of wit as well as the writer of a number of odes, elegies, hymns, fables, and other compositions in verse, of which one, entitled a Hymn to Darkness, is warmly praised by Dr. Johnson, who has given the author a place in his Lives of the Poets. In that work too may be found an account of Hammond, the author of the Love Elegies, who died in 1742, in his thirty-second year, driven mad, and eventually sent to his grave, it is affirmed, by the inexorable cruelty of the lady. a Miss Dashwood, who, under the name of Delia, is the subject of his verses, and who, we are told, survived him for thirty-seven years without finding any one else either to marry or fall in love with her. The character, as Johnson remarks, that Hammond bequeathed her was not likely to attract courtship. Hammond's poetry, however, reflects but coldly the amorous fire which produced all this mischief; it is correct and graceful, but languid almost to the point of drowsiness. Gilbert West was born about 1705, and died in 1756: besides other verse, he published a translation of a portion of the odes of Pindar, which had long considerable reputation, but is not very Pindaric, though a smooth and sonorous performance. The one of his works that has best kept its ground is his prose tract entitled Observations on the Resurrection, a very able and ingenious disquisition, for which the university of Oxford made West a Doctor of Laws. Aaron Hill, who was born in 1685 and died in 1750, and who lies buried in Westminster Abbey, was at different periods of his life a traveller, a projector, a theatrical manager, and a literary man. He is the author of no fewer than seventeen dramatic pieces, original and translated, among which his versions of Voltaire's Zaire and Merope long kept possession of the stage. His poetry is in general both pompous and empty enough; and of all he has written, almost the only passage that is now much remembered is a satiric sketch of Pope, in a few lines, which have some imitative smartness, but scarcely any higher merit. Pope had offended him by putting him in the Dunciad, though the way in which he is mentioned is really complimentary to Hill.

COLLINS; SHENSTONE; GRAY.

By far the greatest of all the poetical writers of this age who, from the small quantity of their productions, or the brevity of each of them separately considered, are styled minor poets, is Collins. William Collins, born in 1720, died at the early age of thirty-six, and nearly all his poetry had been written ten years before his death. His volume of Odes, descriptive and allegorical, was published in 1746; his Oriental Eclogues had appeared some years before, while he was a student at Oxford. Only his unfinished Ode on the Popular Superstitions of the Highlanders was found among his papers after his death, and it is dated 1749. The six or seven last years of his short life were clouded with a depression of spirits which made intellectual exertion impossible. All that Collins has written is full of imagination, pathos, and melody. The defect of his poetry in general is that there is too little of earth in it: in the purity and depth of its beauty it resembles the bright blue sky. Yet Collins had genius enough for anything; and in his ode entitled The Passions he has shown with how strong a voice and pulse of humanity he could, when he chose, animate his verse, and what extensive and enduring popularity he could command.

Gray and Shenstone were both born before Collins, though they both outlived him,—Shenstone dying at the age of fifty in 1763, Gray at that of fifty-five in 1771. Shenstone is remembered for his Pastoral Ballad, his Schoolmistress, and an elegy or two; but there was very little potency of any kind in the music of his slender oaten pipe. Gray's famous Elegy written in a Country Churchyard, his two Pindarics, his Ode on Eton College, his Long Story, some translations from the Norse and Welsh, and a few other short pieces, which make up his contributions to the poetry of his native language, are all admirable for their exquisite finish, nor is a true poetical spirit ever wanting, whatever may be thought of the form in which it is sometimes embodied. When his two celebrated compositions, The Progress of Poesy and The Bard, appeared together in 1757, Johnson affirms that "the readers of poetry were at first content to gaze in mute amazement;" and, although the difficulty or impossibility of understanding them which was then, it seems, felt and confessed, is no longer complained of, much severe animadversion has been passed on them on other accounts. Still, whatever objections may be made to the artificial and unnatural character and over-elaboration of their style, the gorgeous brocade of the verse does not hide the true fire and fancy beneath, or even the real elegance of taste that has arrayed itself so ambitiously. But Gray often expresses himself, too, as naturally and simply in his poetry as he always does in his charming Letters and other writings in prose: the most touching of the verses in his Ode to Eton College, for instance, are so expressed; and in his Long Story he has given the happiest proof of his mastery over the lightest graces and gaieties of song.

Young; Thomson.

Of the remaining poetical names of this age the two most considerable are those of Young and Thomson. Dr. Edward Young, the celebrated author of the Night Thoughts, was born in 1681 and lived till 1765. He may be shortly characterized as, at least in manner, a sort of successor, under the reign of Pope and the new style established by him and Dryden, of the Donnes and the Cowleys of a former age. He had nothing, however, of Donne's subtle fancy, and as little of the gaiety and playfulness that occasionally break out among the quibbles and contortions of Cowley. On the other hand, he has much more passion and pathos than Cowley, and, with less elegance, perhaps makes a nearer approach in some of his greatest passages to the true sublime. But his style is radically an affected and false one; and of what force it seems to possess, the greater part is the result not of any real principle of life within it, but of mere strutting and straining. Nothing can be more unlike the poetry of the Night Thoughts than that of the Seasons. If Young is all art and effort, Thomson is all negligence and nature; so negligent, indeed, that he pours forth his unpremeditated song apparently without the thought ever occurring to him that he could improve it by any study or elaboration, any more than if he were some winged warbler of the woodlands, seeking and caring for no other listener except the universal air which the strain made vocal. As he is the poet of nature, so his poetry has all the intermingled rudeness and luxuriance of its theme. There is no writer who has drunk in more of the inmost soul of his subject. If it be the object of descriptive poetry to present us with pictures and visions the effect of which shall vie with that of the originals from which they are drawn, then Thomson is the greatest of all descriptive poets; for there is no other who surrounds us with so much of the truth of Nature, or makes us feel so intimately the actual presence and companionship of all her hues and fragrances. His spring blossoms and gives forth its beauty like a daisied meadow; and his summer landscapes have all the sultry warmth and green luxuriance of June; and his harvest fields and his orchards "hang the heavy head" as if their fruitage were indeed embrowning in the sun; and we see and hear the driving of his winter snows, as if the air around us were in confusion with their uproar. The beauty and purity of imagination, also, diffused over the melodious stanzas of the Castle of Indolence, make that poem one of the gems of the language. Thomson, whose Winter, the first portion of his Seasons, was published in 1726, died in 1748, in his forty-eighth year. Two years before had died his countryman, the Rev. Robert Blair, born in 1699, the author of the well-known poem in blank verse called The Grave, said to have been first published in 1743. It is remarkable for its masculine vigour of thought and expression, and for the imaginative solemnity with which it invests the most familiar truths; and it has always been one of our most popular religious poems.

ARMSTRONG; AKENSIDE; WILKIE; GLOVER.

Among the more eminent, again, of the second-rate writers of longer poems about this date, the latter part of the reign of George II., immediately after the death of Pope, may be noticed Dr. John Armstrong, who was born in Scotland in 1709, and whose Art of Preserving Health, published in 1744, has the rare merit of an original and characteristic style, distinguished by raciness and manly grace; and Dr. Mark Akenside, likewise a physician, the author, at the age of twenty-three, of The Pleasures of Imagination, published in the same year with Armstrong's poem, and giving another example of the treatment of a didactic subject in verse with great ingenuity and success. Akenside's rich, though diffuse, eloquence, and the store of fanciful illustration which he pours out, evidence a wonderfully full mind for so young a man. Neither Akenside nor Armstrong published any more verse after the accession of George III.; though the former lived till 1770, and the latter till 1779. Wilkie, the author of the rhyming epic called The Epigoniad, who was a Scotch clergyman and professor of natural philosophy at St. Andrews, would also appear from the traditionary accounts we have of him to have been a person of some genius as well as learning, though in composing his said epic he seems not to have gone much farther for his model or fount of inspiration than to the more sonorous passages of Pope's Homer. The Epigoniad, published in 1753, can scarcely be said to have in any proper sense of the word long survived its author, who died in 1772. Nor probably was Glover's blank verse epic of Leonidas, which appeared so early as 1737, much read when he himself passed away from among men, in the year 1785, at the age of seventy-four—although it had had a short day of extraordinary popularity, and is a performance of considerable rhetorical merit. Glover, who was a merchant of London, and distinguished as a city political leader on the liberal side (a circumstance which helped the temporary success of his epic), also wrote two tragedies, Boadicea, which was brought out in 1753; Medea, which appeared in 1761: they have the reputation of being cold and declamatory, and have both been long ago consigned to oblivion. He is best remembered for his ballad of Admiral Hosier's Ghost —which he wrote when he was seven-and-twenty, and was accustomed, it seems, to sing to the end of his life,—though Hannah More, who tells us she heard him sing it in his last days, is mistaken in saying that he was then past eighty.

Scottish Poetry.

Thomson was the first Scotsman who won any conspicuous place for himself in English literature. He had been preceded, indeed, in the writing of English by two or three others of his countrymen; by Drummond of Hawthornden, who has been mentioned in a preceding page, and his contemporaries—the Earl of Stirling, who is the author of several rhyming tragedies and other poems, well versified, but not otherwise of much poetical merit, published between 1603 and 1637, the Earl of Ancrum, by whom we have some sonnets and other short pieces, and Sir Robert Ayton, to whom is commonly attributed the well-known song, " I do confess thou'rt smooth and fair," and who is also the author of a considerable number of other similar effusions, many of them of superior polish and elegance. At a later date, too, Sir George Mackenzie, as already noticed, had written some English prose; as, indeed, Drummond had also done, besides his poetry. But none of these writers, belonging to the century that followed the union of the crowns, can be considered as having either acquired any high or diffused reputation in his own time, or retained much hold upon posterity. Even Drummond is hardly remembered as anything more than a respectable sonnetteer; his most elaborate work, his prose History of the Jameses, has passed into as complete general oblivion as the tragedies and epics of Lord Stirling and the Essays of Sir George Mackenzie. If there be any other writer born in Scotland of earlier date than Thomson, who has still a living and considerable name among English authors, it is Bishop Burnet; but those of his literary performances by which he continues to be chiefly remembered, however important for the facts they contain, have scarcely any literary value. Leighton, the eloquent archbishop of Glasgow, although of Scotch descent, was himself born in London. The poetry of Thomson was the first produce of the next era, in which the two countries were really made one by their union under one legislature, and English became the literary language of the one part of the island as much as of the other.

The Scottish dialect, however, still continued to be employed in poetry. The great age of Scottish poetry, as we have seen, extends from about the beginning of the fifteenth to about the middle of the sixteenth century, the succession of distinguished names comprehending, among others, those of James I., and Henderson, and Holland, and Henry the Minstrel, and Gawin Douglas, and Dunbar, and Sir David Lyndsay.* It is remarkable

* See pp. 167—183.

that this space of a hundred and fifty years exactly corresponds to the period of the decay and almost extinction of poetry in England which intervenes between Chaucer and Surrey. On the other hand, with the revival of English poetry in the latter part of the sixteenth century the voice of Scottish song almost died away. The principal names of the writers of Scottish verse that occur for a hundred and fifty years after the death of Lyndsay are those of Alexander Scot, who was Lyndsay's contemporary, but probably survived him, and who is the author of several short amatory compositions, which have procured him from Pinkerton the designation of the Scottish Anacreon; Sir Richard Maitland of Lethington, who died at a great age in 1586, and is less memorable as a poet than as a collector and preserver of poetry, the two famous manuscript volumes in the Pepysian Library, in which are found the only existing copies of so many curious old pieces, having been compiled under his direction, although his own compositions, which have, with proper piety, been printed by the Maitland Club at Glasgow, are also of some bulk, and are creditable to his good feeling and good sense; Captain Alexander Montgomery, whose allegory of The Cherry and the Slae, published in 1597, is remarkable for the facility and flow of the language, and long continued a popular favourite, its peculiar metre (which, however, is of earlier origin than this poem) having been on several occasions adopted by Burns; and Alexander Hume, who was a clergyman and died in 1600, having published a volume of Hymns, or Sacred Songs, in his native dialect, in 1599. Other Scottish poets of the sixteenth century, of whom nothing or next to nothing is known except the names, and a few short pieces attributed to some of them, are John Maitland Lord Thirlstane (second son of Sir Richard), Alexander Arbuthnot, who was a clergyman, Clapperton, Flemyng, John Blyth, Moffat, Fethy, Balnavis, Sempil, Norval, Allan Watson, George Bannatyne (the writer of the Bannatyne manuscript in the Advocates' Library), who was a canon of the cathedral of Moray, and Wedderburn, the supposed author of the Compendious Book of Godly and Spiritual Songs, of which the first edition in all probability appeared in the latter part of this century, and also, according to one theory, of The Complaint of Scotland, published in 1548.* But it is possible that some of these names may belong to a date anterior to that of Lyndsay. King James, also, before his accession to the English throne, published in Edinburgh two collections of Scottish verse by himself; the first, in 1585, entitled The Essays of a Prentice in

* See p. 191.

the Divine Art of Poesy; the other, in 1591, His Majesty's Poetical Exercises at vacant hours; but the royal inspiration is peculiarly weak and flat.

In the whole course, we believe, of the seventeenth century not even the name of a Scottish poet or versifier occurs. The next that appeared was Allan Ramsay, who was the contemporary of Thomson, and must be accounted the proper successor of Sir David Lyndsay, after the lapse of more than a century and a half. Ramsay was born in 1686, and lived till 1758. He belongs to the order of self-taught poets, his original profession having been that of a barber; his first published performance, his clever continuation of the old poem of Christ's Kirk on the Green (attributed by some to James I. of Scotland, by others to James V.) appeared in 1712; his Gentle Shepherd, in 1725; and he produced besides numerous songs and other shorter pieces from time to time. Ramsay's verse is in general neither very refined nor very imaginative, but it has always more or less in it of true poetic life. His lyrics, with all their frequent coarseness, are many of them full of rustic hilarity and humour; and his well-known pastoral, though its dramatic pretensions otherwise are slender enough, for nature and truth both in the characters and manners may rank with the happiest compositions of its class.

THE NOVELISTS, RICHARDSON, FIELDING, SMOLLETT.

A very remarkable portion of the literature of the middle of the last century is the body of prose fiction, the authors of which we familiarly distinguish as the modern English novelists, and which in some respects may be said still to stand apart from everything in the language produced either before or since. If there be any writer entitled to step in before Richardson and Fielding in claiming the honour of having originated the English novel, it is Daniel Defoe. But, admirable as Defoe is for his inventive power and his art of narrative, he can hardly be said to have left us any diversified picture of the social life of his time, and he is rather a great *raconteur* than a novelist, strictly and properly so called. He identifies himself, indeed, as perfectly as any writer ever did, with the imaginary personages whose adventures he details;—but still it is adventures he deals with rather than either manners or characters. It may be observed that there is seldom or ever anything peculiar or characteristic in the language of his heroes and heroines: some of them talk, or write, through whole volumes, but all in the same style; in fact, as to this matter, every one of them is merely a repetition of Defoe himself. Nor even in professed dialogue is he happy in individualizing his characters by their manner of expressing themselves; there may be the employment occasionally of certain distinguishing phrases, but the adaptation of the speech to the speaker seldom goes much beyond such mere mechanical artifices; the heart and spirit do not flash out as they do in nature; we may remember Robinson Crusoe's man Friday by his broken English, but it is in connexion with the fortunes of their lives only, of the full stream of incident and adventure upon which they are carried along, of the perils and perplexities in which they are involved, and the shifts they are put to, that we think of Colonel Jacque, or Moll Flanders, or even of Robinson Crusoe himself. What character they have to us is all gathered from the circumstances in which they are placed; very little or none of it from either the manner or the matter of their discourses. Even their conduct is for the most part the result of circumstances; any one of them acts, as well as speaks, very nearly as any other would have done similarly situated. Great and original as he is in his proper line, and admirable as the fictions with which he has enriched our literature are for their other merits, Defoe has created no character which lives in the national mind—no Squire Western, or Trullibor, or Parson Adams, or Strap, or Pipes, or Trunnion, or Lesmahago, or Corporal Trim, or Uncle Toby. He has made no attempt at any such delineation. It might be supposed that a writer able to place himself and his readers so completely in the midst of the imaginary scenes he describes would have excelled in treating a subject dramatically. But, in truth, his genius was not at all dramatic. With all his wonderful power of interesting us by the air of reality he throws over his fictions, and carrying us along with him whithersoever he pleases, he has no faculty of passing out of himself in the dramatic spirit, of projecting himself out of his own proper nature and being into those of the creations of his brain. However strong his conception was of other things, he had no strong conception of character. Besides, with all his imagination and invention, he had little wit and no humour—no remarkable skill in any other kind of representation except merely that of the plain literal truth of things. Vivid and even creative as his imagination was, it was still not poetical. It looked through no atmosphere of ideal light at anything; it saw nothing adorned, beautified, elevated above nature; its gift was to see the reality, and no more. Its pictures, therefore, partake rather of the character of fac-similes than that of works of art in the true sense.

On turning our eyes from his productions to those either of Fielding or Richardson, we feel at once the spell of quite another sort of inventive or creative power. Yet no two writers could well be more unlike than the two we have mentioned are to one another both in manner and in spirit. Intellectually and morally, by original constitution of mind as well as in the circumstances of their training and situation, the two great contemporary novelists stood opposed the one to the other in the most complete contrast. Fielding, a gentleman by birth, and liberally educated, had been a writer for the public from the time he was twenty; Richardson, who had nearly attained that age before Fielding came into the world (the one was born in 1689, the other in 1707), having begun life as a mechanic, had spent the greater part of it as a tradesman; and had passed his fiftieth year before he became an author. Yet, after they had entered upon the same new field of literature almost together, they found themselves rivals upon that ground for as long as either continued to write. To Richardson certainly belongs priority of date as a novelist: the first part of his Pamela was published in 1740, the conclusion in 1741; and Fielding's Joseph Andrews, originally conceived with the design of turning Richardson's work into ridicule, appeared in 1742. Thus, as if their common choice of the same species of writing, and their antipathies of nature and habit, had not been enough to divide them, it was destined that the two founders of the now school of fiction should begin their career by having a personal quarrel. For their works, notwithstanding all the remarkable points of dissimilarity between those of the one and those of the other, must still be considered as belonging to the same school or form of literary composition, and that a form which they had been the first to exemplify in our language. Unlike as Joseph Andrews was to Pamela, yet the two resembled each other more than either did any other English work of fiction. They were still our two first novels properly so called—our two first artistically constructed epics of real life. And the identity of the species of fictitious narrative cultivated by the two writers became more apparent as its character was more completely developed by their subsequent publications, and each proceeded in proving its capabilities in his own way, without reference to what had been done by the other. Fielding's Jonathan Wild appeared in 1743; Richardson's Clarissa Harlowe—the greatest of his works—was given to the world in 1748; and the next year the greatest birth of Fielding's genius—his Tom Jones—saw the light. Finally, Fielding's Amelia was published in

1751; and Richardson's Sir Charles Grandison in 1753. Fielding died at Lisbon in 1754, at the age of forty-seven; Richardson survived till 1761, but wrote nothing more.

Meanwhile, however, a third writer had presented himself upon the same field—Smollett, whose Roderick Random had appeared in 1748, his Peregrine Pickle in 1751, and his Count Fathom in 1754, when the energetic Scotsman was yet only in his thirty-fourth year. His Sir Launcelot Greaves followed in 1762, and his Humphrey Clinker in 1771, in the last year of the author's active life. Our third English novelist is as much a writer *sui generis* as either of his two predecessors, as completely distinguished from each of them in the general character of his genius as they are from each other. Of the three, Richardson had evidently by far the richest natural soil of mind; his defects sprung from deficiency of cultivation; his power was his own in the strictest sense; not borrowed from books, little aided even by experience of life, derived almost solely from introspection of himself and communion with his own heart. He alone of the three could have written what he did without having himself witnessed and lived through the scenes and characters described, or something like them which only required to be embellished and heightened, and otherwise artistically treated, in order to form an interesting and striking fictitious representation. His fertility of invention, in the most comprehensive meaning of that term, is wonderful,—supplying him on all occasions with a copious stream both of incident and of thought that floods the page, and seems as if it might so flow on and diffuse itself for ever. Yet it must be confessed that he has delineated for us rather human nature than human life—rather the heart and its universal passions, as modified merely by a few broad distinctions of temperament, of education, of external circumstances, than those subtler idiosyncracies which constitute what we properly call character. Many characters, no doubt, there are set before us in his novels, very admirably drawn and discriminated: Pamela, her parents, Mr. B., Mrs. Jewkes, Clarissa, Lovelace, Miss Howe, Sir Charles Grandison, Miss Byron, Clementina, are all delineations of this description for the most part natural, well worked out, and supported by many happy touches: but (with the exception, perhaps, of the last mentioned) they can scarcely be called original conceptions of a high order, creations at once true to nature and new to literature; nor have they added to that population of the world of fiction among which every reader of books has many familiar acquaintances hardly less real to his fancy and feelings than any he has met with in the actual world, and for the most part much more interesting. That which, besides the story, interests us in Richardson's novels, is not the characters of his personages but their sentiments—not their modes but their motives of action—the anatomy of their hearts and inmost natures, which is unfolded to us with so elaborate an inquisition and such matchless skill. Fielding, on the other hand, has very little of this, and Smollett still less. They set before us their pictures of actual life in much the same way as life itself would have set them before us if our experience had chanced to bring us into contact with the particular situations and personages delineated; we see, commonly, merely what we should have seen as lookers-on, not in the particular confidence of any of the figures in the scene; there are they all, acting or talking according to their various circumstances, habits, and humours, and we are welcome to look at them and listen to them as attentively as we please; but, if we want to know anything more of them than what is visible to all the world, we must find it out for ourselves in the best way we can, for neither they nor the author will ordinarily tell us a word of it. What both these writers have given us in their novels is for the most part their own actual experience of life, irradiated, of course, by the lights of fancy and genius, and so made something much more brilliant and attractive than it was in the reality, but still in its substance the product not of meditation but of observation chiefly. Even Fielding, with all his wit, or at least pregnancy of thought and style—for the quality in his writings to which we allude appears to be the result rather of elaboration than of instinctive perception—would probably have left us nothing much worth preserving in the proper form of a novel, if he had not had his diversified practical knowledge of society to draw upon and especially his extensive and intimate acquaintance with the lower orders of all classes, in painting whom he is always greatest and most at home. Within that field, indeed, he is the greatest of all our novelists. Yet he has much more refinement of literary taste than either Smollett or Richardson; and, indeed, of the works of all the three, his alone can be called classical works in reference to their formal character. Both his style and the construction of his stories display a care and artifice altogether unknown to the others, both of whom, writing on without plan or forethought, appear on all occasions to have made use alike of the first words and the first incidents that presented themselves. Smollett, a practised writer for the press, had the command, indeed, of a style the fluency of which is far from being without force, or rhetorical parade either; but it is animated by no peculiar expressiveness, by no graces either of art or of nature. His power consists in the cordiality of his conception and the breadth and freedom of his delineation of the humorous, both in character and in situation. The feeling of the humorous in Smollett always overpowers, or at least has a tendency to overpower, the merely satirical spirit; which is not the case with Fielding, whose humour has generally a sly vein of satire running through it, even when it is most gay and genial.

STERNE.

But he to whom belongs the finest spirit of whim among all our writers of this class is the immortal author of The Life and Opinions of Tristram Shandy. Sterne, born in Ireland in 1713, had already published one or two unregarded sermons when the first and second volumes of his most singular novel were brought out at York in the year 1759. The third and fourth volumes followed in 1761; the fifth and sixth in 1762; the seventh and eighth not till 1765; the ninth in 1767. The six volumes of his Yorick's Sermons had also come out in pairs in the intervals; his Sentimental Journey appeared in 1768; and his death took place the same year. Sterne has been charged with imitation and plagiarism; but surely originality is the last quality that can be denied to him. To dispute his possession of that is much the same as it would be to deny that the sun is luminous because some spots have been detected upon its surface. If Sterne has borrowed or stolen some few things from other writers, at least no one ever had a better right to do so in virtue of the amount that there is in his writings of what is really his own. If he has been much indebted to any predecessor, it is to Rabelais; but, except in one or two detached episodes, he has wholly eschewed the extravagance and grotesqueness in which the genius of Rabelais loves to disport itself, and the tenderness and humanity that pervade his humour are quite unlike anything in the mirth of Rabelais. There is not much humour, indeed, anywhere out of Shakespeare and Cervantes which resembles or can be compared with that of Sterne. It would be difficult to name any writer but one of those two who could have drawn Uncle Toby or Trim. Another common mistake about Sterne is, that the mass of what he has written consists of little better than nonsense or rubbish—that his beauties are but grains of gold glittering here and there in a heap of sand, or, at most, rare spots of green scattered over an arid waste. Of no writer could this be said with less correctness. Whatever he has done is wrought with the utmost care, and to the highest polish and perfection. With all his apparent caprices of manner, his language is throughout the purest idiomatic English; nor is there, usually, a touch in any of his pictures that could be spared without injury to the effect. And, in his great work, how completely brought out, how exquisitely finished, is every figure, from Uncle Toby, and Brother Shandy, and Trim, and Yorick, down to Dr. Slop, and Widow Wadman, and Mrs. Bridget, and Obadiah himself! Who would resign any one of them, or any part of any one of them?

Goldsmith.

It has been observed, with truth, that, although Richardson has on the whole the best claim to the title of inventor of the modern English novel, he never altogether succeeded in throwing off the inflation of the French romance, and representing human beings in the true light and shade of human nature. Undoubtedly the men and women of Fielding and Smollett are of more genuine flesh and blood than the elaborate heroes and heroines who figure in his pages. But both Fielding and Smollett, notwithstanding the fidelity as well as spirit of their style of drawing from real life, have for the most part confined themselves to some two or three departments of the wide field of social existence, rather abounding in strongly marked peculiarities of character than furnishing a fair representation of the common national mind and manners. And Sterne also, in his more aërial way, deals rather with the oddities and quaintnesses of opinion and habit that are to be met with among his countrymen than with the broad general course of our English way of thinking and living. Our first genuine novel of domestic life is Goldsmith's Vicar of Wakefield, written in 1761, when its author, born in Ireland in 1728, was as yet an obscure doer of all work for the booksellers, but not published till 1766, when his name had already obtained celebrity by his poem of The Traveller. Assuming the grace of confession, or the advantage of the first word, Goldsmith himself introduces his performance by observing, that there are a hundred faults in it; adding, that a hundred things might be said to prove them beauties. The case is not exactly as he puts it: the faults may have compensating beauties, but are incontrovertibly faults. Indeed, if we look only to what is more superficial or external in the work, to the construction and conduct of the story, and even to much of the exhibition of manners and character, its faults are unexampled and astounding. Never was there a story put together in such an inartificial, thoughtless, blundering way. It is little better than such a "concatenation accordingly" as satisfies one in a dream. It is not merely that everything is brought about by such sudden apparitions and transformations as only happen at the call of Harlequin's wand. Of this the author himself seems to be sensible, from a sort of defence which he sets up in one place: "Nor can I go on," he observes, after one of his sharp turns, "without a reflection on these accidental meetings which, though they happen every day, seldom excite our surprise but upon some extraordinary occasion. To what a fortuitous occurrence do we not owe every pleasure and convenience of our lives! How many seeming accidents must unite before we can be clothed or fed! The peasant must be disposed to labour, the shower must fall, the wind fill the merchant's sail, or numbers must want the usual supply." But, in addition to this, probability, or we might almost say possibility, is violated at every step with little more hesitation or compunction than in a fairy tale. Nothing happens, nobody acts, as things would happen, and as men and women would naturally act, in real life. Much of what goes on is entirely incredible and incomprehensible. Even the name of the book seems an absurdity. The Vicar leaves Wakefield in the beginning of the third chapter, and, it must be supposed, resigns his vicarage, of which we hear no more; yet the family is called the family of Wakefield throughout. This is of a piece with the famous bull that occurs in the ballad given in a subsequent chapter:—

> The dew, the blossoms on the tree,
> With charms *inconstant* shine;
> Their charms were his, but, woe to me,
> Their *constancy* was mine.

But why does the vicar, upon losing his fortune, give up his vicarage? Why, in his otherwise reduced circumstances, does he prefer a curacy of fifteen pounds to a vicarage of thirty-five? Are we expected to think this quite a matter of course (there is not a syllable of explanation), upon the same principle on which we are called upon to believe that he was overwhelmed with surprise at finding his old friend Wilmot not to be a monogamist? —the said friend being at that time actually courting a fourth wife. And it is all in the same strain. The whole story of the two Thornhills, the uncle and nephew, is a heap of contradictions and absurdities. Sir William Thornhill is universally known;

and yet in his assumed character of Burchell, without even, as far as appears, any disguise of his person, he passes undetected in a familiar intercourse of months with the tenantry of his own estate. If, indeed, we are not to understand something even beyond this—that, while all the neighbours know him to be Sir William, the Primroses alone never learn that fact, and still continue to take him for Mr. Burchell. But what, after all, is Burchell's real history? Nothing that is afterwards stated confirms or explains the intimation he is made unintentionally to let fall in one of the commencing chapters, about his early life. How, by-the-by, does the vicar come to know, a few chapters afterwards, that Burchell has really been telling his own story in the account he had given of Sir William Thornhill? Compare chapters third and sixth. But, take any view we will, the uncle's treatment of his nephew remains unaccounted for. Still more unintelligible is his conduct in his self-adopted capacity of lover of one of the vicar's daughters, and guardian of the virtue and safety of both. The plainest, easiest way of saving them from all harm and all danger stares him in the face, and for no reason that can be imagined he leaves them to their fate. As for his accidental rescue of Sophia afterwards, the whole affair is only to be matched for wildness and extravagance in Jack the Giant-killer or some other of that class of books. It is beyond even the Doctor of Divinity appearing at the fair with his horse to sell, and in the usual forms putting him through all his paces. But it is impossible to enumerate all the improbabilities with which the story is filled. Every scene, without any exception, in which the squire appears involves something out of nature or which passes understanding:—his position in reference to his uncle in the first place, the whole of his intercourse with the clergyman's family, his dining with them attended by his two women and his troop of servants in their one room, at other times his association there with young farmer Williams (suddenly provided by the author when wanted as a suitor for Olivia), the unblushing manner in which he makes his infamous proposals, the still more extraordinary indulgence with which they are forgiven and forgotten, or rather forgotten without his ever having asked or dreamt of asking forgiveness, all his audacious ruffianism in his attempts to possess himself of the two sisters at once, and finally, and above all, his defence of himself to his uncle at their meeting in the prison, which surely outruns anything ever before attempted in decent prose or rhyme. Nor must that superlative pair of lovers, the vicar's eldest son George and Miss Arabella Wilmot, be overlooked, with the singularly cool and easy way in which they pass from the most violent affection to the most entire indifference, and on the lady's part even transference of hand and heart to another, and back again as suddenly to mutual transport and confidence. If Goldsmith intended George for a representation of himself (as their adventures are believed to have been in some respects the same), we should be sorry to think the likeness a good one; for he is the most disagreeable character in the book. His very existence seems to have been entirely forgotten by his family, and by the author, for the first three years after he left home; and the story would have been all the better if he had never chanced to turn up again, or to be thought of, at all. Was ever such a letter read as the one he is made in duty and affection to write to his father in the twenty-eighth chapter! Yet there is that in the book which makes all this comparatively of little consequence; the inspiration and vital power of original genius, the charm of true feeling, some portion of the music of the great hymn of nature made audible to all hearts. Notwithstanding all its improbabilities, the story not only amuses us while we read, but takes root in the memory and affections as much almost as any story that was ever written. In truth, the critical objections to which it is obnoxious hardly affect its real merits and the proper sources of its interest. All of it that is essential lies in the development of the characters of the good vicar and his family, and they are one and all admirably brought out. He himself, simple and credulous, but also learned and clear-headed, so guileless and affectionate, sustaining so well all fortunes, so great both in suffering and in action, altogether so unselfish and noble-minded; his wife, of a much coarser grain, with her gooseberry-wine, and her little female vanities and schemes of ambition, but also made respectable by her love and reverence for her husband, her pride in, if not affection for, her children, her talent of management and housewifery, and the fortitude and resignation with which she too bears her part in their common calamities; the two girls, so unlike and yet so sister-like; the inimitable Moses, with his black ribbon, and his invincibility in argument and bargain-making; nor to be omitted the chubby-cheeked rogue little Bill, and the "honest veteran" Dick; the homely happiness of that fireside, upon which worldly misfortune can cast hardly a passing shadow; their little concerts, their dances; neighbour Flamborough's two rosy daughters, with their red top-knots; Moses's speculation in the green spectacles, and the vicar's own subsequent adventure (though running somewhat into the extravaganza style) with the same venerable arch-rogue, "with grey hair, and no flaps to his pocket-holes;" the immortal family picture; and, like a sudden thunderbolt falling in the sunshine, the flight of poor passion-driven Olivia, her few distracted words as she stept into the chaise, "O! what will my poor papa do when he knows I am undone!" and the heart-shivered old man's cry of anguish—"Now, then, my children, go and be miserable; for we shall never enjoy one hour more;" —these, and other incidents and touches of the same kind, are the parts of the book that are remembered; all the rest drops off, as so much mere husk, or other extraneous enwrapment, after we have read it; and out of these we reconstruct the story, if we will have one, for ourselves, or, what is better, rest satisfied with the good we have got, and do not mind though so much truth and beauty will not take the shape of a story, which is after all the source of pleasure even in a work of fiction which is of the lowest importance, for it scarcely lasts after the first reading. Part of the charm of this novel of Goldsmith's too consists in the art of writing which he has displayed in it. The style, always easy, transparent, harmonious, and expressive, teems with felicities in the more heightened passages. And, finally, the humour of the book is all good-humour. There is scarcely a touch of ill-nature or even of satire in it from beginning to end— nothing of either acrimony or acid. Johnson has well characterized Goldsmith in his epitaph as *sive risus essent movendi sive lacrymæ, affectuum potens at lenis dominator*—a ruler of our affections, and mover alike of our laughter and our tears, as gentle as he is prevailing. With all his loveable qualities, he had also many weaknesses and pettinesses of personal character; but his writings are as free from any ingredient of malignity, either great or small, as those of any man. As the author, too, of the Traveller and the Deserted Village, published in 1765 and 1771, Goldsmith, who lived till 1774, holds a distinguished place among the poetical writers of the middle portion of the last century. He had not the skyey fancy of his predecessor Collins, but there is an earnestness and cordiality in his poetry which the school of Pope, to which, in its form at least, it belongs, had scarcely before reached, and which make it an appropriate prelude to the more fervid song that was to burst forth among us in another generation.

CHURCHILL.

But perhaps the writer who, if not by what he did himself, yet by the effects of his example, gave the greatest impulse to our poetry at this time, was Churchill. Charles Churchill, born in 1731, published his first poem, The Rosciad, in 1761; and the rest of his pieces, his Apology to the Critical Reviewers—his epistle to his friend Lloyd, entitled Night—The Ghost, eventually extended to four Books—The Prophecy of Famine—his Epistle to Hogarth—The Conference—The Duellist—The Author—Gotham, in three Books—The Candidate—The Farewell—The Times—Independence—all within the next three years and a half. He was suddenly carried off by an attack of fever in November, 1764. If we put aside Thomson, Churchill, after all deductions, may be pronounced, looking to the quantity as well as the quality of his productions, to be the most considerable figure that appears in our poetry in the half-century from Pope to Cowper. But that is, perhaps, rather to say little for the said half-century than much for Churchill. All that he wrote being not only upon topics of the day, but addressed to the most sensitive or most excited passions of the mob of readers, he made an immense impression upon his contemporaries, which, however, is now worn very faint. Some looked upon him as Dryden come to life again, others as a greater than Dryden. As for Pope, he was generally thought to be quite outshone or eclipsed by the new satirist. Yet Churchill, in truth, with great rhetorical vigour and extraordinary fluency, is wholly destitute of either poetry or wit of any high order. He is only, at the most, a better sort of Cleveland, not certainly having more force or pungency than that old writer, but a freer flow and broader sweep in his satire. Of the true fervour and fusing power of Dryden he has nothing, any more than he has of what is best and most characteristic in Pope, to whose wit his stands in the relation or contrast of a wooden pin to a lancet. The most successful ten continuous lines he ever wrote in the same style are certainly not worth the ten worst of Pope's. But, indeed, he scarcely has anywhere ten lines, or two lines, without a blemish. In reading Pope, the constant feeling is that, of its kind, nothing could be better; in reading Churchill, we feel that nearly everything might be better, that, if the thought is good, the setting is defective, but generally that, whatever there may be of merit in either, there are flaws in both.

FALCONER; BEATTIE; MASON.

To the present date belongs Falconer's pleasing descriptive poem, The Shipwreck, the truth, nature, and pathos of which, without much imaginative adornment, have made it a general favourite.

It was first published in 1762, and its author, who was a native of Scotland, was lost at sea in 1769, in his thirty-ninth year. Another poem of this age, by a countryman of Falconer's, is Beattie's Minstrel, the first book of which was published in 1770, the second in 1774. The Minstrel is an harmonious and eloquent composition, glowing with poetical sentiment; but its inferiority in the highest poetical qualities may be felt by comparing it with Thomson's Castle of Indolence, which is perhaps the other work in the language which it most nearly resembles, but which yet it resembles much in the same way as gilding does solid gold, or as coloured water might be made to resemble wine. We may also notice the celebrated Heroic Epistle to Sir William Chambers, which, with several other effusions in the same vein, appeared in 1773, and is now known to have been, what it was always suspected to be, the composition of Gray's friend, Mason, who commenced poet so early as 1748 by the publication of a satire on the University of Oxford, entitled Isis, and afterwards produced his tragedies of Elfrida in 1752 and Caractacus in 1759, and the four Books of his English Garden in 1772, 1777, 1779, and 1781, besides a number of odes and other shorter pieces, some of them not till towards the close of the century. Mason, who died, at the age of seventy-two, in 1797, enjoyed in his day a great reputation, which is now become very small. His satiric verse is in the manner of Pope, but without the wit; and the staple of the rest of his poetry too is mostly words.

THE WARTONS; PERCY; CHATTERTON; MACPHERSON.

There is much more of fancy and true poetry, though less sound and less pretension, in the compositions of Thomas Warton, who first made himself known by a spirited reply to Mason's Isis in 1749, when he was only a young man of twenty-one, and afterwards produced many short pieces, all evidencing a genuine poetic eye and taste. Thomas Warton, however, who lived till 1790, chiefly owes the place he holds in our literature to his prose works—his Observations on the Fairy Queen, his edition of the Minor Poems of Milton, and, above all, his admirable History of English Poetry, which, unfinished as it is, is still perhaps our greatest work in the department of literary history. Of the three quarto volumes the first appeared in 1774, the second in 1778, the last in 1781. Dr. Joseph Warton, the elder brother of Thomas, is also the writer of some agreeable verses; but the book by which his name will live is his Essay on the

Genius and Writings of Pope, the first volume of which was published, anonymously, in 1756, the second not till 1782. He died in 1800, in his seventy-eighth year.

The Wartons may be regarded as the founders of a new school of poetic criticism in this country, which, romantic rather than classical in its spirit (to employ a modern nomenclature), and professing to go to nature for its principles instead of taking them on trust from the practice of the Greek and Roman poets, or the canons of their commentators, assisted materially in guiding as well as strengthening the now reviving love for our older national poetry. But perhaps the publication which was as yet at once the most remarkable product of this new taste, and the most effective agent in its diffusion, was Percy's celebrated Reliques of Ancient English Poetry, which first appeared in 1765. The reception of this book was the same that what is natural and true always meets with when brought into fair competition with the artificial; that is to say, when the latter is no longer new any more than the former:—

> " As one who, long in populous city pent,
> Forth issuing on a summer's morn to breathe
> Among the pleasant villages and farms
> Adjoined, from each thing met conceives delight,
> The smell of grain, or tedded grass, or kine,
> Or dairy, each rural sight, each rural sound ;"

such pleasure took the reader of those rude old ballads in their simplicity, directness, and breezy freshness and force, thus suddenly coming upon him after being sated with mere polish and ornament. And connected with the same matter is the famous imposture of Rowley's poems, by which a boy of seventeen, the marvellous Chatterton, deceived in the first instance a large portion of the public, and, after the detection of the fraud, secured to himself a respectable place among the original poets of his country. Chatterton, who terminated his existence by his own hand in August, 1770, produced the several imitations of ancient English poetry which he attributed to Thomas Rowley, a monk of the fifteenth century, in that and the preceding year. But this was the age of remarkable forgeries of this description: Chatterton's poems of Rowley having been preceded, and perhaps in part suggested, by Macpherson's poems of Ossian. The first specimens of the latter were published in 1760, under the title of Fragments of Ancient Poetry, collected in the Highlands of Scotland, and translated from the Gaelic or Erse language; and they immediately excited both an interest and a controversy, neither the one nor the other of which has quite died away even to the present hour. One circumstance, which has contributed to keep up the dispute about Ossian so much longer than that about Rowley, no doubt, is, that there was some small portion of truth mixed up with Macpherson's deception, whereas there was none at all in Chatterton's; but the Ossianic poetry, after all that has been said about its falsehood of style and substance as well as of pretension, making it out to be thus a double lie, must still have some qualities wonderfully adapted to allure the popular taste. Both Chatterton and Macpherson wrote a quantity of modern English verse in their own names; but nothing either did in this way was worth much: they evidently felt most at ease in their masks.

Dramatic Writers.

The dramatic literature of the earlier part of the reign of George III. is very voluminous, but consists principally of comedies and farces of modern life, all in prose. Home, indeed, the author of Douglas, which came out in 1757, followed that first successful effort by about half a dozen other attempts in the same style, the last of which, entitled Alfred, was produced in 1778; but they were all failures. Horace Walpole's great tragedy, the Mysterious Mother, although privately printed in 1768, was never acted, and was not even published till many years after. The principal writers whose productions occupied the stage were Goldsmith, Garrick, and Foote, who all died in the earlier part of the reign of George III.; and Macklin, Murphy, Cumberland, Colman, Mrs. Cowley, and Sheridan, who mostly survived till after the commencement of the present century. Goldsmith's two capital comedies of the Good-Natured Man, and She Stoops to Conquer, were brought out, the former in 1768, the latter in 1773. But the most brilliant contributions made to our dramatic literature in this age were Sheridan's celebrated comedies of The Rivals, brought out in 1775, when the author was only in his twenty-fifth year, The Duenna, which followed the same year, and The School for Scandal, which crowned the reputation of the modern Congreve, in 1777. After all that had been written, indeed, meritoriously enough in many instances, by his contemporaries and immediate predecessors, these plays of Sheridan's were the only additions that had yet been made to the classic comedy of Congreve, Vanbrugh, and Farquhar; and perhaps we may say that they are still the last it has received. Sheridan's wit is as polished as Congreve's, and its flashes, if not quite so quick and dazzling, have a softer, a more liquid light;

he may be said to stand between the highly artificial point and concentration of Congreve and the Irish ease and gaiety of Farquhar, wanting, doubtless, what is most characteristic of either, but also combining something of each. Sheridan had likewise produced all his other dramatic pieces—The Trip to Scarborough, The Critic, &c.—before 1780; although he lived for thirty-six years after that date.

FEMALE WRITERS.

The direction of so large a portion of the writing talent of this age to the comic drama is an evidence of the extended diffusion of literary tastes and accomplishments among the class most conversant with those manners and forms of social life which chiefly supply the materials of modern comedy. To this period has been sometimes assigned the commencement of the pursuit of literature as a distinct profession in England; now, too, we may say, began its domestic cultivation among us—the practice of writing for the public as the occupation and embellishment of a part of that leisure which necessarily abounds in an advanced state of society, not only among persons possessing the means of living without exertion of any kind, but almost throughout the various grades of those who are merely raised above the necessity of labouring with their hands. Another indication of the same thing is the great increase that now took place in the number of female authors. To the names of Mrs. Cowley, Mrs. Sheridan, Mrs. Brooke, Mrs. Lennox, Miss Sophia Lee, and Miss Frances Burney, afterwards Madame D'Arblay, whose two first novels of Evelina and Cecilia appeared, the former in 1777, the latter in 1782, may be added, as distinguished in other kinds of writing than plays and novels, blind Anna Williams, Dr. Johnson's friend, whose volume of Miscellanies in prose and verse was published in 1766; the learned Miss Elizabeth Carter, whose translation of Epictetus, however, and we believe all her other works, had appeared before the commencement of the reign of George III., although she lived till the year 1806; her friend Miss Catherine Talbot, the writer of a considerable quantity both of prose and verse, now forgotten; Mrs. Montagu (originally Miss Elizabeth Robinson), the pupil of Dr. Conyers Middleton, and the founder of the Blue Stocking Club, whose once famous Essay on the Writings and Genius of Shakespeare was published in 1769, and who survived till the year 1800; Mrs. Chapone (Miss Hester Mulso), another friend of Miss Carter, and the favourite correspondent of Samuel Richardson, whose Letters on the Improvement of the

Mind appeared in 1773; Mrs. Macaulay (originally Miss Catherine Sawbridge, finally Mrs. Graham), the notorious republican historian and pamphleteer, whose History of England from the Accession of James I. to the Restoration was published in a succession of volumes between the years 1763 and 1771, and then excited much attention, though now neglected; and the other female democratic writer, Miss Helen Maria Williams, who did not, however, begin to figure as a politician till after the French Revolution, her only publications that fall to be noticed in this place being some volumes of verse which she gave to the world in 1782 and the two or three following years. Mrs. Hannah More, Mrs. Barbauld, Mrs. Charlotte Smith, Mrs. Inchbald, and some other female writers who did not obtain the height of their reputation till a later date, had also entered upon the career of authorship within the first quarter of a century of the reign of George III. And to the commencement of that reign is to be assigned perhaps the most brilliant contribution from a female pen that had yet been added to our literature, the collection of the Letters of Lady Mary Wortley Montagu, which, although written many years before, were first published in 1763, about a year after Lady Mary's death. The fourth volume, indeed, did not appear till 1767.

PERIODICAL ESSAYISTS.

To the latter part of the reign of George II. belongs the revival of the Periodical Essay, which formed so distinguishing a feature of our literature in the age of Anne. Political writing, indeed, in this form had been carried on from the era of the Examiner, and the Englishman, and the Freeholder, and Defoe's Review and Mercator, and the British Merchant, with little, if any intermission, in various publications; the most remarkable being The Craftsman, in which Bolingbroke was the principal writer, and the papers of which, as first collected and reprinted in seven volumes, extend from the 5th of December, 1726, to the 22nd of May, 1731; nor was the work dropped till it had gone on for some years longer. Some attempts had even been made during this interval to supply the place of the Tatler, Spectator, and Guardian, by periodical papers, ranging, in the same strain, over the general field of morals and manners: Ambrose Philips, for instance, and a number of his friends, in the year 1718 began the publication of a paper entitled "The Free-thinker, or Essays on Ignorance, Superstition, Bigotry, Enthusiasm, Craft, &c., intermixed with several pieces of wit and humour designed to restore the deluded part of mankind to the use of reason and common sense," which attracted considerable attention at the time, and was kept up till the numbers made a book of three volumes, which were more than once reprinted. The Museum was another similar work, which commenced in 1746, and also ran to three volumes—Horace Walpole, Akenside, the two Wartons, and other eminent writers being among the contributors; but nothing of this kind that was then produced has succeeded in securing for itself a permanent place in our literature. The next of our periodical works after The Guardian that is recognized as one of the classics of the language is The Rambler, the first number of which appeared on Tuesday, the 20th of March, 1750, the last (the 208th) on Saturday, the 14th of March, 1752, and all the papers of which, at the rate of two a week, with the exception only of three or four, were the composition of Samuel Johnson, who may be said to have first become generally known as a writer through this publication. The Rambler was succeeded by The Adventurer, edited and principally written by Dr. Hawkesworth, which was also published twice a week, the first number having appeared on Tuesday, the 7th of November, 1752, the last (the 139th) on Saturday, the 9th of March, 1754. Meanwhile The World, a weekly paper, had been started under the conduct of Edward Moore, the author of the Fables for the Female Sex, the tragedy of The Gamester and other dramatic productions, assisted by Lord Lyttelton, the Earls of Chesterfield, Bath, and Cork, Horace Walpole, Soame Jenyns, and other contributors: the first number appeared on Thursday, the 4th of January, 1753; the 209th, and last, on the 30th of December, 1756. And contemporary with The World, during a part of this space, was The Connoisseur, established and principally written by George Colman, in conjunction with Bonnell Thornton, a writer possessed of considerable wit and humour, which, however, he dissipated for the most part upon ephemeral topics, being only now remembered for his share in a translation of Plautus, also undertaken in concert with his friend Colman, the first two of the five volumes of which were published in 1766, two years before his death, at the age of forty-four. The Connoisseur was, like The World, a weekly publication, and it was continued in 140 numbers, from Thursday, the 31st of January, 1754, to the 30th of September, 1756. Mrs. Frances Brooke's weekly periodical work entitled The Old Maid, which subsisted from November, 1755, to July in the following year, is not usually admitted into the collections of the English essayists. The next publication of this class which can be said still to hold a place in our literature is Johnson's Idler, which appeared once a week from Saturday, the 15th of April, 1758, to Saturday, the 5th of April, 1760. And with The Idler closes what may be called the second age of the English periodical essayists, which commences with The Rambler, and extends over the ten years from 1750 to 1760, the concluding decade of the reign of George II. After this occurs another long interval, in which that mode of writing was dropped, or at least no longer attracted either the favour of the public or the ambition of the more distinguished literary talent of the day; for no doubt attempts still continued to be made, with little or no success, by obscure scribblers, to keep up what had lately been so popular and so graced by eminent names. But we have no series of periodical papers of this time, of the same character with those already mentioned, that is still reprinted and read. Goldsmith's Citizen of the World, occupied as it is with the adventures and observations of an individual, placed in very peculiar circumstances, partakes more of the character of a novel than of a succession of miscellaneous papers; and both the letters composing that work and the other delightful essays of the same writer were published occasionally, not periodically or at regular intervals, and only as contributions to the newspapers or other journals of the day,—not by themselves, like the numbers of the Spectator, the Rambler, and the other works of that description that have been mentioned. Our next series of periodical essays, properly so called, was that which began to be published at Edinburgh, under the name of The Mirror, on Saturday, the 23rd of January, 1779, and was continued at the rate of a number a week till the 27th of May, 1780. The conductor and principal writer of The Mirror was the late Henry Mackenzie, who died in Edinburgh, at the age of eighty-six, in 1831, the author of The Man of Feeling, published anonymously in 1771, The Man of the World, 1773, and Julia de Roubigné, 1777, novels after the manner of Sterne, which are still universally read, and which have much of the grace and delicacy of style as well as of the pathos of that great master, although without any of his rich and peculiar humour. The Mirror was succeeded, after an interval of a few years, by The Lounger, also a weekly paper, the first number of which appeared on Saturday, the 5th of February, 1785, Mackenzie being again the leading contributor: the last (the 101st) on the 6th of January, 1787. But with these two publications the spirit of periodical essay-writing, in the style first made famous by Steele and Addison, expired also in Scotland, as it had already done a quarter of a century before in England.

POLITICAL WRITING.—WILKES; JUNIUS.

A hotter excitement, in truth, had dulled the public taste to the charms of those ethical and critical disquisitions, whether grave or gay, which it had heretofore found sufficiently stimulating; the violent war of parties, which, after a lull of nearly twenty years, was resumed on the accession of George III., made political controversy the only kind of writing that would now go down with the generality of readers; and first Wilkes's famous North Briton, and then the yet more famous Letters of Junius, came to take the place of the Ramblers and Idlers, the Adventurers and Connoisseurs. The North Briton, the first number of which appeared on Saturday, the 5th of June, 1762, was started in opposition to The Briton, a paper set up by Smollett in defence of the government on the preceding Saturday, the 29th of May, the day on which Lord Bute had been nominated first lord of the Treasury. Smollett and Wilkes had been friends up to this time; but the opposing papers were conducted in a spirit of the bitterest hostility, till the discontinuance of The Briton on the 12th of February, 1763, and the violent extinction of The North Briton on the 23rd of April following, fifteen days after the resignation of Bute, with the publication of its memorable "No. Forty-five." The celebrity of this one paper has preserved the memory of the North Briton to our day, in the same manner as in its own it produced several reimpressions of the whole work, which otherwise would probably have been as speedily and completely forgotten as the rival publication, and as the Auditors and Monitors, and other organs of the two factions, that in the same contention helped to fill the air with their din for a season, and then were heard of no more than any other quieted noise. Wilkes's brilliancy faded away when he proceeded to commit his thoughts to paper, as if it had dissolved itself in the ink. Like all convivial wits, or shining talkers, he was of course indebted for much of the effect he produced in society to the promptitude and skill with which he seized the proper moment for saying his good things, to the surprise produced by the suddenness of the flash, and to the characteristic peculiarities of voice, action, and manner with which the jest or repartee was set off, and which usually serve as signals or stimulants to awaken the sense of the ludicrous before its expected gratification comes; in writing, little or nothing of all this could be brought into play; but still some of Wilkes's colloquial impromptus that have been preserved are so perfect, considered in themselves, and without regard to the readiness with which they may have been struck out,—are so true and deep, and evince so keen a feeling at once of the ridiculous and of the real,—that one wonders at finding so little of the same kind of power in his more deliberate efforts. In all his published writings that we have looked into—and, what with essays, and pamphlets of one kind and another, they fill a good many volumes—we scarcely recollect anything that either in matter or manner rises above the veriest commonplace, unless perhaps it be a character of Lord Chatham, occurring in a letter addressed to the Duke of Grafton, some of the biting things in which are impregnated with rather a subtle venom. A few of his verses also have some fancy and elegance, in the style of Carew and Waller. But even his private letters, of which two collections have been published, scarcely ever emit a sparkle. And his House of Commons speeches, which he wrote beforehand and got by heart, are equally unenlivened. It is evident, indeed, that he had not intellectual lung enough for any protracted exertion or display. The soil of his mind was a hungry, unproductive gravel, with some gems imbedded in it. The author of the Letters of Junius made his *début* about four years after the expiration of The North Briton, what is believed to be his first communication having appeared in the Public Advertiser on the 28th of April, 1767; but the letters, sixty-nine in number, signed Junius, and forming the collection with which every reader is familiar, extend only over the space from the 21st of January, 1769, to the 2nd of November, 1771. Thus it appears that this celebrated writer had been nearly two years before the public before he attracted any considerable attention; a proof that the polish of his style was not really the thing that did most to bring him into notoriety; for, although we may admit that the composition of the letters signed Junius is more elaborate and sustained than that of the generality of his contributions to the same newspaper under the name of Brutus, Lucius, Atticus, and Mnemon, yet the difference is by no means so great as to be alone sufficient to account for the prodigious sensation at once excited by the former, after the slight regard with which the latter had been received for so long a time. What, in the first instance at least, more than his rhetoric, made the unknown Junius the object of universal interest, and of very general terror, was undoubtedly the quantity of secret intelligence he showed himself to be possessed of, combined with the unscrupulous boldness with which he was evidently prepared to use it. As has been observed, "ministers found, in these letters, proofs of some enemy, some spy, being amongst them." It was immediately perceived in the highest circle of political society that the writer was either actually one of the members of the government, or a person who by some means or other had found access to the secrets of the government. And this suspicion, generally diffused, would add tenfold interest to the mystery of the authorship of the letters, even where the feeling which it had excited was one of mere curiosity, as it would be, of course, with the mass of the public. But, although it was not his style alone, or even chiefly, that made Junius famous, it is probably that, more than anything else, which has preserved his fame to our day. More even than the secret, so long in being penetrated, of his real name: that might have given occasion to abundance of conjecture and speculation, like the problem of the Iron Mask and other similar enigmas; but it would not have prompted the reproduction of the letters in innumerable editions, and made them, what they long were, one of the most popular and generally read books in the language, retaining their hold upon the public mind to a degree which perhaps never was equalled by any other literary production having so special a reference, in the greater part of it, to topics of a temporary nature. The history of literature attests, as has been well remarked, that power of expression is a surer preservative of a writer's popularity than even strength of thought itself; that a book in which the former exists in a remarkable degree is almost sure to live, even if it should have very little else to recommend it. The style of Junius is wanting in some of the more exquisite qualities of eloquent writing; it has few natural graces, little variety, no picturesqueness; but still it is a striking and peculiar style, combining the charm of high polish with great nerve and animation, clear and rapid, and at the same time sonorous,—masculine enough, and yet making a very imposing display of all the artifices of antithetical rhetoric. As for the spirit of these famous compositions, it is a remarkable attestation to the author's power of writing that they were long universally regarded as dictated by the very genius of English liberty, and as almost a sort of Bible, or heaven-inspired exposition, of popular principles and rights. They contain, no doubt, many sound maxims, tersely and vigorously expressed; but of profound or farsighted political philosophy, or even of ingenious disquisition having the semblance of philosophy, there is as little in the Letters of Junius as there is in the Diary of Dodington or of Pepys; and, as for the writer's principles, they seem to be as much the product of mere temper, and of his individual animosities and spites, as even of his partisan habits and passions. He defends the cause of liberty itself in the spirit of tyranny; there is no generosity, or even common fairness, in his mode of combating; the newest lie, or private scandal, of the day serves as well, and as frequently, as anything else to point his sarcasm, or to arm with its vivid lightning the thunder of declamatory invective that resounds through his pages.

JOHNSON.

The character of Junius was drawn, while the mysterious shadow was still occupying the public gaze with its handwriting upon the wall, by one of the most distinguished of his contemporaries, in a publication which made a considerable noise at the time, but is now very much forgotten:—"Junius has sometimes made his satire felt; but let not injudicious admiration mistake the venom of the shaft for the vigour of the bow. He has sometimes sported with lucky malice; but to him that knows his company it is not hard to be sarcastic in a mask. While he walks, like Jack the Giant-killer, in a coat of darkness, he may do much mischief with little strength. . . . . . Junius burst into notice with a blaze of impudence which has rarely glared upon the world before, and drew the rabble after him as a monster makes a show. When he had once provided for his safety by impenetrable secrecy, he had nothing to combat but truth and justice—enemies whom he knows to be feeble in the dark. Being then at liberty to indulge himself in all the immunities of invisibility; out of the reach of danger, he has been bold; out of the reach of shame, he has been confident. As a rhetorician, he has had the art of persuading when he seconded desire; as a reasoner, he has convinced those who had no doubt before; as a moralist, he has taught that virtue may disgrace; and, as a patriot, he has gratified the mean by insults on the high. Finding sedition ascendant, he has been able to advance it; finding the nation combustible, he has been able to inflame it. . . . . It is not by his liveliness of imagery, his pungency of periods, or his fertility of allusions that he detains the cits of London and the boors of Middlesex. Of style and sentiment they take no cognizance: they admire him for virtues like their own, for contempt of order and violence of outrage, for rage of defamation and audacity of falsehood. . . . . Junius is an unusual phenomenon, on which some have gazed with wonder, and some with terror; but wonder and terror are transitory passions. He will soon be more closely viewed, or more attentively examined; and what folly has taken for a comet, that from his flaming hair shook pestilence and war, inquiry will find to be only a meteor formed by the vapours of putrefying democracy, and kindled into flame by the effervescence of interest struggling with conviction; which, after having plunged its followers into a bog, will leave us inquiring why we regard it." Thus wrote, in his ponderous but yet vigorous way, Samuel Johnson, in his pamphlet entitled Thoughts on the late Transactions respecting Falkland's Islands, published in 1771, in answer, as is commonly stated, to Junius's Forty-second Letter, dated the 30th of January in that year. Junius, although he continued to write for a twelvemonth longer, never took any notice of this attack; and Mrs. Piozzi tells us that Johnson "often delighted his imagination with the thoughts of having destroyed Junius." The lively lady, however, is scarcely the best authority on the subject of Johnson's *thoughts*, although we may yield a qualified faith to her reports of what he actually said and did. He may, probably enough, have thought, and said too, that he had beaten or silenced Junius, referring to the question discussed in his unanswered pamphlet; although, on the other hand, it does not appear that Junius was in the habit of ever noticing such general attacks as this: he replied to some of the writers who addressed him in the columns of the Public Advertiser, the newspaper in which his own communications were published, but he did not think it necessary to go forth to battle with any of the other pamphleteers by whom he was assailed, any more than with Johnson.

The great lexicographer winds up his character of Junius by remarking that he cannot think his style secure from criticism, and that his expressions are often trite, and his periods feeble. The style of Junius, nevertheless, was probably to a considerable extent formed upon Johnson's own. It had some strongly marked features of distinction, but yet it resembles the Johnsonian style much more than it does that of any other writer in the language antecedent to Johnson. Born in 1709, Johnson, after having while still resident in the country commenced his connexion with the press by some work in the way of translation and magazine writing, came to London along with his friend and pupil, the afterwards celebrated David Garrick, in March, 1737; and forthwith entered upon a career of authorship which extends over nearly half a century. His poem of London, an imitation of the Third Satire of Juvenal, appeared in 1738; his Life of Savage, in a separate form, in 1744 (having been previously published in the Gentleman's Magazine); his poem entitled The Vanity of Human Wishes, an imitation of Juvenal's Tenth Satire, in 1749; his tragedy of Irene (written before he came up to London) the same year; The Rambler, as already mentioned, between March, 1750, and March, 1752; his Dictionary of the English Language in 1755; The Idler between April, 1758, and April, 1760; his Rasselas in 1759; his edition of Shakespeare in 1765; his Journey to the Western Islands of Scotland in 1775; his Lives of the Poets in 1781; the intervals between these more remarkable efforts having given birth to many magazine articles, verses, and pamphlets, which cannot be here enumerated. His death took place on the 13th of December, 1784. All the works the titles of which have been given may be regarded as having taken and kept their places in our standard literature; and they form, in quantity at least, a respectable contribution from a single mind. But Johnson's mind is scarcely seen at its brightest if we do not add to the productions of his own pen the record of his colloquial wit and eloquence preserved by his admirable biographer, Boswell, whose renowned work first appeared, in two volumes quarto, in 1790; having, however, been preceded by the Journal of the Tour to the Hebrides, which was published the year after Johnson's death. It has been remarked, with truth, that his own works and Boswell's Life of him together have preserved a more complete portraiture of Johnson, of his intellect, his opinions, his manners, his whole man inward and outward, than has been handed down from one age to another of any other individual that ever lived. Certainly no celebrated figure of any past time still stands before our eyes so distinctly embodied as he does. If we will try, we shall find that all others are shadows, or mere outlines, in comparison; or, they seem to skulk about at a distance in the shade, while he is there fronting us in the full daylight, so that we see not only his worsted stockings and the metal buttons on his brown coat, but every feature of that massive countenance, as it is solemnized by meditation or lighted up in social converse, as his whole frame rolls about in triumphant laughter, or, as Cumberland saw the tender-hearted old man, standing beside his friend Garrick's open grave, at the foot of Shakespeare's monument, and bathed in tears. A noble heroic nature was that of this Samuel Johnson, beyond all controversy: not only did his failings lean to virtue's side—his very intellectual weaknesses and prejudices had something in them of strength and greatness; they were the exuberance and excess of a rich mind, not the stinted growth of a poor one. There was no touch of meanness in him: rude and awkward enough he was in many points of mere demeanour, but he had the soul of a prince in real generosity, refinement, and elevation. Of a certain kind of intellectual faculty, also, his endowment was very high. His quickness of penetration, and readiness in every way, were probably as great as had ever been combined with the same solid qualities of mind. Scarcely before had there appeared so thoughtful a sage, and so grave a moralist, with so agile and sportive a wit. Rarely has so prompt and bright a wit been accompanied by so much real knowledge, sagacity, and weight of matter. But, as we have intimated, this happy union of opposite kinds of power was most complete, and only produced its full effect, in his colloquial displays, when, excited and unformalized, the man was really himself, and his strong nature forced its way onward without regard to anything but the immediate object to be achieved. In writing he is still the strong man, working away valiantly, but, as it were, with fetters upon his limbs, or a burden on his back; a sense of the conventionalities of his position seems to oppress him; his style becomes artificial and ponderous; the whole process of his intellectual exertion loses much of its elasticity and life; and, instead of hard blows and flashes of flame, there is too often, it must be confessed, a more raising of clouds of dust and the din of inflated commonplace. Yet, as a writer, too, there is much in Johnson that is of no common character. It cannot be said that the world is indebted to him for many new truths, but he has given novel and often forcible and elegant expression to some old ones; the spirit of his philosophy is never other than manly and high-toned, as well as moral; his critical speculations, if not always very profound, are frequently acute and ingenious, and in manner generally lively, not seldom brilliant. Indeed, it may be said of Johnson, with all his faults and shortcomings, as of every man of true genius, that he is rarely or ever absolutely dull. Even his Ramblers, which we hold to be the most indigestible of his productions, are none of them mere leather or prunello; and his higher efforts, his Rasselas, his Preface to Shakespeare, and many passages in his Lives of the Poets, are throughout instinct with animation, and full of an eloquence which sometimes rises almost to poetry. Even his peculiar style, whatever we may allege against it, bears the stamp of the man of genius; it was thoroughly his own; and it not only reproduced itself, with variations, in the writings of some of the most distinguished of his contemporaries, from Junius's Letters to Macpherson's Ossian, but, whether for good or for evil, has perceptibly influenced our literature, and even in some degree the progress of the language, onwards to the present day. Some of the characteristics of the Johnsonian style, no doubt, may be found in older writers, but, as a whole, it must be regarded as the invention of Johnson. No sentence-making at once so uniformly

clear and exact, and so elaborately stately, measured, and
sonorous, had proceeded habitually from any previous English
pen. The pomposity and inflation of Johnson's composition
abated considerably in his own later writings, and, as the
cumbering flesh fell off, the nerve and spirit increased: the
most happily executed parts of the Lives of the Poets offer almost
a contrast to the oppressive rotundity of the Ramblers, produced
thirty years before; and some eminent writers of a subsequent
date, who have yet evidently formed their style upon his, have
retained little or nothing of what, to a superficial inspection,
seem the most marked characteristics of his manner of expression. Indeed, as we have said, there is perhaps no subsequent
English prose-writer upon whose style that of Johnson has been
altogether without its effect.*

BURKE.

But the greatest, undoubtedly, of all our writers of this age
was Burke, one of the most remarkable men of any age.
Edmund Burke was born in Dublin, in 1730; but he came over
in 1750 to the British metropolis, and from this time he mostly
resided in England till his death, in 1797. In 1756 he published
his celebrated Vindication of Natural Society, an imitation of the
style, and a parody on the philosophy, of Lord Bolingbroke;
and the same year his Philosophical Inquiry into the Origin of
our Ideas of the Sublime and Beautiful. In 1757 appeared
anonymously his Account of the European Settlements in
America. In 1759 came out the first volume of The Annual
Register, of which he is known to have written, or superintended
the writing of, the historical part for several years. His public
life commenced in 1761, with the appointment of private secretary
to the chief secretary for Ireland, an office which carried him
back for about four years to his native country. In 1766 he
became a member of the English House of Commons; and from
that date almost to the hour of his death, besides his exertions as
a front figure in the debates and other business of parliament,
from which he did not retire till 1794, he continued to dazzle
the world by a succession of political writings such as certainly
had never before been equalled in brilliancy and power. We
can mention only those of greatest note:—his Thoughts on the

* Every reader who takes any interest in Johnson will remember the brilliant papers of Lord Macaulay in the Edinburgh Review, for September, 1831,
and Mr. Carlyle, in the twenty-eighth number of Fraser's Magazine, for
April, 1832.

Cause of the Present Discontents, published in 1770; his Reflections on the Revolution in France, published in 1790; his Appeal from the New to the Old Whigs, in 1792; his Letter to a Noble Lord on his Pension, in 1796; his Letters on a Regicide Peace, in 1796 and 1797; his Observations on the Conduct of the Minority, in 1797; besides his several great speeches, revised and sent to the press by himself; that on American Taxation, in 1774; that on Conciliation with America, in 1775; that on the Economical Reform Bill, in 1780; that delivered in the Guildhall at Bristol previous to his election, the same year; that on Mr. Fox's India Bill, in 1783; and that on the Nabob of Arcot's Debts, in 1785. These, perhaps the most splendid of all, which he delivered at the bar of the House of Lords in 1788 and 1789, on the impeachment of Mr. Hastings, have also been printed since his death from his own manuscript.

Burke was our first, and is still our greatest, writer on the philosophy of practical politics. The mere metaphysics of that science, or what we may call by that term for want of a better, meaning thereby all abstract speculation and theorizing on the general subject of government without reference to the actual circumstances of the particular country and people to be governed, he held from the beginning to the end of his life in undisguised, perhaps in undue, contempt. This feeling is as strongly manifested in his very first publication, his covert attack on Bolingbroke, as either in his writings and speeches on the contest with the American colonies or in those of the French Revolution. He was, as we have said, emphatically a practical politician, and, above all, an English politician. In discussing questions of domestic politics, he constantly refused to travel beyond the landmarks of the constitution as he found it established; and the views he took of the politics of other countries were as far as possible regulated by the same principle. The question of a revolution, in so far as England was concerned, he did not hold to be one with which he had anything to do. Not only had it never been actually presented to him by the circumstances of the time; he did not conceive that it ever could come before him. He was, in fact, no believer in the possibility of any sudden and complete re-edification of the institutions of a great country; he left such transformations to Harlequin's wand and the machinists of the stage; he did not think they could take place in a system so mighty and so infinitely complicated as that of the political organization of a nation. A constitution, too, in his idea, was not a thing, like a steam-engine, or a machine for threshing corn, that could be put together and set up in a few weeks or months, and that would work equally well wherever it was set up; he looked upon it rather as something that must in every case grow and gradually evolve itself out of the soil of the national mind and character, that must take its shape in a great measure from the prevalent habits and feelings to which it was to be accommodated, that would not work or stand at all unless it thus formed an integral part of the social system to which it belonged. The notion of a constitution artificially constructed, and merely as it were fastened upon a country by bolts and screws, was to him much the same as the notion of a human body performing the functions of life with no other than such a separable artificial head stuck upon it. A constitution was with him a thing of life. It could no more be set up of a sudden than a full-grown tree could be ordered from the manufacturer's and so set up. Like a tree, it must have its roots intertwisted with the earth on which it stands, even as it has its branches extended over it. In the great fields of politics and religion, occupied as they are with men's substantial interests, Burke regarded inquiries into first principles as worse than vain and worthless, as much more likely to mislead and pervert than to afford instruction or right guidance; and it is remarkable that this feeling, though deepened and strengthened by the experience of his after-life, and, above all, exasperated by the events to which his attention was most strongly directed in his latest days into an intense dread and horror of the confusion and wide-spread ruin that might be wrought by the assumption of so incompetent a power as mere human ratiocination to regulate all things according to its own conceit, was entertained and expressed by him with great distinctness at the outset of his career. It was in this spirit, indeed, that he wrote his Vindication of Natural Society, with the design of showing how anything whatever might be either attacked or defended with great plausibility by the method in which the highest and most intricate philosophical questions were discussed by Lord Bolingbroke. He "is satisfied," he says in his Preface, "that a mind which has no restraint from a sense of its own weakness, of its subordinate rank in the creation, and of the extreme danger of letting the imagination loose upon some subjects, may very plausibly attack everything the most excellent and venerable; that it would not be difficult to criticise the Creation itself; and that, if we were to examine the divine fabrics by our ideas of reason and fitness, and to use the same method of attack by which some men have assaulted revealed religion, we might, with as good colour, and with the same success, make the wisdom and power of God in his Creation appear to many no better than foolishness." But, on the other hand, within the boundary by which he conceived himself to be properly limited and restrained, there never was either a more ingenious and profound investigator or a bolder reformer than Burke. He had, indeed, more in him of the orator and of the poet than of the mere reasoner; but yet, like Bacon, whom altogether he greatly resembled in intellectual character, an instinctive sagacity and penetration generally led him to see where the truth lay, and then his boundless ingenuity supplied him readily with all the considerations and arguments which the exposition of the matter required, and the fervour of his awakened fancy with striking illustration and impassioned eloquence in a measure hardly to be elsewhere found intermingled and incorporated with the same profoundness, extent, and many-sidedness of view. For in this Burke is distinguished from nearly all other orators, and it is a distinction that somewhat interferes with his mere oratorical power, that he is both too reflective and too honest to confine himself to the contemplation of only one side of any question he takes up: he selects, of course, for advocacy and inculcation the particular view which he holds to be the sound one, and often it will no doubt be thought by those who dissent from him that he does not do justice to some of the considerations that stand opposed to his own opinion; but still it is not his habit to overlook such adverse considerations; he shows himself at least perfectly aware of their existence, even when he possibly underrates their importance. For the immediate effect of his eloquence, as we have said, it might have been better if his mind had not been so Argus-eyed to all the various conflicting points of every case that he discussed—if, instead of thus continually looking before and after on all sides of him, and stopping, whenever two or more apparently opposite considerations came in his way, to balance or reconcile them, he could have surrendered himself to the one view with which his hearers were prepared strongly to sympathise, and carried them along with him in a whirlwind of passionate declamation. But, "born for the universe," and for all time, he was not made for such sacrifice of truth, and all high, enduring things, to the triumph of an hour. And he has not gone without his well-earned reward. If it was objected to him in his own day that, "too deep for his hearers," he

"still went on refining,
And thought of convincing while they thought of dining,"

that searching philosophy which pervades his speeches and writings, and is there wedded in such happy union to glowing words and poetic imagery, has rescued them alone from the neglect and oblivion that have overtaken all the other oratory and political pamphleteering of that day, however more loudly lauded at the time, and has secured to them an existence as extended as that of the language, and to their eloquence and wisdom whatever admiration and whatever influence and authority they may be entitled to throughout all coming generations. The writings of Burke are, indeed, the only English political writings of a past age that continue to be read in the present. And they are now perhaps more studied, and their value, both philosophical and oratorical, better and more highly appreciated, than even when they were first produced. They were at first probably received, even by those who rated them highest and felt their power the most, as little more than mere party appeals—which, indeed, to a considerable extent most of them were, for their author, from the circumstances of his position and of the time, was of necessity involved in the great battle of faction which then drew into its maelstrom everything littlest and greatest, meanest and loftiest—and, as was his nature, he fought that fight, while that was the work to be done, like a man, with his whole heart, and mind, and soul, and strength. But it can hardly be said in prosaic verity, as it has been said in the liveliness and levity of verse, that he "to party gave up what was meant for mankind." He gave up nothing to his party, except his best exertions for the time being, and for the end immediately in view, while he continued to serve under its banner. He separated himself from his party, and even from the friends and associates with whom he had passed his life, when, whether rightly or wrongly, he conceived that a higher duty than that of fidelity to his party-banner called upon him to take that course. For that Burke, in leaving the ranks of the opposition in the year 1790, or rather in declining to go along with the main body of the opposition in the view which they took at that particular moment of the French Revolution, acted from the most conscientious motives and the strongest convictions, we may assume to be now completely admitted by all whose opinions anybody thinks worth regarding. The notion that he was bought off by the ministry —he who never to the end of his life joined the ministry, or ceased to express his entire disapprobation of their conduct of the war with France—he, by whom, in fact, they were controlled and coerced, not he by them—the old cry that he was paid to attack the French Revolution, by the pension, forsooth, that was bestowed upon him five years after—all this is now left to the rabid ignorance of your mere pothouse politician. Those who have really read and studied what Burke has written know that there was nothing new in the views he proclaimed after the breaking out of that mighty convulsion, nothing differing from or inconsistent with the principles and doctrines on the subject of government he had always held and expressed. In truth, he could not have joined in the chorus of acclamation with which Fox and many of his friends greeted the advent of the French Revolution without abandoning the political philosophy of his whole previous life. As we have elsewhere observed, "his principles were altogether averse from a purely democratic constitution of government from the first. He always, indeed, denied that he was a man of aristocratic inclinations, meaning by that one who favoured the aristocratic more than the popular element in the constitution: but he no more for all that ever professed any wish wholly to extinguish the former element than the latter..... The only respect in which his latest writings really differ from those of early date is, that they evince a more excited sense of the dangers of popular delusion and passion, and urge with greater earnestness the importance of those restraining institutions which the author conceives, and always did conceive, to be necessary for the stability of governments and the conservation of society. But this is nothing more than the change of topic that is natural to a new occasion."* Or, as he has himself finely said, in defending his own consistency—" A man, who, among various objects of his equal regard, is secure of some, and full of anxiety for the fate of others, is apt to go to much greater lengths in his preference of the objects of his immediate solicitude than Mr. Burke has ever done. A man so circumstanced often seems to undervalue, to vilify, almost to reprobate and disown, those that are out of danger. This is the voice of nature and truth, and not of inconsistency and false pretence. The danger of anything very dear to us removes, for the moment, every other affection from the mind. When Priam has his whole thoughts employed on the body of his Hector, he repels with indignation, and drives from him with a thousand reproaches, his surviving sons, who with an officious piety crowded about him to offer their assistance. A good critic would say that this is a masterstroke, and marks a deep understanding of nature in the father of poetry. He would despise a Zoilus, who would conclude

* Art. on Burke, in Penny Cyclopædia, vi. 35.

from this passage that Homer meant to represent this man of affliction as hating, or being indifferent and cold in his affections to, the poor relics of his house, or that he preferred a dead carcase to his living children."*

As a specimen of Burke's spoken eloquence we will give from his Speech on the case of the Nabob of Arcot, delivered in the House of Commons on the 28th of February, 1785, the passage containing the description of Hyder Ali's devastation of the Carnatic:—

When at length Hyder Ali found that he had to do with men who either would sign no convention, or whom no treaty and no signature could bind, and who were the determined enemies of human intercourse itself, he decreed to make the country possessed by these incorrigible and predestinated criminals a memorable example to mankind. He resolved, in the gloomy recesses of a mind capacious of such things, to leave the whole Carnatic an everlasting monument of vengeance, and to put perpetual desolation as a barrier between him and those against whom the faith which holds the moral elements of the world together was no protection. He became at length so confident of his force, so collected in his might, that he made no secret whatsoever of his dreadful resolution. Having terminated his disputes with every enemy, and every rival, who buried their mutual animosities in their common detestation against the creditors of the Nabob of Arcot,† he drew from every quarter whatever a savage ferocity could add to his new rudiments in the arts of destruction; and, compounding all the materials of fury, havoc, and desolation, into one black cloud, he hung for a while on the declivities of the mountains. Whilst the authors of all the evils were idly and stupidly gazing on this menacing meteor, which blackened all their horizon, it suddenly burst, and poured down the whole of its contents upon the plains of the Carnatic. Then ensued a scene of woe, the like of which no eye had seen, no heart conceived, and which no tongue can adequately tell. All the horrors of war before known or heard of were mercy to that new havoc. A storm of universal fire blasted every field, consumed every house, destroyed every temple. The miserable inhabitants, flying from their flaming villages, in part were slaughtered; others, without regard to sex, to age, to the respect of rank, or sacredness of function, fathers torn from children, husbands from wives, enveloped in a whirlwind of cavalry, and amidst the goading spears of drivers, and the trampling of pursuing horses, were swept into captivity in an unknown and hostile land. Those who were able to evade this tempest fled to the walled cities. But, escaping from fire, sword, and exile, they fell into the jaws of famine.

The alms of the settlement, in this dreadful exigency, were certainly liberal; and all was done by charity that private charity could do; but it

---

* Appeal from the New to the Old Whigs.
† The designs upon Hyder, which provoked this retaliation on his part, are represented in the speech as the scheme of the Nabob's English creditors.

was a people in beggary, a nation which stretched out its hands for food. For months together these creatures of sufferance, whose very excess and luxury in their most plenteous days had fallen short of the allowance of our austerest fasts, silent, patient, resigned, without sedition or disturbance, almost without complaint, perished by an hundred a day in the streets of Madras; every day seventy at least laid their bodies in the streets, or on the glacis of Tanjore, and expired of famine in the granary of India. I was going to awake your justice towards this unhappy part of our fellow-citizens by bringing before you some of the circumstances of this plague of hunger. Of all the calamities which beset and waylay the life of man, this comes the nearest to our heart, and is that wherein the proudest of us all feels himself to be nothing more than he is: but I find myself unable to manage it with decorum; these details are of a species of horror so nauseous and disgusting; they are so degrading to the sufferers and to the hearers; they are so humiliating to human nature itself; that, on better thoughts, I find it more advisable to throw a pall over this hideous object, and to leave it to your general conceptions.

For eighteen months without intermission, this destruction raged from the gates of Madras to the gates of Tanjore; and so completely did these masters in their art, Hyder Ali and his ferocious son, absolve themselves of their impious vow, that, when the British armies traversed, as they did, the Carnatic for hundreds of miles in all directions, through the whole line of their march they did not see one man, not one woman, not one child, not one four-footed beast of any description whatever. One dead, uniform silence reigned over the whole region.

It is a mistake to suppose that either imagination or passion is apt to become weaker as the other powers of the mind strengthen and acquire larger scope. The history of all the greatest poetical minds of all times and countries confutes this notion. Burke's imagination grew with his intellect, by which it was nourished, with his over-extending realm of thought, with his constantly increasing experience of life and knowledge of every kind; and his latest writings are his most splendid as well as his most profound. Undoubtedly the work in which his eloquence is at once the most highly finished, and the most impregnated with philosophy and depth of thought, is his Reflections on the French Revolution. But this work is so generally known, at least in its most striking passages, that we may satisfy ourselves with a single short extract:—

You will observe, that, from Magna Charta to the Declaration of Rights, it has been the uniform policy of our constitution to claim and assert our liberties as an *entailed inheritance*, derived to us from our forefathers, and to be transmitted to our posterity; as an estate specially belonging to the people of this kingdom, without any reference whatever to any other more general or prior right. By this means our constitution preserves an unity in so great a diversity of its parts. We have an inheritable crown; an inheritable peerage; and a House of Commons and a people inheriting privileges, franchises, and liberties from a long line of ancestors.

This policy appears to me to be the result of profound reflection; or rather the happy effect of following nature, which is wisdom without reflection, and above it. A spirit of innovation is generally the result of a selfish temper and confined views. People will not look forward to posterity, who never look backward to their ancestors. Besides, the people of England well know, that the idea of inheritance furnishes a sure principle of conservation, and a sure principle of transmission, without at all excluding a principle of improvement. It leaves acquisition free: but it secures what it acquires. Whatever advantages are obtained by a state proceeding on these maxims are locked fast as in a sort of family settlement: grasped as in a kind of mortmain for ever. By a constitutional policy, working after the pattern of nature, we receive, we hold, we transmit our government and our privileges, in the same manner in which we enjoy and transmit our property and our lives. The institutions of policy, the goods of fortune, the gifts of Providence, are handed down, to us and from us, in the same course and order. Our political system is placed in a just correspondence and symmetry with the order of the world, and with the mode of existence decreed to a permanent body composed of transitory parts; wherein, by the disposition of a stupendous wisdom, moulding together the great mysterious incorporation of the human race, the whole at one time is never old, or middle-aged, or young, but, in a condition of unchangeable constancy, moves on through the varied tenor of perpetual decay, fall, renovation, and progression. Thus, by preserving the method of nature in the conduct of the state, in what we improve we are never wholly new; in what we retain we are never wholly obsolete. By adhering in this manner, and on these principles, to our forefathers, we are guided, not by the superstition of antiquarians, but by the spirit of philosophic analogy. In this choice of inheritance we have given to our frame of polity the image of a relation in blood; binding up the constitution of our country with our dearest domestic ties; adopting our fundamental laws into the bosom of our family affections; keeping inseparable, and cherishing with the warmth of all their combined and mutually reflected charities, our state, our hearths, our sepulchres, and our altars.

Through the same plan of a conformity to nature in our artificial institutions, and by calling in the aid of her unerring and powerful instincts to fortify the fallible and feeble contrivances of our reason, we have derived several other, and those no small, benefits from considering our liberties in the light of an inheritance. Always acting as if in the presence of canonized forefathers, the spirit of freedom, leading in itself to misrule and excess, is tempered with an awful gravity. This idea of a liberal descent inspires us with a sense of habitual native dignity, which prevents that upstart insolence almost inevitably adhering to and disgracing those who are the first acquirers of any distinction. By this means our liberty becomes a noble freedom. It carries an imposing and majestic aspect. It has a pedigree and illustrating ancestors. It has its bearings and its ensigns armorial. It has its gallery of portraits; its monumental inscriptions; its records, evidences, and titles. We procure reverence to our civil institutions on the principle upon which nature teaches us to revere individual men; on account of their age, and on account of those from whom they are descended. All your sophisters cannot produce any thing better adapted to preserve a rational and manly freedom than the course that we have pursued, who have chosen our nature rather than our speculations, our breasts rather than our inventions, for the great conservatories and magazines of our rights and privileges.

The Reflections appeared in 1790. We shall not give any extract from the Letter to a Noble Lord on the attacks made upon him in the House of Lords by the Duke of Bedford and the Earl of Lauderdale, which, as it is one of the most eloquent and spirited, is also perhaps the most generally known of all Burke's writings. The following passage from another Letter, written in 1795 (the year before), to William Elliot, Esq., on a speech made in the House of Lords by the Duke of Norfolk, will probably be less familiar to many of our readers:—

I wish to warn the people against the greatest of all evils—a blind and furious spirit of innovation, under the name of reform. I was indeed well aware that power rarely reforms itself. So it is undoubtedly when all is quiet about it. But I was in hopes that provident fear might prevent fruitless penitence. I trusted that danger might produce at least circumspection; I flattered myself, in a moment like this, that nothing would be added to make authority top-heavy; that the very moment of an earthquake would not be the time chosen for adding a story to our houses. I hoped to see the surest of all reforms, perhaps the only sure reform, the ceasing to do ill. In the meantime, I wished to the people the wisdom of knowing how to tolerate a condition which none of their efforts can render much more than tolerable. It was a condition, however, in which every thing was to be found that could enable them to live to nature, and, if so they pleased, to live to virtue and to honour.

I do not repent that I thought better of those to whom I wished well than they will suffer me long to think that they deserved. Far from repenting, I would to God that new faculties had been called up in me, in favour not of this or that man, or this or that system, but of the general vital principle, that whilst in its vigour produced the state of things transmitted to us from our fathers; but which, through the joint operations of the abuses of authority and liberty, may perish in our hands. I am not of opinion that the race of men, and the commonwealths they create, like the bodies of individuals, grow effete, and languid, and bloodless, and ossify, by the necessities of their own conformation and the fatal operation of longevity and time. These analogies between bodies natural and politic, though they may sometimes illustrate arguments, furnish no argument of themselves. They are but too often used, under the colour of a specious philosophy, to find apologies for the despair of laziness and pusillanimity, and to excuse the want of all manly efforts when the exigencies of our country call for them most loudly.

How often has public calamity been arrested on the very brink of ruin by the seasonable energy of a single man! Have we no such man amongst us? I am as sure as I am of my being that one vigorous mind, without

2 E

office, without situation, without public functions of any kind (at a time when the want of such a thing is felt, as I am sure it is), I say, one such man, confiding in the aid of God, and full of just reliance in his own fortitude, vigour, enterprise, and perseverance, would first draw to him some few like himself, and then that multitudes, hardly thought to be in existence, would appear, and troop about him.

If I saw this auspicious beginning, baffled and frustrated as I am, yet, on the very verge of a timely grave, abandoned abroad and desolate at home, stripped of my boast, my hope, my consolation, my helper, my counsellor, and my guide (you know in part what I have lost, and would to God I could clear myself of all neglect and fault in that loss), yet thus, even thus, I would rake up the fire under all the ashes that oppress it. I am no longer patient of the public eye; nor am I of force to win my way, and to justle and elbow in a crowd. But, even in solitude, something may be done for society. The meditations of the closet have affected senates with a subtle frenzy, and inflamed armies with the brands of the furies. The cure might come from the same source with the distemper. I would add my part to those who would animate the people (whose hearts are yet right) to new exertions in the old cause.

Novelty is not the only source of zeal. Why should not a Maccabeus and his brethren arise to assert the honour of the ancient laws, and to defend the temple of their forefathers, with as ardent a spirit as can inspire any innovator to destroy the monuments of the piety and the glory of ancient ages? It is not a hazarded assertion, it is a great truth, that, when once things are gone out of their ordinary course, it is by acts out of the ordinary course they can alone be re-established. Republican spirit can only be combated by a spirit of the same nature: of the same nature, but informed with another principle, and pointed to another end. I would persuade a resistance both to the corruption and to the reformation that prevails. It will not be the weaker, but much the stronger, for combating both together. A victory over real corruptions would enable us to baffle the spurious and pretended reformations. I would not wish to excite, or even to tolerate, that kind of evil which invokes the powers of hell to rectify the disorders of the earth. No! I would add my voice, with better, and, I trust, more potent charms, to draw down justice, and wisdom, and fortitude from heaven, for the correction of human vice, and the recalling of human error from the devious ways into which it has been betrayed. I would wish to call the impulses of individuals at once to the aid and to the control of authority. By this, which I call the true republican spirit, paradoxical as it may appear, monarchies alone can be rescued from the imbecility of courts and the madness of the crowd. This republican spirit would not suffer men in high place to bring ruin on their country and on themselves. It would reform, not by destroying, but by saving the great, the rich, and the powerful. Such a republican spirit we, perhaps fondly, conceive to have animated the distinguished heroes and patriots of old, who knew no mode of policy but religion and virtue. These they would have paramount to all constitutions; they would not suffer monarchs, or senates, or popular assemblies, under pretences of dignity, or authority, or freedom, to shake off those moral riders which reason has appointed to govern every sort of rude power. These, in appearance loading them by their weight, do by that pressure augment their essential force. The momentum is increased by the extraneous weight. It is true in moral, as it is in mechanical science. It is true, not only in the draught but in the race. These riders of the great, in effect, hold the reins which guide them in their course, and wear the spur that stimulates them to the goals of honour and of safety. The great must submit to the dominion of prudence and of virtue, or none will long submit to the dominion of the great.

From the second of the Letters on a Regicide Peace, or to transcribe the full title, Letters addressed to a Member of the present Parliament on the Proposals for Peace with the Regicide Directory of France,* published in 1796, we give as our last extract the following remarkable observations on the conduct of the war:—

It is a dreadful truth, but it is a truth that cannot be concealed; in ability, in dexterity, in the distinctness of their views, the Jacobins are our superiors. They saw the thing right from the very beginning. Whatever were the first motives to the war among politicians, they saw that in its spirit, and for its objects, it was a *civil war*; and as such they pursued it. It is a war between the partisans of the ancient, civil, moral, and political order of Europe, against a sect of fanatical and ambitious atheists, which means to change them all. It is not France extending a foreign empire over other nations; it is a sect aiming at universal empire, and beginning with the conquest of France. The leaders of that sect secured the *centre of Europe*; and, that assured, they knew that, whatever might be the event of battles and sieges, their cause was victorious. Whether its territory had a little more or a little less pecled from its surface, or whether an island or two was detached from its commerce, to them was of little moment. The conquest of France was a glorious acquisition. That once well laid as a basis of empire, opportunities never could be wanting to regain or to replace what had been lost, and dreadfully to avenge themselves on the faction of their adversaries.

They saw it was a *civil war*. It was their business to persuade their adversaries that it ought to be a *foreign* war. The Jacobins everywhere set up a cry against the new crusade; and they intrigued with effect in the cabinet, in the field, and in every private society in Europe. Their task was not difficult. The condition of princes, and sometimes of first ministers too, is to be pitied. The creatures of the desk, and the creatures of favour, had no relish for the principles of the manifestoes.[1] They promised no governments, no regiments, no revenues from whence emoluments might arise by perquisite or by grant. In truth, the tribe of vulgar politicians are the lowest of our species. There is no trade so vile and mechanical as

---

* There are four Letters in all; of which the two first appeared in 1796 (a surreptitious edition being also brought out at the same time by Owen, a bookseller of Piccadilly), the third was passing through the press when Burke died, in July, 1797, and the fourth, which is unfinished, and had been written, so far as it goes, before the three others, after his death.

[1] Of the Emperor and the King of Prussia, published in August, 1792.

government in their hands. Virtue is not their habit. They are out of themselves in any course of conduct recommended only by conscience and glory. A large, liberal, and prospective view of the interests of states passes with them for romance; and the principles that recommend it for the wanderings of a disordered imagination. The calculators compute them out of their senses. The jesters and buffoons shame them out of everything grand and elevated. Littleness in object and in means to them appears soundness and sobriety. They think there is nothing worth pursuit but that which they can handle—which they can measure with a two-foot rule—which they can tell upon ten fingers.

Without the principles of the Jacobins, perhaps without any principles at all, they played the game of that faction. . . . They aimed, or pretended to aim, at *defending* themselves against a danger from which there can be no security in any *defensive* plan. . . . This error obliged them, even in their offensive operations, to adopt a plan of war, against the success of which there was something little short of mathematical demonstration. They refused to take any step which might strike at the heart of affairs. They seemed unwilling to wound the enemy in any vital part. They acted through the whole as if they really wished the conservation of the Jacobin power, as what might be more favourable than the lawful government to the attainment of the petty objects they looked for. They always kept on the circumference; and, the wider and remoter the circle was, the more eagerly they chose it as their sphere of action in this centrifugal war. The plan they pursued in its nature demanded great length of time. In its execution, they who went the nearest way to work were obliged to cover an incredible extent of country. It left to the enemy every means of destroying this extended line of weakness. Ill success in any part was sure to defeat the effect of the whole. This is true of Austria. It is still more true of England. On this false plan even good fortune, by further weakening the victor, put him but the farther off from his object.

As long as there was any appearance of success, the spirit of aggrandizement, and consequently the spirit of mutual jealousy, seized upon all the confederated powers. Some sought an accession of territory at the expense of France, some at the expense of each other, some at the expense of third parties; and, when the vicissitude of disaster took its turn, they found common distress a treacherous bond of faith and friendship.

The greatest skill, conducting the greatest military apparatus, has been employed; but it has been worse than uselessly employed, through the false policy of the war. The operations of the field suffered by the errors of the cabinet. If the same spirit continues when peace is made, the peace will fix and perpetuate all the errors of the war. . . . .

Had we carried on the war on the side of France which looks towards the Channel or the Atlantic, we should have attacked our enemy on his weak or unarmed side. We should not have to reckon on the loss of a man who did not fall in battle. We should have an ally in the heart of the country, who, to one hundred thousand, would at one time have added eighty thousand men at the least, and all animated by principle, by enthusiasm, and by vengeance; motives which secured them to the cause in a very different manner from some of those allies whom we subsidized with millions. This ally (or rather this principal in the war), by the confession of the regicide himself, was more formidable to him than all his other foes united. Warring there, we should have led our arms to the capital of wrong. Defeated, we could not fail (proper precautions taken) of a sure retreat. Stationary, and only supporting the royalists, an impenetrable barrier, an impregnable rampart, would have been formed between the enemy and his naval power. We are probably the only nation who have declined to act against an enemy, when it might have been done, in his own country; and who, having an armed, a powerful, and a long victorious ally in that country, declined all effectual co-operation, and suffered him to perish for want of support. On the plan of a war in France, every advantage that our allies might obtain would be doubtful in its effect. Disasters on the one side might have a fair chance of being compensated by victories on the other. Had we brought the main of our force to bear upon that quarter, all the operations of the British and imperial crowns would have been combined. The war would have had system, correspondence, and a certain connection. But, as the war has been pursued, the operations of the two crowns have not the smallest degree of mutual bearing or relation.[1]

Metaphysical and Ethical Writers.

The most remarkable metaphysical and speculative works which had appeared in England since Locke's Essay were, Dr. Samuel Clarke's Sermons on the Evidences of Natural and Revealed Religion, 1705, in which he expounded his famous à priori argument for the existence of a God; Berkeley's Theory of Vision, 1709; his Principles of Human Knowledge, 1710, in which he announced his argument against the existence of matter; his Dialogue between Hylas and Philonous, 1713; his Alciphron, or the Minute Philosopher, 1732; his Analyst, 1734; the Earl of Shaftesbury's Characteristics of Men, Manners, Opinions, and Times, first published in the form in which we now have them in 1713, after the author's death; Mandeville's Fable of the Bees, or Private Vices Public Benefits, 1714; Dr. Francis Hutcheson's Inquiry into the Ideas of Beauty and Virtue, 1725; Andrew Baxter's Inquiry into the Nature of the Human Soul, 1730; Bishop Butler's Sermons preached at the Rolls Chapel, 1726; and his Analogy of Religion, Natural and Revealed, to the Constitution and Course of Nature, 1736. David Hume, who was born in 1711, and died in 1776, and who has gained the highest place in two very distinct fields of intellectual and literary enterprise, commenced his literary life by the pub-

[1] These prophetic views are very similar to those that were urged twelve years later in a memorable article in the Edinburgh Review, known to be by a great living orator. (See No. XXV., Don Cevallos on the French Usurpation of Spain.)

lication of his Treatise on Human Nature, in 1739. The work, which, as he has himself stated, was projected before he left college, and written and published not long after, fell, to use his own words, "dead-born from the press;" nor did the speculations it contained attract much more attention when republished ten years after in another form under the title of Philosophical Essays concerning Human Understanding; but they eventually proved perhaps more exciting and productive, at least for a time, both in this and in other countries, than any other metaphysical views that had been promulgated in modern times. Hume's Inquiry concerning the Principles of Morals appeared in 1752, his Natural History of Religion in 1755; and with the latter publication he may be regarded as having concluded the exposition of his sceptical philosophy. Among the most distinguished writers on mind and morals that appeared after Hume within the first quarter of a century of the reign of George III. may be mentioned Hartley, whose Observations on Man, in which he unfolded his hypothesis of the association of ideas, were published in 1749; Lord Kames (Henry Home), whose Essays on the Principles of Morality and Natural Religion were published in 1752; Adam Smith, whose Theory of Moral Sentiments was published in 1759; Reid, whose Inquiry into the Human Mind on the Principles of Common Sense was published in 1764; Abraham Tucker (calling himself Edward Search, Esq.), the first part of whose Light of Nature Pursued was published in 1768, the second in 1778, after the author's death; and Priestley, whose new edition of Hartley's work, with an Introductory Dissertation, was published in 1775; his Examination of Dr. Reid's Inquiry, the same year; and his Doctrine of Philosophical Necessity, in 1777. We may add to the list Campbell's very able Dissertation on Miracles, in answer to Hume, which appeared in 1763; and Beattie's Essay on Truth, noticed in a former page, which appeared in 1770, and was also, as everybody knows, an attack upon the philosophy of the great sceptic.

HISTORICAL WRITERS:—HUME; ROBERTSON; GIBBON.

In the latter part of his literary career Hume struck into altogether another line, and the subtle and daring metaphysician suddenly came before the world in the new character of an historian. He appears, indeed, to have nearly abandoned metaphysics very soon after the publication of his Philosophical Essays. In a letter to his friend Sir Gilbert Elliott, which,

though without date, seems from its contents, according to
Mr. Stewart, to have been written about 1750 or 1751, he says,
"I am sorry that our correspondence should lead us into these
abstract speculations. I have thought, and read, and composed
very little on such questions of late. Morals, politics, and
literature have employed all my time." The first volume of
his History of Great Britain, containing the Reigns of James I.
and Charles I., was published, in quarto, at Edinburgh, in 1754;
the second, containing the Commonwealth and the Reigns of
Charles II. and James II., at London, in 1757. According to
his own account the former was received with "one cry of
reproach, disapprobation, and even detestation;" and after the
first ebullitions of the fury of his assailants were over, he adds,
"what was still more mortifying, the book seemed to sink into
oblivion: Mr. Miller told me that in a twelvemonth he sold only
forty-five copies of it." He was so bitterly disappointed, that,
he tells us, had not the war been at that time breaking out
between France and England, he had certainly retired to some
provincial town of the former kingdom, changed his name, and
never more returned to his native country. However, after a
little time, in the impracticability of executing this scheme of
expatriation, he resolved to pick up courage and persevere, the
more especially as his second volume was considerably advanced.
That, he informs us, "happened to give less displeasure to the
Whigs, and was better received: it not only rose itself, but
helped to buoy up its unfortunate brother." The work, indeed,
seems to have now rapidly attained extraordinary popularity.
Two more volumes, comprehending the reigns of the princes of
the House of Tudor, appeared in 1759; and the remaining two,
completing the History, from the Invasion of Julius Cæsar to
the accession of Henry VII., in 1762. And several new editions
of all the volumes were called for in rapid succession. Hume
makes as much an epoch in our historical as he does in our
philosophical literature. His originality in the one department
is as great as in the other; and the influence he has exerted
upon those who have followed him in the same path has been
equally extensive and powerful in both cases. His History,
notwithstanding some defects which the progress of time and of
knowledge is every year making more considerable, or at least
enabling us better to perceive, and some others which probably
would have been much the same at whatever time the work had
been written, has still merits of so high a kind as a literary
performance that it must ever retain its place among our few
classical works in this department, of which it is as yet perhaps

the greatest. In narrative clearness, grace, and spirit, at least, it is not excelled, scarcely equalled, by any other completed historical work in the language; and it has besides the high charm, indispensable to every literary performance that is to endure, of being impressed all over with the peculiar character of the author's own mind, interesting us even in its most prejudiced and objectionable passages (perhaps still more, indeed, in some of these than elsewhere) by his tolerant candour and gentleness of nature, his charity for all the milder vices, his unaffected indifference to many of the common objects of human passion, and his contempt for their pursuers, never waxing bitter or morose, and often impregnating his style and manner with a vein of the quietest but yet truest and richest humour. One effect which we may probably ascribe in great part to the example of Hume was the attention that immediately began to be turned to historic composition in a higher spirit than had heretofore been felt among us, and that ere long added to the possessions of the language in that department the celebrated performances of Robertson and Gibbon. Robertson's History of Scotland during the Reigns of Queen Mary and of King James VI. was published at London in 1759; his History of the Reign of the Emperor Charles V., in 1769; and his History of America, in 1776. Robertson's style of narration, lucid, equable, and soberly embellished, took the popular ear and taste from the first. A part of the cause of this favourable reception is slily enough indicated by Hume, in a letter which he wrote to Robertson himself on the publication of the History of Scotland :—" The great success of your book, besides its real merit, is forwarded by its prudence, and by the deference paid to established opinions. It gains also by its being your first performance, and by its surprising the public, who are not upon their guard against it. By reason of these two circumstances justice is more readily done to its merit, which, however, is really so great, that I believe there is scarce another instance of a first performance being so near perfection." * The applause, indeed, was loud and universal, from Horace Walpole to Lord Lyttelton, from Lord Mansfield to David Garrick. Nor did it fail to be renewed in equal measure on the appearance both of his History of Charles V. and of his History of America. But, although in his own day he probably bore away the palm from Hume in the estimation of the majority, the finest judgments even then discerned, with Gibbon, that there was something higher in " the careless inimitable graces " of the latter than in his rival's more elaborate regularity, flowing

* Account of the Life and Writings of Robertson, by Dugald Stewart.

and perspicuous as it usually is; and, as always happens, time has brought the general opinion into accordance with this feeling of the wiser few. The first volume of Gibbon's History of the Decline and Fall of the Roman Empire appeared in 1776, a few months before the death of Hume, and about a year before the publication of Robertson's America; the second and third followed in 1781; the three additional volumes, which completed the work, not till 1788. Of the first volume, the author tells us, "the first impression was exhausted in a few days; a second and third edition were scarcely adequate to the demand; and a scarcely diminished interest followed the great undertaking to its close, notwithstanding the fear which he expresses in the preface to his concluding volumes that "six ample quartos must have tried, and may have exhausted, the indulgence of the public." A performance at once of such extent, and of so sustained a brilliancy throughout, perhaps does not exist in ancient or modern historical literature; but it is a hard metallic brilliancy, which even the extraordinary interest of the subject and the unflagging animation of the writer, with the great skill he shows in the disposition of his materials, do not prevent from becoming sometimes fatiguing and oppressive. Still the splendour, artificial as it is, is very imposing; it does not warm, as well as illuminate, like the light of the sun, but it has at least the effect of a theatrical blaze of lamps and cressets; while it is supported everywhere by a profusion of real erudition such as would make the dullest style and manner interesting. It is remarkable, however, that, in regard to mere language, no one of these three celebrated historical writers, the most eminent we have yet to boast of, at least among those that have stood the test of time, can be recommended as a model. No one of the three, in fact, was of English birth and education. Gibbon's style is very impure, abounding in Gallicisms; Hume's, especially in the first edition of his History, is, with all its natural elegance, almost as much infested with Scotticisms; and, if Robertson's be less incorrect in that respect, it is so unidiomatic as to furnish a still less adequate exemplification of genuine English eloquence. Robertson died at the age of seventy-one, in 1793; Gibbon, in 1794, at the age of fifty-seven.

POLITICAL ECONOMY; THEOLOGY; CRITICISM AND BELLES LETTRES.

Besides his metaphysical and historical works, upon which his fame principally rests, the penetrating and original genius of Hume also distinguished itself in another field, that of economical speculation, which had for more than a century before his time to some extent engaged the attention of inquirers in this country. There are many ingenious views upon this subject scattered up and down in his Political Discourses, and his Moral and Political Essays. Other contributions, not without value, to the science of political economy, for which we are indebted to the middle of the last century, are the Rev. R. Wallace's Essay on the Numbers of Mankind, published at Edinburgh in 1753; and Sir James Steuart's Inquiry into the Principles of Political Economy, which appeared in 1767. But these and all other preceding works on the subject have been thrown into the shade by Adam Smith's celebrated Inquiry into the Nature and Causes of the Wealth of Nations, which, after having been long expected, was at last given to the world in the beginning of the year 1776. It is interesting to learn that this crowning performance of his friend was read by Hume, who died before the close of the year in which it was published: a letter of his to Smith is preserved, in which, after congratulating him warmly on having acquitted himself so as to relieve the anxiety and fulfil the hopes of his friends, he ends by saying, "If you were here at my fireside, I should dispute some of your principles.... But these, and a hundred other points, are fit only to be discussed in conversation. I hope it will be soon, for I am in a very bad state of health, and cannot afford a long delay." Smith survived till July, 1790.

A few other names, more or less distinguished in the literature of this time, we must content ourselves with merely mentioning:—in theology, Warburton, Lowth, Horsley, Jortin, Madan, Gerard, Blair, Geddes, Lardner, Priestley; in critical and grammatical disquisition, Harris, Monboddo, Kames, Blair, Jones; in antiquarian research, Walpole, Hawkins, Burney, Chandler, Barrington, Steevens, Pegge, Farmer, Vallancey, Grose, Gough; in the department of the belles lettres and miscellaneous speculation, Chesterfield, Hawkesworth, Brown, Jenyns, Bryant, Hurd, Melmoth, Potter, Francklin, &c.

THE LATTER PART OF THE EIGHTEENTH CENTURY.

COWPER.

THE death of Samuel Johnson, in the end of the year 1784, makes a pause, or point of distinction, in our literature, hardly less notable than the acknowledgment of the independence of America, the year before, makes in our political history. It was not only the end of a reign, but the end of kingship altogether, in our literary system. For King Samuel has had no successor; nobody since his day, and that of his contemporary Voltaire, who died in 1778, at the age of eighty-five, has sat on a throne of literature either in England or in France.

It is a remarkable fact that, if we were to continue our notices of the poets of the last century in strict chronological order, the first name we should have to mention would be that of a writer, who more properly belongs to what may almost be called our own day. Crabbe, whose Tales of the Hall, the most striking production of his powerful and original genius, appeared in 1819, and who died so recently as 1832, published his first poem, The Library, in 1781: some extracts from it are given in the Annual Register for that year. But Crabbe's literary career is divided into two parts by a chasm or interval, during which he published nothing, of nearly twenty years; and his proper era is the present century.

One remark, however, touching this writer may be made here: his first manner was evidently caught from Churchill more than from any other of his predecessors. And this was also the case with his contemporary Cowper, the poetical writer whose name casts the greatest illustration upon the last twenty years of the eighteenth century. William Cowper, born in 1731, twenty-three years before Crabbe,—we pass over his anonymous contributions to his friend the Rev. Mr. Newton's collection of the Olney Hymns, published in 1776,—gave to the world the first volume of his poems, containing those entitled Table-Talk, The Progress of Error, Truth, Expostulation, Hope, Charity, Conversation, and Retirement, in 1782; his famous History of John Gilpin appeared the following year, without his name, in a publication called The Repository; his second volume, containing The Task, Tirocinium, and some shorter pieces, was published in 1785; his translations of the Iliad and the Odyssey in 1791; and his death took place on the 25th of April, 1800. It is recorded that Cowper's first volume attracted little attention: it certainly appears to have excited no perception in the mind or eye of the public of that day that a new and great light had arisen in the poetical firmament. The Annual Register for 1781, as we have said, gives extracts from Crabbe's Library; a long passage from his next poem, The Village, is given in the volume for 1783; the volume for 1785 in like manner treats its readers to a quotation from The Newspaper, which he had published in that year; but, except that the anonymous History of John Gilpin is extracted in the volume for 1783 from the Repository, we have nothing there of Cowper's till we come to the volume for 1786, which contains two of the minor pieces published in his second volume. Crabbe was probably indebted for the distinction he received in part to his friend and patron Burke, under whose direction the Register was compiled; but the silence observed in regard to Cowper may be taken as not on that account the less conclusive as to the little or next to no impression his first volume made. Yet surely there were both a force and a freshness of manner in the new aspirant that might have been expected to draw some observation. Nor had there of late been such plenty of good poetry produced in England as to make anything of the kind a drug in the market. But here, in fact, lay the main cause of the public inattention. The age was not poetical. The manufacture of verse was carried on, indeed, upon a considerable scale, by the Hayleys and the Whiteheads and the Pratts and others (spinners of sound and weavers of words not for a moment to be compared in inventive and imaginative faculty, or in faculty of any kind, any more than for the utility of their work, with their contemporaries the Arkwrights and Cartwrights); but the production of poetry had gone so much out, that, even in the class most accustomed to judge of these things, few people knew it when they saw it. It has been said that the severe and theological tone of this poetry of Cowper's operated against its immediate popularity; and that was probably the case too; but it could only have been so, at any rate to the same extent, in a time at the least as indifferent to poetry as to religion and morality. For, certainly, since the days of Pope, nothing in the same style had been produced among us to be compared with these poems of Cowper's for animation, vigour, and point, which are among the most admired qualities of that great writer, any more than for the cordiality, earnestness, and fervour which are more peculiarly their own. Smoother versification we had had in great abundance; more pomp and splendour of rhetorical declamation, perhaps, as in Johnson's paraphrases from Juvenal; more warmth and glow of imagination, as in Goldsmith's two poems, if they are to be considered as coming into the competition. But, on the whole, verse of such bone and muscle had proceeded from no recent writer,—not excepting Churchill, whose poetry had little else than its coarse strength to recommend it, and whose hasty and careless workmanship Cowper, while he had to a certain degree been his imitator, had learned, with his artistical feeling, infinitely to surpass. Churchill's vehement invective, with its exaggerations and personalities, made him the most popular poet of his day: Cowper, neglected at first, has taken his place as one of the classics of the language. Each has had his reward—the reward he best deserved, and probably most desired.

As the death of Samuel Johnson closes one era of our literature, so the appearance of Cowper as a poet opens another. Notwithstanding his obligations both to Churchill and Pope, a main characteristic of Cowper's poetry is its originality. Compared with almost any one of his predecessors, he was what we may call a natural poet. He broke through conventional forms and usages in his mode of writing more daringly than any English poet before him had done, at least since the genius of Pope had bound in its spell the phraseology and rhythm of our poetry. His opinions were not more his own than his manner of expressing them. His principles of diction and versification were announced, in part, in the poem with which he introduced himself to the public, his Table-Talk, in which, having intimated his contempt for the " creamy smoothness " of modern fashionable verse, where sentiment was so often

> sacrificed to sound,
> And truth cut short to make a period round,

he exclaims,

> Give me the line that ploughs its stately course
> Like a proud swan, conquering the stream by force;
> That, like some cottage beauty, strikes the heart,
> Quite unindebted to the tricks of art.

But, although he despised the " tricks " of art, Cowper, like every great poet, was also a great artist; and, with all its in that day almost unexampled simplicity and naturalness, his style is the very reverse of a slovenly or irregular one. If his verse be not so highly polished as that of Pope,—who, he complains, has

> Made poetry a mere mechanic art,
> And every warbler has his tune by heart,—

it is in its own way nearly as "well disciplined, complete, compact," as he has described Pope's to be. With all his avowed admiration of Churchill, he was far from being what he has called that writer—

> Too proud for art, and trusting in mere force.

On the contrary, he has in more than one passage descanted on "the pangs of a poetic birth"—on

> the shifts and turns,
> The expedients and inventions multiform,
> To which the mind resorts, in chase of terms,
> Though apt, yet coy, and difficult to win;—

and the other labours to be undergone by whoever would attain to excellence in the work of composition. Not, however, that, with all this elaboration, he was a slow writer. Slowness is the consequence of indifference, of a writer not being excited by his subject—not having his heart in his work, but going through it as a mere task; let him be thoroughly in earnest, fully possessed of his subject and possessed by it, and, though the pains he takes to find apt and effective expression for his thoughts may tax his whole energies like wrestling with a strong man, he will not write slowly. He is in a state of active combustion—consuming away, it may be, but never pausing. Cowper is said to have composed the six thousand verses, or thereby, contained in his first volume, in about three months.

Not creative imagination, nor deep melody, nor even, in general, much of fancy or grace or tenderness, is to be met with in the poetry of Cowper; but yet it is not without both high and various excellence. Its main charm, and that which is never wanting, is its earnestness. This is a quality which gives it a power over many minds not at all alive to the poetical; but it is also the source of some of its strongest attractions for those that are. Hence its truth both of landscape-painting, and of the description of character and states of mind; hence its skilful expression of such emotions and passions as it allows itself to deal with; hence the force and fervour of its denunciatory eloquence, giving to some passages as fine an inspiration of the moral sublime as is perhaps anywhere to be found in didactic poetry. Hence, we may say, even the directness, simplicity, and manliness of Cowper's diction—all that is best in the form, as well as in the spirit, of his verse. It was this quality, or temper of mind, in short, that principally made him an original poet; and, if not the founder of a new school, the pioneer of a new era, of English poetry. Instead of repeating the unmeaning conventionalities and faded affectations of his predecessors, it led him to turn to the actual nature within him and around him, and there to learn both the truths he should utter and the words in which he should utter them.

After Cowper had found, or been found out by, his proper audience, the qualities in his poetry that at first had most repelled ordinary readers rather aided its success. In particular, as we have said, its theological tone and spirit made it acceptable in quarters to which poetry of any kind had rarely penetrated, and where it may perhaps be affirmed that it keeps its ground chiefly perforce of this its most prosaic peculiarity; although, at the same time, it is probable that the vigorous verse to which his system of theology and morals has been married by Cowper has not been without effect in diffusing not only a more indulgent toleration but a truer feeling and love for poetry throughout what is called the religious world. Nor is it to be denied that the source of Cowper's own most potent inspiration is his theological creed. The most popular of his poems, and also certainly the most elaborate, is his Task; it abounds in that delineation of domestic and every-day life which interests everybody, in descriptions of incidents and natural appearances with which all are familiar, in the expression of sentiments and convictions to which most hearts readily respond: it is a poem, therefore, in which the greatest number of readers find the greatest number of things to attract and attach them. Besides, both in the form and in the matter, it has less of what is felt to be strange and sometimes repulsive by the generality; the verse flows, for the most part, smoothly enough, if not with much variety of music; the diction is, as usual with Cowper, clear, manly, and expressive, but at the same time, from being looser and more diffuse, seldomer harsh or difficult than it is in some of his other compositions; above all, the doctrinal strain is pitched upon a lower key, and, without any essential point being given up, both morality and religion certainly assume a countenance and voice considerably less rueful and vindictive. But, although The Task has much occasional elevation and eloquence, and some sunny passages, it perhaps nowhere rises to the passionate force and vehemence to which Cowper had been carried by a more burning zeal in some of his earlier poems. Take, for instance, the following fine burst in that entitled Table-Talk:—

> Not only vice disposes and prepares
> The mind, that slumbers sweetly in her snares,
> To stoop to tyranny's usurped command,
> And bend her polished neck beneath his hand
> (A dire effect, by one of Nature's laws,
> Unchangeably connected with its cause);
> But Providence himself will intervene
> To throw his dark displeasure o'er the scene.
> All are his instruments; each form of war,
> What burns at home, or threatens from afar,
> Nature in arms, her elements at strife,
> The storms that overset the joys of life,
> Are but his rods to scourge a guilty land,
> And waste it at the bidding of his hand.
> He gives the word, and mutiny soon roars
> In all her gates, and shakes her distant shores;
> The standards of all nations are unfurled;
> She has one foe, and that one foe the world:
> And, if he dooms that people with a frown,
> And mark them with a seal of wrath pressed down,
> Obduracy takes place; callous and tough
> The reprobated race grows judgment-proof;
> Earth shakes beneath them, and heaven wars above;
> But nothing scares them from the course they love.
> To the lascivious pipe, and wanton song,
> That charm down fear, they frolic it along,
> With mad rapidity and unconcern,
> Down to the gulf from which is no return.
> They trust in navies, and their navies fail—
> God's curse can cast away ten thousand sail!
> They trust in armies, and their courage dies;
> In wisdom, wealth, in fortune, and in lies;
> But all they trust in withers, as it must,
> When He commands, in whom they place no trust.
> Vengeance at last pours down upon their coast
> A long-despised, but now victorious, host;
> Tyranny sends the chain, that must abridge
> The noble sweep of all their privilege;
> Gives liberty the last, the mortal shock;
> Slips the slave's collar on, and snaps the lock.

And, even when it expresses itself in quite other forms, and with least of passionate excitement, the fervour which inspires those earlier poems occasionally produces something more brilliant or more graceful than is anywhere to be found in The Task. How skilfully and forcibly executed, for example, is the following moral delineation in that called Truth:—

> The path to bliss abounds with many a snare;
> Learning is one, and wit, however rare.

The Frenchman first in literary fame—
(Mention him, if you please. Voltaire?—The same)
With spirit, genius, eloquence, supplied,
Lived long, wrote much, laughed heartily, and died.
The Scripture was his jest-book, whence he drew
Bon mots to gall the Christian and the Jew;
An infidel in health; but what when sick?
Oh—then a text would touch him at the quick.
View him at Paris in his last career;
Surrounding throngs the demigod revere;
Exalted on his pedestal of pride,
And fumed with frankincense on every side,
He begs their flattery with his latest breath,
And, smothered in 't at last, is praised to death.

   Yon cottager, who weaves at her own door,
Pillow and bobbins all her little store;
Content though mean, and cheerful if not gay,
Shuffling her threads about the livelong day,
Just earns a scanty pittance, and at night
Lies down secure, her heart and pocket light;
She, for her humble sphere by nature fit,
Has little understanding, and no wit,
Receives no praise; but, though her lot be such,
(Toilsome and indigent) she renders much;
Just knows, and knows no more, her Bible true—
A truth the brilliant Frenchman never knew;
And in that charter reads with sparkling eyes
Her title to a treasure in the skies.

   O happy peasant! O unhappy bard!
His the mere tinsel, hers the rich reward;
He praised perhaps for ages yet to come,
She never heard of half a mile from home;
He lost in errors his vain heart prefers,
She safe in the simplicity of hers.

Still more happily executed, and in a higher style of art, is the following version, so elaborately finished, and yet so severely simple, of the meeting of the two disciples with their divine Master on the road to Emmaus, in the piece entitled Conversation:—

It happened on a solemn eventide,
Soon after He that was our surety died,
Two bosom friends, each pensively inclined,
The scene of all those sorrows left behind,
Sought their own village, busied as they went
In musings worthy of the great event:
They spake of him they loved, of him whose life,
Though blameless, had incurred perpetual strife,
Whose deeds had left, in spite of hostile arts,
A deep memorial graven on their hearts.

> The recollection, like a vein of ore,
> The farther traced, enriched them still the more;
> They thought him, and they justly thought him, one
> Sent to do more than he appeared to have done;
> To exalt a people, and to place them high
> Above all else; and wondered he should die.
> Ere yet they brought their journey to an end,
> A stranger joined them, courteous as a friend,
> And asked them, with a kind, engaging air,
> What their affliction was, and begged a share.
> Informed, he gathered up the broken thread,
> And, truth and wisdom gracing all he said,
> Explained, illustrated, and searched so well
> The tender theme on which they chose to dwell,
> That, reaching home, The night, they said, is near
> We must not now be parted,—sojourn here.
> The new acquaintance soon became a guest,
> And, made so welcome at their simple feast,
> He blessed the bread, but vanished at the word,
> And left them both exclaiming, 'Twas the Lord!
> Did not our hearts feel all he deigned to say?
> Did not they burn within us by the way?

For one thing, Cowper's poetry, not organ-toned, or informed with any very rich or original music, any more than soaringly imaginative or gorgeously decorated, is of a style that requires the sustaining aid of rhyme: in blank verse it is apt to overflow in pools and shallows. And this is one among other reasons why, after all, some of his short poems, which are nearly all in rhyme, are perhaps what he has done best. His John Gilpin, universally known and universally enjoyed by his countrymen, young and old, educated and uneducated, and perhaps the only English poem of which this can be said, of course at once suggests itself as standing alone in the collection of what he has left us for whimsical conception and vigour of comic humour; but there is a quieter exercise of the same talent, or at least of a kindred sense of the ludicrous and sly power of giving it expression, in others of his shorter pieces. For tenderness and pathos, again, nothing else that he has written, and not much that is elsewhere to be found of the same kind in English poetry, can be compared with his Lines on receiving his Mother's Picture:—

> O that those lips had language! Life has passed
> With me but roughly since I heard thee last.
> Those lips are thine—thy own sweet smile I see,
> The same that oft in childhood solaced me:
> Voice only fails, else how distinct they say,
> "Grieve not, my child, chase all thy fears away!"

COWPER.

The meek intelligence of those clear eyes
(Blest be the art that can immortalize,
The art that baffles Time's gigantic claim
To quench it) here shines on me still the same.
  Faithful remembrancer of one so dear,
O welcome guest, though unexpected here!
Who bid'st me honour with an artless song,
Affectionate, a mother lost so long.
I will obey, not willingly alone,
But gladly, as the precept were her own:
And, while that face renews my filial grief,
Fancy shall weave a charm for my relief,
Shall steep me in Elysian reverie,
A momentary dream that thou art she.
  My mother! when I learned that thou wast dead,
Say, wast thou conscious of the tears I shed?
Hovered thy spirit o'er thy sorrowing son,
Wretch even then, life's journey just begun?
Perhaps thou gav'st me, though unfelt, a kiss;
Perhaps a tear, if souls can melt in bliss—
Ah that maternal smile! it answers—Yes.
I heard the bell tolled on thy burial day,
I saw the hearse that bore thee slow away,
And, turning from my nursery window, drew
A long, long sigh, and wept a last adieu!
But was it such?—It was.—Where thou art gone,
Adieus and farewells are a sound unknown:
May I but meet thee on that peaceful shore,
The parting word shall pass my lips no more!
Thy maidens, grieved themselves at my concern,
Oft gave me promise of thy quick return.
What ardently I wished I long believed,
And, disappointed still, was still deceived;
By expectation every day beguiled,
Dupe of to-morrow even from a child,
Thus many a sad to-morrow came and went,
Till, all my stock of infant sorrow spent,
I learned at last submission to my lot,
But, though I less deplored thee, ne'er forgot.
  Where once we dwelt our name is heard no more,
Children not thine have trod my nursery floor;
And where the gardener Robin, day by day,
Drew me to school along the public way,
Delighted with my bauble coach, and wrapped
In scarlet mantle warm, and velvet-capped,
'Tis now become a history little known
That once we called the pastoral house our own.
Short-lived possession! but the record fair,
That memory keeps of all thy kindness there,
Still outlives many a storm, that has effaced
A thousand other themes less deeply traced.

Thy nightly visits to my chamber made,
That thou might'st know me safe and warmly laid;
Thy morning bounties ere I left my home,
The biscuit, or confectionary plum;
The fragrant waters on my cheeks bestowed
By thy own hand, till fresh they shone and glowed:
All this, and, more endearing still than all,
Thy constant flow of love, that knew no fall,
Ne'er roughened by those cataracts and breaks,
That humour interposed too often makes;
All this still legible in memory's page,
And still to be so to my latest age,
Adds joy to duty, makes me glad to pay
Such honours to thee as my numbers may;
Perhaps a frail memorial, but sincere,
Not scorned in heaven, though little noticed here.
  Could Time, his flight reversed, restore the hours,
When, playing with thy vesture's tissued flowers,
The violet, the pink, and jessamine,
I pricked them into paper with a pin,
(And thou wast happier than myself the while,
Would'st softly speak, and stroke my head, and smile)
Could those few pleasant days again appear,
Might one wish bring them, would I wish them here?
I would not trust my heart;—the dear delight
Seems so to be desired, perhaps I might.—
But no:—what here we call our life is such,
So little to be loved, and thou so much,
That I should ill requite thee to constrain
Thy unbound spirit into bonds again.
  Thou, as a gallant bark from Albion's coast
(The storms all weather'd and the ocean crossed),
Shoots into port at some well-havened isle,
Where spices breathe, and brighter seasons smile,
There sits quiescent on the floods, that show
Her beauteous form reflected clear below,
While airs impregnated with incense play
Around her, fanning light her streamers gay;
So thou, with sails how swift! hast reached the shore
"Where tempests never beat, nor billows roar."¹
And thy loved consort on the dangerous tide
Of life long since has anchored by thy side.
But me, scarce hoping to attain that rest,
Always from port withheld, always distressed—
Me howling blasts drive devious, tempest-tossed,
Sails ripped, seams opening wide, and compass lost;
And day by day some current's thwarting force
Sets me more distant from a prosperous course.
Yet O the thought that thou art safe, and he!
That thought is joy, arrive what may to me.

¹ Garth.

> My boast is not, that I deduce my birth
> From loins enthroned, and rulers of the earth;
> But higher far my proud pretensions rise—
> The son of parents passed into the skies.
>   And now farewell.—Time unrevoked has run
> His wonted course; yet what I wished is done.
> By contemplation's help, not sought in vain,
> I seem to have lived my childhood o'er again;
> To have renewed the joys that once were mine,
> Without the sin of violating thine;
> And, while the wings of fancy still are free,
> And I can view this mimic show of thee,
> Time has but half succeeded in his theft—
> Thyself removed, thy power to soothe me left.

This is no doubt, as a whole, Cowper's finest poem, at once springing from the deepest and purest fount of passion, and happy in shaping itself into richer and sweeter music than he has reached in any other. It shows what his real originality, and the natural spirit of art that was in him, might have done under a better training and more favourable circumstances of personal situation, or perhaps in another age. Generally, indeed, it may be said of Cowper, that the more he was left to himself, or trusted to his own taste and feelings, in writing, the better he wrote. In so far as regards the form of composition, the principal charm of what he has done best is a natural elegance, which is most perfect in what he has apparently written with the least labour, or at any rate with the least thought of rules or models. His Letters to his friends, not written for publication at all, but thrown off in the carelessness of his hours of leisure and relaxation, have given him as high a place among the prose classics of his country as he holds among our poets. His least successful performances are his translations of the Iliad and Odyssey, throughout which he was straining to imitate a style not only unlike his own, but, unfortunately, quite as unlike that of his original—for those versions of the most natural of all poetry, the Homeric, are, strangely enough, attempted in the manner of the most artificial of all poets, Milton.

DARWIN.

Neither, however, did this age of our literature want its artificial poetry. In fact, the expiration or abolition of that manner among us was brought about not more by the example of a fresh and natural style given by Cowper, than by the exhibition of the opposite style, pushed to its extreme, given by his contemporary Darwin. Our great poets of this era cannot be accused of hurrying into print at an immature age. Dr. Erasmus Darwin, born in 1721, after having risen to distinguished reputation as a physician, published the Second Part of his Botanic Garden, under the title of The Loves of the Plants, in 1789: and the First Part, entitled The Economy of Vegetation, two years after. He died in 1802. The Botanic Garden, hard, brilliant, sonorous, may be called a poem cast in metal—a sort of Pandemonium palace of rhyme, not unlike that raised long ago in another region,—

> where pilasters round
> Were set, and Doric pillars, overlaid
> With golden architrave ; nor did there want
> Cornice, or frieze, with bossy sculptures graven :
> The roof was fretted gold.

The poem, however, did not rise exactly "like an exhalation." "The verse," writes its sprightly biographer, Miss Anna Seward, "corrected, polished, and modulated with the most sedulous attention; the notes involving such great diversity of matter relating to natural history; and the composition going forward in the short recesses of professional attendance, *but chiefly in his chaise, as he travelled from one place to another* ; the Botanic Garden could not be the work of one, two, or three years; it was ten from its primal lines to its first publication." If this account may be depended on, the Doctor's supplies of inspiration must have been vouchsafed to him at the penurious rate of little more than a line a day. At least, therefore, it cannot be said of him, as it was said of his more fluent predecessor in both gifts of Apollo, Sir Richard Blackmore, that he wrote "to the rumbling of his chariot wheels." The verse, nevertheless, does in another way smack of the travelling-chaise, and of "the short recesses of professional attendance." Nothing is done in passion and power; but all by filing, and scraping, and rubbing, and other painstaking. Every line is as elaborately polished and sharpened as a lancet; and the most effective paragraphs have the air of a lot of those bright little instruments arranged in rows, with their blades out, for sale. You feel as if so thick an array of points and edges demanded careful handling, and that your fingers are scarcely safe in coming near them. Darwin's theory of poetry evidently was, that it was all a mechanical affair—only a higher kind of pin-making. His own poetry, however, with all its defects, is far from being merely mechanical. The Botanic Garden is not a poem which any man of ordinary intelligence could have produced by sheer care and industry, or such faculty of writing as could be acquired by serving an apprenticeship to the trade of poetry. Vicious as it is in manner, it is even there of an imposing and original character; and a true poetic fire lives under all its affectations, and often blazes up through them. There is not much, indeed, of pure soul or high imagination in Darwin; he seldom rises above the visible and material; but he has at least a poet's eye for the perception of that, and a poet's fancy for its embellishment and exaltation. No writer has surpassed him in the luminous representation of visible objects in verse; his descriptions have the distinctness of drawings by the pencil, with the advantage of conveying, by their harmonious words, many things that no pencil can paint. His images, though they are for the most part tricks of language rather than transformations or new embodiments of impassioned thought, have often at least an Ovidian glitter and prettiness, or are striking from their mere ingenuity and novelty —as, for example, when he addresses the stars as "flowers of the sky," or apostrophizes the glowworm as "Star of the earth, and diamond of the night." These two instances, indeed, thus brought into juxtaposition, may serve to exemplify the principle upon which he constructs such decorations: it is, we see, an economical principle; for, in truth, the one of those figures is little more than the other reversed, or inverted. Still both are happy and effective enough conceits—and one of them is applied and carried out so as to make it more than a more momentary light flashing from the verse. The passage is not without a tone of grandeur and meditative pathos:—

>Roll on, ye stars! exult in youthful prime,
>Mark with bright curves the printless steps of time;
>Near and more near your beamy cars approach,
>And lessening orbs on lessening orbs encroach;—
>Flowers of the Sky! ye too to age must yield,
>Frail as your silken sisters of the field!
>Star after star from heaven's high arch shall rush,
>Suns sink on suns, and systems systems crush,
>Headlong, extinct, to one dark centre fall,
>And death and night and chaos mingle all!
>—Till o'er the wreck, emerging from the storm,
>Immortal Nature lifts her changeful form,
>Mounts from her funeral pyre on wings of flame,
>And soars and shines, another and the same.

There is also a fine moral inspiration, as well as the usual rhetorical brilliancy, in the following lines:—

>Hail, adamantine Steel! magnetic Lord!
>King of the prow, the ploughshare, and the sword!

True to the pole, by thee the pilot guides
His steady helm amid the struggling tides,
Braves with broad sail the immeasurable sea,
Cleaves the dark air, and asks no star but thee!

BURNS.

It was in October or November of the year 1786 that the press of the obscure country town of Kilmarnock gave to the world, in an octavo volume, the first edition of the Poems, chiefly in the Scottish Dialect, of Robert Burns. A second edition was printed at Edinburgh early in the following year. Burns, born on the 25th of January, 1759, had composed most of the pieces contained in this publication in the two years preceding its appearance: his life—an April day of sunshine and storm—closed on the 21st of July, 1796; and in his last nine or ten years he may have about doubled the original quantity of his printed poetry. He was not quite thirty-seven and a half years old when he died—about a year and three months older than Byron. Burns is the greatest peasant-poet that has ever appeared; but his poetry is so remarkable in itself that the circumstances in which it was produced hardly add anything to our admiration. It is a poetry of very limited compass—not ascending towards any "highest heaven of invention," nor even having much variety of modulation, but yet in its few notes as true and melodious a voice of passion as was ever heard. It is all light and fire. Considering how little the dialect in which he wrote had been trained to the purposes of literature, what Burns has done with it is miraculous. Nothing in Horace, in the way of curious felicity of phrase, excels what we find in the compositions of this Ayrshire ploughman. The words are almost always so apt and full of life, at once so natural and expressive, and so graceful and musical in their animated simplicity, that, were the matter ever so trivial, they would of themselves turn it into poetry. And the same native artistic feeling manifests itself in everything else. One characteristic that belongs to whatever Burns has written is that, of its kind or in its own way, it is a perfect production. It is perfect in the same sense in which every production of nature is perfect, the humblest weed as well as the proudest flower; and in which, indeed, every true thing whatever is perfect, viewed in reference to its species and purpose. His poetry is, throughout, real emotion melodiously uttered. As such, it is as genuine poetry as was ever written or sung. Not, however, although its chief and best inspiration is passion rather than imagination, that any poetry ever was farther from being a mere Æolian warble addressing itself principally to the nerves. Burns's head was as strong as his heart; his natural sagacity, logical faculty, and judgment were of the first order; no man, of poetical or prosaic temperament, ever had a more substantial intellectual character. And the character of his poetry is like that of the mind and the nature out of which it sprung—instinct with passion, but not less so with power of thought—full of light, as we have said, as well as of fire. More of matter and meaning, in short, in any sense in which the terms may be understood, will be found in no verses than there is in his. Hence the popularity of the poetry of Burns with all classes of his countrymen—a popularity more universal, probably, than any other writer ever gained, at least so immediately; for his name, we apprehend, had become a household word among all classes in every part of Scotland even in his own lifetime. Certainly at the present day, that would be a rare Lowland Scotchman, or Scotchwoman either, who should be found never to have heard of the name and fame of Robert Burns, or even to be altogether ignorant of his works. It has happened, however, from this cause, that he is not perhaps, in general, estimated by the best of his productions. Nobody, of course, capable of appreciating any of the characteristic qualities of Burns's poetry will ever think of quoting even the best of the few verses he has written in English, as evidence of his poetic genius. In these he is Samson shorn of his hair, and become as any other man. But even such poems as his Cotter's Saturday Night, and his tale of Tam o' Shanter, convey no adequate conception of what is brightest and highest in his poetry. The former is a true and touching description in a quiet and subdued manner, suitable to the subject, but not adapted to bring out much of his illuminating fancy and fusing power of passion: the other is a rapid, animated, and most effective piece of narrative, with some vigorous comedy, and also some scene-painting in a broad, dashing style, but exhibiting hardly more of the peculiar humour of Burns than of his pathos. Of a far rarer merit, much richer in true poetic light and colour, and of a much more original and distinctive inspiration, are many of his poems which are much less frequently referred to, at least out of his own country. Take, for instance, that entitled 'To a Mouse, on turning her up in her Nest with the Plough, November, 1785:—

Wee,[1] sleekit,[2] cow'rin',[3] timorous beastie,[4]
O what a panic 's in thy breastie!'
Thou need na[5] start awa[6] sa hastie,
　　Wi' bickerin' brattle![7]
I wad be laith[8] to rin[9] an' chase thee,
　　Wi' murderin' pattle.[10]

I'm truly sorry man's dominion
Has broken nature's social union,
An' justifies that ill opinion
　　Which makes thee startle
At me, thy poor earth-born companion,
　　An' fellow mortal.

I doubt na, whiles,[11] but thou may thieve;
What then? Poor beastie, thou maun[12] live!
A daimen icker[13] in a thrave[14]
　　'S a sma'[15] request:
I'll get a blessin' wi' the lave,[16]
　　An' never miss 't.

Thy wee bit housie,[17] too, in ruin!
Its silly wa's the win's are strewin'![18]
An' naething, now, to big a new ane,[19]
　　O' foggage[20] green!
An' bleak December's winds ensuin',
　　Baith snell[21] and keen!

Thou saw the fields laid bare an' waste,
An' weary winter comin' fast;
An' cozie[22] here, beneath the blast,
　　Thou thought to dwell;
Till crash! the cruel coulter passed
　　Out through thy cell.

That wee bit heap o' leaves an' stibble[23]
Has cost thee monie[24] a weary nibble!
Now thou 's[25] turned out, for a' thy trouble,
　　But house or hald,[26]
To thole[27] the winter's sleety dribble;
　　An' cranreuch cald.[28]

---

[1] Little.　　[2] Sleek.　　[3] Cowering.
[4] Diminutives of "beast," and "breast."　　[5] Not.
[6] Away.　　[7] With scudding fury.　　[8] Would (should) be loth.
[9] Run.　　[10] With murderous ploughstaff.　　[11] Sometimes.
[12] Must.　　[13] An occasional ear of corn.
[14] A double shock.　　[15] Is a small.　　[16] Remainder.
[17] Triple diminutive of house—untranslatable into English.
[18] Its weak walls the winds are strewing.
[19] Nothing now to build a new one.　　[20] Moss.　　[21] Biting.
[22] Snug.　　[23] Very small quantity of leaves and stubble.　　[24] Many.
[25] Thou is (art).　　[26] Without house or hold.　　[27] Endure.
[28] Hoar-frost cold.

> But, Mousie,[1] thou art no thy lane[2]
> In proving foresight may be vain:
> The best-laid schemes o' mice an' men
>   Gang aft a-gley,[3]
> An' leave us nought but grief and pain,
>   For promised joy.
>
> Still thou art blest compared wi' me!
> The present only toucheth thee:
> But och I[4] I backward cast my ee[5]
>   On prospects drear;
> An' forward, though I canna[6] see,
>   I guess an' fear.

A simple and common incident poetically conceived has never been rendered into expression more natural, delicately graceful, and true. Of course, however, our glossarial interpretations can convey but a very insufficient notion of the aptness of the poet's language to those to whom the Scottish dialect is not familiar. Such a phrase as "bickering brattle," for instance, is not to be translated. The epithet "bickering" implies that sharp, explosive, fluttering violence, or impetuosity, which belongs to any sudden and rapid progressive movement of short continuance, and it expresses the noise as well as the speed. It is no doubt the same word with the old English "bickering," but used in a more extensive sense: a "bicker" means commonly a short irregular fight, or skirmish: but Milton has "bickering flame," where, although the commentators interpret the epithet as equivalent to *quivering*, we apprehend it includes the idea of *crackling* also. Darwin has borrowed the phrase, as may be seen in one of our extracts given above. Nor is it possible to give the effect of the diminutives, in which the Scottish language is almost as rich as the Italian. While the English, for example, has only its *manikin*, the Scotch has its *mannie, mannikie, bit mannie, bit mannikie, wee bit mannie, wee bit mannikie, little wee bit mannie, little wee bit mannikie*; and so with *wife, wifie, wifikie*, and many other terms. Almost every substantive noun has at least one diminutive form, made by the affix *ie*, as *mousie, housie*. We ought to notice also, that the established or customary spelling in these and other similar instances does not correctly represent the pronunciation:—the vowel sound is the soft one usually indicated by *oo*; as if the words were written *moosie, hoosie, cooroo*, &c. It is an advantage that the Scottish dialect possesses, somewhat akin to that possessed by the Greek in the time of Homer, that, from having been comparatively but little employed in literary

---

[1] Diminutive of "mouse." [2] Not alone. [3] Go oft awry.
[4] Ah. [5] Eye. [6] Cannot.

composition, and only imperfectly reduced under the dominion of grammar, many of its words have several forms, which are not only convenient for the exigencies of verse, but are used with different effects or shades of meaning. In particular, the English form is always available when wanted; and it is the writer's natural resource when he would rise from the light or familiar style to one of greater elevation or earnestness. Thus, in the above verses, while expressing only half-playful tenderness and commiseration, Burns writes "Now thou 's turned out" (pronounce *oot*), in his native dialect; but it is in the regular English form, "Still thou art blest," that he gives utterance to the deeper pathos and solemnity of the concluding verse.

The proper companion to this short poem is that addressed To a Mountain Daisy, on turning one down with the Plough, in April, 1786; but in that the execution is not so pure throughout, and the latter part runs somewhat into commonplace. The beginning, however, is in the poet's happiest manner:—

Wee, modest, crimson-tipped flow'r,
Thou 's met me in an evil hour;
For I maun crush amang the stour[1]
    Thy tender stem;
To spare thee now is past my pow'r,
    Thou bonnie[2] gem.

Alas! its no[3] thy neebor[4] sweet,
The bonnie lark, companion meet!
Bending thee 'mang the dewy weet[5]
    Wi' spreckled[6] breast,
When upward springing, blythe, to greet
    The purpling east.

Cauld blow the bitter-biting north
Upon thy early, humble, birth;
Yet cheerfully thou glinted[7] forth
    Amid the storm,
Scarce reared above the parent earth
    Thy tender form.

The flaunting flowers our gardens yield
High sheltering woods and wa's maun[8] shield;
But thou beneath the random bield[9]
    O' clod or stane[10]
Adorns the histie[11] stubble-field,
    Unseen, alane.

---

[1] Dust (pronounce *floor, hoor, stoor, poor*).
[2] Lovely. [3] Not. [4] Neighbour. [5] Wet. [6] Speckled.
[7] Peeped, or rather glanced (glanced'st). [8] Walls must.
[9] Shelter. [10] Stone. [11] Dry and rugged.

There, in thy scanty mantle clad,
Thy snawy¹ bosom sun-ward spread,
Thou lifts thy unassuming head
    In humble guise;
But now the share uptears thy bed,
    And low thou lies!

Such is the fate of artless maid,
Sweet floweret of the rural shade!
By love's simplicity betrayed,
    And guileless trust,
Till she, like thee, all soiled is laid
    Low i' the dust.

Such is the fate of simple bard,
On life's rough ocean luckless-starred!
Unskilful he to note the card
    Of prudent lore,
Till billows rage, and gales blow hard,
    And whelm him o'er!

Such fate to suffering worth is given,
Who long with wants and woes has striven,
By human pride or cunning driven
    To misery's brink,
Till, wrenched of every stay but heaven,
    He, ruined, sink!

Even thou who mourn'st the Daisy's fate,
That fate is thine—no distant date;
Stern Ruin's ploughshare drives, elate,
    Full on thy bloom,
Till crushed beneath the furrow's weight
    Shall be thy doom!

The most brilliant comic power, again, animates the pieces entitled Scotch Drink, Death and Dr. Hornbook, the Holy Fair, the Ordination, and others of his more irreverent or reckless effusions. As a picture of manners, however, his Hallowe'en is Burns's greatest performance—with its easy vigour, its execution absolutely perfect, its fulness of various and busy life, the truth and reality throughout, the humour diffused over it like sunshine and ever and anon flashing forth in changeful or more dazzling light, the exquisite fooling and rendering both of the whole human spirit of the scene, and also of its accessories in what we can scarcely call or conceive of as inanimate nature while reading such lines as the following:—

    Whiles² ow'r³ a linn⁴ the burnie⁵ plays,
    As through the glen⁶ it wimpled;⁷

¹ Snowy.   ² Sometimes.   ³ Over.   ⁴ Waterfall.
   ⁵ Rivulet.   ⁶ Dale.   ⁷ Nimbly meandered.

Whiles round a rocky scar[1] it strays;
 Whiles in a wiel[2] it dimpled;
Whiles glittered to the nightly rays,
 Wi' bickering, dancing dazzle;
Whiles cookit[3] underneath the braes,
 Below the spreading hazel.

But this poem is too long for quotation, and is besides well known to every reader who knows anything of Burns. We will rather present our English readers with one or two shorter pieces that may serve to illustrate another quality of the man and of his poetry—the admirable sagacity and good sense, never separated from manliness and a high spirit, that made so large a part of his large heart and understanding. All the more considerate nature of Burns speaks in the following Epistle to a Young Friend, dated May, 1786:—

I lang hae[4] thought, my youthfu' friend,
 A something to have sent you,
Though it should serve nae[5] other end
 Than just a kind memento;
But how the subject-theme may gang
 Let time and chance determine;
Perhaps it may turn out a sang,
 Perhaps turn out a sermon.

Ye 'll try the world soon, my lad,
 And, Andrew dear, believe me,
Ye 'll find mankind an unco squad,[6]
 And muckle[7] they may grieve ye:
For care and trouble set your thought,
 Ev'n when your end 's attained;
And a'[8] your views may come to nought,
 Where every nerve is strained.

I 'll no[9] say men are villains a';
 The real, hardened wicked,
Wha hae nae[10] check but human law,
 Are to a few restricked;[11]
But oh! mankind are unco[12] weak,
 An' little to be trusted;
If self the wavering balance shake,
 It 's rarely right adjusted!

Yet they wha fa'[13] in fortune's strife,
 Their fate we should na[14] censure;

---

[1] Cliff.   [2] Small whirlpool.
[3] Slily disappeared by dipping down, skulked. [Dr. Currie interprets it, "appeared and disappeared by fits."]   [4] Long have.   [5] No.
[6] Strange crew.   [7] Much.   [8] All.   [9] Not.   [10] Who have no
[11] Restricted.   [12] Very, strangely.   [13] Who fall.   [14] Not.

BURNS.

For still the important end of life
  They equally may answer:
A man may hae an honest heart,
  'Though poortith¹ hourly stare him;
A man may tak² a neebor's³ part,
  Yet hae nae cash to spare him.

Aye free aff han'⁴ your story tell,
  When wi' a bosom crony;⁵
But still keep something to yoursel⁶
  You scarcely tell to ony.⁷
Conceal yoursel as weel's⁸ ye can
  Frae⁹ critical dissection;
But keek¹⁰ through every other man
  Wi' sharpened, slee¹¹ inspection.

The sacred lowe¹² o' weel-placed love,
  Luxuriantly indulge it;
But never tempt the illicit rove,
  Though naething should divulge it:
I wave the quantum o' the sin,
  The hazard of concealing;
But oh! it hardens a' within,
  And petrifies the feeling!

To catch dame Fortune's golden smile,
  Assiduous wait upon her;
And gather gear by every wile
  That's justified by honour;
Not for to hide it in a hedge,
  Not for a train attendant;
But for the glorious privilege
  Of being independent.

The fear o' hell's a hangman's whip
  To haud¹³ the wretch in order;
But where ye feel your honour grip,
  Let that aye be your border;
Its slightest touches—instant pause;
  Debar a' side pretences;
And resolutely keep its laws,
  Uncaring consequences.

The great Creator to revere
  Must sure become the creature;
But still the preaching cant forbear,
  And even the rigid feature:

---

¹ Poverty.   ² Take.   ³ Neighbour's.
⁴ Off-hand. ⁵ Intimate associate. ⁶ Yourself. ⁷ Any.
⁸ As well as. ⁹ From. ¹⁰ Look slily. ¹¹ Sly.
¹² Flame. ¹³ Hold.

> Yet ne'er with wits profane to range
> Be complaisance extended;
> An Atheist's laugh 's a poor exchange
> For Deity offended.
> When ranting round in pleasure 's ring
> Religion may be blinded;
> Or, if she gie¹ a random sting,
> It may be little minded;
> But when on life we 're tempest-driven—
> A conscience but a canker—
> A correspondence fixed wi' heaven
> Is sure a noble anchor.
>
> Adieu, dear, amiable youth!
> Your heart can ne'er be wanting;
> May prudence, fortitude, and truth,
> Erect your brow undaunting!
> In ploughman phrase, "God send you speed,"
> Still daily to grow wiser;
> And may you better reck the rede²
> Than ever did the adviser.

This poem, it will be observed, is for the greater part in English; and it is not throughout written with all the purity of diction which Burns never violates in his native dialect. For instance, in the fourth stanza the word "censure" is used to suit the exigencies of the rhyme, where the sense demands some such term as deplore or regret; for, although we might censure the man himself who fails to succeed in life (which, however, is not the idea here), we do not censure, that is blame or condemn, his fate; we can only lament it; if we censure anything, it is his conduct. In the same stanza, the expression "stare him" is, we apprehend, neither English nor Scotch: usage authorizes us to speak of poverty staring a man in the face, but not of it staring him, absolutely. Again, in the tenth stanza, we have "Religion may be blinked," apparently, for may be blinked, disregarded, or looked at as with shut eyes.* We notice these things, to prevent an impression being left with the English reader that they are characteristic of Burns. No such vices of style, we repeat, are to be found in his Scotch, where the diction is uniformly as natural and correct as it is appropriate and expressive.

In a far more elevated and impassioned strain is the poem

¹ Give.
² "Himself the primrose path of dalliance treads,
And recks not his own rede."—Shakespeare, Hamlet.
* Unless, indeed, we may interpret the word as meaning deprived of the power of seeing.

entitled The Vision. It is too long to be quoted entire; but the
following extracts will be sufficiently intelligible:—

> The sun had closed the winter day,
> The curlers quat¹ their roaring play,
> An' hungered mawkin² ta'en her way
>   To kail-yards³ green,
> While faithless snaws⁴ ilk⁵ step betray
>   Whare⁶ she has been.
>
> The thresher's weary flingin' tree⁷
> The lee-lang⁸ day had tired me;
> And, when⁹ the day had closed his e'e¹⁰
>   Far i' the west,
> Ben i' the spence,¹¹ right pensivelie,
>   I gaed¹² to rest.
>
> There, lanely,¹³ by the ingle-cheek,¹⁴
> I sat and eyed the spewing reek,¹⁵
> That filled wi' hoast-provoking smeek¹⁶
>   The auld clay biggin';¹⁷
> An' heard the restless rattons¹⁸ squeak
>   About the riggin'.¹⁹
>
> All in this mottie,²⁰ misty clime,
> I backward mused on wasted time,
> How I had spent my youthfu' prime,
>   An' done nae thing
> But stringin' blethers²¹ up in rhyme,
>   For fools to sing.
>
> Had I to guid advice but harkit,²²
> I might, by this,²³ hae led a market,
> Or strutted in a bank an' clarkit²⁴
>   My cash account:
> While here, half-mad, half-fed, half-sarkit,²⁵
>   Is a' the amount.
>
> I started, muttering Blockhead! Coof!²⁶
> And heaved on high my waukit loof,²⁷
> To swear by a' yon starry roof,
>   Or some rash aith,²⁸
> That I henceforth would be rhyme-proof
>   Till my last breath—

---

¹ Quitted. ² The hare. ³ Colewort gardens.
⁴ Snows. ⁵ Every. ⁶ Where [pronounce whar]
⁷ Flail. ⁸ Live-long. ⁹ When. ¹⁰ Eye.
¹¹ Within in the sitting apartment. ¹² Went. ¹³ Lonely.
¹⁴ Fireside. ¹⁵ Smoke issuing out. ¹⁶ Cough-provoking smoke.
¹⁷ The old clay building, or house. ¹⁸ Rats. ¹⁹ The roof of the house.
²⁰ Full of motes. ²¹ Nonsense, idle words. ²² Hearken.
²³ By this time. ²⁴ Written. ²⁵ Half-shirted.
²⁶ Fool. ²⁷ My palm thickened (with labour). ²⁸ Oath.

When click! the string the snick¹ did draw;
And jee! the door gaed to the wa';
An' by my ingle-lowe I saw,
    Now bleezin'² bright,
A tight, outlandish hizzie,³ braw,
    Come full in sight.

Ye need na doubt I held my whisht;⁴
The infant aith, half-formed, was crushed;
I glowr'd as eerie's I'd been dushed⁵
    In some wild glen;
When sweet, like modest worth, she blushed
    And steppit ben.⁶

Green, slender, leaf-clad holly boughs
Were twisted, gracefu', round her brows;
I took her for some Scottish Muse
    By that same token;
An' come to stop those reckless vows
    Would soon been⁷ broken.

A hair-brained, sentimental trace
Was strongly marked in her face;
A wildly witty, rustic grace
    Shone full upon her;
Her eye, even turned on empty space,
    Beamed keen with honour.

. . . . .

With musing, deep, astonished stare,
I viewed the heavenly-seeming fair;
A whispering throb did witness bear
    Of kindred sweet:
When, with an elder sister's air,
    She did me greet:—

"All hail! my own inspired bard!
In me thy native Muse regard!
Nor longer mourn thy fate is hard,
    Thus poorly low!
I come to give thee such reward
    As we bestow.

"Know the great Genius of this land
Has many a light aërial band,
Who, all beneath his high command,
    Harmoniously,
As arts or arms they understand,
    Their labours ply.

. . . . .

---

¹ Latch.   ² Blazing.   ³ Hussy.   ⁴ ...
⁵ I stared as frightened as if I had been attacked by a bull...
⁶ Walked into the room.   ⁷ Which would soon ha...

BURNS.

"Of these am I—Coila my name;
And this district as mine I claim,
Where once the Campbells, chiefs of fame,
  Held ruling power :—
I marked thy embryo tuneful flame
  Thy natal hour.

"With future hope I oft would gaze
Fond on thy little early ways,
Thy rudely carolled chiming phrase
  In uncouth rhymes,
Fired at the simple, artless lays
  Of other times.

"I saw thee seek the sounding shore,
Delighted with the dashing roar ;
Or, when the North his fleecy store
  Drove through the sky,
I saw grim nature's visage hoar
  Struck thy young eye.

"Or, when the deep-green-mantled earth
Warm cherished every floweret's birth,
And joy and music pouring forth
  In every grove,
I saw thee eye the general mirth
  With boundless love.

"When ripened fields and azure skies
Called forth the reapers' rustling noise
I saw thee leave their evening joys,
  And lonely stalk
To vent thy bosom's swelling rise
  In pensive walk.

"When youthful love, warm-blushing, strong
Keen-shivering shot thy nerves along,
Those accents, grateful to thy tongue,
  The adored name,
I taught thee how to pour in song,
  To soothe thy flame.

"I saw thy pulse's maddening play
Wild send thee pleasure's devious way,
Misled by fancy's meteor ray,
  By passion driven ;
But yet the light that led astray
  Was light from heaven.

. . . . .

"To give my counsels all in one,
Thy tuneful flame still careful fan ;

> Preserve the dignity of man
>   With soul erect;
> And trust the universal plan
>   Will all protect.
>
> "And wear thou this"—she solemn said,
> And bound the holly round my head:
> The polished leaves and berries red
>   Did rustling play;
> And, like a passing thought, she fled
>   In light away.

These extracts, as extracts in every case must be, are only indications or hints of what is to be found in the body of poetry from which they are taken; and in this instance, from various causes, the impression so conveyed may probably be more than usually inadequate—for the strangeness of the dialect must veil much of the effect to an English reader, even when the general sense is apprehended; and, besides, their length, their peculiarly Scottish spirit and character, and other considerations have prevented us from quoting the most successful of Burns's pieces in some of the styles in which he most excelled. But still what we have transcribed may serve to give a more extended and a truer notion of what his poetry really is than is commonly entertained by strangers, among whom he is mostly known and judged of from two or three of his compositions, which perhaps of all that he has produced are the least marked by the peculiar character of his genius. Even out of his own country, his Songs, to be sure, have taken all hearts—and they are the very flame-breath of his own. No truer poetry exists in any language, or in any form. But it is the poetry of the heart much more than of either the head or the imagination. Burns's songs do not at all resemble the exquisite lyrical snatches with which Shakspeare, and also Beaumont and Fletcher, have sprinkled some of their dramas—enlivening the busy scene and progress of the action as the progress of the wayfarer is enlivened by the voices of birds in the hedgerows, or the sight and scent of wild-flowers that have sprung up by the road-side. They are never in any respect exercises of ingenuity, but always utterances of passion, and simple and direct as a shout of laughter or a gush of tears. Whatever they have of fancy, whatever they have of melody, is born of real emotion—is merely the natural expression of the poet's feeling at the moment, seeking and finding vent in musical words. Since "burning Sappho" loved and sung in the old isles of Greece, not much poetry has been produced so thrillingly tender as some of the best of these songs. Here, for example, is one, rude enough perhaps in language and versification,—but every line, every cadence is steeped in pathos:—

>Ye banks, and braes, and streams around
> The castle o' Montgomery,
>Green be your woods, and fair your flowers,
> Your waters never drumlie![1]
>There summer first unfauld her robes,
> And there the langest tarry!
>For there I took the last farewell
> O' my sweet Highland Mary.
>
>How sweetly bloomed the gay green birk,[2]
> How rich the hawthorn's blossom,
>As underneath their fragrant shade
> I clasp'd her to my bosom!
>The golden hours on angel wings
> Flew o'er me and my dearie;
>For dear to me as light and life
> Was my sweet Highland Mary.
>
>Wi' mony a vow and locked embrace
> Our parting was fu' tender;
>And, pledging aft to meet again,
> We tore oursels asunder;
>But oh! fell death's untimely frost,
> That nipt my flower sae early!
>Now green 's the sod, and cauld 's the clay,
> That wraps my Highland Mary!
>
>O pale, pale now those rosy lips
> I aft hae kissed sae fondly!
>And closed for aye the sparkling glance
> That dwelt on me sae kindly!
>And mouldering now in silent dust
> That heart that lo'ed[3] me dearly!
>But still within my bosom's core
> Shall live my Highland Mary.

These compositions are so universally known, that it is needless to give any others at full length; but we may throw together a few verses and half-verses gathered from several of them:—

>When o'er the hill the eastern star
> Tells bughtin'[4] time is near, my joe;
>And owsen[5] frae the furrowed field
> Return sae dowf[6] and weary, O;

---

[1] Turbid with mud.   [2] Birch.   [3] Loved.
[4] Folding.   [5] Oxen.   [6] Dull, spiritless

Down by the burn, where scented birks
  Wi' dew are hanging clear. my joe,
I'll meet thee on the len-rig,[1]
  My ain[2] kind dearie, O.

In mirkest[3] glen, at midnight hour,
  I'd rove, and ne'er be eerie,[4] O,
If through that glen I gaed[5] to thee,
  My ain kind dearie, O.
Although the night were ne'er sae wild,
  And I were ne'er sae weary, O,
I'd meet thee on the lea-rig,
  My ain kind dearie, O.

  .   .   .   .   .

  .   .   .   .   .

I hae sworn by the heavens to my Mary,
  I hae sworn by the heavens to be true;
And sae may the heavens forget me,
  When I forget my vow!

O plight me your faith, my Mary,
  And plight me your lily-white hand;
O plight me your faith, my Mary,
  Before I leave Scotia's strand.

We hae plighted our troth, my Mary,
  In mutual affection to join;
And cursed be the cause that shall part us!
  The hour, and the moment o' time!

O poortith[6] cauld, and restless love, .
  Ye wreck my peace between ye;
Yet poortith a' I could forgive,
  An' 'twere na for my Jeanie.

O why should fate sic[7] pleasure have
  Life's dearest bands untwining?
Or why sae sweet a flower as love
  Depend on fortune's shining?

  .   .   .   .

  .   .   .   .

To thy bosom lay my heart,
  There to throb and languish;
Though despair had wrung its core,
  That would heal its anguish.

---

[1] Grassy ridge.   [2] Own.   [3] Darkest.
[4] Frightened by dread of spirits.   [5] Went.   [6] Poverty.   [7] Such.

Take away those rosy lips,
  Rich with balmy treasure:
Turn away thine eyes of love,
  Lest I die with pleasure.

* * * * *

Here's a health to ane I lo'e dear,
  Here's a health to ane I lo'e dear;
Thou art sweet as the smile when fond lovers meet,
  And soft as their parting tear, Jessy!

Although thou maun[1] never be mine,
  Although even hope is denied,
'Tis sweeter for thee despairing
  Than aught in the world beside, Jessy!

* * * * *

Ae[2] fond kiss, and then we sever;
  Ae fareweel, alas, for ever!

* * * *

Had we never loved sae kindly,
Had we never loved sae blindly,
Never met, or never parted,
We had ne'er been broken-hearted.
Fare thee weel, thou first and fairest!
Fare thee weel, thou best and dearest!

* * * * *

Ae fond kiss, and then we sever;
Ae fareweel, alas, for ever!

* * * * *

In all, indeed, that he has written best, Burns may be said to have given us himself,—the passion or sentiment which swayed or possessed him at the moment,—almost as much as in his songs. In him the poet was the same as the man. He could describe with admirable fidelity and force incidents, scenes, manners, characters, or whatever else, which had fallen within his experience or observation; but he had little proper dramatic imagination, or power of going out of himself into other natures, and, as it were, losing his personality in the creations of his fancy. His blood was too hot, his pulse beat too tumultuously, for that; at least he was during his short life too much the sport both of his own passions and of many other stormy influences to acquire such power of intellectual self-command and self-suppression. What he might have attained to if a longer earthly

[1] Must.   [2] One.

existence had been granted to him—or a less tempestuous one—who shall say? Both when his genius first blazed out upon the world, and when its light was quenched by death, it seemed as if he had been born or designed to do much more than he has done. Having written what he wrote before his twenty-seventh year, he had doubtless much more additional poetry in him than he gave forth between that date and his death at the age of thirty-seven—poetry which might now have been the world's for ever if that age had been worthy of such a gift of heaven as its glorious poet.

THE NINETEENTH CENTURY.

It might almost seem as if there were something in the impressiveness of the great chronological event formed by the termination of one century and the commencement of another that had been wont to act with an awakening and fructifying power upon literary genius in these islands. Of the three last great sunbursts of our literature, the first, making what has been called the Elizabethan age of our dramatic and other poetry, threw its splendour over the last quarter of the sixteenth and the first of the seventeenth century; the second, famous as the Augustan age of Anne, brightened the earlier years of the eighteenth; the nineteenth century was ushered in by the third. At the termination of the reign of George III., in the year 1820, there were still among us, not to mention minor names, at least nine or ten poetical writers, each (whatever discordance of opinion there might be about either their relative or their absolute merits) commanding universal attention from the reading world to whatever he produced:—Crabbe (to take them in the order of their seniority), Wordsworth, Coleridge, Southey, Scott, Campbell, Moore, Byron, Shelley, and perhaps we ought to add Keats, though more for the shining promise of his great but immature genius than for what he had actually done. Many other voices there were from which divine words were often heard, but these were oracles to whom all listened, whose inspiration all men acknowledged. It is such crowding and clustering of remarkable writers that has chiefly distinguished the great literary ages in every country: there are eminent writers at other times, but they come singly or in small numbers, as Lucretius, the noblest of the Latin poets, did before the Augustan age of Roman literature; as our own Milton and Dryden did in the interval between our Elizabethan age and that of Anne; as Goldsmith, and Burke, and Johnson, and then Cowper, and Burns, in twos and threes, or one by one, preceded and as it were led in the rush and crush of our last revival. For such single swallows, though they do not make, do yet commonly herald the summer; and accordingly those remarkable writers who have thus appeared between one great age of literature and another have mostly, it may be observed, arisen not in the earlier but in the later portion of the interval—have been not the lagging successors of the last era, but the precursors of the next. However the fact is to be explained or accounted for, it does indeed look as if Nature in this, as in other things, had her times of production and of comparative rest and inactivity—her autumns and her winters—or, as we may otherwise conceive it, her alternations of light and darkness, of day and night. After a busy and brilliant period of usually some thirty or forty years, there has always followed in every country a long term during which the literary spirit, as if overworked and exhausted, has manifested little real energy or power of life, and even the very demand and taste for the highest kind of literature, for depth, and subtlety, and truth, and originality, and passion, and beauty, has in a great measure ceased with the supply—a sober and slumbrous twilight of imitation and mediocrity, and little more than mechanical dexterity in bookmaking, at least with the generality of the most popular and applauded writers.

After all, the reawakening of our English literature, on each of the three occasions we have mentioned, was probably brought about mainly by the general political and social circumstances of the country and of the world at the time. The poetical and dramatic wealth and magnificence of the era of Elizabeth and James came, no doubt, for the most part, out of the passions that had been stirred and the strength that had been acquired in the mighty contests and convulsions which filled, here and throughout Europe, the middle of the sixteenth century; another breaking up of old institutions and re-edification of the state upon a new foundation and a new principle, the work of the last sixty years of the seventeenth century, if it did not contribute much to train the wits and fine writers of the age of Anne, at least both prepared the tranquillity necessary for the restoration of elegant literature, and disposed the public mind for its enjoyment; the poetical dayspring, finally, that came with our own century was born with, and probably in some degree out of, a third revolution, which shook both established institutions and the minds and opinions of men throughout Europe as much almost as the Reformation itself had done three centuries and a half before. It is also to be observed that on each of these three occasions the excitement appears to have come to us in part from a foreign literature which had undergone a similar reawakening, or put forth a new life and vigour, shortly before our own: in the Elizabethan age the contagion or impulse was caught from the literature of Italy; in the age of Anne from that of France; in the present period from that of Germany.

THE LAST AGE OF THE GEORGES.
WORDSWORTH.

This German inspiration operated most directly, and produced the most marked effect, in the poetry of Wordsworth. Wordsworth, who was born in 1770, has preserved in the editions of his collected works some of his verses written so long ago as 1786; and he also continued to the last to reprint the two earliest of his published poems, entitled An Evening Walk, addressed to a Young Lady, from the Lakes of the North of England, and Descriptive Sketches, taken during a pedestrian tour among the Alps, both of which first appeared in 1793. The recollection of the former of these poems probably suggested to somebody, a few years later, the otherwise not very intelligible designation of the Lake School, which has been applied to this writer and his imitators, or supposed imitators. But the Evening Walk and the Descriptive Sketches, which are both written in the usual rhyming ten-syllabled verse, are perfectly orthodox poems, according to the common creed, in spirit, manner, and form. The peculiarities which are conceived to constitute what is called the Lake manner first appeared in the Lyrical Ballads; the first volume of which was published in 1798, the second in 1800.

In the Preface to the second volume of the Lyrical Ballads, the author himself described his object as being to ascertain how far the purposes of poetry might be fulfilled "by fitting to metrical arrangement a selection of the real language of men in a state of vivid sensation." It might, perhaps, be possible to defend this notion by the aid of certain assumptions as to what is implied in, or to be understood by, a state of vivid sensation, which it may be contended is only another phrase for a state of poetical excitement: undoubtedly the language of a mind in such a state, selected, or corrected, and made metrical, will be poetry. It is almost a truism to say so. Nay, we might go farther, and assert that, in the circumstances supposed, the selection and the adaptation to metrical arrangement would not be necessary; the language would flow naturally into something of a musical shape (that being one of the conditions of poetical expression), and, although it might be improved by correction, it would have all the essentials of poetry as it was originally produced. But what is evidently meant is, that the real or natural language of any and every mind when simply in a state of excitement or passion is necessarily poetical. The respect in which the doctrine differs from that commonly held is, that it assumes more passion or vivid sensation to be in all men and in all cases substantially identical with poetical excitement, and the language in which passion expresses itself to be consequently always poetry, at least after it has undergone some purification or pruning, and been reduced to metrical regularity. As for this qualification, we may remark that it must be understood to mean nothing more than that the language of passion is improved with reference to poetical effect by being thus trained and regulated: otherwise the statement would be contradictory and would refute itself; for, if passion, or vivid sensation, always speaks in poetry, the metrical arrangement and the selection are unnecessary and unwarrantable; if these operations be indispensable, the language of vivid sensation is not always poetry. But surely it is evident from the nature of the thing that it is altogether a misconception of what poetry is to conceive it to be nothing more than the language naturally prompted by passion or strong emotion. If that were all, all men, all women, and all children would be poets. Poetry, in the first place, is an art, just as painting is an art; and the one is no more to be practised solely under the guidance of strong emotion than the other. Secondly, poetical emotion is something as distinct from mere ordinary passion or excitement as is musical emotion, or the feeling of the picturesque or the beautiful or the grand in painting or in architecture; the one may and often does exist where there exists nothing of the other. Nobody has ever thought of defining music to be merely the natural vocal utterance of men in a state of vivid sensation, or painting to be nothing more than their natural way of expressing themselves when in such a state by lines and colours: no more is poetry simply their real language, or expression by words, when in such a state. It makes no difference that words are a mode of expression of which men have much more generally the use than they have the use of either colours or musical sounds; if all men could sing or could handle the brush, they still would not all be musicians and painters whenever they were in a passion.

It is true that even in the rudest minds emotion will tend to make the expression more vivid and forcible; but it will not for all that necessarily rise to poetry. Emotion or excitement alone will not produce that idealization in which poetry consists. To have that effect the excitement must be of a peculiar character, and the mind in which it takes place must be peculiarly gifted. The mistake has probably arisen from a confusion of two things which are widely different—the real language of men in a state of excitement, and the imaginative imitation of such language in the artistic delineation of the excitement. The latter alone will necessarily or universally be poetical; the former may be the veriest of prose. It may be said, indeed, that it is not men's real language, but the imitation of it, which is meant to be called poetry by Wordsworth and his followers—that, of course, their own poetry, even when most conformable to their own theory, can only consist of what *they conceive* would be the real language of persons placed in the circumstances of those from whom it professes to proceed. But this explanation, besides that it leaves the theory we are examining, considered as an account or definition of poetry, as narrow and defective as ever, still assumes that poetical imitation is nothing more than transcription, or its equivalent—such invention as comes as near as possible to what literal transcription would be; which is the very misapprehension against which we are arguing. It is equally false, we contend, to say that poetry is nothing more than either the real language of men in a state of excitement, or the mere imitation, the closer the better, of that real language. The imitation must be an idealized imitation—an intermingling of the poet with his subject by which it receives a new character; just as, in painting, a great portrait, or other picture from nature, is never a fac-simile copy, but always as much a reflection from the artist's own spirit as from the scene or object it represents. The realm of nature and the realm of art, although counterparts, are nevertheless altogether distinct the one from the other; and both painting and poetry belong to the latter, not to the former.

We cannot say that Wordsworth's theory of poetry has been altogether without effect upon his practice, but it has shown itself rather by some deficiency of refinement in his general manner than by very much that he has written in express conformity with its requisitions. We might affirm, indeed, that its principle is as much contradicted and confuted by the greater part of his own poetry as it is by that of all languages and all times in which poetry has been written, or by the universal past experience of mankind in every age and country. He is a great poet, and has enriched our literature with much beautiful and noble writing, whatever be the method or principle upon which he constructs, or fancies that he constructs, his compositions. His Laodamia, without the exception of a single line, his Lonely Leech-gatherer, with the exception of very few lines; his Ruth, his Tintern Abbey, his Feast of Brougham, the Water Lily, the greater part of the Excursion, most of the Sonnets, his great Ode on the Intimations of Immortality in Early Childhood, and many of his shorter lyrical pieces, are nearly as unexceptionable in diction as they are deep and true in feeling, judged according to any rules or principles of art that are now patronized by anybody. It is true, indeed, that it will not do to look at anything that Wordsworth has written through the spectacles of that species of criticism which was in vogue among us in the last century; we believe that in several of the pieces we have named even that narrow and superficial doctrine (if it could be recalled from the tomb) would find little or nothing to object to, but we fear it would find as little to admire; it had no feeling or understanding of the poetry of any other era than its own,—neither of that of Homer, nor that of the Greek dramatists, nor that of our own Elizabethan age,—and it certainly would not enter far into the spirit either of that of Wordsworth or of any of his eminent contemporaries or successors. It is part, and a great part, of what the literature of Germany has done for us within the last sixty years, that it has given a wider scope and a deeper insight to our perception and mode of judging of the poetical in all its forms and manifestations; and the poetry of Wordsworth has materially aided in establishing this revolution of taste and critical doctrine, by furnishing the English reader with some of the earliest and many of the most successful or most generally appreciated examples and illustrations of the precepts of the new faith. Even the errors of Wordsworth's poetical creed and practice, the excess to which he has sometimes carried his employment of the language of the uneducated classes, and his attempts to extract poetical effects out of trivial incidents and humble life, were fitted to be rather serviceable than injurious in the highly artificial state of our poetry when he began to write. He may not have succeeded in every instance in which he has tried to glorify the familiar and elevate the low, but he has nevertheless taught us that the domain of poetry is much wider and more various than it used to be deemed, that there is a great deal of it to be found where it was formerly little the fashion to look for anything of the kind, and that the poet does not absolutely require for the exercise of his art and the display of his powers what are commonly called illustrious or distinguished characters, and an otherwise dignified subject, any more than long and learned words. Of all his English contemporaries Wordsworth stands foremost and alone as the poet of common life. It is not his only field, nor perhaps the field in which he is greatest; but it is the one which is most exclusively his own. He has, it is true, no humour or comedy of any kind in him (which is perhaps the explanation of the ludicrous touches that sometimes startle us in his serious poetry), and therefore he is not, and seldom attempts to be, what Burns was for his countrymen, the poetic interpreter, and, as such, refiner as well as embalmer, of the wit and merriment of the common people: the writer by whom that title is to be won is yet to arise, and probably from among the people themselves: but of whatever is more tender or more thoughtful in the spirit of ordinary life in England the poetry of Wordsworth is the truest and most comprehensive transcript we possess. Many of his verses, embodying as they do the philosophy as well as the sentiment of this every-day human experience, have a completeness and impressiveness, as of texts, mottoes, proverbs, the force of which is universally felt, and has already worked them into the texture and substance of the language to a far greater extent, we apprehend, than has happened in the case of any contemporary writer.

Wordsworth, though only a few years deceased, for he survived till 1850, nearly sixty years after the publication of his first poetry, is already a classic; and, extensively as he is now read and appreciated, any review of our national literature would be very incomplete without at least a few extracts from his works illustrative of the various styles in which he has written. As a specimen of what may be called his more peculiar manner, or that which is or used to be more especially understood by the style of the Lake School of poetry, we will begin with the well-known verses entitled The Fountain, a Conversation, which, in his own classification, are included among what he designates Poems of Sentiment and Reflection, and are stated to have been composed in 1799:—

> We walked with open heart, and tongue
> Affectionate and true,
> A pair of friends, though I was young,
> And Matthew seventy-two.
>
> We lay beneath a spreading oak,
> Beside a mossy seat;
> And from the turf a fountain broke,
> And gurgled at our feet.
>
> "Now, Matthew!" said I, "let us match
> This water's pleasant tune
> With some old border-song, or catch
> That suits a summer's noon;
>
> Or of the church-clock and the chimes
> Sing here, beneath the shade,
> That half-mad thing of witty rhymes
> Which you last April made!"
>
> In silence Matthew lay, and eyed
> The spring beneath the tree;
> And thus the dear old man replied,
> The grey-haired man of glee:

ENGLISH LITERATURE AND LANGUAGE.

"No check, no stay, this streamlet fears;
　How merrily it goes!
'Twill murmur on a thousand years,
　And flow as now it flows.

And here, on this delightful day,
　I cannot choose but think
How oft, a vigorous man, I lay
　Beside this fountain's brink.

My eyes are dim with childish tears,
　My heart is idly stirred,
For the same sound is in my ears
　Which in those days I heard.

Thus fares it still in our decay:
　And yet the wiser mind
Mourns less for what age takes away
　Than what it leaves behind.

The blackbird amid leafy trees,
　The lark above the hill,
Let loose their carols when they please,
　Are quiet when they will.

With nature never do they wage
　A foolish strife; they see
A happy youth, and their old age
　Is beautiful and free:

But we are pressed by heavy laws;
　And often, glad no more,
We wear a face of joy, because
　We have been glad of yore.

If there be one who need bemoan
　His kindred laid in earth,
The household hearts that were his own,
　It is the man of mirth.

My days, my friend, are almost gone,
　My life has been approved,
And many love me; but by none
　Am I enough beloved."

"Now, both himself and me he wrongs,
　The man who thus complains!
I live and sing my idle songs
　Upon these happy plains,

And, Matthew, for thy children dead
　I'll be a son to thee!"
At this he grasped my hand, and said,
　"Alas! that cannot be!"

We rose up from the fountain-side;
And down the smooth descent
Of the green sheep-track did we glide;
And through the wood we went;

And, ere we came to Leonard's Rock,
He sang those witty rhymes
About the crazy old church-clock,
And the bewildered chimes.

The following, entitled The Affliction of Margaret, dated 1804, and classed among the Poems founded on the Affections, is more impassioned, but still essentially in the same style:—

Where art thou, my beloved son,
Where art thou, worse to me than dead?
Oh find me, prosperous or undone!
Or, if the grave be now thy bed,
Why am I ignorant of the same,
That I may rest; and neither blame
Nor sorrow may attend thy name?

Seven years, alas! to have received
No tidings of an only child;
To have despaired, have hoped, believed,
And been for evermore beguiled;
Sometimes with thoughts of very bliss!
I catch at them, and then I miss;
Was ever darkness like to this?

He was among the prime in worth,
An object beauteous to behold;
Well born, well bred; I sent him forth
Ingenuous, innocent, and bold:
If things ensued that wanted grace,
As hath been said, they were not base;
And never blush was on my face.

Ah! little doth the young one dream,
When full of play and childish cares,
What power is in his wildest scream,
Heard by his mother unawares!
He knows it not, he cannot guess:
Years to a mother bring distress;
But do not make her love the less.

Neglect me! no, I suffered long
From that ill thought; and, being blind,
Said, "Pride shall help me in my wrong:
Kind mother have I been, as kind
As ever breathed:" and that is true;
I've wet my path with tears like dew,
Weeping for him when no one knew.

My son, if thou be humbled, poor,
Hopeless of honour and of gain,
Oh! do not dread thy mother's door;
Think not of me with grief and pain:
I now can see with better eyes;
And worldly grandeur I despise,
And Fortune with her gifts and lies.

Alas! the fowls of heaven have wings,
And blasts of heaven will aid their flight:
They mount—how short a voyage brings
The wanderers back to their delight!
Chains tie us down by land and sea;
And wishes, vain as mine, may be
All that is left to comfort thee.

Perhaps some dungeon bears thee groan,
Maimed, mangled, by inhuman men;
Or thou, upon a desert thrown,
Inheritest the lion's den;
Or hast been summoned to the deep,
Thou, thou and all thy mates, to keep
An incommunicable sleep.

I look for ghosts; but none will force
Their way to me:—'tis falsely said
That there was ever intercourse
Between the living and the dead;
For, surely, then I should have sight
Of him I wait for day and night
With love and longings infinite.

My apprehensions come in crowds;
I dread the rustling of the grass;
The very shadows of the clouds
Have power to shake me as they pass;
I question things, and do not find
One that will answer to my mind;
And all the world appears unkind.

Beyond participation lie
My troubles, and beyond relief:
If any chance to heave a sigh,
They pity me, and not my grief.
Then come to me, my Son, or send
Some tidings that my woes may end;
I have no other earthly friend!

Here is another from the same class, and still in the same style, dated 1708. The verses are very beautiful; they bear some resemblance to the touching old Scotch ballad called Lady Anna Bothwell's Lament, beginning

Balow, my boy, lie still and sleep;
It grieves me sair to see thee weep—

of which there is a copy in Percy's Reliques, and others, differing considerably from that, in other collections:—

Her eyes are wild, her head is bare,
The sun has burned her coal-black hair;
Her eyebrows have a rusty stain,
And she came far from over the main.
She has a baby on her arm,
 Or else she were alone:
And underneath the haystack warm,
 And on the greenwood stone,
She talked and sung the words among,
And it was in the English tongue.

"Sweet babe, they say that I am mad,
But nay, my heart is far too glad;
And I am happy when I sing
Full many a sad and doleful thing:
Then, lovely baby, do not fear!
I pray thee, have no fear of me;
But safe as in a cradle, here,
My lovely baby, shalt thou be:
To thee I know too much I owe;
I cannot work thee any woe.

A fire was once within my brain;
And in my head a dull, dull pain;
And fiendish faces, one, two, three,
Hung at my breast, and pulled at me;
But then there came a sight of joy,
It came at once to do me good;
I waked, and saw my little boy,
My little boy of flesh and blood;
Oh joy for me that sight to see!
For he was there, and only he.

Suck, little babe, oh suck again!
It cools my blood, it cools my brain;
Thy lips I feel them, baby! they
Draw from my heart the pain away.
Oh! press me with thy little hand;
It loosens something at my chest;
About that tight and deadly band
I feel thy little fingers prest.
The breeze I see is in the tree:
It comes to cool my babe and me.

Oh! love me, love me, little boy!
Thou art thy mother's only joy;

ENGLISH LITERATURE AND LANGUAGE.

And do not dread the waves below
When o'er the sea-rock's edge we go;
The high crag cannot work me harm,
Nor leaping torrents when they howl;
The babe I carry on my arm
He saves for me my precious soul;
Then happy lie; for blest am I;
Without me my sweet babe would die.

Then do not fear, my boy! for thee
Bold as a lion will I be:
And I will always be thy guide,
Through hollow snows and rivers wide.
I'll build an Indian bower; I know
The leaves that make the softest bed:
And if from me thou wilt not go,
But still be true till I am dead,
My pretty thing, then thou shalt sing
As merry as the birds in spring.

Thy father cares not for my breast,
'Tis thine, sweet baby, there to rest;
'Tis all thine own!—and, if its hue
Be changed, that was so fair to view,
'Tis fair enough for thee, my dove!
My beauty, little child, is flown,
But thou wilt live with me in love;
And what if my poor cheek be brown?
'Tis well for thee, thou canst not see
How pale and wan it else would be.

Dread not their taunts, my little life;
I am thy father's wedded wife;
And underneath the spreading tree
We two will live in honesty.
If his sweet boy he could forsake,
With me he never would have stayed;
From him no harm my babe can take;
But he, poor man! is wretched made;
And every day we two will pray
For him that 's gone and far away.

I'll teach my boy the sweetest things,
I'll teach him how the owlet sings.
My little babe! thy lips are still,
And thou hast almost sucked thy fill.
—— Where art thou gone, my own dear child?
What wicked looks are those I see?
Alas! alas! that look so wild,
It never, never came from me:
If thou art mad, my pretty lad,
Then I must be for ever sad.

Oh! smile on me, my little lamb!
For I thy own dear mother am.
My love for thee has well been tried:
I've sought thy father far and wide.
I know the poisons of the shade,
I know the earth-nuts fit for food:
Then, pretty dear, be not afraid:
We'll find thy father in the wood.
Now laugh and be gay, to the woods away!
And there, my babe, we'll live for aye."

But much, perhaps we might say the greater part, of Wordsworth's poetry is in a very different style or manner. Take, for example, his noble Laodamia, dated 1814, and in the later editions placed among what he calls Poems of the Imagination, though formerly classed as one of the Poems founded on the Affections:—

"With sacrifice before the rising morn
Vows have I made by fruitless hope inspired;
And from the infernal Gods, 'mid shades forlorn
Of night, my slaughtered Lord have I required:
Celestial pity I again implore:—
Restore him to my sight—great Jove, restore!"

So speaking, and by fervent love endowed
With faith, the suppliant heavenward lifts her hands;
While, like the sun emerging from a cloud,
Her countenance brightens—and her eye expands;
Her bosom heaves and spreads, her stature grows;
And she expects the issue in repose.

O terror! what hath she perceived? O joy!
What doth she look on? Whom doth she behold?
Her Hero slain upon the beach of Troy?
His vital presence? his corporeal mould?
It is—if sense deceive her not—'tis He!
And a God leads him, winged Mercury!

Mild Hermes spake—and touched her with his wand
That calms all fear; "Such grace hath crowned thy prayer,
Laodamia! that at Jove's command
Thy husband walks the paths of upper air:
He comes to tarry with thee three hours' space;
Accept the gift, behold him face to face!"

Forth sprang the Impassioned Queen her Lord to clasp;
Again that consummation she assayed;
But unsubstantial form eludes her grasp
As often as that eager grasp was made.
The Phantom parts—but parts to re-unite,
And re-assume his place before her sight.

"Protesilaus, lo! thy guide is gone!
Confirm, I pray, the Vision with thy voice:
This is our palace,—yonder is thy throne;
Speak, and the floor thou tread'st on will rejoice.
Not to appal me have the Gods bestowed
This precious boon; and blest a sad abode."
"Great Jove, Laodamia! doth not leave
His gifts imperfect:—Spectre though I be,
I am not sent to scare thee or deceive;
But in reward of thy fidelity.
And something also did my worth obtain;
For fearless virtue bringeth boundless gain.
Thou knowest, the Delphic oracle foretold
That the first Greek who touched the Trojan strand
Should die; but me the threat could not withhold:
A generous cause a victim did demand;
And forth I leapt upon the sandy plain;
A self-devoted chief—by Hector slain."
"Supreme of Heroes—bravest, noblest, best!
Thy matchless courage I bewail no more,
Which then, when tens of thousands were deprest
By doubt, propelled thee to the fatal shore:
Thou found'st—and I forgive thee—here thou art—
A nobler counsellor than my poor heart.
But thou, though capable of sternest deed,
Wert kind as resolute, and good as brave;
And he, whose power restores thee, hath decreed
That thou should'st cheat the malice of the grave;
Redundant are thy locks, thy lips as fair
As when their breath enriched Thessalian air.
No Spectre greets me,—no vain Shadow this;
Come, blooming Hero, place thee by my side!
Give, on this well-known couch, one nuptial kiss
To me, this day, a second time thy bride!"
Jove frowned in heaven: the conscious Parcae threw
Upon those roseate lips a Stygian hue.
"This visage tells thee that my doom is past:
Nor should the change be mourned, even if the joys
Of sense were able to return as fast
And surely as they vanish.—Earth destroys
Those raptures duly—Erebus disdains:
Calm pleasures there abide—majestic pains.
Be taught, O faithful Consort, to control
Rebellious passion: for the Gods approve
The depth, and not the tumult of the soul;
A fervent, not ungovernable love.
Thy transports moderate; and meekly mourn
When I depart, for brief is my sojourn."—

WORDSWORTH.

"Ah, wherefore?—Did not Hercules by force
Wrest from the guardian monster of the tomb
Alcestis, a reanimated corse,
Given back to dwell on earth in vernal bloom?
Medea's spells dispersed the weight of years,
And Aeson stood a youth 'mid youthful peers.

The Gods to us are merciful—and they
Yet further may relent: for mightier far
Than strength of nerve and sinew, or the sway
Of magic potent over sun and star,
Is love, though oft to agony distrest,
And though his favourite seat be feeble woman's breast.

But if thou goest I follow"—"Peace!" he said—
She looked upon him and was calmed and cheered;
The ghastly colour from his lips had fled;
In his deportment, shape, and mien appeared
Elysian beauty, melancholy grace,
Brought from a pensive, though a happy place.

He spake of love, such love as Spirits feel
In worlds whose course is equable and pure;
No fears to beat away—no strife to heal—
The past unsighed for, and the future sure;
Spake of heroic acts in graver mood
Revived, with finer harmony pursued;
Of all that is most beauteous—imaged there
In happier beauty; more pellucid streams,
An ampler ether, a diviner air,
And fields invested with purpureal gleams;
Climes which the sun, who sheds the brightest day
Earth knows, is all unworthy to survey.

Yet there the soul shall enter which hath earned
That privilege by virtue.—"Ill," said he,
"The end of man's existence I discerned,
Who from ignoble games and revelry
Could draw, when we had parted, vain delight,
While tears were thy best pastime day and night:

And while my youthful peers before my eyes
(Each hero following his peculiar bent)
Prepared themselves for glorious enterprise
By martial sports,—or, seated in the tent,
Chieftains and kings in council were detained;
What time the fleet at Aulis lay enchained.

The wished-for wind was given:—I then revolved
The oracle upon the silent sea;
And, if no worthier led the way, resolved
That, of a thousand vessels, mine should be
The foremost prow in pressing to the strand,—
Mine the first blood that tinged the Trojan sand.

Yet bitter, oftimes bitter, was the pang
When of thy loss I thought, beloved wife!
On thee too fondly did my memory hang,
And on the joys we shared in mortal life,—
The paths which we had trod—these fountains, flowers;
My new-planned cities, and unfinished towers.

But should suspense permit the foe to cry,
'Behold, they tremble!—haughty their array,
Yet of their number no one dares to die?'
In soul I swept the indignity away:
Old frailties then recurred:—but lofty thought,
In act embodied, my deliverance wrought.

And thou, though strong in love, art all too weak
In reason, in self-government too slow;
I counsel thee by fortitude to seek
Our blest reunion in the shades below.
The invisible world with thee hath sympathised;
Be thy affections raised and solemnised.

Learn, by a mortal yearning, to ascend—
Seeking a higher object. Love was given,
Encouraged, sanctioned, chiefly for that end;
For this the passion to excess was driven—
That self might be annulled; her bondage prove
The fetters of a dream, opposed to love."[1]

Aloud she shrieked! for Hermes reappears!
Round the dear shade she would have clung—'tis vain:
The hours are past—too brief had they been years;
And him no mortal effort can detain:
Swift, towards the realms that know not earthly day,
He through the portal takes his silent way,
And on the palace floor a lifeless corse she lay.

She—who, though warned, exhorted, and reproved,
Thus died, from passion desperate to a crime—
By the just Gods, whom no weak pity moved,
Was doomed to wear out her appointed time,
Apart from happy ghosts, that gather flowers
Of blissful quiet 'mid unfading bowers.

Yet tears to mortal suffering are due;
And mortal hopes defeated and o'erthrown
Are mourned by man,—and not by man alone,

---

[1] The reader of Milton will remember the same idea in the eighth book of Paradise Lost:—

"Love refines
The thoughts, and heart enlarges; hath his seat
In reason, and is judicious; is the scale
By which to heavenly love thou may'st ascend."

As fondly he believes.—Upon the side
Of Hellespont (such faith was entertained)
A knot of spiry trees for ages grew
From out the tomb of him for whom she died;
And ever, when such stature they had gained
That Ilium's walls were subject to their view,
The trees' tall summits withered at the sight;
A constant interchange of growth and blight.

In the same grand strain is very much especially of Wordsworth's later poetry. Neither puerility nor over familiarity of diction, with whatever other faults they may be chargeable, can well be attributed to either the Excursion, or the Sonnets, or the Odes. But it is, on the other hand, a misconception to imagine that this later poetry is for the most part enveloped in a haze through which the meaning is only to be got at by initiated eyes. Nothing like this is the case. The Excursion, published in 1814, for instance, with the exception of a very few passages, is a poem that he who runs may read, and the greater part of which may be apprehended by readers of all classes as readily as almost any other poetry in the language. We may say the same even of The Prelude, or Introduction to the Recluse (intended to consist of three Parts, of which The Excursion is the second, the first remaining in manuscript, and the third having been only planned), which was begun in 1799 and completed in 1805, although not published till a few months after the author's death in 1850; an elaborate poem, in fourteen books, of eminent interest as the poet's history of himself, and of the growth of his own mind, as well as on other accounts, and long before characterized by Coleridge, to whom it is addressed, as

"An Orphic song indeed,
A song divine of high and passionate thoughts
To their own music chanted."*

---

* In reference, no doubt, to Wordsworth's own lines, in the First Book of the Poem:—

"Some philosophic song
Of Truth that cherishes our daily life;
With meditations passionate from deep
Recesses in man's heart, immortal verse
Thoughtfully fitted to the Orphean lyre."

And here, again, we have the echo of Milton's line, in the Third Book of Paradise Lost:—

"With other notes than to the Orphean lyre."

COLERIDGE.

In all that constitutes artistic character the poetry of Coleridge is a contrast to that of Wordsworth. Coleridge, born in 1772, published the earliest of his poetry that is now remembered in 1796, in a small volume containing also some pieces by Charles Lamb, to which some by Charles Lloyd were added in a second edition the following year. It was not till 1800, after he had produced and printed separately his Ode to the Departing Year (1796), his noble ode entitled France (1797), his Fears in Solitude (1798), and his translations of both parts of Schiller's Wallenstein, that he was first associated as a poet and author with Wordsworth, in the second volume of whose Lyrical Ballads, published in 1800, appeared, as the contributions of an anonymous friend, Coleridge's Ancient Mariner, Foster Mother's Tale, Nightingale, and Love. "I should not have requested this assistance," said Wordsworth, in his preface, "had I not believed that the poems of my friend would, in a great measure, have the same tendency as my own, and that, though there would be found a difference, there would be found no discordance, in the colours of our style; as our opinions on the subject of poetry do almost entirely coincide." Coleridge's own account, however, is somewhat different. In his Biographia Literaria, he tells us that, besides the Ancient Mariner, he was preparing for the conjoint publication, among other poems, the Dark Ladie and the Christabel, in which he should have more nearly realized his ideal than he had done in his first attempt, when the volume was brought out with so much larger a portion of it the produce of Wordsworth's industry than his own, that his few compositions, "instead of forming a balance, appeared rather an interpolation of heterogeneous matter;" and then he adds, in reference to the long preface in which Wordsworth had expounded his theory of poetry, "With many parts of this preface in the sense attributed to them, and which the words undoubtedly seem to authorize, I never concurred; but, on the contrary, objected to them as erroneous in principle and contradictory (in appearance at least) both to other parts of the same preface, and to the author's own practice in the greater number of the poems themselves."

Coleridge's poetry is remarkable for the perfection of its execution, for the exquisite art with which its divine spirit is endowed with formal expression. The subtly woven words, with all their sky colours, seem to grow out of the thought or emotion, as the flower from its stalk, or the flame from its feeding oil. The music of his verse, too, especially of what he has written in rhyme, is as sweet and as characteristic as anything in the language, placing him for that rare excellence in the same small band with Shakespeare, and Beaumont and Fletcher (in their lyrics), and Milton, and Collins, and Shelley, and Tennyson. It was probably only quantity that was wanting to make Coleridge the greatest poet of his day. Certainly, at least, some things that he has written have not been surpassed, if they have been matched, by any of his contemporaries. And (as indeed has been the case with almost all great poets) he continued to write better and better the longer he wrote; some of his happiest verses were the produce of his latest years. To quote part of what we have said in a paper published immediately after Coleridge's death :—" Not only, as we proceed from his earlier to his later compositions, does the execution become much more artistic and perfect, but the informing spirit is refined and purified—the tenderness grows more delicate and deep, the fire brighter and keener, the sense of beauty more subtle and exquisite. Yet from the first there was in all he wrote the divine breath which essentially makes poetry what it is. There was ' the shaping spirit of imagination,' evidently of soaring pinion and full of strength, though as yet sometimes unskilfully directed, and encumbered in its flight by an affluence of power which it seemed hardly to know how to manage : hence an unselecting impetuosity in these early compositions, never indicating anything like poverty of thought, but producing occasionally considerable awkwardness and turgidity of style, and a declamatory air, from which no poetry was ever more free than that of Coleridge in its maturer form. Yet even among these juvenile productions are many passages, and some whole pieces, of perfect gracefulness, and radiant with the purest sunlight of poetry. There is, for example, the most beautiful delicacy of sentiment, as well as sweetness of versification and expression, in the following lines, simple as they are :—

> Maid of my love, sweet Genevieve!
> In beauty's light you glide along;
> Your eye is like the star of eve,
> And sweet your voice as Seraph's song.
> Yet not your heavenly beauty gives
> This heart with passion soft to glow:
> Within your soul a voice there lives!
> It bids you hear the tale of woe.
> When, sinking low, the sufferer wan
> Beholds no hand outstretched to save,

> Fair, as the bosom of the swan
> That rises graceful o'er the wave,
> I've seen your breast with pity heave;
> And therefore love I you, sweet Genevieve!

And the following little picture, entitled Time, Real and Imaginary, is a gem worthy of the poet in the most thoughtful and philosophic strength of his faculties:—

> On the wide level of a mountain's head
> (I knew not where, but 'twas some fairy place),
> Their pinions, ostrich-like, for sails outspread,
> Two lovely children ran an endless race;
>   A sister and a brother!
>   That far outstripped the other;
> Yet ever runs she with reverted face,
> And looks and listens for the boy behind:
>   For he, alas! is blind!
> O'er rough and smooth with even step he passed,
> And knows not whether he be first or last.

In a different manner, and more resembling that of these early poems in general, are many passages of great power in the Monody on the Death of Chatterton, and in the Religious Musings, the latter written in 1794, when the author was only in his twenty-third year. And, among other remarkable pieces of a date not much later, might be mentioned the ode entitled France, written in 1797, which Shelley regarded as the finest ode in the language; his Fire, Famine, and Slaughter, written, we believe, about the same time; his ode entitled Dejection; his blank verse lines entitled The Nightingale; his Rime of the Ancient Mariner, and his exquisite verses entitled Love, to which last for their union of passion with delicacy, and of both with the sweetest, richest music, it would be difficult to find a match in our own or any language.

"Of Coleridge's poetry, in its most matured form and in its best specimens, the most distinguishing characteristics are vividness of imagination and subtlety of thought, combined with unrivalled beauty and expressiveness of diction, and the most exquisite melody of verse. With the exception of a vein of melancholy and meditative tenderness, flowing rather from a contemplative survey of the mystery—the strangely mingled good and evil—of all things human, than connected with any individual interests, there is not in general much of passion in his compositions, and he is not well fitted, therefore, to become a very popular poet, or a favourite with the multitude. His love itself, warm and tender as it is, is still Platonic and spiritual in its tenderness, rather than a thing of flesh and blood. There is nothing in his poetry of the pulse of fire that throbs in that of Burns; neither has he much of the homely every-day truth, the proverbial and universally applicable wisdom, of Wordsworth. Coleridge was, far more than either of these poets, 'of imagination *all* compact.' The fault of his poetry is the same that belongs to that of Spenser; it is too purely or unalloyedly poetical. But rarely, on the other hand, has there existed an imagination in which so much originality and daring were associated and harmonized with so gentle and tremblingly delicate a sense of beauty. Some of his minor poems especially, for the richness of their colouring combined with the most perfect finish, can be compared only to the flowers which spring up into loveliness at the touch of 'great creating nature.' The words, the rhyme, the whole flow of the music seem to be not so much the mere expression or sign of the thought as its blossoming or irradiation—of the bright essence the equally bright though sensible effluence."*

In most of Coleridge's latest poetry, however, along with this perfection of execution, in which he was unmatched, we have more body and warmth—more of the inspiration of the heart mingling with that of the fancy. The following lines are entitled Work without Hope, and are stated to have been composed 21st February, 1827:—

> All nature seems at work. Slugs leave their lair—
> The bees are stirring—birds are on the wing—
> And winter, slumbering in the open air,
> Wears on his smiling face a dream of spring!
> And I, the while, the sole unbusy thing,
> Nor honey make, nor pair, nor build, nor sing.
>
> Yet well I ken the banks where amaranths blow,
> Have traced the fount whence streams of nectar flow.
> Bloom, O ye amaranths! bloom for whom ye may,
> For me ye bloom not! Glide, rich streams, away!
> With lips unbrightened, wreathless brow, I stroll:
> And would you learn the spells that drowse my soul?
> Work without hope draws nectar in a sieve,
> And hope without an object cannot live.

To about the same date belongs the following, entitled Youth and Age:—

> Verse, a breeze mid blossoms straying,
> Where Hope clung feeding, like a bee—

---

* Printing Machine, No. 12, for 16th August, 1834.

Both were mine! Life went a maying
With Nature, Hope, and Poesy,
   When I was young!
When I was young?—Ah, woeful when!
Ah! for the change 'twixt now and then!
This breathing house not built with hands,
This body that does me grievous wrong,
O'er airy cliffs and glittering sands
How lightly then it flashed along:—
Like those trim skiffs, unknown of yore,
On winding lakes and rivers wide,
That ask no aid of sail or oar,
That fear no spite of wind or tide!
Nought cared this body for wind or weather
When youth and I lived in't together.

Flowers are lovely; love is flower-like;
Friendship is a sheltering tree;
O! the joys that came down shower-like,
Of Friendship, Love, and Liberty,
   Ere I was old!
Ere I was old?—Ah, woeful ere,
Which tells me, Youth's no longer here!
O Youth! for years so many and sweet
'Tis known that thou and I were one;
I'll think it but a fond conceit—
It cannot be, that thou art gone!
Thy vesper-bell hath not yet tolled:—
And thou wert aye a masker bold!
What strange disguise hast now put on,
To make believe that thou art gone?
I see these locks in silvery slips,
This drooping gait, this altered size:
But springtide blossoms on thy lips,
And tears take sunshine from thine eyes!
Life is but thought: so think I will
That Youth and I are house-mates still.

Dew-drops are the gems of morning,
But the tears of mournful eve!
Where no hope is, life's a warning
That only serves to make us grieve,
   When we are old:
That only serves to make us grieve,
With oft and tedious taking leave;
Like some poor nigh-related guest,
That may not rudely be dismist,
Yet hath outstayed his welcome while,
And tells the jest without the smile.

The following may have been written a few years later.

It winds up a prose dialogue between two girls and their elderly male friend the Poet, or Improvisatore, as he is more familiarly styled, who, after a most eloquent description of that rare mutual love, the possession of which he declares would be more than an adequate reward for the rarest virtue, to the remark, "Surely, he who has described it so well must have possessed it?" replies, "If he were worthy to have possessed it, and had believingly anticipated and not found it, how bitter the disappointment!" and then, after a pause, breaks out into verse thus :—

> Yes, yes! that boon, life's richest treat,
> He had, or fancied that he had;
> Say, 'twas but in his own conceit—
>   The fancy made him glad!
> Crown of his cup, and garnish of his dish,
> The boon prefigured in his earliest wish,
> The fair fulfilment of his poesy,
> When his young heart first yearned for sympathy!
> But e'en the meteor offspring of the brain
>   Unnourished wane;
> Faith asks her daily bread,
> And fancy must be fed.
> Now so it chanced—from wet or dry,
> It boots not how—I know not why—
> She missed her wonted food; and quickly
> Poor fancy staggered and grew sickly.
> Then came a restless state, 'twixt yea and nay,
> His faith was fixed, his heart all ebb and flow;
> Or like a bark, in some half-sheltered bay,
> Above its anchor driving to and fro.
> That boon, which but to have possest
> In a belief gave life a zest—
> Uncertain both what it had been,
> And if by error lost, or luck;
> And what it was;—an evergreen
> Which some insidious blight had struck,
> Or annual flower, which, past its blow,
> No vernal spell shall e'er revive!
> Uncertain, and afraid to know,
>   Doubts tossed him to and fro:
> Hope keeping Love, Love Hope, alive,
> Like babes bewildered in the snow,
> That cling and huddle from the cold
> In hollow tree or ruined fold.
> Those sparkling colours, once his boast,
>   Fading, one by one away,
> Thin and hueless as a ghost,
>   Poor fancy on her sick-bed lay;

Ill at a distance, worse when near,
Telling her dreams to jealous fear!
Where was it then, the sociable sprite
That crowned the poet's cup and decked his dish!
Poor shadow cast from an unsteady wish,
Itself a substance by no other right
But that it intercepted reason's light;
It dimmed his eye, it darkened on his brow:
A peevish mood, a tedious time, I trow!
    Thank heaven! 'tis not so now.

O bliss of blissful hours!
The boon of heaven's decreeing,
While yet in Eden's bowers
Dwelt the first husband and his sinless mate!
The one sweet plant, which, piteous heaven agreeing,
They bore with them through Eden's closing gate!
Of life's gay summer tide the sovran rose!
Late autumn's amaranth, that more fragrant blows
When passion's flowers all fall or fade;
If this were ever his in outward being,
Or but his own true love's projected shade,
Now that at length by certain proof he knows
That, whether real or a magic show,
Whate'er it was, it is no longer so;
Though heart be lonesome, hope laid low,
Yet, lady, deem him not unblest;
The certainty that struck hope dead
Hath left contentment in her stend:
    And that is next to best!

And still more perfect and altogether exquisite, we think, than anything we have yet given, is the following, entitled Love, Hope, and Patience, in Education:—

O'er wayward childhood would'st thou hold firm rule,
And sun thee in the light of happy faces;
Love, Hope, and Patience, these must be thy graces,
And in thine own heart let them first keep school.
For, as old Atlas on his broad neck places
Heaven's starry globe, and there sustains it,—so
Do these upbear the little world below
Of Education,—Patience, Love, and Hope.
Methinks, I see them grouped in seemly show,
The straitened arms upraised, the palms aslope,
And robes that touching, as adown they flow,
Distinctly blend, like snow embossed in snow.

O part them never! If Hope prostrate lie,
    Love too will sink and die.

But Love is subtle, and doth proof derive
From her own life that Hope is yet alive;
And, bending o'er with soul-transfusing eyes,
And the soft murmurs of the mother dove,
Woos back the fleeting spirit, and half supplies:—
Thus Love repays to Hope what Hope first gave to Love.

Yet haply there will come a weary day,
    When overtasked at length
Both Love and Hope beneath the load give way.
Then, with a statue's smile, a statue's strength,
Stands the mute sister, Patience, nothing loth,
And both supporting does the work of both.

SOUTHEY.

Coleridge died in 1834; his friend Southey, born three years later, survived to 1843. If Coleridge wrote too little poetry, Southey may be said to have written too much and too rapidly. Southey, as well as Coleridge, has been popularly reckoned one of the Lake poets; but it is difficult to assign any meaning to that name which should entitle it to comprehend either the one or the other. Southey, indeed, was, in the commencement of his career, the associate of Wordsworth and Coleridge; a portion of his first poem, his Joan of Arc, published in 1796, was written by Coleridge; and he afterwards took up his residence, as well as Wordsworth, among the lakes of Westmoreland. But, although in his first volume of minor poems, published in 1797, there was something of the same simplicity or plainness of style, and choice of subjects from humble life, by which Wordsworth sought to distinguish himself about the same time, the manner of the one writer bore only a very superficial resemblance to that of the other; whatever it was, whether something quite original, or only, in the main, an inspiration caught from the Germans, that gave its peculiar character to Wordsworth's poetry, it was wanting in Southey's; he was evidently, with all his ingenuity and fertility, and notwithstanding an ambition of originality which led him to be continually seeking after strange models, from Arabian and Hindoo mythologies to Latin hexameters, of a genius radically imitative, and not qualified to put forth its strength except while moving in a beaten track and under the guidance of long-established rules. Southey was by nature a conservative in literature as well as in politics, and the eccentricity of his Thalabas and Kehamas was as merely spasmodic as the Jacobinism of his Wat Tyler. But even Thalaba and

Kehama, whatever they may be, are surely not poems of the Lake school. And in most of his other poems, especially in his latest epic, Roderick, the Last of the Goths, Southey is in verse what he always was in prose, one of the most thoroughly and unaffectedly English of our modern writers. The verse, however, is too like prose to be poetry of a very high order; it is flowing and eloquent, but has little of the distinctive life or lustre of poetical composition. There is much splendour and beauty, however, in the Curse of Kehama, the most elaborate of his long poems.

Scott.

Walter Scott, again, was never accounted one of the Lake poets; yet he, as well as Wordsworth and Coleridge, was early a drinker at the fountain of German poetry; his commencing publication was a translation of Bürger's Lenore (1796), and the spirit and manner of his original compositions were, from the first, evidently and powerfully influenced by what had thus awakened his poetical faculty. His robust and manly character of mind, however, and his strong nationalism, with the innate disposition of his imagination to live in the past rather than in the future, saved him from being seduced into either the puerilities or the extravagances to which other imitators of the German writers among us were thought to have, more or less, given way; and, having soon found in the popular ballad-poetry of his own country all the qualities which had most attracted him in his foreign favourites, with others which had an equal or still greater charm for his heart and fancy, he henceforth gave himself up almost exclusively to the more congenial inspiration of that native minstrelsy. His poems are all lays and romances of chivalry, but infinitely finer than any that had ever before been written. With all their irregularity and carelessness (qualities which in some sort are characteristic of and essential to this kind of poetry), that element of life in all writing, which comes of the excited feeling and earnest belief of the writer, is never wanting; this animation, fervour, enthusiasm,—call it by what name we will,—exists in greater strength in no poetry than in that of Scott, redeeming a thousand defects, and triumphing over all the reclamations of criticism. It was this, no doubt, more than anything else, which at once took the public admiration by storm. All cultivated and perfect enjoyment of poetry, or of any other of the fine arts, is partly emotional, partly critical; the enjoyment and appreciation are only perfect when these two qualities are blended; but most of the poetry that had been produced among us in modern times had aimed at affording chiefly, if not exclusively, a critical gratification. The Lay of the Last Minstrel (1805) surprised readers of all degrees with a long and elaborate poem, which carried them onward with an excitement of heart as well as of head which many of them had never experienced before in the perusal of poetry. The narrative form of the poem no doubt did much to produce this effect, giving to it, even without the poetry, the interest and enticement of a novel; but all readers, even the least tinctured with a literary taste, felt also, in a greater or less degree, the charm of the verse, and the poetic glow with which the work was all alive. Marmion (1808) carried the same feelings to a much higher pitch; it is undoubtedly Scott's greatest poem, or the one at any rate in which the noblest passages are found; though the more domestic attractions of the Lady of the Lake (1810) made it the most popular on its first appearance. Meanwhile, his success, the example he had set, and the tastes which he had awakened in the public mind, had affected our literature to an extent in various directions which has scarcely been sufficiently appreciated. Notwithstanding the previous appearance of Wordsworth, Coleridge, Southey, and some other writers, it was Scott who first in his day made poetry the rage, and with him properly commences the busy poetical production of the period we are now reviewing; those who had been in the field before him put on a new activity, and gave to the world their principal works, after his appearance; and it was not till then that the writer who of all the poets of this age attained the widest blaze of reputation, eclipsing Scott himself, commenced his career. But what is still more worthy of note is, that Scott's poetry impressed its own character upon all the poetry that was produced among us for many years after; it put an end to long works in verse of a didactic or merely reflective character, and directed the current of all writing of that kind into the form of narrative. Even Wordsworth's Excursion (1814) is for the most part a collection of tales. If Scott's own genius, indeed, were to be described by any single epithet, it would be called a narrative genius. Hence, when he left off writing verse, he betook himself to the production of fictions in prose, which were really substantially the same thing with his poems, and in that freer form of composition succeeded in achieving a second reputation still more brilliant than his first.

We cannot make room for the whole of the battle in Marmion;

and the following extracts, which describe the fighting, lose part of their effect by being separated from the picture of Marmion's death-scene, with the pathos and touching solemnity of which they are in the original canvas so finely intermingled and relieved; but, even deprived of the advantages of this contrast, most readers will probably agree with a late eloquent critic, that, "of all the poetical battles which have been fought from the days of Homer, there is none comparable for interest and animation—for breadth of drawing and magnificence of effect—with this."*—

> Blount and Fitz-Eustace rested still
> With Lady Clare upon the hill;
> On which (for far the day was spent)
> The western sun-beams now were bent.
> The cry they heard, its meaning knew,
> Could plain their distant comrades view:
> Sadly to Blount did Eustace say,
> "Unworthy office here to stay!
> No hope of gilded spurs to-day,—
> But see! look up—on Flodden bent,
> The Scottish foe has fired his tent."
>   And sudden, as he spoke,
> From the sharp ridges of the hill,
> All downward to the banks of Till
>   Was wreathed in sable smoke.
> Volumed and fast, and rolling far,
> The cloud enveloped Scotland's war,
>   As down the hill they broke;
> Nor martial shout, nor minstrel tone,
> Announced their march; their tread alone,
> At times one warning trumpet blown,
>   At times a stifled hum,
> Told England, from his mountain throne
>   King James did rushing come.—
> Scarce could they hear, or see, their foes
> Until at weapon point they close.
> They close, in clouds of smoke and dust,
> With sword-sway, and with lance's thrust;
>   And such a yell was there
> Of sudden and portentous birth,
> As if men fought upon the earth
>   And fiends in upper air;
> O life and death were in the shout,
> Recoil and rally, charge and rout,
>   And triumph and despair.
> Long looked the anxious squires; their eye
> Could in the darkness nought descry.

* Jeffrey, in Edinburgh Review.

SCOTT.

At length the freshening western blast
Aside the shroud of battle cast,
And, first, the ridge of mingled spears
Above the brightening cloud appears;
And in the smoke the pennons flew,
As in the storm the white sea-mew.
Then marked they, dashing broad and far,
The broken billows of the war,
And plumed crests of chieftains brave,
Floating like foam upon the wave;
 But nought distinct they see:
Wide raged the battle on the plain;
Spears shook and falchions flashed amain;
Fell England's arrow-flight like rain;
Crests rose, and stooped, and rose again,
 Wild and disorderly.
Amid the scene of tumult, high
They saw Lord Marmion's falcon fly:
And stainless Tunstall's banner white,
And Edmund Howard's lion bright,
Still bear them bravely in the fight;
 Although against them come
Of gallant Gordons many a one,
And many a stubborn Badenoch man,
And many a rugged border clan,
 With Huntley, and with Home.

Far on the left, unseen the while,
Stanley broke Lennox and Argyle;
Though there the western mountaineer
Rushed with bare bosom on the spear,
And flung the feeble targe aside,
And with both hands the broadsword plied.
'Twas vain:—but Fortune, on the right,
With fickle smile cheered Scotland's fight.
Then fell that spotless banner white,
 The Howard's lion fell;
Yet still Lord Marmion's falcon flew
With wavering flight, while fiercer grew
 Around the battle-yell.
The Border slogan rent the sky!
A Home! a Gordon! was the cry:
 Loud were the clanging blows;
Advanced,—forced back,—now low, now high,
 The pennon sunk and rose;
As bends the bark's mast in the gale,
When rent are rigging, shrouds, and sail,
 It wavered 'mid the foes.
No longer Blount the view could bear:
" By Heaven, and all its saints! I swear,

"I will not see it lost!"
Fitz-Eustace, you with Lady Clare
May bid your beads, and patter prayer,—
I gallop to the host."
And to the fray he rode amain,
Followed by all the archer train.
The fiery youth, with desperate charge,
Made, for a space, an opening large,—
The rescued banner rose;—
But darkly closed the war around;
Like pine-tree, rooted from the ground,
It sunk among the foes.
Then Eustace mounted too, yet staid,
As loth to leave the helpless maid,
When, fast as shaft can fly,
Bloodshot his eyes, his nostrils spread,
The loose rein dangling from his head,
Housing and saddle bloody red,
Lord Marmion's steed rushed by;
And Eustace, maddening at the sight,
A look and sign to Clara cast,
To mark he would return in haste,
Then plunged into the fight.

. . . . .

The war, that for a space did fail,
Now trebly thundering swelled the gale,
And Stanley! was the cry:—
A light on Marmion's visage spread,
And fired his glazing eye:
With dying hand, above his head,
He shook the fragment of his blade,
And shouted "Victory!"—
"Charge, Chester, charge! On, Stanley, on!"
Were the last words of Marmion.

By this, though deep the evening fell,
Still rose the battle's deadly swell;
For still the Scots, around their king,
Unbroken, fought in desperate ring.
Where's now their victor vaward wing?
Where Huntley, and where Home?
O, for a blast of that dread horn,
On Fontarabian echoes borne,
That to King Charles did come,
When Roland brave, and Olivier,
And every paladin and peer,
On Roncesvalles died!

Such blast might warn them, not in vain,
To quit the plunder of the slain,
And turn the doubtful day again,

SCOTT.

While yet on Flodden side,
Afar, the Royal standard flies,
And round it toils, and bleeds, and dies
  Our Caledonian pride!
In vain the wish—for far away,
While spoil and havoc mark their way,
Near Sybil's Cross the plunderers stray.—
"O lady," cried the Monk, "away!"
  And placed her on her steed,
And led her to the chapel fair
  Of Tilmouth upon Tweed.

. . . . .

But, as they left the darkening heath,
More desperate grew the strife of death.
The English shafts in volleys hailed;
In headlong charge their horse assailed;
Front, flank, and rear the squadrons sweep
To break the Scottish circle deep,
  That fought around their king:
But yet, though thick the shafts as snow,
Though charging knights like whirlwinds go,
Though billmen ply the ghastly blow,
  Unbroken was the ring;
The stubborn spearmen still made good
Their dark impenetrable wood,
Each stepping where his comrade stood
  The instant that he fell.
No thought was there of dastard flight;
Linked in the serried phalanx tight,
Groom fought like noble, squire like knight,
  As fearlessly and well;
Till utter darkness closed her wing
O'er their thin host and wounded king.
Then skilful Surrey's sage commands
Led back from strife his shattered bands;
  And from the charge they drew,
As mountain waves from wasted lands
  Sweep back to ocean blue.
Then did their loss his foemen know;
Their king, their lords, their mightiest low,
They melted from the field as snow,
When streams are swollen and south winds blow,
  Dissolves in silent dew.

Tweed's echoes heard the ceaseless plash,
  While many a broken band,
Disordered, through her currents dash,
  To gain the Scottish land;
To town and tower, to down and dale,
To tell red Flodden's dismal tale,

And raise the universal wail.
Tradition, legend, tune, and song
Shall many an age that wail prolong:
Still from the sire the son shall hear
Of the stern strife, and carnage drear,
  Of Flodden's fatal field,
Where shivered was fair Scotland's spear,
  And broken was her shield!

Scott, born in 1771, died in 1832.

CRABBE; CAMPBELL; MOORE.

Crabbe, Campbell, and Moore, were all known as poetical writers previous to the breaking forth of Scott's bright day: Crabbe had published his first poem, The Library, so far back as in 1781, The Village in 1783, and The Newspaper in 1785; Campbell, his Pleasures of Hope in 1799; Moore, his Anacreon in 1800. But Campbell alone had before that epoch attracted any considerable share of the public attention; and even he, after following up his first long poem with his Hohenlinden, his Battle of the Baltic, his Mariners of England, and a few other short pieces, had laid aside his lyre for some five or six years. Neither Crabbe nor Moore had as yet produced anything that gave promise of the high station they were to attain in our poetical literature, or had even acquired any general notoriety as writers of verse. No one of the three, however, can be said to have caught any part of his manner from Scott. Campbell's first poem, juvenile as its execution in some respects was, evinced in its glowing impetuosity and imposing splendour of declamation the genius of a true and original poet, and the same general character that distinguishes his poetry in its maturest form, which may be described as a combination of fire and elegance; and his early lyrics, at least in their general effect, are not excelled by anything he subsequently wrote, although the tendency of his style towards greater purity and simplicity was very marked in all his later compositions. It was with a narrative poem—his Pennsylvanian Tale of Gertrude of Wyoming—that Campbell (in 1809) returned to woo the public favour, after Scott had made poetry, and that particular form of it, so popular; and, continuing to obey the direction which had been given to the public taste, he afterwards produced his exquisite O'Connor's Child and his Theodric: the former the most passionate, the latter the purest, of all his longer poems. Crabbe, in like manner, when he at last, in 1807, broke his silence of twenty years, came forth with a volume, all that was now in which consisted of narrative poetry, and he never afterwards attempted any other style. Narrative, indeed, had formed the happiest and most characteristic portions of Crabbe's former compositions; and he was probably led now to resume his pen mainly by the turn which the taste and fashion of the time had taken in favour of the kind of poetry to which his genius most strongly carried him. His narrative manner, however, it is scarcely necessary to observe, has no resemblance either to that of Scott or to that of Campbell. Crabbe's poetry, indeed, both in its form and in its spirit, is of quite a peculiar and original character. It might be called the poetry of matter-of-fact, for it is as true as any prose, and, except the rhyme, has often little about it of the ordinary dress of poetry; but the effect of poetry, nevertheless, is always there in great force, its power both of stirring the affections and presenting vivid pictures to the fancy. Other poets may be said to exalt the truth to a heat naturally foreign to it in the crucible of their imagination; he, by a subtler chemistry, draws forth from it its latent heat, making even things that look the coldest and deadest sparkle and flash with passion. It is remarkable, however, in how great a degree, with all its originality, the poetical genius of Crabbe was acted upon and changed by the growth of new tastes and a new spirit in the times through which he lived,—how his poetry took a warmer temperament, a richer colour, as the age became more poetical. As he lived, indeed, in two eras, so he wrote in two styles: the first, a sort of imitation, as we have already observed, of the rude vigour of Churchill, though marked from the beginning by a very distinguishing quaintness and raciness of its own, but comparatively cautious and commonplace, and dealing rather with the surface than with the heart of things; the last, with all the old peculiarities retained, and perhaps exaggerated, but greatly more copious, daring, and impetuous, and infinitely improved in penetration and general effectiveness. And his poetical power, nourished by an observant spirit and a thoughtful tenderness of nature, continued to grow in strength to the end of his life; so that the last poetry he published, his Tales of the Hall, is the finest he ever wrote, the deepest and most passionate in feeling as well as the happiest in execution. In Crabbe's sunniest passages, however, the glow is still that of a melancholy sunshine: compared to what we find in Moore's poetry, it is like the departing flush from the west, contrasted with the radiance of morning poured out plentifully over earth and sky, and making all things laugh in light. Rarely has there been seen so gay, nimble, airy a wonder-worker in verse as

Moore; rarely such a conjuror with words, which he makes to serve rather as wings for his thoughts than as the gross attire or embodiment with which they must be encumbered to render them palpable or visible. His wit is not only the sharpest and brightest to be almost anywhere found, but is produced apparently with more of natural facility, and shapes itself into expression more spontaneously, than that of any other poet. But there is almost as much humour as wit in Moore's gaiety; nor are his wit and humour together more than a small part of his poetry, which, preserving in all its forms the same matchless brilliancy, finish, and apparent ease and fluency, breathes in its tenderer strains the very soul of sweetness and pathos. Moore, after having risen to the ascendant in his proper region of the poetical firmament, at last followed the rest into the walk of narrative poetry, and produced his Lalla Rookh (1817): it is a poem, with all its defects, abounding in passages of great beauty and splendour; but his Songs are, after all, probably, the compositions for which he will be best remembered.

No poetry of this time is probably so deeply and universally written upon the popular heart and memory as Campbell's great lyrics; these, therefore, it is needless to give here; some things that he has written in another style will have a greater chance of being less familiar to the reader. With all his classic taste and careful finish, Campbell's writing, especially in his earlier poetry, is rarely altogether free for any considerable number of lines from something hollow and false in expression, into which he was seduced by the conventional habits of the preceding bad school of verse-making in which he had been partly trained, and from which he emerged, or by the gratification of his ear lulling his other faculties asleep for the moment; even in his Battle of the Baltic, for instance, what can be worse than the two lines—

> But the might of England flushed
> To anticipate the scene?

And a similar use of fine words with little or no meaning, or with a meaning which can only be forced out of them by torture, is occasional in all his early compositions. In the Pleasures of Hope, especially, swell of sound without any proportionate quantity of sense, is of such frequent occurrence as to be almost a characteristic of the poem. All his later poetry, however, is of much purer execution; and some of it is of exquisite delicacy and grace of form. A little incident was never, for example, more perfectly told than in the following verses:—

> The ordeal's fatal trumpet sounded,
>   And sad pale Adelgitha came,
> When forth a valiant champion bounded,
>   And slew the slanderer of her fame.
>
> She wept, delivered from her danger;
>   But, when he knelt to claim her glove—
> "Seek not," she cried, "oh! gallant stranger,
>   For hapless Adelgitha's love.
>
> "For he is in a foreign far land
>   Whose arm should now have set me free;
> And I must wear the willow garland
>   For him that's dead or false to me."
>
> "Nay! say not that his faith is tainted!"
>   He raised his vizor—at the sight
> She fell into his arms and fainted;
>   It was indeed her own true knight.

Equally perfect, in a higher, more earnest style, is the letter to her absent husband, dictated and signed by Constance in her last moments, which closes the tale of Theodric:—

> "Theodric, this is destiny above
> Our power to baffle; bear it then, my love!
> Rave not to learn the usage I have borne,
> For one true sister left me not forlorn;
> And, though you're absent in another land,
> Sent from me by my own well-meant command,
> Your soul, I know, as firm is knit to mine
> As these clasped hands in blessing you now join:
> Shape not imagined horrors in my fate—
> Even now my sufferings are not very great;
> And, when your grief's first transports shall subside,
> I call upon your strength of soul and pride
> To pay my memory, if 'tis worth the debt,
> Love's glorying tribute—not forlorn regret:
> I charge my name with power to conjure up
> Reflection's balmy, not its bitter, cup.
> My pardoning angel, at the gates of heaven,
> Shall look not more regard than you have given
> To me; and our life's union has been clad
> In smiles of bliss as sweet as life e'er had.
> Shall gloom be from such bright remembrance cast?
> Shall bitterness outflow from sweetness past?
> No! imaged in the sanctuary of your breast,
> There let me smile, amidst high thoughts at rest;
> And let contentment on your spirit shine,
> As if its peace were still a part of mine:
> For, if you war not proudly with your pain,
> For you I shall have worse than lived in vain.

> But I conjure your manliness to bear
> My loss with noble spirit—not despair;
> I ask you by our love to promise this,
> And kiss these words, where I have left a kiss,—
> The latest from my living lips for yours."
>   Words that will solace him while life endures:
> For, though his spirit from affliction's surge
> Could ne'er to life, as life had been, emerge,
> Yet still that mind, whose harmony elate
> Rang sweetness even beneath the crush of fate,—
> That mind in whose regard all things were placed
> In views that softened them, or light that graced,—
> That soul's example could not but dispense
> A portion of its own blest influence;
> Invoking him to peace and that self-sway
> Which fortune cannot give, nor take away;
> And, though he mourned her long, 'twas with such woe
> As if her spirit watched him still below.

It is difficult to find a single passage, not too long for quotation, which will convey any tolerable notion of the power and beauty of Crabbe's poetry, where so much of the effect lies in the conduct of the narrative—in the minute and prolonged but wonderfully skilful as well as truthful pursuit and exposition of the course and vicissitude of passions and circumstances: but we will give so much of the story of the Elder Brother, in the Tales of the Hall, as will at least make the catastrophe intelligible. We select this tale, among other reasons, for its containing one of those pre-eminently beautiful lyric bursts which seem to contrast so strangely with the general spirit and manner of Crabbe's poetry. After many years, the narrator, pursuing another inquiry, accidentally discovers the lost object of his heart's passionate but pure idolatry living in infamy:—

>   Will you not ask, how I beheld that face,
> Or read that mind, and read it in that place?
> I have tried, Richard, ofttimes, and in vain,
> To trace my thoughts, and to review their train—
> If train there were—that meadow, grove, and stile,
> The fright, the escape, her sweetness, and her smile;
> Years since elapsed, and hope, from year to year,
> To find her free—and then to find her here!
>   But is it she?—O! yes; the rose is dead,
> All beauty, fragrance, freshness, glory, fled;
> But yet 'tis she—the same and not the same—
> Who to my bower a heavenly being came;
> Who waked my soul's first thought of real bliss,
> Whom long I sought, and now I find her—this.

CRABBE.

I cannot paint her—something I had seen
So pale and slim, and tawdry and unclean;
With haggard looks, of vice and woe the prey,
Laughing in languor, miserably gay:
Her face, where face appeared, was amply spread,
By art's warm pencil, with ill-chosen red,
The flower's fictitious bloom, the blushing of the dead:
But still the features were the same, and strange
My view of both—the sameness and the change,
That fixed me gazing, and my eye enchained,
Although so little of herself remained;
It is the creature whom I loved, and yet
Is far unlike her—would I could forget
The angel or her fall; the once adored
Or now despised! the worshipped or deplored!
" O! Rosabella!" I prepared to say,
" Whom I have loved;" but Prudence whispered, Nay,
And Folly grew ashamed—Discretion had her day.
She gave her hand; which, as I lightly pressed,
The cold but ardent grasp my soul oppressed;
The ruined girl disturbed me, and my eyes
Looked, I conceive, both sorrow and surprise.

. . . .

If words had failed, a look explained their style;
She could not blush assent, but she could smile:
Good heaven! I thought, have I rejected fame,
Credit, and wealth, for one who smiles at shame?
She saw me thoughtful—saw it, as I guessed,
With some concern, though nothing she expressed.
" Come, my dear friend, discard that look of care," &c.

. . . .

Thus spoke the siren in voluptuous style,
While I stood gazing and perplexed the while,
Chained by that voice, confounded by that smile.
And then she sang, and changed from grave to gay,
Till all reproach and anger died away.

———

" My Damon was the first to wake
  The gentle flame that cannot die;
My Damon is the last to take
  The faithful bosom's softest sigh:
The life between is nothing worth,
  O! cast it from thy thought away;
Think of the day that gave it birth,
  And this its sweet returning day.

" Buried be all that has been done,
  Or say that nought is done amiss;

> For who the dangerous path can shun
>   In such bewildering world as this?
> But love can every fault forgive,
>   Or with a tender look reprove;
> And now let nought in memory live,
>   But that we meet, and that we love."

And then she moved my pity; for she wept,
And told her miseries, till resentment slept;
For, when she saw she could not reason blind,
She poured her heart's whole sorrows on my mind
With features graven on my soul, with sighs
Seen, but not heard, with soft imploring eyes,
And voice that needed not, but had, the aid
Of powerful words to soften and persuade.
    "O! I repent me of the past;" &c.

. . . . . .

Softened, I said, "Be mine the hand and heart,
If with your world you will consent to part."
She would—she tried.—Alas! she did not know
How deeply-rooted evil habits grow:
She felt the truth upon her spirits press,
But wanted ease, indulgence, show, excess,
Voluptuous banquets, pleasures—not refined,
But such as soothe to sleep the opposing mind—
She looked for idle vice, the time to kill,
And subtle, strong apologies for ill.
And thus her yielding, unresisting soul
Sank, and let sin confuse her and control:
Pleasures that brought disgust yet brought relief,
And minds she hated helped to war with grief.

. . . . . .

I had long lost her; but I sought in vain
To banish pity;—still she gave me pain.

. . . . . .

—————— There came at length request
That I would see a wretch with grief oppressed,
By guilt affrighted—and I went to trace
Once more the vice-worn features of that face,
That sin-wrecked being! and I saw her laid
Where never worldly joy a visit paid:
That world receding fast! the world to come
Concealed in terror, ignorance, and gloom;
Sin, sorrow, and neglect; with not a spark
Of vital hope,—all horrible and dark.—
It frightened me!—I thought, and shall not I
Thus feel?—thus fear?—this danger can I fly?
Do I so wisely live that I can calmly die?

. . . . . .

Still as I went came other change—the frame
And features wasted, and yet slowly came
The end; and so inaudible the breath,
And still the breathing, we exclaimed—'Tis death!
But death it was not: when indeed she died
I sat and his last gentle stroke espied:
When—as it came—or did my fancy trace
That lively, lovely flushing o'er the face?
Bringing back all that my young heart impressed!
It came—and went!—She sighed, and was at rest!

From Moore, whose works are more, probably, than those of any of his contemporaries in the hands of all readers of poetry, we will make only one short extract. Here is the exquisitely beautiful description in the Fire Worshippers, the finest of the four tales composing Lalla Rookh, of the calm after a storm, in which the heroine, the gentle Hinda, awakens in the war-bark of her lover Hafed, the noble Gheber chief, into which she had been transferred from her own galley while she had swooned with terror from the tempest and the fight:—

How calm, how beautiful comes on
The stilly hour when storms are gone!
When warring winds have died away,
And clouds, beneath the dancing ray,
Melt off, and leave the land and sea
Sleeping in bright tranquillity—
Fresh as if day again were born,
Again upon the lap of morn!
When the light blossoms, rudely torn
And scattered at the whirlwind's will,
Hang floating in the pure air still,
Filling it all with precious balm,
In gratitude for this sweet calm:—
And every drop the thunder-showers
Have left upon the grass and flowers
Sparkles, as 'twere that lightning gem
Whose liquid flame is born of them!
When, 'stead of one unchanging breeze,
There blow a thousand gentle airs,
And each a different perfume bears,—
As if the loveliest plants and trees
Had vassal breezes of their own,
To watch and wait on them alone,
And waft no other breath than theirs!
When the blue waters rise and fall,
In sleepy sunshine mantling all;
And even that swell the tempest leaves
Is like the full and silent heaves

Of lovers' hearts when newly blest—
Too newly to be quite at rest!
Such was the golden hour that broke
Upon the world, when Hinda woke
From her long trance, and heard around
No motion but the water's sound
Rippling against the vessel's side,
As slow it mounted o'er the tide.—
But where is she?—her eyes are dark,
Are wildered still—is this the bark,
The same that from Harmozia's bay
Bore her at morn—whose bloody way
The sea-dog tracks?—No! strange and new
Is all that meets her wondering view
Upon a galliot's deck she lies,
  Beneath no rich pavilion's shade,
No plumes to fan her sleeping eyes,
  Nor jasmin on her pillow laid.
But the rude litter, roughly spread
With war-cloaks, is her homely bed,
And shawl and sash, on javelins hung,
For awning o'er her head are flung.
Shuddering she looked around—there lay
  A group of warriors in the sun
Resting their limbs, as for that day
Their ministry of death were done;
Some gazing on the drowsy sea,
Lost in unconscious reverie;
And some, who seemed but ill to brook
That sluggish calm, with many a look
To the slack sail impatient cast,
As loose it flagged before the mast.

Crabbe, born in 1754, lived till 1832; Campbell, born in 1777, died in 1844; Moore, born in 1780, died in 1851.

BYRON.

Byron was the writer whose blaze of popularity it mainly was that threw Scott's name into the shade, and induced him to abandon verse. Yet the productions which had this effect—the Giaour, the Bride of Abydos, the Corsair, &c., published in 1813 and 1814 (for the now idolatry was scarcely kindled by the two respectable, but somewhat tame, cantos of Childe Harold, in quite another style, which appeared shortly before these effusions).

were, in reality, only poems written in what may be called a variation of Scott's own manner—Oriental lays and romances, Turkish Marmions and Ladies of the Lake. The novelty of scene and subject, the exaggerated tone of passion in the outlandish tales, and a certain trickery in the writing (for it will hardly now be called anything else), materially aided by the mysterious interest attaching to the personal history of the noble bard, who, whether he sung of Giaours, or Corsairs, or Laras, was always popularly believed to be "himself the great sublime he drew," wonderfully excited and intoxicated the public mind at first, and for a time made all other poetry seem spiritless and wearisome; but, if Byron had adhered to the style by which his fame was thus originally made, it probably would have proved transient enough. Few will now be found to assert that there is anything in these earlier poems of his comparable to the great passages in those of Scott—to the battle in Marmion, for instance, or the raising of the clansmen by the fiery cross in the Lady of the Lake, or many others that might be mentioned. But Byron's vigorous and elastic genius, although it had already tried various styles of poetry, was, in truth, as yet only preluding to its proper display. First, there had been the very small note of the Hours of Idleness; then, the sharper, but not more original or much more promising, strain of the English Bards and Scotch Reviewers (a satirical attempt in all respects inferior to Gifford's Baviad and Mæviad, of which it was a slavish imitation); next, the certainly far higher and more matured, but still quiet and commonplace, manner of the first two cantos of Childe Harold; after that, suddenly the false glare and preternatural vehemence of these Oriental rhapsodies, which yet, however, with all their hollowness and extravagance, evinced infinitely more power than anything he had previously done, or rather were the only poetry he had yet produced that gave proof of any remarkable poetic genius. The Prisoner of Chillon and Parisina, The Siege of Corinth and Mazeppa, followed, all in a spirit of far more truth, and depth, and beauty than the other tales that had preceded them; but the highest forms of Byron's poetry must be sought for in the two concluding cantos of Childe Harold, and in what else he wrote in the last seven or eight years of his short life.

SHELLEY.

Yet the greatest poetical genius of this time, if it was not that of Coleridge, was, probably, that of Shelley. Byron died in

1824, at the age of thirty-six; Shelley in 1822, at that of twenty-nine. What Shelley produced during the brief term allotted to him on earth, much of it passed in sickness and sorrow, is remarkable for its quantity, but much more wonderful for the quality of the greater part of it. His Queen Mab, written when he was eighteen, crude and defective as it is, and unworthy to be classed with what he wrote in his maturer years, was probably the richest promise that was ever given at so early an age of poetic power, the fullest assurance that the writer was born a poet. From the date of his Alastor, or The Spirit of Solitude, the earliest written of the poems published by himself, to his death, was not quite seven years. The Revolt of Islam, in twelve cantos, or books, the dramas of Prometheus Unbound, The Cenci, and Hellas, the tale of Rosalind and Helen, The Masque of Anarchy, The Sensitive Plant, Julian and Maddalo, The Witch of Atlas, Epipsychidion, Adonais, The Triumph of Life, the translations of Homer's Hymn to Mercury, of the Cyclops of Euripides, and of the scenes from Calderon and from Goethe's Faust, besides many short poems, were the additional produce of this springtime of a life destined to know no summer. So much poetry, so rich in various beauty, was probably never poured forth with so rapid a flow from any other mind. Nor can much of it be charged with either immaturity or carelessness: Shelley, with all his abundance and facility, was a fastidious writer, scrupulously attentive to the effect of words and syllables, and accustomed to elaborate whatever he wrote to the utmost; and, although it is not to be doubted that if he had lived longer he would have developed new powers and a still more masterly command over the several resources of his art, anything that can properly be called unripeness in his composition had, if not before, ceased with his Revolt of Islam, the first of his poems which he gave to the world, as if the exposure to the public eye had burned it out. Some haziness of thought and uncertainty of expression may be found in some of his later, or even latest, works; but that is not to be confounded with rawness; it is the dreamy ecstasy, too high for speech, in which his poetical nature, most subtle, sensitive, and voluptuous, delighted to dissolve and lose itself. Yet it is marvellous how far he had succeeded in reconciling even this mood of thought with the necessities of distinct expression: witness his Epipsychidion (written in the last year of his life), which may be regarded as his crowning triumph in that kind of writing, and as, indeed, for its wealth and fusion of all the highest things—of imagination, of expression, of music,—one of the greatest miracles ever wrought in poetry. In other styles, again, all widely diverse, are the Cenci, the Masque of Anarchy, the Hymn to Mercury (formally a translation, but essentially almost as much an original composition as any of the others). It is hard to conjecture what would have been impossible to him by whom all this had been done.

It will suffice to give one of the most brilliant and characteristic of Shelley's shorter poems—his Ode, or Hymn, as it may be called, To a Skylark, written in 1820:—

> Hail to thee, blithe spirit,
>   Bird thou never wert,
> That from heaven, or near it,
>   Pourest thy full heart
> In profuse strains of unpremeditated art.
>
> Higher still and higher
>   From the earth thou springest;
> Like a cloud of fire
>   The blue deep thou wingest,
> And singing still dost soar, and soaring ever singest.
>
> In the golden lightning
>   Of the sunken sun,
> O'er which clouds are brightening,
>   Thou dost float and run;
> Like an embodied Joy whose race is just begun.
>
> The pale purple even
>   Melts around thy flight;
> Like a star of heaven
>   In the broad daylight,
> Thou art unseen, but yet I hear thy shrill delight,
>
> Keen as are the arrows
>   Of that silver sphere,
> Whose intense lamp narrows
>   In the white dawn clear,
> Until we hardly see, we feel that it is there.
>
> All the earth and air
>   With thy voice is loud,
> As, when night is bare,
>   From one lonely cloud
> The moon rains out her beams, and heaven is overflowed.
>
> What thou art we know not:
>   What is most like thee?
> From rainbow clouds there flow not
>   Drops so bright to see
> As from thy presence showers a rain of melody.

Like a poet hidden
　In the light of thought,
Singing hymns unbidden,
　Till the world is wrought
To sympathy with hopes and fears it heeded not:

Like a highborn maiden
　In a palace tower,
Soothing her love-laden
　Soul in secret hour
With music sweet as love, which overflows her bower:

Like a glow-worm golden
　In a dell of dew,
Scattering unbeholden
　Its aërial hue
Among the flowers and grass, which screen it from the view:

Like a rose embowered
　In its own green leaves,
By warm winds deflowered,
　Till the scent it gives
Makes faint with too much sweet those heavy-winged thieves:

Sound of vernal showers
　On the twinkling grass,
Rain-awakened flowers,
　All that ever was
Joyous and clear and fresh, thy music doth surpass.

Teach us, sprite or bird,
　What sweet thoughts are thine;
I have never heard
　Praise of love or wine
That panted forth a flood of rapture so divine.

Chorus hymeneal,
　Or triumphal chant,
Matched with thine would be all
　But an empty vaunt—
A thing wherein we feel there is some hidden want.

What objects are the fountains
　Of thy happy strain?
What fields, or waves, or mountains?
　What shapes of sky or plain?
What love of thine own kind? what ignorance of pain?

With thy clear keen joyance
　Languor cannot be:
Shadow of annoyance
　Never came near thee:
Thou lovest; but ne'er knew love's sad satiety.

Waking or asleep,
  Thou of death must deem
Things more true and deep
  Than we mortals dream,
Or how could thy notes flow in such a crystal stream?

We look before and after,
  And pine for what is not;
Our sincerest laughter
  With some pain is fraught;
Our sweetest songs are those that tell of saddest thought.

Yet if we could scorn
  Hate, and pride, and fear;
If we were things born
  Not to shed a tear,
I know not how thy joy we ever should come near.

Better than all measures
  Of delightful sound,
Better than all treasures
  That in books are found,
Thy skill to poet were, thou scorner of the ground!

Teach me half the gladness
  That thy brain must know,
Such harmonious madness
  From my lips would flow,
The world should listen then, as I am listening now.

KEATS.

Keats, born in 1796, died the year before Shelley, and, of course, at a still earlier age. But his poetry is younger than Shelley's in a degree far beyond the difference of their years. He was richly endowed by nature with the poetical faculty, and all that he has written is stamped with originality and power; it is probable, too, that he would soon have supplied, as far as was necessary or important, the defects of his education, as indeed he had actually done to a considerable extent, for he was full of ambition as well as genius; but he can scarcely be said to have given full assurance by anything he has left that he would in time have produced a great poetical work. The character of his mental constitution, explosive and volcanic, was adverse to every kind of restraint and cultivation; and his poetry is a tangled forest, beautiful indeed and glorious with many a majestic oak and sunny glade, but still with the unpruned, untrained savagery everywhere, constituting, apparently, so much of its essential character as to be inseparable from it, and indestructible without the ruin at the same time of everything else. There is not only the absence of art, but a spirit antagonistic to that of art. Yet this wildness and turbulence may, after all, have been only an affluence of true power too great to be soon or easily brought under regulation,—the rankness of a tropic vegetation, coming of too rich a soil and too much light and heat. Certainly to no one of his contemporaries had been given more of passionate intensity of conception (the life of poetry) than to Keats. Whatever he thought or felt came to him in vision, and wrapped and thrilled him. Whatever he wrote burns and blazes. And his most wanton extravagances had for the most part a soul of good in them. His very affectations were mostly prompted by excess of love and reverence. In his admiration and worship of our Elizabethan poetry he was not satisfied without mimicking the obsolete syllabication of the language which he found there enshrined, and, as he conceived, consecrated. Even the most remarkable of all the peculiarities of his manner—the extent, altogether, we should think, without a parallel in our literature, to which he surrenders himself in writing to the guidance of the mere wave of sound upon which he happens to have got afloat, often, one would almost say, making ostentation of his acquiescence and passiveness—is a fault only in its excess, and such a fault, moreover, as only a true poet could run into. Sound is of the very essence of song; and the music must always in so far guide the movement of the verse, as truly as it does that of the dance. It only is not the all in all. If the musical form be the mother of the verse, the sense to be expressed is the father. Yet Keats, by what he has thus produced in blind obedience to the tune that had taken possession of him—allowing the course of the composition to be directed simply by the rhyme sometimes for whole pages—has shown the same sensibility to the musical element in poetry, and even something of the same power of moulding language to his will, which we find in all our greatest poets—in Spenser especially, whose poetry is ever as rich with the charm of music as with that of picture, and who makes us feel in so many a victorious stanza that there is nothing his wonder-working mastery over words cannot make them do for him. Keats's Endymion was published in 1817; his Lamia,* Isabella, Eve of St.

* "If any one," Leigh Hunt has said, "could unite the vigour of Dryden with the ready and easy variety of pause in the works of the late Mr. Crabbe and the lovely poetic consciousness in the *Lamia* of Keats, in which the lines seem to take pleasure in the progress of their own beauty, like sea-nymphs luxuriating through the water, he would be a perfect master of rhyming heroic verse."

Agnes, and the remarkable fragment, Hyperion, together in 1820, a few months before his death. The latter volume also contained several shorter pieces, one of which, of great beauty, the Ode to a Nightingale, may serve as a companion to Shelley's Skylark:—

>My heart aches, and a drowsy numbness pains
> My sense, as though of hemlock I had drunk,
>Or emptied some dull opiate to the drains
> One minute past, and Lethe-ward had sunk:
>'Tis not through envy of thy happy lot,
> But being too happy in thine happiness,—
>   That thou, light-winged Dryad of the trees,
>   In some melodious plot
>   Of beechen green, and shadows numberless,
> Singest of summer in full-throated ease.
>
>O for a draught of vintage that hath been
> Cooled a long age in the deep-delved earth,
>Tasting of Flora and the country green,
> Dance, and Provençal song, and sun-burnt mirth!
>O for a beaker full of the warm South,
> Full of the true, the blissful Hippocrene,
>   With beaded bubbles winking at the brim,
>   And purple-stained mouth;
>   That I might drink, and leave the world unseen,
> And with thee fade away into the forest dim:
>
>Fade far away, dissolve, and quite forget
> What thou among the leaves hast never known,
>The weariness, the fever, and the fret
> Here, where men sit and hear each other groan;
>Where palsy shakes a few, sad, last grey hairs;
> Where youth grows pale, and spectre-thin, and dies;
> Where but to think is to be full of sorrow
>   And leaden-eyed despairs;
>   Where beauty cannot keep her lustrous eyes,
> Or new love pine at them beyond to-morrow.
>
>Away! away! for I will fly to thee,
> Not charioted by Bacchus and his pards,
>But on the viewless wings of Poesy,
> Though the dull brain perplexes and retards!
>Already with thee! Tender is the night,
> And haply the Queen-moon is on her throne,
>   Clustered around by all her starry fays;
>   But here there is no light
>   Save what from heaven is with the breezes blown
> Through verdurous glooms and winding mossy ways.

I cannot see what flowers are at my feet,
  Nor what soft incense hangs upon the boughs,
But in embalmed darkness guess each sweet
  Wherewith the seasonable month endows
The grass, the thicket, and the fruit-tree wild;
  White hawthorn, and the pastoral eglantine;
  Fast-fading violets, covered up in leaves;
    And mid-day's eldest child,
The coming musk-rose, full of dewy wine,
The murmurous haunt of flies on summer eves.

Darkling I listen, and, for many a time,
  I have been half in love with easeful Death,[1]
Called him soft names in many a mused rhyme,
  To take into the air my quiet breath;
Now more than ever seems it rich to die,
  To cease upon the midnight with no pain,
  While thou art pouring forth thy soul abroad
    In such an ecstasy!
Still would'st thou sing, and I have ears in vain—
  To thy high requiem become a sod.

Thou wast not born for death, immortal Bird!
  No hungry generations tread thee down;
The voice I hear this passing night was heard
  In ancient days by emperor and clown;
Perhaps the self-same song hath found a path
  Through the sad heart of Ruth, when, sick for home
  She stood in tears amid the alien corn;
    The same that oft-times hath
Charmed magic casements, opening on the foam
Of perilous seas, in faery lands forlorn.

Forlorn! the very word is like a bell
  To toll me back from thee to my soul's self!
Adieu! the fancy cannot cheat so well
  As she is famed to do, deceiving elf.
Adieu! adieu! thy plaintive anthem fades
  Past the near meadows, over the still stream,
  Up the hill-side; and now 'tis buried deep
    In the next valley-glades:
Was it a vision, or a waking dream?
Fled is that music:—do I wake or sleep?

---

[1] Shelley had probably this line in his ear, when in the Preface to his Adonais, which is an elegy on Keats, he wrote—describing "the romantic and lonely cemetery of the Protestants" at Rome, where his friend was buried—"The cemetery is an open space among the ruins, covered in winter with violets and daisies. It might make one in love with death, to think that one should be buried in so sweet a place."

HUNT.

These last names can hardly be mentioned without suggesting another—that of one who has only the other day been taken from us. Leigh Hunt, the friend of Shelley and Keats, had attracted the attention of the world by much that he had done, both in verse and prose, long before the appearance of either. His Story of Rimini, published in 1816, being, as it was, indisputably the finest inspiration of Italian song that had yet been heard in our modern English literature, had given him a place of his own as distinct as that of any other poetical writer of the day. Whatever may be thought of some peculiarities in his manner of writing, nobody will now be found to dispute either the originality of his genius, or his claim to the title of a true poet. Into whatever he has written he has put a living soul; and much of what he has produced is brilliant either with wit and humour, or with tenderness and beauty. In some of the best of his pieces too there is scarcely to be found a trace of anything illegitimate or doubtful in the matter of diction or versification. Where, for example, can we have more unexceptionable English than in the following noble version of the Eastern Tale?—

> There came a man, making his hasty moan,
> Before the Sultan Mahmoud on his throne,
> And crying out—" My sorrow is my right,
> And I *will* see the Sultan, and to-night."
> "Sorrow," said Mahmoud, "is a reverend thing;
> I recognise its right, as king with king;
> Speak on." "A fiend has got into my house,"
> Exclaimed the staring man, "and tortures us;
> One of thine officers—he comes, the abhorred,
> And takes possession of my house, my board,
> My bed:—I have two daughters and a wife,
> And the wild villain comes, and makes me mad with life."
> "Is he there now?" said Mahmoud:—" No; he left
> The house when I did, of my wits bereft;
> And laughed me down the street, because I vowed
> I 'd bring the prince himself to lay him in his shroud.
> I 'm mad with want—I 'm mad with misery,
> And, oh thou Sultan Mahmoud, God cries out for thee!"
>
> The Sultan comforted the man, and said,
> "Go home, and I will send thee wine and bread "
> (For he was poor), "and other comforts. Go:
> And, should the wretch return, let Sultan Mahmoud know."

In three days' time, with haggard eyes and beard,
And shaken voice, the suitor re-appeared,
And said, "He's come."—Mahmoud said not a word,
But rose and took four slaves, each with a sword,
And went with the vexed man. They reach the place,
And hear a voice, and see a female face,
That to the window fluttered in affright:
"Go in," said Mahmoud, "and put out the light;
But tell the females first to leave the room;
And, when the drunkard follows them, we come."

The man went in. There was a cry, and hark.
A table falls, the window is struck dark:
Forth rush the breathless women; and behind
With curses comes the fiend in desperate mind.
In vain: the sabres soon cut short the strife,
And chop the shrieking wretch, and drink his bloody life.

"Now *light* the light," the Sultan cried aloud.
'Twas done; he took it in his hand, and bowed
Over the corpse, and looked upon the face;
Then turned and knelt beside it in the place,
And said a prayer, and from his lips there crept
Some gentle words of pleasure, and he wept.

In reverent silence the spectators wait,
Then bring him at his call both wine and meat;
And when he had refreshed his noble heart,
He bade his host be blest, and rose up to depart.

The man amazed, all mildness now, and tears,
Fell at the Sultan's feet, with many prayers,
And begged him to vouchsafe to tell his slave
The reason, first, of that command he gave
About the light; then, when he saw the face,
Why he knelt down; and lastly, how it was
That fare so poor as his detained him in the place.

The Sultan said, with much humanity,
"Since first I saw thee come, and heard thy cry,
I could not rid me of a dread, that one
By whom such daring villanies were done
Must be some lord of mine, perhaps a lawless son.
Whoe'er he was, I knew my task, but feared
A father's heart, in case the worst appeared;
For this I had the light put out; but when
I saw the face, and found a stranger slain,
I knelt, and thanked the sovereign arbiter,
Whose work I had performed through pain and fear;
And then I rose, and was refreshed with food,
The first time since thou cam'st, and marr'dst my solitude."

Other short pieces in the same style are nearly as good—such as those entitled The Jaffar and The Inevitable. Then there are the admirable modernizations of Chaucer—of whom and of Spenser, whom he has also imitated with wonderful cleverness, no one of all his contemporaries probably had so true and deep a feeling as Hunt. But, passing over likewise his two greatest works, The Story of Rimini and The Legend of Florence (published in 1840), we will give one other short effusion, which attests, we think, as powerfully as anything he ever produced, the master's triumphant hand, in a style which he has made his own, and in which, with however many imitators, he has no rival:—

THE FANCY CONCERT.

They talked of their concerts, their singers, and scores,
And pitied the fever that kept me in doors;
And I smiled in my thought, and said, " O ye sweet fancies,
And animal spirits, that still in your dances
Come bringing me visions to comfort my care,
Now fetch me a concert,—imparadise air."

Then a wind, like a storm out of Eden, came pouring
Fierce into my room, and made tremble the flooring,
And filled, with a sudden impetuous trample
Of heaven, its corners; and swelled it to ample
Dimensions to breathe in, and space for all power;
Which falling as suddenly, lo! the sweet flower
Of an exquisite fairy-voice opened its blessing;
And ever and aye, to its constant addressing,
There came, falling in with it, each in the last,
Flageolets one by one, and flutes blowing more fast,
And hautboys and clarinets, acrid of reed,
And the violin, smoothlier sustaining the speed
As the rich tempest gathered, and buz-ringing moons
Of tambours, and huge basses, and giant bassoons;
And the golden trombone, that darteth its tongue
Like a bee of the gods; nor was absent the gong,
Like a sudden fate-bringing oracular sound
Of earth's iron genius, burst up from the ground,
A terrible slave come to wait on his masters
The gods, with exultings that clanged like disasters;
And then spoke the organs, the very gods they,
Like thunders that roll on a wind-blowing day;
And, taking the rule of the roar in their hands,
Lo! the Genii of Music came out of all lands;
And one of them said, " Will my lord tell his slave
What concert 'twould please his Firesideship to have?"

Then I said, in a tone of immense will and pleasure,
"Let orchestras rise to some exquisite measure;
And let their be lights and be odours; and let
The lovers of music serenely be set;
And then, with their singers in lily-white stoles,
And themselves clad in rose-colour, fetch me the souls
Of all the composers accounted divinest,
And, with their own hands, let them play me their finest."

Then, lo! was performed my immense will and pleasure,
And orchestras rose to an exquisite measure;
And lights were about me and colours; and set
Were the lovers of music, all wondrously met;
And then, with their singers in lily-white stoles,
And themselves clad in rose-colour, in came the souls
Of all the composers accounted divinest,
And, with their own hands, did they play me their finest.

Oh! truly was Italy heard then, and Germany,
Melody's heart, and the rich brain of harmony;
Pure Paisiello, whose airs are as new
Though we know them by heart, as May-blossoms and dew
And nature's twin son, Pergolesi; and Bach,
Old father of fugues, with his endless fine talk;
And Gluck, who saw gods; and the learned sweet feeling
Of Haydn; and Winter, whose sorrows are healing;
And gentlest Corelli, whose bowing seems made
For a hand with a jewel; and Handel, arrayed
In Olympian thunders, vast lord of the spheres,
Yet pious himself, with his blindness in tears,
A lover withal, and a conqueror, whose marches
Bring demi-gods under victorious arches;
Then Arne, sweet and tricksome; and masterly Purcell,
Lay-clerical soul; and Mozart universal,
But chiefly with exquisite gallantries found,
With a grove in the distance of holier sound;
Nor forgot was thy dulcitude, loving Sacchini;
Nor love, young and dying, in shape of Bellini;
Nor Weber, nor Himmel, nor Mirth's sweetest name,
Cimarosa; much less the great organ-voiced fame
Of Marcello, that hushed the Venetian sea;
And strange was the shout, when it wept, bearing thee,
Thou soul full of grace as of grief, my heart-cloven,
My poor, my most rich, my all-feeling Beethoven.
O'er all, like a passion, great Pasta was heard,
As high as her heart, that truth-uttering bird;
And Banti was there; and Grassini, that goddess!
Dark, deep-toned, large, lovely, with glorious boddice;
And Mara; and Malibran, stung to the tips
Of her fingers with pleasure; and rich Fodor's lips

And, manly in face as in tone, Angrisani;
And Naldi, thy whim; and thy grace, Tramezzani;
And was it a voice?—or what was it?—say—
That, like a fallen angel beginning to pray,
Was the soul of all tears and celestial despair!
Paganini it was, 'twixt his dark-flowing hair.

So now we had instrument, now we had song—
Now chorus, a thousand-voiced one-hearted throng;
Now pauses that pampered resumption, and now—
But who shall describe what was played us, or how?
'Twas wonder, 'twas transport, humility, pride;
'Twas the heart of the mistress that sat by one's side;
'Twas the graces invisible, moulding the air
Into all that is shapely, and lovely, and fair,
And running our fancies their tenderest rounds
Of endearments and luxuries, turned into sounds;
'Twas argument even, the logic of tones;
'Twas memory, 'twas wishes, 'twas laughters, 'twas moans;
'Twas pity and love, in pure impulse obeyed;
'Twas the breath of the stuff of which passion is made.

And these are the concerts I have at my will;
Then dismiss them, and patiently think of your "bill."—
(*Aside*) Yet Lablache, after all, makes me long to go, still.

Leigh Hunt died, at the age of seventy-five, in 1859,—the last survivor, although the earliest born, of the four poets, with the other three of whom he had been so intimately associated, and the living memory of whom he thus carried far into another time, indeed across an entire succeeding generation.* To the last, even in outward form, he forcibly recalled Shelley's fine picture of him in his Elegy on Keats, written nearly forty years before:—

"What softer voice is hushed over the dead?
Athwart what brow is that dark mantle thrown?
What form leans sadly o'er the white death-bed,
In mockery of monumental stone,
The heavy heart heaving without a moan?
If it be he, who, gentlest of the wise,
Taught, soothed, loved, honoured the departed one;
Let me not vex, with inharmonious sighs,
The silence of that heart's accepted sacrifice."

---

* Hunt—Byron—Shelley—Keats, born in that order (in 1784, 1788, 1793, and 1796), died in exactly the reverse, and also at ages running in a series contrary throughout to that of their births; Keats, at 25, in 1821,—Shelley, at 29, in 1822,—Byron, at 36, in 1824, Hunt, at 75, in 1859.

Other Poetical Writers of the Earlier Part of the Nineteenth Century.

The names that have been mentioned are the chief of those belonging, wholly or principally, to the earlier part of the present century, or to that remarkable literary era which may be regarded as having expired with the reign of the last of the Georges. Many others, however, also brighten this age of our poetical literature, which cannot be here noticed.

On the whole, this space of somewhat less than half a century, dating from the first appearance of Cowper and Burns, must be pronounced to be the most memorable period in the history of our poetical literature after the age of Spenser and Shakespeare. And if, in comparing the produce of the two great revivals, the one happening at the transition from the sixteenth century into the seventeenth, the other at that from the eighteenth into the nineteenth, we find something more of freshness, freedom, raciness, and true vigour, warmth, and nature, in our earlier than in our recent poetry, it is not to be denied, on the other hand, that in some respects the latter may claim a preference over the former. It is much less debased by the intermixture of dross or alloy with its fine gold — much less disfigured by occasional pedantry and affectation — much more correct and free from flaws and incongruities of all kinds. In whatever regards form, indeed, our more modern poetry must be admitted, taken in its general character, to be the more perfect; and that notwithstanding many passages to be found in the greatest of our elder poets which in mere writing have perhaps never since been equalled, nor are likely ever to be excelled; and notwithstanding also something of greater boldness with which their position enabled them to handle the language, thereby attaining sometimes a force and expressiveness not so much within the reach of their successors in our own day. The literary cultivation of the language throughout two additional centuries, and the stricter discipline under which it has been reduced, may have brought loss or inconvenience in one direction, as well as gain in another; but the gain certainly preponderates. Even in the matter of versification, the lessons of Milton, of Dryden, and of Pope have no doubt been upon the whole instructive and beneficial; whatever of misdirection any of them may have given for a time to the form of our poetry passed away with his contemporaries and immediate followers, and now little or nothing but the good remains—the example of the superior care and uniform finish, and also something of sweetest and deepest music, as well as much of spirit and brilliancy, that were unknown to our earlier poets. In variety and freedom, as well as in beauty, majesty, and richness of versification, some of our latest writers have hardly been excelled by any of their predecessors; and the versification of the generality of our modern poets is greatly superior to that of the common run of those of the age of Elizabeth and James.

Prose Literature.

Among the most distinguished ornaments of the prose literature of this recent era were some of the chief poetical writers of the time. Southey and Scott were two of the most voluminous prose writers of their day, or of any day; Coleridge also wrote much more prose than verse; both Campbell and Moore are considerable authors in prose; there are several prose pieces among the published works of Byron, of Shelley, and of Wordsworth; both Leigh Hunt and Wilson perhaps acquired more of their fame, and have given more wide-spread delight, as prose writers than as poets; Charles Lamb's prose writings, his golden Essays of Elia, and various critical papers, abounding in original views and the deepest truth and beauty, have made his verse be nearly forgotten. Among the other most conspicuous prose writers of the period we have been reviewing may be mentioned, in general literature and speculation, Sidney Smith, Hazlitt, Jeffrey, Playfair, Stewart, Alison, Thomas Brown; in political disquisition, Erskine, Cobbett, Mackintosh, Bentham, Brougham (alone, of so many, still preserved to us, with his laurels won in every field of intellectual contest, both mentally and physically one of the most *vital* of the sons of men); in theological eloquence, Horsley, Wilberforce, Foster, Hall, Irving, Chalmers; in history, Fox, Mitford, Lingard, James Mill, Hallam, Turner; in fictitious narrative, Miss Edgeworth, Mrs. Opie, Miss Owenson (Lady Morgan), Mrs. Brunton, Miss Austen, Madame d'Arblay (Miss Burney), Godwin, Maturin. The most remarkable prose works that were produced were Scott's novels, the first of which, Waverley, appeared in 1814.* A powerful influence upon literature was also exerted from the first by the Edinburgh Review, begun in 1802; the Quarterly Review, begun in 1809; and Blackwood's Magazine, established in 1817.

* With the second title of 'Tis Sixty Years Since, the work professing (in the Introductory Chapter) to have been written, as it really was in part, nine years before.

PROGRESS OF SCIENCE.

A few of the most memorable facts connected with the progress of scientific discovery in England, during this period, may be very briefly noted. In astronomy Herschel continued to pursue his observations, commenced a short time before 1781, in which year he discovered the planet Uranus; in 1802, appeared in the Philosophical Transactions his catalogue of 500 new nebulæ and nebulous stars; in 1803 his announcement of the motions of double stars around each other; and a long succession of other important papers, illustrative of the construction of the heavens, followed down to within a few years of his death, at the age of eighty-four, in 1822. In chemistry, Davy, who had published his account of the effects produced by the respiration of nitrous oxide (the laughing gas) in 1800, in 1807 extracted metallic bases from the fixed alkalis, in 1808 demonstrated the similar decomposability of the alkaline earths, in 1811 detected the true nature of chloride (oxymuriatic acid), and in 1815 invented his safety lamp; in 1804 Leslie published his Experimental Enquiry into the Nature and Properties of Heat; in 1808 the Atomic Theory was announced by Dalton; and in 1814 its development and illustration were completed by Wollaston, to whom both chemical science and optics are also indebted for various other valuable services.

LITERATURE OF THE PRESENT DAY.

WHAT is properly the History of our Literature closes with the age or generation preceding the present; for history takes cognizance only of that which is past. What of literary production has taken place within the last thirty years, much or most of it by writers who are still alive, is hardly yet ripe for impartial appreciation. We may call this period the Victorian era. If we compare its poetical literature with that of the immediately preceding period of the same length, which will take us back to the beginning of the century, and may be called the last age of the Georges, confining ourselves to writers of established reputation, or whose names are universally more or less familiar, we shall find about the same number, between forty and fifty, in each; but differently distributed in the two cases in respect of their degrees of eminence. While of those of the Georgian thirty years we may reckon about ten as belonging to the first rank, and about as many more as belonging to the second, leaving only twenty-five for the third, of the equal number belonging to the subsequent portion of the century we cannot account more than three, or at most four, as being of the first rank, leaving, with again ten or eleven of the second, about thirty who must be assigned to the third or lowest. The difference, then, between the two periods will be, that in the poetical literature of the first we have ten writers of the highest and only twenty-five who must be held to belong to the lowest of the three ranks, and that in that of the second we have only three or four of the highest with about thirty of the lowest. This enumeration takes account of the leading poetical writers who have arisen in the American division of the English race, two or three of whom may be reckoned as of the second rank, though certainly not one as of the first.

In the prose literature of the two periods, however, we should probably find the above proportions more than reversed. The literary greatness of the Victorian age has hitherto manifested itself mostly in the works of our writers in prose. It is as if the one age were distinguished for its production of gold, the other for its production of silver. Probably in no other period, moreover, has there been seen so much activity of female genius and talent as we have had in the present, displaying itself princi-

2 L

pally, indeed, in fictitious narrative; but yet ranging, too, in several instances, above or beyond that. Of the writers in verse, however, who have attained any considerable distinction in the two periods, while about ten are women in the first, there are only five or six in the second.

Yet it is a memorable distinction of the present age, and one which belongs to no other in any literature (unless, indeed, we are to except that in which Sappho flourished), that one of its greatest writers in verse is a woman. And, if we put aside the possible case of Sappho, of whom so little remains that, exquisite as that little is held to be by all who are best able to judge, we are left to estimate her in the main merely from her fame among her countrymen—which, however, resounds through all the after ages of Greece—probably Elizabeth Barrett (Mrs. Browning) is entitled to be regarded as the greatest woman poet that has yet appeared in any language. With whatever her poetry may be chargeable whether of defect or of excess—whatever it either wants which it should have, or has which it should not have— there are two vital elements, and they are the chief ingredients of the poetical, in which it is never wanting;—subtlety of imagination and force of conception and feeling. In not much modern verse shall we find more of Greek intensity than in the following lines, entitled "A Child's Grave at Florence (A. A. E. C.; born July, 1848; died November, 1849)":—

> Of English blood, of Tuscan birth,
> What country should we give her?
> Instead of any on the earth,
> The civic Heavens receive her.
>
> And here, among the English tombs,
> In Tuscan ground we lay her,
> While the blue Tuscan sky endomes
> Our English words of prayer.
>
> A little child!—how long she lived
> By months, not years, is reckoned:
> Born in one July, she survived
> Alone to see a second;
>
> Bright-featured, as the July sun
> Her little face still played in,
> And splendours, with her birth begun,
> Had had no time for fading.
>
> So, LILY, from those July hours,
> No wonder we should call her;
> She looked such kinship to the flowers,
> Was but a little taller.

LITERATURE OF THE PRESENT DAY.

A Tuscan lily,—only white,
 As Dante, in abhorrence
Of red corruption, wished aright
 The lilies of his Florence.[1]

We could not wish her whiter,—her
 Who perfumed with pure blossom
The house!—a lovely thing to wear
 Upon a mother's bosom!

This July creature thought perhaps
 Our speech not worth assuming;
She sat upon her parents' laps,
 And mimicked the gnats humming;

Said "father," "mother,"—then left off,
 For tongues celestial fitter.
Her hair had grown just long enough
 To catch heaven's jasper-glitter.

Babes! Love could always hear and see[2]
 Behind the cloud that hid them.
"Let little children come to me,
 And do not thou forbid them."

So, unforbidding, have we met,
 And gently here have laid her,
Though winter is no time to get
 The flowers that should o'erspread her.

We should bring pansies quick with spring,
 Rose, violet, daffodilly,
And also, above everything,
 White lilies for our Lily.

Nay, more than flowers this grave exacts,—
 Glad, graceful attestations
Of her sweet eyes and pretty acts,
 With calm renunciations.

Her very mother with light feet
 Should leave the place too earthy,
Saying, "The angels have thee, sweet,
 Because we are not worthy."

But winter kills the orange buds,
 The gardens in the frost are,
And all the heart dissolves in floods,
 Remembering we have lost her!

Poor earth, poor heart,—too weak, too weak,
 To miss the July shining!
Poor heart!—what bitter words we speak[3]
 When God speaks of resigning!

---

[1] The emphasis on the *his*; and in the next line on the *we* and the *her*.
[2] The *always* emphasised. [3] The *we* emphatic.

Sustain this heart in us that faints,
 Thou God, the self-existent!
We catch up wild at parting saints,
 And feel thy heaven too distant.

The wind that swept them out of sin
 Has ruffled all our vesture:
On the shut door that let them in
 We beat with frantic gesture,—

To us—us also—open straight!
 The outer life is chilly—
Are we too, like the earth, to wait
 Till next year for our Lily?

—Oh, my own baby on my knees,
 My leaping, dimpled treasure,
At every word I write like these
 Clasped close, with stronger pressure!

Too well my own heart understands,—
 At every word beats fuller—
My little feet, my little hands,[1]
 And hair of Lily's colour!

—But God gives patience, Love learns strength,
 And Faith remembers promise,
And Hope itself can smile at length
 On other boys gone from us.

Love, strong as Death, shall conquer Death,
 Through struggle made more glorious.
This mother stills her sobbing breath,
 Renouncing, yet victorious.

Arms, empty of her child, she lifts,
 With spirit unbereaven,—
"God will not all take back his gifts;
 My Lily's mine in heaven!

"Still mine! maternal rights serene
 Not given to another!
The crystal bars shine faint between
 The souls of child and mother.

"Meanwhile," the mother cries, "content!
 Our love was well divided.
Its sweetness following where she went,
 Its anguish stayed where I did.

"Well done of God, to halve the lot,
 And give her all the sweetness;
To us, the empty room and cot,—
 To her, the Heaven's completeness.

[1] The *my* strongly emphasised, both times, of course.

"To us, this grave—to her, the rows
  The mystic palm-trees spring in,
To us, the silence in the house,—
  To her, the choral singing.

"For her, to gladden in God's view,—
  For us, to hope and bear on!—
Grow, Lily, in thy garden new,
  Beside the rose of Sharon.

"Grow fast in heaven, sweet Lily clipped,
  In love more calm than this is,—
And may the angels dewy-lipped
  Remind thee of our kisses!¹

"While none shall tell thee of our tears,
  These human tears now falling,
Till, after a few patient years,
  One home shall take us all in.

"Child, father, mother,—who left out?
  Not mother, and not father!—
And when, our dying couch about,
  The natural mists shall gather,

"Some smiling angel close shall stand,
  In old Corregio's fashion,
And bear a LILY in his hand,
  For death's ANNUNCIATION."

Mrs. Browning's Aurora Leigh has some serious and pervading faults, both in manner and in spirit,—too much evidence of effort and ambition, both in the thought and the language, exploding occasionally in mere tricks of style, oftener putting us off with wit instead of poetry, and generally over-charging and over-straining the expression, together with a constantly recurring tone of dictation and sarcasm, which is the more unpleasant inasmuch as it does not seem natural to the writer, and, what is perhaps worst of all, a visibly uneasy consciousness, or at least apprehension, never long absent, that her task is after all beyond her strength; but, with all its faults, it may fairly claim to be, so far as is known, the greatest poetical work ever produced by a woman. Yet it is still all over and all through, in form and in substance, as evidently a product of the female mind as any other long poem by a woman that we possess. It is, indeed, we should say, pre-eminently feminine in character. It would be almost as impossible to take it for the work of a man as to take the Iliad for the work of a woman.

Born in Tuscany, the child of an English father and an Italian mother, who died when she was four years old, Aurora thus

¹ The over emphatic.

vividly describes what she felt when, left an orphan by her father having been also taken away, and sent for by his relations, she first looked upon her new country with her native one fresh in her memory :—

> The train swept us on.
> Was this my father's England? the great isle?
> The ground seemed cut up from the fellowship
> Of venture, field from field, as man from man;
> The skies themselves looked low and positive,
> As almost you could touch them with a hand,
> And dared to do it they were so far off
> From God's celestial crystals; all things blurred,
> And dull and vague. Did Shakspeare and his mates
> Absorb the light here?—not a hill or stone
> With heart to strike a radiant colour up
> Or active outline on the indifferent air.

Gradually, however, she comes to appreciate something of the tamer landscape :—

> Not a grand nature. Not my chestnut-woods
> Of Vallombrosa, cleaving by the spurs
> To the precipices. Not my headlong leaps
> Of waters, that cry out for joy or fear
> In leaping through the palpitating pines,
> Like a white soul tossed out to eternity
> With thrills of time upon it. Not indeed
> My multitudinous mountains, sitting in
> The magic circle, with the mutual touch
> Electric, panting from their full deep hearts
> Beneath the influent heavens, and waiting for
> Communion and commission. Italy
> Is one thing, England one.
>   On English ground,
> You understand the letter—ere the fall
> How Adam lived in a garden. All the fields
> Are tied up fast with hedges, nosegay-like;
> The hills are crumpled plains, the plains parterres,
> The trees, round, woolly, ready to be clipped,
> And if you seek for any wilderness
> You find, at best, a park. A nature tamed
> And grown domestic like a barn-door fowl,
> Which does not awe you with its claws and beak
> Nor tempt you to an eyrie too high up,
> But which, in cackling, sets you thinking of
> Your eggs to-morrow at breakfast, in the pause
> Of finer meditation.
>   Rather say,
> A sweet familiar nature, stealing in

As a dog might, or child, to touch your hand
Or pluck your gown, and humbly mind you so
Of presence and affection, excellent
For inner uses, from the things without.

Ere long her heart opens to it all:—

Whoever lives true life will love true love.
I learnt to love that England. Very oft,
Before the day was born, or otherwise
Through secret windings of the afternoons,
I threw my hunters off and plunged myself
Among the deep hills, as a hunted stag
Will take the waters, shivering with the fear
And passion of the course. And when at last
Escaped, so many a green slope built on slope
Betwixt me and the enemy's house behind,
I dared to rest, or wander, in a rest
Made sweeter for the step upon the grass,
And view the ground's most gentle dimplement,
(As if God's finger touched but did not press
In making England) such an up and down
Of verdure,—nothing too much up or down,
A ripple of land; such little hills, the sky
Can stoop to tenderly and the wheatfields climb;
Such nooks of valleys lined with orchises,
Fed full of noises by invisible streams;
And open pastures where you scarcely tell
White daisies from white dew,—at intervals
The mythic oaks and elm-trees standing out
Self-poised upon their prodigy of shade,—
I thought my father's land was worthy too
Of being my Shakspeare's.

Equally brilliant and cordial with this picture of English nature is this other of the artificial in France (whatever may be exactly the meaning of some parts of it). We give the passage as rewritten, and very considerably altered from its original form, for the fourth edition of the poem:—

I mused
Up and down, up and down, the terraced streets,
The glittering boulevards, the white colonnades
Of fair fantastic Paris, who wears trees
Like plumes, as if man made them, spire and tower
As if they had grown by nature, tossing up
Her fountains in the sunshine of the squares,
As if in beauty's game she tossed the dice,
Or blew the silver down-balls of her dreams
To sow futurity with seeds of thought
And count the passage of her festive hours.

The city swims in verdure, beautiful
As Venice on the waters, the sea-swan.
What bosky gardens, dropped in close-walled courts
As plums in ladies' laps who start and laugh :
What miles of streets that run on after trees,
Still carrying all the necessary shops,
Those open caskets with the jewels seen !
And trade is art, and art's philosophy,
In Paris. There's a silk for instance, there,
As worth an artist's study for the folds
As that bronze opposite ! nay, the bronze has faults,
Art's here too artful,—conscious as a maid
Who leans to mark her shadow on the wall
Until she lose a 'vantage in her step.
Yet Art walks forward, and knows where to walk ;
The artists also are idealists,
Too absolute for nature, logical
To austerity in the application of
The special theory—not a soul content
To paint a crooked pollard and an ass,
As the English will because they find it so
And like it somehow.—There the old Tuileries
Is pulling its high cap down on its eyes,
Confounded, conscience-stricken, and amazed
By the apparition of a new fair face
In those devouring mirrors. Through the grate
Within the gardens, what a heap of babes,
Swept up like leaves beneath the chestnut-trees
From every street and alley of the town,
By the ghosts perhaps that blow too bleak this way
A-looking for their heads! dear pretty babes,
I wish them luck to have their ball-play out
Before the next change. Here the air is thronged
With statues, poised upon their columns fine
As if to stand a moment were a feat,
Against that blue ! What squares, what breathing-room
For a nation that runs fast,—ay, runs against
The dentist's teeth at the corner in pale rows,
Which grin at progress in an epigram.

We add one passage more, wonderful for the imaginative subtlety with which it is conceived and worked out,—Aurora's account of her mother's picture, which hung upon the wall of the silent house, "among the mountains above l'elago," to which her father had retired after losing her, with his child and their faithful old Assunta :—

The painter drew it after she was dead,
And when the face was finished, throat and hands,

Her cameriera carried him, in haste
Of the English-fashioned shroud, the last brocade
She dressed in at the Pitti; "he should paint
No sadder thing than that," she swore, "to wrong
Her poor signora." Therefore very strange
The effect was. I, a little child, would crouch
For hours upon the floor with knees drawn up,
And gaze across them, half in terror, half
In adoration, at the picture there,—
That swan-like supernatural white life
Just sailing upward from the red stiff silk
Which seemed to have no part in it, nor power
To keep it from quite breaking out of bounds.
For hours I sat and stared. Assunta's awe
And my poor father's melancholy eyes
Still pointed that way. That way went my thoughts
When wandering beyond sight. And as I grew
In years, I mixed, confused, unconsciously,
Whatever I last read or heard or dreamed,
Abhorrent, admirable, beautiful,
Pathetical, or ghastly, or grotesque,
With still that face . . . which did not therefore change,
But kept the mystic level of all forms,
Hates, fears, and admirations was by turns
Ghost, fiend, and angel, fairy, witch, and sprite,
A dauntless Muse who eyes a dreadful Fate,
A loving Psyche who loses sight of Love,
A still Medusa with mild milky brows
All curdled and all clothed upon with snakes
Whose slime falls fast as sweat will; or anon
Our Lady of the Passion, stabbed with swords
Where the Babe sucked; or Lamia in her first
Moonlighted pallor, ere she shrunk and blinked
And shuddering wriggled down to the unclean;
Or my own mother, leaving her last smile
In her last kiss upon the baby-mouth
My father pushed down on the bed for that,—
Or my dead mother, without smile or kiss,
Buried at Florence.

There are only two other names in the poetical literature of the present age that can be held to stand incontestably in the first rank;—Tennyson and Robert Browning. Diverse in much, they have nevertheless also much in common. They are both of them profound and subtle thinkers as well as richly endowed with the divine faculty of poetry in special; thinkers, and also workers; and so each has made himself a consummate artist in addition to whatever he might otherwise have been of a great poet. Tennyson, our present English King of Song, crowned as such not more by official nomination than by the general voice, has won to himself the personal attachment of his countrymen in a degree that has been rarely equalled in the history of literature. Among ourselves, Scott is the only other great writer who ever was held during his lifetime in anything like the same universal love and honour. The poetry of Tennyson has charmed all hearts by something more than its artistic qualities. It is as full of nobleness as of beauty. The laurel when he resigns it to another will again be acknowledged by all to be "greener from the brows of him that uttered nothing base." Everywhere his verse, whether tender or lofty, whether light-hearted or sad, breathes the kindest and manliest nature. Not only the chief of his shorter poems, but his In Memoriam and his Idylls of the King, are familiar to all readers. The following is in his simplest and quietest manner, but it is very perfect:—

> In her ear he whispers gaily,
>   "If my heart by signs can tell,
> Maiden, I have watched thee daily,
>   And I think thou lov'st me well."
> She replies, in accents fainter,
>   "There is none I love like thee."
> He is but a landscape-painter,
>   And a village maiden she.
> He to lips that fondly falter
>   Presses his without reproof;
> Leads her to the village altar,
>   And they leave her father's roof.
> "I can make no marriage present:
>   Little can I give my wife.
> Love will make our cottage pleasant,
>   And I love thee more than life."
> They by parks and lodges going,
>   See the lordly castles stand:
> Summer woods, about them blowing,
>   Made a murmur in the land.
> From deep thought himself he rouses,
>   Says to her that loves him well,
> "Let us see these handsome houses
>   Where the wealthy nobles dwell."
> So she goes by him attended,
>   Hears him lovingly converse,
> Sees whatever fair and splendid
>   Lay betwixt his home and hers;
> Parks with oak and chestnut shady,
>   Parks and ordered gardens great,
> Ancient homes of lord and lady,
>   Built for pleasure and for state.

LITERATURE OF THE PRESENT DAY.

All he shows her makes him dearer:
  Evermore she seems to gaze
On that cottage growing nearer,
  Where they twain will spend their days.
O but she will love him truly!
  He shall have a cheerful home;
She will order all things duly,
  When beneath his roof they come.
Thus her heart rejoices greatly,
  Till a gateway she discerns
With armorial bearings stately,
  And beneath the gate she turns;
Sees a mansion more majestic
  Than all those she saw before:
Many a gallant gay domestic,
  Bows before him at the door.
And they speak in gentle murmur,
  When they answer to his call,
While he treads with footstep firmer,
  Leading on from hall to hall.
And, while now she wonders blindly,
  Nor the meaning can divine,
Proudly turns he round and kindly,
  "All of this is mine and thine."
Here he lives in state and bounty,
  Lord of Burleigh, fair and free,
Not a lord in all the county
  Is so great a lord as he.
All at once the colour flushes
  Her sweet face from brow to chin:
As it were with shame she blushes,
  And her spirit changed within.
Then her countenance all over
  Pale again as death did prove;
But he clasped her like a lover,
  And he cheered her soul with love.
So she strove against her weakness,
  Though at times her spirits sank:
Shaped her heart with woman's meekness
  To all duties of her rank:
And a gentle consort made he,
  And her gentle mind was such
That she grew a noble lady,
  And the people loved her much.
But a trouble weighed upon her,
  And perplexed her, night and morn,
With the burden of an honour
  Unto which she was not born.
Faint she grew, and ever fainter,
  As she murmured, "Oh, that he

Were once more that landscape-painter
 Which did win my heart from me!"
So she drooped and drooped before him,
 Fading slowly from his side:
Three fair children first she bore him,
 Then before her time she died.
Weeping, weeping, late and early,
 Walking up and pacing down,
Deeply mourned the Lord of Burleigh,
 Burleigh House, by Stamford Town.
And he came to look upon her,
 And he looked at her and said,
" Bring the dress and put it on her,
 That she wore when she was wed."
Then her people, softly treading,
 Bore to earth her body, drest
In the dress that she was wed in,
 That her spirit might have rest.

By way of contrast to this true English ballad, and to exemplify Tennyson's extent of range, we will give now a few lines from the Ode on the Death of the Duke of Wellington, which make one of the great passages in the poetry of the world:—

—This is England's greatest son,
He that gained a hundred fights,
Nor ever lost an English gun;
This is he that far away
Against the myriads of Assaye
Clashed with his fiery few and won;
And underneath another sun,
Warring on a later day,
Round affrighted Lisbon drew
The treble work, the vast designs
Of his laboured rampart-lines,
Where he greatly stood at bay,
Whence he issued forth anew,
And ever great and greater grew,
Beating from the wasted vines
Back to France her banded swarms,
Back to France with countless blows,
Till o'er the hills her eagles flew
Past the Pyrenean pines,
Followed up in valley and glen
With blare of bugle, clamour of men,
Roll of cannon and clash of arms,
And England pouring on her foes.
Such a war had such a close.
Again their ravening eagle rose

In anger, wheeled on Europe-shadowing wings,
And barking for the thrones of kings;
Till one that sought but Duty's iron crown
On that loud sabbath shook the spoiler down;
A day of onsets of despair!
Dashed on every rocky square
Their surging charges foamed themselves away;
Last, the Prussian trumpet blew;
Through the long tormented air
Heaven flashed a sudden jubilant ray,
And down we swept and charged and overthrew.[1]
So great a soldier taught us there
What long-enduring hearts could do,
In that world's earthquake, Waterloo!

Pope is singular among our modern poets as having written nothing in blank verse; we do not remember that Tennyson has published so much as a sentence of prose. Not even, we believe, the shortest preface, dedication, or foot-note. In this as in other ways he has treated the public with almost ceremonious respect. Being by nature and vocation a poet, he declines to show himself without his singing robes about him. He will not make himself common, as he will do nothing carelessly or in haste. Nor has Browning either ever attempted to palm off careless work upon his readers. His Paracelsus, published when he was only three-and-twenty, marvellous as it was for the depth and completeness of the conception, was perhaps still more remarkable for the delicacy and perfection of the execution, peculiar as the manner was in some respects. And everything that he has produced since, even when departing farthest from established models, has been elaborated and finished with the same masterly skill. But, although he too has now made himself a great name, he has never attained, and is not likely ever to attain, the universal popularity of Tennyson, the general admiration at once of the few and of the many. There is scarcely anything in his poetry that is specially English. What of it is not distinctly of another country is either cosmopolitan or not of the earth at all. He has no special sympathies with the people whose language he writes, or with anything belonging to them—either their literature, their history, their political institutions, or any feeling that makes the national heart beat highest. It is irksome to most people to read English poetry, however fine artistically regarded, with so little in it of an English heart. Yet much of Browning's poetry, considered simply as poetry, is

[1] The emphasis on *we*, as perhaps also on *their* four lines above.

certainly, both in the soul of passionate vision that animates it and in grace and expressiveness of form, as exquisite as anything that has been produced in our day. He is often complained of as difficult to understand; and no doubt the train of thought is sometimes remote and subtle, and the language wrought to a corresponding degree of compression and fineness of edge, doing its work like the lancet or like the lightning. But this is equally true of much of Tennyson's poetry. Neither is to be read running. Browning, however, is so great a master of words that there is nothing he cannot make them do for him, no manner of using them in which he is not at home. Here is a portion (we must not be so unconscionable as to appropriate the whole) of one poem of his which is as simple and easy in style as it is airy and brilliant, and is in every way fitted to charm both old and young.—"The Pied Piper of Hamelin; A Child's Story," as it is entitled, "(written for, and inscribed to, W. M. the younger.)":—

  Hamelin town 's in Brunswick,
   By famous Hanover city;
  The river Weser, deep and wide,
   Washes its walls on the southern side;
  A pleasanter spot you never spied;
   But when begins my ditty,
  Almost five hundred years ago,
   To see the townsfolk suffer so
  From vermin, was a pity.

    Rats!
  They fought the dogs, and killed the cats,
   And bit the babies in the cradles,
  And ate the cheeses out of the vats,
   And licked the soup from the cooks' own ladles,
  Split open the kegs of salted sprats,
  Made nests inside men's Sunday hats,
  And even spoiled the women's chats,
   By drowning their speaking
   With shrieking and squeaking
  In fifty different sharps and flats.

  At last the people in a body
   To the Town Hall came flocking:
  "'Tis clear," cried they, "our Mayor's a noddy;
   "And as for our Corporation—shocking
  "To think we buy gowns lined with ermine
  "For dolts who can't or won't determine
  "What's best to rid us of our vermin!
  "You hope, because you're old and obese
  "To find in the furry civic robe ease?

LITERATURE OF THE PRESENT DAY.

"Rouse up, Sirs! Give your brains a racking
"To find the remedy we're lacking,
"Or, sure as fate, we'll send you packing!"
At this the Mayor and Corporation
Quaked with a mighty consternation.

An hour they sat in council;
  At length the Mayor broke silence:
"For a guilder I'd my ermine gown sell;
  "I wish I were a mile hence!
"It's easy to bid one rack one's brain—
"I'm sure my poor head aches again,
"I've scratched it so, and all in vain.
"Oh, for a trap, a trap, a trap!"
Just as he said this, what should hap
At the chamber door but a gentle tap?
"Bless us," cried the Mayor, "what's that?"
(With the Corporation as he sat,
Looking little, though wondrous fat;
Nor brighter was his eye, nor moister
Than a too-long-opened oyster,
Save when at noon his paunch grew mutinous
For a plate of turtle green and glutinous)
"Only a scraping of shoes on the mat?
"Anything like the sound of a rat
"Makes my heart go pit-a-pat!"

"Come in!" the Mayor cried, looking bigger:
And in did come the strangest figure!
His queer long coat from heel to head
Was half of yellow and half of red;
And he himself was tall and thin,
With sharp blue eyes, each like a pin,
And light loose hair, yet swarthy skin,
No tuft on cheek nor beard on chin,
But lips where smiles went out and in—
There was no guessing his kith and kin!
And nobody could enough admire
The tall man and his quaint attire:
Quoth one: "It's as my great-grandsire,
"Starting up at the trump of Doom's tone,
"Had walked this way from his painted tombstone."

He advanced to the council-table:
And, "Please your honours," said he, "I'm able,
"By means of a secret charm, to draw
"All creatures living beneath the sun,
"That creep, or swim, or fly, or run,
"After me so as you never saw!
"And I chiefly use my charm
"On creatures that do people harm,

ENGLISH LITERATURE AND LANGUAGE.

"The mole, and toad, and newt, and viper;
"And people call me the Pied Piper."
(And here they noticed round his neck
A scarf of red and yellow stripe,
To match with his coat of the selfsame cheque;
And at the scarf's end hung a pipe;
And his fingers, they noticed, were ever straying
As if impatient to be playing
Upon this pipe, as low it dangled
Over his vesture so old-fangled).
"Yet," said he, "poor piper as I am,
"In Tartary I freed the Cham,
"Last June, from his huge swarms of gnats;
"I eased in Asia the Nizam
"Of a monstrous brood of vampire-bats:
"And, as for what your brain bewilders,
"If I can rid your town of rats
"Will you give me a thousand guilders?"
"One? fifty thousand!" was the exclamation
Of the astonished Mayor and Corporation.

Into the street the Piper stept,
  Smiling first a little smile,
As if he knew what magic slept
  In his quiet pipe the while;
Then, like a musical adept,
To blow the pipe his lips he wrinkled,
And green and blue his sharp eyes twinkled
Like a candle-flame where salt is sprinkled;
And ere three shrill notes the pipe uttered,
You heard as if an army muttered;
And the muttering grew to a grumbling;
And the grumbling grew to a mighty rumbling;
And out of the houses the rats came tumbling.
Great rats, small rats, lean rats, brawny rats,
Brown rats, black rats, grey rats, tawny rats,
Grave old plodders, gay young friskers,
  Fathers, mothers, uncles, cousins,
Cocking tails and pricking whiskers,
  Families by tens and dozens,
Brothers, sisters, husbands, wives—
Followed the piper for their lives.
From street to street he piped advancing,
And step for step they followed dancing,
Until they came to the river Weser,
Wherein all plunged and perished—
Save one, who, stout as Julius Cæsar,
Swam across and lived to carry
(As he the manuscript he cherished)
To Rat-land home his commentary,

Which was, "At the first shrill notes of the pipe,
"I heard a sound as of scraping tripe.
"And putting apples, wondrous ripe,
"Into a cider-press's gripe:
"And a moving away of pickle-tub boards,
"And a leaving ajar of conserve-cupboards,
"And a drawing the corks of train-oil-flasks,
"And a breaking the hoops of butter-casks:
"And it seemed as if a voice
"(Sweeter far than by harp or by psaltery
"Is breathed) called out, Oh rats, rejoice!
"The world is grown to one vast drysaltery!
"So munch on, crunch on, take your nuncheon,
"Breakfast, supper, dinner, luncheon!
"And just as a bulky sugar-puncheon,
"All ready staved, like a great sun shone
"Glorious scarce an inch before me,
"Just as methought it said, Come, bore me!
"—I found the Weser rolling o'er me."

You should have heard the Hamelin people
Ringing the bells till they rocked the steeple;
"Go," cried the Mayor, "and get long poles!
"Poke out the nests and block up the holes!
"Consult with carpenters and builders,
"And leave in our town not even a trace
"Of the rats!"—when suddenly up the face
Of the Piper perked in the market-place,
With a "First, if you please, my thousand guilders!"

But for the manner in which this fair demand was received by the rulers of the delivered town, and all that thence ensued, the reader must be left to resort to the poet's own pages. We give as a specimen of another kind the concluding lines of Paracelsus's long and eloquent dying declamation:—

Love's undoing
Taught me the worth of love in man's estate,
And what proportion love should hold with power
In his right constitution; love preceding
Power, and with much power always much more love;
Love still too straitened in its present means,
And earnest for new power to set it free.
I learned this, and supposed the whole was learned:
And thus, when men received with stupid wonder
My first revealings, would have worshipped me,
And I despised and loathed their proffered praise—
When, with awakened eyes, they took revenge
For past credulity in casting shame
On my real knowledge, and I hated them—

It was not strange I saw no good in man,
To overbalance all the wear and waste
Of faculties, displayed in vain, but born
To prosper in some better sphere: and why?
In my own heart love had not been made wise
To trace love's faint beginnings in mankind,
To know even hate is but a mask of love's,
To see a good in evil, and a hope
In ill-success; to sympathize, be proud
Of their half-reasons, faint aspirings, dim
Struggles for truth, their poorest fallacies,
Their prejudice, and fears, and cares, and doubts;
Which all touch upon nobleness, despite
Their error, all tend upwardly though weak,
Like plants in mines which never saw the sun,
But dream of him, and guess where he may be,
And do their best to climb and get to him.
All this I knew not, and I failed. Let men
Regard me, and the poet dead long ago
Who once loved rashly; and shape forth a third,
And better-tempered spirit, warned by both:
As from the over-radiant star too mad
To drink the light-springs, beamless thence itself—
And the dark orb which borders the abyss,
Ingulfed in icy night,—might have its course
A temperate and equi-distant world.
Meanwhile, I have done well, though not all well.
As yet men cannot do without contempt—
'Tis for their good, and therefore fit awhile
That they reject the weak, and scorn the false,
Rather than praise the strong and true, in me.
But, after, they will know me! If I stoop
Into a dark tremendous sea of cloud,
It is but for a time; I press God's lamp
Close to my breast—its splendour, soon or late,
Will pierce the gloom: I shall emerge one day!

And thus the finished music of the poem returns to the same note from which it had sprung up on its grand parabolic sweep, and the self-willed and daring but always noble as well as brilliant visionary to the words with which he had broken away long ago from his two friends Festus and Michal:—

I go to prove my soul!
I see my way as birds their trackless way—
I shall arrive! what time, what circuit first,
I ask not: but, unless God send his hail
Or blinding fire-balls, sleet, or stifling snow,
In some time—his good time—I shall arrive:
He guides me and the bird. In his good time!

If there be a fourth name belonging to this period, the middle portion of the present century, which after-times will recognize as that of a poet of the first class, it is that of the late Thomas Hood. No one of his contemporaries has surpassed him either in perfection of workmanship or in originality of conception. Upon whatever he has written he has stamped the impress of himself, and as with a diamond signet. Nor, although his most distinctive manner is comic, is he at all inferior to himself when he adopts a different style, as he has done in several of his best-known poems. As in other instances, indeed,—for example, in Horace and in Burns—what gives their peculiar character and charm to his most pathetic touches is essentially the same thing which makes the brilliancy of his comic manner. All that is most characteristic of him in expression and thought is to be discerned in the curious felicity of the following exquisitely beautiful and tender lines:—

> We watched her breathing through the night,
>   Her breathing soft and low,
> As in her breast the wave of life
>   Kept heaving to and fro.
>
> So silently we seemed to speak,
>   So slowly moved about,
> As we had lent her half our powers
>   To eke her living out.
>
> Our very hopes belied our fears,
>   Our fears our hopes belied—
> We thought her dying when she slept,
>   And sleeping when she died.
>
> For when the morn came dim and sad,
>   And chill with early showers,
> Her quiet eyelids closed—she had
>   Another morn than ours.

INDEX.

A.

ACCENTUAL verse, 113, 124
Addison, Joseph, 357
Akenside, Dr. Mark, 379
Alchemists, 71
Aldred, Archbishop, Curse of, 87
Alfred the Great, 13
Alliterative verse, 110
Ancren Riwle, 98
Andrews, Bishop, 278
Anglo-Saxon, or Saxon, 20
Anne, age of, 457, 458
Anselm, 32, 34, 41
Arabic learning, 29
Arabic numerals, 71
Arbuthnot, Dr. John, 362
Armstrong, Dr. John, 379
Ascham, Roger, 188
Atterbury, Bishop, 363

B.

Bacon, Francis, 275
Bacon, Roger, 73, 88
Baker, Sir Richard, 310
Bale's Kynge Johan, 207
Barbour, John, 157
Barclay, Alexander, 191
Barrow, Dr. Isaac, 338
Baxter, Richard, 337
Beattie, James, 394
Beaumont, Francis, 266, 281, 331
Ben Jonson, 270
Bible, Translation of the, 273
Blackmore, Sir Richard, 365
Blank verse, 210
Bolingbroke, Lord, 364
Browne, Sir Thomas, 306
Browne, William, 296
Browning, Mrs., 514
Browning, Robert, 525

Brunne, Robert de, 105
Buckhurst, Lord, vide Sackville, T.
Bunyan, John, 338
Burke, Edmund, 408
Burnet, Bishop, 345
Burnet, Thomas, 346
Burns, Robert, 440
Burton, Robert, 277
Butler, Samuel, 323
Byron, Lord, 490

C.

Campbell, Thomas, 480
Carew, Thomas, 287
Cartwright, William, 284
Celtic Languages and Literature, 7
Chapman, George, 251
Charles I., 297
Chatterton, Thomas, 395
Chaucer, Geoffrey, 121
Chaucer's prose, 165
Chillingworth, William, 301
Chroniclers, 162
Churchill, Charles, 239
Cibber, Colley, 370
Clarendon, Lord, 333
Classical learning, 41
Cleveland, John, 289
Coleridge, S. T., 474
Collins, William, 328
Commonwealth Literature, 310
Compound English, 121
Congreve, William, 369
Conquests, the Norman, 24
Corbet, Bishop, 285
Cowley, Abraham, 321
Cowper, William, 427
Crabbe, George, 427, 488, 492
Cranmer, Archbishop, 186
Cudworth, Dr. Ralph, 337

INDEX.

D.

Daniel, Samuel, 242, 279
Darwin, Erasmus, 437
Davies, Sir John, 253
Defoe, Daniel, 369
Denham, Sir John, 288
Donne, Dr. John, 254, 27
Dorset, Earl of, vide Sackville, T.
Douglas, Gawin, 195
Drama, end of the old, 280
Drama, the regular, 200
Dramatists of Eighteenth Century, 369, 398
Dramatists of Seventeenth Century, 331
Drayton, Michael, 248
Drummond, Sir William, 253
Dryden, John, 328
Dunbar, William, 196
Dyer, John, 371

E.

Edwards, Richard, 211
Eighteenth Century, latter part of, 427
Elizabethan Literature, 198
Elizabethan Poetry, 237
Elizabethan Prose Writers, 219, 272
Elyot, Sir Thomas, 186
English as a literary tongue, 82
English after the Conquest, 58
English Language, 10, 28
English, Original (Saxon or Anglo-Saxon), 20
English, Revolutions of, 84
Essayists, Periodical, 396
Euphuism, 219
Europe, Languages of Modern, 1

F.

Fairfax, Edward, 252
Falconer, William, 393
Fanshawe, Sir Richard, 253
Farquhar, George, 369
Female Writers, 397
Ferrex and Porrex, 208
Fielding, Henry, 384
Fletcher, Giles, 242
Fletcher, John, 266, 281, 331
Fletcher, Phineas, 242
Ford, John, 272
Fortescue, Sir John, 171
French Language in England, 48, 79
French School of Poetry, 286
Fuller, Thos., 303

G.

Gammer Gurton's Needle, 205
Garth, Sir Samuel, 365
Gay, John, 362
Georges, last Age of the, 439
Gibbon, Edward, 425
Gloucester, Robert of, 104
Glover, Richard, 379
Goldsmith, Oliver, 388
Gorboduc, Tragedy of, 208
Gower, John, 155
Gray, Thomas, 377
Greene, Robert, 213, 221

H.

Hales, John, 301
Hall, Bishop, 275
Hall, Joseph, 249
Harington, Sir John, 252
Harrington, Sir James, 308
Hawes, Stephen, 191
Henry the Minstrel, 178
Henryson, Robert, 179
Herbert, George, 283
Herrick, Robert, 284
Heywood, John, 194, 202
Historical Writers, 278
Hobbes Thomas, 334
Hood, Thomas, 531
Hooker, Richard, 275
Hume, David, 422
Hunt, Leigh, 505

J.

James I. of Scotland, 177
Johnson, Samuel, 404
Junius, 402

K.

Keats, John, 501
Knolles, Richard, 270
Kyd, Thomas, 216

L.

Langue d'Oc and Langue d'Oyl, 53
Latimer, Bishop, 186
Latin after the Conquest, 46
Latin Chroniclers, 47
Latin Literature of Britain, early, 3
Layamon, 89
Learned tongues, the, 75
Leighton, Archbishop, 312
Locke, John, 348
Lodge, Thomas, 216

INDEX.   535

Lovelace, Richard, 287
Lydgate, John, 175
Lyly, John, 215, 219, 221
Lyndsay, Sir David, 196

M.

Malory, Sir Thomas, 173
Mandevill, Sir John, 153
Mandeville, Bernard de, 359
Manayng, Robert, 105
Marlowe, Christopher, 214
Marvel, Andrew, 325
Mason, William, 394
Massinger, Philip, 271
Mathematical Studies, 68
Metaphysical Writers, 421
Milton, John, Poetry of, 312
Milton, John, Prose of, 299
Minor Poets of Eighteenth Century, 370
Minot, Lawrence, 106
Miracle Plays, 201
Mirror for Magistrates, 198
Misogonus, 205
Mixed English, 121
Moore, Thomas, 489, 495
Moral Plays, 201
More, Dr. Henry, 337
More, Sir Thomas, 184

N.

Nash, Thomas, 223
Nevile, Henry, 316
Newspapers, 309
Nineteenth Century, 457
Nineteenth Century, early part of, 510

O.

Occleve, Thomas, 174
Oriental Learning, 77
Ormulum, the, 95
Ossian, Macpherson's, 385

P.

Parnell, Dr. Thomas, 364
Pecock, Bishop, 169
Peele, George, 212
Percy's Reliques, 395
Piers Ploughman, 110
Political Economy, 426
Pope, Alexander, 353
Present day, Literature of, 513
Printing in England, 167
Prior, Matthew, 363
Prose, English, 164, 188

Q.

Quarles, Francis, 283

R.

Raleigh, Sir Walter, 278
Ralph Roister Doister, 203
Randolph, Thomas, 285
Religious Poets, 283
Revolution, Effects of, 341
Revolution, Survivors of, 342
Richardson, Samuel, 382
Ridley, Bishop, 186
Robertson, William, 424
Roman de la Rose, 137
Romance, Metrical, 102
Roy, William, 194

S.

Sackville, Thomas, 199, 208
Saxon, or Anglo-Saxon, 20
Scholarship, English, Earliest, 12
Scholastic Philosophy, 30, 67
Scott, Sir Walter, 482
Scottish Poetry, 380
Scottish Poets, 176, 195
Scottish Prose Writers, 180
Second English, 85
Sedley, Sir Charles, 327
Semi-Saxon, 85
Shaftesbury, Earl of, 359
Shakespeare's Dramatic Contemporaries, 265
Shakespeare, William, 257, 258
Shelley, P. B., 497
Shenstone, William, 377
Shirley, James, 280
Sidney, Sir Philip, 220
Skelton, John, 192
Smollett, Tobias, 385
South, Dr. Robert, 347
Southey, Robert, 481
Spenser, Edmund, 224
Steele, Sir Richard, 357
Sterne, Laurence, 382
Suckling, Sir John, 288
Surrey, Earl of, 196
Swift, Jonathan, 349
Sylvester, Joshua, 242

T.

Taylor, Jeremy, 302
Tennyson, Alfred, 521

Theological Elizabethan Writers, 274
Third English, 121
Thomson, James, 328
Tillotson, Archbishop, 340

U.

Udall, Nicholas, 203
Universities and Schools, 34, 73

V.

Vanbrugh, Sir John, 389

W

Waller, Edmund, 323
Warner, William, 238
Warton, Thomas and Joseph, 384
Wiclif, John de, 165
Wilkes, John, 401
Wilkie, William, 379
Wilson, Thomas, 189
Wither, George, 290
Wordsworth, William, 458
Wyatt, Sir Thomas, 197
Wynton, Andrew of, 178

Y.

Young, Dr. Edward, 377

THE END.

www.ingramcontent.com/pod-product-compliance
Lightning Source LLC
Chambersburg PA
CBHW031942290426
44108CB00011B/639